THE FIRE IS UPON US

THE
FIRE
IS
UPON
US

Nicholas
Buccola

James Baldwin,
William F. Buckley Jr.,
and the Debate
over Race in America

Princeton University Press
Princeton and Oxford

Published by Princeton University Press

41 William Street, Princeton, New Jersey 08540

6 Oxford Street, Woodstock, Oxfordshire OX20 1TR

press.princeton.edu

ISBN 978-0-691-18154-7
ISBN (e-book) 978-0-691-19739-5

British Library Cataloging-in-Publication Data is available

Editorial: Rob Tempio and Matt Rohal
Production Editorial: Brigitte Pelner
Production: Merli Guerra
Publicity: James Schneider (US) and Kate Farquhar-Thomson (UK)
Copyeditor: Cindy Milstein

Jacket Images: (Left) William F. Buckley. Courtesy of Nick Machalaba /
Penske Media. (Right) James Baldwin. Courtesy of Steve Schapiro
Corbis Premium Collection

This book has been composed in Arno

Printed on acid-free paper ∞

Printed in the United States of America

1 3 5 7 9 10 8 6 4 2

This book is dedicated to my mom and dad,
whose love seems limitless,
and to Mark E. Kann (1947–2016)
and Scott B. Smith (1963–2017),
who taught me so much about
teaching, scholarship, and friendship

The White community in the South is entitled to take such measures as are necessary to prevail, politically and culturally . . . because, for the time being, it is the advanced race.

—WILLIAM F. BUCKLEY JR., "WHY THE SOUTH MUST PREVAIL" (1957)

Interviewer: "[In *The Fire Next Time*], you talk about a people being led to their doom by an attitude of mind. . . . What do you say now about the fire?"

James Baldwin: "The fire is upon us."

—JAMES BALDWIN INTERVIEWED BY JOHN HALL, TRANSATLANTIC REVIEW (1970)

Contents

Illustrations

THE FIRE IS UPON US

Prologue

On the evening of February 18, 1965, the Cambridge Union was abuzz with excitement. The debating hall of the Union, which was modeled after the British House of Commons, was packed with more than seven hundred people. Students and guests at the idyllic campus of the University of Cambridge filled every spot available on the benches and in the galleries, and still more sat in the aisles and on the floor. As the world's oldest and most prestigious debating society, the Cambridge Union had often been the site of public attention, but this evening had the promise of something extraordinary. Just a few days earlier, the Union had marked its 150th anniversary with an event that featured the Archbishop of Canterbury and several members of parliament, but the energy in the air on this night was different.[1] The people in the debating hall of the Union sensed that they were about to witness an intellectual clash for the ages.

As the crowd poured in, the space became hotter, stuffier, and further in violation of the fire code. More than forty-five minutes before the official start time of the debate, Union officials had to set up crash barriers to prevent more people from entering the debating hall. Once the barriers were in place, an overflow audience of more than five hundred people dispersed to other rooms on the Union premises in order to watch the proceedings on closed-circuit televisions. The British Broadcasting Corporation (BBC) was on hand to record the event, and the BBC commentator, a Conservative member of parliament named Norman St. John Stevas, reported that "in all the years he had known the Union"— he had been a member when he was a student at Cambridge decades earlier—he had never seen it so well attended.[2]

At approximately 8:45 p.m. Union president Peter Fullerton—an undergraduate studying history—emerged through the doors of the hall to lead the debaters to their seats. Behind Fullerton were two student

debaters—David Heycock and Jeremy Burford—and the two guest debaters for the evening: James Baldwin and William F. Buckley Jr. Both
guests of honor were about forty years old, both were American, and both
had risen to prominence as writers, but that was about all they had in
common. Baldwin was the grandson of slaves and had risen from the Harlem ghetto to become one of the world's most famous writers. He was,
in the words of his friend Malcolm X, "*the* poet" of the civil rights revolution, the leading literary voice of the movement that was—at that very
moment—engaged in a struggle to radically alter the nature of American society.[3] Baldwin believed that the soul of the country was desperately in need of redemption, and he had devoted his voice and pen to
hasten the nation's deliverance.

Buckley may as well have been from another planet. He was born into
immense wealth and emerged from his elite upbringing to become one
of the country's leading conservative polemicists. Through his *National
Review* magazine, his thrice-weekly newspaper column, and frequent appearances on radio, television, and the lecture circuit, Buckley spread
his conservative message. At the heart of that message was the belief that
American society was basically good, and that it was the sacred duty of
conservatives to defend it from any ideas, personalities, or movements
that were deemed threats to it. In the years prior to their meeting at Cambridge, Buckley had made it entirely clear that he viewed Baldwin and
the movement he represented as subversive to everything that made
America great.

As Baldwin and Buckley walked up the aisle to their seats, the students
in the debating hall of the Union were probably struck by more superficial differences between the two men. Baldwin was, in the words of his
friend Maya Angelou, built like a "dancer"—standing only five foot six
and not weighing much more than 130 pounds—and his most striking
features were undoubtedly his large, brown "frog eyes."[4] Buckley stood
over half a foot taller than Baldwin, and his dark hair was—on this
occasion—combed neatly from left to right. As Baldwin made his way
to the speaker's bench to his left, he greeted the mostly white audience
with a beaming smile that revealed a pronounced gap between his two
front teeth. Just a couple of steps behind him, Buckley ambled through

the crowd and toward the speaker's bench to the right. He carried a clipboard in his hand, and his feline smile was accompanied by a twinkle from his piercing blue eyes.

There was no mistaking what drew such a large crowd that night: students and guests were packed into the Union in order to see Baldwin, who was second in international prominence only to Martin Luther King Jr. as the voice of the black freedom struggle. It can be difficult for contemporary readers to appreciate the heights to which Baldwin's star had ascended by the mid-1960s. The writer William Styron was not embellishing much when he said that Baldwin was, in those days, "among the 5 or 6 most famous people in the world[.] More famous than [Frank] Sinatra. Or Henry Kissinger. Or Shirley Temple." He was so famous, Styron joked, "he had to wear white-face for disguise."[5] In his novels, plays, and essays, Baldwin had explored the depths of the human soul through tales that forced readers to examine the racial, religious, and sexual mythologies that dominated their lives. Just two years prior to the Cambridge debate, readers the world over had been electrified by Baldwin's jeremiad *The Fire Next Time*, which was the most important piece of writing to emerge out of the civil rights movement. Now the students at Cambridge were going to get a chance to see the poet-prophet in the flesh.

While Baldwin's presence alone would have probably produced the fervor of the evening, those in attendance might also have been drawn by the promise of the fireworks that were likely to be ignited by having him share the platform with a conservative. Although Buckley had not yet achieved international fame, he was by then, in the words of the writer Norman Mailer, "the leading young Conservative in the [United States], and in fact the most important Conservative in the public eye after Barry Goldwater."[6] The students did not know much about Buckley, but the buzz prior to the debate was that he would be a worthy foe for Baldwin. Rumor had it that he had been a star debater at Yale and one of the leading champions of the Goldwater candidacy in the United States. What might happen when a proud right-winger went toe to toe with a confirmed radical?

The motion before the house—"The American dream is at the expense of the American Negro"—was crafted to invite Baldwin and Buckley to go beyond defending their divergent positions on the civil rights movement. Baldwin had established himself as one of the movement's leading champions, and Buckley was known to be one of its most vociferous critics, but Union officials hoped the motion would inspire their guests to engage more fundamental questions about the relationship between the ideals of the American dream—for example, freedom, equality, and opportunity—and what Baldwin had called "the racial nightmare" that was tearing the country apart.[7] In a sense, this was the perfect motion for Baldwin and Buckley to debate. The core of Baldwin's indictment of his compatriots was that their mythology—including the American dream—had enabled them to avoid coming to terms with the injustice of their past and present. Unless they could accept the truth of their past and take responsibility for it in the present, Baldwin argued, the American dream would remain a nightmare for many.

Buckley, on the other hand, considered himself to be a guardian of the ideals at the core of the American dream. The American experiment had been, he thought, a tremendous success, and the "responsibility of leadership" fell to elites like him to protect the ideas, norms, and institutions that had made it so. The United States, he believed, had become an "oasis of freedom and prosperity" because it was a society rooted in certain "immutable truths." Among these truths were the belief that the "rights and responsibilities of self-government" ought to be entrusted to those who had demonstrated themselves worthy of power and the idea that "security"—in a social and economic sense—should be "individually earned," not provided by the government.[8]

Buckley's prominence on the American right wing had something to do with his message—a combination of devout religiosity, strident antiegalitarianism, and deep opposition to the welfare state—but it also had to do with his incredible success as a communicator and popularizer of conservative ideas.[9] The ideas themselves often took a back seat to the unique style with which he delivered them. "No other actor," Mailer observed of Buckley, "can project simultaneous hints that he is in the act of playing Commodore of the Yacht Club, Joseph Goebbels, Robert Mitchum, Maverick, Savonarola, the nice prep-school kid next door, and the snows of yesteryear."[10] Just about everyone who knew

Buckley personally reported that he was immensely charming and generous, but those who entered into public debate with him had a different story to tell.[11] Before a debate, Buckley could be found exchanging idle chitchat and laughter with his interlocutor, but when the lights came up, he unleashed his inner Torquemada.[12]

And so the stage was set for an epic clash between an unapologetic radical and one of the founding fathers of American conservatism. Baldwin, son of Harlem turned literary voice of the civil rights movement, was about to square off with Buckley, son of privilege turned "Saint Paul of the conservative movement."[13] The tension in the room was palpable as Union president Fullerton rose to invite the first speaker to address the house.

While Baldwin and Buckley were eating their predebate dinner with Union officials, a twenty-two-year-old civil rights organizer named James Orange was arrested for "disorderly conduct" in Marion, Alabama. Orange worked for King's Southern Christian Leadership Conference (SCLC) and this would not be the first time he would find himself in an Alabama jail. While King and many of his colleagues had been challenging segregation and disenfranchisement about twenty-seven miles away in Selma, Orange had been doing the same in the small town of Marion. A couple of weeks prior to the Cambridge debate, Orange led a school boycott in Marion to protest the arrest of sixteen people who had engaged in a sit-in at a segregated restaurant. Orange, who was described as a "formidable man who stood well over six feet tall and weighed three hundred pounds," led an "army" of seven hundred students to the jail, where they sang freedom songs until they were arrested and hauled away in buses.[14]

On the morning of the Cambridge debate, Orange led another school boycott, and by the early afternoon, he was once again incarcerated. Right around the same time Baldwin and Buckley were entering the debating hall of the Cambridge Union, an FBI agent reported via radio that a "new crew" had arrived in Marion to pick up where Orange left off.[15] A few hours later, this new crew stood before a crowd of several hundred people in Zion United Church, which was just one block from the jail cell that held Orange. Leaders in the church formulated a plan to protest Orange's arrest. Those assembled would "march to the jailhouse in a line, two by two, and sing freedom songs."[16] Reverend James Dobynes would be on the front line of the march, and if stopped by police, would lead the group in prayer before returning to the church.

Soon after the four hundred civil rights protesters began their short march to the jail, their leaders sensed they were in for trouble. After making it only half a block, the marchers were confronted by a blockade of law enforcement officers who ordered them "to disperse or to return to the church."[17] As planned, Dobynes knelt to lead the group in prayer before returning to the church, but as he lowered his head, a state trooper bludgeoned him with a club. The Alabama law enforcement officers on the scene had the foresight to keep the news media on the other side of the square and unofficially "deputized" some local segregationist ruffians to keep the reporters at bay in the event violence broke out. Soon after the state troopers attacked Dobynes, the reporters began to make their move across the square, only to be met by the segregationist mob, which proceeded to assault them and destroy their cameras. In the midst of the assault, the correspondent from the *New York Times* reported that "Negroes could be heard screaming and loud whacks rang through the square."[18]

Jimmie Lee Jackson—a twenty-six-year-old church deacon—sought refuge from this horror, along with his mother and his injured eighty-two-year-old grandfather, in Mack's Café. State troopers followed the family into the café, and began beating Jackson, his mother, and his grandfather with clubs. At some point in the melee, a state trooper shot Jackson twice in the stomach. A few days later, Jackson would die from his wounds.[19]

The fact that the Baldwin-Buckley debate occurred on the same day as the Marion protests and the mortal wounding of Jackson captures rather perfectly what this book is about. What happened the night Baldwin and

Buckley squared off at Cambridge is a climactic chapter in this narrative, but this book is about far more than the debate itself. As fate would have it, Baldwin and Buckley were almost exact contemporaries, and so they came of age—intellectually speaking—at the same time (the late 1940s) and reached the height of their prominence at nearly the same moment (the mid-1960s). Right in the middle of that timeline, the two movements that each man would do so much to shape—the civil rights movement and conservative movement, respectively—were born. This is the story of how two of the most consequential postwar American intellectuals responded to the civil rights revolution. My focus in what follows is on their ideas rather than the interesting personal lives each man led.[20] My aim is to explain what they believed, why they believed it, and what we might be able to learn from their clash over civil rights.[21]

The story of how Baldwin and Buckley responded to the civil rights revolution is worth telling in its own right, but I am also inspired by the enduring relevance of the themes of their decades-long debate. The American people have still not woken up from the "racial nightmare" that occupied Baldwin's mind during so much of his life. Dramatic gaps persist between white and black economic success, educational attainment, and homeownership.[22] Black Americans are far more likely to be stopped, searched, arrested, beaten, or killed by law enforcement.[23] In the midst of this continuing racial nightmare, the conservative movement that Buckley did so much to create and champion has coalesced around a politics of racial resentment and nationalist authoritarianism. While some of the rhetoric and policy debates have evolved, the core issues that divided Baldwin and Buckley remain as relevant as ever.

Chapter 1

The Ghetto and the Mansion, 1924–46

Imagine waking to find yourself trapped in a small room with all the windows shut. As you try to breathe in such a space, which is occupied by several of your siblings, you are likely to feel an "insistent, maddening, claustrophobic pounding" in your "skull." This is a room you want to leave, but you know that what awaits you outside threatens to suffocate you in other ways. Your parents have probably already gone to work, leaving you to take care of your younger brothers and sisters. Outside the apartment are streets marked by congestion and a catalog of catastrophe. This, James Baldwin tells us, is what it often felt like to be trapped in the "Harlem ghetto" of his youth.[1]

Now imagine waking up to find yourself in a large room in a mansion with over one hundred other rooms. As you make your way into the day, you find that there are servants attending to your every need and desire. As you step outside the mansion, you are confronted with seemingly endless natural space to explore. You look forward to the time when you will be free to do so, but you know that first, a nice breakfast awaits you, and then a day carefully planned by your numerous tutors to include plenty of nourishment for your mind and soul as well. This, William F. Buckley Jr. tells us, is what it felt like to grow up on one of his family's estates.

Although Baldwin and Buckley did not begin making waves on the intellectual scene until the late 1940s, their arrivals did not occur ex nihilo. In their youth, both men were shaped by the environments in which they found themselves and the intellectual influences that were exerted on them. As such, it is worthwhile to consider a few relevant matters about the early years of Baldwin and Buckley.[2]

Emma "Berdis" Jones was a Marylander by birth who made her way north during the Great Migration of African Americans out of the South in the first quarter of the twentieth century. On August 2, 1924, she gave birth to her first child, James, at Harlem Hospital. His biological father remains a mystery, but when James was still a toddler, his mother married David Baldwin, the son of slaves who had recently made his way north from New Orleans. Berdis and David would have eight more children, the youngest of which would be born on the day David died in 1943.

Baldwin's relationships with his mother and stepfather would be of vital importance to his intellectual development, but before we consider these relationships we must examine the environment in which the Baldwin family found itself: Harlem of the 1920s and 1930s. By the time Baldwin was born, Harlem was well on its way to becoming the country's largest black ghetto. What was once a relatively diverse neighborhood—with many Italians, Irish, and Jews—was by the end of the 1920s almost 100 percent black and brown.[3] Harlem was, of course, the site of an incredible artistic scene that reached its apex with the "Renaissance" of the 1920s, but during Baldwin's childhood it became the hub of a great deal of economic privation, with many residents out of work, and those who were able to find a job were paid about 25 percent less than their white counterparts.[4]

The cost of living in Harlem only compounded the economic distress most families experienced. As Baldwin often noted later in life, it is incredibly expensive to be poor.[5] The formal and informal enforcement of racial boundaries in housing made it possible for ghetto landlords to charge more for less. By the mid-1930s, most Harlemites lived in housing that was in desperate need of repair, and lacked central heating and indoor plumbing. And yet in the words of one historian, "Rents remained higher than economically comparable neighborhoods" around the city. The most economically depressed parts of Harlem were, furthermore, desperately overcrowded, with "820 people per acre, or about three times the Manhattan average."[6] Due to these conditions and inadequate health

FIGURE 1.1. 125th Street in Harlem, circa 1935 (Bettmann Collection / Getty Images)

care, the "mortality rate in central Harlem was 40 percent higher than the city average during the early years of the Depression, while the infant mortality rate was twice the city average."[7]

It was in this environment that David and Berdis Baldwin attempted to raise James and his siblings. David was a day laborer and lay Pentecostal preacher, and Berdis worked as a housekeeper. Like most Harlemites, they often struggled to find work, and when they did, they were paid less than their white counterparts in the city. When they were unable to find enough work to feed themselves and their children, they sought relief from the government. Like many other black families, they were frequently demoralized by the almost all-white staff of the Home Relief Bureau, which visited the homes of would-be recipients to determine their worthiness for support. Not surprisingly, blacks were denied benefits at a far greater rate than white applicants.[8]

This was the Harlem in which Baldwin was born and raised, and it had a profound impact on the thinker he would become. Baldwin believed that coming to grips with the conditions of the "Harlem ghetto" was important to be sure, but there was an even more crucial task to be undertaken. We must come to grips, he thought, with the very existence of the Harlem ghetto and ghettos like it in every other American city. How did these spaces come into being, and why do they continue to exist? What does this indicate about the moral lives of those who created and maintained them, and what do these ghettos do to the moral lives of those who are trapped within them? These would be some of the questions that haunted Baldwin from his childhood to his dying day.

A little over a year after Baldwin was born and in the same city, Aloïse Steiner Buckley gave birth to William.[9] "Billy," as he would be called throughout his childhood, was the sixth of ten children born to Will Buckley and Aloïse. Will and Aloïse were both southerners, though of different types. Will was a Texan, who had made, lost, and regained fortunes in the real estate and oil businesses in the United States and abroad. Aloïse was born into a well-to-do family in New Orleans.[10] Will was a frenetic type, constantly on the move in pursuit of his next big financial conquest and, by the time Billy was born, could be counted among the nouveau riche. Aloïse came from "old money," her grandfathers served in the Confederate Army during the Civil War, and she was firmly rooted in the values and mores of the "Old South."[11]

The environment of Billy's upbringing makes for a stark contrast with the Harlem of Baldwin's youth. A year prior to his birth, Buckley's father purchased "Great Elm," a forty-seven-acre estate in Sharon, Connecticut. The estate featured a large mansion and extensive staff to tend to the large family's every need.[12] Life at Great Elm was carefully regimented, with clear hierarchies, duties, and schedules.[13] Save for a two-year stint living in Paris with his family and a year at a British boarding school, Billy's central childhood experience was the "unmitigated pleasures" of Great Elm. The freedom and joy of the summer, he observed

FIGURE 1.2. Great Elm, the Buckley estate in Sharon, Connecticut
(LIFE Picture Collection / Getty Images)

in autobiographical writings, continued "almost seamlessly" once the "school year" began because "we were taught by tutors right there in the same rooms in which we played when indoors during summer." "When school began for us at the end of September," Buckley explained, "we continued to ride horseback every afternoon, we swam two or three times every day," and "our musical tutors continued to come to us just as they had during the summer, and some us would rise early and hunt pheasants at our farm before school."[14] As his brother Reid put it, "To us children, Sharon was heaven on earth."[15]

When not enjoying the vast outdoors of the estate, the Buckley children received a demanding, if unconventional, education. Billy was primarily homeschooled through the eighth grade (with the exception of one year in a British boarding school). The family employed two full-time teachers, and hired a number of part-time tutors, coaches, and instructors to fill out the academic and extracurricular program.[16] According to Billy's sister, Aloise, her father's "theory of childrearing" was straightforward: "He brought up his sons and daughters with the quite simple objective that they become absolutely perfect." To achieve that end, he saw to it that his children receive professional instruction in, well, just about everything.[17]

The education of the Buckley children continued informally around the dinner table, where the family would engage in spirited discussions of everything under the sun.[18] Everyone in the family, Reid explained later, was "passionately opinionated" and cared deeply about not only the substance of an opinion but also the style with which it was delivered. "No opinion," Reid recalled, "was by our reckoning worth the name that wasn't worth holding with all our hearts and souls, so that every meal we argued ferociously about novels and poetry and the latest 'flick' we had seen."[19] Reid remembered the family being "quarrelsome" about many things, but it is worth noting that politics and religion were not among them. On these matters, the family was in complete agreement.[20]

Within the environments thus described, the minds of Baldwin and Buckley were shaped—first and foremost—by their relationships to their parents. Both men grew up in households that were basically patriarchal, but they viewed their mothers as important moral teachers. Baldwin would devote far more of his autobiographical writing to reflections on his stepfather than he would to thoughts on his mother, but he often credited her with teaching him the meaning of resilience and what it meant to love another human being. She lived and wanted her children to live, he recalled, by the golden rule, and she taught "that people have to be loved for their faults as well as their virtues, their ugliness as well as their beauty." Although Baldwin would grapple with questions of faith throughout his life, he would identify his mother as a true Christian, in the best sense possible. She sacrificed for others, forgave them for their sins, and most important, she knew what it meant to love another human being. Berdis's lessons about the meaning of love ended up being the anchor of Baldwin's "personal ideology" for the rest of his life.[21]

Buckley, like Baldwin, thought of his mother as a kind of moral exemplar. The virtue that Buckley saw as most central to his mother's character was her piety. She was "as devoted a child of God as I have ever known," he remembered, who "worshipped God as intensely as the saint transfixed." Aloïse expressed her devotion by regular attendance at mass and prayed frequently in a quest to understand the "rules" God wanted human beings to follow in the world. As Buckley watched his mother act on her understanding of those rules, he was struck by the "vivacity," "humor," and personal charm she exhibited with everyone she encountered.[22] It is clear that these elements of her personality—both her public sense of devotion to God and capacity for charm—had a great impact on Buckley, who would follow in his mother's footsteps in both respects.

One other aspect of Aloïse's personality is especially relevant to the themes of this book. Buckley recalled that "although Father was the unchallenged authority at home, Mother was unchallengeably in charge of arrangements in a house crowded with ten children and as many tutors, servants, and assistants."[23] As Buckley watched his mother govern her households (the family would also acquire an estate in South Carolina and spend extended periods abroad), there can be little doubt that he absorbed some crucial lessons about the possibility of beneficent hierarchies, racial and otherwise. Aloïse, Reid would confess, was "a racist" in the sense that she "assumed that white people were intellectually superior to black people," but he explained, "She truly loved black people and felt securely comfortable with them from the assumption of her superiority in intellect, character, *and station*." Blacks were, to her, "dear, kind, simple people," and she felt, Reid explained, a sense of noblesse oblige to those who remained loyal to the family over the years.[24] Hers was a genteel, maternal racism, and there can be little doubt that it shaped her children's worldviews. As we will see again and again in the pages that follow, few things rankled Buckley more than the conflation of racial attitudes like those of his mother with those of racists motivated by hatred. It was possible, he would insist, to reject racial egalitarianism while at the same time treating those of other races humanely. When he made such claims, there can be little doubt he had his mother in mind.

Most of what we need to know about the early intellectual development of Buckley and Baldwin can be gleaned from how each man viewed his father. From an early age, Billy idolized his father. Indeed, by the age of five, he was so taken with his father that he announced that he would abandon his given middle name, Francis, in order to become William Frank Buckley Jr.[25] Although Will was away from the family quite a bit on business and was described as a relatively shy presence, there can be no doubt that he was a dominant influence in the household. He believed he was a "self-made man," and this self-perception undoubtedly played some role in the ideology he would develop and impart to his children. Devout Catholicism was one strand in Will's creed, but the other strands were focused on worldly concerns. Will was, at his core, an individualist. He believed that individuals could impose their will on the world and achieve great things. This core belief in individualism led Will to shudder at the rise of leftist movements around the world and to view American progressivism with deep skepticism. Will's suspicion of state power led him to staunchly oppose Franklin Delano Roosevelt and the New Deal, and it played some part in his embrace of the America First Committee's opposition to US intervention in World War II.[26]

It is safe to say that Will's embrace of the America First Committee's position was rooted only in part in his resistance to state power because his anti-Semitism played some role as well. In his writings later in life, Buckley was relatively open about this failing of his father; perhaps in part because it seems to be an inheritance he was able to shed at a fairly early age.[27] When reflecting on his father's anti-Semitism, Buckley told biographer John Judis that he recalled someone telling him "he would leave the room if ever someone in it said something about the Jews which he had heard routinely at his own dinner table." "That exactly expresses the situation," Buckley explained to Judis, "in my home."[28]

Aloïse was the most consistent presence in the organization of the particulars of the unconventional education the Buckley children received at the family's estates, yet Will's impact was felt not only during disquisitions at the dinner table but also in the recruitment of occasional guests who would speak to the children about matters moral and political. The man who had the most lasting impact on this front was the individualist intellectual Albert Jay Nock, who taught the Buckley children to distrust democracy and embrace the idea that "a Remnant" of elites ought to govern society.[29] Another influence worth noting, though not an intellectual to be sure, was the segregationist South Carolina politician Strom Thurmond, who the family got to know during its winter stays in the palmetto state. Will's love for Thurmond was so strong he once told him "he knew of no other politician whose views he entirely approved of."[30]

Buckley, "born to absolutes" and "nurtured on dogma," did not accept everything his parents taught him, but the basic outline of his worldview was set at a young age.[31] This worldview consisted of an amalgamation of devout Catholicism, antidemocratic individualism, hostility to collectivism in economics, and a strong devotion to hierarchy—including racial hierarchy—in the social sphere.[32] Although Buckley did not end up aspiring to follow in his father's professional footsteps, he did devote himself to conserving most of the key components of his father's point of view. "As a writer, speaker and debater," Aloise wrote, "his son, Bill, was the essence of all W.F.B. himself had stood and fought for politically."[33] On the level of the personal relationship between father and son, then, we see another stunning contrast with Baldwin, whose life's work was devoted in part to articulating why his father's worldview ought to be rejected.

The "man I called my father," Baldwin once wrote, "really *was* my father in every sense except the biological, or literal one. He formed me, and he raised me, and he did not let me starve."[34] Over the course of his life, Baldwin was—personally, philosophically, and creatively—simultaneously haunted and fascinated by David Baldwin Sr. His reflections on the meaning of David's life and the impact of his relationship to him would be the central themes of Baldwin's writing. He would come to view his father as a complex figure for whom he had some sympathy, but his life would always serve, fundamentally, as a cautionary tale of how not to live. David was, in short, the embodiment of bitterness and self-hatred, and for this reason, Baldwin came to reject his teachings with just about every fiber of his being.

Although a great deal of Baldwin's writing about his father would focus on matters spiritual and psychological, the physical facts of David's life should not be ignored. David, like so many others in the first generation of "free men," left the South in search of greater opportunity in the North, only to find a life that kept him at the margins of society. He was often unable to find work, and even when he did have a job, his work was back-breaking and the rung he occupied on the economic ladder was thoroughly demoralizing. "I remember my father had trouble keeping us alive," Baldwin told an interviewer in 1963. "I understand him much better now. Part of his problem was he couldn't feed his kids."[35]

One of the ways David dealt with his status at the margins of society was to shield himself with a rigid armor of religiosity. In an open letter to his nephew that was published in 1962, Baldwin explained the connection between his father's marginalization and his faith when he wrote that his father "had a terrible life; he was defeated long before he died because, at the bottom of his heart, he really believed what white people said about him. This is one of the reasons he became so holy."[36] The church, he explained to an interviewer, was the "only means" his parents had to express "their pain and their despair."[37] David was convinced that it was only holiness that could protect him and his family from the cruel world that surrounded them. This led him to express his love in an "outrageously demanding and protective way," and to be extraordinarily "bitter" in his outlook and "indescribably cruel" in his personal relationships. David's bitterness was rooted in the "humiliation" he felt in his everyday life, and it led him to view those he thought the authors of that humiliation—all white people—with suspicion. It also extended to his fellow blacks, though, most of whom he viewed as insufficiently holy. At home, David attempted to rule the family in an authoritarian fashion that left James and his siblings in a constant state of fear. "I do not remember, in all those years," he wrote in 1955, "that one of his children was ever glad to see him come home."[38]

As young Baldwin watched his father, he saw a great deal that he wanted to avoid. His father was "menaced" by the world around him, and this was a fate Jimmy recognized he could not easily circumvent.[39] But he did not want to follow the route his father had chosen as his way through this menacing world. David, as far as his son could tell, had allowed the cruel world to overtake him, and so cruelty itself became the core of his being, the means by which he would defend and define himself. As David grasped for a lever of power in a world in which he was essentially powerless, the only one he could find was composed of a deadly combination of fear and loathing. In exchange for the small sense of pride this gave him in his life, he was forced to sacrifice his "dignity" or, as Baldwin would put it later, "the health of his soul."[40] This was a price that even a young Baldwin knew was far too high.

In 1929 Baldwin began school at P.S. 24, and it did not take long for him to gain recognition as a student with enormous potential. Outside school, he read constantly (with a special fondness for Harriet Beecher Stowe and Charles Dickens) and began experimenting with writing.[41] He became obsessed with the power of words to connect human beings across time and space. Books were, for him, not merely an escape but also a means to make sense of his experience. Over the next several years, Baldwin's love of the creative arts expanded to film and theater, and he was fortunate enough to find several teachers—most notably Bill Miller and Countee Cullen—who took an interest in his intellectual development and encouraged him to cultivate his love of reading, writing, and the arts.[42] Miller took Baldwin to see live theater and the movies, and offered the Baldwin family financial support in especially tough economic times. Cullen, one of the great poets of the Harlem Renaissance, was one of Baldwin's teachers at Frederick Douglass Junior High School and encouraged him to apply to attend the prestigious DeWitt Clinton High

School in the Bronx.[43] Without the support and encouragement of these two teachers, the world may have never gotten to know Baldwin.

At the age of fourteen, while many of his peers were beginning to experiment with alcohol, tobacco, sex, and petty crime, Baldwin sought refuge in the church. After a dramatic conversion experience, he went beyond merely "joining the church as another worshipper." Instead, he "intended to best" his "father on his own ground" by becoming "a preacher—a young minister."[44] For the next three years, Baldwin's sermons proved to be a bigger draw than his father's, and he was permitted to spend a great deal of time alone in order to write his sermons. With this solitude, he was able to devote himself to his love of reading and writing.

Later in life, when Baldwin reflected on his escape into the church, he concluded that it was rooted in a quest to find some means by which to protect himself from the power of his father along with the "vast and merciless" world around him. As a "handle" or "gimmick" to help him navigate the environment in which he found himself, "the church racket," as Baldwin called it, proved to be the one to which his "capabilities" were best suited.[45] Even as a young man, Baldwin had a way with words and a flair for the dramatic. He was a natural in the pulpit, and although the armor provided by the church was of little value in the face of the unbelievable cruelty around him, it was something, and something, he concluded, was better than nothing.

Baldwin's exit from the church will be discussed in great detail later in this book, but for now suffice it to say that the seeds of doubt were planted by a broadening of his intellectual horizons and the hypocritical deeds of the "true believers" he saw around him. Though not as sudden as the conversion experience that drew him into the church, Baldwin's conversion experience out of the church was just as profound. The "fortress" of his faith, he wrote later, had been "pulverized."[46]

Right around the same time Baldwin was falling away from the church, he was introduced to Beauford Delaney, the man one biographer calls "the most important influence in his life."[47] Delaney was a black painter who lived in Greenwich Village, and it did not take Baldwin long to see he was a kindred spirit. Delaney became a sort of father-mentor figure in Baldwin's life and had an enduring impact on how the budding writer would see the world. Indeed, as Baldwin would explain later, it was "the reality" of Delaney's "seeing that caused me to begin to see." Delaney, Baldwin noticed, was "*seeing* all the time"; he was, in other words, a "witness" who was able to use all that he saw as fuel for his creativity. Although his medium was different, Delaney taught Baldwin what it meant to be an artist. His work, Baldwin said later, brings about "a new experience of reality" for those who are able to see it. The ability to bring about a new experience of reality is not only a great "triumph" for an artist, Delaney showed Baldwin, but also is a transformative act of love. "No greater lover," Baldwin noted of Delaney, "ever held a brush." Baldwin's time with Delaney fueled his dreams that he might be able one day to do with his pen what the great painter did with his brush.[48]

Although Baldwin was not a stellar student in high school, he did thrive in the endeavors that held his attention. The most notable of these was his editorship of the *Magpie*, the school's literary magazine. Baldwin had been writing creatively for about as long as he had been able to read, and the *Magpie* allowed him to share his talents with others. His teachers were quite impressed. One called him a "talented and modest boy, who will surely go far," and another declared him to be "an intellectual giant."[49]

After years of homeschooling and one year of boarding school in England, Buckley was sent to an elite prep school called Millbrook. While there, he excelled academically, thrived in debate, and made a name for himself by being "obnoxiously Catholic" and vociferously conservative.[50] Buckley promoted the America First Committee's opposition to US intervention in World War II at Millbrook, a place where they were "distinctly unpopular."[51] Buckley's parents noted their pride in their fifteen-year-old son's "attitude of having strong convictions and of not being too bashful to express them." Indeed, Buckley's forthrightness was on full display when he "appeared uninvited at a faculty meeting" at Millbrook in order to criticize a faculty member who had "deprived him of the right to express his political views in class" before he "proceeded to expound to the stunned faculty on the virtues of isolationism, the dignity of the Catholic church and the political ignorance of the school staff."[52]

Buckley did not mind finding himself on the deviant side of political arguments. He cared far less about being popular than he did about being right. His upbringing led him to feel at home in the position of "outsider." This was the Buckley way. "In the largely Episcopalian and mainline Protestant, Anglo-Saxon Connecticut," Reid wrote, "we were Catholics, Irish, and Southern." In the South, where the family spent its winters, the Buckleys were considered Yankees. This upbringing, Reid concluded, made the Buckley children "pretty fair polemicists," and Billy was the best of the bunch. With so many arguments to be had, the Buckleys "never wasted time doubting [their] convictions."[53] While at Millbrook, Buckley was confronted with challenge after challenge to his worldview, but this led him to cling even tighter to his creed.

Buckley graduated from Millbrook in 1943, and in 1944—after a brief deferment due to a sinus problem—he was inducted into the US Army and was eventually accepted into officer candidate school at Fort Benning in Georgia.[54] Thanks to the many winters he spent in Camden, South Carolina, Buckley was probably not too shocked by what he found when he reported for duty. The army into which Buckley was inducted was segregated, and black soldiers from the period wrote about the harshness of the conditions. "It is no secret," noted a corporal at a southern army camp in 1944, "that the Negro soldier in the South is as much persecuted as his civilian brother." The conditions in his camp, he continued, "are intolerable, and may be considered on par with the worst conditions throughout the South since 1865." The treatment of blacks in the American military during World War II was made all the more bitter by the fact that the United States was at war with a German regime that preached a doctrine of racial hierarchy. This cruel irony was not lost on black soldiers. On a crowded troop train in Texas, one reported that "the colored soldiers were fed behind a Jim Crow curtain at one end of the dining car. In the main section, along with the white folks, a group of German war prisoners dined—and no doubt fed their illusions of race superiority on that Jim Crow curtain."[55]

None of the cruelty of segregation seems to have had any effect on Buckley, who actually reported to his parents that the practices at Fort Benning were far too racially progressive for his taste. "There are also some Negroes here," he wrote to his father. "This I don't particularly like, but there's nothing much I can do about it. I haven't had to do much with any of them yet, but I imagine they are the highest type of Negroes."[56]

Right around the same time Buckley was lamenting the fact that he was being forced to share Fort Benning with black soldiers, Baldwin was learning, in a new way, what it meant to be black in America. After he graduated from high school, he was able to avoid military service as the oldest child in a family that was in financial distress.[57] He found work at various defense plants in New Jersey, and it was there that he had his first extensive encounters with white southerners. Throughout his childhood and teenage years, Baldwin had come face-to-face with racism when he was confronted by police or "the housewives, taxi-drivers, elevator boys, dishwashers, bartenders, lawyers, doctors, and grocers" who were all prone to use "the color line" as an "outlet" for their "frustrations and hostilities."[58] But in New Jersey, Baldwin was introduced to racism of a different sort. In his interaction with the southerners and those policing the color line in the New Jersey suburbs, he discovered a brand of racism that was more belligerent and virulent than what he had encountered in New York City. Baldwin's first reaction to this behavior was disbelief. "I simply did not know," he wrote later, "what was happening. I did not know what I had done, and I shortly began to wonder what *anyone* could possibly do, to bring about such unanimous, active, and unbearably vocal hostility."[59]

In addition to confronting this sort of belligerent racial hostility, Baldwin was introduced to a more passive, almost-robotic racism. During his time in New Jersey, he became accustomed to seeing and hearing the phrase "We don't serve Negroes here." After several "dreadful" encounters with servers at such establishments, Baldwin finally "snapped" on what would be his last night in New Jersey. He and a friend went to the movies and wanted to get a bite to eat afterward. When they were denied service at a restaurant aptly named "the American Diner," Baldwin said he felt "a click at the nape of my neck as though some interior string connecting my head to my body had been cut," and he walked into "an enormous, glittering, and fashionable restaurant" nearby. He sat down at a table and eventually a server appeared: "She did not ask me what I wanted, but repeated, as though she had learned it somewhere, 'We don't serve Negroes here.' She did not say it with the blunt, derisive hostility to which I had grown accustomed, but, rather, with a note of apology in her voice, and fear." The racism of this white waitress was more enraging to Baldwin than the belligerence he dealt with on a daily basis at the defense plants. He detected in her voice that she *knew* (in a way that the belligerent racist did not) that she was treating him unjustly and that she also knew that there was good reason to be fearful. She could see "the fever" in Baldwin's eyes in a way that those others could not. This made him "more cold and more murderous than ever." He picked up a water mug on the table and "hurled it with all my strength at her. She ducked and it missed her and shattered against the mirror behind the bar."[60]

That night, Baldwin eluded the mob and the police that pursued him, and he realized that he needed to escape far more than that. He recognized not only that he could have been murdered that night but perhaps more disturbingly, he also saw that his rage had almost led him to murder someone else. "I saw nothing very clearly but I did see this: that my life, my *real* life, was in danger, and not from anything other people might do but from the hatred I carried in my own heart."[61]

In 1943 Baldwin returned to Harlem, where his father was nearing death. David had been physically ill for some time and had begun to exhibit signs of mental illness. Baldwin believed that his father's physical and mental illnesses were worsened by the bitterness that dominated his life. When it became clear that he was a danger to himself and others, David was committed to a hospital for the mentally ill and, on July 28, died—as many Harlemites did—of complications from tuberculosis.[62] Later that same day, Baldwin's mother gave birth to her last child, Paula Maria.

After a brief stay with his family in Harlem, Baldwin escaped to Greenwich Village, where he tried to make ends meet with a series of odd jobs, the most important of which was as a waiter at a restaurant called the Calypso. At the Calypso and in the Village generally, Baldwin engaged in self-exploration on several levels. Intellectually, his time at the Calypso afforded him opportunities to interact with an incredible roster of regulars who would achieve prominence on the political and artistic scene, including C. L. R. James, Claude McKay, Alain Locke, Paul Robeson, Burt Lancaster, Marlon Brando, and Eartha Kitt.[63] Baldwin loved to talk and, like Buckley, loved to argue. The setting and clientele of the Calypso was, in some ways, an ideal place for the aspiring writer to entertain ideas and expand his intellectual horizons.

Baldwin's time in the Village was also an important phase in the development of his sexual identity. He had several relationships that ranged in length from one night to several months with both men and women, and although the Village was more hospitable than most places to those who were labeled as "queer," Baldwin was not entirely sure where he fit in. He was not "attracted to men whom he considered to be pretentiously effeminate" and so he often found himself "with the more ambiguous sort, and he suffered the abuse that derived from their shame."[64] Although Baldwin was more sexually attracted to men than he was to women, he fell in love with several women during this period and did not feel comfortable then—or ever—with the idea of putting a label on his sexual identity.[65] When asked about his sexual preference, Baldwin was fond of saying, "Love is where you find it."[66]

It was during these years in the Village that Baldwin would make the connections that would help him gain entrée to the New York literary scene. In December 1943, he met and befriended a young black leftist named Eugene Worth. It was through this relationship that Baldwin was introduced to several New York intellectuals who would give him his start as a professional writer. Worth, Baldwin explained later, would introduce him to the "people who were to take me to Saul Levitas, of *The New*

Leader, Randall Jarrell, of *The Nation*, Elliot Cohen and Robert Warshow, of *Commentary*, and Philip Rahv, of *Partisan Review*."[67] Baldwin's introduction to these leading New York editors was crucial to his development because it was through them that he was able to learn how one might make a living as a writer. Levitas would eventually suggest "a book review per week as a useful discipline" to force Baldwin to his writing desk in order to meet regular deadlines.[68] For Baldwin, who was trying to make ends meet and enjoying a vibrant social life, the goal of one review a week ended up being a bit out of reach. He did, though, accept Levitas's invitation to take up book reviewing and through these short pieces was able to establish himself as an estimable literary provocateur.

In the thick of these bohemian years in the Village, Baldwin would catch another break that proved to be of the utmost importance. While he was working at the Calypso, Baldwin was in the early stages of writing what would become his first novel, *Go Tell It on the Mountain*, and would occasionally read aloud from his works in progress during bull sessions with the patrons and employees of the restaurant. One such patron was sufficiently impressed with what she heard that she decided to introduce him to Richard Wright, the Mississippi-born black novelist who had electrified the literary scene with his novel *Native Son*. In winter 1945, Baldwin met with Wright, who looked at some of his work and decided to recommend him for a literary fellowship, which he received.[69]

But things would get worse for Baldwin before they got better. He had a difficult time making progress with his writing, and in 1946, his friend Worth committed suicide. In later years, Baldwin would identify this event as a crucial turning point in his life. He had fallen in love with Worth, and although the two were "never lovers," this relationship proved to be of great significance.[70] Worth became a symbol of idealism for Baldwin. He had been a member of the Young People's Socialist League and dreamed of a revolution that would bring about justice on earth. And yet at every turn, the world told Worth that his revolution would never come and that the color of his skin made him less than fully human. This was more than a dreamer like Worth could possibly bear. And so in 1946, he threw himself off the George Washington Bridge.[71]

Although Baldwin would never adopt Worth's idealism—he remained a member of the Young People's Socialist League only long enough to conclude "it may be impossible to indoctrinate me"—he thought the story of his fallen friend revealed something significant about the sickness of the country's soul and what he might need to do to save his own. What kind of a country, he asked himself, drives a compassionate young man like Worth to self-destruction? And what must I do, he wondered, to avoid the same fate?

Chapter 2

Disturbing the Peace, 1946–54

In fall 1946, Buckley took up residence in New Haven, Con-necticut, to begin his freshman year at Yale, and a growing number of New York intellectuals were taking notice of an "intensely serious," "delicate," "intuitive," "rash," "impractical," "rebellious," and "mercurial" young man named James Baldwin.[1] Some of these intellectuals were so taken with this young man that they started inviting him to review books for the magazines they edited, and within months, his byline would begin appearing on American newsstands.[2]

As Buckley and Baldwin reached these pivotal moments, they were attempting to figure out how to make their way in the world. Buckley's time in the army proved to be critical on this front. His insulated upbringing had set him back socially, and at Millbrook he often dismissed anyone who deviated from his religious or political views as "stupid." This did not make him many friends. In a letter to his mother, Buckley reported that his time in the army had allowed him to learn "the importance of tolerance and the importance of proportion about all matters." Buckley decided to try to better understand those with alternative perspectives and perhaps even befriend them.[3] As we will see in a moment, it does not appear that Buckley became any less dogmatic while at Yale, but he did demonstrate enhanced social skills that would end up being crucial in his ascent to positions of influence on campus and after graduation.

Baldwin seemed to his friends in the Village to be always bouncing between "grief" and "delight." The writer Norman Mailer described him a few years later as "sensitive, like an exposed nerve." Baldwin's sensitivity and proclivity to depression were probably at the root of his tendency to move "swiftly, constantly, like a flickering light."[4] It was almost as if Baldwin thought that so long as he kept moving, the grief and rage that haunted him might not be able to catch up. When he was not on the move, Baldwin was writing, the vocation that would launch him to international prominence and help him keep his demons at bay.

⸻

Baldwin did not waste any time using his literary criticism to make bold pronouncements about the role of the writer in society. [5] The writer, he declared, ought to help their reader understand themselves, others, and the world around them. In order to do that, the writer must be a "realist" whose prose is free from the subterfuge of sentimentality and ideology. In his first published piece—a 1947 review for the *Nation* magazine of Maksim Gorky's *Best Short Stories*—he brought his realist lens to bear on the famous Russian author and objected to his tendency to be "frequently sentimental" instead of engaging in "honest exploration of those provinces, the human heart and mind, which have operated, historically and now, as the no man's land between us and our salvation."[6]

Baldwin's extension of realism to nonfiction writing was on display later in 1947 in another review for the *Nation*. In *There Once Was a Slave*, Shirley Graham told, as her subtitle described it, "The Heroic Story of Frederick Douglass." Douglass was the most prominent African American political leader of the nineteenth century, and Graham was certainly not the first—or the last—to consider his role in history to be a heroic one. For her efforts, Graham had received the Julian Messner Award "for having written the best book combatting racial intolerance in America." The stature of the subject and author—Graham was a well-respected writer and activist who would later marry W.E.B. DuBois, the "dean" of African American intellectuals—might have led many a reviewer to approach the book with a great deal of deference. In his assessment of Graham, the audacious twenty-three-year-old Baldwin was anything but deferential. The central problem with the book, he argued, was that it was not really a biography of Douglass at all. It was not, in other words, a genuine attempt to tell the truth about a real human being. Instead, Graham used Douglass to communicate a certain set of ideas about "the position of the Negro in America today." Graham, Baldwin explained, "is so obviously determined to Uplift the Race that she makes Douglass a quite unbelievable hero and has robbed him of dignity and humanity alike." In "her frenzied efforts" to make Douglass "a symbol of Freedom" and "an example of what the Negro Race can produce," Graham "has reduced a significant, passionate human being to the obscene level of a Hollywood caricature."[7]

Baldwin's critique of Graham was not only literary; it was also political. The Julian Messner Award notwithstanding, he was doubtful that a book like Graham's (even if widely read) could make "any contribution to interracial understanding" or the "battle against intolerance."[8] Such racial progress, the young Baldwin argued, was more likely to be promoted by a different sort of writing: "Relations between Negroes and whites demand honesty and insight; they must be based on the assumption that there is one race and that we are all a part of it."[9] Treating human beings as symbols, even when done for a good cause, is a major obstacle to interracial understanding and justice.

⁓

While Baldwin was getting his start as a literary critic in New York, Buckley was on his way to establishing himself as "the most visible figure" in Yale's class of 1950.[10] Buckley had arrived in New Haven in September 1946 as an almost-twenty-one-year-old freshman, recently honorably discharged from the US Army. The incoming class of which Buckley was a part was three times the size of the typical one because, as he explained later, "one of Yale's contributions to the war effort had been to make a comprehensive promise to matriculate, once the war was over, every single student it had accepted from the graduating secondary-school classes during the war." So Buckley and many members of his class arrived on campus with a different attitude than the typical "apple-cheeked freshmen straight out of high school or prep school." As Buckley remembered it, one of the most dramatic differences between the veterans and nonveterans at Yale was the former's sense of urgency. "We were in something of a hurry to get on," he wrote later, "get some learning, get married, get started in life."[11] But it was not just a sense of urgency that distinguished many of these veterans, according to Raymond

Price Jr., who was one year behind Buckley at Yale; it was also a sense of "purpose."[12]

There is little question about Buckley's sense of purpose when he arrived on campus. His worldview was dominated by two commitments above all: Christianity and right-wing politics. Buckley's faith in Christianity was deep, and although Catholics were a distinct minority at Yale (about 13 percent of the student body), he expected the institution, in the words of its then president Charles Seymour, to advance the "tremendous validity and power of the teaching of Christ."[13] Buckley used the term "individualism" as a catchall for the right-wing political philosophy that he had inherited from his parents and had fortified by his encounters with Albert Jay Nock. Although the precise contours of this philosophy were yet to be developed, certain core tenets were already there during his early college years. He was a staunch defender of the free enterprise system and an anti-Communist, and was opposed to the expanded role government had taken on during the New Deal.

While at Yale, Buckley ended up pursuing a "divisional" major in the social sciences. He did not have any desire to utilize his coursework to rethink the religious and political commitments that had been inculcated in his household for as long as he could remember. During his freshman year, one of his instructors encouraged him to take a course in metaphysics. "I have God and my father," Buckley replied. "That's all I need."[14]

Although the substance of Buckley's worldview seemed unlikely to change during his stay in New Haven, his mind did receive a considerable jolt when he encountered political science professor Willmoore Kendall during the fall semester of his sophomore year. Kendall was a relatively young, tall, and charismatic Oklahoman who had recently arrived at Yale after a stint as an intelligence officer. Buckley would later describe Kendall as "a genius of sorts."[15] He graduated from college at the age of eighteen, spent time at Oxford as a Rhodes scholar, and made several important contributions to the field of political theory before his fortieth birthday. Kendall was learned, opinionated, and conservative. Buckley had found himself a mentor.

Kendall influenced Buckley on many levels. Substantively, the most important thing Kendall taught Buckley was that the idea of an "open society"—which had recently been popularized by the Austrian thinker Karl Popper—was a dangerous illusion. Rather than promoting an ethos of epistemic humility, open inquiry, and critical thought, Kendall advocated the enforcement of a "public orthodoxy," which he defined later as "that tissue of judgments defining the good life and indicating the meaning of human existence, which is held commonly by the members of any given society, who see in it the charter of their way of life and ultimate justification of their society."[16]

Kendall's philosophical commitment to the idea of public orthodoxy manifested itself politically in his fervent anti-Communism, or as he would call it later, "egghead McCarthyism."[17] Kendall had, once upon a time, been a Trotskyist, but by the time Buckley met him, he was well along on his journey to the Far Right. The story that Buckley loved to tell about Kendall's anti-Communism went something like this. In the midst of the latest Red Scare, Kendall's Yale colleagues were shocked and appalled by the jailing of several leaders of the Communist Party. After he listened to his fellow political scientists express their righteous indignation for two hours, Kendall stood up at a faculty meeting and reenacted a conversation he claimed to have had with a "colored janitor" on campus. "Is it true professor," Kendall imitated the janitor, "dat dere's people in New York City who want to . . . destroy the guvamint of the United States?" Kendall responded in the affirmative, and the janitor said, "Well, why don't we lock 'em up?" This janitor, Kendall told his faculty colleagues, demonstrated more "political wisdom" than they could muster in hours of moralistic alarmism about the issues at hand.[18] The janitor was, in his way, simply calling for the enforcement of the public orthodoxy.[19]

Buckley was able to see that Kendall's iconoclasm was not making him many friends on the Yale campus.[20] This drew him even closer to his mentor. Buckley had plenty of experience alienating those around him with deviant political views and admired Kendall's willingness to defend his positions, no matter what the social costs. Indeed, Buckley reported later that he thought Kendall might be "a conservative *because* he was surrounded by liberals." He was, at his core, a nonconformist who seemed to take some pleasure in being "socially disruptive."[21] Although Buckley would never endorse social disruption for its own sake, there was something immensely appealing to him about the adoption of an antiestablishment posture while in the thick of the establishment. You may not prove to be the most popular guy on the scene, but you sure would be able to have a lot of fun.

While Buckley was learning at the knee of Professor Kendall, Baldwin was continuing to establish himself on the New York literary scene. As a literary critic, he was using the work of others to figure out what it meant to be "an honest man and a good writer."[22] In the midst of his many review assignments for publications such as the Nation and the New Leader, Baldwin also wrote short fiction and essays. In 1948, he received a significant break when Commentary magazine invited him to write an essay about Harlem. Commentary had been founded in 1945 by the American Jewish Committee as a journal of "significant thought and opinion, Jewish affairs and contemporary issues."[23] Given this focus, the editors were especially interested in Baldwin's thoughts on the relationship between blacks and Jews in Harlem. The piece that resulted, "The Harlem Ghetto," marks the beginning of Baldwin's prolific career as an essayist. By the end of his life, many scholars would conclude that the essay was not only his best genre but that he also would go down in history as one of the finest essayists in the English language. "The Harlem Ghetto" features stylistic and substantive dimensions that would become fixtures of Baldwin's oeuvre. Baldwin dealt with his assigned topic in a way that combined gritty accounts of life on the ground in Harlem with bird's-eye reflections on human nature and social life. Substantively, he utilized the piece to offer insights on the moral psychology at the root of American race relations. These insights would prove to be the theoretical anchor of his work for decades to come.

One of the most striking things about "The Harlem Ghetto" is the fact that Baldwin does not address the assigned topic—the relationship between blacks and Jews in Harlem—until the last third of the essay. He did not believe one could really understand the relationship the editors wanted him to examine without first having a sense of the broader context of life in Harlem—its atmosphere, leaders, and culture. This would be a signature Baldwin move. In order to understand social and political phenomena, one must pan out from the specific matter at hand in order to get a sense of the broader context. One could not begin to comprehend the relationship between blacks and Jews in Harlem, Baldwin thought, without first getting a sense of the spaces in which they interacted.

Baldwin's Harlem was "pervaded by a sense of congestion, rather like the insistent, maddening claustrophobic pounding in the skull that comes from trying to breathe in a very small room with all of the windows shut." The press in Harlem, he argued, was generally lowbrow and marked by an emphasis on violence. "Negroes live violent lives, unavoidably," he explained. "A Negro press without violence is therefore not possible." Political leaders in Harlem, Baldwin reported to his mostly white readers, are much like the political leaders any place else: some fight nobly to "make life somewhat easier for parents" in the neighborhood while others are "far more concerned with their careers than with the welfare of Negroes."[24]

After providing the reader with a sense of what life was like in "The Harlem Ghetto," Baldwin turned his attention to the assigned topic: the relationship between blacks and Jews in the neighborhood. He began by pointing out that on a certain level of abstraction, there is a sense of connection blacks feel to Jews as a result of their shared history of marginalization and the fact that the religious experience of many blacks is deeply rooted in Old Testament texts. "The more devout Negro," Baldwin wrote, "considers that he *is* a Jew, in bondage, to a hard taskmaster and waiting for a Moses to lead him out of Egypt." This somewhat-abstract sense of connection, Baldwin declared, was no match for the actual power relationships between blacks and Jews in the neighborhood. "Jews in Harlem," Baldwin observed, "are small tradesmen, rent collectors, real estate agents, and pawnbrokers." For blacks, then, they were often the *face* of exploitation and oppression. It is, he continued, "the Jew whom the Negro hates most," for his hatred of the Jew "is an aspect of his humiliation whittled down to a manageable size and then transferred; it is the

best form the Negro has for tabulating vocally his long record of grievances against his native land." This hatred is compounded by the sense
that "the Jew should know better." For most Jews, though, the call of
conscience was all too often muted by the harsh realities of trying to
"climb higher on the American social ladder." On such a quest, there
is "nothing to gain from identification with any minority even more
unloved than he."[25]

In what would become another hallmark of his writing, Baldwin concluded the essay by offering a solution that was more spiritual than it
was political. "Sociological investigations and committee reports" have
identified the symptoms of "the cancer," and "recreational centers" and
the like have been proposed as treatment. This treatment may keep the
symptoms at bay in a limited way for a short time, but it cannot address
the root problem: "the furious, bewildered rage of people" who constantly
feel "the unendurable frustration of always being everywhere, inferior."
Until this root problem is addressed, the seeds of hatred will find ready
soil. "Just as society must have a scapegoat, so hatred must have a symbol. Georgia has the Negro and Harlem has the Jew."[26]

Buckley expected that while at Yale, he would be supplied with knowledge that would deepen his faith and better equip him to defend his conservative ideas. The student body was fairly conservative, and there were
right-wing professors here and there, but Buckley found the atmosphere
of the campus to be generally indifferent or hostile to his core commitments.[27] In the face of this perceived hostility, he found several outlets
through which to express his opposition. From his freshman year forward, he worked his way up the pecking order at the *Yale Daily News*,
and this, as we will see in a moment, would prove to have lasting consequences for him and Yale. In addition, he was one of three freshmen chosen for the debate team and thrived in this role throughout his college
career. Buckley had acquired his debating skills at the family dinner table
and developed them in the Forum, the debate program at Millbrook. His
friend Alistair Horne reported later that Buckley's extreme political views

often put him on the losing side of debates at Millbrook—even though he had demonstrated superior "forensic skill"—but "defeat and unpopularity only seemed to sharpen his appetite." Despite his out-of-the-mainstream views, Horne reports, Buckley was "judged easily the best Junior speaker of the year" and continued his forensic excellence throughout his senior year.[28]

At Yale, Buckley continued to hone his skills as a debater. He teamed up with L. Brent Bozell Jr.—who would go on to play an important role in his personal and professional life—to make up one of the most formidable teams the campus had ever seen. Bozell was judged by most to be the better speaker of the two, but Buckley found his niche as a master of rebuttal and ridicule. According to his coach, Buckley had "a flair for the dramatic" and knew how get under the skin of his opponents.[29] He was not particularly good at defending his own views—something Professor Kendall kidded him about "unmercifully"—but he knew how to go for the "jugular" of his opponent's argument.[30]

In addition to participating in debates with other students, the audacious Buckley would soon be invited to debate Yale faculty on a local radio program. One of his regular sparring partners was Yale law professor Thomas I. Emerson. Although Emerson was an elite scholar and almost two decades older than Buckley, he often found himself overwhelmed by the young man's forensic skills. "He was a rather formidable debater," Emerson said later, "and he was much better than I was. He used to talk circles around me, by and large." Years later, Emerson concluded Buckley was so effective because he was a master at appealing to the instincts and self-interest of the audience, and "finding the weakness of the liberal side." Furthermore, he was a skilled "hit-and-run debater. He would make his points very rapidly, very decisively; and before anyone could really reply he'd take off on another point, so that one could never get around to answering him."[31]

While Baldwin's writing career was getting off the ground and Buckley was establishing himself as a star debater at Yale, the country's racial and party politics were undergoing significant change. In 1947, Jackie Robinson became the first African American player in major league baseball since the late nineteenth century. His arrival in the major leagues was greeted with adulation by some and scorn by others. Later that year, a committee appointed by President Harry S. Truman proposed "the creation of a civil rights division in the Department of Justice, a permanent Federal Employment Practices Commission with enforcement powers; ending segregation in the armed forces; and federal legislation to punish lynching, secure voting rights, and [abolish] segregation in interstate transport."[32] Truman endorsed many of the committee's recommendations, but he faced strong opposition from southern Democrats in Congress. A. Philip Randolph, the president of the predominantly African American labor union known as the Brotherhood of Sleeping Car Porters, met with Truman and encouraged him to take executive action to end segregation in the armed forces. When the Democratic Party held its convention in Philadelphia in July 1948, the stage was set for a fight between racial progressives and conservatives. After a vigorous debate on the floor, progressives succeeded in getting several civil rights planks added to the platform, including a commitment to "eradicate all racial, religious and economic discrimination" by guaranteeing "the right to live, the right to work, the right to vote, [and] the full and equal protection of the laws."[33]

The adoption of these planks led a large contingent of southern delegates to walk out of the convention, and eventually, these people would form the States' Rights Democratic Party (aka the Dixiecrats) and nominate arch segregationist Strom Thurmond as their presidential candidate. The Dixiecrats adopted several planks in their platform that indicated precisely why they had seceded from the Democrats, including statements of opposition to "governmental interference" with "private employment," "the elimination of segregation," and "the repeal of miscegenation statutes" as well as declarations of support for "the racial integrity of each race," "home-rule," and "local self-government."[34] In his speech accepting the Dixiecrat nomination for president, Thurmond warned his audience that the "danger" before the country was "deadly in its seriousness." The choice before us, he said, was resistance to civil rights or a slide toward totalitarianism: "There is no question but that this follows in detail the pattern used in Germany and Italy by the dictators to destroy the liberties of those people."[35]

Around the same time, another group of disaffected Democrats met to nominate a candidate of their own. Henry A. Wallace of Iowa had served as vice president under Franklin Delano Roosevelt before being replaced on the ticket by the more conservative Truman in 1944. Wallace then served as secretary of commerce for Roosevelt and stayed on under Truman for about a year until the president dismissed him from office. The Progressive Party nominated Wallace as a left-wing alternative to Truman. Among other things, the Progressives called for an end to "all forms of discrimination in the armed services and Federal employment," and demanded "full equality" for people of all races as well as "federal anti-lynch, anti-discrimination, and fair-employment-practices legislation, . . . legislation abolishing segregation in interstate travel, [and] the enactment of a universal suffrage law."[36] Wallace toured the South during the campaign, and made a point of acting on the egalitarianism of his platform by speaking to unsegregated crowds as well as refusing to patronize segregated restaurants and hotels.[37]

With the Dixiecrats out the door and the major competition for votes focused on progressives of various party identifications, Truman acted quickly on civil rights on his return to Washington, DC, after the Democratic Convention. On July 26, he issued two executive orders—9980 and 9981—that established "a Fair Employment Board to promote non-discriminatory employment practices in the federal civil service," and declared "equal treatment and opportunity" in the armed forces to be "presidential policy."[38]

In the midst of this political tumult, Baldwin penned an essay on the Progressive Party called "Journey to Atlanta" for the *New Leader*. At first glance, it would seem that the Progressive Party would be attractive to the young, former socialist. Baldwin's reflections on the party, though, turned out to be anything but adulatory and reveal a great deal about the sort of lens through which he tended to view politics.

Rather than devoting the essay to a close reading of the Progressive Party platform or utterances of Wallace, Baldwin's "Journey" relied on what he believed to be the richest repository of truth: experience. Personal experience would eventually become Baldwin's primary source for much of his nonfiction writing, but in "Journey" he relied on the next best thing: the experiences of two younger brothers, who were invited by the Wallace campaign to perform their musical act at Progressive Party events in Atlanta. The basic idea, Baldwin's brother David reported, "was that we were supposed to sing," the music would attract a crowd, and then the party would "take over to make speeches and circulate petitions." David kept a "blow-by-blow account" of the journey, and this account served as the basis of his brother Jimmy's essay for the *New Leader*.[39]

"Journey" begins with Baldwin reflecting on what the Progressive Party phenomenon looked like through the eyes of a typical African American. "Of all Americans," Baldwin wrote, "Negroes distrust politicians most" because "they are always aware of the enormous gap between election promises and their daily lives." The "fatalistic indifference" to politics that results is exasperating to the "American liberal" whose faith in "education" fuels a profound hope in the possibilities of politics. This liberal viewed the "fatalistic indifference" of African Americans as a manifestation of "political irresponsibility" and immaturity. Baldwin, however, saw matters differently. This attitude was the "product of experience, experience which no amount of education can quite efface." The political experience of African Americans had been harsh. Their "one major devastating gain," of course, was emancipation. This was, without a doubt, a victory, but Baldwin reminded the reader that in the end, it was a victory won not by the "humanitarian impulses" of the vocal minority of abolitionists but instead by the force of arms. In the wake of this victory, the window of opportunity provided by Reconstruction closed in what was—politically, socially, and economically speaking—the blink of an eye. Despite "hard, honest struggles to improve the position of the Negro people, their position has not, in fact, changed so far as most of them are concerned."[40]

Baldwin was not oblivious to the counterargument likely to be raised to this line of thought. If we consider racial progress from the "historical perspective," a critic might say, do we not have reason to be hopeful? Doesn't the arc of history seem to be bending "toward ever greater democracy?" The young Baldwin's response to these questions reveals what would prove to be an enduring part of his moral vision. Even if this "historical perspective" captures important truths, Baldwin found himself wondering, What are the real consequences for "a Negro growing up in any one of this country's ghettos?"[41] Baldwin's moral expectations were, in short, about as demanding as one can imagine. From this moral position, Baldwin was able to acknowledge political, social, and economic progress on the macrolevel while at the same time forbidding us to avert our eyes from the appalling injustice in the life of the average teenager in Harlem. It is through the eyes of this teenager that Baldwin demanded we view the world.

When Wallace and the Progressive Party came along in 1948, Baldwin said, the people of Harlem had good reason to be skeptical. "Journey" is a simultaneously comic and tragic account of how the gap between "promise and performance" played out for Baldwin's brothers on their musical tour for the Progressives. The promise of private accommodations and square meals, for example, ended up being cots at the YMCA dormitory and plates of "limp vegetables."[42] The Progressive Party activists had all the right beliefs, but they seemed to have difficulty acting on them. On their return to New York, the band members could not help but laugh at the gaps between the journey they had envisioned and the one that actually occurred. Baldwin intended for their story to serve as a parable for the false hope of politics. Even the best of intentions and most extravagant promises were unlikely to bring about significant change in the lives of young men like Baldwin's brothers.

Buckley was also skeptical of the Wallace campaign, but for different reasons. He supported the Republican nominee Thomas Dewey, but it was Wallace who garnered most of his attention.[43] What interested Buckley about Wallace was the former vice president's strong support from the Far Left, including the Communist Party. Given these dubious associations, Buckley was incensed when he learned that several members of the Yale faculty were Wallace supporters. Indeed, the aforementioned Professor Emerson was running for governor of Connecticut on the Wallace ticket. Buckley utilized his considerable debating skills to draw attention to these deviations from the American orthodoxy (as he understood it), and even infamously teamed up with Kendall to accuse Professor Nathaniel S. Colley of transferring "his loyalty to the Soviet Union" and declaring that the "Wallace *movement* was inspired and dominated by the Communist Party."[44]

The Colley affair and Emerson candidacy were, for Buckley, manifestations of a deeper problem: Why were some of the leading intellectuals in the country being seduced by Wallace's message? Perhaps more important, what were these men teaching in their classrooms? Yes, it was true that an overwhelming number of Buckley's classmates were supporters of Dewey, but it did not bode well for the future to have the leaders of tomorrow educated by men like Colley and Emerson.[45] Buckley was fast becoming obsessed with the nexus between higher education and political culture. Leftist professors were corrupting the young, and this could have the long-term effect of undermining the public orthodoxy. Someone had to sound the alarm, and Buckley would soon acquire a major platform to do just that.

⁓

A little over a week after President Truman narrowly defeated Dewey, Baldwin was on a boat to Europe. In August, he had turned twenty-four and decided he could no longer take living in the United States. He worried that if he stayed, he would follow his father and his friend Worth down the path of self-destruction. He chose instead to follow the path that had been taken by Richard Wright and other black artists by fleeing to Paris. Baldwin hoped that physically removing himself from New York would provide him with the critical distance he needed to write about his life there. Furthermore, the move would supply him with a fresh set of experiences, on which he might draw in his writings. It did not take long for any romantic illusions he may have had about Paris to evaporate, but the move proved to be a fruitful one.

In February 1949, Buckley took over as "chairman" (or editor in chief) of the *Yale Daily News*. Although Buckley had already developed a reputation for strident views and occasional ferocity in political combat, he was also respected—if somewhat begrudgingly—by most of his peers and professors. This had something to do with his considerable personal appeal. Even Professor Emerson, who Buckley had more or less called a traitor, found him to be "affable and quite charming and even attractive in some ways."[46] But it also had to do with the fact that Buckley demonstrated considerable skill as a communicator and provocateur. Friends and enemies alike found a kind of magnetism in Buckley's personality. Even those who did not like what he had to say wanted to keep hearing him say it. When the time came to elect a new chair of the *Yale Daily News*, Buckley was the obvious choice.

On taking over as chair, Buckley announced that he would have "no squeamishness about editorial subject matter," and within weeks, he was using his column to voice "support for a House Un-American Activities Committee initiative to force registration of American communists."[47] In addition to anti-Communism, Buckley's favorite political theme was to resist calls to "liberalize" the Republican Party in the wake of five straight losses in presidential elections and the decades-long Democratic domination of Congress. The party, he argued, must cling to "the principles of free enterprise" and "anti-New Dealism," even if it means continued failure at the polls. "We would prefer a Party," he declared, "that is a long-time election loser, but that never forsakes genuine opposition to thinly-adulterated socialism."[48]

Buckley's commentaries on national and international politics attracted the attention of students and faculty to be sure, but it was his forays into campus politics that became the stuff of legend. In a five-hundred-student sociology lecture, a popular, liberal professor named

Raymond Kennedy called Catholicism "a bundle of voodoo mumbo jumbo."[49] According to Clifford Brokaw, who was on the editorial staff at the *Yale Daily News*, "Buckley went catatonic" when he heard the remark and soon thereafter sat down at his typewriter to hammer out a series of essays about why he thought the Kennedy episode was so troubling. In an editorial called "For a Fair Approach," he took Kennedy to task for using his classroom to create a "cult of anti-religion" at Yale. Kennedy, Buckley argued in the piece, used "bawdy and slapstick humor," "ridicule and slant," and other "pernicious techniques" to undermine the religious convictions of his students. Buckley conceded that as a man, Kennedy "is entitled to his own beliefs in regard to the existence of God," but as a professor at Yale, he had an obligation to promote the "tenets of Christianity."[50]

Buckley's anti-Kennedy editorials would prove to be only a prelude to a more systematic critique of Yale, but before he would sit down to pen his full indictment of the institution, he utilized his position to stage some political theater to showcase his views on the state of higher education. As chair, he was responsible for planning and hosting the *Yale Daily News* annual banquet. Yale President Seymour had announced his retirement, and Buckley proposed to use the banquet to provide him with quite a send-off by inviting the presidents of Harvard, Princeton, MIT, the University of Pennsylvania, and Columbia (General Dwight David Eisenhower) to visit New Haven in order to honor him. With a distinguished lineup, it is no surprise that the event attracted significant media attention, including coverage by the *New York Times*.[51] What none of these distinguished academic leaders realized was that they were mere pawns in Buckley's quest to advance his ideological agenda. Rather than simply playing the role of master of ceremonies, the twenty-five-year-old Buckley took the opportunity to deliver the keynote address with the elite university presidents serving as little more than warm-up acts. "In the name of freedom of inquiry," Buckley declared, "American colleges" ignore eternal "truths" and "hire renowned scholars who proceed to devote their time to advancing their own theories about Christianity, which at best they epitomize as sociologically useful, [and] at worst as superstition and fraud."[52]

The banquet was a fitting conclusion to Buckley's illustrious tenure as chair of the *Yale Daily News*, during which, in the words of one Yale administrator, he had made it "the most lively college newspaper in the country, past or present."[53]

It was during his early days in Paris that Baldwin would write his first truly groundbreaking piece. His early reviews, essays, and stories led many in the intelligentsia to call him "promising," but with "Everybody's Protest Novel," Baldwin arrived. In the essay, he offered a harsh critique of Harriet Beecher Stowe's *Uncle Tom's Cabin*, a book he read repeatedly and cherished when he was a child. In "Protest," he defended the thesis that the book he had once loved was a "very bad novel" as a result of its "self-righteous[ness]" and "virtuous sentimentality." Baldwin defined "sentimentality" as "the ostentatious parading of excessive and spurious emotion," and he contended that it "is the mark of dishonesty and the inability to feel." The "wet eyes of the sentimentalist," he explained, "betray his aversion to experience, his fear of life and his arid heart." Not only is sentimentality dishonest, it is also dangerous: sentimentality "is always . . . the signal of secret and violent inhumanity, the mask of cruelty." Stowe is best understood, Baldwin argued, as "an impassioned pamphleteer" who believed that "God and salvation" were her personal property, and thought that saints and sinners were as easy to identify as black and white.[54]

The "protest novel" is often spared the sort of criticism it deserves, Baldwin surmised, because it is shielded by its righteousness. Who among us really wants to take someone like Stowe to task for her failures as an artist? The end in cases such as hers is frequently thought to justify the means. Indeed, we are not only willing to forgive, Baldwin said, but also are eager to celebrate artists such as Stowe and the works they produce. The righteous among us get a "definite thrill of virtue" when we read such books, and their presence gives us hope that "salvation" is coming. "As long as such books are being published," Baldwin was told by an American liberal, "everything will be all right."[55]

Like his critiques of Gorky and Graham, Baldwin's dismantling of *Uncle Tom's Cabin* had both artistic and political dimensions. Although he was in sympathy with Stowe's end, he found her means to be artistically disastrous and morally dangerous. His central artistic point is captured in what he called "the business of the novelist," which he described as facing up to the "complexity" of human nature because it is "only within this web of ambiguity, paradox, this hunger, danger, [and] darkness" that we can "find . . . ourselves."[56] This artistic point is intimately related to a moral one: Baldwin worried that sentimentalism had the potential to undermine our sense of "devotion to the human being, his freedom and fulfillment; freedom which cannot be legislated, fulfillment which cannot be charted."[57] This, he said, was his "prime concern" and "his frame of reference." In protest literature, this sense of human dignity is "diminished" and often sacrificed at the altar of an abstract "cause." In the construction of "the cause," we attempt to make "life fit neatly into pegs" by forcing people and things into tidy categories. The spirit of the cause is "hot, self-righteous, fearful, [and] bloodthirsty." It is this spirit that seeks "to exorcise evil by burning witches" and "activates" the "lynch mob."[58]

In the conclusion to "Protest," Baldwin made a shocking shift in his argument by turning his critical eye to Wright, the Mississippi-born writer who had helped him get his start by recommending him for a Saxton Fellowship in 1947.[59] At the time, Wright occupied a place in American letters to which Baldwin aspired, and the older writer's expatriation from New York to Paris played some role in Baldwin's decision to find his way to the "city of lights." His various debts to Wright notwithstanding, Baldwin worried that the writer may have repeated some of Stowe's sins, though in a different key. Baldwin contended that Bigger Thomas, the main character in Wright's acclaimed novel *Native Son*, was a "descendant" of Stowe's "Uncle Tom." Although Bigger and Tom are about as different as characters can possibly be, they are connected, Baldwin said, by the fact that their humanity was subsumed by the ideological preoccupations of their creators. Both characters symbolize the "failure of the protest novel" because they do not embody the "beauty, dread, [and] power" of real human experience.[60]

Buckley was offered another platform to express his views when he was invited to serve as the undergraduate speaker for the class of 1950's Alumni Day, an annual gathering of Yale graduates. Two days before he was scheduled to deliver the address, he submitted the text of his speech to the University News Bureau. It took no more than two hours for the Yale administration to conclude that his address was not suitable for the occasion. In the speech, Buckley had planned to "unburden" himself "of one of the problems" that was "uppermost" in his mind—a problem that he believed was the central "dilemma of mid-twentieth century liberal American education." Buckley then intended to provide a brief sketch of Yale's history, from its founding in 1701 as an institution with a clear mission to train Congregationalist ministers to the moment he was writing, "when the University seems to have no mission." The sense of mission that once guided the institution had been abandoned in the name of "free and untrammeled inquiry" along with a "policy of educational *laissez faire.*" This policy, Buckley concluded, was an abdication of responsibility by Yale's faculty, administration, trustees, and alumni. Their responsibility, simply stated, was to formulate an "educational credo" that could be inculcated into the minds of students during their time at Yale. In Buckley's formulation, the credo would hold that "Yale considers active Christianity the first basis of enlightened thought and action," and "communism, socialism, collectivism, and government paternalism inimical to the dignity of the individual."[61] After some back and forth with the administration about the speech, Buckley refused to rewrite it but offered to withdraw from the program. This offer was hastily accepted. As is so often the case in history, this attempt to suppress unwelcome ideas only led to those ideas getting much more attention.[62]

The administration was not able to prevent Buckley from taking the rostrum one last time before graduation because the Yale Class Council had selected him to deliver the Class Day oration at the conclusion of the academic year in 1950. Buckley's address, which he called "Today We Are Educated Men," contains echoes of ideas he had developed previously and the seeds of things to come. As "Yale men," Buckley told those assembled, we take on the "responsibility of leadership." Unfortunately, he said, this was not a responsibility for which Yale had prepared them. The moral relativism that had been ingrained at Yale was the equivalent of teaching "two and two make three" as well as "the shortest distance between two points is a crooked line," and "from this morass we are" expected "to extract a workable, enlightened synthesis to govern our thoughts and actions, for today we are educated men. As an alternative to this relativism, Buckley encouraged his classmates to take their bearings in "certain immutable truths" about God and man, stop "apologizing" for their shared "beliefs" and "traditions," and resist the temptation to adopt the progressive's fetish for "change." Instead of accepting demands for "bold new measures" and "audacious steps forward," Buckley urged his classmates to cling to "negativism" because "America has grown and has prospered . . . by rewarding initiative and industry, by conceding to her citizens not only the rights and responsibilities of self-government, but also the right and responsibilities of self-care, of individually earned security."[63]

Buckley concluded the speech by acknowledging "deficiencies in American life" such as "suffering, injustice and want." In language that is quintessentially conservative and anticipates precisely how he would later respond to radicals like Baldwin, Buckley said we must not allow these deficiencies to upset our moorings. "Our greatest efforts," he said, must be devoted to "preserving the framework" and "principles" that have made "our country an oasis of freedom and prosperity." In a blaze of rhetorical fireworks, Buckley ended the speech with a string of words that made up the core of his conservative creed: we must use our education "to enhance our *devotion* to the good in *what we have,* to reinforce *our allegiance* to our principles, to convince us that our outlook *is* positive: that the *retention* of the best features of our way of life is the most enlightened and noble of goals."[64]

With "The Harlem Ghetto" and "Journey to Atlanta," Baldwin had launched what would be a prolific career as an author of political essays. He still considered himself to be primarily a writer of fiction, though, and continued to work on his first novel and offer criticism of the fiction of others. "Everybody's Protest Novel" had established Baldwin as a serious literary provocateur, and in 1951, he published a sequel essay titled "Many Thousands Gone" that picked up where he had left off.[65] This time around, the target of Baldwin's critical eye was Wright's *Native Son*. "Thousands" is, in part, a continuation of Baldwin's critique of the sins of sentimental political fiction, but it is also something more. In the essay, Baldwin offered his most sustained analysis yet of the moral psychology of race relations in the United States.

"Our estrangement" from the American Negro, Baldwin told the mostly white readers of *Partisan Review*, is a symptom of "our estrangement from *ourselves*."[66] Our trouble, Baldwin insisted, was our failure to accept the humanity of black people. In the typical American mind, "the Negro" is less a human being than he is a social symbol. He is not a man; he is "a problem" that consists of a bundle of "statistics, slums, rapes, injustices, [and] remote violence." On a good day, "the Negro" is a sign of "our" social progress. Our relationship to "the Negro" is based on how he makes *us* feel—scared, "virtuous, outraged, helpless." Baldwin's argument was straightforward: if we were able to strip away the layers of statistics and myths, we would find that underneath it all, those we call Negroes are real human beings with the same hopes, fears, virtues, and vices as anyone else, most of whom "want only their proper place in the sun and the right to be left alone, like any other citizen of the republic." Our failure to get beyond seeing "the Negro" in symbolic, sociological, and sentimental terms has had terrible consequences not only for "him" but for "us" as well: "Our dehumanization of the Negro then is indivisible from our dehumanization of ourselves: the loss of our own identity is the price we pay for the annulment of his."[67]

With this as his foundation, Baldwin started in on *Native Son*. Like his critique of *Uncle Tom's Cabin* (and in a slightly different way, his dismissal of Graham's biography of Douglass), Baldwin's concerns were both artistic and moral. That "artist," he wrote, "is strangled who is forced to deal with human beings solely in social terms." Wright's main character, Bigger Thomas, seemed to Baldwin to be less like a real human being than like "a monster created by the American republic" and it was therefore not possible for Wright to discuss a vital dimension of the life of his characters—"this dimension being the relationship that Negroes bear to one another, that depth of involvement and unspoken recognition of shared experience which creates a way of life." Without the ability to address this dimension, he left the reader with the impression "that in Negro life there exists no tradition, no field of manners, no possibility of ritual or intercourse."[68]

This artistic failure to describe the complex reality of Bigger's life had profound moral consequences. Wright had created a character who, like Stowe's "Uncle Tom," comes across as something *other* than human. Stowe gave us "Tom the Angel," and Wright had given us "Bigger the Monster." To the extent that the reader accepts Wright's argument that Bigger had been created by the sins of the republic, he may have succeeded in making the reader feel guilty and perhaps even afraid, but Baldwin doubted he succeeded in helping the reader *see themselves* in the eyes of "the other." Baldwin expressed skepticism about the potential of this sort of fiction to bring about that worthwhile moral end and, in his conclusion, called for telling different kinds of stories—stories that might "liberate us" from "dehumanizing images and stereotypes," and "for the first time, to clothe this phantom with flesh and blood, to deepen, by our understanding of him and his relationship to us, our understanding of ourselves and of all men."[69]

In spring 1950, Buckley graduated from Yale. That summer, he married Patricia Taylor, the daughter of one of Canada's wealthiest men.[70] Buckley had been hired by Yale to serve as an instructor for a beginning Spanish class, and his continued proximity to campus proved to be helpful for a major project he had begun. He had decided to use the themes of his undelivered Alumni Day speech as the basis for a book-length indictment of the reigning educational philosophy of his alma mater. Buckley worked on the book—with editorial assistance from his former professor Kendall and the libertarian pamphleteer (and Nock disciple) Frank Chodorov—over the next several months, completed it in January 1951, and it was published with the title *God and Man at Yale* by the Henry Regnery Company in October of that year.[71]

In the preface of *God and Man*, Buckley said he arrived at Yale with "a firm belief in Christianity and a profound respect for American institutions and traditions," and expected to find "allies against secularism and collectivism" standing at the lecterns of his classes in New Haven. To his surprise, he discovered that the dominant "educational philosophy" and "educational policy" at Yale seemed to him to be at best noncommittal about "the role of man in the universe" and "the role of man in society," and at worst, he found that many of those entrusted with the education of Yale students were openly hostile to "faith in God" and "the individual's capacity to work out his own destiny without recourse to the state." Buckley's aim in *God and Man* was "to expose what I regard as an extraordinarily irresponsible educational attitude that, under the protective label of 'academic freedom' has produced one of the most extraordinary incongruities of our time: the institution that derives its moral and financial support from Christian individualists and then addresses itself to the task of persuading the sons of these supporters to be atheistic socialists." To be clear, Buckley's objection was not that the students were being indoctrinated but rather that they were being indoctrinated with the wrong ideas. In his view, "the faculty of Yale is morally and constitutionally responsible to the trustees of Yale, who are in turn responsible to the Yale alumni, and thus duty bound to transmit to their students the wisdom, insight, and value judgments which in the trustees' opinion will enable the American citizen to make the optimum adjustment to the community and to the world."[72]

Buckley made it clear that his reflections on Yale had implications far beyond the institution itself. "I myself," he wrote, "believe that the duel between Christianity and atheism is the most important in the world. I further believe that the struggle between individualism and collectivism is the same struggle reproduced on another level."[73] Buckley then offered a telling disclaimer. *God and Man*, he informed his readers, was *not* an "apologia" for Christianity and individualism. Instead, he started with "the assumption that Christianity and freedom are 'good',* without ever worrying that by so doing, I am being presumptuous." In the footnote indicated by the * after "good," Buckley explained that "in point of fact, the argument I shall advance does not even require that free enterprise and Christianity be 'good,' but merely that the educational overseers of a private university should consider them to be 'good.'"[74] In other words, what mattered for his argument was who had the power, not necessarily who had the truth.

Before proceeding to an explanation of how Buckley built his case in the subsequent chapters of *God and Man*, a few words must be said about the significance of the themes he introduced in the preface. First, it is worth noting the "Manichaeanism" of Buckley's worldview, with "Christian individualism" on the side of good and atheistic socialism (or collectivism or Communism) on the side of evil.[75] This Manichaeanism would become a permanent fixture in Buckley's understanding of both domestic and international politics in the years ahead, and would play a crucial role in how he would view Baldwin. Second, it is worth noting the role Buckley saw for himself in the Manichaean struggle between good an evil. *God and Man* represents Buckley's answer to the call to responsibility he issued in his Class Day oration. We, he told his classmates, have an obligation to serve as guardians of the *known goods* against those progressives and revolutionaries who promise to deliver *unknown betters*. Finally, Buckley's caveat and footnote about "the good" are tremendously important. Although he would go on to become one of the most prolific political writers of the twentieth century, Buckley would never be comfortable offering systematic defenses of his ideas.[76] Most of Buckley's writing *assumed* the truth of his core commitments, and focused instead on revealing the dangers posed by personalities, philosophies, and policies he deemed to be threats to them. Furthermore, Buckley's footnote on the status of "the good" in his arguments should not be ignored. While he would later fashion himself as a staunch critic of moral relativism, there is something quite relativist about his starting point in *God and Man*.[77] In the footnote cited above, Buckley seemed to be saying that the truth of Christianity and individualism was not relevant to the argument at hand. Rather, what mattered was that those with the power—and Buckley would be sure to add, responsibility—*believed* these doctrines to be true. Buckley was, in sum, philosophically absolutist, but operationally relativist.[78] This understanding of the relationship between power and truth is worth emphasizing because it would have significant consequences for his later views of civil rights.

After this stirring preface, Buckley set out to provide evidence in support of his claims about the prevailing attitudes toward religion and individualism at Yale. Buckley's thesis in his chapter on religion was that "Yale, corporately speaking, is neither pro-Christian" nor "neutral toward religion." In support of this thesis, Buckley surveyed the courses and professors at Yale that contribute most to the religious "atmosphere" of the institution to see whether the course or professor being examined "fortifies or shatters the average student's respect for Christianity." Buckley's survey led him to conclude that most of the Yale faculty "in those fields of study that treat most often with religion" were at best neutral and at worst hostile to "religious values." In due course, he accused a history professor of practicing "bigoted atheism" and retold the story of Professor Kennedy, who "subverted the faith of numbers of students who, guilelessly, entered [his] course hoping to learn sociology and left with the impression that faith in God and the scientific approach to human problems are mutually exclusive." The "failure to Christianize Yale," Buckley concluded, was due "to the shibboleths of 'academic freedom' "—a theme to which he would return later in the book.[79]

Buckley's chapter on "Individualism at Yale" focused less on the personalities and views of professors than on the content of textbooks used in the Department of Economics. His thesis in the chapter is that "the net influence of Yale economics" is "thoroughly collectivistic." Buckley found it worth noting again that it was beyond his scope "to rebut the arguments of the collectivist" because the truth of what he had to say was not the heart of the matter; the central issue was what the alumni and trustees "want[ed] taught." "Individualism is dying at Yale," he concluded, "and without a fight."[80]

With his diagnosis of the problems established, Buckley devoted the rest of *God and Man* to his prescription. The responsibility to save Yale resided with the Yale alumni who had "the power," "right," and *duty* "to interfere when they are in disagreement with Yale's educational policy."[81] To suggest that alumni, through the board of trustees, ought to control the "atmosphere" on campus and the content of what was being taught in the classroom was to jump onto "the third rail of American higher education": the doctrine of academic freedom. In the 1940 *Statement of Principles of Academic Freedom and Tenure*, which was developed by the American Association of University Professors and the Association of American Colleges and Universities, this doctrine is broken into two major components: "Teachers are entitled to full freedom in research and in the publication of results. . . . [And] teachers are entitled to freedom in the classroom in discussing their subject."[82] Buckley's primary objection was to the second idea, which he said had become accepted "as a matter of reflex action" thanks to "liberal propaganda."[83] Rather than embracing a doctrine of "laissez-faire education" in the classroom, the alumni had the right, power, and duty to control *who* does the teaching, and *what* is being taught. What was revolutionary about this proposal, Buckley insisted, was not that this power would be exerted—it already was—but instead *who* would be exerting it and to what ends.

Buckley argued that it was silly to suppose that professors were actually hired "without consideration of their personal convictions." After all, Yale would not knowingly hire someone who was "anti-Negro" or "anti-Semitic," he noted, because these views are "look[ed] upon" as "false values." The decision not to hire a racist is based on a "value judgment," and when such a decision is made, no one cries foul in the name of academic freedom. With this and several other examples as his basis, Buckley contended it was his task "not so much to argue that limits should be *imposed*, but that existing limits should be narrowed" to exclude atheists and collectivists along with the "racists, totalitarians, and Stalinists."[84]

In making his case for narrowing the range of acceptable faculty hiring and classroom instruction, Buckley acknowledged that those doing the narrowing would not be doing so from the firm foundation of absolute truth. What mattered, he said, was not that Christianity was "the Truth" but rather that it appeared to be true "in the eyes of Christians." Individualism, he conceded, "is not regarded as truth, even by the majority of its most ardent supporters." Again, that is of no consequence. What did matter was that "we"—those with the power, right, and duty to say so—"believe in it," and as a result, "we are entitled to say, [it] is, if not truth, the nearest thing we have to truth, no closer thing to truth in the field of social relations having appeared on the horizon."[85]

What would the "educational philosophy" defended in *God and Man* look like in practice? Buckley sketched the following scene. Students would not "be shielded from the thought and writings of men with different values" from the reigning orthodoxy but instead the faculty role would go beyond analyzing and discussing these ideas; they must also challenge them: "While reading and studying Marx or Hitler, Laski or the Webbs, Huxley or Dewey, I should expect the teacher to 'deflate' the arguments advanced." The failure to do so would be for the educator "to foreswear a democratic responsibility and to earn for himself the contemptible title of dilettante and solipsist."[86] Buckley's Manichaeanism is evident in the list of thinkers he believed faculty members would be duty bound to deflate. There is John Dewey, a democratic theorist and defender of a "new individualism," cheek by jowl with Adolf Hitler, one of the greatest mass murderers of the twentieth century.

By the time *God and Man* was published in October 1951, Buckley had left New Haven for Mexico City for a brief tour of duty in the Central Intelligence Agency. With the Korean War heating up, Buckley—with the assistance of Professor Kendall—took a "draft-avoidance route that was popular with Yale grads" by pursuing intelligence work.[87] Buckley's "cover" was that he was in Mexico to look after some of his father's oil investments there. In fact, he was in all likelihood sent to monitor radical political activities in the country.[88] His commanding officer in Mexico City was E. Howard Hunt, who would go on to achieve infamy in the Watergate scandal.[89]

While Buckley was engaged in covert operations for his country, Yale was engaged in some covert (and overt) operations of its own. The Yale administration had gotten word about *God and Man*, and in the words of writer Dwight McDonald, it "reacted with all the grace and agility of an elephant cornered by a mouse" by first enlisting a wealthy alum to attempt to talk Buckley out of publishing the manuscript, and after that failed, recruiting McGeorge Bundy—a Yale alum, distinguished academic, self-proclaimed "believer in God, [and] Republican"—to dismiss Buckley in the *Atlantic Monthly* as a "twisted" and "ignorant" extremist.[90] Yale's countermeasures only proved to enhance the attention *God and Man* received, and although the book received mostly harsh reviews, Regnery Publishing could hardly keep up with the demand for copies. With *God and Man*, Buckley had arrived on the American cultural scene. This would not be the last time he would be dismissed by "the establishment," but he had certainly proven to be difficult to ignore.

While literary critics and polemicists rained down a shower of scorn on Buckley, Baldwin was attempting to complete a semiautobiographical novel that avoided the pitfalls of protest literature. At the end of 1951 and beginning of 1952, Baldwin was tucked away in a small chalet in the Swiss Alps attempting to finish the book. Baldwin's experiences in the Swiss town Loèche-les-Bains would become the basis for the essay "Stranger in the Village," which would be published in *Harper's* in 1953. In the essay, Baldwin described the peculiar experience of spending those months in a place where, as far as he could tell, none of the natives had ever laid eyes on a black man before. For the six hundred villagers, Baldwin was nothing less than "a living wonder."[91] Baldwin drew on the experience of living as a stranger among the villagers in order to reflect on his status as a stranger within Western civilization.[92] Although he felt quite estranged from the villagers, the isolation proved to be precisely what he needed to finish the novel he had labored over—off and on—for eight long years. It was there, on a snowy peak in Switzerland, that *Go Tell It on the Mountain* was completed.

In *Mountain*, Baldwin set out to tell a story that transcended the constraints of protest literature. Although a reader might find much worthy of protest in his story, his primary aim was to narrate the tale of a family in Harlem—the Grimes family—in a way that captured the complexity, terror, and beauty of real human lives. In telling their story, he would address racial issues, but he wanted to write more than a "race novel." He also wanted to capture the religious lives of his characters in a way that avoided stereotype. And he wanted to write a novel that was attentive to the power of setting—both Harlem and the South—without losing sight of the agency of his characters.[93]

The Grimes family patriarch, Gabriel, bore a striking resemblance to Baldwin's father. Gabriel is described as devout and rigid in his faith, and brutally judgmental and abusive in his life. He justified his brutality by saying "God's way" is a "narrow way," and it was his responsibility to keep his family on the path of righteousness. Although Gabriel is judgmental and brutal to everyone he meets, we learn he is especially so with his stepson John because he is a "bastard child" and therefore "the Devil's son."[94] What we learn from the many flashbacks to Gabriel's life in the South is that his attitude toward John has far less to do with the provenance of his stepson than it does with Gabriel's own history.

As a young man, Gabriel drank too much and lived a less than reputable life. After he was "saved by the Lord," he became a preacher and married Deborah, a devout woman in his flock. While Deborah was wasting away in her sick bed, Gabriel had a torrid love affair with a younger woman named Esther. As a result of their dalliance, Esther became pregnant, and Gabriel stole money from his ailing wife to enable his mistress to move north to give birth to their child. Esther died giving birth to their son, Royal, who ended up living a short, unfortunate life before dying in a barroom brawl. Gabriel eventually confessed his sins to Deborah before she passed away. With her death, Gabriel alone knew the truth—or so he thought.

I provide this brief description of what Langston Hughes would privately call the "low down story" at the heart of *Mountain* because the tale of Gabriel—who he *was* in the South and who he *is* in Harlem—is an allegory that demonstrates Baldwin's belief in the power of history and mythology in the lives of human beings.[95] The space John occupied in Gabriel's mind was not rooted in anything his stepson had done but rather in Gabriel's own desperate attempt to avoid accepting his own history. Gabriel's psychological need to have "the Devil's son" in his life is analogous to America's need to have "the Negro" in its national psyche. Just as his hatred of John allowed Gabriel to avoid coming to terms with his past, so too does the hatred of "the Negro" allow Americans to avoid coming to terms with their history.

Although Baldwin successfully avoided the pitfalls of the "protest novel," he did not shy away from addressing the effects of racism on the lives of his characters. Many themes in the novel struck at the essence of the American dream: the idea that each individual should be free to author their own life in a land of opportunity. When the young John is fantasizing about what his life might be, he sees before him not the seemingly limitless roads described in the mythology of the American dream but rather a "*Broadway*"—the term he uses to capture life on "the Avenue," which was marked by poverty, "sins of the flesh," and "the unconquerable odor of dust, and sweat, and urine, and homemade gin"—and the "*narrow way*" of his father, which promised only "humiliation," "hunger," and "toil."[96] The only roads available to John were those to hell, and there was little doubt that his race was a major reason why.

Baldwin's critique is made all the more damning by the fact that the novel's primary setting is the North, where blacks like John's parents had migrated in large numbers to escape the racist brutality of the South. John had read that in the South, "white people cheated [colored people] of their wages, and burned them, and shot them—and did worse things, said his father, which the tongue could not endure to utter."[97] And yet all the family members in *Mountain* who came "North in search of the American Dream" would see their hopes "dashed by the failure of the American nation" to see through the "myth of racial inferiority."[98] The story of how this nightmare played out in the lives of Baldwin's characters is powerful, but perhaps none of these tales is as disturbing as that of Richard, who was John's biological father. Richard is described as a "very thin and beautiful, and nervous" man who displayed an irreverence and sassiness "that fell just short of insolence," and he was an intellectually curious sort, who was always reading books and going to museums.[99] In other words, Richard was a lot like Baldwin himself.[100] Soon after John's mother, Elizabeth, discovered she was pregnant with Richard's baby, Richard was falsely accused of robbing a white man's store. After he was locked up and beaten by police, Richard fell into a state of despair, and without ever learning of Elizabeth's pregnancy, took his own life. In the amount of time that elapsed between Richard's arrest and his suicide, we learn that his hopelessness was rooted in what Baldwin would later call the "nightmare" of racism.[101] No matter what he did—how hard he worked, what books he read, or what relationships he cultivated—he would, in the eyes of people like the white store owner and police, be just another "black bastard."[102]

In 1952, Buckley resigned from the Central Intelligence Agency and returned to the United States from Mexico. Later that year, Baldwin got a loan from Marlon Brando (who he had met through a mutual friend) that enabled him to make a journey across the Atlantic in order to negotiate a deal with Alfred Knopf to publish *Mountain*. The United States to which Buckley and Baldwin returned was dominated by the international and domestic politics of the Cold War. Internationally, the country was still embroiled in war in Korea, where, according to President Truman, American troops were attempting to thwart "Communists in the Kremlin" who were "engaged in a monstrous conspiracy to stamp out freedom all over the world."[103] At home, Senator Joseph McCarthy of Wisconsin—a stocky veteran of World War II with media savvy and a drinking problem—had emerged as a major force on the national political stage. In 1950, McCarthy had delivered a now-famous speech to the Women's Republican Club of Wheeling, West Virginia, in which he claimed that the federal government was "infested with Communists," and brandished a piece of paper that he said had the names of government officials who were Communists, fellow travelers, or other "security risks."[104] The senator announced that he was on a mission to expose these traitors, and see to it that they were removed from their positions and possibly imprisoned.

The rise of McCarthyism brings into relief the question on Buckley's mind at the time: What united the American Right? At that moment in history, the Republican Party was defined, in large part, by varying degrees of opposition to the major domestic and foreign policies of Roosevelt and his successor, Truman. The battle for control of the party had, for the preceding decade or so, pitted a conservative faction that tended to be more anti–New Deal in its domestic policy and more isolationist in its foreign policy against a liberal faction that was more at peace with the New Deal and more internationalist in its foreign policy. Senator Robert A. Taft of Ohio was recognized as the leader of the conservative wing, and Governor Thomas Dewey of New York led the liberals. In the 1944 and 1948 presidential elections, the party had chosen Dewey over Taft as its standard-bearer, and in 1952, the Republicans found themselves at a crossroads: they had missed a golden opportunity to oust Truman in 1948 (when segments of his party splintered leftward with Wallace and rightward with Thurmond), and 1952 appeared, once again, to be a promising year. Truman's second term approval rating had plummeted to an average of 36.5 percent (compared to a 55.6 percent average during his first term), and he decided not to run for reelection.[105] With no obvious candidate available to reunite the fractured party, the Democrats looked vulnerable indeed. On the Republican side, the major contenders at first appeared to be the conservative Taft and moderate governors Earl Warren of California and Harold Stassen of Minnesota. Since mid-1951, though, bipartisan "Ike Clubs" had been started around the country in order to draft General Eisenhower into the presidential race. Eisenhower was well regarded by figures in both major parties (Truman had even tried to recruit him to run at the top of the Democratic ticket in 1948), and he decided to accept the invitation to run as a Republican because he objected to Taft's noninterventionist foreign policy views.[106] Eisenhower's positions on many issues were somewhat mysterious at the outset, but he soon became the favored choice of the liberal wing led by Dewey. On July 11, 1952, delegates at the Republican National Convention in Chicago nominated Eisenhower on the first ballot, and he was able to assuage some conservatives by choosing Richard M. Nixon, a young, strongly anti-Communist senator from California, as his running mate. During his pursuit of the nomination, Eisenhower also accrued a political debt to Warren, and in a decision that would prove fateful for the history of American racial politics, he would end up repaying that debt by nominating Warren to be chief justice of the US Supreme Court in 1953.

Leaders of the Democratic Party were determined to avoid the factionalism that tore them asunder in 1948. None of the men the *New York Times* called the "leading Democratic presidential possibilities"—Senator Estes Kefauver of Tennessee, former diplomat and Secretary of Commerce Averell Harriman of New York, or Senator Richard Russell of Georgia—had sufficient support to secure the nomination, and the delegates at the convention ended up choosing a compromise candidate: Governor Adlai Stevenson of Illinois. The *New York Times* reported that Stevenson was considered acceptable to the southern delegations because he "long has been against Federal compulsion or even Federal action except as a last resort in the field of racial discrimination in employment." The southern delegations pledged their loyalty to the party, and that loyalty was rewarded with the nomination of Senator John J. Sparkman of Alabama, a populist whose economic views were likely to be pleasing to Progressives who had supported Wallace and whose views on race—he had called Truman's civil rights program a "colossal blunder"—were probably pleasing to those who had supported Thurmond.[107]

Although by 1952 neither major political party was ready to take bold action on civil rights, the National Association for the Advancement of Colored People's (NAACP) Legal Defense and Education Fund was slowly chipping away at the legal regime of Jim Crow. Since the late 1930s, lawyers at the fund—led initially by Charles Hamilton Houston and then Thurgood Marshall—had been executing an incremental strategy to undermine de jure segregation in public education. Marshall was the grandson of a slave who had a keen strategic mind and a reputation for hosting great parties after scoring legal victories. Recognizing that a direct challenge to the constitutionality of the doctrine of "separate but equal" would be unwise, and that white resistance to desegregation would be significant for primary and secondary schools, the lawyers at the fund first focused their attention on segregation in higher education, and successfully litigated cases in Maryland (1936), Missouri (1938), Texas (1950), and Oklahoma (1950).[108]

In a number of these foundational cases, Marshall and his team cleverly painted the Supreme Court and defenders of segregation into a corner that demonstrated separation and equality were fundamentally incompatible. Early in 1951, Marshall was ready to go for the jugular: in a bundle of cases from South Carolina, Virginia, Delaware, Kansas, and the District of Columbia, the NAACP's fund challenged the constitutionality of segregation in primary and secondary schools, where there were dramatic funding disparities between black and white schools. This bundle of cases became known as *Brown v. Board of Education of Topeka, Kansas*, and just after Eisenhower's landslide victory over Stevenson in November 1952, the Supreme Court heard oral arguments. In June 1953, the Court ordered a second round of oral arguments to take place in October. Although the Court was leaning toward ruling in favor of the plaintiffs represented by the fund, the justices were divided under the weak leadership of Chief Justice Fred Vinson. When Vinson died suddenly of a heart attack in September—an event fellow Justice Felix Frankfurter suggested might be counted as evidence for the existence of God—President Eisenhower found himself in an awkward spot.[109] He had promised his former rival for the Republican nomination, the progressive governor of California, Warren, the next vacancy on the Supreme Court, but when he made this promise he had not expected that vacancy to be the seat of the chief justice. Warren held Eisenhower to his word, and once confirmed, was able to use his considerable political skill to unite the Court to sign onto a unanimous opinion in *Brown* that declared "in the field of public education the doctrine of 'separate but equal' has no place. Separate educational facilities are inherently unequal."[110]

In the ongoing war over racial justice in the United States, *Brown* was a major victory for progressives. A few years prior to the decision,

Marshall had expressed hope that a constitutional victory of this sort was just what the country needed to finally deliver on the promises of emancipation and Reconstruction. After all, he said, it is not as if "the majority of Americans are lawless people who will not follow the law as interpreted by the Supreme Court."[111] Perhaps Marshall was right about the majority of Americans, but what he was not able to anticipate was just how "lawless" some defenders of Jim Crow were prepared to get.

Chapter 3

Joining the Battle, 1955–61

While *Brown v. Board* was working its way through the court system, Buckley was looking for his professional niche. He knew he wanted to devote himself to "political questions" and the most obvious way to do so—besides running for elected office—was through journalism.[1] But the options for a right-wing writer of Buckley's style were limited to three major conservative journals of opinion: *Human Events*, the *Freeman*, and *American Mercury*. In the early 1950s, Buckley published essays with all three (including one on the racial politics of the "Little Black Sambo" stories), and received job offers from both the *Freeman* and *American Mercury*.[2] He accepted the *American Mercury*'s offer to become associate editor because it was a more well-established commodity, it had a much larger circulation, and he was promised journalistic autonomy.[3] Buckley ended up spending only a few months at the *American Mercury*, penning three major pieces, and departing after editorial disagreement with his superiors.[4]

Buckley then teamed up with his old Yale debating partner and now brother-in-law L. Brent Bozell Jr. to write a book-length defense of McCarthyism. The book, *McCarthy and His Enemies*, was something short of a "full-throated" defense of the senator himself. Buckley sensed, though, that whatever McCarthy's faults, he was being mistreated by the same "establishment" that had reacted so negatively to *God and Man at Yale*. He therefore took it to be his duty "to get to the bottom of the McCarthy story" and tell the American people the truth.[5]

Buckley and Bozell described "the problem" to which McCarthy was responding in the following stark terms: the Communists have an "ambition to occupy the world," and "conceivably a single individual could shift the balance of power" between the Kremlin and "free world." Faced with such a dire threat to national security, what had the federal government done? According to Buckley and Bozell, not nearly enough, and the rise of McCarthy, they argued, is best understood in the context of this failure. The bulk of *McCarthy* is devoted to an analysis of the Wheeling speech, a critique of State Department policy on "loyalty risks" in the years prior to McCarthy's rise, and detailed discussions of the nine accusations McCarthy had made public. Buckley and Bozell conceded that McCarthy's tactics were sometimes problematic (e.g., he was often "guilty of exaggeration"), but they believed his cause was just. The idea that McCarthy had put the country in the "grip of a reign of terror," they contended, was "palpable nonsense," and he was best understood as the imperfect enforcer of a completely justifiable national orthodoxy: "Adherents of Communism are . . . [to be] excluded from positions of public trust and popular esteem."[6] The influence of Buckley's Yale mentor, Kendall, is palpable here. Buckley and Bozell were defending the right of the majority to enforce the "public orthodoxy," which rejected Communism as an acceptable worldview. The idea of an "open society," Kendall insisted, was rife with fallacies. Any sane society was a closed society, and it was the right of the people to determine the nature of its exclusiveness.

In response to the "to a hammer everything looks like a nail" critique—which in this case manifested itself in concerns that non-Communists on the Left were being unfairly targeted by McCarthy—Buckley and Bozell were incredulous: the Left continued to dominate the universities, media, and government so if the senator *was* attempting to marginalize non-Communist liberals, he was failing miserably.[7] The "conformity" McCarthy and his supporters were trying to enforce, they argued, was quite broad, quite mild, and quite necessary. After all, Buckley and Bozell asked, should the American government allow individuals who were committed to its overthrow into positions of power and responsibility?

It is worth considering how these arguments fit with some of the themes of *God and Man at Yale*. Of particular importance is what *McCarthy* indicates about the Manichaeanism and relativism that were central to the assertions in Buckley's indictment of Yale. At first glance it would seem that the *McCarthy* book is in tension with my claim that Buckley's worldview is best described as Manichaean. After all, they were adamant

FIGURE 3.1. Buckley in 1954, after agreeing to serve as a television proxy for Senator Joseph McCarthy (AP Photo / Arnold Walter)

that liberals were *not* the targets of "*McCarthy*'s call to conformity." Whether or not this was true of the authors themselves, though, was a bit more ambiguous. After shielding McCarthy from the charge that he had targeted liberals, they wrote, "But it may well be we have not heard the last of [the] idea of [narrowing] the limits of tolerable opinion so as to exclude left-wing Liberals." "Some day," they explained, "the patience of America may at last be exhausted, and we will strike out against the Liberals. Not because they are treacherous like Communists, but because . . . we conclude 'that they are mistaken in their predictions, false in their analyses, wrong in their advice, and through the results of their actions injurious to the interests of the nation.'"[8] Nowhere in the passage did the authors indicate that such a slide would be problematic, and this reveals a willingness to slip toward the sort of Manichaeanism that is evident in *God and Man*. In addition, Buckley and Bozell suggested that such a slide might be due to the exhaustion of "the patience of America." Like his references to "the Alumni" in *God and Man*, Buckley located the source of the "truth" to be enforced in the views of a collective, which is the essence of relativism.[9]

During his 1952 visit to the United States, Baldwin said he stayed long enough to "show [*Mountain*] to my family, and to sell it," and then he "hauled on out of there" and made his way back to Paris, where he continued to write fiction and nonfiction. In 1954, Baldwin returned to the United States with hopes of finding a professional theater company willing to stage his play *The Amen Corner* while he worked on his second novel (*Giovanni's Room*) and a rather unlikely project for a twenty-nine-year old: his "memoir."[10] In fact, the "memoir" project was what would become his first published essay collection, *Notes of a Native Son*—a book he put together with the help of his "high school buddy" Sol Stein, then an editor at Beacon Press.[11] *Notes* was to consist of ten essays (most of which were previously published) that were divided into three parts: literary and film criticism, reflections on the experience of being black in America, and reflections on the experience of being an American in Europe. Several of the essays included in *Notes* have been discussed above (e.g., "The Harlem Ghetto," "Journey to Atlanta," and "Everybody's Protest Novel").

Baldwin's stepfather, David, is the centerpiece of "Notes of a Native Son." Baldwin said that David, like the character Gabriel in *Mountain*,

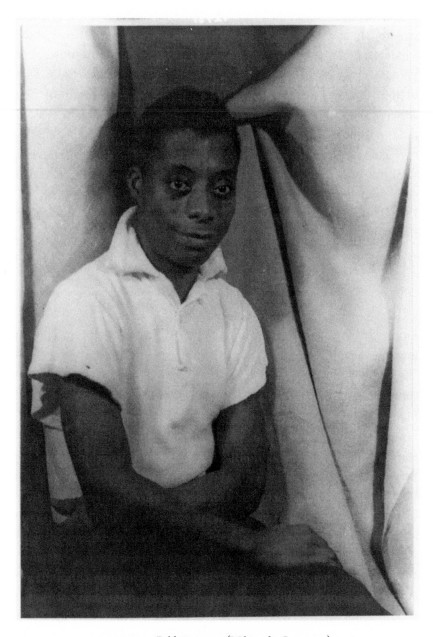

FIGURE 3.2. Baldwin in 1955 (Wikimedia Commons)

"could be chilling in the pulpit and indescribably cruel in his personal life and he was certainly the most bitter man I have ever met"; he treated other blacks in the neighborhood "with the most uncharitable asperity" and distrusted all white people.[12] While it is clear that one of the themes of the essay is Baldwin's struggle to avoid the "intolerable bitterness" that consumed his father, it is far less an indictment of the man than it is a quest to understand him and the circumstances that created him.[13]

The terror of being at "the mercy of the reflexes the color of one's skin caused in other people" allowed Baldwin to understand—but not accept—the hatred that filled his father's heart. What must it have been like, he asked himself, for his father to be in a world that so despised him? How did it feel for him to send his children, "whom he could barely feed," out into the streets of Harlem, with its "steady parade of . . . muggings, stabbings, assaults, gang wars, and accusations of police brutality?"[14] Is it really any surprise that David, like so many other Harlem parents, "felt a directionless, hopeless bitterness, as well as that panic which can scarcely be suppressed when one knows that a human being one loves is beyond one's reach and in danger?"[15]

Baldwin's ability to reach a deeper understanding of his father empowered him to be able to do something David was never able to do: resist the temptation to allow hatred and bitterness to take over his soul. Again, Baldwin started by trying to understand this temptation: "One of the reasons people cling to their hates so stubbornly is because they sense, once hate is gone, that they will be forced to deal with pain." But this, Baldwin could see, would not do, for hatred "could destroy so much," and it "never failed to destroy the man who hated and this was an immutable law." Instead of clinging to hate, Baldwin concluded, we must "hold on to the things that matter" and hold in our minds two ideas "which seem to be in opposition":

> acceptance without rancor of life as it is, and men as they are; in light of this idea, it goes without saying that injustice is a commonplace. But this did not mean that one could be complacent, for the second idea was of equal power: that one must never, in one's life, accept these injustices as commonplace but must fight them with all one's strength.[16]

A visitor to a well-stocked newsstand in November 1955 might have thumbed through that month's *Harper's* and seen the Baldwin essay just described (which was originally published under the title "Me and My House"). If this reader continued exploring the offerings on the racks, they may have seen *National Review*, a new magazine, with Buckley as its founding editor.

Although Buckley had found considerable success as an author—both *God and Man* and *McCarthy* made it onto best-seller lists—he was bored and frustrated with the glacial pace of book publishing.[17] He was an impatient man, not cut out to be anyone's employee, and wanted to have an impact on the day-to-day world of politics. What Buckley really wanted—though still under the age of thirty—was a magazine of his own.[18] Buckley recognized that magazines such as the *Nation* and *New Republic* played important roles in defining and promoting liberal and progressive ideas in the first half of the twentieth century, and his aim was to create a magazine that could do the same for conservatism in the second half of the century.[19] In order to accomplish this goal, Buckley needed to raise money for the enterprise and recruit an editorial staff. The daunting nature of the first task was diminished significantly by a $100,000 ($750,000 in today's dollars) gift from his father for the magazine, and Buckley proved to have a knack for fund-raising.[20] But it was in the execution of the second task—recruiting editors and writers for the magazine—that Buckley demonstrated strategic gifts that would have lasting consequences for the conservative movement he would play such a crucial part in shaping.[21]

It has become commonplace in the contemporary scholarship on the conservative movement to describe Buckley's project at *National Review* as "fusionist"—that he sought to fuse various factions on the Right into a coherent intellectual and political movement. While there is a great deal of truth in this idea, it is important to distinguish what we know from hindsight from the actual editorial choices Buckley faced at the time. In putting together an editorial team and recruiting writers for the magazine, Buckley may have had a grand plan in mind, but his more immediate task was to make several choices about how he wanted the magazine to respond to the central issues of the day: the Cold War, the proper scope of government involvement in economic life, the status of morality and religion in Western culture, and the question of civil rights (which had become a major topic of discussion in the wake of the *Brown* decision).

In the founding documents Buckley drafted for potential investors in *National Review* (which he reprinted in the first issue), he declared that the magazine's writers would "stand athwart history, yelling Stop, when no one is inclined to do so." He proclaimed that "the century's most blatant force of satanic utopianism is communism," and "coexistence with communism [was] neither desirable nor possible, nor honorable," and therefore those at the magazine considered themselves to be "irrevocably at war" with the Communists and their sympathizers.[22] In order to help make this case in the magazine, Buckley recruited James Burnham, a dapper, former Communist philosophy professor turned self-styled "futurist" and global strategist. Burnham's regular column in the magazine was called the Third World War. To offer additional reflections on the Cold War, Buckley had his heart set on Whittaker Chambers, a portly ex Communist who had become famous in 1948 when he appeared before the House Un-American Activities Committee to accuse former State Department official Alger Hiss of working with him as a Communist spy. Chambers had written a monumental autobiography called *Witness* in which he described his life as a Communist agent, provided greater explanation of the charges against Hiss, and explained the existential threat posed by the Soviets. Chambers was in ill health and worried that the magazine might be too radical for his taste, so he declined Buckley's overtures (though he would write for the magazine later).[23]

On questions related to the proper "relationship of the state to the individual" in economic life, the magazine declared itself "without reservations, on the libertarian side." The "job of the central government," the editors announced in their statement of convictions, is "to protect its citizens' lives, liberty, and property," and all "other activities of government tend to diminish freedom and hamper progress." In making these claims, Buckley hoped to distinguish the magazine from the "well-fed Right" that had "made its peace with the New Deal."[24] The most prominent libertarian in the founding group was Frank Meyer, an insomniac and former Communist who had established his right-wing bona fides writing for the *American Mercury* and *Freeman*.[25] Meyer worried that the Communist Party might target him for assassination as a result of his defection so he set up shop in rural Woodstock, New York, and developed the habit of sleeping during the day so he would be up at night when he guessed the assassins might strike. Meyer's regular column, Principles and Heresies, focused on academic journals, and he would end up running the magazine's book review section as well. Meyer has been credited by most historians of conservatism as the intellectual godfather of the "fusionist" project.[26] The libertarian commitment to freedom, he insisted, was inextricably bound to the traditionalist commitment to virtue and piety because authentic righteousness can only be realized by the free choices of individuals rather than coerced by the state.[27]

Although what we now call "social issues" did not have the same status in US politics of the mid-1950s, questions about the place of morality and religion in American (and broader Western) culture were being discussed, especially among the intelligentsia.[28] Some of this had to do with a sense that the cultural and religious moorings of the West had an important role to play in the Cold War, but it also had a more philosophical dimension to it: in the shadow of recent totalitarian mayhem, what moral truths might light the way to a more just future? On these questions, the "Mission Statement" made it clear that *National Review* was on "the conservative side," defending "fixed postulates" and "the organic moral order" against the advocates of "relativism" and "scientific utopias."[29] Conservatives, the editors claimed, understood that "truth is neither arrived at nor illuminated by monitoring election results, . . . but by other means, including a study of human experience."[30] In order to guide readers on their quest to separate truth from fad, Buckley recruited Kendall to serve as a senior editor and Russell Kirk, a former professor at Michigan State University who made a name for himself with the 1953 publication of *The Conservative Mind*, to contribute to the magazine. Kirk was identified with the traditionalist wing of the American Right due to his emphasis on stability, community, and order.[31]

By the end of 1955, the question of civil rights was clearly on the ascendance in national political life and yet National Review's founding documents made no explicit mention of these issues. There is a good case to be made that Buckley's reservations about "radical social experimentation" and his dismissal of "social engineers" with "Ph.Ds in social architecture" were veiled jabs at those who were seeking to replace the tradition of Jim Crow with a "grand design" produced by "the liberal intellectual imagination."[32] Whether this implication was intended or not, Buckley would soon make it abundantly clear where the magazine stood on the question of civil rights and thus set himself on a collision course with Baldwin.

Just weeks before Buckley's debut issue of National Review and Baldwin's "Me and My House" hit the newsstands, Emmett Louis Till, a black fourteen-year-old from Chicago, traveled to visit relatives in rural Mississippi. During his trip, he went with friends to get some candy from a store in the town of Money. While in the store, Till encountered a white woman who reported that he "got fresh" and "whistled at her." Whatever Till said and did was perceived by the woman to be a great offense against southern norms. She proceeded to go home to report the "crime" to her husband, Roy Bryant, who then enlisted his half brother, J. W. Milam, to help him kidnap, torture, and murder Till.

On receiving the news in Chicago of her son's death, Till's mother, Mamie Till-Bradley, sobbed, "I cannot think. I just can't think. He didn't do anything to deserve that.... How could anyone do this terrible thing to him?"[33] When Till's remains were transported back to Chicago and his mother viewed his mutilated body, she did not see anyone she recognized. Till had been beaten so severely that his head was swollen to nearly twice its original size. Painful though it was, Till-Bradley believed that it was important for the world to see what had been done to her son, so she ordered an open casket at his funeral.

FIGURE 3.3. Emmett Till before he was murdered (Wikimedia Commons)

"No other lynching in recent years," a newspaper reported at the time, "had aroused the indignation that this crime against a handicapped, 14-year old boy had." The murder received national news coverage, and the gruesome photographs of Till's remains inspired citizens to send "thousands of letters, wires, and telephone messages to President Eisenhower, Attorney General Herbert Brownell, and congressmen from all states."[34]

The trial of Till's killers a month later had the air of a horrific sequel to the Scopes trial of three decades earlier, as reporters from all over the country traveled south to behold a grotesque exhibition of southern intransigence. The lynching of African Americans was nothing new in the South—several thousand lynchings had been reported since the end of the Civil War—but the "lack of witnesses," one newspaper reported, had

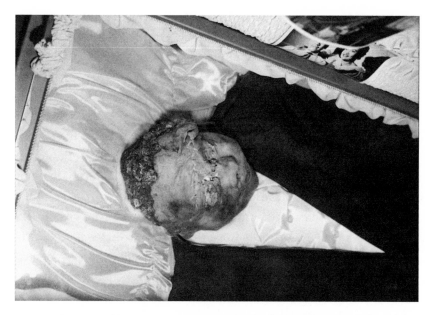

FIGURE 3.4. Emmett Till after he was murdered (Wikimedia Commons)

often been an impediment to investigations.[35] Such was not the case with the Till murder: the boy's uncle, Mose Wright, had answered the door the night Bryant and Milam kidnapped him. Wright shocked everyone in the courtroom, in the words of journalist Murray Kempton, when he "stood on his tiptoes to the full limit of his sixty-four years and his five feet three inches," and "pointed his black, workworn finger straight at the huge and stormy head of J.W. Milam and swore that this was the man who dragged fourteen-year old Emmett Louis Till out of his cotton field cabin the night the boy was murdered."[36]

When the all-white jury exited the segregated courtroom, one visiting reporter thought that "in the face of overwhelming evidence against the lynchers, and their own admission that they had kidnapped the boy ('but had turned him loose unharmed')," the jury deliberations should be clear-cut. Indeed, they were, but not in the direction that seemed so obvious to the reporter: after just one hour, the jury returned to acquit both men. One juror reported afterward that the deliberations "wouldn't have taken them *that* long had they not stopped to drink pop first."[37]

The Till case became a symbol not only of the unspeakable horror of racist violence in the South and the legal regime that condoned it but also of larger political questions about "outside agitators" who were accused of "trying to destroy the social order of the South." As one "red-necked [sheriff's] deputy" explained to *Nation* magazine reporter Dan Wakefield as they gazed at the large crowd that assembled outside the courthouse during the trial, the "dress up Negroes" gathered there "were strangers. Ninety-five percent of them's not ours. Ours is out picking cotton and tending to their own business." Indeed, this sort of thinking had been the linchpin of the legal defense offered on behalf of Bryant and Milam: the whole case was the product of "some sinister group" (rumored outside the courtroom to be the NAACP) that was seeking to upset the "racial traditions of the South." If the defendants were convicted of the crime, defense attorney J. W. Kellum asked the jury, "where under the shining sun is the land of the free and the home of the brave?"[38]

A few months after the acquittal, Buckley's old boss at the *American Mercury*, William Bradford Huie, purchased the rights to Bryant and Milam's version of what really happened that night. The original plan, the men reported, was to beat and "scare some sense into Till," but when he refused to cower in response to the pistol-whipping delivered by the men, Milam was moved to go further: "I just decided it was time a few people got put on notice," he explained to Huie. "As long as I live and can do anything about it, niggers are gonna stay in their place. Niggers ain't going to vote where I live. . . . They ain't gonna go to school with my kids."[39] With these ideas running through his head, he and Bryant continued to beat Till, forced him to undress, shot him, used barbed wire to tie his body to a seventy-five-pound piece of farm equipment, and threw him into the Tallahatchie River.

⁓

About three hundred miles southeast of the Till murder trial, African Americans in Montgomery, Alabama, were moving out of what Milam called "their place." Just weeks after the Till verdict, a black woman named Mary Louise Smith was arrested for violating the city's public bus segregation laws. In Montgomery, buses were segregated—as they were in most of the South—with blacks relegated to the back and whites allowed to sit in the front. The ordinance in Montgomery, though, was especially degrading because bus drivers were given discretionary powers to enforce a "floating" color line. Smith's arrest, conviction, and punishment (a nine dollar fine) were not the first under this law, but her case occurred in a new context. The local NAACP and local black church leaders had been gearing up to pursue a legal fight against the ordinance. The activists decided for various reasons that the Smith case was not an ideal vehicle for this challenge so she paid her fine and they waited for another opportunity.[40]

That opportunity came on December 1, 1955, when Rosa Parks, a soft-spoken, bespectacled seamstress who moonlighted as a secretary for the local chapter of the NAACP, stepped onto a public bus after a full day of work at the Montgomery Fair Department Store. Before long, all thirty-six seats on the bus were filled with twenty-two blacks and fourteen whites, and the driver, J. P. Blake, noticed that a white man was without a seat. Blake called on the four black passengers sitting behind the last row of white passengers to vacate the row so the man could sit down. According to southern norms, the whole row had to be vacated because the white man could not be expected to share it with blacks. None of the four passengers moved. After the driver approached them and made his demand more forcefully, three of the passengers did as instructed, but Parks persisted until she was arrested. When E. D. Nixon, Parks's boss at the NAACP, asked her if she would be willing to allow her arrest to serve as a vehicle to challenge the ordinance, her husband pleaded with her to refuse: "The white folks," he said, "will kill you, Rosa." Parks was undeterred. "If you think it will mean something to Montgomery and do some good," she told Nixon, "I'll be happy to go along with it."[41]

In order to "do some good" in Montgomery, Nixon and other local black leaders decided to pursue the legal challenge to the ordinance while at the same time orchestrating a mass boycott of the public bus system in the city. When they met after Parks's arrest to form the Montgomery Improvement Association to organize their efforts, they chose a twenty-six-year-old Baptist minister named Martin Luther King Jr. as their president.[42] This was not merely the filing of a legal challenge; it was a crucial step in the development of a *movement* to combat racial injustice.

During the brief window of time between the Till verdict and the uprising in Montgomery, Baldwin headed back to Europe on a quest to find a publisher for his second novel, *Giovanni's Room*. He reached an agreement in November with Michael Joseph of London to publish the novel in the United Kingdom, and soon after that, secured a contract with Dial Press to publish the book in the United States.

At first glance, *Giovanni* appears to be a significant departure from the road Baldwin had traveled as a writer. Why, many of his mentors and business associates had asked, would a "promising Negro writer" write a novel about a gay love affair in Paris between a white American and an Italian? Several people who had worked with Baldwin on previous projects—such as Alfred Knopf—declined to collaborate with him on *Giovanni* because they viewed it as an ill-conceived project that might derail the young author's career. In the face of such resistance, Baldwin persisted, insisting that those who dismissed his new book as an "all-white gay novel" were missing the point.[43] For Baldwin, *Giovanni* was not about race, sexual orientation, class, or nationality; it was about matters that transcended all such categories. At its core, *Giovanni*—which at one point had the working title of *Fable for Our Children*—is a book about morality, although not the petty moralism of what one does in the bedroom but rather something much more profound: the essentially human struggle to treat oneself and others with dignity.[44]

The protagonist in the story is a wayward, young American named David, who the reader finds in pursuit of the many pleasures of Parisian nightlife. His life changes, though, when he meets and falls in love with an Italian bartender named Giovanni. The novel tells the tale of their affair from its enchanted beginning to its bitter end. The details of the story make it clear that Baldwin's primary interest was not the fact that David and Giovanni were both men. Instead, what interested Baldwin is "what happens to you if you're afraid to love anybody."[45] In David, Baldwin provided a portrait of moral failure. Although he was in love with Giovanni, he was terrified by this love because it promised to set him free. Rather than choosing love and the freedom it entails, David chose the faux purity and safety of a more conventional yet relatively loveless relationship with his girlfriend, Hella. By making this choice, David demonstrated himself to be, in the words of his friend Jacques, "a really despicable" person because he was "contemptuous of other people's pain"—a character flaw that turns out to be a manifestation of something deeper.[46] David's contempt was really for *all* other people and was rooted in the deep contempt he had for himself.

If love, freedom, and dignity made up what we might call the "holy trinity" of Baldwin's moral catechism, David was a sinner indeed.[47] In order to love, Baldwin would claim repeatedly in his writings, people must be free enough to "act on what they know," but this is a "very difficult" thing to do. "To act," he would write later, "is to be committed and to be committed is to be in danger."[48] David did not want to brave the perils that come with love and freedom, so he chose the path of false innocence and safety. In making this choice, he assaulted the dignity of all those who were close to him, and picked a life of torment and self-loathing. To be clear, Baldwin did not pretend the life of love and freedom was without turmoil—it is a life that is "hard to bear"—but it is a more honorable sort of turmoil than that which afflicted David.[49]

Baldwin's exploration of David's deeply disordered soul has clear implications for the philosophical perspective from which he would reflect on civil rights. He had followed the activity in Montgomery closely, and the murder of Till as well as the acquittal of his killers would "fester in his mind for years to come."[50] These events and the growing southern backlash against the Supreme Court's *Brown* desegregation decision led Baldwin to feel a growing sense of duty to engage more directly with the American racial situation. He began developing long-term plans to do that in fiction and nonfiction book projects, and soon was given immediate opportunities to reflect on these issues in two short pieces commissioned by the *Nation* and *Partisan Review*.

The *Nation* had invited Baldwin to review two recently published books: Daniel Guérin's *Negroes on the March*, and J. C. Furnas's *Goodbye to Uncle Tom*. Baldwin called his review essay "The Crusade of Indignation," and in it we find him attempting to work out what it might mean to examine contemporary American race relations through his realist lens. In the Marxist Guérin's *Negroes on the March*, Baldwin found an example of how *not* to think seriously about these issues. Guérin's book was subtitled *A Frenchman's Report on the American Negro Struggle*, and Baldwin's reaction may as well have been called "Everybody's Protest Report." "A man whose vision of the world," Baldwin declared, "remains as elementary as Mr. Guérin's can hardly be trusted to help us understand it." Rather than offering an honest assessment of "the Negro struggle," Guérin used the book as a "shrill diatribe against the capitalist system," and in so doing, pretended that "labor's interests" are always identical to "the Negro's interests." In the end, Baldwin dismissed Guérin's book as a "desperate cliché."[51]

Like Baldwin's realist critique of protest fiction, there were at least two layers at work here: one descriptive and one normative. Descriptively, someone like Guérin was unable to tell the truth about the Negro struggle because he lacked "any sense of history, except as something to be manipulated" to fit the contours of his ideology. The normative dimension of Baldwin's critique was even more damning. Ideological thinking such as Guérin's is dangerous because "respect for the human personality" is subsumed by dreams of the "economic utopia" to come. In the face of Guérin's way of thinking, Baldwin confessed, "I cannot avoid a certain chill when I think of the probable fate of dissenters in his vari-colored brave new world."[52]

Guérin's "ungenerousness" with anyone or anything that did not fit with his ideology was rooted, Baldwin thought, in a "social indignation" that "so frequently leads to the death of personal humility."[53] This is the idea that Baldwin used to tie Guérin's failure to Furnas's relative success in *Goodbye, Uncle Tom*, a book that offered nuanced and philosophical reflections on the historical roots of American racial attitudes. Furnas, like Baldwin years before, found a great deal that was problematic in Stowe's *Uncle Tom's Cabin*. What interested Furnas was not only how the book shaped the politics of its era but also how it continued to impact American racial sensibilities. Fundamentally, Furnas's problem with *Uncle Tom's Cabin* was that it lacked moral complexity and "flatters" the reader's mind, thus "discouraging that mind from any tendency to think through the matter for itself." It is, Baldwin continued, a book that permits the reader "to avoid the risks of thought."[54] Furnas's "unsentimental insistence" that we think through our racial past, present, and future in a way that is rooted in our common humanity—rather than through symbols, ideals, angels, and demons—was welcomed by Baldwin as a far more promising path than the Manichaean thinking of either Guérin or Stowe.

In "Crusade," Baldwin had rather harsh words about two groups with whom he had considerable sympathy: critics of capitalism in the twentieth century and abolitionists in the nineteenth century. What are we to make of this? Baldwin's political philosophy was elusive or, as he would say later, "dynamic."[55] In his 1955 "Autobiographical Notes," he wrote, "I think all theories are suspect, that the finest principles may have to be modified, or may even be pulverized by the demands of life."[56] Ideological thinking like Guérin's or sentimental thinking like Stowe's—however attractive or comforting in theory—are of little value in the real world. We must, Baldwin declared in his critique of Guérin, recognize the "sadly persistent fact" that "freedom, justice, [and] democracy are not common concepts; on the contrary, they are rare. . . . It takes enormous and, above all, individual effort to arrive at the respect for other people that these words imply." Even in the context of something as morally just as Reconstruction after the Civil War, Baldwin said, "clarity is needed, as well charity, however difficult this may be to imagine, much less sustain, toward the other side."[57] It is through this sort of clarity and charity, not "righteous zeal," that Baldwin thought we might be able to find the "moral center" we need to make sense of our racial problems and deal with them responsibly.[58]

Baldwin's *Partisan Review* piece emerged as the result of comments about "the recent troubles in the South" by William Faulkner, the Mississippi-born, Pulitzer prizewinning author of acclaimed novels such as *The Sound and the Fury* and *As I Lay Dying*.[59] Faulkner defended "a middle of the road" position in the debates over race. He conceded that slavery and racial discrimination were "morally bad," and that "the Negroes are right" to claim that they deserve "social equality" and "justice." But "moral truths," Faulkner continued, do not end the argument because sometimes, "truth says this and the fact says that." According to "the squire of Oxford," the relevant facts in the South were these: southern whites are "an emotional people," they do not "like enforced integration," and they are willing to fight another Civil War to resist interference with their way of life. Faulkner's prescription for this volatile situation was to tell blacks to "go slow," take a "long-term view," and "be patient" and "calm," and one day their legitimate claim to equality would be realized. Given Faulkner's moral concessions and self-proclaimed moderation, it is shocking to find that several times during the interview, he made it entirely clear that he would be ready to "fight for Mississippi against the United States even if it meant going out into the street and shooting Negroes."[60]

When *Partisan Review* editor Philip Rahv read Faulkner's comments, he had the inspired idea of asking Baldwin to write a response. Baldwin called the essay that resulted "Faulkner and Desegregation," and in it he sought to do something more than simply refute the famous writer's moral and political arguments. The more urgent task, Baldwin thought, was to try to understand Faulkner and others like him. What did the world look like through the eyes of white southerners who thought of themselves as middle of the road on the racial question?

"Any real change," Baldwin began the essay, "implies the breakup of the world as one has always known it, the loss of all that gave one an identity, the end of safety." In the face of such change, our natural response is to "cling" to what we think we know and what we think we "possess." Those resisting change are less often evil than they are terrified, and when such a person is confronted with a challenge to the very ordering of the universe they have always known, they will respond with defenses and rationalizations that are—like Faulkner's—"almost entirely and helplessly dishonest, when not, indeed, insane." It is tempting to laugh at or dismiss these dishonest and absurd rationalizations, but Baldwin insisted we must not; they "demand our attention" because they reveal important truths about our inner lives. "Faulkner," Baldwin declared, "means everything he says, means them all at once, and with very nearly the same intensity."[61] We can learn something not only about Faulkner and those like him but also about ourselves if we try to determine how such seemingly incoherent thinking is possible.

Baldwin's explanation of the white southern mind contains echoes of themes explored in *Mountain* and *Giovanni*. The white southerner, he said, is striving to achieve a coherent "moral identity," but they are having an awfully rough time because they cling to "two entirely antithetical doctrines, two legends, two histories"—one that is centered around "the beliefs and principles expressed in the Constitution," and the other "which has not yet dared free itself of the necessity of naked and brutal oppression." These antithetical legends clashed in the Civil War, and "the North, in winning the war, left the South only one means of asserting its identity and that means was the Negro." Northerners, Baldwin concluded, emerged from the conflict with a sense of "moral superiority" and were able to say, in effect, "we have done our part" to fix "the Negro Problem."[62] The southerners, of course, could not make such a claim, and so the achievement of moral identity would prove to be a far more complicated matter.

The glimpse into Faulkner's middle-of-the-road southern mind was, for Baldwin, revealing indeed. In Baldwin's view, Faulkner—"among so many others!"—was stuck, and wanted those demanding social progress to "go slow" so he might have time to figure out how to "lift himself above his ancient, crippling bitterness . . . , cease fleeing from his conscience, and achieve . . . [his moral] identity." If the Negro must move from "his place" in my moral world, Faulkner seemed to be saying, I need time to figure out how to reorient myself. Baldwin's insistence that we must try to understand minds like Faulkner's does not free us from the obligation of moral judgment. In the end, this plea for more time was, in Baldwin's view, an evasion of responsibility. "There is never time in the future in which we will work out our salvation," he concluded the essay. "The challenge is in the moment, the time is always now."[63]

——————

While Baldwin saw symptoms of "insanity" in Faulkner's response to the tumult in the South, Buckley took to the pages of *National Review* to conclude just the opposite. In a short editorial called "Voices of Sanity," he praised Faulkner and the legal scholar Alpheus T. Mason for announcing their skepticism about the Supreme Court's desegregation decisions. Faulkner, Buckley announced, "is *against* segregated schooling; but he is convinced that the issue is political, not racial, and involves inalienable rights of member states," and therefore would be willing to "shoot Negroes" to defend those rights. What Faulkner and Mason (who had been critical of the legal reasoning of the Court's *Brown* decision) reveal is that "the issue is subtle," and it is a mistake to "pitch the question except in polar moral terms."[64] This idea echoed a claim Buckley had advanced just a week earlier when he wrote that "it is not altogether clear whether a moral issue is at stake" in the segregation controversy, and the "moral fervor attached to the Court decision itself is unconvincing and, at worst, hypocritical." In these early pieces, Buckley was careful to avoid making any moral arguments in favor of or against segregation. This led, he claimed, to attacks from both sides, with segregationists accusing him of having a desire "to 'mongrelize' the race," and integrationists reporting that they read his editorials with "mounting horror, indignation, and disgust."[65] By "dogged[ly] insist[ing]" that *other things* than Jim Crow are at stake," Faulkner and Mason were, Buckley concluded, "voices of sanity."[66]

Just what, in Buckley's mind, were the "other things" that trumped moral qualms about Jim Crow? His writing on civil rights in the late 1950s and the pieces he commissioned on the subject for *National Review* can help us answer this question. As Buckley biographer Carl Bogus has pointed out, at nearly the exact same moment in late 1955 two movements emerged that would shape the rest of the American century: "the conservative movement was born on November 19, 1955, the publication date of the first issue of *National Review,*" and two weeks later the arrest of Parks and its aftermath effectively launched the civil rights movement.[67] As Buckley rose to national prominence at the helm of his new magazine in the midst of racial upheaval, he made it entirely clear how he believed thoughtful conservatives ought to react. With few exceptions, Buckley and his writers responded to the civil rights movement with skepticism and hostility. History did not have to play out the way it did. Buckley had full editorial control over the path *National Review* would take, and there were plenty of prominent figures on the American Right who were consistently progressive on civil rights, but Buckley chose to use his platform to promote a program of resistance and this would have lasting consequences for the conservative movement.[68]

But not just any program of resistance would do. Buckley was determined to use the pages of *National Review* to fashion a sophisticated conservative case against civil rights. As he would explain it later, when he reflected on *National Review*'s first ten years in print, "In race relations, we have been extremely articulate, non-racist while not attempting a dogmatic racial egalitarianism either."[69] He wanted the magazine to avoid racism *and* resist racial egalitarianism. This proved to be a delicate balance indeed.

In the early years of *National Review*, Buckley and his colleagues developed a case against the civil rights movement that consisted of four major categories of argument: constitutionalist, authoritarian, traditionalist, and racial elitist. Each of these categories was undergirded by an assumption of cultural (if not congenital) white supremacy.[70] According to the constitutionalist argument, the civil rights movement was to be resisted because it threatened the American constitutional system. The authoritarian response to black liberation struggle emphasized the threat it posed to the social order. According to traditionalist reasoning, the civil rights movement was to be resisted because it interfered with "the Southern way of life." And finally, there was a great deal of racial elitism and paternalism, which was occasionally buttressed with crude racial pseudoscience, to be found in the pages of *National Review*. Racial elitists maintained that the civil rights movement was to be resisted because "advanced," or "civilized," white people have the right and duty to "civilize" the less "advanced," or "civilized," black people.[71] In order to understand how Buckley thought about race, each of these categories must be considered in turn.

In the early days of *National Review*, Buckley and his writers often attacked the civil rights movement with a constitutionalist argument that emphasized the threat it posed to the ordered liberty promised by the American system of government. The basic assertion went something like this: the major aim of the American constitutional system is to safeguard personal freedom, and in order to achieve that goal, governmental power is carefully divided horizontally (between the branches of the federal government) and vertically (between federal, state, and local governments). In order to protect personal freedom in the long run, short-term political desires may have to be thwarted if their achievement would require disruption of this constitutional structure. As Buckley put it in one of the early issues of *National Review*, "Political decentralization" is a "mechanical safeguard to freedom," and it is not wise to tinker with constitutional machinery.[72]

National Review's application of this argument to the civil rights movement varied depending on the most urgent controversy. Soon after the magazine was launched, Buckley and his fellow editors declared "the Supreme Court's decision in the key segregation cases (*Brown* and *Bolling*) to be one of the most brazen acts of judicial usurpation in our history" because the Court had assumed a power (the determination of educational policy) that it did not rightfully possess.[73] The editors of *National Review* were careful to point out that the usurpation in question was not merely horizontal in nature (i.e., that this was an inappropriate action because it was undertaken by the judiciary), but more important, that it was a violation of the vertical division of power within the federal system. "We are [also]," they explained, "opposed to congressional intervention in the school segregation issue."[74]

Buckley's constitutionalist critique of *Brown* anticipated many ideas that were defended in the March 1956 congressional resolution known as the "Southern Manifesto," a document signed by nineteen senators (including every southern senator save for three) and seventy-seven members of the House of Representatives.[75] The manifesto condemned the "unwarranted decision of the Supreme Court in the public school cases" as a "clear abuse of judicial power" that was "destroying the amicable relations that have been created through ninety years of patient effort by good people of both races."[76]

National Review gave the manifesto a stamp of approval a month later when it published a piece by Forrest Davis called "The Right to Nullify." Davis—a former Washington editor for the *Saturday Evening Post* and former adviser to Senator Robert Taft—called *Brown* an "edict" and "legislative fiat" that upset "centuries-old traditions" of educating children separately as well as protecting school auditoriums as safe spaces for the expression of white civic pride.[77] Davis conceded that the "impulses" and "desires of Negroes" that moved the Court to act should not be minimized, but something larger was at stake: "the merits and bounds of federal power over the local concerns of citizens." He dismissed as utopian nonsense the idea that there was a constitutional imperative to secure equality before the law, and concluded by asserting that white southerners had every right to feel "aggrieved" and "frustrated," and that the "statesmen" who authored the Southern Manifesto and populated the Citizens' Councils that had mobilized on the grassroots level were right to declare that they have "substantial warrant for seeking to nullify the [*Brown*] decision short of rebellion."[78]

Buckley's approval of the Southern Manifesto is especially revealing of the fine line he was attempting to walk on race. The leaders of the southern resistance in Congress received considerable praise in *National Review*, mostly through the column of Washington correspondent Sam M. Jones, a veteran reporter from Virginia who was a former aide to Senator McCarthy, and considered to be a "faithful and understanding friend" by George Lincoln Rockwell, who would go on to become the "commander" of the American Nazi Party.[79] As *National Review*'s Man on the Hill, Jones used his column—which was featured on the inside cover of the magazine from its founding until 1958—as a space to promote the ideas of arch segregationists in Congress. In early 1956, he wrote a glowing piece about Senator Thurmond of South Carolina, a Buckley family friend who received a gift subscription to *National Review* from Buckley Sr. In 1956, Will Buckley wrote to Thurmond to tell him that he would love the magazine because, among other things, "[Bill] is for segregation and backs it in every issue."[80] In his puff piece on Thurmond, Jones dubbed the senator "a latter day Patrick Henry" ready to lead another "Dixiecrat rebellion" against "the leadership of the Democratic Party" if it failed to resist "the edict that races *must* mix, in schools or elsewhere."[81] In case there was any doubt about what Jones had in mind when he wrote of "mixing," he made himself entirely clear in a later column that featured an interview with Senator Russell of Georgia. The interview took place while Thurmond was on the Senate floor attempting to filibuster the Civil Rights Act of 1957 (which will be discussed below). "Do the people of the South," Jones asked, "fear political domination by the Negro or miscegenation or both?" In response, Russell said white southerners feared both, but that "we feel even more strongly about miscegenation or racial amalgamation." To help his readers connect the dots, Jones's next question was, "Do you believe that school integration would be a step toward mass miscegenation in the South?"[82] Russell responded, of course, in the affirmative.

Buckley's own writing about these southern "statesmen" differed in spirit and substance from the fawning adulation offered by Jones. Buckley was uncomfortable with the inclusion of racially incendiary rhetoric about miscegenation in *National Review*. Indeed, in an interoffice memo to the other editors of the magazine, Buckley lamented the fact that Jones seemed to incorporate commentary on miscegenation into so many of his columns.[83] Buckley seemed willing, though, to set these qualms aside because he viewed southern segregationists as potentially useful allies in the advancement of the conservative agenda. Perhaps earlier than most, he saw great potential in a "southern strategy" to advance the conservative cause. The southerners, Buckley reasoned, might be shoved into the conservative camp by the overreach of the Supreme Court. In a 1956 editorial called "Return to States' Rights," Buckley revealed his hopes for bringing southerners into the conservative coalition. The South, he wrote, had a long tradition of defending states' rights from the "brilliant" pro-slavery politician John C. Calhoun to the present. The trouble with contemporary "states-righters," Buckley contended, was that they were inconsistent opportunists. They were solid states' righters on the question of race, but "when the federal government proposes to lavish its economic charms on a particular state, resistance vanishes." Buckley expressed hope that the Court's action in *Brown* "may have the effect of shaking inchoate states-righters out of their opportunistic stupor." He was prepared to stand shoulder to shoulder with them in their defense of states' rights on racial matters, but he wanted them to embrace the states' rights position in other areas as well. Now that federal intervention had "struck hard at traditions deeply rooted and very deeply cherished" in the South, Buckley hoped southerners might be pushed to embrace a "reasoned, principled and consistent" view of "the broad and—potentially—dynamic concept of decentralized political authority."[84]

Given the potential strategic value of southerners in Congress—something a young Arizona Senator named Barry Goldwater had noted in his diary as early as 1952—Buckley's courtship is not too surprising.[85] But in "The Right to Nullify," Davis also singled out for praise the members of the Citizens' Councils throughout the South.[86] Wasn't that a step too far for Buckley, who claimed to be trying to promote a "nonracist" conservative position on civil rights?[87] After all, the Citizens' Council movement—which had grown from a dozen members in Sunflower County, Mississippi, in the immediate aftermath of *Brown* to a large and powerful organization with chapters throughout the South—was widely understood to be the "uptown" or "Rotary Club" version of the Ku Klux Klan.[88] The councilmen, as they liked to be called, talked "a great deal about the difference between their organization and the Ku Klux Klan," reporter Dan Wakefield noted in the mid-1950s, but "the difference is slight." The tall, mustachioed council leader William J. Simmons—who had once studied French literature at the Sorbonne—explained their raison d'être in this way: "The South has a large nigger population," and "anyone with two eyes in his head and roughly normal vision can look around him and see that there is a vast and permanent difference between the white and colored people." This difference, Simmons argued, will "forever prohibit them from living on terms of equality in the same society."[89]

The councilmen took it to be their task to prevent the federal government from forcing southerners to accept "terms of equality" not of their choosing. The council, Simmons explained later, was there to stop "Big Government" from forcing the South down the road to "mongreliza-tion."[90] According to Simmons, segregation was fully consistent with "terms of equality" they could accept: "Why should the nigger feel any more discriminated against than the white man for associating with his own kind? White people who are segregated don't seem to resent it," he said with a chuckle to an interviewer.[91] At a council rally in Montgom-ery, Alabama, in February 1956, Mississippi senator James Eastland ad-dressed a crowd of twelve thousand councilmen, many of whom were gripping a handbill in their sweaty palms that read, "We hold these truths to be self-evident, that all whites are created equal with certain rights, among these are life, liberty, and the pursuit of dead niggers."[92]

Councilmen were also quick to point out that the tactics they used—newsletters, television and radio programs, and economic pressure—were quite different from the means favored by the Klan.[93] But again, Wakefield found these differences to be largely superficial:

> The klansmen hid their faces with sheets and paraded their deeds in the open. The Councilmen hid many of their deeds, or at least many of the deeds their words would inspire, behind memos and mimeographs and parade their faces in the open. But whether the means be a memo or a fiery cross, the end is the same—a climate of distrust and fear that breeds unsolved murders and threats of more.[94]

The last time Wakefield had been in Mississippi, it was to cover the Till trial. He had seen firsthand what the climate of distrust and fear had wrought.

In summer 1958, James Jackson Kilpatrick, a *National Review* contribu-tor and Virginia newspaper editor who has rightly been dubbed one of American history's leading "salesmen for segregation," put Buckley in touch with Simmons, who was the editor and publisher of the Citizens' Council newsletter, the *Citizen*.[95] Kilpatrick, who by then had close work-ing relationships with both men, thought the match could be beneficial for both the council and *National Review*. If a relatively mainstream con-servative organ like *National Review* provided any positive press for the council, it might help the organization muster greater credibility on the

NOTICE!

TO ALL WHITE CITIZENS
GREETINGS:

STOP

Buying FORD CARS and TRUCKS
and other Ford Products

For years and years a considerable portion of the profits from the sale of Ford cars, trucks and other Ford products have been funneled into tax free foundations. MILLIONS and MILLIONS and MILLIONS of dollars of Ford profits have been distributed to integration and civil rights organizations to fight the white people of the SOUTH, by forcing them to associate with negroes.

It is time to dry up at least one source of the money that is being used to destroy our Southern way of life.

DON'T BUY A FORD EVER AGAIN

For additional copies of this circular, write

CITIZENS' COUNCIL OF GREATER NEW ORLEANS, INC.

509 Delta Building   New Orleans Louisiana 70112

FIGURE 3.5. Citizens' Council Poster, circa 1960 (Wikimedia Commons)

national scene. For *National Review*, which was struggling financially, a connection with the council held out the promise of more subscribers and donors, among other things. On July 10, 1958, Kilpatrick wrote to Buckley with some exciting news:

> Bill Simmons, the major domo of the entire Citizens Council movement in the South, happened to pass through Richmond a week or so ago, and came by the house for dinner. In the course of our conversation, I brought up *National Review*'s troubles, and asked if he could promote NR in his editorial columns. He said he would be glad to, and volunteered to work out some arrangement with you for use of their 65,000 name mailing list if it would be of help to you.[96]

A few weeks later, after a phone conversation with Buckley, Simmons agreed to send the mailing list to *National Review*.[97] In addition, Simmons sent Buckley a letter in which he praised *National Review* for "making a highly significant and material contribution to the cause of political and social sanity."[98] Along with the letter, Simmons provided Buckley with copies of recent editions of the *Citizen* so he would be able to see first-hand what the organization was all about. These editions—like all other editions of the periodical—were devoted almost exclusively to advancing the segregationist cause through editorials, letters, and racist cartoons.[99] In his response to Simmons, Buckley said he was grateful for the support and the mailing list, and looked forward to reaching out to the supporters of the Citizens' Council "only because I feel that our position on states' rights is the same as your own and that we are therefore, as far as political decentralization is concerned, pursuing the same ends."[100]

There are a couple of ways to interpret Buckley's cozying up to the Citizens' Council.[101] One explanation is that whatever qualms he had about the council's racism were trumped by his desire to use its mailing list to increase the circulation of his magazine.[102] This explanation cannot be dismissed altogether since the magazine was struggling to stay afloat, but there is more to the story than that. Perhaps more important, Buckley had developed a deep respect for Kilpatrick so when the Virginian offered his endorsement of the council, he was likely persuaded that the alliance would be worthwhile. Buckley and Kilpatrick met in 1956 when Henry Regnery—the publisher of Buckley's first two books—sent Buckley a copy of Kilpatrick's states' rights manifesto, *The Sovereign States*, which Regnery published as well.[103] Regnery introduced Kilpatrick to Buckley as "one of the new leaders in southern conservatism and states' rights."[104] Indeed, Kilpatrick—or "Kilpo" as he was known to friends and associates—had used his perch as the editor of the *Richmond News Leader* to become, in the words of historian George Nash, "the principal journalistic and constitutional theorist of [the] 'massive resistance'" campaign that had emerged in Virginia in response to *Brown*.[105] It did not take long for Buckley and Kilpatrick to realize that they were ideological soul mates who could trust and rely on one another in their professional lives.[106] When, in 1957, Kilpatrick was looking to hire a new associate editor to work for him at the *Richmond News Leader*, he reached out to Buckley for a recommendation: "What I need is a writer with conservative views," he wrote to his friend, "who is 'right' on the school question in the South, and on matters of constitutional government."[107] Buckley later called Kilpatrick "the primary editorialist on our side of the fence. . . . In fact, I sometimes jocularly refer to him as 'Number One.'"[108] Kilpatrick was, in sum, the embodiment of what Buckley took to be a responsible conservative position on civil rights; he was deeply committed to the segregationist cause, but instead of defending it with demagogic rhetoric, he offered relatively sophisticated jurisprudential arguments.

It was for this reason that Buckley relied on Kilpatrick to offer *National Review*'s showcase response to the 1957 Little Rock school integration crisis, which became a symbol of the white southern resistance to the implementation of *Brown*.[109] In the face of a federal court order demanding the integration of Central High School, Arkansas governor Orval Faubus called in the National Guard to prevent black students from attending. The nine students, once turned away, were met with angry white mobs in the streets surrounding Central High School. Some in the mob became violent and assaulted a black journalist who was there to cover the story. In response to this conflagration of racial tension, President Eisenhower attempted to persuade Faubus to relent, and when he proved to be intransigent, the president ordered the 101st Airborne Division of the US Army to escort the black students into the school.

"The nine Negro pupils," Kilpatrick declared in his *National Review* essay on the crisis, "are not really very important in all this." What really mattered, he insisted, were the "two great [jurisprudential] conflicts" at the heart of the controversy: "a conflict of powers" and "a conflict of rights." The conflict of powers issue, Kilpatrick claimed, was a clear-cut one: in the face of angry mobs unwilling to accept the integration of the "Little Rock Nine," the government's primary obligation was to "keep the peace," and the "police power" belonged primarily to the states, not the federal government.[110]

Kilpatrick's discussion of the "question of rights" in the Little Rock case takes us to the second category of argument emphasized by *National Review* on civil rights: authoritarianism. In this context, authoritarianism means a decided preference for the exercise of authority in pursuit of some political goal (e.g., social order) over competing claims of individual rights. Although *National Review*'s constitutionalist arguments offered in opposition to the civil rights movement were usually framed in broadly libertarian terms, the magazine's libertarianism had its limits.[111] More specifically, when the freedom of the individual (especially when that individual was a person of color) was thought to be a threat to their preferred social order, Buckley and most of his writers in this period took a decidedly authoritarian turn. Kilpatrick's language in the Little Rock piece made this entirely clear. On one side of the conflict, "the people have a community right to peace and tranquility, the right to freedom from tumult and lawlessness."[112] Just so there was no doubt about how this right applied to the case at hand, Kilpatrick added, "The white parents of the South have some rights relating to the quiet education of their children under surroundings which they desire." On the other side of the conflict, "the Supreme Court has created certain 'rights' for Negro students . . . [including] the right to attend a non-segregated public school." Kilpatrick insisted that this was at best a pseudo right because the Court did a "lawless thing" by creating a right nowhere to be found in the Constitution. "Race-mixing of certain schools," Kilpatrick concluded ominously, "now leads to knifings, dynamitings [*sic*], and other forms of violence. . . . By far the worst is yet to come."[113]

There is a clear tension between the apparently libertarian framing of the constitutionalist argument—political decentralization is a safeguard of individual liberty—and the antilibertarian implications of the authoritarian position. In order to address this, Buckley complemented the common authoritarian rejoinder—there can be no liberty without social order—with two other categories of argument: traditionalism and racial elitism. These categories are crucial to making sense of Buckley's early views on race and civil rights.

Although Buckley often invoked the constitutionalist and authoritarian arguments in defense of his opposition to federal intervention on civil rights, there was more to his position than these appeals to the proper role of government and the desire for social order. In addition, Buckley wanted his magazine to offer an affirmative defense of the southern "way of life," especially on matters of race. In order to make the case for southern traditionalism, Buckley turned to several southern agrarian writers, but none played so prominent a role as Richard M. Weaver, whose "The Regime of the South" was among Buckley's favorite pieces ever published in *National Review*.[114] In order to get a sense of the "traditionalist" argument against civil rights, it is worthwhile to consider the ideas of Weaver in some detail.

Weaver was a native of North Carolina who had lived in several southern states including Kentucky, Tennessee, and Louisiana. He was a quiet, intense, "bulldog of a man" who taught composition and rhetoric at a number of institutions before finding his professional home at the University of Chicago in 1945.[115] In 1948, he would make a huge splash on the intellectual scene with his book *Ideas Have Consequences*. This text would soon be identified—along with Friedrich Hayek's *Road to Serfdom*, Kirk's *The Conservative Mind*, and Chambers's *Witness*—as one of the four pillars of the American conservative movement.[116] *Ideas Have*

Consequences is a complex little book, but for our purposes, it is enough to know what Weaver declared on the first page: the corruption of our way of thinking was bringing about "the dissolution of the West."[117]

Buckley had been introduced to Weaver's ideas when he was studying under Kendall at Yale. When *Ideas Have Consequences* appeared, Kendall took to the pages of the prestigious *Journal of Politics* to nominate Weaver for "the captaincy of the anti-Liberal team."[118] In 1955, when Buckley was filling out the staff of regular writers for *National Review*, Kendall suggested Weaver as a natural fit.[119] And so in the first issue of *National Review*, Weaver's name was on the masthead of the new magazine. Weaver was a frequent book reviewer and occasional essayist for the magazine, and would prove to be one of Buckley's go-to guys on race matters.

Weaver's first significant piece on civil rights for *National Review* was a review essay with the subtle title "Integration Is Communization." In the piece, Weaver argued that the Communists were "skilled enough in warfare" to realize that a full frontal assault on American political, cultural, and economic institutions was a losing strategy so they adopted the approach of edging Americans toward Communism by "indirect methods." The "opening tactic" in this strategy was the "racial collectivism" of school integration. The US Supreme Court, Weaver declared, was nothing more than a "running dog of the Kremlin."[120]

In "The Regime of the South," Weaver's approach was more philosophical, subtle, and rooted in the notion that ideas do indeed have consequences. Weaver began the essay by diagnosing American culture with anomie, which he described as a "condition of society in which the guidelines of belief and behavior have disappeared, so that frustration and chaos reach dangerous levels." The proper remedy for this cultural sickness, he argued, "will have to be regime"—a term meant to capture not only "the government and the laws" but also "beliefs, traditions, customs, habits, and observances, many of which affect the minutiae of daily living." The regime in which we live matters, Weaver asserted, because it sustains us by providing "every man, high and low, some sense of being at home. It tends, moreover, to diminish the sense of being 'low' by sustaining a sense of belonging." Furthermore, each man's station is the product of the "voluntary preferences of many individuals, acting and interacting out of respect for some basic values," instead of "top-heavy government."[121]

With that philosophical foundation established, Weaver turned to the matter at hand: Why is the "regime of the South . . . under heavy assault by Liberalism?" The answer, Weaver maintained, had a lot more to do with the pathologies of liberalism than any wrongdoing by southerners. "Liberalism," he declared, "is the death-wish of modern civilization" due to its "incapacity for commitment, its nihilistic approach, . . . its almost pathological fear of settled principle, [and its desire] to destroy everything and conserve nothing." The Southern regime, which was rooted in a "love of life" and "positive arrangements that enrich the enjoyment of life," enraged the nihilistic liberal who has attempted to sustain himself on little more than "a diet of self-questioning." Weaver contended that the southern regime "holds up a mirror to the Liberal. He hates what he sees there, and strikes out in anger against the bearer of the unpleasing image."[122]

According to Weaver, the recent liberal assault on the regime of the South—the attempts to integrate schools and enfranchise African Americans—was the latest battle in a long-running war. There was, of course, the Civil War in which the North rebelled against the South's constitutional commitment to self-determination and then the North's attempt to reconstruct the South in its own image. But then there was the attack on "fundamentalism" that was so dramatically illustrated by the Scopes trial in the 1920s. And then the assault on the "sharecropping system" and, most recently, "poll tax." None of these things, Weaver complained, were worth getting "excited over."[123] Instead, all these things were best understood as mere tools that liberals have found convenient to use in order to lash out against the South for daring to have a soul-sustaining and life-affirming regime.

Weaver's rhetorical strategy in this piece—and most of his others on the South—was to talk about race without actually saying much of anything about it. The only major reference to race in the entirety of "The Regime of the South" is a passing mention of the idea that the "South has had the enormously difficult problem of accommodating a large minority distinct in race and culture." It does not take much reading between the lines to understand how the philosophical discussion at the beginning of the essay might apply to the status of African Americans in the South. If we read race back into the philosophical explanation of regime, it is clear Weaver was trying to argue that the southern system "recognizes its capacity to give every man," regardless of race, "some sense of being at home" and "tends, moreover, to diminish the sense of being 'low'" in the racial hierarchy "by sustaining the sense of belonging."[124]

Buckley found a great deal to like in Weaver's defense of the southern regime, which was, in short, a philosophical defense of the views of hierarchy, racial and otherwise, that dominated the household in which he grew up. Like another southern writer he hired during the era, Anthony Harrigan, Buckley "believed that progress resulted not from equality of condition, but from fruitful inequalities."[125] On the question of race, this meant the acceptance of, in the words of Weaver's teacher and occasional *National Review* contributor Donald Davidson, "tough-minded, pragmatic solution[s]" to racial issues, which were "the most difficult of all problems."[126]

Over the first few years of *National Review*'s existence, Buckley mostly relied on writers like Kilpatrick, Jones, Weaver, and Harrigan to offer this multipronged case against civil rights. Buckley's own voice on these issues came through loud and clear in summer 1957 in an editorial titled, "Why the South Must Prevail."[127] Although the editorial was unsigned at the time, the piece oozes with Buckley's distinctive style, and he later confessed to having been its author. "Why the South" is Buckley's own "Southern Manifesto." The constitutionalist, authoritarian, and traditionalist arguments were all useful to him, but in "Why the South" he revealed what he took to be the heart of the matter: whites had the right as well as duty to subordinate and govern blacks because they were, "for the time being," the advanced race. Most contemporary readers would call this view "white supremacist," and that would not be wrong, but white supremacy was implicit in each of the categories already discussed. Buckley's willingness to subordinate the rights of black people to the constitutionalist cause of decentralization, the demand for social order, or southern tradition were all rooted in a political calculus that put a lesser value on black lives. The view he defended in "Why the South" was also white supremacist, but it is distinctive because it is more explicitly so, and he provided a more detailed explanation of his racial elitism.

The proximate inspiration for the publication of "Why the South" was the Senate vote on the Civil Rights Act of 1957. The legislative battle over the bill—filibusters and all—had gone on for some time, and what remained was a weak bill that did little to protect the rights of anyone. One of the most contentious issues in the bill was a provision that empowered federal judges to rule on civil rights cases rather than allowing them to be heard by juries.[128] Supporters of civil rights favored this provision because federal judges seemed more likely to enforce these laws than all-white southern juries. Segregationists in Congress (with the help of allies like Goldwater) killed the provision, and Buckley declared this to be a "conservative victory" because it provided a mechanism for "a jury to modify or waive the law in such circumstances as, in the judgment of the jury, require so grave an interposition between the law and its violator."[129] In other words, Buckley was taking Davis's "Right to Nullify" argument a step further: southerners need not rely solely on state and local politicians to interpose themselves between the federal law and their way of life; the people themselves may do it through acts of jury nullification. At first glance, it is rather surprising to find the conservative Buckley defending a radical idea so apparently at odds with the rule of law. Context, though, is everything. Buckley's defense of jury nullification was *all about* the Civil Rights Act of 1957, which promised (though did not quite deliver on that promise) to bolster protections for southern blacks. Buckley was defending the idea of jury nullification for one reason and one reason only: the "white community," he declared, must be empowered to excuse government officials who refuse to recognize the legal rights of black people.[130]

In his defense of this position, Buckley mentioned some of the constitutionalist, authoritarian, and traditionalist ideas described above, but only in passing; the core of his case was an explicit defense of white supremacy and call for racialized paternalism. The "central question" at hand, Buckley wrote, "is whether the White community in the South is entitled to take such measures as are necessary to prevail, politically and culturally, in areas where it does not dominate numerically."[131] Buckley argued that this question should not be answered "by merely consulting the catalogue of rights of American citizens, born Equal" but rather by considering "the claims of civilization." It is "more important," he explained, "for any community, anywhere in the world, to affirm and live by civilized standards, than to bow to the demands of the numerical majority." The white community is entitled to dominate blacks in the South because it is "for the time being . . . the advanced race."[132] Not only did Buckley endorse jury nullification as a means to protect "civilization" against "Negro backwardness," but he refused to condemn those whites who were willing to pay "the terrible price of violence" in order to protect their power.[133]

After advancing this rationale for white domination, Buckley did consider one counterargument to his thesis: the idea of universal suffrage. This notion, he declared, was at best a myth—we exclude all sorts of people from voting (e.g., minors)—and at worst a rhetorical tool for demagogues. "Universal suffrage," he retorted, is an unwise and potentially dangerous idea. A critic might ask if it is not—like decentralization—a "mechanical safeguard of freedom." Buckley's response would have been, I think, a mixed one. Democratic institutions can indeed be safeguards to freedom, but only if those institutions are operated by enlightened and responsible citizens. In his view, southern blacks were not sufficiently enlightened to exercise such responsibility.

Buckley concluded the piece with an elitist and paternalist call to white southerners to meet the "grave moral challenge" presented by their superior position. They must resist the temptation, Buckley insisted, to exploit African Americans as a "servile class," and instead employ "humane and charitable means" to civilize them so that one day they might achieve "genuine cultural equality."[134] In sum, Buckley believed white supremacy was a temporary, not a permanent, condition; it would one day come to an end as a result of paternalistic measures taken by southern whites. The determination of what those measures would be and when they had brought about "cultural equality" sufficient to recognize the political rights of blacks should, in Buckley's view, be left completely up to the "white community" of the South.[135]

Two weeks after Buckley published "Why the South," Bozell—his former Yale debate partner, his brother-in-law, the coauthor of *McCarthy and His Enemies*, and one of his associate editors at *National Review*—offered a full-page critique of it in an essay called "The Open Question." Bozell, unlike Buckley, was a lawyer by training, and this background shines through in his critique. In the piece, Bozell rejected Buckley's framing of the "central question" at stake as a conflict between "Universal Suffrage" and "Civilization." Bozell expressed some doubt as to whether "southern civilization hangs on the thread of Negro disfranchisement [*sic*]," but what he found more objectionable was Buckley's use of the straw man of "Universal Suffrage." "If that were true," he wrote, "I would hold my breath," but something far more important hung in the balance: "There is a law—[the Fifteenth Amendment guaranteeing the right to vote]—involved, and a Constitution, and the editorial gives White Southerners leave to violate them both in order to keep the Negro politically impotent." For Bozell, this was a sin not just against constitutionalism but also against the heart of conservatism. The rule of law, he declared, "is indispensable for the well-ordered society and a minimal requirement for the preservation of conservative values" so it must be defended even when a particular piece of legislation might be at odds with one's immediate political preferences. It should be noted that Bozell, like Buckley, rejected the legitimacy of the *Brown* decision and was perfectly comfortable with southern resistance to this "judicial usurpation." "But where the law is clear, as in the case of the Fifteenth Amendment," true conservatives ought to affirm its majesty by pledging their rhetorical, moral, and political support to those on its side.[136]

In the same issue of *National Review* in which Bozell published this piece, Buckley responded with "A Clarification" of his argument, in which he reiterated central points of "Why the South" and made two new assertions. First, he claimed that "the Fourteenth and Fifteenth Amendments"—two of the three so-called Civil War amendments that promise, among other things, "equal protection of the laws" and the right to vote—"are regarded by much of the South as inorganic accretions to the original document, grafted upon it by a victor-at-war by force." His second new argument was that the South could and should live up to the "spirit of the Constitution" along with "the letter of the Fifteenth Amendment" by "enacting [disenfranchisement] laws that apply equally to blacks *and* whites."[137] Without saying so, Buckley seems to have conceded to Bozell that conservatives ought to affirm the majesty of the Constitution. This concession, though, did not undermine Buckley's endorsement of flouting the Fifteenth Amendment because apparently it was not *really* part of the Constitution. Because they were established "by force," the Civil War amendments lacked the legitimacy of the rest of the Constitution and therefore southerners could feel free to disregard them. It is worth noting that Buckley failed to mention the first of the Civil War amendments, which abolished slavery, but his logic seems to suggest the reinstitution of slavery might have been permissible if white southerners deemed it necessary to advance civilization.

Buckley's other suggestion—that the South should enact racially "neutral" disenfranchisement laws—is one that he would defend repeatedly over the next several years, including in his debate with Baldwin.[138] Although Buckley thought the idea might shield him from accusations of racism, it actually helps us see the centrality of white supremacy to his anti–civil rights philosophy. His first instinct was to disregard the Constitution as an unwelcome obstacle to the goal of white domination. When he was called out for his disrespect for the rule of law, he embraced color-blind disenfranchisement as the next best way to sustain white supremacy. His goal was to maintain white domination of the South, one way or the other.

⁓

At the very time when Buckley and his colleagues were debating the finer points of just how far southern resistance ought to go, Baldwin was staring into the eyes of a fifteen-year-old boy who was among the first black students to attend a recently integrated high school in North Carolina. Baldwin had made his way to this young man's living room "on assignment" to write pieces on the racial situation in the South for *Harper's* and *Partisan Review*.[139] It was his first trip to the South, and he said his journey was fueled by "intrigue and terror." Baldwin was taken with the boy's "very large eyes," which not only "spoke but . . . registered volumes."[140] Baldwin's preoccupation with the eyes of his subjects has great significance. The eyes speak in many ways, but perhaps most important, they hold the key to intersubjective understanding. Baldwin's quest was to get as close as he could to seeing the world through the eyes of his "characters"—fictional and nonfictional—and his primary goal as a writer was to provide his reader with the chance to do the same.

What had this boy's very large eyes seen lately? Baldwin learned that G, as he called him in the piece to protect his anonymity, had been subjected to "name-calling," "threatening phone calls," human barricades meant to keep him out of school, and physical assaults at the hands of other students. As Baldwin listened to this nightmare, he began to wonder "how [G] managed to face what surely was the worst moment of his day—the morning, when he opened his eyes and realized that it was all to be gone through again."[141] G proved to be rather taciturn about how all this made him feel, and Baldwin began to suspect that this was because his mother, "Mrs. R," was present for the interview. It was his mother, after all, who had been one of only a few dozen parents (in a city with a black population of fifty thousand) to submit an application for him to attend the school. She had sent him marching toward that white barricade.

As Baldwin reflected on the precarious situation into which Mrs. R had thrust G, he wondered what "prompted her" to take this audacious step.[142] Perhaps because Baldwin had helped raise his younger siblings, he had long been drawn to—and haunted by—what the world must look like through the eyes of a black parent. In "Notes of a Native Son," he had described looking around the church at his father's funeral and pondering "the impossibility every parent in that room faced: how to prepare the child for the day when the child would be despised and how to *create* in the child—by what means?—a stronger antidote to this poison than one had found for oneself."[143] Mrs. R was one such parent, and when she was presented with the chance to get G out of the failed institution that was his former school, she could not refuse. "My boy's a good boy," she told Baldwin, "and I wanted to see him have a chance."[144]

After speaking with G and his mother, Baldwin's next stop was a visit with the principal of G's new school, a young, white southerner who seemed "bewildered and in trouble." What interested Baldwin was not so much this man's view of the merits of *Brown v. Board* or his thoughts on the details of North Carolina's "pupil-assignment" integration program but rather what it was like for him to play what was undoubtedly a difficult role in the drama that was developing in the South. After some back and forth, it became clear that although integration was "simply contrary to everything he'd ever seen or believed," he had no "hatred or ill-will" toward black people, and most important, felt he had "a job to do." Furthermore, he told Baldwin, "race relations in his city were 'excellent' and had not been strained by recent developments." Baldwin took this man at his word; he was no virulent racist or arch segregationist; instead, he was the sort of southern moderate whose role in the maintenance of the Jim Crow regime had been passive and almost robotic. In a sense, the principal's racial attitudes were reminiscent of the waitress in New Jersey who had so enraged Baldwin a decade earlier. Only now, the more mature Baldwin was able to manage "the fever"; instead of throwing something at the principal or storming out of the room, he found himself rather liking the man and wanting to understand him. The principal struck him as "gentle" and "honorable," but also delusional. He, along with so many others not only in the South but also in the entire country, had deluded himself into denying "the life, the aspirations, the universal humanity hidden behind the dark skin," and by so doing, stayed insulated from "any pangs of conscience" that might force a painful reexamination of his entire sense of reality. Perhaps the most powerful moment of the interview occurred toward its end when Baldwin looked into the principal's eyes and said, "[It must be] very hard for *you* to face a child and treat him unjustly because of something for which he is no more responsible than—than *you* are." In the "anguish," "pain," and "bewilderment" that filled the man's eyes at that moment, Baldwin caught a glimpse of "the impossibility"—a term he invoked again here—that so haunted those parents in Harlem.[145]

From Charlotte, Baldwin made his way to the "rust red earth of Georgia." As his plane descended, he wondered if the ground of Georgia had "acquired its color from the blood that had dripped down from [the] trees" after the lynching and castration of so many black men throughout its history. Baldwin began his *Partisan Review* piece, "Nobody Knows My Name: A Letter from the South," with this startling image, which served as a visual expression of his thesis in the essay: the "dispute" over "whether black children had the same rights, or capacities, for education as did the children of white people" had "nothing to do with education," and everything to do with "political power" and "sex."[146]

The centrality of sex in the racial upheaval was far more complicated than simply white fear of "race-mixing," such as was trumpeted repeatedly by Jones in *National Review*. As Baldwin would point out again and again, the races had already been mixing in the South for a long time. The "people who have made the region what it is today"—"the master who had coupled with his slave," the white youth "nursed and raised by [his] black Mammy," and that youth grown up feeling ashamed "after his first experiment with black flesh"—are racked by pain and bitterness because everywhere they look they see "flesh of their flesh," the reality of which they feel compelled to deny.[147] The rejection of black humanity was the cement that held this fortress of denial together.

The most poignant personal encounter Baldwin described in "Nobody" took place in Atlanta with an old black man, who directed him to his "first segregated bus." Like so many of his encounters, Baldwin was especially moved by the man's eyes, which "seemed to say that what I was feeling [as I boarded the bus] he had been feeling, at a much higher pressure, all his life. But my eyes would never see the hell his eyes had seen." The man's life, Baldwin surmised, had been dominated "by the power of white people" in the name of "paternalism." Even with the most humane and charitable of "superiors," such an arrangement denies the "subordinate" class of an essential element of human dignity. "It is not a pretty thing to be a father," Baldwin wrote, "and be ultimately dependent on the

power and kindness of some other man for the well-being of your house."
When men find themselves with such power over other men, they seldom act humanely, and so the man under his control could "at any instant" see all that he has and all that he loves "taken from him."[148] This
was the point that Buckley seemed unable to understand: even the most
benevolent of superiors denies those they dominate of their dignity.

"Nobody" reveals sharp contrasts between the reactions of Baldwin
and Buckley to the racial situation in the South. Before I consider their
deep differences, though, a word must be said about an important simi-
larity. In these early writings, both Baldwin and Buckley expressed disdain for the tendency of white northerners to take a "holier than thou"
attitude toward white southerners on the racial question. Baldwin had
long poked at this pretension in his works of criticism, including "Everybody's Protest Novel" and "Many Thousands Gone." In "Nobody," he
declared that the only major difference between segregation in the North
and South was that down there, it's "official." In Baldwin's formulation,
"Segregation is unofficial in the North and official in the South, a crucial
difference that does nothing, nevertheless, to alleviate the lot of most
Northern Negroes."[149] In the same year that the book *Nobody Knows My
Name* was published, Buckley pointed out that the "Jim Crowism" of the
North is simply "more sophisticated" than that of the South—a fact that
hardly makes it morally superior.[150]

Some of the differences between Buckley and Baldwin in their early
assessments of the burgeoning civil rights movement were obvious, and
others were less so. While Buckley's colleagues at *National Review* were
praising senators like Thurmond and Russell as "statesmen," and Buckley was trying to figure out how to ally with them, Baldwin was describing how the words of these men went through the air and into the ears
of black parents who were then "unable to sleep at night."[151] While Baldwin was writing of the insanity of the political lives of men beholden to
the whims of Citizens' Councils, Buckley was soliciting subscriptions
from the supporters of the councils and commissioning contributors like
Kilpatrick who were considered heroes by councilmen.

This last point invites us to consider differences between Buckley and
Baldwin that are more complex than their divergent views of southern

senators and the Citizens' Council. The philosophy at the core of Buckley's understanding of freedom might best be described as inegalitarian libertarianism. Buckley often called himself a libertarian, and by this he meant—as he put it in the debut issue of *National Review*—that the proper role of government in peacetime "should be limited to the protection of its citizens' lives, liberty, and property."[152] If a government is limited in this way, it is properly called libertarian. Later in life, Buckley would describe the position he embraced in the early 1960s as that of a "presumptive libertarian," by which he meant that there should be "a presumption in favor of liberty for the private sector."[153]

But Buckley's libertarian conception of freedom was, from the beginning, fused with inegalitarianism. He believed that only some people were sufficiently "advanced" to be free. Those who are not sufficiently advanced should not, on Buckley's account, be left completely outside the bounds of the libertarian promise—they ought, for example, to be protected in their person and property—but their liberty should be circumscribed until they reach the proper level of development. We saw above that an assumption of white supremacy was blended into every layer of Buckley's resistance to civil rights and therefore it is not surprising to find that there is a strong racial component to his inegalitarian libertarianism.

In the conclusion to "Nobody," Baldwin offered a different view of freedom. This is not to say that Baldwin rejected the importance of libertarian protections; he did not. In fact, he said time and again that the protection of the basic rights of all people would be a giant leap forward for American civilization. The achievement of this goal is a necessary component of justice, but this is not the whole of it. For Baldwin, the realization of this promise of freedom (as well as other important social, political, and economic promises) was impossible without first achieving freedom from the delusions that allow us to deny the humanity of others. "Human freedom," Baldwin declared, "is a complex, difficult—and private—thing. If we can liken life, for a moment, to a furnace, then freedom is the fire which burns away illusion."[154] The process of liberation must begin within each individual through fearless self-examination. It is only through such examination that we might be able to understand what Baldwin and millions of individuals like him meant when they said, "Nobody knows my name."[155]

Soon after his elevation to a leadership role with the Montgomery Improvement Association, King began his meteoric rise from local to regional to national to international prominence as the face of the black freedom struggle. During this rise, King attracted many admirers and enemies. Less than two months after the Montgomery bus boycott started, King's home was bombed, as was the house of his colleague Ralph Abernathy a few nights later. Against the advice of many friends and supporters, King stayed in Montgomery and continued to agitate. By the end of 1956, the Supreme Court ruled that the bus segregation laws were unconstitutional, and King was among the first passengers to ride on the newly integrated Montgomery City Bus Lines.[156]

King's status as a national leader was established in early 1957 when he was named chair of the organization that would come to be known as the SCLC, and his visage—along with an image of him preaching—was featured on the February 18 issue of *Time* magazine. In spring 1957, King delivered his first address at the Lincoln Memorial (on black voting rights), and about a month later, he met with Vice President Nixon to discuss civil rights.[157] So by the time Baldwin met King in the late 1950s, he had good reason to feel "overwhelmed" by entering a room occupied by such a "world-famous man."[158]

When Baldwin met King, he was less intrigued by "his public role" than by "his private life." This intrigue, Baldwin was quick to point out, was not directed at the "juicy tidbits" of King's private life (which would soon become the obsession of FBI director J. Edgar Hoover). Instead, he was interested in King's "private life" in this sense: he wanted to know "how it felt to be standing where he stood, how he bore it, what complex of miracles had prepared him for it." It was not long into their first conversation, which became the basis for Baldwin's essay "The Dangerous Road before Martin Luther King," that he realized that the preacher could be rather guarded about such matters, and so their dialogue drifted in the direction of the public questions this "slight and vulnerable" preacher was trying to address. The most important of these, Baldwin contended, was not whether segregation was going to die but rather "how long, how violent, and how expensive the funeral is going to be."[159] A leader like King, Baldwin surmised, could not answer this issue for "the Republic," but he was playing a crucial role in presenting all Americans with opportunities to reflect on the question and motivating some Americans to move toward an answer.

At the heart of King's philosophy, Baldwin found the idea that "bigotry was a disease and that the greatest victim of this disease was not the bigot's object, but the bigot himself," who was "not ruled by hatred, but by terror."[160] What was at stake in the struggle, therefore, was not only the liberation of the oppressed but perhaps even more profoundly, the liberation of the oppressors. In this idea, Baldwin found King offering a Christianized version of something he had articulated powerfully several years earlier in "Many Thousands Gone": "Our dehumanization of the Negro then is indivisible from our dehumanization of ourselves: the loss of our own identity is the price we pay for our annulment of his."[161]

The second set of ideas of King's that Baldwin saw as especially powerful were his commitments to nonviolence, love, and community. Baldwin's conception of love was not identical to King's, his devotion to nonviolence was not quite as deep as King's, and as someone who "liked to do things alone," Baldwin was never quite as drawn to community (or at least not in the same way) as King. For King, though, these ideas ran deep. Baldwin detected that this was more than mere rhetoric; it was "a way of life."[162]

With this philosophy as his guide, King had "succeeded in a way no Negro before him has managed to do, to carry the battle into the individual heart and make its resolution the province of individual will." But Baldwin thought King was in a "difficult position" because he found himself in between "official leadership" in the upper echelons of power (from presidents to members of Congress and so on) and the young activists at the grass roots who Baldwin believed had "begun nothing less than a moral revolution."[163] One of the central challenges before King, then, was to occupy a space in the middle of the road between the power elite and the young people agitating in the streets. To borrow a felicitous phrase from Buckley's colleague Weaver, King was discovering that "the middle of the road is not the safest place to be."[164]

⌒

During his first journey to the South, Baldwin also had occasion to interact with some of these young revolutionaries. Throughout the late 1950s, young black people throughout the region had engaged in small protests against segregation by entering and occupying spaces reserved for "whites only." Before 1960, few of these activities "made the news, all faded from public notice, and none had the slightest catalytic effect anywhere else." In February 1960, a sit-in in Greensboro, North Carolina, proved to be something different. The sit-in began when four black students from North Carolina Agricultural and Technical College sat down at a whites-only lunch counter at a Woolworths department store, where they were denied service, but they refused to give up their seats. They stayed in the seats until the store closed, and when the store opened the next day, they made their way back to those seats at the lunch counter. Within days, the "Greensboro Four" were joined by hundreds of supporting protesters and "copycat" protests were initiated in other cities. Within two months, what started as a small-scale protest had grown into a full-scale movement, with activities taking place in dozens of cities throughout the South.[165]

In "They Can't Turn Back," which was published in *Mademoiselle* magazine in August 1960, Baldwin described his encounter with students involved in sit-in protests in Tallahassee, Florida, earlier that year. Baldwin's narrative about the conflagration of protests sweeping through the South is not a simple tale of heroes and villains. It is, rather, marked by an attention to the inner lives of the people involved as well as nuanced reflections about the profundity of what was at stake in the struggle. As he spoke with students in Tallahassee, he found himself wondering how what was happening around them affected their confrontation "with problems yet more real, more dangerous and more personal than these: who they are, what they want, how they are to achieve what they want and how they are to reconcile their responsibilities to their parents with their responsibilities to themselves." Baldwin found himself pondering what the world must have looked like through the eyes of J, a student he met who was sympathetic to the protesters, but worried that he might lose his scholarship if he joined in.[166] He wondered whether or not V was justified in feeling "bitter about the failure of the [nonstudent] Negro community" in Tallahassee to join the students in protest. Baldwin considered what it must have been like to have one's protests interrupted by the "baseball bats and knives" of "the members of the White Citizens' Council" as well as "tear gas bombs" of the police. These reflections led him to conclude that "there is something new" about these students that separates them from their elders. They were not the first generation of African Americans to be defiant, but there was something about their challenge that empowered them, unlike most of their forbearers, "to frighten the mob more than the mob" frightened them. What was that something? These young people had parents who taught them "never to bow" your "head to nobody." Directives such as these, Baldwin reported, were not new. Earlier generations of black fathers (including his own) had made similar declarations. The problem, Baldwin said, was that his father's words were often belied by what his children could see in front of them: "But sometimes Daddy's head *was* bowed; frequently Daddy was destroyed." So what had changed? Why might the parents of these students have been able to deliver this message with more confidence to listeners who were more willing to believe it? These students, Baldwin saw, "were born at the very moment at which Europe's domination of Africa was ending." He did not spell out the significance of this fact in much detail, yet there is no mistaking his point: for men of Baldwin's father's generation, the empowerment of black people was little more than a dream, but these young people had grown up with the reality of black liberation elsewhere in the world, and that had filled them with confidence that liberation could happen in the United States. "It seems to me," Baldwin concluded, "that they are the only people in this country now who really believe in freedom." Therefore, they ought not be viewed as a threat but rather as a source of hope. "Insofar as they can make [freedom] real for themselves, they will make it real for all of us. The question with which they present the nation is whether or not we really want to be free."[167]

Buckley and his colleagues at *National Review* had also taken notice of King and the student activists. It is one of the strange coincidences of history that King, who would play such a crucial role in one of the major progressive movements of his era, arrived on the political scene at almost exactly the same moment as *National Review*, which would play such a central part in shaping the American conservative movement.

National Review's initial reaction to King's activities may, at first glance, be rather surprising. In early 1956, city officials in Montgomery resorted to all sorts of tactics to undermine the bus boycotters including fining taxi drivers who undercharged and attempting to stop insurance companies from covering cars used in carpools for the boycotters. In addition, the city indicted King and dozens of others for violating an Alabama statute that forbade the boycotting of businesses. Just before the trial commenced, Buckley and his editorial team published an unsigned paragraph about the case in the This Week news section of the magazine. The editors said that while there was no doubt King and others were guilty of violating the statute, it was a "bad law" that undermined "effective protest." The editors went on to offer a tepid defense of the boycotters: "In free societies," they wrote, "change should be brought about as the result of social, not legal pressure; and that is the kind of pressure Alabama Negroes are in the process of exerting."[168] The editors must have been well aware, though, that in addition to the "social" pressure being applied by the boycott, King and his allies were exerting legal pressure to overturn Montgomery's bus segregation regime. The editors failed to mention this fact and instead seemed determined to carve out a "middle way" that would put them to the left of the white mobs reacting violently to the boycotters as well as those who were using "bad laws" to thwart legitimate social pressure.

About a month later, after King and others were convicted of violating the boycott law, Buckley authored a short piece called "Foul." In it, he reiterated his belief that the law in question was a "bad law—as is any law that penalizes human beings for exercising in legitimate fashion, their right to protest whatever laws or customs they deem offensive." He went on to object to the city's refusal to allow "the Negroes a franchise to operate their own bus line." Buckley surmised that the reason why city officials were so vexed by the boycott was primarily economic: the city really missed the fares of black passengers. If blacks were willing "to assume the economic burden of establishing a separate bus line," Buckley reasoned, "they should be allowed to do so, and the white people of Montgomery, if they have pride, should be quick to allow them to do so."[169] It is worth noting here that Buckley was not willing to go so far as to say that the *city* had an obligation to provide a "separate but equal" bus line; rather, he insisted that blacks would have to be willing to pay for the creation and operation of this line. In the heart of the piece, Buckley was sure to remind readers "that the force of law ought not to be used by the federal government to force integration," and he concluded the piece with this: "By the same token, for the segregation they cherish, the white people must be prepared to pay the whole cost—twenty cents a ride; instead of ten, if need be."[170]

There are a number of revealing things about Buckley's "Foul" editorial. As noted above, it is somewhat surprising that he was supportive of the boycotters. This support, though, was fairly narrow in scope. The scheme he ended up endorsing would have left the demeaning system of racial segregation on city buses in place. Indeed, the editorial had nary a word to say about the justice of the segregation statute itself. Instead, he simply declared that segregation could be maintained if whites had enough "pride" to pay for it. In addition, the idea of a separate, private bus line was marked by greater injustice when we consider it against the backdrop of the significant economic disadvantage in Montgomery of most blacks, who earned less than half the median income of whites and were nearly twice as likely to be unemployed.[171] Whatever the abstract appeal of Buckley's call for blacks to assume the "economic burden" to operate a separate bus line, when we consider it in the context of the real circumstances of the citizens of Montgomery, the proposal loses much of its luster.

It was not until early 1959 that Buckley ran an article-length piece on King in *National Review*. In "The Two Faces of Dr. King," a *National Review* correspondent writing under the pseudonym A. B. H. provided an account of a lecture the reverend gave at Yale University. The tone of the piece was mocking and skeptical. A. B. H. described King as a "clerky little man" whose speaking style was less than inspiring: "Martin Luther King will never rouse a rabble; in fact, I doubt very much whether he could keep a rabble awake, if it were past its bedtime." A. B. H. was not convinced that King's approach was authentically nonviolent because his movement, in the end, depended on the willingness of the federal government "to accomplish integration."[172] The liberal audience at Yale, of course, greeted the conclusion of King's speech with a standing ovation. "I rose too," A. B. H. reported, "and applauded heartily. *I* was applauding Dr. King for not saying 'the truth shall make you free,' because actually it took the Supreme Court, in this case, didn't it?"[173]

About four months after he published this critique of King, Buckley weighed in on the student sit-in movement in a short piece called "Distinguamus," which is the Latin word for "distinction." The distinction Buckley thought ought to be made was between that which was defensible and that which was indefensible in the "activity of young Negroes-on-the-March in the South." The "boycott Negroes have instituted against business concerns which discriminate against Negroes" is, he argued, a "wholly commendable form of protest; it is a form of social assertiveness which we must understand, and can sympathize with." The young people crossed the line, though, when they engaged in sit-ins because, Buckley declared, "a Negro does not have the right to enter a privately owned restaurant whose proprietors choose, for whatever reasons, to bar access to non-whites." The line Buckley claimed to be drawing was between activity that respected "American institutions" and relied on "legitimate, organic progress," and activity that violated "the right guaranteed to an American entrepreneur to refuse to do business with whomever he likes" and therefore must rely on "inventionistic legal argumentation."[174]

It is important to remember that the racial turmoil described above was occurring in a domestic context marked by economic growth—the gross national product rose "in constant 1958 dollars from $355.3 billion in 1950 to $487.7 billion in 1960"—and an international context in which "the Korean war was fading from memory, the Red Scare was weakening," and there seemed to be a growing determination to engage with the Soviets.[175] In 1959, Vice President Nixon visited the Soviet Union, and just a few weeks later Soviet premier Nikita Khrushchev would visit the United States and meet with everyone from President Eisenhower to the movie starlet Marilyn Monroe.[176]

Buckley surveyed this scene with dismay. While he was pleased with the prosperity of the 1950s, he believed that even greater economic heights might have been reached if Eisenhower had rolled back the New Deal state. Buckley was appalled by the administration's attempt to engage Khrushchev (who he viewed as a tyrant) and apoplectic at the idea of allowing the Soviet premier to step onto American soil. In protest of the visit, Buckley "threatened to dye the Hudson River red so that when Krushchev entered New York it would be a river of blood."[177] Buckley did not follow through on this threat, but he did organize an anti-Khrushchev rally, to be held at Carnegie Hall. Before a near-capacity crowd, Buckley delivered a stirring speech in which he declared that Khrushchev's presence was a sign of "the dissipated morale of the nation," which did not bode well for American prospects in the Cold War.[178]

In the context of the prosperity and relative peace of the later Eisenhower years, many scholars began to conclude that the country had reached a strong consensus on the soundness of liberal values.[179] Most Americans, these scholars observed, believed they had essentially figured out how to achieve the good society, and only marginal figures dissented from this ideological harmony. This too incensed Buckley. Those championing this consensus view of American political culture were, indirectly, dismissing the work to which he had devoted the last decade of his life: the use of the spoken and written word—through books, essays, *National Review*, radio, lecture tours, debates, and appearances on radio and television—to establish a viable conservative counterculture. Had all this work been for naught?

In the twilight of the 1950s, this question was at the center of Buckley's mind, and he sought to answer it in his third book, *Up from Liberalism*, which was published in late 1959.[180] Buckley hoped his treatise might emancipate his readers from the intellectual bondage of liberal thinking. Liberal philosophy, he argued, is rooted in an overly optimistic estimation of human nature, unreasonable faith in human progress, and unwise belief in human equality.[181] In order to demonstrate the flaws with this way of looking at the world, Buckley culled together a series of cases in which these principles led liberals to take intellectually and morally irresponsible positions on issues of the day.

Rather than considering the full range of cases Buckley examined in the book, it seems appropriate, given the themes of his debate with Baldwin, to focus on his discussion of the flaws in the typical liberal responses to questions about race and civil rights. Buckley's first complaint was the unwillingness of liberals to engage in serious conversations about the topic. Rather than consider the merits of various conservative objections to civil rights, Buckley contended, liberals tend to view the opposition as monolithic, ascribe "ridiculous" views to this monolith, and dismiss it as unworthy of a serious response. This sort of liberal dismissal was deeply offensive to Buckley because he had devoted his adult life to articulating and promoting the ideas of the "responsible right" in order to demonstrate that on this and other issues, "conservative intellectual" need not be an oxymoron. On racial questions, the liberal tendency to lump and dismiss was especially upsetting because he had been painstakingly trying to carve out an intellectual and political space for nonracist conservative opposition to civil rights. "There are men in the South," Buckley wrote, "and elsewhere whose motives are despicable," and who "encourage a coarse demagogy particularly suited to the temperament of Know Nothingism and the Ku Klux Klan," but there are also, he seemed to be saying, people like me and the southerners I commission to write for *National Review*, "who speak in measured tones, of the grave constitutional crisis brought on by the Supreme Court's recent passion for imposing its will on the folkways of the nation."[182] There is a big difference, Buckley declared to his liberal antagonists, between the sort of thing being said by a robed Klansman on a hillside and the sort of thing being said against civil rights by the tweed-suited Weaver in one of his think pieces for *National Review*.

Beyond this inability or unwillingness to distinguish between crude and sophisticated conservative arguments against civil rights, Buckley objected to the "root assumptions" revealed by liberal thinking on these issues. More specifically, he argued that liberals were far too enthusiastic about democracy. In order to demonstrate this point in connection to the civil rights question, Buckley restated the central assertions of his 1957 "Why the South Must Prevail" editorial. Again, he made it entirely clear what he was defending: white people in the South, he declared, had the right to prevent black people from voting. These white people, Buckley reminded his readers, seem willing "to take whatever measures"— including violations of the law—"are necessary to make certain they have their way." Buckley held this position to be compelling given that "the White community is entitled to put forward a claim to prevail politically because, for the time being anyway, the leaders of American civilization are white—as one would certainly expect given their preternatural advantages, of tradition, training, and economic status."[183] It is worth noting how Buckley expanded on his "Why the South" argument on this point in a slight yet important way by adding the last dozen or so words. He wanted to emphasize that his support for white supremacy was not absolute and permanent; it was contingent and temporary. He went on to explain that he rejected the idea that blacks were biologically inferior.[184] Their inferiority, he said, was "cultural and educational," and as a result, the superior white community had the right and duty to uphold the standards of civilization until blacks could show themselves capable of casting "a thoughtful vote." The superiority of the conservative to the liberal position on these questions, Buckley concluded, was evidenced by the conservative's realistic "sympathy for the [white] Southern position" while the liberal "ruthlessly" applied his "ideological abstractions."[185]

It is worth pausing for a moment to reflect on the relationship between Buckley's racial elitism and his hostility to democracy. In private correspondence after *Up from Liberalism* was published, Buckley told a friend, "I pray every Negro will not be given the vote in South Carolina tomorrow" because such a development would cause him to "lose that repose through which, slowly but one hopes surely, some of the decent instincts of the white man to go to work, fuse with his own myths and habits of mind, and hence a man more likely to know God."[186] Buckley believed that some human beings were not fit for full citizenship and so could not ever accept democracy as anything more than an instrumental good. His hostility to democracy went far deeper than mere concerns about particular processes and institutions; it was rooted in his rejection of a conception of human equality robust enough to allow for full citizenship. These deeply antidemocratic views were fused with his long-held belief in the inferiority of black people to form a philosophy of racial hierarchy that he hoped might be deemed more respectable than what was being peddled by the "coarse" demagogues in the Ku Klux Klan.

In his conclusion to *Up from Liberalism*, Buckley began with a question: "Up where from liberalism?" After devoting most of the two-hundred-page book to his criticisms of liberalism like the ones described above, an attentive reader who made it through to the end might have had good reason to wonder if Buckley would ever reveal a suitable ideological alternative lurking in the shadows. Enter conservatism—sort of. Conservatism was indeed Buckley's preferred ideology, but he admitted that conservatives were largely "bound together" by what they opposed—namely liberalism and Communism. Conservatism, he further admitted, eludes simple definition because it is, by its very nature, leery of "ideologization," defined as the attempt to make the world conform to some sort of rational political plan. These challenges notwithstanding, Buckley attempted in his conclusion to at least move toward a "conservative framework" that might guide future decision making.[187]

One of the most striking things about Buckley's conclusion in *Up from Liberalism* is just how much it differs in spirit from the founding documents of *National Review*, which he had written just a few years earlier. In those documents, you will recall, Buckley embraced a kind of "idealism," declaring himself and his comrades to be "radical conservatives" who had "not made peace with the New Deal."[188] His conclusion in *Up from Liberalism*, by contrast, is marked by sobriety, realism, and, well, peace with the New Deal. The acknowledged inspiration for the conclusion of the book was Chambers, whose morose and brooding worldview had exerted a great deal of influence on Buckley through their robust epistolary relationship throughout the 1950s.[189] Chambers's central insight, Buckley confessed, was that "the rock-core of the Conservative Position can be held realistically only if Conservatism will accommodate itself to the needs and hopes of the masses."[190] Rather than standing athwart the train of history shouting "Stop!" (as Buckley had pledged to do in the founding documents of *National Review*), he seemed to be bowing his head, shrugging his shoulders, and asking, Is there room for one more? "Indeed. The machine must be accepted," he wrote, and conservatives must adopt "a proper kind of realism."[191] These are not the words of a radical.

Despite these concessions, Buckley implored conservatives not to despair; they still had an important role to play in charting the train's course and slowing its velocity. Although they had to adopt a realistic view, they must still stand firm to prevent the country from "fall[ing] over the cliff into liberalism." Conservatives must do this, Buckley instructed, by resisting when liberals try to respond to every problem with a government program. The conservative "program" must be a "No-Program" rooted in the following defiant credo:

> I will not cede more power to the state. . . . I will hoard my power like a miser, resisting every effort to drain it away from me. I will then use *my* power, as *I* see fit. I mean to live my life an obedient man, but obedient to God, subservient to the wisdom of my ancestors; never the authority of political truths arrived at yesterday at the voting booth. That is a program of sorts, is it not?[192]

Buckley's chastened hopes for radical conservatism were buoyed slightly a few months after *Up from Liberalism* was published. He traveled to the 1960 Republican National Convention in Chicago with Marvin Liebman, a publicist who was his collaborator in the anti-Khrushchev rally.[193] While in Chicago, they spent some time with David Francke and Doug Caddy, two college students there to promote their Youth for Goldwater organization. The day after the convention, Buckley had lunch with Francke, Caddy, and Liebman, who "suggested to Caddy and the other students that they set up a new student organization" for young conservatives. Caddy and Francke worked with Liebman to organize a meeting of young conservatives for the purposes of establishing such an organization. Buckley was so excited by the idea that he offered up his parents' estate, Great Elm, as the site for the summit.[194]

In early September, about one hundred students—from forty-four colleges in twenty-four states—arrived at Great Elm for a sort of "constitutional convention" for their new organization, Young Americans for Freedom.[195] In the beautiful environs of the Buckley estate in Sharon, Connecticut, the students listened to lectures by conservative luminaries such as Bozell and Buckley, and discussed how they might create a conservative future. Buckley oversaw the proceedings in the spirit of a sagacious mentor, attendee Lee Edwards remembers. "Many of us," Edwards said, "had one major goal in life: to be just like Bill Buckley." But according to Edwards, Buckley did not use his idol status to dominate the proceedings. Instead, he played a more passive role, as the students worked out what conservative youth ought to do to change the direction of the country.[196]

The organizers had decided that one of their principal tasks during the weekend would be to hammer out a statement of principles that could serve as the founding document of the new organization. Rather than starting from scratch, they asked M. Stanton Evans, a twenty-six-year-old who had "recently been appointed as editor of the *Indianapolis News*," to draft a preliminary document that could be debated and refined at Sharon.[197] Evans's father, Medford Evans, was a regular contributor to many periodicals on the Right, including *National Review*, the John Birch Society's (JBS) *American Opinion*, and the Citizens' Council's *Citizen* (he would become its managing editor in 1962).[198] Buckley thought so highly of Medford that when former President Herbert Hoover asked Buckley to recommend a new director for his Hoover Institution at Stanford University, Buckley included Evans among his short list of four.[199]

Evans the younger accepted this invitation and arrived at the meeting with a draft document that would evolve over the course of the weekend to become the credo of principles known as the "Sharon Statement," which would soon be one of the cornerstone documents of the American conservative movement. The statement that resulted from these proceedings is concise and, although far more earnest in its tone, contains echoes of the founding documents Buckley crafted for *National Review* a few years earlier. The authors identified the period in which they were writing as one marked by "moral and political crises," and declared that in such times one must be anchored by "certain eternal truths." The "truths" then enunciated consist of the several pillars that fit perfectly with the sort of conservatism Buckley and his colleagues had been trying defend in *National Review*: "God-given free will" and the God-granted "right to be free"; the indivisibility of economic and political freedom; government limited to "the preservation of internal order, the provision of National Defense, and the administration of justice"; the "genius of the Constitution" as "the best arrangement yet devised" for simultaneously "empowering" and "restraining" government through the "division of powers" (especially through "the clause that reserves primacy to the several states"); the market economy as the best system to protect freedom and promote prosperity; and the belief that "periods of freedom are rare," "international communism" is the greatest threat to freedom, and therefore it is in the national interest to pursue "victory over rather than coexistence with, this menace."[200]

Taken together, these pillars capture some of the major strands that Buckley had been weaving together in *National Review*: anti-Communism, libertarianism, and traditionalism. But what did these young students have to say about the burgeoning civil rights movement? According to Edwards, who as a twenty-seven-year-old congressional staffer was actually one of the oldest participants in the many hours of deliberations at Sharon, the civil rights issue simply "did not come up."[201] It is not surprising that Buckley, in his role as sagacious mentor, does not seem to have pushed the students to address the issue head-on In fact, the Sharon Statement strikes just the level of abstraction that he thought was advisable on the civil rights question. It was best, Buckley believed, to talk about race without ever actually mentioning race. The Sharon Statement's emphasis on "the primacy of the several states" had become a central trope in the conservative opposition to federal intervention on the civil rights question, and the statement's commitments to "internal order" and "economic freedom" provided rationales for resistance to the integration efforts by state or nonstate actors deemed likely to bring about civil unrest. There was no need to add a separate pillar explicitly endorsing the racial status quo; this commitment was baked into the pillars at the foundation of the American conservative movement.[202]

As the young activists were plotting a conservative future at Great Elm, Baldwin was trying to weave together the complicated plot of his third novel, *Another Country*, while at the same time writing essays and delivering lectures in which he was working out the contours of his own moral and political philosophy. As fate would have it, he found himself doing a great deal of this work just thirty miles southeast of Great Elm, at the country house of the writer William Styron. Baldwin had met Styron, a hard-drinking southerner, a few years earlier, and the two had enjoyed several evenings of imbibing, singing, and talking in the bars and nightclubs of Manhattan and Paris. In late 1960, Baldwin's life was even more tumultuous than usual. He had been on the move constantly—bouncing between bases in Paris and Greenwich Village when not "on assignment" for a magazine or off giving a lecture on a college campus—and his desk was full of half-done essay projects and his sprawling, uncompleted novel. He was, furthermore, low on money and continually distracted by his vibrant social life.

One of his editors at the time, Robert Silvers at *Harper's*, had an idea that he thought might help Baldwin get his life into some semblance of order (and get him to deliver an overdue assignment to the magazine): What if the young writer went out to the country to the relative peace and quiet of Styron's Roxbury home? In September, Silvers presented the idea to Styron and his wife, and they agreed to host Baldwin. Soon thereafter, Baldwin made his way to Roxbury, where he was, off and on, the Styron's houseguest for the next several months. Styron was just getting started with the book project that would become *The Confessions of Nat Turner*, and he and Baldwin spent countless hours drinking, smoking, and talking.[203]

Baldwin's time with the Styrons came in the midst of an immensely productive and tremendously important period in his career. In several pieces written and published in these years—especially "The Discovery of What It Means to Be an American" (1959), "Fifth Avenue, Uptown" (1960), "In Search of a Majority" (1960), "East River, Downtown" (1961), and "The New Lost Generation" (1961)—the contours of his mature moral and political philosophy were taking shape. Just as Buckley provided his readers with a defiant credo in *Up from Liberalism*, Baldwin would use these pieces (most of which would be included in his next collection, *Nobody Knows My Name*) to provide readers with a clear sense of how he viewed the world.

Baldwin's primary aim in these essays was to diagnose what ailed the American soul. The treatment of African Americans was, of course, the key symptom that led him to the conclusion that the country was ill, but it is important to emphasize that Baldwin viewed racism and other ideologies of exclusion as *symptoms* of deeper problems, not causes in themselves. For Baldwin, the root cause of the country's woes was not evil but rather fear. Americans, he believed, are a people who live in a perpetual state of terror. This terror is, at its core, psychological in nature and has to do with our quest—individually and collectively—for a meaningful identity. The American "identity crisis," perhaps paradoxically, is rooted in two things at the core of "American exceptionalism": the perception of social mobility and the fact of pluralism. In an aristocratic society with widely shared values, Baldwin argued, it is easier to have a clear sense of who you are and what is expected of you. In American society, we are told that there exists mobility that enables us to move up and down the social ladder according to our merit, and the fact of religious and cultural pluralism undermines the sense of "universally accepted forms or standards" that can guide us in our quest for meaning.[204] In the United States, we are told we can become whatever we want to become. If we think to ask who we *ought* to become, there are no universal standards to provide us with an answer.

In this moral vacuum, Baldwin told an audience at Kalamazoo College in November 1960, the mythology of the American dream emerged.[205] In response to the question of identity, Americans told one another to aspire to the ideal of the hardworking, pious, and virtuous "conqueror." But what should we conquer? There would be grand projects—for example, the "settling" of the country or defeat of foreign enemies—but on a day-to-day basis the American dream requires that we try to climb the ladder of success. One's "status" on that ladder, Baldwin told his audience at Kalamazoo, "became a kind of substitute for identity."[206]

It is worth noting that Baldwin's frequent discussion of "status" in this period included, but was not limited to, economic status. The "problem of status" had a significant economic dimension, but again, he asked us to peel that layer of explanation away to see what we might find. In his speech at Kalamazoo, Baldwin quoted Plato's *Republic* when he said, "What is honored in a country is cultivated there," and there is no question that money-making is part of the American "national self-image." Moneymaking and money spending are not, though, treated as ends in themselves. We are not, Baldwin said, simple materialists (although we are often condemned as such). "In fact," he maintained, "we are much closer to being metaphysical because nobody has ever expected from things the miracles that we expect."[207] We expect the land we take, the money we make, and the goods we acquire to do far more than supply us with life's necessities; we expect these *things* to give us a sense of meaning.

A purely materialist explanation was also unacceptable to Baldwin because it failed to provide an adequate account of the *social* dimension of "the problem of status in American life." In "In Search of a Majority," Baldwin described the sense in which we are always seeing and judging ourselves, and others, through the lens of status—something that inevitably leads to "social paranoia."[208] We achieve some level of

psychological peace when we feel as though we can peer down at someone else from the rung we occupy, and we aspire to continue our ascent
so we can peer down on yet more of our neighbors. But this sense of
peace is fleeting because we know that at any moment, we might fall and
lose our social status.

This, Baldwin argued, is where "the Negro" comes in. "The Negro" has
been used as a would-be antidote for the "social panic" that is caused by
our constant "fear of losing status":

> When one slips, one slips back not a rung but back into chaos and no
> longer knows who he is. And this reason, this fear, suggests to me one of
> the real reasons for the status of the Negro in this country. In a way, the
> Negro tells us where the bottom is: *because he is there*, and *where* he is,
> beneath us, we know where the limits are and how far we must not fall.
> We must not fall beneath him.[209]

The idea of "the Negro" in American culture has its roots not in biology
but rather in psychology. Americans created "the Negro," and buttressed
that creation with laws, customs, and mores in order to give themselves
some modicum of peace in the midst of perpetual status anxiety. In order
to rationalize this creation, Americans have refused "to look on the Negro
simply as a man." Instead, we have told ourselves that he is, at worst, a
threat, and at best, "a kind of ward," or "a victim" or "problem."[210]

We cling to the affirmative myth of the American dream and the negative myth of "the Negro Problem" because without them, we fear that
we might fall into an abyss of despair. Our fear of this despair is at the root
of our anti-intellectualism and tendency toward moral evasion. "We have
a very deep-seated distrust," Baldwin wrote in 1959, "of real intellectual
effort (probably because we suspect it will destroy . . . that myth of America to which we cling so desperately)."[211] These myths—and the habits
of the mind and heart that perpetuate them—hardly constitute an adequate cure for the sickness of the American soul. They might sometimes
paper over what ails us, but they fail to address our real problems. Beneath
the "conqueror-image" at the core of the American dream, Baldwin told
the audience at Kalamazoo, there are "a great many unadmitted despairs

and confusions, and anguish."[212] Just beneath the surface of these myths, our identities are still in a state of deep crisis. As he would put it later:

> This continent is now conquered, but our habits and our fears remain. And, in the same way that to become a social human being one modifies and suppresses and, ultimately, without great courage, lies to oneself about all one's interior, uncharted chaos, so have we, as a nation, modified and suppressed and lied about all the darker forces in our history. We know, in the case of the person, that whoever cannot tell himself the truth about his past is trapped in it, is immobilized in the prison of his undiscovered self.[213]

Underneath our myths, Baldwin saw, were inescapable realities that tormented oppressed and oppressor alike. The horror experienced by a human being who is the target of southern mob violence is obvious enough, but Baldwin also implored us to consider the terror that likely lurks in the hearts of those perpetrating the violence. The sense of helplessness that weighs down on the occupant of a northern ghetto is "immediately obvious," yet Baldwin also wanted us to think about the well-meaning white policeman who has been charged with the task of law enforcement within those ghettos. What must it be like for him to face, "daily and nightly, people who would gladly see him dead"? All these people are caught within a web of mythology that prevents them from treating one another as human beings. "It is a terrible, an inexorable, law," Baldwin concluded in his 1960 "Fifth Avenue, Uptown" letter, "that one cannot deny the humanity of another without diminishing one's own: in the face of one's victim, one sees himself. Walk through the streets of Harlem and see what we, this nation, have become."[214]

Baldwin's writings in this period reveal that he too wanted to encourage his readers to find their way "up from liberalism," though in a different direction from the one Buckley prescribed. While Buckley objected to the liberal tendency to think every social problem can be solved, Baldwin objected to the very framing of race matters as social problems. This framing, he insisted, doomed even the most well-intentioned liberal solution to failure. "Nothing can be done," Baldwin said in response to liberals who threw up their hands as the housing projects deteriorated, "as long as . . . colored people" are treated as something other than human beings.[215]

So what, in these writings at the dawn of the 1960s, did Baldwin prescribe for the sickness of the American soul? The first step, of course, is to recognize that one is sick. This is no easy task. It is difficult, Baldwin thought, to get enough critical distance from one's "sense of reality" to realize that one is living in a web of lies. But this is precisely what we must do. For Baldwin, self-examination is a basic duty: man "is enjoined," he wrote later, "to conquer the great wilderness that is himself."[216] This duty to oneself is part and parcel of the duty we have to look at ourselves collectively. "The time has come," he wrote in 1959, "God knows, for us to examine ourselves, but we can only do this if we are willing to free ourselves of the myth of America and try to find out what is really happening here."[217] If we take the bold and difficult step of engaging in this sort of self-reflection, Baldwin believed, we would realize we are ill in the ways described above.

Only once we have accepted that we are ill might we be willing to consider the possibility of treatment. The prescriptions Baldwin provided were updated versions of what I described as the "holy trinity" of his moral catechism in my discussion of *Giovanni's Room*: dignity, love, and freedom. The "revolution now occurring in the world," Baldwin wrote of the sit-in protesters in 1960, is animated by one overriding demand: "*Negroes want to be treated like men*: a perfectly straightforward statement, containing only seven words." In order for the dignity of all people to be recognized, we must liberate ourselves—"a man is not a man until he's able and willing to accept his own vision of the world, no matter how radically this vision departs from others"—from the myths that delude and divide us.[218] On this account, freedom is something more than freedom from interference with one's choices (as Buckley described it in *Up from Liberalism*); it is also freedom from delusion.[219]

In addition to self-examination, we are enjoined, Baldwin argued, to attempt to liberate others from delusion. These acts of liberation, he believed, are fundamentally acts of love. In his discussions of these matters, Baldwin often spoke and wrote about the responsibilities of "the artist" or "poet" to his society, but the theory of responsibility he developed has implications for everyone.[220] "The artist," he wrote, "is present to correct the delusions to which we fall prey in our attempts to avoid" coming to grips with reality. This responsibility puts the artist at odds with his society. The "responsible actors" in any society take as their primary duty the perpetuation of the existing social order. The artist, on the other hand, takes as his primary responsibility the revelation of "all that he can possibly discover concerning the mystery of the human being." The "peculiar nature of this responsibility," Baldwin continued, puts the artist in the position of "warring" with his society.But it is a peculiar kind of war: "Societies never know it, but the war of an artist with his society is a lover's war, and he does, at his best, what lovers do, which is to reveal the beloved to himself, and with that revelation, make freedom real."[221]

Baldwin believed that liberating acts of love were also deeply holy acts. "To be with God," he told those assembled at Kalamazoo, "is really to be involved with some enormous, overwhelming desire, and joy, and power which you cannot control, which controls you." The controlling power of God, though, is not an invitation to "control others." Instead, God ought to be understood as a "means of liberation" and an invitation to love one another. But love, as Baldwin understood it, is not easy and sentimental; it is difficult and often painful: "Love does not begin and end the way we think it does. Love is a battle, love is a war; love is a growing up."[222]

Chapter 4

Taking Responsibility, 1961–62

On May 4, 1961, a group of about a dozen civil rights activ-
ists embarked on a journey to test the enforcement of laws banning the
racial segregation of bus terminals throughout the South. The activists,
known as the Freedom Riders, departed from a terminal in Washington,
DC, and traveled without major incident through several states. Ten days
into their journey things changed. On May 14, one of the buses was met
by a mob in Anniston, Alabama. The attackers threw rocks at the bus,
slashed its tires, and firebombed it. Riders on a second bus managed to
make it through the Anniston assault only to meet a larger mob at the
next stop in Birmingham, where several of the Freedom Riders were severely beaten with baseball bats, lead pipes, and bicycle chains. On
May 20, a third group of riders made its way to Montgomery, where it
would meet the worst violence yet. The Freedom Riders were outnumbered by the mob by a ratio of about five to one. In the words of one reporter at the scene, "Using pipes, baseball bats, sticks and fists, the mob
surged on the small group of Freedom Riders, clubbing, punching, chas-
ing and beating both whites and Negroes." As some of the civil rights activists attempted to run away, the mob pursued them and proceeded to
stomp the victims they were able to capture.[1]

Images of the beaten Freedom Riders were being piped into the homes
of many Americans through the increasingly omnipresent medium of
television. It would have been one thing to hear the voice of Jim Zwerg,
who was among the most severely injured by the mob attacks, on a radio
broadcast, or even see a still image of him in a newspaper or magazine.
But it was quite another to see his battered face on the television screen,
speaking through cracked teeth and numerous bandages. What must it
have been like for television viewers as they looked on the "puffed and
swollen" face of nineteen-year-old William F. H. Barbee, who had been
stomped to a pulp by six or seven attackers?[2] Not only did the images of

the Freedom Riders find their way into American living rooms, but so did their defiant words: "We were willing to give our all," Barbee said, "so men of every race, creed and color may be equal before the law. We'll batter your segregation institutions until they crumble to dust."[3]

⌁

Like so many others, Buckley and Baldwin were captivated by the racial violence sparked by the Freedom Riders in the South. Buckley took to the pages of *National Review* to pen an editorial called "Let Us Try, at Least, to Understand." Buckley began the piece with a vignette about what happened a year earlier when George Lincoln Rockwell, the Commander of the American Nazi Party, appeared at a hearing to seek a permit to speak in a predominantly Jewish neighborhood in New York City.[4] "At the hearing," Buckley wrote, Rockwell was greeted by "a mob of Jews who hurled insults at him . . . lunged at him . . . and would, if given the chance, [have] beaten him bloody."[5] Buckley argued that *both* Rockwell and the mob were deserving of our condemnation.

From this confident assessment of the Rockwell case, Buckley's prose then slid right into a discussion of the Freedom Riders (who played the Nazi role in his analogy) along with the white mobs that had recently bombed and beaten them (who played the role of the "Jewish mob" in the analogy). Buckley anticipated an objection to the comparison he was making: the analogy fails due to the drawing of a false moral equivalence. The cause of the Freedom Riders, a critic would say, is morally superior to that of the Nazis, and the righteous indignation of the "Jewish mob" is far more legitimate than that of the southern mob. Buckley acknowledged that as a conservative, he found this sort of critique of moral relativism quite appealing.[6] It was, however, "irrelevant" in this particular case because Jim Crow "does not strike the average white Southerner as wrong."[7] To support his claim, Buckley cited Weaver's "The Regime of the South." As Weaver had argued there, "What the North is asking the South to do is to abandon its regime, the cluster of traditions and conventions and adjustments that make up a way of life that is different from our own."[8] Buckley mocked northern claims to moral superiority ("our

Jim Crowism" is simply a bit "more sophisticated" than the southerners'),
and rejected the idea that "we" had any "right to determine the shape, and
the quality of Southern life." He concluded the piece with this stirring
defense of southern defiance:

> *They* feel that *their* life is for *them* to structure; that the Negro has grown
> up under generally benevolent circumstances, considering where he
> started and how far he had to go; that he is making progress; that the
> coexistence of that progress and the Southern way of life demand, for
> the time being, separation. A conspicuous, theatrical, cinemascopic bus
> ride into the heart of things to challenge with language of unconditional
> surrender this deeply felt belief was met, inevitably, by a spastic re-
> sponse. By violence. Let us try, at least, to understand.[9]

The "conspicuous, theatrical, [and] cinemascopic" nature of the Freedom
Rider project that so appalled Buckley was, as far as Baldwin was concerned, precisely what the country needed. The young activists in the
South were bringing the American racial situation into great relief. Baldwin would not disagree with Buckley's mocking of the "more sophisticated Jim Crowism" of the North. Indeed, less than a year earlier, Baldwin had made the same point in *Esquire* when he wrote that blacks who
move North "do not escape Jim Crow: they merely encounter another,
not-less-deadly variety."[10] Rather than undermining the legitimacy of the
Freedom Rider project, as Buckley suggested, Baldwin argued that this
fact enhanced its importance. In a sense, the project was aimed not at "the
heart of things" in the Deep South but instead at "the heart" of the moderate North. The Freedom Riders were bringing the ugliness of racism
into the living rooms of *all* Americans, and Baldwin hoped that their confrontations with the angry mobs in the South might inspire some of
these Americans to confront the reality of the national racial nightmare.
Buckley spoke of northern racial hypocrisy in order to get people to lay
off the South. Baldwin spoke of it in order to encourage people to lay into
the North.

While the Freedom Riders were traveling the highways of the South in order to bring the question of civil rights back to the center of the nation's consciousness, Baldwin and Buckley were both traveling back and forth between Connecticut—where Buckley lived with his wife and son in Stamford, and Baldwin continued his stint as a kind of writer in residence at Styron's home in Roxbury—and Manhattan—where Buckley spent time at the offices of *National Review* on East Thirty-Seventh Street, and Baldwin still kept an apartment in Greenwich Village. By mid-1961, both men had established themselves as forces to be reckoned with in the world of ideas. In addition to his work at *National Review*, Buckley had begun publishing in more popular magazines such as *Esquire* and *Coronet*. Baldwin was also a frequent contributor to *Esquire* as well as the *New York Times, Encounter*, and the *Partisan Review*. Both men were gaining acclaim on the lecture circuit, visiting college campuses and speaking at events to promote the work of various organizations with which they had political sympathies. They were also gaining popularity as media personalities on radio and television, where they wowed listeners and viewers with their eloquence, wit, and charisma.

Buckley enjoyed this whirlwind of activity, but he also longed for an opportunity to take a step back and reflect on big questions. According to biographer John Judis, he even pondered leaving *National Review* to pursue an academic career. He was talked out of becoming "Professor Buckley," but he did have a plan to satiate his appetite for reflection: he would write a "big book" in which he would explain his conservative political philosophy. In 1961, he signed a contract with Putnam's to write what he hoped would be his magnum opus, *Revolt against the Masses*.[11]

Meanwhile, Baldwin was still working on what he thought might be his magnum opus, the novel *Another Country*, but in fact, 1961 saw the seeds planted for another project that would ultimately claim that mantle in Baldwin's oeuvre. It is fair to say that Baldwin never intended to write what would become *The Fire Next Time*. Instead, the book—which would consist of one short essay ("My Dungeon Shook") and one long essay ("Down at the Cross")—emerged as a result of several literary wheels that were set in motion in 1961. First, William Shawn, the famed editor of the *New Yorker*, commissioned Baldwin to travel to Africa and write about his journey for the magazine. Second, Norman Podhoretz, the editor of *Commentary*, commissioned Baldwin to write a piece about the Nation of Islam (NOI), a fast-growing religious sect that was capturing the attention of many Americans. After a number of twists and turns to which I will return later, these two invitations would lead Baldwin to write what most scholars consider to be his greatest work, and it would be the work that would cast the largest shadow over his debate with Buckley a few years later. Baldwin's road to writing *Fire*, though, starts with the rise of the NOI.

In the black ghetto of Detroit during summer 1930, a mysterious peddler-prophet began to capture the attention of many residents. "My name is W.D. Fard," one man remembered him saying, "and I come from the Holy City of Mecca. More about myself I will not tell you yet, for the time has not yet come." Fard offered whomever would listen tales of his journeys in foreign lands, nutritional advice, theological musings, and "increasingly bitter denunciations of the white race." At first, Fard communicated his ideas on street corners and in house-to-house visits, but eventually he was able to secure a temple for his growing movement, which he called the NOI. By the mid-1930s, Fard had written two manuals for his nearly eight thousand followers, and created an organizational apparatus that included not only places of worship but also educational projects and the Fruit of Islam, "a military organization for the men who were drilled by captains and taught tactics and the use of firearms."[12]

Fard required his followers to abandon their given surnames, which he associated with slavery, and adopt new names that declared their new Muslim identities. This new identity, he taught, required submission to the tenets of his peculiar brand of Islam, which included not only specific guidelines about how to live but also how one ought to view other human beings. As Baldwin would summarize it later, the NOI taught that

At the very beginning of time there was not one white face to be found in all the universe. Black men ruled the earth and the black man was perfect.... Allah allowed the Devil, through his scientists, to carry on infernal experiments, which resulted, finally, in the creation of the devil known as the white man, and later, even more disastrously, in the creation of the white woman. And it was decreed that these monstrous creatures should rule the earth for a certain number of years ... [but] their rule is now ending, and Allah, who never approved of the creation of the white man in the first place (who knows him, in fact, to be not a man at all but a devil), is anxious to restore the rule of peace that the rise of the white man totally destroyed.

In sum, it was essential to the NOI creed that there was "by definition, no virtue in white people," and in fact, they were not *really* people at all.[13]

One of Fard's earliest converts was a petite, Georgia-born man named Elijah Poole, who would take the name Elijah Muhammad when he joined the NOI. Muhammad rose quickly to become Fard's second in command and helped the founder of the sect spread its influence into other black ghettos around the country. In mid-1934, Fard disappeared and Muhammad took control of the movement. Under Muhammad's leadership, scholar C. Eric Lincoln has noted, the sect spread rapidly, and began opening not only new temples around the country but also "schools, apartment houses and grocery stores, restaurants and farms."[14] Perhaps just as important, Muhammad developed a more comprehensive program for the NOI and had a keen eye for identifying talent in his ranks.

One such talent was Malcolm Little, a petty criminal who was introduced to NOI doctrines while serving time. Little had utilized his time in prison to immerse himself in the world of ideas. According to biographer Manning Marable, Little "devoured the writings of influential scholars such as W.E.B. DuBois," and "plowed through Herodotus, Kant, [and] Nietzsche."[15] In addition, Little joined the prison's debate club and honed his rhetorical skills. Little and his siblings had been raised on the black nationalist ideas of Marcus Garvey so when his brother Reginald introduced him to the ideas of the NOI during a visit to the penitentiary, it was not a bridge too far for him to accept some of what he was hearing.

Before long, several of Little's siblings joined the NOI and encouraged him to write to Muhammad to address any remaining doubts he had about the faith. Write Little did—again and again—and Muhammad wrote back—again and again—and soon after he was released from prison in summer 1952, Malcolm Little became Malcolm X and began his meteoric rise within the ranks of the NOI. By the late 1950s—after several peripatetic years of preaching and organizing—Malcolm was widely identified as Muhammad's second in command.[16]

In 1959, the journalist Mike Wallace ran a five-part television documentary series called *The Hate That Hate Produced* that he described as a "study of the rise of black racism."[17] The series generated a great deal of interest in Wallace's predominantly white audience, and so the following week, he repeated highlights from the series along with previously unaired footage. There was no doubt about it; Malcolm X was the star of the show. A massive television audience was introduced for the first time to this tall, charismatic preacher whose forceful delivery of the NOI doctrine proved to be inspiring to some, terrifying to others, and mesmerizing to all.

⸻

Over the years, Baldwin had noticed the growing NOI presence in Harlem, where the sect had established Mosque No. 7 in 1946. Malcolm X had been preaching there since 1956, and ministers were also popular "street corner speakers," where they would often attract large crowds with their incendiary rhetoric. In "Fifth Avenue, Uptown," which was published in *Esquire* in July 1960, Baldwin had noted the growing influence of "Moslems," who were "united by nothing more—and nothing less—than a hatred of the white world and all its works."[18] Baldwin was simultaneously fascinated and frightened by the rise of the NOI. What fascinated him was the relatively warm reception NOI speakers received from Harlemites even though, Baldwin suspected, most of their audience viewed their theology as bizarre and unbelievable. He was frightened by the hatred at the heart of the NOI's message, which he knew might be seductive to the hopeless.

Baldwin, for his part, had been seduced by a different message. He admired and supported King and the SCLC, but the civil rights organizations for which he had the greatest affinity were the Congress of Racial Equality (CORE) and Student Nonviolent Coordinating Committee (SNCC), two nonviolent groups that were engaged in direct action to bring about racial progress.[19] The NOI had been sharply critical of these groups, which it contended were using degrading means— nonviolent resistance—in pursuit of an unworthy end: integration. When television and radio hosts were looking for guests who would deliver the most powerful arguments on each side of this debate, Baldwin and Malcolm X were often at the top of their lists.

In April 1961, Baldwin arrived at the Manhattan studio of NBC television for the taping of an episode of the public affairs show *The Open Mind*. The host of the show, Princeton University historian Eric Goldman, had assembled quite a panel to discuss civil rights. On the program with Baldwin that night would be C. Eric Lincoln, a philosopher who had just published a book on the NOI; the black conservative newspaper columnist George Schuyler, whose "Olympian serenity" had long "infuriated" Baldwin; and none other than Malcolm X himself.[20]

It must have been quite a scene as the four men arrived on the set of *The Open Mind*. Lincoln was a bear of a man who spoke in a deep southern drawl that revealed his Alabama roots. Schuyler was a short but sturdily built northerner whose white hair established his status as the elder statesman in the room. Malcolm dressed, as always, in a dark suit and tie, stood nearly a foot taller than Baldwin, and sported his signature horn-rimmed glasses and close-cropped, reddish hair. Goldman was the only white man on the panel, and looked and sounded the part of the liberal professor.

For the first several minutes of the discussion, Baldwin sat back in silence as Goldman attempted to get Lincoln and Malcolm to define the nature of the "Black Muslim program" while Schuyler lobbed rhetorical grenades accusing the NOI of being "anti-Christian," "anti-white," violent, and delusional. After Malcolm attempted to clarify the nature of the NOI's separatism, Goldman jumped in to invite Baldwin to join the conversation. What, Goldman asked, was *his* "understanding of the

FIGURE 4.1. Martin Luther King Jr. and Malcolm X, circa 1964 (Wikimedia Commons)

purposes of the movement?" The "Muslim movement," Baldwin responded, is best understood in terms of "power," "morality," and "identity." What the NOI promised its followers, he explained, was the acquisition of power in exchange for the acceptance of its peculiar notions of morality and identity. The relative powerlessness of blacks in America, Baldwin argued, was what provided the NOI with fertile ground in which to grow. When an NOI minister tells a would-be recruit in Detroit or Harlem that they are being oppressed, Baldwin said, they have "all the evidence" on their side.[21]

This comment caused Schuyler to turn his ire, for the moment, from Malcolm to Baldwin. He disagreed "violently" with Baldwin's suggestion that "all the evidence" was on the side of the NOI and suggested that it was dangerous to say so because such statements were used to justify the NOI's "campaign of hate against white people." After some back and forth about the evidence on each side of the argument, Baldwin addressed Schuyler's concern about the NOI's "campaign of hate against white people." On this issue, Baldwin and Schuyler found some common ground. The NOI, Baldwin had asserted earlier in the conversation, actually had a great deal in common with the southern segregationists. What the NOI had done, Baldwin contended, is merely taken the ideology of white supremacy, swapped the power positions of white and black, and dressed it up in the garb of their strange moral theology. In Baldwin's words, "What the Muslim movement is doing is simply taking the equipment or the history really of white people with Negroes and turning [it] against white people." Baldwin could not have been more adamant about his opposition to this approach. Whatever the merits of the strategy as a way to enhance one's sense of power, he argued, it was a sure way to destroy one's soul. Muslims should remember, he said, that the doctrine of white supremacy had "done more to destroy white men in this country . . . than it has done to destroy the Negro."[22] Baldwin made this point while acknowledging the physical destruction of slavery, lynching, and the ghettos. Physical destruction, he seemed to be saying, is but one way to perish; he was concerned, primarily, with the threat of the moral destruction that followed inevitably from all philosophies rooted in the denial of universal human dignity.

Baldwin's nuanced position on the NOI and other matters was met with this response from his white liberal host: "Mr. Baldwin," Goldman said, "now you confuse me. One can have two aims if one is a Negro": integration or separation.[23] At this point, Baldwin—probably frustrated—receded from the conversation for another few minutes. When he reflected on encounters like this later, he would admit exasperation with Goldman and his ilk.[24] In the face of the NOI, liberals like Goldman were asking all the wrong questions. He spent nearly the whole hour trying to understand the minute details of the NOI's economic, political, and martial programs. For Baldwin, these details were not worthy of such focus. The NOI programs, Baldwin saw—and his host clearly did not—were really of minor importance in comparison to the details of black life that made the rise of the NOI possible in the first place. When he came back into the conversation, Baldwin confronted Goldman on this point as the host admitted that what he—and presumably his mostly white audience—really wanted "to find out is whether the Muslim movement does hate me or not, and whether it proposes to use force to satisfy that hatred." Baldwin was incredulous. "It is not important," he told Goldman, whether the NOI hates you or not; "that is not at all the question . . . that's irrelevant." *The* question, Baldwin told Goldman, is whether white people—whether they be reactionary or liberal—are ready to face up to "the crimes for which they are responsible" and accept, finally, that the "Negro" is "as human as he is, and that he is losing his humanity insofar as he denies you yours."[25]

———

Just a few days after their appearance on television together, Baldwin and Malcolm X met again at the studios of the WBAI radio station, where they participated in a panel discussion of the sit-in movement with student activist LaVerne McCummings.[26] During the course of the conversation, Malcolm explained that the NOI objected to the passivity and nonviolence of the student activists. "The word 'sit' itself," he noted, "is not an honorable tag. Anybody can sit. An old woman can sit. A coward can sit. A baby can sit. It takes a man to stand." According to Malcolm, the sit-in movement was a manifestation of a lack of racial pride along with a willingness to accept labels and limitations imposed by whites and moderate black leaders. As an alternative, Malcolm called for blacks to embrace the doctrines of the NOI, especially the celebration of racial pride (which was, in his view, ordained by God), and the determination to defend oneself and one's people by any means necessary. This acceptance of violence, Malcolm pointed out, was quintessentially American. After all, American heroes have been, as a rule, violent men. When host John Donald asked Malcolm if his objections to the means of the sit-in movement extended to its "goal" as well, Malcolm responded, "If their goal is integration, it is not a worthwhile one. But if their goal is freedom, justice, and equality, then that's a worthwhile goal."[27]

In response to Malcolm, McCummings provided a brief history of the sit-in movement, and explained that the students were not mobilized because they wanted to drink coffee with whites but rather by a desire to challenge the entire system of degradation and inequality. The sit-ins at lunch counters, he contended, were merely symbols that represented a demand for the realization of a "democratic way of life."[28]

Baldwin entered the conversation with a call for greater analytic and rhetorical precision: "I have a feeling," he said, "that a great many words have been floating around this table which need to be redefined. And that, by the way, is a problem which faces this entire country." In response to McCummings, Baldwin pushed for a more precise definition of integration and, more important, an explanation of *why* it was a worthwhile goal. He expressed skepticism about equality as a sufficient goal for the movement:

> There are a great many people who I am not prepared to accept as my equal. Some of them are white and some of them are black. From my point of view, integration in terms of being raised to the level of a Mississippi cracker is not integration at all. It seems to me the hope of this country and the role the Negro can play in it is to raise these people to a level they have not yet achieved. One has got to reexamine the standards of the country, which not only afflict black people, they afflict the entire country. No one in this country knows any more what it means to be an American. He does not know what he means by freedom. He does not know what he means by equality.[29]

This statement captures something crucial about Baldwin's moral and political philosophy. Baldwin was, of course, committed to the ideas of equality before the law, political equality, and equal rights. He worried, though, about the legitimacy of equality as a goal in the moral realm. He did not want blacks—once made equal legally and politically—to strive to meet the standards by which the white world measured success. Some ways of life, he insisted, were better than others, and the civil rights revolution had the potential to inspire Americans to reimagine the standards by which they lived.

In response to Malcolm, Baldwin had many things to say. First, he contended that if his understanding of courage was not capacious enough to encompass the sorts of risks being taken by McCummings and the other student activists, then his conception of courage was insufficient. Second, in response to Malcolm's call for black power to achieve "freedom, justice, and equality," Baldwin pushed him for more precise definitions and recognition that these ideas might be in tension with each other.

In order to explain these points, Baldwin pointed to the recent "liberation" of African countries from colonial rule. In those places, "white power has been broken," and this made it much more difficult for white men everywhere to define and subordinate nonwhites. In this moment when the white power structure had been destabilized, Baldwin said, "the responsibility" that faces us is to "decide what we want." Using the example of the formerly British African nations, Baldwin argued that it seemed obvious that freedom and power were crucial pillars of self-respect: "An African nation cannot expect to be respected unless it is free, unless it's political destiny is in its own hands, which is what we mean by power." The situation of American blacks, however, was not perfectly analogous to that of the recently liberated African nations. American whites and blacks, he said, were bound together in a unique way: "We have been integrated for a very long time. . . . The history which has produced us we are going to have deal with, in any case, one of these days."[30]

Baldwin maintained that both the sit-in movement and the NOI were important because they were drawing attention to the many blacks perishing around the country through violence and addiction, and the millions "perishing from demoralization, bitterness and hatred." The students had played a crucial role by dramatizing the injustice of the most blatantly racist practices in the society, and the NOI had provided the most unflinching description of the reality of black life. The rage that was being portrayed by the NOI and was fueling the protests throughout the South could, Baldwin warned, "blow this country wide apart."[31]

Baldwin also launched a direct attack on theology generally and NOI doctrine specifically. "To me," he said, "all theologies are suspect" because they encourage human beings to escape reality and construct false identities. As an alternative to theological thinking, Baldwin proposed the "reckless" idea that we attempt to live our lives without the support of mythology and ideology. "I would like to think of myself as being able to face whatever it is I have to face as me," he declared, "without having my identity dependent on something that finally has to be *believed*." He conceded that reliance on religion, race, and culture as the bases of identity might be useful in some circumstances, but we must never lose sight of the fact that this reliance "has something very dangerous in it." As long as we rely on such things to make sense of where we fit into the world and how we ought to act in it, "the confusion . . . and the bloodshed will be great."[32]

To the ears of Malcolm X, these were fighting words. "As a *black* man," he responded, "and *proud* of being a black man, I can't conceive of myself as having any desire to lose my identity."[33] To Malcolm, Baldwin's comments were symptomatic of the unwillingness of many blacks to take pride in their race. To illustrate this point, Malcolm noted that he had recently seen King debate Buckley's colleague Kilpatrick on television, and was appalled when Kilpatrick proclaimed his pride in the white race and King declined to defend "black pride" in response.[34] Malcolm did not object completely to Baldwin's suggestion that the whole question of identity needed to be reexamined, but he objected strenuously to the idea that this new identity be forged in a way that was deracialized and secular. To the contrary, Malcolm called for a radical reconstruction of identity that was deeply rooted in the divine superiority of blackness. Embrace your blackness, Malcolm demanded, and stand up "like a man" and fight for your rights. In choosing to take pride in one's racial identity and the willingness to use force in defense of one's rights, he observed, blacks would be acting in a manner consistent with the pantheon of American heroes from Patrick Henry to those who fought fascism in World War II.

Baldwin was permitted to make one final statement in response to Malcolm. The question of violence versus nonviolence, he argued, was not primarily moral but instead strategic. In the context of racial politics, violence had been and would continue to be a "given," and black leaders ought to be guided by a desire to navigate this violent terrain in a "responsible" way. But where Baldwin chose to focus his concluding comments was on the "question of identity," which he said was the absolute key to everything else (including the question of violence). It is essential, he asserted, to recognize that the black history is simultaneously "one of the ugliest histories in the history of the West" *and* "one of the most remarkable histories that we know of." Coming to grips with this history was, Baldwin maintained, absolutely crucial not only to rethinking the question of identity but also to the reexamination of what we mean by freedom, justice, equality, and courage. In order to demonstrate this point, Baldwin challenged Malcolm's repeated identification of Henry as an American hero who ought to be emulated. "Patrick Henry," Baldwin said with passion, "is not one of *my* heroes. . . . I don't see any reason for me, at this late date, to begin modeling myself on an image which I've always found to be frankly mediocre and not a standard to which I myself could repair."[35] It is a mistake, Baldwin concluded, to look to figures such as Henry for the standards by which we ought to live. What we must do, he told Malcolm and McCummings, is come up with new standards that can guide us once the day of liberation comes.[36] "It seems to me," he declared, "that my responsibility . . . is to begin to prepare for this day because this day *is* coming."[37]

While Malcolm was jousting with Baldwin on radio and television, Muhammad was paying close attention. As Muhammad was listening with interest as Minister Malcolm debated Baldwin, the Federal Bureau of Investigation (FBI) was listening with interest to Muhammad's phone calls. During one such call—only a few weeks after Baldwin and Malcolm's April debates—Muhammad told Malcolm that he thought "Brother Baldwin" was "wonderful" and admired him because "there was no 'Tom' in him." Muhammad said he was so moved by Baldwin's performance on television, "if he had known his telephone number he would have called him as soon as he was through looking at him" and he instructed his minister to "send him his best love" the next time he saw Baldwin in New York.[38] Malcolm then gave Muhammad the telephone number for Baldwin's Greenwich Village apartment. Soon thereafter, Muhammad extended an invitation for Baldwin to join him for dinner at his Chicago mansion on July 16, 1961.[39]

As Baldwin made his way up the steps of Muhammad's mansion on Chicago's South Side, he asked himself a question, Why am I here? What did this self-proclaimed prophet who was striking fear into the hearts of so many Americans want with me? Baldwin's own reasons for accepting the invitation were obvious enough. He was a writer who relied on experience as a primary source for material and had accepted an invitation to write about the NOI for *Commentary*. But he wondered about the precise nature of Muhammad's motivations. What, after watching him spar with Malcolm and others on television, did Muhammad take Baldwin's "usefulness to be?" After all, Baldwin had made it entirely clear that he was not on board with the NOI program, which he viewed as fundamentally sinister. On reflection, though, Baldwin concluded that Muhammad might have been hopeful he would change his mind. Interestingly, Baldwin suspected that Muhammad's hope for his conversion had far less to do with his exchanges with conservatives like Schuyler than it did with his exchanges with liberals like Goldman. While Baldwin had found it necessary to defend the NOI's diagnosis of the race problem against some of Schuyler's criticisms, it was really the "incredible, abysmal, and really cowardly obtuseness" of white liberals like Goldman that most exasperated Baldwin.[40] During the discussion on *The Open Mind*, for example, Goldman seemed unable to understand how Malcolm could possibly diagnose the racial situation in such dire terms and was obsessed with the details of the NOI program—especially the question of violence—that seemed most threatening to him as a white elite.

Muhammad, Baldwin suspected, had sensed his exasperation with liberals like Goldman and thought there might be some hope, as one white member of the audience put it after one of his television appearances, that he may yet become "Mr. James X." So when Baldwin sat to Muhammad's left at his large dining room table, at which they were joined by many NOI

FIGURE 4.2. Nation of Islam leader Elijah Muhammad, circa 1964 (Wikimedia Commons)

followers, Baldwin could not help but feel "he was sizing me up" and figuring out "[my] usefulness" to the movement. The back and forth between the two men was cordial and revealing. Baldwin was sympathetic to Muhammad's diagnosis of the racial problem because "things are as bad as the Muslims say they are."[41] But when Baldwin looked at Muhammad's face just a few inches from his own, he found more to fear in the man than to admire.

When Baldwin reflected on the dinner later, he would identify several reasons why Muhammad left him feeling fearful. First, "whenever Elijah

spoke, a kind of chorus arose from the table, saying, 'Yes, that's right.'"
Baldwin was not a joiner or follower, and the reflexive call and response
of the dinner conversation made him uncomfortable. Furthermore, the
substance of this call and response was inconsistent with Baldwin's core
values. Muhammad repeatedly referred to the "white devils" with whom
Baldwin appeared on television. Baldwin admitted that "the people referred to had certainly made me feel exasperated and useless," but he
rejected the idea that they were "devils." This was the heart of the disagreement between the two men. Muhammad believed whites were
irredeemably evil, and Baldwin knew some whites "who were struggling as hard as they knew how, and with great effort and sweat and
risk, to make the world more human," and moreover, held out hope
that more whites might join them in this struggle. For Muhammad, the
proper response to white racism was rejection and separation. This was
a response Baldwin could not accept. So as he stood on the front steps
of the mansion with Muhammad after dinner, Baldwin felt conflicted.
He "felt very close" to Muhammad because he shared his "pain and his
fury," but because of "what he conceived as his responsibility and what
I took to be mine—we would always be strangers, and possibly, one
day, enemies."[42]

While Baldwin was clarifying his own position in relation to the fringe
of the black freedom struggle, Buckley was attempting to do the same in
relation to the fringe of the American Right. As *National Review* came
to be seen as one of the most prominent tribunes of the right wing,
Buckley was undertaking the crucial task of "editing conservatism."[43] In
other words, Buckley and his colleagues at the magazine were attempting to establish themselves as intellectual bouncers who would get to
decide which groups would be allowed to stay at the conservative party,
and who would be left out in the ideological wilds. When the Russian
émigré novelist Ayn Rand, for example, took individualism a bit too far
for Buckley's taste and committed the mortal sin of rejecting God, he

commissioned Chambers to write such a savage review of her novel *Atlas Shrugged* that Rand refused to ever again be in the same room as Buckley.[44]

The John Birch Society (JBS) presented Buckley with a more complicated case. The society was founded in 1958 by a candy manufacturer named Robert Welch for the purposes of organizing against the worldwide Communist conspiracy. Buckley was sympathetic to just about anyone who was anti-Communist, but it did not take long for him to see that the JBS might be more of a liability than an asset. This had become evident to him in the late 1950s when Welch sent him a copy of his "secret" book, *The Politician*, in which he unveiled the intricacies of Communist infiltration of the US government. Just about everyone, including then president Eisenhower, was in on the plot. The JBS presented a difficult case for Buckley because Welch had been an original donor to *National Review*, and many leading conservative luminaries and financial backers were simultaneously contributing to both Buckley's magazine and Welch's (*American Opinion*). Buckley also had to confront the fact that the JBS was growing to become a powerful force on the American Right, with over sixty thousand members and an "annual revenue of about $1.6 million (the equivalent of about $11 million today)."[45] In the wake of the Cuban Revolution in 1959 and latest Berlin crisis in 1961, Buckley was worried about the trajectory of the Cold War. Could he really afford to alienate the Birchers?

Buckley's reticence to bring fringe elements like Randian objectivists and Birchers into the conservative fold forced him to walk some fine lines. He was worried about alienating potential allies, but he also wanted to fashion a conservative movement that was intellectually serious. In addition to fielding many complaints from readers about his criticisms of Rand and Welch, he was confronted with challenges from readers who thought him too soft on racial questions. In *Up from Liberalism*, you will recall that he had argued that there were "no scientific grounds for assuming congenital Negro disabilities."[46] This view was anathema to many of his readers, especially southerners who may have subscribed thanks to the Citizens' Council endorsement of *National Review* in the late 1950s.

One such southerner wrote to Buckley to complain about his skepticism of the biological basis for white supremacy, and Buckley responded:

> I have no objections whatever to continuing research on the question of the relative congenital superiority or inferiority among the races. But what conclusions of a political kind I should be prepared to draw from the fruits of such research, I am not prepared so say. My own notion, for instance, is that the Jewish race can probably be demonstrated to be more intelligent than the Gentile, on the average; as Gentiles might be shown to be superior to Negroes in intelligence. I guess another way of saying the same thing is that I believe a) there are as yet no conclusive grounds for such generalizations . . . and b) the whole situation is not, frankly, one of my principal concerns.[47]

Private communications such as these might lead us to wonder if Buckley's racial views had softened a bit in the three years since he authored "Why the South Must Prevail." In that piece he had made some clear racial generalizations and had relied on them to draw conclusions of a political kind. Was he beginning to doubt the wisdom of these views?

The short answer is no. In March 1960, Buckley and his fellow editors at *National Review* penned an editorial in which they reminded readers that they believed "in the Deep South the Negroes are, by comparison with the Whites, retarded ('unadvanced,' the National Association for the Advancement of Colored People might put it)," and the "South, then, quite properly rests in White hands." This position of superiority, they reminded readers, "imposes moral obligations of paternalism, patience, protection, devotion, sacrifice." But they mustn't forget that "nobody knows" the "solution to the Negro problem."[48]

In 1961, Buckley was given an opportunity to make this argument to a larger audience when the *Saturday Review* asked him to write an essay in response to the question, "Desegregation: Will It Work?"[49] Buckley's essay, which he would include in his next book under the title "Can We Desegregate, Hesto Presto?," trumpets the "philosophy of no" with which he had concluded *Up from Liberalism*. "What," he began his essay, "is the conservatives' solution to the race problem in the South? I answer there is no present solution to it." Do not listen to the liberals, he implored his readers, who will tell you "there is always a road" to a better place. The conservative is here to remind you that, alas, "some problems are insoluble."[50]

In the course of his argument, Buckley conceded that "the race problem has debasing effects on blacks and whites alike," and the federal government *could* take drastic actions to end segregation and enforce the Fifteenth Amendment. In Buckley's mind, though, the questions of debasement and governmental power were not determinative. Instead, the question was a moral one: "*Should* the government take . . . action to end segregation?" In a fascinating twist, Buckley began his defiant call for resistance to racial progress by citing the words of none other than Baldwin: "You know, the world is hard enough and people is evil enough without all the time looking for it and stirring it up and making it worse." These words were spoken by the character Leona in Baldwin's forthcoming novel *Another Country*, an excerpt of which had appeared in the spring 1960 issue of the *Partisan Review*. This was the first time Buckley would cite Baldwin in print, and he took the opportunity to describe him as a "tormented Negro writer . . . who celebrates his bitterness against the white community mostly in journals of the far political Left."[51] Leona had offered, in Buckley's estimation, valuable advice: don't stir up trouble; you'll only make things worse.

In support of this "don't rock the boat" position on civil rights, Buckley offered two major arguments. First, he questioned whether or not "the average Southern Negro" was really all that unhappy. Negro elites (like Louis Lomax, King, and Baldwin) were "more sensitive, and hence more bitter." We should, Buckley seemed to be suggesting, allow the Negro masses to stay content in their place in "the regime of the South," not rouse them. Second, Buckley wondered if desegregation was really everything it was cracked up to be. Had the results been "unambiguously successful?" If so, we might still have compelling reasons (e.g., "the ideal of [local] self-government" or "traditions of our system") to leave segregation intact, but if not, we would have all the more reason to leave it alone. As an alternative, Buckley endorsed a gradual, organic approach as "the right kind of integration." In order for blacks to be accepted fully, he wrote, they "must advance," and when they have advanced sufficiently, "the myths" about them "will begin to fade." Once the day comes "when the Negroes have finally realized their long dream of attaining the status of the white man," Buckley concluded, "I hope the white man will still be free."[52]

Buckley's invitation to contribute to the popular *Saturday Review* was one of many indicators of his meteoric rise on the American cultural scene. Around the same time the *Saturday Review* essay was published, the North American Newspaper Alliance ran a Buckley column defending conservatism opposite a column critiquing it by his soon-to-be archrival Gore Vidal, a well-to-do writer and provocateur who had established himself as a leading voice of the literary Left. The exchange with Vidal generated a considerable amount of fan mail, including a note from Buckley's friend Dr. Ramon Castroviejo. In response to Castroviejo's missive, Buckley wrote, "Vidal must be nuts. He is also, I am told, a maricon."[53] The exchange with Vidal also helped Buckley secure an invitation to begin writing a syndicated column, which debuted in April 1962. Within a couple of years, his column would appear thrice weekly in over 150 newspapers.[54]

Buckley's rise was accelerated by the fact that he proved to be a compelling presence on television. The 1960 election had revealed how powerful this medium could be in the communication of political ideas. The telegenic John F. Kennedy had just defeated Nixon in part because, to put it bluntly, he looked better on TV. Buckley was not a "natural" in quite the way Kennedy was. Viewers were attracted to Kennedy in part because of his movie star good looks, but Buckley's appeal was of a different sort. Buckley's charm came from the vast collection of mannerisms, gesticulations, affectations, and idiosyncrasies that made him one of a kind. His dark hair was, in those days, neatly parted from left to right and his face was the home of many features that would contribute to his fame. His lively eyebrows bounced up and down as he spoke, and beneath them his blue eyes danced in rhythm with the torrent of multisyllabic words that came flowing out of his mouth. When Buckley unleashed a verbal barb, for example, he had a tendency to accompany it with a lightning-quick bugging of his eyes. Underneath his slender nose was a mouth, the most remarkable features of which were two prominent front teeth and a tongue that frequently darted upward to moisten his lips as he spoke. And perhaps most famously, there was that peculiar *way* he spoke. Buckley's "accent" defies easy categorization, and its origins have been much debated. The combination of the fact that he learned English while at the same time learning Spanish and French from his family's servants and tutors, the influence of the southern accents of his parents, and his boarding school experience in England produced a manner of speaking that was truly unique.[55] Buckley had a stockpile of obscure words that he would sprinkle throughout his columns and speeches, and had a gift for altering the pace and tone of his speech for dramatic effect. He had, in sum, mastered the art of performing conservatism.

Millions of Americans were able to experience Buckley's remarkable television presence when he appeared on the *Tonight Show* with Jack Paar in January 1962. The Paar appearance garnered Buckley a lot of attention, including from the man occupying the oval office. Kennedy, who had appeared on the *Tonight Show* in June 1960, called Paar to tell him that he had done the country the "greatest service" by inviting Buckley and his ilk on his show to express their views. When Kennedy received an honorary degree from Yale a few months later, he noted that not all Yale alumni—including "William F. Buckley Jr. of the class of 1950"—would be pleased that the university was conferring him with such an honor.[56] The fact that everyone from Paar to the president of the United States could use Buckley as a punch line confirmed his status as a major player on the American cultural scene.

Buckley's increased presence in the public eye led to a veritable cavalcade of invitations to lecture and debate around the country. Buckley was a happy warrior who relished the intellectual and performative dimensions of such appearances. He was further motivated by his desire to keep *National Review* afloat so he pledged to devote all his speaking fees to the magazine.[57] Buckley became a fixture on the public speaking circuit—sometimes making seventy appearances in a year—and was a huge draw. Ideological friends and enemies alike found something to enjoy in a Buckley appearance. Conservatives loved seeing such an articulate defense of their views, and reveled in his acerbic and witty attacks on leftists. Ideological opponents often had a grudging admiration of Buckley's style and could not help but be energized by his relentless provocation.[58] Buckley's appeal, in sum, was not just about ideas; it was about entertainment.

The entertainment value of ideas was on full display in 1962, when Buckley was invited to square off in debate against the radical writer Norman Mailer. A publicist named John Golden had come up with the idea for the debate. On September 25, heavyweight boxing champion Floyd Patterson was set to defend his title at Comiskey Park in Chicago. Golden's idea was to give the throngs of people in town for the fight an opportunity to attend an intellectual brawl between Buckley and Mailer. When the two men arrived at the Medinah Temple to debate the "real nature of the right wing in America," they looked out at a capacity crowd of three thousand people.[59] Their messages would reach far beyond those in the crowded venue that night. The editors of *Playboy* magazine, anticipating rhetorical fireworks that might excite their reader's minds while the centerfolds excited their bodies, had agreed to publish a transcription of the debate. Over the course of the next couple of hours, Buckley and Mailer gave the crowd the intellectual pugilism Golden had promised. Buckley delivered a decidedly religious defense of conservatism that night, but he was sure to sprinkle in plenty of jabs at Mailer's obsession with the "world's genital glands."[60]

As fate would have it, Baldwin was also in Chicago to cover the Patterson-Liston fight, and while he was in town, he spent time with Mailer. The two writers had met in Paris in 1956, and although they considered themselves friends, they also viewed each other with a considerable amount of suspicion. Each had criticized the other in print, and their encounter in Chicago ended up being the scene of a "well-publicized falling-out."[61] When they got into a drunken argument at a cocktail party, Baldwin told Mailer that "he'd rather spend his time with a white racist" than someone like Mailer "since with the racist he knew exactly where he stood." Mailer "got sore" and "almost slugged" Baldwin, who ended up—according to the host of the party—in tears.[62] After the Chicago encounter, Baldwin concluded that he and Mailer "temperamentally can't hit it off," and interestingly enough, it was Buckley who would maintain a deeper relationship with "America's angry young man."[63]

~~~~~~~~

Not long after his dinner with Muhammad, Baldwin returned to Paris for a brief stop before embarking for Israel as part of the travel commissioned by the *New Yorker*. Baldwin chronicled his trip in several letters to his agent Robert P. Mills that would later be published in *Harper's* as "Letters from a Journey." In the letters, Baldwin confessed that he was "afraid" to make the trip to Africa. He was worried about what he might find there, and once discovered, what he would be able to say about it. The core of Baldwin's fear, he explained, had to do with "something unutterably painful about the end of oppression." More specifically, Baldwin was overwhelmed by the sense of "responsibility" that comes with liberation. Now that parts of Africa were free, he was terrified by the prospect of abandoning his "dream of Africa" for the reality of the continent that awaited him.[64]

Baldwin was also sure in the letters to update Mills on the progress he was making on *Another Country* and "Down at the Cross," which he hinted had become something more than a report on the NOI. Baldwin decided that rather than proceeding to Africa from Israel, he would head to Istanbul, Turkey, where his friend Engin Cezzar would host him for several months. While in Turkey, he finished *Another Country*, his sprawling third novel in which he told a complex story about love, sexuality, race, and longing.[65] In the novel, Baldwin said later, he attempted "to write the way [jazz musicians] sound."[66]

The other major project on Baldwin's desk, his NOI essay for Podhoretz at *Commentary*, also had a musical feel to it. In this ambitious piece of writing, which would become "Down at the Cross," the long essay that would fill most of the pages of his book *The Fire Next Time*, Baldwin weaved four major strands: an autobiographical account of his teenage years in Harlem; a thoughtful explanation of the rise, appeal, and danger of the NOI; a scathing critique of the "moral history" of "the West"; and an articulation of his philosophy of dignity, love, and liberation. On a first reading, there may seem to be something discordant about the essay as the reader is taken at a steady clip from the streets of Harlem in the 1940s to the dining room table of Muhammad in 1961 to general discussions of the moral failures of Christendom. What at first sounds discordant, though, soon emits a great harmony as Baldwin artfully reveals the ways in which each of the strands of "Cross" is intimately related to every other. In order to pull off this daring literary feat, Baldwin would need several months of writing and revision, and so throughout 1962—as he traveled from Turkey to Switzerland to France to the United States to, finally, many countries in Africa—he would return time and again to crafting the essay that would, in the words of Podhoretz, soon deserve to be "placed among the classics of our language."[67]

"Cross" begins with Baldwin in Harlem at the age of fourteen. In those days, in those streets, Baldwin felt a sense of fear and hopelessness creeping into his life. He was "afraid of the evil within"—his budding sexual desires, and his sense that a life of crime was not merely *a* possibility but rather *the* possibility—and "the evil without." The "evil without" that so terrified Baldwin had its particulars—abuse at the hands of the police, the advances of "the whores and pimps and racketeers on the Avenue," and his tyrannical stepfather—but he was more frightened by "something deeper," more "vast," and more "merciless." What Baldwin had to fear, in other words, was far more than the cops who assaulted him on multiple occasions or the pimps who might try to claim him as "their little boy."[68] These possibilities were terrible enough, but what Baldwin found most troubling was that these threats were made possible by "nameless," "impersonal," and "bottomlessly cruel" structures of power that shaped his life as well as the lives of those around him. Domination does not require a cop with a club standing over you at every instant; something imperceptible will do.

In the face of these circumstances, how can one forge an identity that might serve as protection against a hostile world? Where, in other words, can one find "a handle, a lever, a means of inspiring fear" that can be relied on for survival? Baldwin considered and reflected on several common responses to these questions. Perhaps by getting an education, saving one's pennies, or serving in the military one might be able to fight back against the oppressiveness of the ghetto. Baldwin was doubtful. Whatever the merit of these strategies, none offered armor enough to keep one safe from "the housewives, taxi-drivers, elevator boys, dishwashers, bartenders, lawyers, judges, doctors, and grocers" who so desperately needed an "outlet for their frustrations and hostilities."[69]

Confronted with such a cruel world, Baldwin was not surprised that so many of his peers turned to "wine or whiskey or the needle," or pursued the "dangers of a criminal career." But Baldwin chose a different path by fleeing into the fortress of faith. As he reflected back, he saw much that was "curiously deliberate" in his journey to the church, but at the time it seemed more arbitrary than anything else. The "terror" he felt pushed him to want desperately to be "taken over" by someone or something, and it was little more than "good luck," he wrote, "that I found myself in the church racket instead of some other."[70]

In his quest to survive in a world that had "evolved no terms for [his] existence," Baldwin gave himself to the Lord. In order to make his salvation interesting enough to sustain his attention, he went beyond becoming "merely . . . another worshipper"; he became "a preacher—a Young minister" at several Harlem churches. In "Cross," Baldwin thought through what those years in the pulpit might reveal about questions of authenticity, identity, and power. There is no doubt that Baldwin discovered new dimensions of power in the pulpit, and on a spiritual level, he found that there was nothing like "the power and the glory" he felt when "in the middle of a sermon, I knew that I was somehow, by some miracle, really carrying, as they said, 'the Word'—when the church and I were one." On a personal level, he also experienced a sense of power as a result of his new "status," which granted him a "sudden right to privacy" from his father's interference.[71]

The fortress of Baldwin's faith turned out to be a house of cards. Jesus, Baldwin wrote, "knew all the secrets of my heart . . . but I didn't," and "the bargain we struck, actually, down there at the foot of the cross, was that he would never let me find out." Jesus, however, "failed his bargain," Baldwin continued. "He was a much better man than I took Him for." This is a complex and paradoxical passage. The major secret in Baldwin's heart was that his escape into the church had been utterly "dishonest" and "cunning," and he had come to believe that "the principles governing the rites and customs" of the church were not "Faith, Hope, and Charity" but instead "Blindness, Loneliness, and Terror, the first principle necessarily and actively cultivated in order to deny the two others." When Baldwin was "down there at the foot of the Cross," therefore, he often *felt* as if he had been "released" and "saved," but in fact, he had "escaped from nothing whatever" and was far from safe.[72] Jesus, Baldwin confessed, was too good to allow him to live a lie. And so Baldwin's fortress of faith—such as it was constituted at the time—crumbled to the ground.[73]

Baldwin identified several factors as critical to his overcoming the "blindness" that had simultaneously empowered and "immobilized" him during his three years in the pulpit. First, he had begun reading seriously again, and some of what he read shook his faith. Second, at DeWitt Clinton High School in the Bronx many of Baldwin's best friends were Jewish, and they asked him several discomfiting questions about heaven, hell, and the supposed divine inspiration of the Bible. These conversations led Baldwin to think more deeply about the relationship between his faith and "the question of color." "I knew that, according to many Christians, I was a descendant of Ham, who had been cursed, and that I was therefore predestined to be a slave. This had nothing to do with anything I was, or contained, or could become; my fate had been sealed forever from the beginning of time."[74]

Baldwin's sense that Christian behavior was often at odds with morality was also rooted in his experiences at home and in the Harlem churches in which he preached. Under his own roof, he was witness to the brutality of his father, who "slammed [him] across the face with his great palm" when he invited his Jewish best friend over one afternoon.[75] Outside his home, Baldwin's fellow ministers did little to redeem his faith in Christianity. These men and women were, in his estimation, hypocrites of the worst sort. The hypocrisy of the ministers went deeper than the "houses and Cadillacs" they acquired "while the faithful continue[d] to scrub floors" to a level far more fundamental. The ministers were moral and spiritual hypocrites; they had no love in their hearts, and their religion "was a mask for hatred and self-hatred and despair." The morality the ministers preached, Baldwin thought, seemed to be a far cry from the teachings of Jesus, and they repeatedly excused their flock from the Christian command to "love everybody" while at the same time telling them to "reconcile themselves to their misery on earth."[76]

"The Jimmy" is what writer Sharifa Rhodes-Pitts calls a literary "maneuver" Baldwin mastered in which he moved suddenly from the particular to something much wider or even universal.[77] In "Cross," Baldwin employed this maneuver repeatedly, and we can certainly see it in his move from the criticism of *his* church in Harlem to his critique of Christendom generally. The first full Jimmy takes place about a third of the way into "Cross," when Baldwin pans out to discuss "the historical role of Christianity in the realm of power—that is, politics—and in the realm of morals." He was quick to point out that his critique had little to do with "the disreputable, sun baked Hebrew who gave [the Christian church] his name" but rather with the behavior of those who claimed to act on his behalf.[78] Politically, Baldwin concluded, "Christianity has operated with an unmitigated arrogance and cruelty." To illustrate this point, Baldwin reminded the readers of the startling newsreel footage of "Italian priests and bishops blessing Italian boys who were on their way to Ethiopia," and the fact that "another Christian nation, Germany," was—at the precise moment Baldwin was going through his crisis of faith—then in the process of sending millions of people into the "fiery furnace."[79]

Baldwin wrapped up the first part of "Cross" by arguing that in order to "become a truly moral human being (and let us not ask whether or not this is possible; I think we must *believe* that it is possible), one must first divorce himself from all the prohibitions, crimes, and hypocrisies of the Christian church." Baldwin had sought refuge in the church in order to establish some sense of identity and attain a small modicum of power. Before long, he realized that the "safety" he found in the church was dishonest, immobilizing, and fundamentally immoral. For Baldwin, the church was a false refuge that offered inauthentic empowerment and invited the abdication of moral responsibility. Baldwin reached these conclusions on the basis of personal experience, but on reflection he realized that they were manifestations of more widespread failures of Christianity in the realms of morality and politics. The "God" of Christian practice, Baldwin concluded, was not worthy of our faith. "If the concept of God has any validity or any use," he declared, "it can only be to make us larger, freer, and more loving. If God cannot do this, then it is time we got rid of him."[80]

The second major strand in "Cross" consists of Baldwin's careful consideration of the origins, appeal, and dangers of the NOI. In his memoir *Breaking Ranks*, Podhoretz claims to have "given Baldwin the idea for *The Fire Next Time*."[81] This is only partially true. At some point in 1961, Podhoretz asked Baldwin if he would be willing to write a piece for *Commentary* on the NOI, and Baldwin agreed (verbally) to do so. As Podhoretz explained later, "In those days, nobody signed contracts. You trusted people at their word."[82] The precise details of what happened next are lost to history. In all likelihood, Baldwin began writing his piece on the NOI soon after his meeting with Muhammad in July 1961, and at some point later that year—as he repeatedly postponed his trip to Africa for the *New Yorker*—he came up with the idea of expanding the NOI piece in significant ways.[83] When *The Fire Next Time* was published as a book in 1963, it consisted of both "Cross," which would be published as "Letter from a Region in My Mind" in the *New Yorker* in November 1962, and "My Dungeon Shook," a piece commissioned by the *Progressive* magazine in June 1962 and published in December 1962. In sum, if Podhoretz had "given Baldwin the idea" for anything, it was the middle third of "Cross," which—if history had played out differently—very well could have been published as a stand-alone essay in *Commentary*.

Unfortunately for Podhoretz, history did not play out that way, and Baldwin's reflections on the NOI made their way into print as the second part of "Cross." Setting aside for the moment the ethical questions raised by Baldwin's journalistic betrayal of Podhoretz, this proved to be a brilliant literary move. Just after Baldwin offered the bracing passage on the "validity and usefulness of God," he shifted abruptly to his encounters over the years with the NOI. Although this shift may seem odd at first, it soon becomes clear that Baldwin is asking the reader to reason analogically with him. For those skeptical of his arguments about the shortcomings of Christianity as a source of identity, morality, and power, the analysis of the NOI was intended to provide another illustration of how to think through a similar set of issues by way of what most readers considered to be a bizarre and dangerous cult. In other words, Baldwin knew that most of his readers would have a much easier time casting a critical eye on the NOI than they would on their own mythologies of identity and power. In a sense, the NOI proved to be the perfect vehicle for what Baldwin was trying to accomplish in "Cross." By thinking through the NOI case with him, he hoped his readers might be better able to think through the mythologies that dominated their lives.

Baldwin first became acquainted with the NOI when he saw its ministers preach in the streets of Harlem. Street corner preaching was nothing new to Harlem—or Baldwin—but he noticed some remarkable things about the scenes of NOI sermons. For one thing, police seemed to be "afraid" of interfering with the NOI preachers or breaking up the rapt audience that listened to them. In the search for a "handle" or "lever" in Harlem, Baldwin had argued earlier in "Cross," the point was to find a form of "power" capable of "inspiring fear." It seemed to Baldwin that if the NOI ministers were doing something that made police officers reticent to pull out "a club or a fist or a gun," they had an impressive "handle" indeed.[84]

Baldwin was also struck by the "behavior of the crowd," which responded to the "utter dedication" of the speakers with "silent intensity" and "a kind of intelligence of hope on their faces."[85] This silent intensity, he came to believe, was rooted in the fact that NOI preachers were articulating—in language more stark and compelling than anything else the crowds had ever heard—the roots of black rage. In addition to voicing this rage, the ministers came with a message about what could be done about it. The subject of the speeches was power, wrapped in a thin veil of theology. Join the NOI, the ministers intoned, and you will achieve power when the white man falls.

Baldwin thought the "the explicitness of [the NOI's] symbols and the candor of its hatred" separated it from the mainstream of American society. The use of these symbols to promote hatred, though, was as American as apple pie. What was distinctive about the NOI was its radical inversion of the usual categories. What was usually white, was now black, and what was usually black, was now white. "The dream" and "sentiment" of the NOI, Baldwin concluded, "is old; the color is new."[86]

—————

In response to the "candor" of the NOI's hatred, Baldwin thought white people tended to ask all the wrong questions. What, they asked black Muslims, do you intend to *do* in order to restore the lost Nation of Islam? Are you willing to kill white people in your quest? Just where will your separate nation be? How will your separate economy work? For Baldwin, these questions were far less important than this one: What can we learn about *ourselves* by contemplating the fact that the NOI had grown up in soil that *we* cultivated? In order to respond to this question, Baldwin pulled another Jimmy by panning back out from the scenes of the NOI street preachers in Harlem to ask big questions about how the failures of Western and American culture made the rise of the NOI possible.

Speaking of the West generally, Baldwin argued that time had demonstrated the "Christian world" to be "morally bankrupt and politically unstable." For Baldwin, this indictment had little to do with the moral, religious, and political doctrines that had been rhetorically dominant in the West, but rather with the behavior of Western countries. For the second time in the essay, he referred to the obscene spectacle "when priests of that church which stands in Rome gave God's blessing to Italian boys being sent out to ravage" Ethiopia. And of course, Baldwin found it difficult to accept the idea that Christianity was synonymous with civilization "when a Christian nation surrenders to a foul and violent orgy, as Germany did during the Third Reich." For Baldwin, the fact that the Nazi movement could rise and thrive in Christian Germany was revealing and damning indeed. "In the heart of Europe," millions of people "were sent to a death so calculated, so hideous, and so prolonged that no age before this enlightened one had been able to imagine it, much less achieve and record it." "The fact of the Third Reich alone," Baldwin observed, "makes obsolete forever any question of Christian superiority, except in technological terms."[87] If this was the record of the "White God," it is not surprising that those seduced by the NOI were ready to give the "Black God" a chance.

Closer to home, Baldwin conceded that the United States had not yet "decided to murder its Negroes systematically," but the historical record, morally speaking, was hardly less devastating. The "Negro's past," as he would explain later in the essay, is marked by "rope, fire, torture, castration, infanticide, rape; death and humiliation; fear by day and night, fear as deep as the marrow of the bone." Those blacks proselytized by the NOI preachers knew this history well; the scars it created were etched in their memories, if not on their bodies. Furthermore, Baldwin noted, the Second World War marked "a turning point in the Negro's relation to America":

> To put it briefly, and somewhat too simply, a certain hope died, a certain respect for white Americans faded. . . . You must put yourself in the skin of a man who is wearing the uniform of his country, is a candidate for death in its defense, and who is called a "nigger" by his comrades-in-arms and his officers; . . . and who watches German prisoners of war being treated by Americans with more human dignity than he has ever received at their hands.

In the midst of this "despair" and "torment," the NOI preachers found audiences primed for their message of hope through hate.[88]

At this point in "Cross," Baldwin shifted back to the particular by bringing the reader to the doorstep of Muhammad and describing the July 1961 dinner discussed above. As he reflected on the dinner, Baldwin was struck by several things. First, as he ate with Muhammad on Chicago's South Side—one of the countries many ghettos—Baldwin could not help but agree with the "justice" of the NOI's "indictment" of the "state of the world." Second, Baldwin was impressed by Muhammad's "single-mindedness"; he maintained a laser-like focus on his "prosecution" of the crimes of whites and his advocacy of the view that the NOI provided the only viable path forward for blacks. Third, Baldwin left the dinner convinced that the NOI doctrine was "a recipe for murder," and its roots were not to be found in the warped minds of this or that self-proclaimed prophet but rather in the corrupt ground from which such demagogues spring.[89]

—————

The final part of "Cross" consists of Baldwin's convergence of his strands of critique to show their relationship to each other and his attempt to offer some thoughts about how "to end the racial nightmare." The spirit of Baldwin's diagnosis and prescription is that of a moralist, not a policy wonk. His primary aim was to challenge his audiences to *think* differently, and he hoped that this would inspire them to *act* more justly. In "Cross," the central concepts Baldwin challenged his readers to rethink were power, freedom, love, and responsibility.

Power is at the heart of the essay. There are moments when Baldwin used the term in fairly formal ways, as when he said that white people "had the judges, the juries, the shotguns, the law, in a word, power."[90] But his use of the word "power" varies throughout the essay. One idea that seems to be central to most of his uses of the term is that power has something to do with control: one person's control over another person(s), one group's control over another group, one person's control over oneself, or a group's control over itself. When he referred to power in the latter two ways, he sometimes used it interchangeably with "freedom," understood as individual or collective self-determination. Power, thus understood, is a morally neutral concept. The important questions to ask are, Who has it and who doesn't? What are the consequences of existing power relationships? Should existing power relationships be changed, and if so, how?

One lesson about power that Baldwin was clearly interested in teaching had been taught by many philosophers over the course of time: under conditions where one individual or group has a great deal more power than another individual or group, the powerful will tend to use their power unjustly. "When a white man faces a black man," Baldwin explained, "especially when the black man is helpless, terrible things are revealed. I know. I have been carried into precinct basements often enough." In order to survive, it is necessary to find "a handle" or "lever" because "*only* the fear of your power" can deter those who would abuse you. This basic desire to avoid the terrors of helplessness is why "power is what the powerless want," or as Baldwin put it in a line that would strike Buckley as especially offensive, "The only thing white people have that black people need, or should want, is power."[91] Some modicum of this sort of power, Baldwin argued, was necessary simply to avoid being "beaten over the head by the whites every instant of our brief passage on this planet."[92]

Although it is clear that Baldwin longed for a world in which the powerless were made more powerful, he was careful to point out that not all forms of empowerment were equally good, and indeed some were harmful. The case of the NOI, he argued, demonstrates this complexity. The sect had succeeded in providing many of its members with a "sense of their own worth," which is an absolutely essential element of empowerment because it indicates an unwillingness to accept the definitions and limitations imposed by the powerful. For this, Baldwin admitted the sect deserved some credit. For Baldwin, this sense of empowerment offered by the NOI and its promise of freedom through self-determination, though, came at too high a price. "I am very much concerned that American Negroes achieve their freedom," Baldwin wrote, "but I am also concerned for their dignity, for the health of their souls, and must oppose any attempt that Negroes may make to do to others what has been done to them."[93] Like his escape into the church as a teenager, the hypocrisy he witnessed when he observed his fellow ministers, and the corrupt institutions of Christianity that had been used to justify unspeakable horrors, the sense of identity and power offered by the NOI was rooted in something false and ultimately immoral.

As an alternative to drawing one's power from "totems, taboos, crosses, blood sacrifices, steeples, mosques, races, armies, flags, [and] nations," Baldwin attempted to fashion a more dignified basis for identity that was rooted in freedom, love, and responsibility. He offered this prescription in moral terms that defy ideological categorization. The revolution he imagined was indeed radical, but he went beyond advocating institutional change to argue for the rebirth of our moral lives.

The idea of freedom as self-determination (both for individuals and communities) was, according to Baldwin, but one dimension of freedom. Baldwin also emphasized a conception of freedom as "sensuality," which he defined as the capacity "to respect and rejoice in the force of life, of life itself, and to be *present* in all that one does, from the effort of loving to the breaking of bread." Interestingly, Baldwin said he was introduced to this form of freedom during his days in the church. "There was, in the life I fled," Baldwin wrote, "a zest and a joy and a capacity for facing and surviving disaster that are very moving and rare." Even in the dire circumstances of the ghetto, some members of Baldwin's church community were able to achieve "a freedom that was close to love," a form of freedom, Baldwin explained, "that one hears in some gospel songs, . . . in jazz, and especially in the blues" that is "tart and ironic, authoritative and double-edged." In the spirit of the blues, Baldwin found a model for how one can find sources of joy and renewal, even in the face of disaster and loss. In this "struggle to achieve and reveal and confirm a human identity," Baldwin saw something "very beautiful."[94]

Baldwin's identification of freedom as a form of respecting and rejoicing in the force of life led him to the conclusion that the rebirth of freedom in the United States required all of us, regardless of race, to become a blues people; that is, a people capable of confronting life honestly— free of false identities and corrupting sources of power—and looking on one another as partners in this project.[95] For guidance, Baldwin encouraged his readers to look to history, not to the usual pantheon of military and political heroes, but rather to the "unsung army of black men and women" who make up "a long line of improbable aristocrats—the only genuine aristocrats this country has ever produced."[96] Black history, Baldwin argued, has many lessons to teach all of us about the meaning of freedom and responsibility. In this history, we find the virtues that Baldwin believed were essential to the rebirth of freedom: "resilience," "perception," "charity," "individuality," "intelligence," "spiritual force," and "beauty." Baldwin was careful to point out that he was "proud of these people not because of their color" but instead because of their character.[97]

In order to achieve freedom of this sort, Baldwin contended, we must love one another.[98] His understanding of love was deep and complex, and the love he prescribed was difficult and often unsettling. To love someone, he explained, is to deny them "spiritual and social ease," which "hard as it may sound," is "the most important thing that one human being can do for another." Love requires us to force each other to confront the delusions that we rely on to avoid taking responsibility for our lives. "Love takes off the masks," Baldwin declared, "that we fear we cannot live without and know we cannot live within."[99]

This brings us to the sense of responsibility Baldwin prescribed in the essay. "One is responsible to life," he wrote. "It is the small beacon in that terrifying darkness from which we come and to which we shall return. One must negotiate this passage as nobly as possible." For Baldwin, the meaning of nobility was inextricably bound to the notions of freedom, love, and dignity described above. The future of the country, and indeed far more than that, depends on our willingness to take on this vast responsibility:

> Everything now, we must assume, is in our hands; we have no right to assume otherwise. If we—and now I mean the relatively conscious whites and the relatively conscious blacks, who must, like lovers, insist on, or create, the consciousness of the others—do not falter in our duty now, we may be able, handful that we are, to end the racial nightmare, and achieve our country, and change the history of the world.[100]

The *New Yorker* had given Baldwin a $5,500 advance to write a series of pieces about his travels to Israel and Africa. On the completion of the projects, the magazine had pledged to deliver an additional $6,500. All told, this $12,000 payment ($82,000 in today's dollars) was by far the biggest commission of Baldwin's career. In early 1962—more than two years after the initial commission—he still had yet to make the trip to Africa and had nothing to send the magazine. In February of that year, he wrote to his agent, Robert P. Mills, from his friend Lucien

Hapsburger's Swiss chalet: "I am again reworking the interminable 'Down at the Cross.' . . . You'll see, I imagine, when you read it, why it has been so hard to do."[101] The precise details of what happened next are a bit murky, but Baldwin got the idea to submit "Cross" to the *New Yorker* instead of sending it to Podhoretz at *Commentary*.[102] Baldwin may have felt justified in doing this for several reasons. First, he believed that "Cross" really had become something more than what he had verbally agreed to do for Podhoretz. Second, he felt an urgent need to submit something to the *New Yorker* since it had given him a large advance and he was so far past his deadline. Third, Baldwin was perpetually short on money and knew *Commentary* could not pay him nearly what the *New Yorker* had promised.[103] Indeed, Podhoretz reported later that the most he could have paid Baldwin for the piece was $600.[104] Finally, Baldwin was not convinced that the *New Yorker* would accept "Cross." It was so long (twenty thousand words), so complicated, and not on the topic for which he had been commissioned to write. Sending the piece to the *New Yorker* may have seemed like a perfect solution. By submitting it only to be rejected, he could buy himself a little bit more time with Shawn, and Podhoretz would end up with his piece on the NOI and then some.

When Baldwin returned to New York, Podhoretz reached out to see how close he was to completing the NOI piece for *Commentary*. When they talked on the phone, Podhoretz sensed that Baldwin was hiding something from him and soon his old friend admitted that the essay was on Shawn's desk. Baldwin apologized and assured Podhoretz that the piece would be in his hands as soon as the *New Yorker* rejected it.[105] Shawn, of course, had other ideas. The essay was certainly unconventional and not on the assigned topic, but Shawn was not about to let it pass him by.

When Baldwin received word that the *New Yorker* was accepting the essay for publication, he passed the news along to Podhoretz, who was devastated by the confession. "I was thunderstruck. No greater violation of the ethics of the trade," Podhoretz wrote later, "could be imagined than Baldwin had committed in taking an article he had been invited to write by the editor of one magazine and giving it to the editor of another." When Baldwin and Podhoretz met to discuss the matter, Podhoretz unleashed a torrent of words at Baldwin, not only for his ethical lapse, but for something that he thought played some part in his betrayal: "I said he dared commit such a dastardly act *because* he was a Negro." Who among all these white liberal magazine editors, Podhoretz imagined Baldwin thinking, would hold him accountable for his ethical shortcomings? Baldwin may have been right about most of the New York literati, but Podhoretz announced he had none of the "white guilt" that might motivate such behavior. In fact, Podhoretz declared in a dramatic monologue on the subject, "Neither I nor my ancestors had ever wronged the Negroes; on the contrary, I had grown up in an 'integrated' slum neighborhood where it was the Negroes who persecuted the whites and not the other way around."[106] At the conclusion of the monologue, Baldwin leaned forward, opened his big eyes even wider than usual, and whispered to Podhoretz, "Norman, you must write all of that down."[107] Podhoretz did write it down (along with many other things) in an essay called "My Negro Problem and Ours," and he published it in *Commentary* in early 1963.[108] In the piece, he described the fear, envy, and hatred he developed for blacks when he was growing up in Brooklyn in the 1930s, and confessed that some of those feelings were still with him. While many on the Left were appalled by Podhoretz's confession, Baldwin called it "a tremendous achievement."[109] Podhoretz had done precisely what Baldwin longed for white people to do: he examined his life and told the truth about what he saw.

When "Cross" appeared in the November 17, 1962, issue of the *New Yorker* under the title "Letter from a Region in My Mind," it became an instant sensation. Within days, Baldwin began receiving letters from other literary elites. The Trappist monk and author Thomas Merton wrote to Baldwin to tell him he was "right all down the line" in his treatment of "one of the great realities of our time." Merton went on to say that he believed Baldwin to be "fundamentally" and "genuinely religious."[110] Hannah Arendt, the German Jewish émigré political theorist who caused her own stir in the *New Yorker* with her reports on the trial of the captured

Nazi Adolf Eichmann, wrote to Baldwin with mixed feelings about his piece. She considered the essay to be "a political event of a very high order," but worried about Baldwin's "gospel of love." "In politics," she explained, "love is a stranger," and the virtues Baldwin identified as central to the African American experience, though laudable, will not survive "the hour of liberation by even five minutes." "Hatred and love belong together," she concluded, "and they are both destructive; you can afford them only in the private and, as a people, only so long as you are not free."[111]

In addition to missives from luminaries, the *New Yorker* received hundreds of letters from readers. The vast majority of these letters were positive in nature, and most shared two common features: congratulations to the magazine for the courage to publish the essay and a request to send several extra copies so that the reader might distribute them to friends.[112] The positive letters showered superlatives on the Baldwin piece, which readers described as "superb," "magnificent," "important," "penetrating," "timely," "splendid," "stirring," "profound," "moving," "excellent," "electrifying," "breath-taking," "lucid," "unforgettable," and "jolting." Several readers called it a "masterpiece" and reported that the essay had a greater impact on them than just about anything else they had ever read. One reader declared Baldwin to be "the prophet of our times."[113]

Some of the positive letters are especially remarkable. A half-black, half-Hawaiian teenager thanked Baldwin for helping him think through questions of identity. A Methodist minister echoed Merton's sentiment when he wrote that although "Mr. Baldwin may long ago have left the church," his essay "is one of the most profoundly Christian things that I have ever read." One woman announced that she planned to send a copy of the article to President Kennedy. "It may get no further than assistant 364," she wrote, "but then I surmise that assistant 364 will be that much wiser." From the American heartland, another writer confessed that Baldwin's writing "made the goose pimples stand out on my neck!"[114]

Not all readers wrote to express such adulation. Some wrote to cancel their subscriptions in outrage. "Before Mr. Baldwin drowns in his own tears of rage and self-pity," noted one man from Illinois, "[I] would suggest he spend more time on history than religion." The essay "reflects the exaggerations of a sick mind," remarked a man from Memphis, "and no amount of justification for the sickness of that mind can relieve you of the charge of sensational journalism for having printed it." A letter writer from Michigan called the piece a "schizophrenic tirade" that should be rejected as "subversive." Several readers asserted that Baldwin was anti-white. A letter writer from Arizona dismissed the piece as a "verbose, rambling sentimental diatribe against white citizens," and another wondered if Baldwin "was charged regular space rates for his recent diatribe against the white race." One reader from New York wondered what "motives" the magazine could have had for publishing a piece that so clearly lacked "literary merit." Fred Keefe, the member of the magazine's editorial staff charged with the task of offering polite responses to these letters, could not resist being a bit snarky in his reply to this last writer: "If you are unable to understand and appreciate James Baldwin's 'Letter from a Region in My Mind,' we're afraid we can't help you."[115]

The publication of "Letter from a Region in My Mind" was a literary event of the highest order. It shot Baldwin's already-rising star to the status of international celebrity. He was the proverbial "talk of the town," and Buckley, of course, took notice. Baldwin was already on his radar as a result of the pieces he had published in *Partisan Review*, *Esquire*, and the *New York Times*, but the *New Yorker* essay provoked Buckley to train his intellectual guns on him in a more serious way. Frank Meyer ran the book review section of *National Review*, but there is evidence to suggest that Buckley himself took charge of the magazine's response to Baldwin.[116] Everyone on the literary scene was talking about the Baldwin essay, and few reviewers had a cross word to say about it.[117] Buckley saw an opportunity for *National Review*. In the midst of this near-universal adulation for Baldwin, *National Review* would publish a sophisticated response that revealed the flaws in his views. The plan was clear enough, but whom could Buckley commission to take on this daunting task? Baldwin's essay was not really focused on the South so Weaver seemed like an ill fit.[118]

The essay had little to say about constitutional questions in the area of civil rights so Kilpatrick was not quite right for the job. Buckley understood that Baldwin was operating on another plane—one that was philosophical, religious, and world historical. There was one writer in his orbit who fit the bill perfectly: Garry Wills.

Not long after Wills graduated from college, the young midwesterner sent a writing sample to Buckley and a few other magazine editors. Buckley saw potential in Wills and invited him to visit the *National Review* offices in New York. Buckley hired Wills—who he later called "*National Review*'s first major discovery"—and he soon found his niche at the magazine as a drama critic and, as a devout Catholic who had briefly attended seminary, became one of the go-to writers on questions of religion.[119] By 1961, Wills had completed his PhD in classics at Yale, and in 1962, was hired to teach history at Johns Hopkins University.

Not long after the Baldwin piece was published, Buckley reached out to Wills to see if he might be willing to author a response for *National Review*. Wills accepted the challenge, and in a letter in January 1963, told Buckley, "The only thing I have for the Baldwin piece is a title: What Color is God?"[120] A few weeks later, Wills sent Buckley—who was on his annual ski vacation in Gstaad, Switzerland—a draft of the piece along with a note that called Baldwin an "intimidating adversary." He concluded the letter with these lines: "Write more. Ski less. That's what you deserve for making me take on [a heavyweight] like Baldwin."[121]

While Wills was editing his piece based on feedback he received from Buckley and others, one can only imagine the look of shock on his face when he opened his newspaper one morning in early March to discover that Buckley had devoted his nationally syndicated newspaper column, On the Right, to his own critique of Baldwin. What was more startling was that the column bore some striking resemblances to "What Color Is God?" Under the title "A Call to Lynch the White God," Buckley lamented the "acquiescent reaction" of "book reviewers, intellectuals, [and] café society" to "Baldwin's explosive indictment of white society." To Buckley, the message of Baldwin's *New Yorker* essay was as clear as it was threatening: "Throw over your ways, unseat your God, usher in immediately a world that transcends races, nations, and altars. Or you are through." Buckley was appalled by the "fever pitch of [Baldwin's] hatred, the fullness of his disgust, [and] the totality of his condemnation," and deeply offended by Baldwin's "special contempt" for Christianity, from his description of Jesus as a "sunbaked, disreputable Hebrew" to his suggestion that the "White God" was somehow to blame for slavery and the Holocaust. Buckley accused intellectuals of taking masochistic pleasure in Baldwin's indictments when they should have been standing up to call him an "eloquent menace" who failed to appreciate the good that Christianity had done in the world, citing among other things the influence of Christian ideas in the "bloody war to get rid of slavery" and the "Christian impulse" that inspired the allies to liberate Dachau. The "ideological totalism" Baldwin offered in place of the grand religious and moral traditions of the West, Buckley concluded, was "preposterous and suicidal."[122]

"Well, if I never do more with my [Baldwin] piece," Wills wrote to Buckley the day "A Call to Lynch the White God" appeared, "I shall have the comfort of knowing it served one purpose—as research and raw material for a Buckley column." Wills then proceeded to provide several specific instances in which Buckley had taken ideas and phrases from "What Color Is God?," and imported them into his column. Along the way, Wills was sure to throw a few rhetorical jabs at Buckley by pointing out a number of factual errors in his piece—for example, an incorrect date for the publication of Baldwin's essay, an incorrect source for a Baldwin quote that Wills had included in his piece and Buckley had imported into his, and a note about Buckley's failure to understand the basic plot details of *Giovanni's Room*—and to say that he would never "trot out the sentimental falsehood about the nation's walking through blood to free the slaves." Wills was sufficiently upset about his mentor's transgressions that he announced he was sending the piece elsewhere and warned Buckley that if he chose to reprint the column in *National Review* (one of his common practices at the time), Wills would "submit a strong protest" calling on readers to question "the ethics of an editor's using submitted material as the basis for his own variations on a theme."[123]

Sometime in the next week, Buckley responded to Wills, but his reply is lost to history.[124] On March 9, though, Wills wrote back to Buckley and

began with these words: "Apparently you think my grievance the product of a morbid imagination. We'll let it rest at that. As you say, it's not
worth the sacrifice of more important things." Buckley did agree to keep
"A Call to Lynch the White God" out of *National Review*, pledged to work
with Wills to be sure that "What Color Is God?" was edited in such a way
that it did not seem that Wills was the one who plagiarized Buckley, and
implored Wills to reconsider his decision to place his Baldwin review
elsewhere. Wills was ambivalent on this last point. He expressed hope
that the piece would end up in *National Review* after all, but wondered
if Buckley should "assign the subject to someone else" since Wills was
"soft on the Negro issue, by *NR* standards."[125] According to Jeffery Hart's
history of *National Review*, Wills's "softness" was indeed the subject of
some debate in the magazine's editorial meetings, where the piece "was
resisted by some editors, most emphatically by Frank Meyer."[126] Buckley disagreed with Meyer and would even go so far as to declare a few
years later that "What Color Is God?" was "very possibly our finest hour"
at the magazine.[127]

"James Baldwin is a disarming man," Wills began, "against whom it is
necessary to arm ourselves. Which, oddly enough, may be what he is trying to tell us." The three central questions Wills set out to answer in
"What Color Is God?" were, Why did Baldwin write his "Letter"? What
has the impact been and why? And how should we respond? Baldwin,
Wills pointed out, "is obviously a man who can do anything with words"
and chose to use his words in the *New Yorker* piece to offer an "indictment of Western civilization," and his charges cut far deeper than just "not
living up to our ideals, for lapsing, for sinning, for being bad Christians."
Instead, Baldwin was saying something even more damning: "He says
we do not *have* any ideals: we do not believe in any of the things our religion, our civilization, our country stand for. It is all an elaborate lie, a
lie whose sole and original function is to fortify privilege." In the face of
this morally bankrupt inheritance, Baldwin has called on us to "tear up
all the Bibles, disband all the police forces, take crowbars to the court
buildings and the libraries"; he has called, in sum, for an "immediate se-
cession from our civilization."[128]

In response to this damning indictment, Baldwin "has been met with vast tolerance and sympathy, a vague clucking of tongues over the plight of the Harlem Negroes, a superficial flurry of comment on how brave the *New Yorker* was, and how eloquent Baldwin is, and how wicked Mississippi is."[129] Wills suspected that this might have been frustrating to Baldwin, who may have been wondering, Did they not *hear* me? I have just said that their empty, pathetic lives stand on a foundation of silt, they have nothing we should want other than power, and their way of life may at any moment—and probably deserves to—come burning to the ground. Shouldn't they be mad?

Indeed they should, Wills argued. And the failure of the literati to stand up to Baldwin proved the point of the *New Yorker* essay in at least two ways. First, the reticence of elites to challenge Baldwin revealed that elites did not really respect him. "We are not treating the Negro as an equal," Wills wrote, "until we can be angry at him, until we are willing to grant that his words *mean* something, that they are worth analysis, refinement, and (if need be) refutation." We owe it to Baldwin, ourselves, each other, and future generations to exhibit the "special courage" necessary "to be what one is, yet continue to fight for what one should have been; to oppose a better man than oneself in the service of a better creed than his."[130]

Wills's long review essay constitutes his attempt to display this "special courage" in the face of Baldwin's effort to "destroy" our "whole tradition." In response to Baldwin's critique, Wills wondered if Baldwin might be guilty of overstating his case. Hadn't Western ideas—including Christian ones—played a key role in the movement to abolish slavery? Even more to the point, doesn't "the language of freedom, morality and human dignity" that Baldwin himself so ably utilized depend on "centuries of other men's . . . struggle with each other and with words."[131]

To demonstrate this point, Wills argued that concepts like the Christian understanding of dignity—which holds that "every man . . . has a soul made and saved by God, bought with His blood"—might be put to good use in the quest for black liberation. This doctrine, he insisted, was not as easily "twisted to the purposes of hatred and oppression" as progressive, secular ideas. The "Christianity of the West," he contended, is "our best hope."[132]

In "What Color Is God?" Wills hoped to model the sort of answer he believed Baldwin deserved. "He is an adversary worthy of our best arguments," he concluded, "and one of the uses of the fight is that it may force us to remember what our best arguments are. Once we do that, we have won; and so has he."[133]

———

"You are popular, in a conversational sense," a journalist told Baldwin not long after Wills's review was published, "so much so that a cocktail party in New York without a James Baldwin discussion would be disastrous."[134] While intellectual battles over Baldwin's ideas were playing out in the nation's journals of opinion and among the cocktail party set, battles of other sorts were taking place on the national and international stages. On the home front, civil rights activists continued to agitate, litigate, and lobby while southern whites continued their violent backlash against this organizing. The early 1960s were violent years in the state of Mississippi, for example, where a farmer and civil rights activist named Herbert Lee was murdered by a segregationist state representative named E. H. Hurst.[135] In fall 1962, a black man named James Meredith repeatedly attempted to register for classes at the University of Mississippi (known as Ole Miss). Meredith's efforts to register, which had been authorized by the Fifth Circuit Court of Appeals, were blocked by Governor Ross Barnett, who called on "every public official and private citizen" in the state to resist the "moral degradation" of integration.[136] After Barnett personally blocked Meredith's entry to Ole Miss on two occasions, President Kennedy federalized the Mississippi National Guard and sent Meredith—accompanied by Deputy Attorney General Nicholas Katzenbach and four hundred federal marshals—back to campus on September 30, 1962. As Attorney General Robert Kennedy and Barnett negotiated behind the scenes, a mob of white Mississippians became increasingly agitated on campus. Former army major general Edwin Walker, who had been relieved of his command for subjecting his troops to the political indoctrination of the Far Right, had called for ten thousand volunteers to descend on the state in order to resist.[137] Resist they did, and on the evening of September 30, the Ole Miss campus was racked by violence as protesters and marshals clashed in a sea of bricks, bats, tear gas, and gunfire.[138] At one point in the melee an Ole Miss student who had been sent to negotiate with the marshals, "faced the mob" and said, "Here's the deal. The marshals will quit using tear gas if we'll stop throwing rocks and bricks." The crowd was silent until someone shouted, "Give us the nigger and we'll quit."[139] Walker—who had become a darling of the American right wing and been the subject of a sympathetic interview in *National Review* by Citizens' Council enthusiast Medford Evans—stood tall in his Stetson cowboy hat and urged the protesters to keep fighting the tyrannical federal government.[140]

Meanwhile, Governor Barnett huddled with advisers in Jackson, including none other than William J. Simmons, the Citizens' Council official who had provided Buckley with his mailing list in 1958. Simmons served as the governor's unofficial "prime minister for racial integrity," and when he was not in Barnett's ear, he was just a stone's throw away at the Citizens' Council office across the street from the governor's mansion. In his conversations with the president and attorney general, it was clear that Barnett was looking for a way to diffuse the situation without losing face with ardent supporters like Simmons and the mobs terrorizing the campus. Kennedy decided he had waited long enough for Governor Barnett to pull off this feat so he ordered federal troops stationed in Memphis to quell what one marshal called the "armed insurrection" at Ole Miss. When the dust settled, two people were dead, more than three hundred were injured, and Kennedy ordered that General Walker be committed for a ninety-day psychiatric evaluation.[141]

Buckley's go-to writer on all matters southern, Kilpatrick, was in Mississippi to witness "The Battle at Ole Miss."[142] According to biographer William P. Hustwit, Kilpatrick was determined to provide an account of the unfolding crisis from a pro–states' rights perspective.[143] Reporting from campus before all hell broke loose, Kilpatrick waxed philosophical about the tragic "struggle" between two sides convinced that their point of view is the right one. After Kilpatrick "surveyed the mood on campus," he "predicted violence." From Oxford, Kilpatrick made his way to the capital in Jackson, where he met with Governor Barnett and his advisers, including Kilpatrick's old friend Simmons. Then he took what his biographer called "an extraordinary step for a segregationist newsman" and drove to Kosciusko, Mississippi, to meet with the family of Meredith.[144] After interviewing Meredith's wife and mother, Kilpatrick returned to the capital, where he once again huddled with the Citizens' Council boss, Simmons.[145] The two segregationists swelled with pride as they looked out the window at a mob gathering around the governor's mansion to protect Barnett from federal marshals. "They won't give up," Simmons told Kilpatrick. "They won't ever give up. They're the finest people on earth."[146] By the time they did indeed give up (in that particular battle anyway), Kilpatrick was back in Oxford "in time to see Edwin Walker and the last of the protesters arrested."[147]

Less than two weeks later, Kilpatrick was in New York, where he was set to appear on *The Open Mind* television program to discuss the question, "Is There a Case of School Segregation?" Kilpatrick had just published a book, *The Southern Case for School Segregation*, in which he attempted to defend an affirmative response to that question, and host Eric Goldman had an inspired idea for who ought to take him on in debate: Baldwin. When his friend Podhoretz found out that Baldwin was planning to share the platform with the segregationist newsman, he tried to talk him out of it. "You will dignify Kilpatrick's position," Podhoretz told Baldwin, "by appearing alongside him."[148] Baldwin was undeterred and arrived on the same set where he had squared off with Malcolm X to do rhetorical battle with America's leading "salesman for segregation."[149]

Baldwin decided to take the offensive against Kilpatrick. In *Nobody Knows My Name*, Baldwin had shown a remarkable capacity for empathy for segregationists like the school principal whom he saw as deluded

FIGURE 4.3. *Richmond News Leader* editor and Buckley confidant James Jackson Kilpatrick, circa 1962 (AP Photo / *Richmond Times-Dispatch*)

but apparently trapped by his circumstances. Kilpatrick, Baldwin believed, was a horse of different color. He was a man who had thought deeply about these issues and devoted himself to preserving racial hierarchy. In his opening remarks, Baldwin went for the jugular:

> You may think that there's a distinction between a man who writes a book like your book and the people who castrate Negroes in the streets. But from my point of view it is men like you who write those books who are responsible for those mobs. I accuse you—not of betraying me—I accuse you of betraying the white people of the South. I don't expect from the porter, the farmer, the sharecropper, the poor white man in the South—I don't expect them to do something which demands an active imagination, demands thought, demands something which most people cannot do really, which is to expand their horizons beyond their own interests. But I do expect a man who can write a sentence, who can

think, to teach these people that the time has come for them, *for them.* This has nothing to do with me.

Goldman turned to Kilpatrick: "Mr. Kilpatrick?" Rather than responding to Baldwin's indictment, Kilpatrick criticized him for making a speech instead of engaging in a conversation. "Alright," Baldwin replied, "let's have a conversation."[150]

For the rest of the show, Baldwin played the role of cross-examining prosecutor as Kilpatrick attempted to justify his commitments to white supremacy and racial apartheid. The centerpiece of Kilpatrick's case was that "Negroes" had not made adequate "contributions to Western values" to be considered first-class citizens worthy of integration with white society.[151] The failure of "the Negro" to make significant contributions to Western "law, philosophy, music, architecture, [and] morality" was due to "hereditary characteristics" and "characteristics of environment." White people, Kilpatrick concluded, are "better equipped in every way to preserve [Western] values which may preserve you too, and may preserve whatever it was from civilization that was worth preserving." Baldwin pressed Kilpatrick to be more precise with his language and peppered him with questions. What did he mean, he asked repeatedly, by "Western values"? What evidence did Kilpatrick have to demonstrate the genetic superiority of white people? Who was responsible for establishing the differences in "environment" that led to greater academic and familial problems in the "Negro community"?[152]

Goldman could hardly get a word in edgewise as Baldwin interrogated Buckley's beau ideal of a southern intellectual, and Kilpatrick never seemed able to steady himself in the midst of the rhetorical body blows Baldwin landed from across the table. When Kilpatrick was sufficiently woozy, Baldwin threw his knockout punch. Baldwin looked Kilpatrick in the eyes and told him the last thing he wanted to hear: he was not a true conservative. "My point," Baldwin told him, "is that you are not protecting the values" that you claim are precious to you; "you are destroying them."[153] If Kilpatrick really cared about preserving Christianity, the "Bill of Rights," and "the Western journey," Baldwin declared, he had a "duty at no matter what cost" to "expand" these concepts to include all people. By failing to do so, Baldwin argued, Kilpatrick was doing far more to undermine "American civilization" than any radical could ever do.

⁓

The day after the Baldwin-Kilpatrick discussion aired on NBC, President Kennedy was presented with visual evidence that the Russians were well on their way to establishing operational nuclear facilities in Cuba. As the president and his advisers contemplated the viability of various military options and negotiated with the Soviets, the world was gripped by the real possibility of nuclear war. After thirteen excruciating days of negotiation, the Soviets agreed to remove the missiles in exchange for a promise from the United States not to invade Cuba, and pledge to remove some of its own missiles from Turkey and Italy.[154]

A few days after the resolution of the Cuban missile crisis, George C. Wallace was elected governor of Alabama with a resounding 96.3 percent of the vote.[155] Wallace, who had once been considered relatively liberal on racial issues, ran on an arch segregationist platform. After losing the 1958 gubernatorial race to John T. Patterson, backed by the Ku Klux Klan, Wallace pledged to "never be out-niggered again."[156] When Wallace was inaugurated a few weeks later, he would utter the now-infamous words, "In the name of the greatest people that ever trod this earth, I draw the line in the dust and toss the gauntlet before the feet of tyranny and I say, segregation today, segregation tomorrow, and segregation forever!"[157]

Meanwhile, leaders of the SCLC, NAACP, CORE, and SNCC continued to push the civil rights movement forward through a combination of education, voter registration, litigation, and protest. A coalition of activists in Albany, Georgia, had run into a well-coordinated effort to diffuse the effectiveness of its protests without attracting a great deal of attention. Albany sheriff Laurie Pritchett recognized that the white southern cause was not well served by violent clashes that were likely to catch the eye of the national media and federal officials. So Pritchett's strategy was to enlist the support of law enforcement officials in the surrounding areas to help him house all the prisoners it might be necessary to take. Pritchett demanded his officers exercise restraint in their interactions with the protesters, arrest them quietly, and transport them to a designated detention facility. When one facility filled up, they would move on to the next one. At one time during the Albany campaign, Pritchett had over seven hundred protesters in detention. When King himself was swept up in a mass arrest in July 1962, Pritchett saw to it that he was swiftly released, lest the arrest attract excessive media attention.[158]

The frustrations of the Albany campaign provided valuable lessons to King and his allies. King recognized the value of political theater in the quest to change hearts and minds so when he strategized with other leaders in January 1963, they set out to confront southern officials they knew would be unable to exercise the restraint shown by Pritchett. At that time, Eugene "Bull" Connor was serving as the commissioner of public safety of Birmingham, Alabama. Connor had devoted most of the six decades he had spent on this planet to various campaigns of racial hatred. As a state legislator in the 1930s, he worked assiduously to keep blacks from voting; in 1948, he led the Alabama delegation's walkout of the Democratic National Convention in protest of Truman's civil rights proposals; and he had established himself as a prominent figure in the Citizens' Council movement and allowed white mobs to brutalize Freedom Riders in 1961.[159] Connor was, in sum, precisely the sort of man King needed. And so in early 1963, the Birmingham campaign was born.

Chapter 5

In the Eye of the Storm, 1963–64

On New Year's Day 1963, Baldwin traveled south in order to begin a lecture tour on behalf of CORE.[1] His first stop was Mississippi, where he met Meredith—the student whose very presence had so angered the Ole Miss community only three months earlier—and Medgar Evers, a young, charismatic NAACP official who ran the organization's Jackson office. It did not take long for Baldwin to realize that Evers was a special human being and would become, in Baldwin's mind, a symbol of hope of what the civil rights revolution might be able to achieve. Evers was a well-educated, well-spoken, handsome army veteran who—at the age of only thirty-seven—embodied the sorts of virtues Baldwin celebrated in his writings. Evers was tough and contemplative, and displayed the sort of resilience and determination that Baldwin believed would be necessary to save the country. Baldwin stayed in Evers's home in Jackson—with Medgar, his wife, Myrlie, and the couple's three young children—and accompanied Evers as he investigated a racially motivated murder in rural Mississippi. By staying with Evers, Baldwin caught a glimpse of the man in full: freedom fighter by day and family man by night. As he watched Evers at work and home, Baldwin found himself wondering—as he had when he met King—how this young man was able to bear the weight of the life he had chosen.

By the end of January, Baldwin was back in New York and *The Fire Next Time*—a book containing the *New Yorker* essay "Down at the Cross: A Letter from a Region in My Mind" and a short piece called "My Dungeon Shook: A Letter to My Nephew on the One Hundredth Anniversary of the Emancipation"—had been published by Dial Press. The short piece had appeared originally in the *Progressive* magazine in late 1962 alongside essays by such luminaries as Adlai Stevenson, John Hope Franklin, A. Philip Randolph, and King. Baldwin had a long-standing idea for a writing project that would consist of a series of letters to his younger

FIGURE 5.1. Baldwin with Medgar Evers, January 1963
(Corbis Premium Historical / Getty Images)

brother so when the editor of the *Progressive*, Morris H. Rubin, invited
him to contribute, he accepted eagerly—at a small fraction of his usual
writing fee—and took the opportunity to experiment with the epistolary form.[2] "My Dungeon Shook" reiterates some of the themes of
"Cross," but its personalized framing proved to be especially powerful.
"You can only be destroyed," the thirty-seven-year old writer told his
fourteen-year old nephew, "by believing that you really are what the white
world calls a *nigger*." Overcoming the labels imposed by the white world,
Baldwin admitted, is no easy task. "This innocent country," he wrote, "set
you down in a ghetto in which, in fact, it intended you should perish."
The country did this "because you were black and for *no other reason*."
By "innocent," Baldwin did not mean freedom from guilt for legal or
moral wrongdoing but rather the less common usage of the term that
indicates ignorance or a lack of self-consciousness. Confronted with these
"innocents," Baldwin instructed his nephew, he had a duty to "accept
them with love." This "acceptance" requires honesty and compassion in

order to help these human beings to liberate themselves from the "inhumanity and fear" they have relied on for so long.[3]

Fire became an instant best seller and remained so for forty-one weeks.[4] In 1962 and 1963, Baldwin received thousands of invitations to speak on college campuses, and to religious groups, civic groups, and professional organizations; he was a guest on dozens of radio and television programs; and he was featured in hundreds of print articles in publications around the world.[5] The same week Wills's "What Color Is God?" appeared in *National Review*, Baldwin's face would appear on the cover of *Time* magazine, and a week later, an eleven-page photo-story on his southern lecture tour for CORE was featured in *Life* magazine.

The *Time* cover placed Baldwin's face under the headline "Birmingham and Beyond: The Negro's Push for Equality." The Birmingham campaign had begun in earnest with a sit-in on April 3, and a few days later King and several other leaders were arrested. While imprisoned, King wrote his "Letter from a Birmingham Jail" in response to a statement issued by a group of clergymen that had condemned the Birmingham campaign as "unwise and untimely." In the face of this criticism, King pointed out that African Americans had already "waited for more than 340 years for our constitutional and God-given rights," and in the face of such injustice, nonviolent resistance was morally justified.[6]

Soon after King's release from jail a week later, he and several hundred protesters from SNCC, CORE, and local schools took to the streets to continue their freedom marches. With television cameras rolling and photographers busily snapping shots of the scene, Connor ordered his men to sic police dogs on the protesters, and commanded officers to unleash high-powered fire hoses—powerful enough to rip the bark off trees—on the men, women, and children in the streets.[7] By the end of the first week of May, police had arrested more than 2,400 protesters and injured hundreds. Soon thereafter, "Alabama's ultrasegregationist Governor George Wallace," *Time* reported, "sent 600 men to reinforce Bull Connor's weary cops."[8] On May 11, members of the Ku Klux Klan set off two bombs targeting King allies, sparking a citywide riot overnight.

FIGURE 5.2. Birmingham police abusing protesters, May 1963 (AP Photo / Bill Hudson)

Baldwin watched the scenes in Birmingham with horror. The day after violence descended on the city, he wrote a telegram to Attorney General Robert F. Kennedy, which read in full:

THOSE WHO BEAR THE GREATEST RESPONSIBILITY FOR THE CHAOS IN BIRMINGHAM ARE NOT IN BIRMINGHAM. AMONG THOSE RESPONSIBLE ARE J. EDGAR HOOVER, SENATOR EASTLAND, THE POWER STRUCTURE WHICH HAS GIVEN BULL CONNOR SUCH LICENSE, AND PRESIDENT KENNEDY, WHO HAS NOT USED THE GREAT PRESTIGE OF HIS OFFICE AS THE MORAL FORUM WHICH IT CAN BE. THIS CRISIS IS NEITHER REGIONAL NOR RACIAL. IT IS A MATTER OF THE NATIONAL LIFE OR DEATH. NO TRUCE CAN BE BINDING UNTIL THE AMERICAN PEOPLE AND OUR REPRESENTATIVES ARE ABLE TO ACCEPT THE SIMPLE FACT THAT THE NEGRO IS A MAN.[9]

About a year before he sent this message, Baldwin had met Robert and his brother John at a White House reception to honor Nobel Prize recipients and other distinguished intellectuals. During the first two years of the administration, Baldwin had been deeply disappointed by the president's performance on civil rights. The administration seemed to view the topic as more of an annoyance than anything else, and Baldwin thought the president's rhetoric on the matter was woefully inadequate. "The speech Kennedy made to Mississippi the night Meredith was carried there," Baldwin told interviewers, "was one of the most shameful performances in our history" because the speech was addressed almost exclusively to the wounded egos of segregationists, and from Baldwin's point of view, it seemed like the president had forgotten there were any black people in Mississippi at all.[10]

Robert Kennedy responded to Baldwin's telegram by inviting him to visit his Virginia home a few days later. On the morning of May 23, Baldwin presented himself at the doorstep of the attorney general. During this short meeting, Baldwin emphasized a theme from his telegram: the administration was failing to use the "moral forum" of the presidency to change the conversation about civil rights.[11] Kennedy asked Baldwin if he would assemble a group of prominent civil rights leaders and activists to meet with him in New York the following day.

On May 24, 1963, Baldwin led a star-studded entourage into the Kennedy residence at 24 Central Park South. Baldwin was joined by several friends and business associates as well as the psychologist Kenneth Clark, Edwin Berry of the Chicago Urban League, King's lawyer Clarence Jones, and artists Lena Horne, Harry Belafonte, Rip Torn, and Lorraine Hansberry. Baldwin's entourage also included the man who would end up being the key figure in the meeting: Jerome Smith, a young activist who had participated in the Freedom Rides and bore scars from the experience.[12]

The meeting was a tense and complicated affair. No transcript exists that records precisely what was said, but accounts by Baldwin, Assistant Attorney General Burke Marshall, and White House aide Arthur Schlesinger (who debriefed Kennedy the following day) provide us with a sense of what happened at "the Summit." Soon after the conversation began, Smith informed Kennedy "he was nauseated by the necessity of being in that room."[13] Kennedy seemed to take this statement personally—although Smith had meant that he was sickened by the fact it was necessary to have the meeting at all—and Kennedy "turned away from Jerome as though to say, 'I'll talk to *you*, who are civilized. But who is *he*?'" This raised the ire of Hansberry, the thirty-three-year-old author of the Broadway hit *Raisin in the Sun*, who looked Kennedy in the eyes and said, "The only man you should be listening to is that man over there [gesturing to Smith]. That is the voice of twenty-million people."[14] Smith proceeded to speak passionately about what it was like to face the white mobs in the South, and wondered aloud whether or not he could remain nonviolent in the face of such brutality.

Kennedy appeared unmoved by Smith's testimony or Hansberry's plea, so Baldwin tried a different tack. He knew that the Kennedys were committed cold warriors and recognized that the recent crisis in Cuba was still on their minds. In order to reveal to Kennedy another consequence of the racial situation, Baldwin asked Smith if he "would fight for his country" to liberate Cuba, for example.[15] In response, Smith shouted, "Never! Never! Never!" According to Schlesinger, "This shocked Kennedy, for whom patriotism was absolute," and in Clark's recollection, "Bobby got redder and redder and redder, and in a sense accused Jerome of treason."[16]

With this exchange, the battle lines were drawn. The meeting would not be about what to do in the South or the northern ghettos; it would be a heated argument pitting Kennedy's liberal nationalism against the radical moralism of Baldwin, Smith, Horne, and Hansberry. From that point on, the many other people in the room seem to have faded into the background, and the most indelible memories for both those on the "Kennedy side" and "Baldwin side" center around Hansberry. "Look," she said to Kennedy, "if *you* can't understand what this young man is saying, then we are without any hope.... [T]here's no alternative except going in the streets ... and chaos."[17] "Most of the talk," as Marshall remembered it, "was about getting guns and shooting white people."[18] What stood out in Baldwin's memory was not Hansberry's warning of the violence to come but rather her insistence on a "moral commitment" from the

Kennedys. This moral commitment, she and others in the room argued, would be demonstrated not just by what they *said*—though that mattered too—but also by what they *did*. "We wanted him to tell his brother the president," Baldwin wrote later, "to personally escort to school, on the following day or the day after, a small black girl already scheduled to enter a Deep South school." Anyone who spat on that girl, Baldwin explained, would also be spitting on the president of the United States. In response, Kennedy told those assembled that this "would be a meaningless moral gesture" and he later dismissed the idea as mere "theatrical posturing."[19]

The recollections of the end of the summit are no less interesting. Baldwin recalled that after three hours, the meeting ended with Hansberry standing up, looking at Kennedy, and saying, "I am worried about the state of a civilization which produced that photograph of the white cop standing on that Negro woman's neck in Birmingham." "Then," Baldwin reported, "she smiled. And I am glad that she was not smiling at me."[20] Kennedy, for his part, remembered both Jones and Belafonte approaching him at the meeting's end in order to offer him support and encouragement. He asked Belafonte why he had not defended the administration during the meeting, and Belafonte said, "I couldn't say this to the others. It would affect my position with these people, and I have a chance to influence them along a reasonable way. . . . If I sided with you on these matters, then I would become suspect."[21]

On returning to Washington, DC, Kennedy expressed frustration and despair to Schlesinger. "You can't talk to them," he said. "It was all emotion, hysteria."[22] Given this reaction, Marshall concluded that the meeting had no "influence on the Attorney General" and that it ought to be regarded as a "minor incident" in the scope of history.[23] Schlesinger disagreed: "[Kennedy] began, I believe, to grasp as from the inside the nature of black anguish. He resented the experience, but it pierced him all the same. His tormentors made no sense; but in a way they made all sense."[24] Indeed, Kennedy would later acknowledge that Schlesinger's interpretation proved to be correct. After the emotion of the meeting dissipated, Kennedy told friends about the Smith incident and then confessed, "I guess if I were in his shoes, if I had gone through what he's gone through, I might feel differently about this country."[25]

Baldwin left the Kennedy residence and went directly to the studios of WNDT, where Clark had arranged to interview him as part of his series *Perspectives: The Negro and the American Promise* (in which he would also interview King and Malcolm X). Both Clark and Baldwin were physically and emotionally exhausted, and as they took their seats, lit their cigarettes, and the cameras started to roll, Baldwin admitted "his mind" was "someplace else." As they sat on the spare set and talked about his childhood in Harlem, Baldwin's voice was reduced almost to a whisper. Months of lecturing had taken their toll to be sure, but the more immediate cause was the sense of despair he felt in the wake of the Kennedy meeting. Again and again during the interview he drifted from the particulars of Clark's questions to larger questions about the American soul. "There are days—this is one of them—when you wonder what your role is in this country and what your future is in it . . . [and] how you are going to communicate to the vast, heedless, unthinking, cruel white majority that *you are here*." After Clark attempted to buoy Baldwin's hope by reminding him of the heroism shown by young protesters in the South, Baldwin told Clark that it was not the souls of the revolutionaries that worried him. "I am terrified," he said, "by the moral apathy, the death of the heart that is happening in my country. These people have deluded themselves for so long that they really don't think I am human. . . . And this means that they have become . . . moral monsters." As these last two words came out of his mouth, Baldwin's large, anguished eyes were cast down at the table in front of him. When Clark began asking his next question, Baldwin leaned back, brought his right hand to his forehead, and said, "It's a terrible indictment, but I mean every word I say."[26]

As hell broke loose in Birmingham, Buckley surveyed the scene with dismay. He and his staff at *National Review* were suspicious of "professional agitators" intent on stirring up trouble in the South, but Buckley also worried about the rise of racist demagogues like Barnett and Wallace. His ideal in this period would have been a southern scene dominated by men like Kilpatrick, who might promote gradual and paternalistic reform. Buckley believed prudent leaders animated by a combination of noblesse oblige and constitutional principle might civilize the region over time. Instead of the civil rights movement's call for "Freedom Now," Buckley's slogan might be, "Some Freedom . . . one day . . . when we decide you're ready."

Barnett and Wallace, Buckley surmised, were not the sorts of men who could manage gradual amelioration of race relations in the South. In the wake of "The Mess in Mississippi" that ensued when Meredith attempted to register for classes at Ole Miss, Buckley expressed his disdain for Governor Barnett. Echoing his "Return to States' Rights" editorial of several years prior, he wondered how we could trust that Barnett was genuinely committed to the doctrine of federalism when he demonstrated such a voracious "appetite for federal patronage" on all matters other than civil rights. Buckley also reported that Barnett furthered the case for his own hypocrisy when it was uncovered that years earlier, while dining at a restaurant in Hartford, Connecticut, he nearly got himself arrested for throwing a tantrum on discovering that there was an African American diner on the premises. Can a man who "tries to tell citizens of Connecticut what they can do and what they can't do," Buckley asked, really be counted as an advocate of "states' rights?"[27]

For a moment, many of Buckley's southern admirers may have worried that he had gone soft on the segregation issue. They would be reassured, however, by the last two paragraphs of the column. The "vagaries of Mr. Barnett" notwithstanding, Buckley still believed there was a principled case to be made for the states' rights position. "Whatever it is [that] provides the passion"—be it "genuine hatred and fear of the Negro race," as the critics contend, or a "devoted belief in the institution of segregation as uniquely meeting the social needs of the moment"—Buckley concluded, "the *political* cause [of home rule] is admirable."[28]

Buckley's reflections on the southern segregationists, when compared to his handling of the JBS, reveal something significant about the strategy he employed as he "edited conservatism." In both cases, Buckley was careful to emphasize the vices of the leaders of these movements while being sure to praise the goodwill of many of their followers. In "The Question of Robert Welch," for example, Buckley took Welch to task for "distorting reality" as well as "refusing to make crucial moral and political distinction[s]," but his followers were praised as "some of the most energetic, self-sacrificing, and dedicated anti-Communists in America."[29] A few months later, as he laid into Governor Barnett, he was careful not to criticize "the average white Southerner," who Buckley identified as an important ally in an "admirable" political cause.[30] Buckley was indeed "editing conservatism," but he was being careful not to edit it out of existence.

Not long after Buckley penned these words, he embarked on an extended tour of Africa. Over the previous several years, he had commissioned several essays for *National Review* on political developments on the continent, and to a one, these pieces cast doubt on the wisdom of self-determination for African peoples. Erik von Kuehnelt-Leddihn—an Austrian monarchist writer whom Buckley called "the world's most fascinating man"—reported from Africa for *National Review* to warn against "highly irrational and frequently semi-religious democratism" along with "the craze and criminal folly of 'democracy' and 'anticolonialism.'"[31] Anthony Lejeune complained from Ghana that European liberals had abdicated "all responsibility" for the dire "consequences" of decolonization.[32]

Views such as these were fully consistent with Buckley's own positions. Over the years, he had several occasions to weigh in on events in Africa, but perhaps never so infamously as when he commented on the Sharpeville massacre in South Africa. In spring 1960, thousands protested apartheid "pass laws"—the internal passport system that imposed severe limitations on the freedom of people of color—outside a police station in Sharpeville. In the midst of the protest, South African police opened fire on the crowd and killed sixty-nine people, including several children.[33] Buckley's response echoed many of the themes of his writings on the

American South, especially his arguments about the Freedom Riders. Killing all those unarmed people in Sharpeville was "surely wrong," but that does not dispose of the "moral problem" at the heart of the situation. "The whites are determined to stay in Africa," he explained, "and these terms call for the ghettoization of blacks." In order to defend this position, "whites are prepared to use machine guns against a mob organized to resist *apartheid*" because "they understood those machine guns to be firing in defense of the homeland." Although their means were "barbaric," Buckley declared, the "whites are entitled . . . to pre-eminence in South Africa."[34]

In a January 1961 profile for *Esquire* magazine, Dan Wakefield asked Buckley when Africans would be prepared for self-government, and Buckley responded, "When they stop eating each other."[35] Later that year, Buckley was censured by the National Student Association for calling the Congolese "semi-savages" during a speech on behalf of Young Americans for Freedom.[36] In a series of pieces written about Africa in late 1962 and early 1963, he expressed these views in more detail. Just a few days after Baldwin's "Letter from a Region in My Mind" was published in the *New Yorker*, readers of Buckley's syndicated column received a "Letter from Cape Town" in which he assumed a posture almost identical to the one that dominated his reflections on the American South. The question of apartheid, Buckley explained, may seem "morally outrageous" to outsiders, but we must try to see the matter through the eyes of the white South Africans. They are "outnumbered four to one," and the system of apartheid seems to them to be all that stands between "life and death." Buckley asked readers to "imagine the feeling . . . under the skin of people who live south just a few hundred miles of a roaring black nationalism which seeks to have its pogromatic way all over the continent."[37]

In a report from Mozambique a week later, Buckley called on "America and the West" to "depart" from "dogmatic anti-colonialism and realize the nature of the beast." Buckley conceded that in Mozambique, the Portuguese dominated "the natives" and treated them as "grown-up children," but "African nationalism" had proven to be "self-discrediting" so we ought to be hesitant to turn against the colonizers.[38]

On January 15, 1963—the day after Wallace delivered his "Segregation Forever" inaugural address in Alabama—Buckley published a long feature essay in *National Review* reflecting on his recent "South African Fortnight." In the piece, he described the arbitrary and degrading features of the South African racial caste system in some depth before confessing that he was not prepared to pass moral judgment on it. Like his assessment of the American racial situation, he contended that it was not, above all, a matter of morality. People keep asking if the system of apartheid is humane, but that, Buckley declared, is the wrong question. The important question is "whether it will work." He concluded the piece by stopping short of approving of apartheid, but he expressed sympathy for its defenders: "I know it is a sincere people's effort to fashion the land of peace they want so badly."[39]

Not long after Birmingham blew up, Buckley sat down at his typewriter to weigh in on what was at stake. In a piece called "Birmingham and After," he encouraged those on all sides of the conflict to practice the virtue of prudence. Although the right to peaceably assemble is protected by the Constitution, he noted, this right is not absolute and can be trumped by concerns for "public order." Buckley then recycled the argument he had made in his Freedom Riders essay by comparing the protesters to Rockwell and the American Nazi Party. Although he was again careful to avoid drawing a moral equivalence between the aims of the civil rights activists and those of the Nazis, he suggested that the analogy was revealing. When Rockwell and his goons provoke Jewish people, he told his readers, we do not have a hard time *understanding* why Jewish people react violently. "What we need to ponder," Buckley suggested, "is why the Southern Community . . . [is] as hostile to these [civil rights] demonstrators as New Yorkers are to Rockwell." Like his explanation of the white South African's attachment to apartheid, he explained that for the white southerner, this was a matter of life and death. "They feel that the demonstrators"—who they know are "capable of lionizing James Baldwin"—"have their eyes on the jugular vein of Southern life"; more specifically, they feel that the demonstrators are trying to destroy the idea that "the management of the South's destiny, at least for the time being," ought to be in the hands of "the white majority."[40]

Buckley concluded with this advice to white southerners: start behaving more prudently or you will hand over your power to the "Federal Government, whose symbol is the paratrooper with bayonet."[41] Prudent behavior in the South, he hoped, would cause federal authorities to back off, and a "dialogue between the best people here" (people more like himself than Baldwin) and the best people "there" (people more like Kilpatrick than Barnett) might steer the region toward gradual progress rather than into the abyss of "chaos."[42]

The events in Birmingham had a galvanizing effect on President Kennedy's interest in civil rights.[43] Word came out of Washington that the administration was about to step up its efforts to protect the rights of African Americans, including the right to vote. In early June, Buckley took to the pages of National Review to cast doubt on Kennedy's motives and attack the idea of universal suffrage. President Kennedy, Buckley suggested, was moved not by "a charitable concern for Negro rights" but rather a "selfish apprehension about next year's elections."[44] Not only were his motives questionable, Buckley continued, but the policy being pursued was deeply unwise. In his explanation, Buckley echoed some of the arguments he had made six years earlier in "Why the South Must Prevail," but this time around his antidemocratic position cut even deeper.[45] Although he had hinted at this in earlier writings, the early June piece on "The Vote in the South" made his position crystal clear: the South should lead the way in "conservative reform" by amending its laws and constitutions to constrict the right to vote even further. The South should administer "objective voter qualifications tests" to *all* would-be voters regardless of race—so as to shift more power into the hands of better-educated white elites, and away from poor whites likely to be seduced by the Barnetts and Wallaces of the world. Buckley acknowledged that even with "impartial adamance" by officials, the de facto impact of this reform would be to keep a far higher percentage of blacks from voting than whites, but this, in his mind, would lift the cloud of racism from the system. Better yet, such a "color-blind" strategy might establish the southerners as national leaders, "pioneering against the mobocracy which is threatening the stability of our society, coarsening our politics, and undermining the vision of the authors of our Federalist Papers."[46]

But Buckley's call for color blindness in the disenfranchisement of voters was *not* an embrace of color blindness generally. Indeed, the very same week he offered the voter qualification proposal, he authored a column critiquing Baldwin's "Call to Colorblindness." Baldwin's goal, Buckley informed his readers, "is nothing less than the *evanescence* of color. He wants the day to come . . . when color consciousness will disappear, when you and I, entering a room, will not have noticed even at the time we leave, who there, if anyone, was black, who was white."[47] Baldwin proposed that this goal could be accomplished, Buckley argued, if "the white population . . . give their power to the negroes, . . . renounce their civilization, . . . [and] despise their God."[48]

Buckley expressed concern about what might happen if the "Negro community" adopted the "raw nervous temperament" and "resentment of racial tribulations" that animated Baldwin. He made reference to Baldwin's recent meeting with Robert Kennedy and reported that the attorney general had apparently "laughed" in response to the call for the president to personally escort black students into segregated schools. To Buckley, this was "no laughing matter"; it was a "tragic matter." It was tragic in the sense that Baldwin wanted what he could not possibly have and was "arousing appetites that simply cannot be satisfied."[49] And so what, Buckley wondered, would Baldwin have us do in the face of this tragic impasse? What, he asked, are we supposed to do to cure the "meanness" of racist whites, like those who had victimized Baldwin over the years? Shall we, Buckley queried provocatively, "shoot them?" Is this what Baldwin was warning against when he prophesied "the fire next time?"[50]

On the same day that Buckley published "The Call to Colorblindness," Baldwin declared war on the FBI. Baldwin had long been a subject of interest to the FBI—his file was started in 1958 and ended up being over eighteen hundred pages—but the agency's focus on him seems to have sharpened just after his May 1963 meetings with Robert Kennedy. In the margin of a newspaper article about the New York meeting, the FBI's second in command, Clyde Tolson, wrote, "What do our files show on James Baldwin?" The next day, an agent prepared a memo that described Baldwin's political activities over the course of the previous decade. Of particular interest to the agent were Baldwin's criticisms of the House Un-American Activities Committee, his support for integration in the United States as well as revolutionary movements in the developing world, and his criticisms of FBI director Hoover. At the conclusion of the informational synopsis, the agent noted under "ACTION," "Information concerning Baldwin and other individuals who participated in the recent conference with the Attorney General is being incorporated into informative memoranda for dissemination to the Attorney General." The "informative memoranda" prepared for the attorney general emphasized only two points: "Baldwin is a homosexual, and on a recent occasion made derogatory remarks in reference to the Bureau." The focus on Baldwin's sexuality is not surprising given Hoover's obsession with such matters—in 1964, he would write on a document in Baldwin's file, "Isn't Baldwin a known pervert?"—and his agents were known to sometimes refer to Baldwin as "Martin Luther Queen."[51]

Baldwin was aware that he was under surveillance by the FBI. He suspected that his phone in New York had been tapped, and in late May, two of his friends reported that FBI agents attempted to enter his New York apartment.[52] In response, he decided to make a public statement about the bureau's abuse of power and disordered priorities. The bureau got advance notice that Baldwin had a statement in the works through its extensive wiretaps. In a conversation between King associates Stanley Levinson and Clarence B. Jones (who was also present at Baldwin's New York meeting with Kennedy), agents heard more about the plans for the March on Washington and were tipped off about Baldwin's upcoming statement. Jones said Baldwin had told him he was about to drop an "atomic bomb," rhetorically speaking, on the FBI. And so he did. In early June, Baldwin released a searing statement against the bureau in which he implored its agents to quit harassing civil rights activists and start investigating southern racist groups.[53]

———

On June 11, 1963, Alabama governor Wallace arranged to stage some political theater. A federal judge had issued a final order granting the admittance of three black students to the University of Alabama. In a carefully orchestrated media event, Wallace walked through a gauntlet of television cameras, photographers, and adoring fans to the doorway of the Foster Auditorium, where two of the students were supposed to complete their registration for courses. When the students got to the doorway accompanied by Deputy Attorney General Nicholas Katzenbach and several federal marshals, Wallace—flanked by Alabama state troopers in their baby-blue helmets—delivered an oration on states' rights and concluded by declaring, "I, George C. Wallace, as Governor of the state of Alabama, . . . do hereby denounce and forbid this illegal and unwarranted action by the central government."[54] Soon thereafter, President Kennedy issued an executive order that federalized the Alabama National Guard, and a few hours later the Thirty-First Division arrived and ordered Wallace to step aside.

That evening, President Kennedy spoke to the nation about civil rights. In the address, he declared that the country was confronting a "moral crisis," and the teachings of the Declaration of Independence, Constitution, and scriptures all pointed in one direction: "Every American ought to have the right to be treated as he would wish to be treated, as one would wish his children to be treated." In order to make this a reality, Kennedy called on Congress to take its boldest action on civil rights since Reconstruction: a law that would give "all Americans the right to be served in facilities which are open to the public—hotels, restaurants, theaters, retail stores, and similar establishments"—and would further empower the federal government to protect the rights of all. If Congress failed to act, Kennedy warned, the "only remedy" for "Negro citizens" would be "in the street."[55] Perhaps "the Summit" was not such a failure after all.

On the same day as Kennedy's civil rights address, two interesting invitations were mailed to Baldwin. The same federal government that had him under FBI surveillance—and would soon declare him to be "a dangerous individual who could be expected to commit acts inimical to the national defense"—was hoping he might be the keynote speaker at an upcoming meeting of the Department of Health, Education, and Welfare.[56] In the same batch of mail, Baldwin received a letter from a scholar at Brandeis University named Jacob Cohen inviting him to contribute to a book called *The Undelivered Fireside Addresses of President John F. Kennedy.* The idea for the book was to have contributors write the speeches they wished President Kennedy would give on a variety of subjects. Cohen hoped Baldwin would author the speech on civil rights.[57]

Just a few hours after Kennedy's televised message on civil rights, a sniper in the streets of Jackson, Mississippi, would send a message of a different sort. Myrlie Evers watched the address on television and waited up with her three children to celebrate the president's speech with her husband, Medgar. Like so many nights, Medgar worked late, attending a mass civil rights meeting and strategizing with other leaders in the movement until after midnight. On that night, Evers was doing just the sort of work that inspired such awe in Baldwin when he met the thirty-seven-year-old civil rights leader earlier that year. When Evers finally arrived home just after 1:00 a.m. on June 12, a sniper's bullet stopped him from walking through his front door. One of his neighbors awoke to the sounds of Evers's three young children screaming, "Daddy! Daddy! Daddy!" At a mass meeting the next night, Myrlie told a crowd of some five hundred people gathered at Pearl Street Church that "nothing can bring Medgar back, but the cause can live on."[58]

Baldwin was devastated by the news of the Evers assassination, which was the first of so many that would happen throughout the 1960s. On a personal level, Baldwin's heart was broken because his brief interaction with Evers had led him to conclude that he exhibited just the sort of nobility that the country so desperately needed. On a philosophical level, Baldwin was less interested in ruminating on the sort of evil that filled the heart of the segregationist who pulled the trigger than he was on the responsibility that all Americans shared in the perpetuation of a world in which something like this was likely to happen. Evers's blood was on all our hands, and Baldwin wanted us to hear the screams of his children as well as the moans of despair that filled Pearl Street Church on the night after this hero had fallen.

Over the next several months, Baldwin would devote himself to two projects that would serve, in part, as his eulogies for Evers: *Nothing Personal* and *Blues for Mister Charlie*.[59] *Nothing Personal* was a collaborative venture with the celebrated photographer Richard Avedon, who was a friend of Baldwin's since their days at DeWitt Clinton High School. The book consists of dozens of photographs Avedon had taken, alongside text written by Baldwin. Most of the Avedon photographs are portraits of prominent Americans including Eisenhower, Malcolm X, Adlai Stevenson, Marilyn Monroe, Linus Pauling, and Wallace. Avedon arranged some of the photographs to make for striking contrasts. One could open the book, for example, to find a photograph of Rockwell being saluted by four of his American Nazi Party followers facing a portrait of the poet Allen Ginsberg, standing completely naked, waving at the camera with one hand while the other covered his crotch. In perhaps the most striking sequence of photographs, Avedon included several black-and-white images of patients at a state asylum for the mentally ill followed by color photos of beaming, healthy Americans frolicking on a beach.

Baldwin's accompanying essay is an extended reflection on the power of mythology to prevent us from confronting reality. The connection to the Evers's assassination was clear: Baldwin's essay was an attempt to examine the nature of the society that could produce an assassin like Byron de la Beckwith. It was no surprise to Baldwin that Beckwith was an active member of the Citizens' Council, but he was careful not to make the same mistake he saw so many make in their analyses of the NOI. What mattered to Baldwin, in other words, was not whether the Citizens' Council preached violence or what state officials like Governor Barnett were saying about the assassination but rather how *we* created such a virulent atmosphere of hatred.[60]

In *Nothing Personal*, Baldwin argued that "the root" of the question and "key" to unlocking the answer is the symbiotic relationship between identity and mythology.[61] The American myth goes something like this: in the beginning, "heroes came looking for freedom," and they had to battle "strangers" and "barbarians" to settle and civilize the virgin land. In order to accomplish these monumental tasks, it was necessary to commit unspeakable crimes, and find and exploit cheap labor. No one likes to admit that their success and prosperity is the result of murder, rape, and plunder, so it was necessary to create myths that served to rationalize and obfuscate these crimes. We convinced ourselves, for instance, that the natives we displaced and slaves we exploited were not fully human, and that our crimes—in most cases—made them better off than they were before. It is vital to this mythology that we maintain the idea that these others are "strangers" because the identities we create for them play a crucial role in pacifying those of us not fortunate enough to share the power of the "brutal and cynical oligarchy." Although many whites—from the poor farmers to the salespeople types like Beckwith—are never allowed to possess real power, they are able to take comfort in the fact that they are not "strangers." Their whiteness is, in short, a safety net that protects them from ever falling to the bottom of the ladder. For a thoroughly mediocre man like Beckwith, race functioned as one of his only sources of power.[62] He may not have risen far in white society, but he could go to bed at night feeling a sense of pride in the color of his skin.

The reliance on racial mythology to establish one's identity was, according to Baldwin, a recipe for disaster. "It is," he wrote, "the very nature of a myth that those who are its victims and, at the same time, its perpetrators, should, by virtue of these two facts, be rendered unable to examine the myth, or even to suspect, much less recognize, that it is a myth which controls and blasts their lives." When we are trapped by mythology, we "can never be free." For Baldwin, a figure like Beckwith is best understood not as an especially evil human being who took his extreme views too far but rather as the natural outgrowth of a society in which "we live by lies."[63]

As readers thought through Baldwin's diagnosis of the American soul while examining the photographs of Wallace, Rockwell, and other merchants of hate, it must have been difficult to find much optimism in *Nothing Personal*. But a few of Avedon's photographs (e.g., of civil rights activists and countercultural icons like Ginsberg) and some of Baldwin's prose did inspire hope that we might free ourselves from "our striking addiction to irreality." "It is necessary," Baldwin declared, "while in darkness, to know that there is light somewhere, to know that in oneself, waiting to be found, there is light." Baldwin argued that in order to find that light, we must come to grips with our past and "use it" as the basis "to build a self again." Only if we are willing to do this, he believed, could we transcend our "youth," false innocence, and corruption to achieve a new sense of self that would allow us to "say Yes to life" and "save each other."[64]

Later in 1963, Baldwin completed *Blues for Mister Charlie*, a play that was born in his mind in the months after the murder of Till. The Till case, he wrote in the notes for *Blues*, "pressed on my mind so hard" and "would not let me go." In *Blues*, Baldwin set for himself the task of exploring the minds of the "wretched" human beings who killed Till, Evers, and six young people in Birmingham. "We have a duty," Baldwin declared, "to try to understand" because although "we probably cannot hope to liberate him, [we can] begin working toward the liberation of his children."[65]

Blues tells the story of the murder of a young black man named Richard at the hands of Lyle Britten, a poor white man. The murder occurs at the beginning of the play, and the rest bounces back and forth between flashbacks to times preceding the murder and the aftermath of the crime.

Among those responding to the crime are the victim's father, Meridian Henry, who is a preacher of a King-like doctrine of nonviolence, and Lorenzo, a student whose radical rhetoric is a combination of SNCC activism and Malcolm X's militancy. By late 1963, the ideas of both Meridian and Lorenzo represented different regions in Baldwin's mind. He found himself drawn to King personally and attracted to nonviolence as a pragmatic strategy, but he also identified with the righteous anger of the more militant factions in the movement. The back and forth between Meridian and Lorenzo can be read, in part, as Baldwin's attempt to work out the most promising strategy for liberation.

Baldwin portrayed Lyle as a relatively harmless and even sweet man when he was among whites. We see him teasing his wife, tending to their baby, and joking with friends. But when Lyle speaks about or interacts with blacks, all that sweetness melts away and he becomes a different person. We learn that Lyle has raped many black women and killed at least one black man in the past. We also learn that Lyle is a poor man and full of resentment about his status in society. Rather than directing this resentment toward his white "betters" who perpetuate the system that keeps him down, it is always directed "downward" toward "the niggers."[66]

In response to what Lyle did to Richard, Lorenzo doubts the wisdom of continuing down the path of nonviolence. At what point, he ponders, is it time to fight fire with fire? When he is warned against stooping down to the level of the Lyles of the world, Lorenzo retorts, "I don't want to be better than they are, why should I be better than they are? And better at what? Better at being a doormat, better at being a corpse?"[67] With this statement, Lorenzo challenged a central argument in Baldwin's philosophy. In "Down at the Cross," for example, Baldwin insisted that the sacrifice of one's dignity was too high a price to pay for freedom. The challenge was to achieve freedom with one's dignity still intact, but Lorenzo wondered if this was really possible when up against people like Lyle and, more dauntingly, the society that created him.

Soon after President Kennedy delivered his televised address on civil rights, he submitted a proposal to Congress on the subject.[68] Just as he had promised in his speech, the legislation addressed not only voter qualification issues but also discrimination in "hotels, motels, restaurants, theaters, and all other public accommodations engaged in interstate commerce." Furthermore, the legislation authorized and empowered the attorney general to file suits to enforce desegregation laws, and withdraw federal funds from those practicing discrimination.[69] This relatively ambitious proposal faced a steep climb in Congress, where southern Democrats had successfully filibustered or hollowed out every meaningful piece of civil rights legislation since Reconstruction.

In the wake of Kennedy's speech and civil rights proposal as well as the internal tumult over Wills's review of Baldwin and the external tumult in the streets of the South, Buckley asked his senior colleagues at *National Review* to prepare memos for him on "how we should handle the Negro problem."[70] Buckley seems to have wanted to get his colleagues to take a step back and reassess what the magazine's (and conservative movement's) position ought to be on these issues. Buckley was probably trying to come to grips with the fact that his preferred way forward—gradual progress on "the Negro problem" guided by nonracist yet not dogmatically egalitarian whites—did not seem viable. Buckley was also grappling with the question of how best to confront the prospect of the first serious civil rights bill since Reconstruction. Would this one go the way of all the others, and either be filibustered to death or hollowed out by unfriendly amendments? What if it wasn't? What should principled conservatives do? By mid-1963, there were already strong indications that Senator Barry Goldwater would seek the Republican nomination for president in 1964, and Buckley was thinking about the relationship between the civil rights issue and possible electoral coalitions that could put Goldwater into the White House. And finally, as Buckley was trying to keep his magazine afloat, and attempting to build and hold together the coalition of groups that made up the nascent conservative movement, he was interested in staking out a position on civil rights that was distinctive from the racist Right, but that did not alienate it completely. He had reached the same conclusion about the racist Right as he had about

Governor Barnett: I may not like where their political energy comes from, but I want it on my side.

In response to Buckley's request, *National Review* senior editor William F. Rickenbacker began his memo informally:

> A couple of nights ago, after a particularly good supper, I stuck my head into the kitchen and said to our handygal, "Mae, that was a most good supper." Mae doubled over, clapped her hand to her mouth, and went into uncontrollable giggles. "What's wrong?" I asked. "Ain't nothing—huh huh ho ha hee hee—izz just the way you sayed it."

Rickenbacker told this story because he believed that the central challenge confronting conservatives on "the Negro problem" was one of framing, or "the way" they "sayed it." The major goals of conservatives, he argued, should be to discourage "revolution," encourage black economic progress, and convince blacks that they will achieve their desired "place" in society not by "pushing and shoving" but rather if they are "willingly granted access to whites by whites, for the common pleasure and advantage of all." Rickenbacker advised Buckley to steer clear of those who defend ideas of racial superiority, and said the magazine ought to condemn media outlets that "persist in giving front-page treatment to every least altercation between Negroes and whites," because this foments conflict and therefore borders on sedition.[71]

Meyer's memo is also worthy of note. Meyer had just used his Principles and Heresies column to provide his "basic analysis of the situation" in an essay called "The Negro Revolution."[72] Meyer made it clear in the piece that he had no love for Baldwin, Malcolm X, *or* King, all of whom "inflamed" the "masses" with "unmeasured and apparently unlimited demands." Black people had suffered "undoubted wrongs," Meyer conceded, but "those wrongs cannot be righted by destroying the foundation of a free and constitutional society." In case there was any doubt, Meyer made it entirely obvious what he was trying to say: although he accepted "the innate value of every created human being" and idea that "every American citizen" is entitled to "equal treatment before the law," he would fight with every fiber of his being against the civil rights bill being pushed by Kennedy because it threatened to deprive "private citizens of the protection of their property," lower "the standards of an already enfeebled educational system," and destroy "the constitutional separation of powers."[73]

At the start of his memo, Meyer referred Buckley to the "basic analysis" he offered in "The Negro Revolution" and added several "tentative proposals" for his consideration. First, Meyer insisted that the demand for equality before the law must be subordinate to "the maintenance of constitutional order." Second, in the wake of the riots in Birmingham and other cities around the country, Meyer worried about what ought to be done if a "revolutionary situation" should arise. In that event, "we must emphatically stand for the preservation of the ordered republic (an armed guard for Congress, extraordinary measures to preserve peace and suppress violence in our cities, etc)." Third, Meyer encouraged Buckley to seek out and partner with "Negro leadership opposed to the revolutionary spirit." Finally, Meyer said the magazine ought to speak for itself on the civil rights bill rather than feeling tethered to the position taken by "our friends in Congress or by Goldwater."[74] For *National Review*, he counseled, politics must be subordinate to principle; anything else would be heretical.

In *The Making of the President: 1964*, Theodore H. White reported that during summer 1963, there were 758 significant civil rights demonstrations across the country in 75 American cities and 13,786 arrests were made as a result.[75] Behind the scenes, civil rights leaders led by A. Philip Randolph and Bayard Rustin plotted to maintain pressure on the powers that be with a mass demonstration in the nation's capital.[76] Randolph had planned the original March on Washington in 1941 in order to challenge segregation in the armed forces and the defense industry, but canceled it after negotiations with the Roosevelt administration led to the issuance of Executive Order 8802, which prohibited discrimination on the basis of "race, creed, color, or national origin" in all programs related to "defense production" as well as for all defense contractors working with the federal government.[77] Kennedy hoped that he, like Roosevelt, might be able to talk Randolph into canceling the march because he feared an outbreak of violence and worried that it could further diminish the chances of the already-stalled civil rights bill. But this time Randolph, who served as chair of the march, and Rustin, who organized a coalition of activists from organizations including the Negro American Labor Council, SCLC, CORE, and SNCC, would not be deterred.

As the summer wore on, Buckley and Baldwin had the civil rights bill and upcoming march on their minds. In an August 3 column on the bill, Buckley conceded that many of the "[Negro] protests" that had taken place throughout the summer were "warranted," but he continued to express skepticism about the aims being sought by the protesters. The issue "goes to the heart of political philosophy: should a Constitution be an instrument for impressing on the community at large the people's general, and even specific ideas of morality?" Against the idea that the Constitution should be used to "bring Paradise" to the people, Buckley argued in favor of the relativist notion that "each community [has] the right to govern its own affairs, according to its own individual lights." South Carolinians and New Yorkers tend to have different moral views, and ought to be free to decide for themselves how they will live together. "The states' rights argument," Buckley concluded, "is deemed by a lot of impatient and right-minded idealists to be a plea for continued racism. It is not. It is a plea for the survival of the federal system, which was once considered, by idealists, to be a glory in itself."[78]

In an August 17 piece called "Count Me Out," Buckley offered direct criticisms of the March on Washington, which he suggested would be an "unruly" and "mobocratic" affair that could do great damage to "interracial progress" as well as "our free institutions."[79] The march was a threat to interracial progress, he argued, because it had been framed in the popular press as a demonstration about the pending civil rights bill, which Buckley believed to be an unwise piece of legislation that could do more harm than good. He was doubtful of what good that law—or any law—could do to improve race relations. "The Negro problem," he wrote, "cannot be solved with the most artful piece of legislation. Solomon himself could not come up with a law of the land which would drain the resentments of James Baldwin."[80] Law was doomed to fail, he contended, because people cannot—and should not—be forced to accept one another. With this assertion, Buckley mobilized the key insight of Meyer's "fusionism": virtue can only be practiced if one is free to choose between virtue and vice.[81] Civil rights legislation would force people to treat one another as equals, thus denying them the opportunity to choose this path for themselves. Whatever the appeal of fusionism as a philosophical concept, it was undoubtedly appealing politically for conservatives eager to maintain the status quo.

The "stampede of several hundred thousand people into Washington who lust after a single piece of legislation," Buckley suggested, posed a threat to "our free institutions" because it substituted the "shock drug" of "mobocratic pressures" for sober, deliberative reflection that focused on matters such as the "constitutional genealogy" and likely "sociological effect" of the legislation in question. Buckley did not rule out the legitimacy of all mass demonstrations, but this one was unacceptable. "Mass demonstrations," he observed, "should be reserved for situations about which there is simply no doubting the correct moral course," and he continued to insist that the cause of civil rights was morally dubious.[82]

On the day Buckley's "Count Me Out" column appeared in newspapers across the country, Baldwin was back in Paris drumming up support for the March on Washington from American expatriates. Baldwin led a meeting of prominent Americans abroad at a Paris jazz club, and a few days later, "led a procession of Americans to the embassy in Paris with a petition backing the March."[83] The petition, which was written by Baldwin, predicted that the march would be one of the most important "demonstrations for human dignity within living memory" and the marchers would be teaching their fellow compatriots valuable lessons about the meaning of the "American Revolution." "It is in our awareness of what this struggle means," the petition concluded, "and the degree of our dedication to it, that our futures, and the future of the world depends."[84]

Two days before the march, Baldwin was back on a plane, crossing the Atlantic to attend the demonstration. On August 28, 1963, Baldwin and other artists including Belafonte, Hansberry, Burt Lancaster, Marlon Brando, Paul Newman, Ossie Davis, Ruby Dee, Bob Dylan, Sidney Poitier, Charlton Heston, and Dick Gregory joined over two hundred thousand peaceful marchers as they made their way from an opening rally at the Washington Monument to a full program of speeches at the Lincoln Memorial. The three broadcast networks had twenty-eight cameras rolling, and hundreds of print journalists and photographers were on hand to chronicle the event.[85]

It was a hot day, and Baldwin was dressed in a dark suit and aviator sunglasses. In one of the most famous photographs from the march, Baldwin was captured with a beaming smile as Brando engulfed him in an embrace with one arm while his other arm brandished a cattle prod he brought with him to remind people of police brutality in the South.

At one point in the proceedings, several of the artists—including Belafonte, Dee, Davis, and Gregory—made statements to the vast crowd assembled on the National Mall. Baldwin, though, was nowhere near the microphone. Instead, photographs show him sitting stoically in the crowd, watching intently. Interestingly, it was Lancaster—the handsome, white movie star—who was introduced by Davis to read the Paris petition Baldwin had written. For Malcolm X, this was a clear slight of Baldwin and exposed "The Farce on Washington" for what it really was. In his "Message to the Grassroots" a few months later, Malcolm said:

> [The March on Washington] was a sell out. It was a takeover. When James Baldwin came in from Paris, they wouldn't let him talk 'cause they couldn't make him go by the script. Burt Lancaster read the speech that Baldwin was supposed to make; they wouldn't let Baldwin get up there, 'cause they know Baldwin's liable to say anything.[86]

Some have speculated that Baldwin was excluded from a prominent role "out front"—just as Rustin had been—because of his sexual orientation.[87] Others have contended that it had more to do with what King adviser Stanley Levinson described as Baldwin's tendency toward "a kind of poetic exaggeration" that made his message off-putting for

FIGURE 5.3. Baldwin with Marlon Brando at the March on Washington, August 1963 (Wikimedia Commons)

moderates.[88] For these and perhaps still other reasons, the man that Malcolm called "the poet of the civil rights revolution" was kept away from the spotlight at the march.[89]

By the time King got up to deliver his famous "I Have a Dream" speech, Baldwin was with Poitier, Belafonte, Brando, Heston, and the writer Joseph Mankiewesz in a television studio, where they would be on a panel to discuss the significance of the march from the perspective of "Hollywood." As Baldwin recalled later, before they sat down to record their conversation, he and the other artists in the studio huddled around a television in silence, "listening to Martin, feeling the passion of the people flowing up to him and transforming him, transforming us."[90]

Two and a half weeks after this awesome display of hope and solidarity, Birmingham was once again racked by violence. On September 15, four young black girls were killed at the 16th Street Baptist Church when members of the Ku Klux Klan bombed the place of worship just before the Sunday morning service. Later that day, two white teenagers—who had attended a different church that morning—went to a segregationist rally, and as they made their way home on a "red motorbike with Confederate stickers," saw two black teenagers approaching on a bicycle (with one on the seat and the other on the handlebars). One of the white teens, Larry Joe Sims, pulled out a .22 caliber pistol and fired two shots—one into the head and one into the chest—of Virgil Ware, thirteen, who died at the scene. As news of the explosion at the church spread, fights began to break out in the streets of Birmingham. Whites and blacks threw rocks at each other, and when the police arrived at the scene of these fights it was commonplace—given the reputation of the police force—for blacks to attempt to flee. Johnny Robinson, a sixteen-year-old black teenager, attempted to run down an alley to escape one such scene, and an officer shot him in the back with a shotgun.[91]

Baldwin was in California on yet another lecture tour when a CORE worker called to alert him to the news from Birmingham. The March on Washington was, for him, a dramatic exercise of the First Amendment right to petition the government for a redress of grievances. The news that "four young black girls had been blown into eternity . . . was the first answer we received to our petition."[92] For Baldwin, it is important to note, this answer was offered not just by the cowardly men who bombed the church but rather by "*the republic*."[93] Baldwin was absolutely devastated by this news, which constituted the second major body blow—after the Evers assassination—to his sense of hope for the country.

Biographer Alvin Felzenberg has identified the Birmingham church bombing as "a major turning point" in Buckley's thinking on civil rights.[94] The event is reported to have moved him to tears.[95] Buckley took to the pages of *National Review* to announce that with the tragedy, Governor "Wallace's factitious popularity quite literally exploded in his face." But if Birmingham was indeed a "turning point" in Buckley's thinking, it was not a turn on a dime. If anything, it may have been more akin to the beginning of a subtle course correction. There is no reason to doubt that the incident shook Buckley to his core. Although he sometimes found it difficult to muster much sympathy for "agitators" struck down by violence in the South, the murder of innocent children—one of whom was about the same age as Buckley's almost-eleven-year-old son, Christopher—crossed a line. In addition, he was hoping to see "the passing [of] George Wallace's star," who was, in his view, giving segregationists a bad name.[96]

But it is worth noting that in his reflections on Birmingham, Buckley was hesitant in three crucial respects. First, he wrote that although it was *"widely assumed* that [Wallace's] noisy opposition [to integration] was responsible for galvanizing the demon who went to church [to kill] little children in the name of racial integrity," he wondered if maybe the bomb was planted by a Communist or "crazed Negro" determined to spark civil unrest.[97] Second, he was unwilling to acknowledge that the *cause* of racial segregation played some role in motivating this sort of violence. Indeed, although Buckley criticized Wallace for "his reliance on the Federal Government in matters of material interest to his state," and "his refusal to permit local school boards to make their own decisions on the matter of integration or segregation," he also showered scorn on "revolutionary assaults on the status quo, and contempt for the law, which are traceable to the Supreme Court's manifest contempt for the settled traditions of constitutional practice" in the desegregation cases. It never seems to have occurred to Buckley that the central premise of segregation—that some human beings are *less than* other human beings—also played some part in legitimizing the logic of violence. Third—and perhaps most damning—Buckley lamented the fact that the bombing might "set back the cause of white people."[98] Like his critiques of the failed "statesmanship" of Barnett and Wallace, he seemed most worried *not* about the victims of racism but instead that racists might undermine the likelihood that the white South would ultimately "prevail."

Buckley's frustrations with the failed political leadership of southern seg-regationists were compounded by his sense that they were squandering a golden opportunity to help bring about a "revolt against the masses." For years he had longed to write a book in which he would describe and defend this revolt, which he hoped would bring about "the imposition of norms" as well as "the restoration of natural, and compassionate, hi-erarchy."[99] Back in 1961, Buckley had signed a contract with Putnam's to write a "big book" on the idea. He had been unable to get much traction on the project over the years, but in late 1963, he worked with *National Review* colleagues Hugh Kenner and James Burnham to get some ideas on paper.[100] In Buckley's notes for the project, it is clear that the prob-lem described above—what to do with the potentially useful political energy of those animated by racial animus—was at the forefront of his mind. "The Negro question," he wrote to Burnham, "*may* cause a revolt against the masses for the wrong reasons," but "does it matter?" Buckley could see that rising racial tensions might lead to a white backlash in support of more authoritarian norms and institutions. The trouble was that many of those fueling the white backlash were motivated by racism—which struck him as regrettable—instead of by a commit-ment to the "restoration of hierarchy."[101] Buckley never did get around to finishing *The Revolt against the Masses*, but he did answer the ques-tion he posed for himself in his notes: no, it did not matter that "the Negro question" caused a revolt against the masses for the "wrong rea-sons."[102] What mattered most to Buckley was hastening the revolt, one way or the other.

Right around the same time Buckley was working out his defense of the "revolt against the masses," President Kennedy traveled to Dallas, Texas, to rally Democrats and fund-raise for his 1964 reelection campaign. Ken-nedy was greeted by throngs of supporters, but also by plenty of animus from the political fringes. From the Right, activists had taken out a full-page advertisement in the *Dallas Morning News* questioning Kennedy's handling of the Cold War, and allies of the reactionary ex general Walker distributed handbills that placed faux mug shots of the president over the text "WANTED FOR TREASON" along with a list of seven charges, including that he had "given support and encouragement to the Communist inspired racial riots" and had "illegally invaded a sovereign state with federal troops."[103] But it was from the other political fringe—the Far Left—that the president's assassin, Lee Harvey Oswald, would emerge. From the sixth floor of a Dallas book depository, Oswald struck the president down with three shots from a high-powered rifle, and within hours, Kennedy was dead.

Baldwin called his sister, Gloria, and research secretary, David Leeming, at an office space he had recently rented on West End Avenue in New York. "Turn on the radio," he said. "Kennedy's been shot." This assassination, he told them, was "only the beginning."[104] There would be, he predicted, more political violence ahead. Baldwin told a reporter that he did not consider "President Kennedy a friend of the Negro," but he did consider his death a "tremendous loss" because Kennedy was an exceptional figure in American political history. "You could argue with him," Baldwin explained. "You could talk with him. He was alive. Do you know what I mean? He could hear. He began to see."[105]

A few days later, Baldwin sat down to write a letter to Bobby Kennedy on behalf of himself, Hansberry, Belafonte, Poitier, and Horne. In addition to offering his condolences, Baldwin urged Kennedy to continue the struggle for civil rights. He told Bobby that with the death of his brother, it fell to him to assume the mantle of civil rights leadership within the political establishment. To fail to take up that mantle, he told Kennedy in the bluntest possible terms, would be to betray his brother's vision of universal human brotherhood. To conclude the letter, Baldwin suggested that the suffering he experienced as a result of the death of his brother might allow Bobby to achieve a deeper understanding of black suffering. Black Americans know suffering all too well and they would share Kennedy's pain in the days ahead. Together, Baldwin hoped, they might unite in a common struggle to liberate all Americans.[106]

Buckley's response to the Kennedy assassination was more detached. Kennedy had become, to his mind, a sort of idol of the "intelligentsia," and so many of that class wept not for him but rather for themselves. His death meant, Buckley surmised, that they might "have to learn again to act for themselves. And, God help us, to *think* for themselves." In the wake of the tragedy, Buckley urged his readers to stay sober in their assessment of the man and sing him only "the praises he is due." For Buckley, this meant applauding the president's "courage, dignity, fortitude, tough-mindedness," [and] . . . "style and energy," but also remembering that— before the assassin's bullets struck him down—many Americans had been hoping for Kennedy's "retirement . . . from public life" one year hence.[107] We must not let the unfortunate demise of the president, Buckley declared, distract from the goals of the conservative movement.

Buckley had long been hoping that the man leading the campaign to retire Kennedy from public life would be Senator Goldwater of Arizona. Two years before the assassination, Buckley took to the pages of the popular magazine *Coronet* to muse about "If Goldwater Were President." Goldwater's strident conservatism, straight talk, and carefully cultivated frontier charm had made him one of the most recognizable figures on the American Right. Like Buckley, he had long been intrigued by the prospect of an alliance between conservative Republicans and southern Democrats. Just months after taking his seat in the Senate in March 1953, he lamented the number of "New Dealers and Fair Dealers" in both parties, and wrote in his diary, "I sense a realignment of Southern conservative Democrats with Democrats and Republicans of the West and Middle West."[108] And so, despite the protestations of Goldwater himself, legions of conservatives had been trying to recruit him to run for president since the late 1950s.[109]

Buckley and his colleagues at *National Review* were in the thick of the "Draft Goldwater" movement. Bozell was particularly enthusiastic about it and was enlisted to ghostwrite a small book that would distill the essence of Goldwater's political philosophy. Goldwater acquiesced in the plan, pending his final approval of the manuscript. Bozell's 127-page book, based on Goldwater speeches, was published in spring 1960 under the title *The Conscience of a Conservative*. The book, which Buckley thought was a bad idea, ended up being a huge success, climbing up the best seller lists and going into reprint after reprint.[110] Goldwater traveled the country barnstorming on behalf of conservative principles and candidates, and Draft Goldwater clubs were popping up everywhere from college campuses to the suburbs.

Once it became clear that Nixon would be the Republican nominee in 1960, Goldwaterites then set their sights on getting their man the vice presidential nomination. In the end, this scheme failed as well, and the party nominated moderate Henry Cabot Lodge. But the Goldwater troops shook the convention with their unbridled enthusiasm and devotion to hard-core conservatism. Although the moderates carried the day at the 1960 Republican National Convention, the tremors caused by the Goldwaterites proved to be a prelude to a tectonic shift in American politics over the next several years.

So by the time Buckley took to the pages of *Coronet* in late 1961 to fantasize about what might have been, he was certainly not the first to imagine this particular "dream walking."[111] Buckley noted that as a candidate, there were many things to like about Goldwater. He was "amiable, good-looking, fluent, earnest, a veteran, an active jet pilot, one part Jewish, a practicing Christian, head of a handsome family, a successful businessman, a best-selling author, a syndicated columnist, and a tough campaigner." More important to Buckley, Goldwater was a "radical conservative": he was radical in that he aimed to "change the face of the nation," but he was conservative in the nature of the change he would pursue. "He would reorient America," Buckley declared, "in the direction of minimum government and maximum personal responsibility." According to Buckley, Goldwater's domestic agenda was derived from "two central beliefs": "that the Constitution enumerates the powers of Congress" and "human freedom is best served by keeping government small." If Goldwater "had his way," Buckley explained, the farmer would wait in vain for their subsidy check, the labor union boss would not get favors from the government, the industrialist would not get their "cozy little tariff," the unemployed would get no help from the federal government, and "the Little Rock Negroes" would not get "their paratroopers."[112]

On this last point, Goldwater presented an interesting case. As Buckley quoted him in the piece, "I believe justice and morality require that persons of different races attend the same school. But I'm not going to impose my ideas of morality and justice on other people. The Constitution gave me no warrant to tell South Carolinians how to run their schools."[113] Unlike so many politicians who said this sort of thing disingenuously, Goldwater had a record in Arizona that supported his contention that he was morally opposed to racial discrimination. When he operated the Goldwater Department Store, he was willing to sell his wares to anyone, regardless of color. He had worked to desegregate the Arizona Air National Guard. He hired a black legislative assistant and pushed to have the Senate cafeteria desegregated so she could eat with other Senate employees. He had been a regular contributor to NAACP chapters in Arizona.[114] But Goldwater was uncompromising in his interpretation of the Constitution, and refused to support judicial, congressional, or executive action that he did not believe was clearly prescribed by the constitutional text. He was, in sum, offering just the sort of argument Buckley preferred on civil rights: nonracist resistance. Buckley had found his new Mr. Conservative.

Buckley worked behind the scenes not only to promote Goldwater's prospects but also to shape public perception of him. In a telling letter to Kilpatrick in early 1963, Buckley asked his friend to write a piece on "The Roots of Goldwater's Popularity in the South." But Buckley requested, if Kilpatrick's "conscience" would allow it, an opinion piece with a particular twist—one that stressed "it is something more than [Goldwater's] laissez-faire position on the Negro problem that endears him in the South."[115] Kilpatrick was "delighted" to manufacture something along those lines.[116]

The drumbeat of the Draft Goldwater movement continued steadily for the three-plus years from the end of the 1960 Republican National Convention to the assassination of President Kennedy in November 1963. Before the assassination, Goldwater was still not overly enthusiastic about the run, and the death of his friend Kennedy—with whom he had served in the Senate—made him all the more reluctant. Yet the Goldwaterites proved to be an unstoppable force, and in January 1964, Goldwater declared his candidacy for the Republican nomination: "I will not change my beliefs to win votes," he said. "I will offer a choice, not an echo."[117]

Even before Goldwater officially announced his candidacy, Buckley met with the senator's campaign brass in order to offer his services. It seems the role he envisioned for himself was as an unofficial liaison between the conservative intellectual community—which he had gotten to know quite well in his capacity as editor of National Review and in his work with several right-wing organizations—and the senator's policy team. Buckley would wait in vain for Goldwater's political handlers to take him up on his offer. To make matters worse, someone from the campaign leaked news of Buckley's ill-fated meeting to the press in order to show that Goldwater was not "too far right." Just weeks after Baldwin was kept from the spotlight at the March on Washington, Buckley was, as the New York Times would report, "repelled" from boarding the ship he helped build.[118]

Meanwhile, back in Washington, President Lyndon Baines Johnson—a tall, fast-talking Texan who had been a lion in the Senate for years prior to his ascent to the vice presidency—had decided to become a champion for the cause of civil rights. Johnson's history on the issue was a checkered one, but in his speech to a joint session of Congress just five days after the assassination, Johnson said, "We have talked long enough in this country about equal rights. We have talked for 100 years or more. It is time now to write the next chapter, and to write it in the books of law."[119] When the civil rights bill was under consideration in Congress, Attorney General Kennedy was a forceful advocate in testimony before key committees.[120] On January 23, 1964, the House of Representatives passed the civil rights bill, but the bill faced a seemingly insurmountable hurdle in the Senate, where southern Democrats—in alliance with conservative Republicans like Goldwater—were determined to stop it.[121] While southerners like Eastland, Thurmond, and Russell had long track records of racially incendiary rhetoric that explained their position on the bill, Goldwater claimed that he could not support the bill so long as it included provisions requiring integration in public accommodations and equal employment opportunity, both of which he considered to be unconstitutional. When the time came for a vote on the bill in June, Goldwater was one of only six Republicans in the Senate to vote against it.

Despite the cold shoulder from the campaign, Buckley soldiered on in the Goldwater cause. Early in the contest, he authored a series of pieces called Answers for Conservatives in which he offered talking points in response to dozens of questions frequently posed to Goldwater supporters. A few months later, Buckley went to bat in defense of Goldwater's decision to oppose the civil rights bill. Indeed, Buckley argued that the senator's position was more than defensible; it was a "profile in courage"—a phrase he borrowed from a book by the late president Kennedy in which he profiled "a half dozen political figures in the history of the United States who, pursuing their consciences, did the devastatingly unpopular thing."[122]

In the months prior to the Republican National Convention, Buckley was confronted with many questions about the connections between the Goldwaterites and the Wallace movement. In the spring, Wallace had challenged President Johnson in the Democratic primaries in Wisconsin, Indiana, and Maryland. Although Johnson won all three states, Wallace performed remarkably well, winning 34 percent of the vote in Wisconsin, 30 percent in Indiana, and 43 percent in Maryland.

In his syndicated column and National Review, Buckley celebrated the "white revolt" that was sweeping the nation. He was happy to accept the fact that many Wallace supporters would find their way into the Goldwater camp because, he insisted, they were not motivated by racism. A coalition of northerners and southerners, he explained, were "awakening" to the "danger to individual liberty" posed by "the new and radical plans" aimed at "breaking up traditional American patterns for racial assimilation and conciliation." Buckley maintained that these voters were not motivated by a dislike of black people but instead by a dislike of the ideas of figures like "James Baldwin and Bayard Rustin," who "despise the American way of life and our civilization," and "challenge root and branch the American approach to free civil order."[123] These voters feel "resentful" about race matters, Buckley conceded, but they are "not racists."[124]

Wallace's rise, Buckley argued later, was not due to his racism but rather because of his "successful dramatization of the loss of freedom and maneuverability in the individual states when the federal government begins to take over local problems." Race, Buckley claimed, simply had nothing to do with it. After all, he noted, Wallace "hardly mentioned the word Negro" in his campaigns in Wisconsin, Indiana, and Maryland.[125] Indeed, as Wallace moved onto the national stage, he had made a strategic decision to eschew explicit racist appeals. Such appeals, he realized, were gratuitous; every voter already knew his reason for being. Better instead to speak in the code of "law and order," "big government," and "states' rights."[126] Voters knew full well what he had in mind.[127]

Although Buckley disliked Wallace personally, he found himself in agreement with the governor on the question of civil rights. "The Brown Decade," Buckley argued, had proven that the voices of resistance—from the Citizens' Council to the editors of National Review—were right. "Brown," he declared, "is an abysmal failure" that "has drastically lowered the standard of education and conduct for both Negro and white children, and has deepened the mutual alienation of the races." Not only was Brown a failure "strictly on its own terms" but it had proven to be incredibly costly for the country too. It helped spawn "the ludicrously named 'civil rights movement,'" Buckley complained, and empowered "the least responsible of the Negro leaders," who in turn "arouse[d] white resistance." "Race relations in this country are ten times worse than in 1954," and the time had come, Buckley concluded, for conservatives to turn back the clock.[128]

For over a decade, Buckley had been laboring to bring about a day when a conservative could serve as the standard-bearer of his party. That day had arrived. In June, his excitement leapt off the pages of a memo he circulated to the staff of National Review, announcing plans for a special edition of the magazine to be released at the Republican National

FIGURE 5.4. Civil rights protest at the 1964 Republican National Convention in San Francisco (Wikimedia Commons)

Convention. On the cover, in big, bold print, the edition would say, "A PROGRAM FOR THE GOLDWATER ADMINISTRATION." In the pages that followed, he and his staff would share their fantasies of what the future might hold. Buckley asked Burnham, for example, to imagine a new course for American foreign policy and tapped none other than Kilpatrick to "advance some proposals" on the domestic front. Among other things, Kilpatrick predicted that when it came to race relations, a president Goldwater would rely on "moral suasion" rather than "state regulation."[129]

In mid-July, the Republicans gathered at the Cow Palace in San Francisco to nominate Goldwater for the presidency of the United States. Just as his candidacy had effectively been launched by the words of *National Review*'s Bozell in spring 1960, the most memorable words of his acceptance speech came from the pen of a contributor to the magazine named Harry Jaffa: "Extremism in defense of liberty is no vice. And . . . moderation in pursuit of justice is no virtue."[130] Although Goldwater declined Wallace's offer to serve as his running mate and "endorsed without reservation" a plank in the party platform calling for the "full implementation of the Civil Rights Act of 1964," the senator's vote against the bill sent a clear message to what used to be the solidly Democratic South.[131] In the words of Kilpatrick, the South was now "Goldwater country."[132] Activists in the civil rights movement agreed with Kilpatrick's assessment. By nominating Goldwater, the GOP was making a play to become the party of choice for racial reactionaries.[133]

And so outside the Cow Palace, protesters greeted Republican delegates with the largest civil rights demonstration since the March on Washington to voice their displeasure with the fact that the party of Lincoln had decided to rely on the spirit of Jefferson Davis to fuel it into the future.

———

Just days after the Civil Rights Act of 1964 was signed into law, three civil rights workers—James Chaney, Andrew Goodman, and Michael Schwerner—disappeared in Philadelphia, Mississippi. Goodman and Schwerner were white New Yorkers who had come south—along with hundreds of others—to volunteer as part of the Freedom Summer project to "register voters, work in community centers, and teach in 'Freedom Schools.'"[134] The three civil rights workers had been investigating a church bombing in rural Mississippi when Klansmen—with the assistance of local law enforcement—kidnapped and murdered them.[135]

With the news out of Mississippi, Buckley again utilized his syndicated column to reflect on the meaning of racist violence in the South. In the face of the latest atrocities, he recycled his oft-used refrain: let us try to understand. This time around, he left Rockwell and the Nazis on the rhetorical sidelines, and instead asked his reader to imagine that hundreds of "campaigners for the States' Rights movement of George Wallace" made their way into Harlem "to evangelize their position." A violent reaction from the citizens of Harlem, he argued, would likely result were such an invasion to occur. For Buckley, the outcome of political violence in the Mississippi case (and his imagined one)—though regrettable—was predictable. The more interesting question to him was whether or not the *cause* for which the civil rights workers died was a worthwhile one. This, too, was an easy question for Buckley to answer. The Freedom Summer workers were appalled by the fact that only 9 percent of African Americans in Mississippi were registered to vote. But why? "Unlike the democratic absolutists," Buckley declared, "some of us are capable of rejoicing at the number of people who do *not* exercise the technical right to vote."[136] What was most tragic about the latest murders in Mississippi, Buckley concluded, was that the victims died in pursuit of a cause that was not only unworthy but also fundamentally unwise.

While the Republicans were meeting in San Francisco two days after this column appeared in *National Review*, Americans were reminded of something on which Baldwin and Buckley had long agreed: US racial problems were national, not merely regional, in scope. On July 16, a white apartment superintendent named Patrick Lynch decided to do his best Connor impression by hosing down several black teenagers who were sitting on the stoop of one of his buildings on the Upper East Side of Manhattan. According to witnesses, Lynch accompanied the blast of his hose with the words, "Dirty niggers, I'll wash you clean!"[137] In response, the young people and some passersby began throwing bottles and garbage can lids at Lynch. An off-duty police lieutenant named Thomas Gilligan intervened and shot a fifteen-year-old black teenager named James Powell, who had gotten in the mix as he walked to summer school.[138] Over the next several days, riots racked Harlem, where one person was killed, dozens were injured, and hundreds more were arrested.[139]

When the Democratic Party met in Atlantic City a few weeks later to nominate Johnson, race proved to be a central issue as well. In protest of the racial reactionaries who controlled the South, a black farmhand named Fannie Lou Hamer led a contingent of civil rights activists called the Mississippi Freedom Democratic Party to the convention. Hamer proposed that the Democratic Party seat her delegation in the place of the "Goldwaterite, segregationist" Mississippi delegation, the head of which had called the NAACP a collection of "Niggers, Alligators, Apes, Coons, and Possums."[140] Hamer's dramatic testimony before the credentials committee of the Democratic Party—in which she described being fired, arrested, and beaten as a result of her attempts to register to vote—was broadcast to millions of Americans watching the convention on television. "If the Freedom Democratic Party is not seated," she declared, "I question America. Is this America, the land of the free and the home of the brave . . . ?"[141]

As the campaign wore on and the likelihood of a Goldwater victory dimmed considerably, Buckley turned his attention to safeguarding the reputation of the conservative movement. The "vile campaign," as Buckley called it, had inspired charges that Goldwater and his supporters were fascists and racists. The baseball legend Jackie Robinson, who identified as a Republican, reported that "the stench of fascism" was in the air when he attended the national convention in San Francisco.[142] King echoed this sentiment when he said saw "dangerous signs of Hitlerism in the Goldwater campaign."[143] Baldwin, who spent much of the summer and fall traveling around Europe to attend several openings of his plays, declared that the Goldwater nomination was "a scandal for the United States" and the Republican National Convention "showed what the nation really thinks of us 20 million Negroes." Although Baldwin still harbored a deep distrust of all politicians, he pledged to "do as much as it is in my power" to support the Johnson campaign. If Goldwater managed to win the election, Baldwin announced, he would leave the United States for good.[144]

Much to Buckley's chagrin, the Anti-Defamation League had even sponsored the creation of a book, *Danger on the Right*, in which its authors cataloged the groups offering support to Goldwater, from "rabble-rousing" right-wingers like the Citizens' Council to "radical" rightists like Robert Welch to "extreme conservatives" like Buckley and his cadre at *National Review*.[145] This sort of thing irked Buckley more than just about anything else in his professional life.[146] For more than a decade, he had been trying to "edit conservatism" to draw clear lines between respectable, intellectually serious conservatives like himself and the "bigots, kooks, and anti-Semites" who filled the pages of *Danger on the Right*.[147] Buckley was incensed to be placed cheek by jowl with the likes of Rockwell, Welch, and Gerald L. K. Smith.

Perhaps in part to push back against the conflation of his position (and Goldwater's) with the racists of the Far Right, Buckley ordered a "Special Report"—consisting of four feature essays—on "The Race Issue and the Campaign" to be published in the September 22 edition of *National Review*. In reality, the "Special Report" was really about "The Race Issue and the Conservative Movement" because Buckley had already spoken several times about "the impending defeat of Barry Goldwater."[148] The "Special Report" is a revealing moment in the development of Buckley's evolving views of race. It is telling both in terms of what Buckley chose to include and what he chose to leave out. None of the essays focused on the civil rights issues in the South. None of them attempted to rebut the accusations of racism against Goldwater and his supporters. Instead, Buckley looked toward the future. The focus of the report, he wrote in his introduction, was on "a growing disillusion with white Democratic voters who are, many of them, beginning to look at the Democratic Party as a vehicle for one very special interest, rather than as the vehicle" of the working class and lower middle class.[149] In order to help his readers think through what the future might hold on "the race issue," Buckley enlisted Ralph Toledano to muse on white backlash, Arlene Croce to write an essay on busing in New York, Richard Wheeler to report on housing discrimination legislation in California, and none other than Wills to offer some philosophical reflections on the matter. The Toledano essay set up the overall theme of "backlash," and was followed by the one-two punch offered by Croce predicting "Suburbia" would "explode" in response to school busing and Wheeler describing Democrats as "insufferably intolerant of anyone who harbors doubts" about fair housing laws.[150]

As he braced himself and his movement for defeat in the Goldwater battle, Buckley was thinking strategically and playing "the long game" on race. When he was assigning articles for the "Special Report," he saw no need to turn to his deep bench of southern apologists. Although the *policy* battle on civil rights seemed to be heading in the wrong direction, an important *political* battle had been won in the South. Just a week before the "Special Report" was published, this political victory was highlighted by the announcement of South Carolina senator Thurmond—a lifelong Democrat, save for his brief foray into third-party politics—that he would join the Republican Party and vote for Goldwater.[151] The Democratic Party was no longer a comfortable home for figures like Thurmond because, as Buckley put it in a column on the matter, "the egalitarians have moved in," leaving little room for those committed to "states' rights."[152] In the column, Buckley fantasized about a mass migration of southern politicians from the Democratic to the Republican Party. Buckley's dream would come true; it just took a matter of years rather than the matter of weeks he had envisioned.[153]

So instead of dwelling on the ongoing racial turmoil in the South, Buckley used the "Special Report" to focus on the grievances of white working-class and suburban voters all over the country who were feeling abandoned by the Democratic Party. These voters, he could see, were the ones the Republican Party would need to woo in future elections. As he looked toward the future, he called on Wills to conclude the "Special Report" with thoughts about the "objectives of the good society" that ought to guide the country on the race problem.[154] In response to this call, Wills defended Goldwater's intuition that race relations were better left to the "tribunal" of "the heart" than that of "the courtroom," but said that "the white community" was in need of "a series of peremptory electric shocks to be awakened and kept awake to its duties." In his reflections on the black community, the impact of Baldwin on Wills—though not explicitly acknowledged—is evident. As "the Negro, feeling his way into new areas of self-awareness, dignity, and pride . . . pushes outward" into the realms of greater social, political, and economic power, Wills thought it was worthwhile to reflect on the example provided by the NOI. The black Muslims did an important service, Wills thought, by offering a "living refutation of the old charge that the Negro cannot live a life of sobriety, industry, and pride himself." But the black Muslim program must ultimately be rejected because it relied on the "pitiful stimuli" of racial hatred and antagonism.[155]

There is one more thing worth noting about what Buckley chose *not* to include in his "Special Report." In the wake of charge after charge that Goldwater and the conservative movement were racist, the "Special Report" seemed to present Buckley with an opportune time to exercise his power as the "keeper of the tablets" for the conservative movement.[156] As we think back on Buckley's role as the "editor of conservatism," several key moments stand out such as his commissioning of Chambers and Wills to write Rand out of the movement, or his own series of essays attempting to purge first Welch and then the entire JBS from the ranks of the respectable Right.[157] And yet on the question of race, we search in vain for that moment when Buckley stood up and offered an unequivocal rejection of racist politics.[158] Privately, he had been willing to write back to racist readers who complained he was too soft when discussing innate racial differences or too hard on the Ku Klux Klan, but he refused to go public to offer a forceful and unequivocal repudiation of racist elements in the right wing.[159] Perhaps this is because he already knew what the rest of the country would soon discover: that the racist Right was now an indispensable part of the conservative coalition.[160]

On Election Day, Buckley wired Goldwater a three-word message: "Rooting for you!"[161] Most of the country, however, was not. In one of the greatest electoral landslides in US history, Johnson carried forty-four states and the District of Columbia, earning 486 electoral votes to Goldwater's 52.[162] The popular vote was 61.1 percent for Johnson and 38.5 percent for Goldwater. The senator was only able to carry his home state of Arizona by about 5,000 votes, and the only other states he won were in the Deep South. To add insult to injury, Buckley lost $1,000 in a bet with television host David Susskind (who would have owed Buckley $5,000 if Goldwater won).[163]

In the wake of this electoral catastrophe, Buckley did not despair. Goldwater had "broken up the Democratic stranglehold in the South," and twenty-seven million Americans had revealed themselves to be friends of the conservative cause.[164] For a movement builder like Buckley, this was but one battle in a much longer war. During the course of this battle, he identified new strategies that he thought might serve conservatives well in the years ahead. But before he would begin testing those strategies in the electoral arena, he had another fight on the horizon; he would soon be invited to meet "the eloquent menace" Baldwin face-to-face.

Chapter 6

"What Concerns Me Most": Baldwin at Cambridge

On Monday, January 4, Bill Kolins, a publicist at Corgi Books in London, called Robert Lantz, Baldwin's agent, to present him with a proposition. Corgi was set to publish the paperback version of *Another Country* in the United Kingdom in February, and Kolins wanted to launch the book with a bang. With Baldwin's star power at an all-time high, Corgi proposed to orchestrate the most extensive publicity campaign in its history. The goal, Kolins explained, would be to bring Baldwin to London for the release of the book and saturate the media landscape with his presence for several days. Kolins envisioned print advertisements, public talks, interviews, and receptions. Baldwin was, at that moment, one of the biggest literary celebrities in the world, and Corgi wanted to give him the star treatment and, of course, sell books.

Lantz called Baldwin, who was back in France, to see if he would be up for a trip to the United Kingdom. Baldwin agreed in principle even though he was—and had been for some time—quite ill with a series of viral infections that often left him bedridden. Baldwin's physical symptoms were coupled with a deep spiritual malaise. In August 1964, Baldwin marked his fortieth birthday with a sense of uncertainty about his personal and professional life. On the personal front, the love of his life, Lucien Happersberger, had fallen for Diana Sands, the actress playing Juanita in the Broadway run of *Blues for Mister Charlie*, and the frenetic pace of Baldwin's life made it difficult for him to sustain meaningful contact with the same group of friends and family for long. Baldwin had many friends in many places, but his transatlantic commuting took a toll on his relationships, and it was next to impossible for him to ever feel at home.

On the professional front, Baldwin—though at the height of his fame—was now the target of more virulent criticism than he had ever faced. *Another Country* was met with mixed reviews, and the book's explicit sexuality and drug use made it a subject of controversy on campuses and in communities throughout the United States. With the arrival of *Blues for Mister Charlie* on Broadway, Baldwin fulfilled a long-held dream of seeing one of his plays reach the pinnacle of the theater scene, but the production was rife with offstage drama.[1] When the play opened in April, it was also met with mixed reviews, including an especially harmful dig at Baldwin by the writer Philip Roth, who panned the play in the *New York Review of Books*.[2] After the tumultuous preproduction, lukewarm critical reception, and financial difficulties due to Baldwin's insistence that ticket prices be kept low, the producers gave the show notice of closing only one month after it opened.[3] A group of artists and philanthropists rallied to raise money to keep the play running for a few more months, but the Broadway run closed for good on August 29.[4]

In December 1964, *Nothing Personal* was the subject of a brutal review by the critic Robert Brustein in the *New York Review of Books*.[5] Brustein had issues with the book itself—he thought that Avedon's photographs transformed his subjects into "repulsive knaves, fools, and lunatics," and said Baldwin's prose sounded like it came from "a punchy and pugnacious drunk awakening from a boozy doze during a stag movie"—but perhaps more disturbing, he saw the book as a sign of Baldwin's artistic decline.[6] Baldwin, Brustein declared, had once been a source of "direct and biting criticism of American life," but this "once courageous and beautiful dissent" had degenerated into the "slippery prose" of a "showbiz moralist."[7]

In addition to these personal and professional woes, Baldwin was concerned about the fate of the world. Although there was some hope to be found in the passage of the Civil Rights Act of 1964 and Johnson's landslide victory over Goldwater, the recent violence in the South and Harlem were merely the most blatant manifestations of the enduring sickness of the American soul. In early August, Baldwin issued a statement to the *New York Post* about the riots in Harlem. He noted that the only people who were not surprised by the events were the residents of

Harlem and other northern ghettos. These people, Baldwin reminded his readers, experience a demoralizing "contrast" every day when they make their way from the "intolerable conditions" under which they live to "the white world" in which most of them work.[8] Those Americans who are not trapped in the ghetto are able to avert their eyes from these conditions and remain ignorant of those who experience them every day. In addition, Baldwin said the people of Harlem had little reason to "respect the Law" because it was "overwhelmingly clear" that "the Law" had "no respect for them." Instead of blaming militant leaders and Communists for civil disorder, Baldwin urged his readers to think about the impact of "the rise of Governor Wallace and still more the candidacy of Senator Goldwater" on the morale of marginalized people. The Johnson victories over Wallace and Goldwater, though welcome news, did not vanquish the "forces responsible for this despair and common danger."[9]

After Lantz received Baldwin's consent, he wrote to Kolins at Corgi Books: "Mr. Baldwin will be happy to make the trip" to London, but he will "do only major interviews, and possibly one reception at which he could meet not only press people, but also other distinguished writers."[10] Lantz also requested that Corgi arrange to fly Baldwin's sister, Gloria Davis, from New York to London to accompany him on the tour. Davis was then in her brother's employ, and he liked to have her as company during his travels. "You need someone to get you going places," he explained to a biographer, "to keep your appointments, you know, to—act as a buffer between you and the *world*."[11] Corgi agreed to this arrangement, and Kolins got to work setting up many appointments for Davis to help her brother keep.

While Baldwin attempted to recover physically and spiritually in the south of France, Buckley was undertaking a restorative project of his own. In the wake of the Goldwater defeat, he used his voice and pen to argue against the idea that the landslide marked the death of the conservative movement. In making this case, Buckley had to walk some fine lines. He still held Goldwater in high regard, but he thought the campaign was disastrous. Some of this, of course, was a result of what Buckley viewed as shameful fearmongering by Goldwater's critics, who successfully prevented an intellectually serious exchange of liberal versus conservative ideas by reframing the race as one of crazed fanaticism (Goldwater) versus the relatively sane status quo (Johnson). But Goldwater's enemies were not the only ones to blame, Buckley argued. Some responsibility belonged to the candidate himself and, of course, his "political counselors." In one postelection speech, Buckley referred to the "glorious ineptitude" revealed by Goldwater's willingness do things such as rail against Medicare while among the retirees of Florida and criticize the Tennessee Valley Authority while in the bosom of Tennessee.[12] Given the unfair accusations against Goldwater from the Left, and impolitic habits of the candidate and his handlers, it would be a mistake, Buckley contended, to view the election result as a referendum on conservatism.

As Buckley looked ahead, racial issues were still at the forefront of his mind. The December 1, 1964, issue of *National Review* provided readers with a "Special Report" on "What Now for Republicans?" and a series of essays in which "Leading Conservatives Discuss the Future," but the feature cover story in the issue was announced in big, bold print: "NEGROES, INTELLIGENCE, AND PREJUDICE" by Ernest van den Haag. Van den Haag, a conservative sociologist at Fordham University who bore a striking resemblance to the title character in the recent hit film *Dr. Strangelove*, was a regular contributor to *National Review* and friend of Buckley's. He had been called as an expert witness to discuss the "sociological-psychological impact of segregation" in the South, and his ideas so pleased the Citizens' Council that it asked him to summarize his testimony on its television program.[13] Buckley had long championed van den Haag's pseudoscientific work on race, even devoting a full-page paean to it in a 1961 issue of *National Review*.[14] In his 1964 piece, van den Haag used a tongue-in-cheek, question-and-answer format to offer criticisms of liberal social scientists who seemed more driven by "egalitarian ideologies" than by scientific truth. It is a bizarre piece of writing thanks in part to the question-and-answer format, but the overall thrust of the argument was this: social scientists should not be afraid to establish criteria for evaluating human beings, determine the differences between racial groups based on that criteria, report the racial differences captured by their results, and prescribe appropriate policy changes based on their findings. Among other things, van den Haag concluded "at least for the time being, the needs of Negro children would be best met . . . by *separate* education geared to meet the obstacles presented by lack of opportunity and unfavorable environment."[15] It is no wonder the Citizens' Council greeted van den Haag's ideas with such enthusiasm.

In an issue that was focused on the future of conservatism, it may seem surprising that Buckley made the editorial choice to feature this provocative piece by van den Haag. Buckley sensed that the essay was likely to ruffle some feathers so he circulated it all over town to intellectuals such as Daniel Bell and Irving Kristol to invite them to respond to van den Haag in print. There was something about the van den Haag piece that Buckley thought was extremely important, but he did not provide a definitive explanation as to why that might be the case. One possibility is that Buckley saw the piece as a fitting follow-up to the "Special Report" on the "Race Issue" he had commissioned only months earlier. The theme of that series—with the exception of the Wills piece, which was more nuanced—was that whites *were* lashing back against the excesses of racial egalitarianism because they resented being told that their privilege was the result of racist legal and social practices. Buckley enlisted van den Haag to tell these aggrieved whites that there was a social scientific basis for their indignation. They were being accused of racial prejudice when in fact, van den Haag was telling them, their desire for separation was justified by "scientific truth."[16]

The intellectuals to whom Buckley sent the piece were not impressed. Bell, who was a distinguished sociologist at Columbia, asked Buckley, in effect, Where are you going with this, Bill? "The existence of any genetically-determined differences between races . . . ," he told Buckley, "has little bearing on the social and moral treatment of members of different races."[17] Kristol, then an editor at Basic Books, called the van den

Haag piece thoroughly "ideological" and suggested to Buckley that "the evidence for an average lower intelligence among Negroes is probably no stronger than the evidence of an average higher intelligence among Jews. So what? The evidence is skimpy; its implications, dubious."[18]

A few weeks after the van den Haag piece was published, Buckley used the space of his column to weigh in on recent events in Mississippi, where a second jury failed to convict Beckwith, whose fingerprints were found on the gun that was used in the assassination of Evers. In addition, local officials were resisting a federal push to prosecute twenty-one individuals thought to have played some role in the murder of civil rights workers Chaney, Goodman, and Schwerner. Buckley acknowledged that there seemed to be "precious little" justice in Mississippi "when white people persecute black people," and the state had "a despicable record of indifference to crime and humiliation." "The trouble," Buckley argued, is that "there are jurors in the South who do not recognize that a crime against a Negro falls under the generic category of 'crime.'" This was a problem, but it was not immediately obvious to Buckley what ought to be done about it. One thing that should *not* be done, he insisted, was to empower the federal government to intervene to promote greater justice for African Americans. To do so, Buckley maintained, would be to infringe on "the best part of Southern life": the right of white southerners to govern themselves. Remarkably, Buckley's arguments on this front were almost identical to what they had been when he launched the magazine nearly a decade earlier. We ought to "deeply distrust government's assumption of any great power" because decentralization, he continued to assert, was an essential safeguard of liberty, the experiences of southern blacks and slain civil rights workers notwithstanding.[19]

With federal coercion off the table as a legitimate option, Buckley suggested that the best approach might be "communication" with the "decent citizens" of Mississippi. Alas, the channels of communication had been gummed up by "fanatical egalitarianism" and "abstract moralizing" by "the Federal Government and the Supreme Court and the moral intelligentsia," who "have no understanding of the best part of Southern life—the part that caused William Faulkner . . . to say that he would take up a rifle and shoot any federal marshal whose presence challenged

Mississippi's right to govern itself."[20] Like his celebration of Faulkner when he uttered these words nearly a decade earlier, Buckley had nary a word of criticism to say about them. This is not surprising since he thought Faulkner was basically justified.[21] The right of white southerners to govern themselves was sacrosanct, and it was perfectly *understandable* to Buckley—though not completely *defensible*—that those with this power would be willing to kill if they sensed it was slipping away.

⁓

Buckley and Baldwin may have never met were it not for the persistence and insubordination of Kolins, the publicist assigned to promote *Another Country* for Corgi Books. Although Baldwin's agent, Lantz, had agreed to a tour that would include only limited engagements, Kolins was determined to develop a far more robust itinerary. During the first week of January, he began working the phones to fill every nook and cranny of Baldwin's week in London. Somewhat naughtily, he seems to have kept the details of the itinerary hidden from Lantz and Davis until the last minute.

One of Kolins's phone calls in January went to the Cambridge Union in order to see if it might be willing to host Baldwin. Peter Fullerton, an undergraduate studying history and Union president at the time, told Kolins that he was unwilling to host Baldwin for a mere book promotion event.[22] The Union, he explained, was a *debating* society so it would be an inappropriate venue for such an event. But Fullerton was not about to let the opportunity to host Baldwin pass the Union by so he presented Kolins with a counterproposal: Would Baldwin be willing to participate in a debate on a "motion which reflected the themes of his writing?"[23] Kolins tentatively accepted this counterproposal, Fullerton explained later, without really knowing what he was committing his client to do. The precise details of where they left their phone call are lost to history, but it seems likely that Fullerton pledged to work out particulars—a date, opponent, and motion—and share them with Kolins as they became available.

While Kolins was making big plans for Baldwin's trip to London, the famous author was sick in bed. On January 12, biographer David Leeming notes, Baldwin's "fever had reached its rather alarming peak," and his sense of his own mortality was heightened by the news that his friend Hansberry had succumbed to pancreatic cancer at the age of only thirty-four.[24] About a week later, Kolins shared flight and hotel details with Lantz, who in turn sent them on to Baldwin and Davis. During the last week of January, Davis reached out to Kolins directly to thank him for making the travel arrangements and request a more detailed itinerary for the week. She made sure to let Kolins know about Baldwin's fragile health and expressed concern about overcommitting him on the tour. She put her trust in Kolins to exercise restraint in putting together Baldwin's schedule.[25]

Kolins does not seem to have been fazed by the requests from Lantz and Davis to keep Baldwin's itinerary light. He was, after all, a publicist. His primary concern was to get Baldwin as much exposure to the British public as possible. And so he carried on finalizing details for press conferences, television interviews, receptions, and appearances at Cambridge and Oxford.

———

While Kolins was scrambling to fill up Baldwin's schedule, Fullerton was working to come up with a motion for debate and find a worthy opponent for Baldwin. In the early days of the Union, historian Percy Cradock notes, "subjects for debate would be chosen by the whole meeting some weeks in advance."[26] By the early twentieth century, though, the officers of the Union began to play a more central role in choosing topics for debate and drafting resolutions. In this case, the more centralized decision-making process was helpful due to the relatively short amount of time available to plan for the Baldwin visit.

As he set out to draft a resolution, Fullerton was animated by an essential principle of formal debate: the resolution ought to be framed in such a way that one can imagine reasonable arguments being offered on both sides. In Fullerton's words, one wants to come up with something that is a relatively "open question."[27] One of the obligations of the debate organizers, he said, was to try to avoid stacking the deck against one side or the other. By 1965, there were still a great number of Americans who were overtly hostile to civil rights, but the tide seemed to be turning against them. The images of nonviolent civil rights protesters being brutalized by mobs and police were changing the hearts and minds of many, the March on Washington proved to be a public relations success, the passage of the Civil Rights Act of 1964 was a significant legislative triumph, and Johnson's landslide victory over Goldwater added to the sense that the defenders of Jim Crow were on the wrong side of history.

Cambridge was a relatively conservative place in 1965. Fullerton noted that the same Union that would be hosting Baldwin had, just weeks earlier, overwhelmingly passed a vote of confidence in the conservative government that was just about to be voted out of office.[28] When it came to racial politics, matters seemed to be moving in a progressive direction. The British had been active participants in the European colonialist "scramble for Africa" during the nineteenth century and long held extensive "colonial possessions" throughout the continent. From 1952 to 1960, the British were at war with rebels in Kenya, and in 1960, during what historian David Birmingham has called a "burst of decolonization," seventeen former African colonies—including the formerly British territory of Nigeria—were recognized by the United Nations as independent members. By the end of the Kenyan rebellion, Birmingham observes, "all shades of British opinion" were convinced that "political decolonization accompanied by economic partnership was the only viable way of maintaining European influence in Africa."[29]

On the domestic front, British racial politics were turbulent as well. In the late 1950s, there had been many acts of violence committed against Afro-Caribbean immigrants in the United Kingdom, including the murder of an Antiguan immigrant named Kelso Cochrane.[30] According to historian Kennetta Hammond Perry, the experience of many black Britons was not far from that of African Americans living under Jim Crow: many housing advertisements specified "Europeans only," "No Coloured," or "White Tenants Only," and many employers were "unwilling to train, hire, and/or recognize the legitimacy of the educational credentials or working knowledge of the Afro-Caribbean laborers."[31] For the students at Cambridge in 1965, issues of racial tension were not altogether foreign. They were coming of age at a time when their country's relationship to Africa was undergoing a dramatic transformation and the status of black Britons was a matter of significant debate.

If somehow British racial politics had escaped the attention of Cambridge students prior to 1965, Fullerton was sure to get them thinking about race matters with a debate he hosted just a few weeks prior to Baldwin versus Buckley. In the recent elections, the controversial Tory politician Peter Griffiths had just earned a seat in the House of Commons from Smethwick. Among other things, Griffiths was accused of relying on the slogan "If you want a nigger for a neighbor, vote Labour" in his quest to unseat Paul Gordon Walker, who was then foreign secretary in the Labour government of Harold Wilson.[32] Fullerton invited the infamous Griffiths to the Union to defend his views. On his arrival at the Union hall, Griffiths was confronted by over two hundred protesters and about forty police officers there to keep the peace.[33]

In this climate, Fullerton's general sense was that he would have to come up with a motion that went beyond something like, "This house believes the civil rights movement in the United States is a good thing." Such a resolution would, he thought, set up an impossible task for those asked to oppose the motion. As he set out to come up with a more "balanced" resolution, Fullerton may have also been guided by something he had said to Baldwin's publicist: the topic was to be drawn from the "themes of Baldwin's writings."[34] Fullerton had read and admired Baldwin's three novels, but the themes of those texts were far too nuanced to provide the basis for a debate resolution. Instead, Fullerton thought it made sense to turn to Baldwin's essays, of which he had read several. Fullerton had read *The Fire Next Time* and remembered the provocative prose of the book, and it is likely that this text provided him with the inspiration he needed.

"The Negroes of this country," Baldwin had warned in *Fire*, "may never be able to rise to power, but they are very well placed indeed to precipitate chaos and bring down the curtain on the American dream." Americans, he explained, "do not dare to examine" the "nature" of the dream and "are far from having made it a reality." "We are controlled here," Baldwin wrote, "by our confusion far more than we know, and the American dream has therefore become something much more closely resembling a nightmare."[35]

This passage may have inspired Fullerton to generate many questions. What is the relationship between the American dream and the "American Negro"? Has the American dream been made possible by American racism? Is the ideology of the American dream an obstacle to racial progress or might it be useful in the quest for racial justice? Perhaps after reflecting on questions such as these, Fullerton came up with the following motion: "Resolved: The American dream is at the expense of the American Negro."

Meanwhile, Fullerton had another important task before him: he had to find a suitable guest to speak opposite Baldwin. Although the students were at the center of activity at the Union, in 1887 a decision was made that would forever change the institution: "When questions of great interest are under debate, it is desirable that strangers distinguished as orators and politicians who are entitled to speak with authority on such questions should be invited to take part in debate." With this policy in place, Cambridge students had remarkable success attracting guest speakers including former US president Theodore Roosevelt, Ethiopian emperor Haile Selassie, and British prime minister Winston Churchill.[36]

Fullerton's first thought was to invite a sitting US senator to debate Baldwin. Although he cannot recall precisely which senators he contacted, he does remember that he sought out individuals who were known to be either hostile to (e.g., Thurmond of South Carolina) or skeptical of (e.g., Goldwater of Arizona) the civil rights movement.[37] An invitation to someone like Thurmond would have been consistent with

Fullerton's reputation for inviting provocative and even inflammatory speakers like Griffiths. Senator after senator, though, declined the invitation to share the platform with Baldwin.

At some point during the mad scramble to find a debater to oppose Baldwin, Fullerton's friend and fellow Union member Michael Tugendhat offered a suggestion: What about Buckley? Fullerton, like most Englishmen in 1965, had scant idea who Buckley was, but Tugendhat would soon have him convinced that he was just the person for the job. In 1963, Tugendhat traveled to the United States for a vacation. While there, a family friend introduced him to Buckley, who by then had become the country's leading conservative polemicist. Tugendhat is unable to recall how much he learned about Buckley's political philosophy or his views of civil rights during their meeting or in the months that followed, but he must have learned enough to conclude that Buckley would be a good candidate to take on Baldwin.[38] It is unclear whether Tugendhat and Fullerton did additional research on Buckley before extending the invitation, but if they did, they would have become all the more convinced that he was a perfect fit for the role. Fullerton asked Tugendhat to extend an invitation to Buckley, who as luck would have it, was just wrapping up his annual vacation to Gstaad, Switzerland. Buckley was never one to turn down an opportunity to debate and likely was eager to take on Baldwin, whose ideas he viewed as nothing less than a threat to Western civilization.

Right around the same time Buckley would have been receiving the invitation from Cambridge, he used his On the Right column to fire another shot across the bow at Baldwin. In an essay with the subtle title "Hate America," Buckley offered his reactions to Baldwin and Avedon's *Nothing Personal*. The piece is less an original review than it is a celebration of the Brustein essay discussed above, which was published in the "left-wing literary journal" the *New York Review of Books*.[39] Brustein's willingness to "let loose" on the "pop liberalism" of Baldwin and Avedon's "non-book," Buckley declared, stood out as a rare exception to "America's astonishing inability to get upon its hind legs and fight back for itself." Much of the Buckley piece consists of extensive quotations from the "eminent" and "honorable" Brustein, but Buckley was sure to sprinkle in a few thoughts of his own. To "provide a suitable text for his Hate-America album," Buckley wrote, Avedon "bought the services of the Number-1 America-hater, James Baldwin," who was hired for the job because he "can really belt out a social protest." Brustein's review was, according to Buckley, an act of great intellectual courage because he utilized the pages of a journal read mostly by Americans on the ideological Left to take Avedon and Baldwin to task for their artistic as well as political failures. Alas, Buckley concluded, Brustein and the editors who decided to run his piece were a distinct minority on the American Left, which consisted mostly of people who spent their time disdaining "their country and, in so doing, undermin[ing] confidence in America," "love for America," and "honorable American self-pride."[40]

On the first of February, Baldwin wrote to Lantz to provide an update on his health and spirits. "I'm trying to be good," he said, "and follow the doctor's orders." Among other things, Baldwin reported that the doctor had ordered him to eat copious amounts of yogurt. "I've gobbled down so much yogurt—which I detest—that I'm thinking of joining the White Citizens' Council when I return." The illness had sapped his energy, he confessed, and left him feeling "unbelievably depressed," and certain that "I am not now, and never have been, and never will be, any good as a writer at all."[41]

The next day, Buckley was out skiing the slopes of Switzerland with his wife, Pat, when she had a terrible accident that broke her leg in five places.[42] Buckley reported to friends later that the doctors predicted it would take two years before her leg was back to normal again. After the injury, it must have been tempting to back out of his commitment to the Cambridge Union. Instead, he planned his trip so that he would be away from his wife for the smallest amount of time possible by booking travel from Zurich to London for the day of the debate, and his return trip for early the next morning.

A few days later, Lantz's assistant, Helen Merrill, sent Baldwin a full-page advertisement for *Another Country* from London's *Bookseller* magazine in order to give him "an idea of how important your forthcoming visit is."[43] "Corgi Books," the advertisement announced, "is preparing the biggest promotion campaign in its history for *Another Country*." As a postscript to her note, Merrill added her voice to the chorus of concern about the itinerary Kolins was putting together: "The schedule in England looks so heavy that I suggested to Gloria to tell Corgi it should be somewhat curtailed."[44]

On February 11—exactly one week before the debate—Lantz sent a one-sentence cable to Kolins (on which he cc'ed Baldwin): "Have advised Baldwin strongly against participating in debate with Buckley. Please cancel it for him."[45] As Lantz would explain to Baldwin biographer William J. Weatherby later, he worried that Baldwin and Buckley would be a combustible mix. Buckley, he explained, "gets under your skin" so only those who can "stay cool" should share a stage with him. "Jimmy," Lantz told Weatherby, "was never cool and amused about the world's problems, he was always aroused."[46] The details of what happened next are murky, but Fullerton does not recall any attempts by Corgi to cancel the debate. The event had already been publicized widely, and Fullerton had arranged for the BBC to film and broadcast the debate. One can only speculate as to why the event was not canceled. In all likelihood, Baldwin was less worried about it than was his agent. He was feeling a bit better physically and likely was unfazed by Buckley's reputed prowess as a debater. When friends like Podhoretz had tried to talk him out of debating Kilpatrick a couple of years earlier, he persisted, and mopped the floor with him— rhetorically speaking. What reason did he have to be afraid of Buckley? In fact, according to Leeming, Baldwin's love of argument led him to rather like opportunities such as this. He was even more attracted, in some ways, to engagements with conservatives and reactionaries because, unlike liberals and moderates, they were often willing to be more honest about their disdain for the civil rights revolution.[47] Although Baldwin had not written about Buckley, he was well aware of him and probably was eager to do to him what he had done to Kilpatrick in late 1962.[48]

What Baldwin was less sure about was what a debate at the Cambridge Union entailed. Whereas Buckley had been participating in formal debates for nearly a quarter of a century, most of Baldwin's intellectual battles had occurred around the tables of places like the White Horse Tavern in Greenwich Village or Café Flor in Paris. Sit-down discussions for radio and television programs were about as "formal" as Baldwin's debates had gotten, and it appears he let Kolins know that he wanted a bit more instruction as to what he was agreeing to do.

Kolins got back in touch with Fullerton and made two requests. First, he asked Fullerton if he would be willing to dine with Baldwin the night he arrived in London (February 16) in order to provide him with a more detailed explanation of the format and norms of Union debate. Fullerton, who was excited to meet the famous writer, accepted this invitation without hesitation. Kolins's second request was a bit more complicated. In addition to the debate itself, Baldwin and Buckley were expected to attend a dinner at the Union before the debate. Traditionally, Fullerton reports, guest speakers and Union officers dined together just prior to the debate itself. When hosting special guest speakers, Fullerton would usually have the guests seated on each side of him, near the center of a long dining room table. Kolins requested, Fullerton recalls, that Baldwin be spared much social interaction with Buckley beforehand. Fullerton does not remember if Kolins provided much explanation for this request, but he granted it.[49] Instead of having Baldwin and Buckley sit on either side of him at the center of the table, Fullerton agreed to have them sit at opposite ends of the long table so they would be unable to engage each other at all during dinner.

We will never know why Kolins made this request, but given the insistence from Baldwin's agent and sister that he not be overtaxed, it seems likely that Kolins considered it a compromise to make the visit to the Union a bit less onerous. Lantz and Davis—like most other literate Americans—had probably gotten to know a bit about Buckley's personality through his syndicated column and frequent media appearances. They knew he could be acerbic, and it was difficult to imagine him sitting in close proximity to Baldwin during dinner and not throwing a rhetorical jab or two. If the traditional seating arrangement had been followed, Baldwin would have been sitting approximately the same distance he had been sitting from Kilpatrick a couple of years earlier. During that experience, he cross-examined Kilpatrick like a prosecutor, and though the experience must have been gratifying, it must also have been exhausting. In essence, Kolins may have been trying to limit the amount of time Baldwin would have to engage with Buckley, thus sparing him some precious physical, intellectual, and emotional energy.

The Saturday edition of *Varsity*, the Cambridge student newspaper, featured a quarter-page advertisement for the debate. Fullerton reports that the Union did not place advertisements for its debates so it seems likely that it was ordered by Kolins in order to ensure a capacity crowd would be on hand. In the same edition of *Varsity*, there was a short article previewing the debate under the headline "Baldwin Tackles Rightist." The "well-known novelist and advocate of civil rights," the article explained, "will be speaking at the Union next Thursday" opposite a representative of the "other extreme of the American political scene," Buckley, "who was Barry Goldwater's original backer." The editors of *Varsity* also alerted students to two other pieces of information likely to pique their interest: the debate would be televised by the BBC, and for the second time in the term, crash barriers would be set up at the Union "in anticipation of the reaction in Cambridge to such a controversial debate."[50]

In the days leading up to the debate, Baldwin was—for the first time in many months—enjoying a "prolonged period of quiet." When he felt well enough to do so, he worked on short stories for a collection he had agreed to publish with Dial Press. During these days of convalescence in the south of France, Leeming reports, Baldwin was "well taken care of,

FIGURE 6.1. Articles and advertisements from *Varsity*, the Cambridge student newspaper (Cambridge University)

FIGURE 6.1. *Varsity* articles and ads-2

FIGURE 6.1. *Varsity* articles and ads-3

FIGURE 6.1. *Varsity* articles and ads-4

FIGURE 6.1. Baldwin-Buckley debate ad in *Varsity*

FIGURE 6.1. Article on Union's 150th Anniversary in *Varsity*

FIGURE 6.1. Article on Union's 150th Anniversary in *Varsity*

having the use of a house belonging to [the author] Harold Robbins, including a resident cook who was 'feeding [him] as though [he] were a prize hog.' "[51]

On Tuesday, February 16, Baldwin boarded a plane and sat down in the first-class cabin for the two-hour flight from Nice to London. On his arrival at Heathrow International Airport in the late afternoon, he was greeted by Kolins, who took him to the beautiful, Georgian-style White-hall Hotel in central Bloomsbury, just across the street from the British Museum. Soon after, Kolins took Baldwin to meet Fullerton for dinner. Kolins and Baldwin peppered Fullerton with questions about the Union, and Fullerton, in turn, peppered Baldwin with questions about his books.[52]

Less than forty-eight hours later, Buckley was on his way from Zurich to London. He had planned his trip in a way that would minimize the time he had to be away from his injured wife. Since she had been discharged from hospital, he wrote to a friend later, "I have had to more or less help

FIGURE 6.2. Baldwin at work, circa 1965 (Michael Ochs Archives / Getty Images)

nurse her night and day."[53] Buckley's concerns about his wife's health were heightened just two days prior to the debate when she was readmitted to the hospital with a pleurisy.

Before leaving for London, Buckley did have time to fire off a few missives to *National Review* editors and contributors, including one to his old friend Kilpatrick. A few months earlier, Buckley had written to Kilpatrick privately and editorialized publicly to push southerners to stand up in opposition to "the dismal list of church bombings and burnings in the Deep South."[54] In his published writing on the subject, Buckley could not resist pointing out the plausibility of the claim that *some* of this destruction was the work of "civil rights or Communist" provocateurs, but he doubted they could be to blame for all the violence. "The destruction of churches," he declared, "is a primary symbol of barbarism." He called on white southerners—especially those who, like Kilpatrick, were "segregationist in principle"—to form a public committee "to rouse public sentiment against this desecration and promote official action to find the criminals responsible."[55] In the *Richmond News Leader*, Kilpatrick reprinted Buckley's *National Review* editorial and wrote one of his own called "Shame of the South," reiterating many of the arguments in even more dramatic language. He called the assailants "rednecked hoodlums" and said the "conscience of the South" needed to speak with "one clear voice to cry 'shame!'"[56] A week before the debate, Kilpatrick wrote to follow up with Buckley "on one of your oldest and best ideas." The "Richmond Ministerial Association," Kilpatrick announced, would "embark formally upon the fundraising plan you had in mind for bombed-out and burned churches."[57] On the morning of the debate, Buckley wrote to Kilpatrick to express his excitement about this "wonderful news" and promised *National Review* would "give it the attention it deserves."[58]

On the afternoon of Thursday, February 18, Buckley and Baldwin arrived in Cambridge. Buckley came to town in a black Austin limousine and made his way to Green Street, where he had arranged to meet up with Tugendhat, the student responsible for his invitation. Baldwin arrived in what Fullerton called the "gaudiest limousine I had ever seen."[59] The size of the vehicle may have been necessary to accommodate the large entourage that accompanied Baldwin. In addition to Kolins and Davis, Baldwin was joined by several other friends and associates.[60] Fullerton remembers Kolins as a "smallish" American "with a limp," who was extremely "protective" of his client. Fullerton recalls Davis being "beautiful and charming," an account corroborated by Baldwin biographer Fern Marja Eckman, who in the mid-1960s described Davis as "pencil-slim, poised, pretty, [and] chic."[61] Fullerton greeted Baldwin and his entourage, and took them on a tour of the Union before a six o'clock press conference in the Union library. "I don't have much confidence in what the Civil Rights Act can do for the American Negro," Baldwin told the assembled reporters. "It is one thing to have a law. It is another thing to have a law that works."[62]

After the press conference, Fullerton showed Baldwin the debating chamber. Perhaps struck by the awesomeness of the venue, Baldwin requested a quiet room where he might have some time to gather his thoughts before dinner. It was there that Baldwin likely reviewed and edited handwritten debate notes he had prepared on hotel stationery. When Fullerton came back to retrieve Baldwin for the dinner prior to the debate, Kolins stopped him and said Baldwin needed more time.

When Buckley arrived at the Union, he was greeted by friends he had invited to watch him debate Baldwin. The actor James Mason, whom Buckley had befriended on the slopes of Switzerland, was there as was Alastair Horne, the British historian who Buckley had met a quarter of a century earlier while both were high school students at Millbrook.[63] It must have been quite a scene when Buckley and the Union officers, all dressed in formal tuxedos, watched the dining room doors open and saw Baldwin enter the room—apparently disobeying Union norms—dressed in a blue suit with a red tie, with his entourage in tow. None of the Union officers remember any signs of personal animus being expressed as Baldwin was introduced to Buckley, but after they met they were—as Fullerton had promised—seated at opposite ends of the long dining room table. Buckley sensed something was up. "Either at his request," Buckley would write later, "or because the host intuited an ungovernable personal animosity by Baldwin to me, we were placed at opposite ends of a long table."[64]

As the Union officers and debaters ate their dinner, students crammed into every nook and cranny of the debating chamber. In addition to filling all the spots available on the benches in the chamber, students sat in vacant spaces they could find on the floor, and still others went upstairs to the galleries. By eight o'clock, the hall was so jam-packed with students that officials had to set up crash barriers in order to prevent more students from trying to get in. More than five hundred students who were turned away at the barriers made their way to other rooms in the Union where they would be able to watch the proceedings on closed-circuit televisions. Although the windows of the Union were opened to let in some cool winter air, the chamber grew stuffy as the combination of hundreds of warm bodies and the klieg lights from the BBC filled the space with heat.

In one of the galleries upstairs, Norman St. John Stevas, a Cambridge graduate and conservative member of Parliament who had a distinguished career as an academic before entering politics, was on hand to serve as a commentator for the BBC recording of the debate. "Well here we are in the debating hall of the Cambridge Union," he said to the television audience. "Hundreds of undergraduates and myself waiting for what could be one of the most exciting nights in the whole of 150 years of Union history." Probably the only empty seats in the chamber were directly behind Stevas as he recorded this introduction, perhaps because they were reserved for the guests of Baldwin and Buckley. "I don't think I've ever seen the Union so well attended," he said. "There are undergraduates *everywhere*; they're on the benches, they're on the floor, they're in the galleries and there are a lot more outside clamoring to get in." Stevas then introduced the resolution and format for the debate. Two student speakers would start the debate—with one speaking on each side—before the crowd would get a chance to hear from the "distinguished guest[s]: the novelist Mr. James Baldwin," who has achieved "worldwide fame," and Mr. William Buckley, "very well known as a conservative in the United States," who was one of the "earliest supporters of Senator Goldwater." After this introduction, Stevas turned in his seat so he could peer down from the gallery and said, "Any moment now, the president will be leading in his officers and his distinguished guests, he'll take his chair, and the debate will begin."[65]

At a quarter to nine o-clock, Fullerton entered the debating chamber, and the audience greeted him with warm applause. The path from the entrance of the chamber to the platform was a narrow one with students seated on the floor forced to tuck their legs in to make room for the entering VIPs. The packed hall into which they entered was a mixture of old and new. The space bore many signs of the Union history, from its ornate architecture and furniture to the historical photographs on the wall behind the elevated platform with the president's chair at its summit. Straight ahead of Fullerton as he approached the chair was a beautiful wooden table with lecterns for the debaters at each end of it. The lecterns faced each other—just like in the House of Commons—and between the lecterns, on the side nearest to the entrance, was a pitcher of water with glasses for the speakers. On the far side of the table, closer to the president's chair, there was a small space for the Union secretary to keep records of the debate proceedings. On each side of the speaker's table there were spaces left vacant on front-row benches for the debaters. Built into the debater's bench, there was a small writing desk attached on a swivel so the participants had someplace to take and keep notes. The benches were situated so that when the debaters were seated in their spots, they would—if they looked straight ahead—be staring into each other's eyes across an aisle of only a few feet.

As Fullerton made his way to the platform amid the applause of the crowd, he was followed first by David Heycock—the student who was proposing the motion along with Baldwin—then Baldwin himself, then Jeremy Burford—the student who was opposing the motion along with Buckley—and then Buckley himself, followed by three more Union officers. The crowd that greeted the debaters was predominantly white and male, but there was greater diversity in the room than there had been throughout most of the Union's history. In February 1963, the Oxford Union had voted to begin allowing female members, and after a couple failed attempts, the Cambridge Union voted to follow suit in November of that year.[66] The debating chamber that had for decades been dominated by only white faces now included the black and brown faces of many African and Indian students.[67]

Once everyone was seated and the applause subsided, Fullerton rose and rang a bell to indicate the beginning of the debate. "The motion before the house tonight is: the American dream is at the expense of the American Negro. Proposer is Mr. David Heycock of Pembroke College and the opposer is Mr. Jeremy Burford of Emmanuel College. Mr. James Baldwin will speak third, Mr. William F. Buckley Jr. will speak fourth. Mr. Heycock has the ear of the house." With that, Heycock rose from his seat next to Baldwin and walked to the lectern to the right of the president's chair. Heycock was dressed in his formal wear, and his long brown hair was combed from left to right above his boyish face. A senior literature major, Heycock started his speech by explaining that it was his "great honor" and duty as the first speaker to introduce the guest debaters. "Mr. William Buckley," he said, "has the reputation of possibly being the most articulate conservative in the United States of America." This led many members of the audience to chuckle, and Buckley smiled before joining the students in laughter when Heycock informed them that the title of Buckley's first book was *God and Man and Yale* [*sic*]." Heycock got another laugh out of the crowd when he listed many of the figures Buckley had taken on in print and debate, and said that none of them had emerged "unscathed from their confrontation" with him. "Mr. James Baldwin," Heycock said as he turned to his right where the author was sitting, "is hardly in need of introduction." Baldwin's large eyes looked nervously in Heycock's direction as he described the author's many accomplishments, but by the end of the brief introduction, his face opened into a wide smile.

With the introductions complete, Heycock launched into his brief speech in support of the motion.[68] Heycock's argument was rooted in a relatively romantic view of the American dream. At its core, he said, America was indeed a land of "freedom and equality" where "artificial barriers to fulfillment and achievement are unheard of," and in which "a man may begin his life as a rail-splitter and end it as president." After setting up this ideal vision, Heycock turned to his critique: "Imagine, however, Mr. President, that *the condition of this utopia* has been the persistent and quite deliberate exploitation of one-ninth of its inhabitants. . . . Imagine this, Mr. President, and you have what is in my opinion the bitter reality of the American dream."

To support this claim, Heycock referred his audience to recent news out of Selma, Alabama, where the SCLC was working to register voters in order to push the idea that the promise of civil rights could not be fulfilled until blacks in the South were empowered to vote. When King and more than 700 others were arrested in Selma in January, Heycock pointed out, there were more blacks in jail than there were on the voting rolls of Dallas County (where Selma is located). In fact, there were twice as many blacks in jail as were registered to vote in the county (only 335 out of a population of 32,700). As Heycock reached the climax of his speech, his long brown hair began to creep down into his eyes, but he was unfazed, asserting:

American society has felt fit to use Negro labor, it has felt fit to use the blood of the Negro in two world wars, it has felt fit to laugh at his jokes, and yet as far as I am concerned it has never felt fit to give the American Negro a fair deal, and for this reason, Mr. President, I would beg leave to propose the motion that the American dream is at the expense of the American Negro.

With that, Heycock returned to his seat amid polite applause, and Fullerton rose, rang the bell, and called Burford to oppose the motion. Burford was a tall, broad-shouldered South African who had already received a bachelor's degree from the University of Cape Town before coming to Cambridge to study law. He was a confident and skilled debater. The previous term, his side had convinced the Union that it ought to oppose revolution in South Africa, and just two months after the Buckley-Baldwin debate, he would place second in the International University Debating Contest.[69] While Heycock's small stature put him in close proximity to his notes on the lectern, Burford looked through his glasses at notes that were positioned at a lectern that only came up to his hips. Burford's speech was revealing not just for what he said but perhaps more important, how the audience reactions helped Baldwin and Buckley get a better sense of the room. The speech was greeted, as Buckley would say later that night, with "considerable mirth," and at first, this audience reaction was playful in nature. "It is not our purpose to oppose civil rights," Burford told the crowd, "it is our purpose to oppose *this motion.*" The crowd chuckled lightly at this and one student yelled, "Here! Here!" To this, Burford turned, cracked a grin, and said, "Thank you, sir. Come and collect your fee afterwards." The audience responded with laughter and applause, and Baldwin shot Burford a smile from across the aisle. After this moment of levity, though, Burford—despite his best efforts— lost his command of the room. His rhetorical strategy was to concede much of Heycock's argument and admit that racial discrimination constituted a major blot on the American dream, and that indeed, the American dream would be much stronger under conditions of true "equality and freedom of opportunity." To this point in his speech, Burford seemed to be heading in the right direction, but the students began to get a bit antsy when he attempted to show that the American dream had the net effect of improving race relations generally and the treatment of blacks specifically. In order to support this contention, Burford said that "the average per capita income of Negroes in American is exactly the same as the average per capita income of people in Great Britain." In response to this, there was biting laughter, a few heckles from the audience, and a few students stood up in their places. These standing students were practicing a Union custom that dated back to 1939, which in the words of Union historian Stephen Parkinson, "allowed members to offer interruptions to main speakers with questions or points of information."[70] It was the prerogative of the speaker to call on these students or ignore them, and at this point in his speech, Burford called on a student, who asked if his point about black wealth referred to "real income" or "money income." Burford admitted he referred only to money income and had not intended to "disguise that fact." In response to this, several members of the audience mocked Burford with laughter. To make matters worse, Burford then began rattling off more statistics about the relative wealth of American blacks and was greeted—again and again—by a crowd that found his numbers incredibly amusing. As seemingly every other sentence was being met with derisive laughter, Baldwin looked genuinely embarrassed for Burford and shot a glance across the aisle at Buckley.

Before sitting down, Burford collected himself and delivered a strong conclusion. "Negro inequality," he said, "has *hindered* the American dream, and I would say that the American dream has been very important indeed in furthering civil rights and in furthering the freedom of the American Negro. Mr. President, sir, I beg to oppose the motion." With that, the audience applauded politely, and Burford returned to his spot on the bench next to Buckley.

Fullerton then rose again and rang the bell to welcome the speaker that the crowd had come to see: "It is now with very great pleasure and a very great sense of honor that I call Mr. James Baldwin to speak third to this motion." With this, Baldwin leaped off the bench, smiled at Heycock, and made his way to the lectern. As the audience greeted him with applause, he took a sip of water, scanned the chamber, and reached into the breast pocket of his jacket to retrieve the notes he had written on hotel stationery. When Buckley wrote and spoke about the debate later he would—without fail—say that Baldwin was *greeted* with a standing ovation by the students that night. As he put it during his next visit to the Union in 1972 to debate the economist John Kenneth Galbraith, "I am very happy to be here again. . . . The last time I was here, before I opened my mouth, the gentleman who was opposing [*sic*] the resolution received a standing ovation—and that was before he opened *his* mouth."[71] This comment was met with great laughter and applause, and functioned in his writing about the debate as a key indicator of the great bias the crowd had in favor of Baldwin (and against him) that night. The trouble with Buckley's claim is that it is not true; the students applauded as Baldwin stood up to speak (as they did for every other speaker that night), but there was no standing ovation at the start of his speech.[72] Either Buckley's memory was playing tricks on him or he was not about to let the truth get in the way of a good one-liner.[73]

When the applause subsided, Baldwin began speaking slowly as he placed his hands behind his back: "I find myself, not for the first time, in the position of a kind of Jeremiah."[74] With that opening, he signaled to the audience that what he had in store for them was something other than the typical Union debate speech.[75] Baldwin was announcing that he—who had grown up in the pews and pulpits of Harlem storefront churches—was about to deliver a sermon, and a particular kind of sermon at that. The Old Testament prophet Jeremiah was known as a preacher of mournful lamentations.[76] "To whom can I speak and give warning?" asked Jeremiah. "Who will listen to me? Their ears are closed so they cannot hear. The word of the Lord is offensive to them; they find no pleasure in it. But I am full of the wrath of the LORD, and I cannot hold it in."[77] Baldwin was announcing that he had come to Cambridge that night to deliver a "jeremiad."[78]

As a preface to his sermon, Baldwin offered a few thoughts on how one's "system of reality" shaped one's reaction to the question, Is the American dream at the expense of the American Negro? In his notes he had written, "(A) This is a loaded question. Our reaction to it, and our response to it, are bound to be determined by the most private and inaccessible assumptions—in other words, by our sense of reality." As Baldwin attempted to find the right words to explain what he meant, he put his hands in his pockets and directed his eyes upward toward those seated in the gallery. When the words came to him, he looked in Buckley's direction and said, "It would seem to me that the proposition before the house ... is a question, hideously loaded, and one's response to that question, one's reaction to that question, has to depend on, in effect, on where you find yourself in the world." As Baldwin uttered these words, Buckley looked at him intently with his pen raised to his mouth. Baldwin was making a point he had made many times before in his writings and discussions with figures as disparate as Malcolm X and Kilpatrick: identity and power are intimately related, and they are at the heart of our trouble. As Baldwin began expounding on this central idea in his philosophy, he raised his voice a bit, picked up the pace of his speech, and began gesturing more actively with his hands. "The Mississippi or the Alabama sheriff," he explained, "who really does believe when he's facing a Negro boy or girl"—as Baldwin said this, he held out his hand to indicate he was imagining the world through the eyes of the white sheriff, confronted with a civil rights protester an arm's length away—"that this woman, this man, this child *must be insane* to attack the system to which he owes his entire identity." For such a man, the proposition before the house was nonsensical. How could anything *really* be at the expense of the American Negro? That made about as much sense to the Alabama sheriff as saying that the harvest was at "the expense" of a beast of burden.

Baldwin, on the other hand, had to speak as "one of a people" who paid a heavy price for this "white supremac[ist]" system of reality. Before one could really address the proposition before the house, Baldwin told the students, one had to address two more elementary questions: Is it legitimate for one civilization to "overtake, subjugate, and in fact to destroy another"? And how does one's response to that question depend on one's "point of view"? This is a question seldom addressed and even less often answered in a serious way. Indeed, one of the central functions of myth-making is to prevent us from having to grapple with fundamental questions such as these.

But Baldwin was there to confront his audience—like an Old Testament prophet—with questions that they did not want to hear, much less answer. He was there to force them to confront the consequences of white supremacy for its victims and perpetrators. The victims, of course, had been subject to a "bloody catalog of oppression" that included untold numbers of rapes and murders, but Baldwin thought this was not the worst of it. The greatest crime committed against the victims of white supremacy was the destruction of their sense of self-worth. In order to explain this point, Baldwin—still a preacher at heart—used repetition to reveal how one's sense of value could crumble over time. He heightened the effect of this message by shifting from referring to the victim of white supremacy as "him" to the use of the word "you." Like so much of his writing, he was attempting to get his audience to see the world—if but for a moment—through the eyes of the other:

> It comes as a *great shock* around the age of five or six or seven to discover the flag to which *you* have pledged allegiance . . . has not pledged allegiance to *you*.
>
> It comes as a *great shock* to discover that Gary Cooper killing off the Indians—while *you* were rooting for Gary Cooper—that the Indians were *you* [*audience laughter*].
>
> It comes as a *great shock* to discover the country which is *your* birthplace, and to which you owe *your* life and *your* identity, has not in its whole system of reality evolved any place for *you*.

As Baldwin delivered these powerful lines, Buckley gazed across the aisle with an inscrutable look on his face. In another "misremembering" about that night, Buckley recalled that Baldwin read "prepared remarks" to the Cambridge students.[79] And yet in most of what has been described so far and in most of what came after, Baldwin did not so much as peek down at his notes, and even if he had, the notes were far from a prepared text. After a few glances in the relatively modulated beginning of his speech, he seemed to slide into full "preacher mode," forgetting about his notes and letting the spirit guide him.[80]

After the victim of white supremacy moves from these various shocks throughout childhood into adulthood, Baldwin said things only get worse as the process of demoralization "accelerates and accelerates" toward psychic catastrophe. One must endure "the catalog of disaster—the policemen, the taxi drivers, the waiters, the landlady, the landlord, the banks, the insurance companies, the millions of details twenty-four hours of every day that you are a worthless human being." As Baldwin enumerated this list, he thrust his left hand out in rhythm with each item, and his teeth seemed to clinch tighter and tighter with indignation. When he got to the end of the list, he said emphatically, "It is not" the catalog of disaster that one experiences as an individual that is most terrifying about white supremacy but rather the fact that one can see the cycle of subjugation and demoralization taking hold in the next generation.

Everything that Baldwin had said leading up to this moment in the speech was relevant to the motion, but his comments about the intergenerational impact of white supremacy constituted the first direct hit he made on the mythology of the American dream, which holds that even if one generation is not able to enjoy the fruits of opportunity, it can die knowing that it has laid the foundation for the next generation to see the dream fulfilled. But this was not a hope to which most American blacks could cling. As you see despair creeping into the minds of your kids, Baldwin told the audience, it occurs to you that "nothing you have done, and as far as you can tell, *nothing you can do*, will save your son or your daughter from meeting the same disaster and coming to the same end."

With this statement, Baldwin came to a moment of transition in his speech and, for the first time in several minutes, glanced down at his notes. Although he had not sketched out ideas on the theme of "expense," his eye may have caught the top of the first page of the hotel stationery, where he had titled the document "The American Dream and the American Negro ($\rightarrow$ at the Expense Of)." Perhaps Baldwin had given some thought to what he was about to do, but it was *not* in his prepared notes, and it seems he may have decided in the moment as he reflected on the meaning of "expense" in this context:

> I am stating very seriously, and this is not an overstatement; *I* picked the
> cotton, and *I* carried it to market, and *I* built the railroads, under

someone else's whip, for nothing. For nothing. The southern oligarchy . . . was created by *my* labor and *my* sweat, and the violation of *my*
women, and the murder of *my* children. This, in the land of the free and
home of the brave.

When Cambridge undergraduate Christie Davies—a former Union president in the audience who had participated in an Oxford Union debate
with Malcolm X in 1964—heard these words, he thought to himself, "He's
won." By personalizing the debate in this way, Davies explained later, Baldwin moved beyond "rational argument" to something more visceral.[81]
How could the Cambridge students vote against Baldwin when a vote
against him would be a vote against generations of victims of racial
oppression?

Baldwin's "*I* picked the cotton" line of reasoning demands closer scru-
tiny. The first thing to note is his striking shift from the second to the
first person. He started the speech by asking the audience to imagine what
the world might look like through the eyes of a subjugated human being.
Now, in the second part of the speech, as he discussed one facet of "expense," he used the first person in an arresting and slightly peculiar way.
He claimed to be speaking "literally" when he said he exerted the labor
that established the power structure in the United States. At first glance,
this seems like an odd thing to say since Baldwin did not *literally* pick the
cotton and so on.[82] Was Baldwin overstating his case? Rather than dismissing this move as a mere "rhetorical device"—as Buckley would when
it was his turn to speak—we ought to think about what Baldwin could
have meant.

Baldwin's personalization of the exploitation of black labor seems best
understood as an attempt to make vivid the *legacy* of slavery and Jim Crow
in American political, social, and economic life. "Legacy," historian David
Blight has said, "is the place where the past and the present meet."[83] What
was "literal" about Baldwin's statement was that the past of racial exploitation was very much alive in the present.[84] Who paid the price for the
building of the country? This could not conceivably have been accomplished, Baldwin explained, without an abundance of "cheap labor"
provided by African Americans. That cheap labor was crucial to creating

structures of power that continued to shape the material, political, and psychological prospects of all Americans.

Baldwin then moved from this "literal" sense in which the American dream was at the expense of the American Negro to a consideration of the psychic costs of American mythology. What, he asked his audience, did American racial mythology cost—especially in moral terms—those who were the supposed beneficiaries of white supremacy? At the beginning of the speech, you will recall that Baldwin invited his audience to see the world for a moment through the eyes of the "Mississippi or Alabama sheriff," to whom the motion before the house would have been totally nonsensical. For a man such as this, the blacks rising up in the South "must be *insane* to attack the system to which he owes his entire identity." With these words, Baldwin was trying to reveal the empathy he felt for these bewildered souls who—like Faulkner—were terrified by the loss of "safety" that follows with "the breakup of the world" as they had always known it."[85]

At this point in the speech, Baldwin asked the audience to return to the mind of "the oppressor" in order to try to understand the costs of white supremacy for those who were supposed to be empowered by the doctrine. In late 1962, as he tried to convince his nephew of his duty to accept others—even those filled with hatred—Baldwin emphasized this theme. "Try to imagine," Baldwin wrote to his nephew, "how you would feel if you woke up one morning to find the sun shining and all the stars aflame. You would be frightened because it is out of the order of nature. Any upheaval in the universe is terrifying because it so profoundly attacks one's sense of one's own reality."[86]

When Baldwin returned to these ideas in the part of his Cambridge speech devoted to the concept of expense, his emphasis shifted from identity to morality.[87] He wanted to bring his audience's attention to the moral consequences of rooting one's identity in racial mythology. The myth of racial hierarchy may seem to be at "the expense of the American Negro" much in the same way that a joke can be at the expense of a particular person or group of people, but in fact this mythology was far more morally costly for those who imagined themselves superior. To demonstrate this point, Baldwin returned to a theme he had developed over several years of thinking, writing, and speaking: the idea that racial hierarchy functions as a crucial psychological safety net within the mythology of the American dream. Although the rhetoric of the American dream is often framed in *absolute* terms—that is, it is about achieving a certain standard of material wealth, freedom, and happiness—the reality of the American dream relies on the power of one's status *relative* to others. Individuals can *feel* that they are participating in the American dream so long as they can convince themselves that they are better off than others in society. "What is happening in the poor woman, the poor man's mind," Baldwin told the students at Cambridge, is this:

> They have been raised to believe, and by now they helplessly believe, that no matter how terrible their lives may be, and their lives have been quite terrible, and no matter how far they fall, no matter what disaster overtakes them, they have one enormous knowledge and consolation which is like a heavenly revelation: at least they are not black.

This way of thinking, Baldwin said, was one of the "worst" things that could happen to a human being. In the shadow of this claim, we can see the affirmative philosophy that Baldwin had been developing over his nearly two decades in public life. Reliance on the construct of race for one's identity was the worst thing that could happen to a human being because it undermined the possibility of achieving "freedom and fulfillment."[88] The human being who forges an identity on the basis of race, Baldwin insisted, was thoroughly unfree and therefore could never possibly find fulfillment.

Baldwin illustrated this point with the example of Dallas County sheriff Jim Clark, who in the weeks preceding the debate had been pictured in newspapers around the world assaulting African American women who were trying to register to vote in Alabama. Clark had become, along with Connor, a symbol of southern brutality, and Baldwin used him as an illustration for precisely this reason. Even Clark, who had been behaving monstrously, was human. "I'm sure he loves his wife, his children. I'm sure you know," he told the laughing students, "he likes to get drunk." Clark was, in other words, quite a bit like the character Lyle in *Blues for Mister Charlie*; he could go from tenderness toward his white friends and family in one minute to utter brutality to black people in the next. A man like this "doesn't know what drives him to use the club, to menace with a gun, and to use a cattle prod." Baldwin then evoked images that some of the students—and certainly many in the television audience—had seen: Clark stomping through the streets of Alabama with a billy club in one hand and cattle prod in the other. "Something awful must have happened to a human being," Baldwin said forcefully as he looked directly at Buckley, "to be able to put a cattle prod against a woman's breast. . . . What happens to the woman is ghastly. What happens to the man who does it is, in some ways, much, much worse." Here Baldwin reiterated an idea he had been defending since at least 1951: one cannot dehumanize another without at the same time dehumanizing oneself.[89] The "moral lives" of powerful men like Clark *and* relatively powerless "poor, [white] Alabama ladies," Baldwin declared, "have been destroyed by the plague called color."

In addition to serving as a safety net for those afflicted by status anxiety, Baldwin believed the construct of race played a crucial role in enabling people to deny their history. The emphasis on racial separation is meant to construct barriers, he argued, that allow whites a way "to deny the only kin they have." Here Baldwin referred to an idea he underscored in many of his writings as well as his discussions with Malcolm X. "The problem in America" is not that we haven't figured out how to solve the "conundrum" of integration but rather "that we have been integrated for a very long time." Baldwin asked his audience to put him "next to any African and you will see what I mean." And then he turned to a line he had been using on a regular basis to personalize the history of "integration" and remind people—in a rather jarring way—of the brutality through which that integration came about: "My grandmother," he said, "was not a rapist!" When someone has "absolute power" over you, your status is not only that of a "slave, but also [that] of a concubine."

As Baldwin reflected on these matters, he reminded his audience of the context in which all this was taking place. These crimes were occurring in 1965, and not in an authoritarian regime but rather one that "espouses" the "notion" that it is the beacon of "freedom" in the world. There was something absurd and grotesquely hypocritical about this, and

Baldwin could not help but express skepticism about recent signs of encouragement. Yes, the Civil Rights Act of 1964 was the law of the land, yet "we had an amendment—the Fifteenth Amendment—nearly a hundred years ago. I hate to again sound like an Old Testament prophet," Baldwin told the students, "but if the amendment was not honored then, I don't have any reason to believe that the civil rights bill will be honored now." What more could black people possibly do to "earn" recognition as equal citizens under the law? "If one has got to prove one's title to the land," Baldwin said while gesturing emphatically with his left hand, "isn't four hundred years enough? Four hundred years, at least three wars. The American soil is full of the corpses of my ancestors. Why is my freedom or my citizenship, or my right to live there, how is it conceivably a question *now*?" In a similar vein, Baldwin pointed out—a bit later in the speech—that when Bobby Kennedy said "it was conceivable that in forty years in America we might have a negro president," many whites viewed this as a "very emancipated statement." But American blacks greeted this statement with "laughter," "bitterness," and "scorn":

> From the point of view of the man in the Harlem barbershop, Bobby Kennedy only got here yesterday, and now he's already on his way to the presidency. We've been [here] four hundred years and now he tell[s] *us* that *maybe* in forty years, *if you're good*, we may let you become president.

With these arguments, Baldwin struck again at some mythologies bound up in the American dream. Indeed, as his debate partner Heycock had said in his speech, the United States is supposed to be a land "in which artificial barriers to fulfillment and achievement are unheard of." People are supposed to be able to rise according to their merit. For African Americans, Baldwin was reminding his audience, the country was anything but a land of equal opportunity and meritocracy.

In the last part of his speech, Baldwin addressed the themes of hesitation and hope. He expressed "political hesitation" despite the Civil Rights Act and "Johnson landslide" because he still wondered if the country as well as its leaders had the *will* to bring about meaningful change. While Mississippi burned, many politicians pleaded, "We can't do anything." Instead of confronting the "terrible" conditions of the northern ghettos, most Americans carried on in a state of "bland ignorance" that was rooted, ultimately, in a denial of the humanity of those trapped there.

Although Baldwin was quite cognizant of the limits of politics, he did believe that with sufficient moral change and political will, progress was possible. If the white people in the South were the ones being deprived of their rights on a massive scale, he told the students, the federal government "would find some way to do something about it." In addition to the capacity to act to protect the rights of those threatened by racial violence and subordination, Baldwin expressed hope in the ability of the American people to resume and extend the unfinished project of Reconstruction. "The city of New York was able," he said, "to reconstruct itself, tear down buildings and raise great new ones, downtown and for money," and so too it would be able—if the people demanded it—to devote resources to reconstructing the infrastructure of Harlem without at the same time engaging in "Negro removal." Baldwin's hope for radical reconstruction was not based on a grand ideology or in a deep commitment to any particular policy agenda. Instead, Baldwin's hope was rooted in the idea, as he put it in 1963, of tapping into "the vast amount of energy" in the country so that we might "change and save ourselves," and ultimately "achieve the American Revolution."[90]

Baldwin then turned his attention to a central theme from "Down at the Cross" that may have been the inspiration for the motion before the house that night. "The Negroes of this country," Baldwin had written there, "may never be able to rise to power, but they are very well placed indeed to precipitate chaos and ring down the curtain on the American dream."[91] His aim in this passage and the conclusion to his Cambridge speech was to play the role of "warning prophet": we are on the road to destruction and can only avoid that fate if we change course. Those who are trapped in the ghettos of the country realize that there are plenty of places that are "bigger, cleaner, whiter, richer, [and] safer," and they were coming to recognize that it was not ordained by God that they be relegated to lives of despair while others were blessed with luxury. They had begun to free themselves from the sense that power relationships were fixed in place when they saw black Africans emerge on "the stage of the world." Baldwin was careful to avoid lionizing African leaders who had emerged as "heroes" for many American blacks. He was every bit as skeptical of sentimentality and romanticism in politics as he was in literature. The rise of black power in Africa, he admitted, "created, and will create, a great many conundrums." As mentioned earlier, while he was preparing to visit Africa for the first time in 1962, he confessed to his agent Bob Mills that he was afraid to sojourn to the continent because this would force him to abandon the "dream" of Africa and begin "judging" the "black people" there "solely as people."[92] "One of the great things that the white world does not know," Baldwin told those assembled at Cambridge, "but I think I do know, is that black people are just like everybody else. . . . We are also mercenaries, dictators, murderers, [and] liars. We are human too." Baldwin believed that the acquisition of power was an essential first step for any oppressed people, but he was always alert to the fact that power could be used for good or ill. He was pleased to see Africans reclaiming power from those who had oppressed them, although he recognized that *some* would use their newfound power immorally. To expect anything else would be to expect something superhuman.

The American people had in their midst a population of several million long-oppressed and demoralized black people who had gained from African examples "a sense of [themselves] beyond a savage or a clown." Changes in power, they realized, were possible. The American case was different, though. While the dream of many African blacks—to oversimplify for a moment—was to reclaim power from those who had colonized them, American blacks were confronted with the task of attempting to assume power *alongside* their white neighbors, who weren't going anywhere. The time for waiting had run out, and the demand was for "freedom now!" The question now was whether or not Americans were ready to exert their power to bring about political, social, and economic change, or if their intransigence would light the fuse that would cause the cities to blow up. Baldwin made it entirely clear he did "care" about his "countrymen" and the prospect of violence was what "concern[ed]" him "most." And time was short. "We are sitting in this room," he said, "and we are—at least we like to think we are—relatively civilized, and we can talk to each other at least on certain levels, so that we could walk out of here assuming that the measure of our enlightenment, or at least our politeness, has some effect on the world. It may not." With these lines, Baldwin was making a truly haunting suggestion. We like to think that reasoned discourse is at the heart of our political lives. We tell ourselves that if we are sufficiently enlightened and well mannered, we can live together—despite our disagreements—in a relatively "civilized" way. But Baldwin's travels over the previous several years—especially in the northern ghettos—had led him to wonder about the viability of these assumptions. This struck him especially powerfully when he spoke to teenagers, like the one he met in San Francisco in 1963 who told him, "I ain't got no flag; I ain't got no country."[93] "I am a grown man," Baldwin said, "and perhaps I can be reasoned with, I certainly hope I can be. But I don't know, and neither does Martin Luther King, *none of us* know, how to deal with those other people whom the white world has so long ignored, who don't believe anything the white world says and don't entirely believe anything I or Martin say."[94] This point brings us back to a somewhat-cryptic comment Baldwin made early in his speech. In his discussion of the impact of white supremacy on "the subjugated," Baldwin said the system destroys a "father's authority" over his son. The concept of authority, in this context as well as that of his comments about the persuasive power of leaders like himself and King, is better understood as akin to legitimacy than command. Baldwin was not trying to say that fathers ought to command their sons—given his own history, this would be an especially peculiar thing to say—and that figures like himself and King ought to control how younger people chose to pursue their liberation. Instead, what worried him was the complete breakdown of the ability to communicate in a way that one's words were respected as plausible and legitimate. Baldwin's primary political goal was to help bring about a state of affairs in which people might "achieve their freedom" while at the same time maintaining "their dignity." Over the years, he had tried to achieve this goal with words, but he sensed that discourse itself was losing its authority. In the vacuum left where words used to be, Baldwin warned, there would be blood.

The window of salvation and redemption was closing, but Baldwin still clung to some hope, and it was on the wings of this hope that he concluded his speech:

> Until the moment comes when we, the Americans, the American people, are able to accept the fact that I have to accept, for example, that my ancestors are both white and black, that on that continent we are trying to forge a new identity for which we need each other, and that I am not a ward of America, I am not an object of missionary charity, I am one of the people who built the country. Until this moment, there is scarcely any hope for the American dream because the people who are denied participation in it, by their very presence, will wreck it. And if that happens, it's a very grave moment for the West. Thank you.

As Baldwin turned and headed toward his seat next to Heycock, the audience erupted in enthusiastic applause. Just as he had at the conclusion of Heycock's and Burford's speeches, Fullerton rose from his president's chair, which was elevated above the speaker's platform, in order to ring his bell for the next speaker. Fullerton was especially conscious of rising to his feet quickly to introduce the next speaker because the representatives from the BBC had told him it was important to move things along throughout the night. Soon after Fullerton got up, the students followed suit, enveloping Baldwin in a standing ovation for nearly a minute. As the students applauded, BBC commentator Stevas spoke over the clapping to tell the television audience, "Tremendously moving moment now, the whole of the Union standing and applauding this magnificent speech by James Baldwin. I've never seen this happen before in the Union in all the years I have known it." About halfway through the standing ovation, Baldwin rose to his feet to acknowledge the crowd. He glanced up at the balcony, perhaps to catch a glimpse of his sister and his other guests, and his face lit up with an enormous grin as he looked at Fullerton and around the chamber.

Fullerton, for his part, was feeling rather embarrassed. It was indeed rare for speakers to receive standing ovations in the Union, and he worried that his decision to stand up while still clapping might have given some in the crowd the idea of standing as well. This bothered him because as the president of the Union, he thought it appropriate for him to preside over the debate in a neutral manner, and wondered if Buckley and Burford might have thought that he was *leading* the standing ovation. It bothered him enough that years later he wrote to Buckley to apologize.[95]

As the students were engulfing Baldwin in ecstatic applause, Buckley stayed seated with his hands in his lap and surveyed the scene with alarm. Couldn't these students see through Baldwin's rhetoric to the threat he posed to their fundamental commitments? Had they not read his writings? First these students had the audacity to laugh mockingly at his debate partner, Burford, and now they were greeting the radical Baldwin with rapturous applause. "I realized," he wrote later, "that this was not going to be *my* night." But rather than attempting to placate the crowd by finding some common ground with Baldwin, Buckley came out swinging. He knew he was going to lose the vote that night, yet he was not about to surrender his pride.

Chapter 7

"The Faith of Our Fathers": Buckley at Cambridge

The standing ovation for Baldwin must have felt like an eternity to Buckley. He remained seated, leaning back, with his legs crossed and a pen to his mouth. In part because the ovation was lasting so long and in part because he felt responsible for it, Fullerton actually sat down in the midst of the applause, probably hoping his classmates would do the same. When the clapping finally subsided, Fullerton rose, rang the bell, and said, "I am now very grateful and very pleased to be able to call Mr. William F. Buckley Jr. to speak fourth to this motion."

With that, Buckley rose from the bench where he was seated next to Burford, grabbed the clipboard on which he had his notes, and made his way slowly to the lectern. He looked down at the ground and let a dramatic silence hang in the air before he uttered a word.[1] Buckley came out swinging: "Gentlemen, it seems to me that of all the indictments Mr. Baldwin has made of America here tonight and in his copious literature of protest"—these last three words must have caused Baldwin to wince a little since he had devoted nearly two decades to criticizing protest literature—"the one thing that is most striking involves, in effect, the refusal of the American community to treat him other than as a Negro." As Buckley uttered these words, he switched back and forth between looking down at the ground and then back up at the students. Nonverbally, he was already showing himself to be different from Baldwin. While Baldwin stayed at the lectern and faced forward or slightly to his right for most of his speech, Buckley was proving to be a wanderer. He moved a long way from the speaker's table repeatedly and turned during the course of his speech to address students seated on all sides of the chamber. With his opening line, he set many in the audience up for a surprise thumb aimed directly at their collective eye. For someone on the progressive side of the spectrum, the assumption would be that this indictment is striking because to be "treated as a Negro" in the United States often meant to be treated, as Baldwin put it in his speech, as if "you are a worthless human being."[2] Buckley, much to the shock of his audience, intended to argue just the opposite: "The American community," he explained, "almost everywhere [Baldwin] goes, treats him with a kind of *unction*"—this last word oozed out of Buckley's mouth slowly and was accompanied by a devious smile—"a kind of *satisfaction* at posturing carefully before his flagellations of our civilization, that indeed, quite properly commands the contempt he so eloquently showers upon us." Rather than being treated poorly as a result of his race, Buckley was saying, Baldwin was treated with obsequiousness at every turn, even though he was engaged in the business of flogging "our civilization." With this idea, Buckley was offering the first of many indications that his speech would be shaped by Wills's "What Color Is God?" Intellectuals, Wills had contended, were actually showing Baldwin a great deal of *disrespect* by greeting him with such uncritical adulation. This was disrespectful because his arguments did not merit such treatment, and he was being paid such deference *because he was black*. To treat him with respect, Wills had insisted, would be to confront the challenge he posed by offering the best arguments we had in defense of "our civilization."

As he stood before the students at Cambridge, Buckley thought that he was taking up the challenge that Wills had issued. "It is impossible in my judgment," Buckley said, turning his gaze from the ground to Baldwin, "to deal with the indictment of Mr. Baldwin unless one is prepared to deal with him as a white man." On hearing this, Baldwin, who sat just feet from Buckley with his head resting on his left fist, opened his large eyes wide and raised his eyebrows in an expression that was a mixture of surprise and disbelief. "The fact that your skin is black," Buckley explained, "is utterly irrelevant to the arguments that you raise." Buckley was now looking directly at Baldwin when he said, "The fact that you sit here as is your rhetorical device and lay the entire weight of the Negro ordeal on your own shoulders is irrelevant to the argument that we are here to discuss." The identities of the debaters, Buckley was insisting, were irrelevant; the only thing that ought to matter is the merit of their arguments.

Given the topic before the Union, Buckley maintained that the focus ought to be on the "gravamen"—one of his favorite obscure vocabulary words that means "essence"—"of Mr. Baldwin's charges against America," which "are not so much . . . that our ideals are insufficient, but that we have no ideals." As Buckley uttered these last few words, his eyes lit up with a smile, and he rose onto his tiptoes. Here again, the influence of Wills on Buckley's thinking is evident. In "What Color Is God?" Wills made much the same point when he wrote, "[Baldwin] says we do not *have* any ideals: we do not believe in any of the things our religion, our civilization, our country stand for. It is all an elaborate lie, a lie whose sole and original function is to fortify privilege."[3] Baldwin, as interpreted by Wills and Buckley, was convinced that America was not a land of ideals but rather "ideology" in the pejorative sense. Americans were not moved by genuine moral and political commitments but instead, as Buckley explained to the Cambridge students, just used idealistic language as "some sort of a superficial coating"—Buckley's right hand went in a circular motion at this point, giving the audience the image that he was, right before its eyes, applying a coat of ideology—"which we come up with at any given moment in order to justify whatever commercial or noxious experiment we are engaged in."

Is it really true that Baldwin rejected the very existence of American ideals? The answer is a bit more complicated than Buckley made it out to be. While it is certainly true that Baldwin believed Americans espoused ideals—such as "freedom," "equality," and "democracy"—that they had failed to really comprehend, let alone achieve, he also believed that there could be real value in the ideals themselves. But you cannot have one thing without the other. In order for ideals to be consequential, we must do the hard work of thinking through what they mean and what a real commitment to them would entail in the world. As Baldwin had written about a decade earlier, "The concepts contained in words like 'freedom,' 'justice,' [and] 'democracy' are not common concepts; on the contrary they are rare. . . . It takes enormous and, above all, individual effort to arrive at the respect for other people that these words imply."[4]

Baldwin took the reflection on ideals seriously and hoped his readers would do the same. In "Nobody Knows My Name," he explained, "Any honest examination of national life proves how far we are from the standard of human freedom with which we began. The recovery of this standard demands of everyone who loves this country a hard look at himself."[5] By the time he penned "Down at the Cross" a couple years later, he was perhaps even more skeptical about the authenticity of the American commitment to freedom, but he still viewed it as a valuable ideal. "I have met only a very few people," he wrote, "and most of them were not Americans—who had any real desire to be free. Freedom is hard to bear."[6]

But Buckley—whether he had read these words or not—was not buying it. Indeed, it would be fair to say that he believed Baldwin was doing a bit of "superficial coating" of his own. Baldwin's occasional calls to "recover" American ideals were ideological subterfuge, he thought, meant to hide a nefarious agenda. "Mr. Baldwin can," Buckley told the students, "writing his book, *The Fire Next Time*, in which he threatens America"—on hearing these words, Baldwin's brow furrowed, and in the vertical creases coming up between his eyebrows one can see genuine befuddlement at what he just heard come out of Buckley's mouth. His expression seems to say, "I did *what* in *The Fire Next Time*?" Baldwin's face would contort even more when Buckley delivered his next line: "[Baldwin] didn't, in writing that book, speak with the British accents that he used exclusively tonight." As Baldwin heard these words, his eyebrows went up, and he opened his large eyes about as far as possible. Many of the students were also taken aback by this peculiar accusation, and a smattering of boos, hisses, and coughs filled the chamber along with a few shouts of "Shame!" Fullerton, perhaps recalling the heckling Griffiths had received at the Union a month earlier, admonished the crowd to refrain from interrupting the speaker. Although it is impossible to know for sure, it seems likely that many students assumed that Buckley was claiming that Baldwin had literally been affecting a British accent to play to the crowd. In fact, Buckley—whose own "accent" was often described as "British"—had something else in mind. Over the years, Buckley had developed the habit of using the word "accents" in a rather-unorthodox way. "Our own intellectuals," he told a college audience about a month before the

Cambridge debate, "speak a derivative speech; speak in European accents." Buckley's use of "accents" in this way was something more akin to "moral vocabulary" than the way the term is used in ordinary conversation. In this context, then, Buckley was accusing Baldwin of shrouding his subversive agenda in language that he thought would be appealing to his British audience. Baldwin's true aim, Buckley insisted, was to convince his listeners to "jettison our entire civilization." In order to support this claim, Buckley then paraphrased a line from *The Fire Next Time* that he viewed as the most revealing of Baldwin's true colors: "The only thing that the white man has that the negro should want is power."[7]

Buckley then drew the two central points of his introduction together by saying that rather than treating Baldwin with the "unctuous servitude" to which he was accustomed—and that animated, he suspected, the standing ovation Baldwin had received minutes earlier—he had something else in mind. "I propose to pay him the honor this night," Buckley pointed at Baldwin with another devious smile on his face. "I'm going to speak to you without any reference whatever to those surrounding protections which you are used to in virtue of the fact that you are a Negro, and in virtue of the fact that your race has dreadfully suffered at the hands of my race." This is what Buckley had meant when he said he would treat Baldwin as he would a "white man"; he would treat him as someone without "surrounding protections." As Buckley turned and pointed at him, Baldwin put his hands down on the bench and pushed himself up, giving the impression—but for a moment—that he might rise to his feet. He did not and instead shot a cold, half grin at Buckley. "I am treating you," Buckley concluded his introduction, "as a fellow American; as a person whose indictments of our civilization are unjustified."

Is "our civilization" worthy of indictment? Buckley seemed to admit as much in the first moments of his speech when he said that "our civilization . . . commands the contempt which [Baldwin] so eloquently showers upon us." But as Buckley launched into the body of his speech, he sought to downplay the significance of this indictment. It was true that American history was full of many "luridities of oppression," but so too was the history of every other country. The English, he reminded his audience, had long excluded Catholics and Jews from the franchise, and had long persecuted the Irish. "The untouchables," he continued, "have a hard life in India," and blacks had long been the perpetrators of violence (as well as its victims) in Africa. Indeed, luridities of oppression were deeply rooted in the "sociological facts of human nature," which show that people tend to "group together," and when they are able to "amass power," they oppress those who are less powerful. The luridities committed by whites against blacks in the United States were, Buckley argued, thoroughly unexceptional and therefore hardly grounds for rejection of "American civilization." To hammer this point home, Buckley contended that there was far "more blood shed trying to bring emancipation to the Irish here in the British Isles than has been shed by all of the people . . . who have been lynched as a result of the delirium of . . . race supremacy in the United States in the days since Reconstruction." Buckley—always the skilled debater—chose his words carefully here by drawing a comparison between English-Irish violence and post-Reconstruction racial violence in the United States, thus leaving off the ledger the centuries of bloodshed under the institution of slavery and the more than half a million killed in the war necessary to bring about its end.

Throughout this part of his speech, Buckley asked a series of rhetorical questions. "Shall we" discuss *this* luridity or *that* one? Buckley asked the students again and again. Like Burford, Buckley was confronted with the sight of several students rising from the benches, hoping to be acknowledged so that they might ask a question. To this point in the speech, Buckley had ignored these students, but he decided to call on one here. "Point of information, sir," the student said. "Why don't we discuss the motion?" This was greeted with laughter and applause in the chamber. It was true that Buckley had yet to say much of anything about the motion, but he did not let that stop him from coming up with a clever comeback. "To respond to your question," he joked, "I was not given your instructions on how to comport myself before being invited here." The students appreciated the quickness of Buckley's wit, and greeted this response with laughter and applause. It seems, though, that Buckley thought the student had a point, and he shifted his attention away from the luridities of oppression throughout history to the contemporary American case.

The central question before the house was *not* whether there were "systems we all recognize as evil" at work in the United States but rather, "What in fact shall we do about it?" More specifically, Buckley asked, "What shall we try to do to eliminate those psychic humiliations which I join Mr. Baldwin in believing are the very worst aspects of discrimination?"[8] Here Buckley took a slight rhetorical detour to remind the students of their "withering laughter" in response to "the statistics of Mr. Burford" on the "material progress" of blacks in the United States. Buckley scolded the students for this reaction, which he thought unjustified. After all, Buckley explained, "material progress" is a significant measure of well-being and not all "capitalization" in American history was the result of "Negro travail." He conceded, though, that these statistics did, in a sense, miss an important point. Even if blacks had achieved economic parity with whites, we would still have a "dastardly situation" on our hands because of the "humiliations" to which blacks were subjected.

To this juncture in the speech, Buckley seemed to have conceded two important things. First, he had acknowledged that American blacks had been subjected to many luridities of oppression at the hands of whites. Second, he admitted that blacks were subjected to psychic humiliation as a result of racial subordination. Buckley coupled both concessions, however, with classic conservative rejoinders. In the case of the luridities of oppression, he reminded the students of the essentially fallen nature of humans and resulting universality of suffering. This is a useful conservative trope because it posits the inescapability of travail and therefore makes all utopian projects seem foolish. After acknowledging the dastardliness of the psychic humiliations to which blacks in general and Baldwin in particular had been subjected over the years, Buckley called on the students to resist the temptation to respond to this evil too abruptly or radically. "I am asking you not to make politics as the crow flies," Buckley said, invoking a phrase from the conservative British philosopher Michael Oakeshott.[9] Buckley's point in this context echoed the one he had made a decade and a half earlier in his Class Day oration, just before he graduated from Yale. On that occasion in 1950, Buckley urged his fellow graduates to be cognizant of "the deficiencies in

American life" without being tempted by radical solutions to correct them. "The retention of the best features of our way of life," he told them, "is the most enlightened and noble of goals." In 1965, facing another group of college students, Buckley's message was the same: in politics, the shortest distance between two points is not always the wisest route to take.

After warning the students against making "politics as the crow flies," Buckley returned to his refrain of "what shall we do?" In a line that the students found rather amusing, he asked them what "instructions" they had for him to "take back to the United States." Buckley personalized the problem of racist psychic humiliation by reminding the students that Baldwin himself had been subjected to ill treatment at the hands of police officers and others. At this point, Buckley turned toward the students seated behind the lectern and raised his voice slightly, "I know! I know from your faces that you share with me the feeling of *compassion* and the feeling of *outrage* that this kind of thing should have happened." As he said this, two students sitting in the front row smiled in disbelief at what they were hearing before one of them covered his face in embarrassment. Like his other concessions, Buckley moved quickly to pivot away from the wrongs done to blacks and back to the idea that there were no easy solutions to the problem. What, he asked, ought to be done to the police officers and others who have mistreated Baldwin? And what ought to be done "to change the warp and woof of moral thought in society in such a fashion as to try to make it happen less and less"? This was *the* question that needed to be answered, and Buckley devoted the next part of his speech to explaining what he took to be the unwise answer given by Baldwin.

Early in his speech, Buckley had provided a preview of his interpretation of Baldwin's agenda when he contended that the author was calling on "us to jettison our entire civilization." This was a theme that Buckley—following Wills—had developed in just about every piece he had written about Baldwin prior to the debate. At this point in the speech, Buckley sought to offer some evidence in support of this reading. Buckley said later that the warmth with which Baldwin was received led him to conclude that the students had scant familiarity with his work and he felt it was his responsibility to warn them about the author's radical commitments. The first step in his argument on this matter was to reveal what Baldwin had said about the "civilization" he intended to "throw . . . over." In *The Fire Next Time*, Buckley claimed, Baldwin argued that "our civilization rests on the rantings of a Hebrew, sunbaked fanatic called Jesus." This formulation was nearly identical to the one Buckley had offered in "A Call to Lynch the White God," where he claimed Baldwin had "special contempt for our religion—founded by Christ, a sunbaked, disreputable fanatic." The relevant line in *Fire*—which Buckley misquoted in both his column and Cambridge speech—actually says, "The real architect of the Christian church was not the disreputable, sunbaked Hebrew who gave it his name but the mercilessly fanatical and self-righteous St. Paul."[10] More on Paul in a moment, but for the time being, let's consider what Baldwin actually said about Jesus. There is little doubt his description of Jesus is striking. Indeed, in a letter dated just two days before the debate, a woman from Fairfax, Virginia, had written to Baldwin to ask about the line in question. The writer reported she was in a book club with several other women and the group was reading *Fire*. At the last meeting, she told Baldwin, she was "the only one who maintained you were not anti-Christ." She asked him for help responding to her fellow book lovers and wondered if he might explain just what he meant by "disreputable, sunbaked Hebrew."[11]

The first thing worth noting is that Baldwin did not—as Buckley claimed in both misquotes—call Christ a "fanatic"; that was a label he saved for Saint Paul. Baldwin did not intend for the adjectives "disreputable" and "sunbaked" to be read as insults, though this appears to be the way Buckley read them, and they seem to have given the readers in Fairfax some pause. The use of "sunbaked" appears to be a reference to something Baldwin had said earlier in the same paragraph in *Fire*, when he reminded his readers that Jesus "came out of a rocky piece of ground in what is now known as the Middle East."[12] This was significant for Baldwin because it was an "elementary historical detail" that many Christians seem to have forgotten after centuries of Europeanizing and whitening Christ to make him the blond-haired, blue-eyed man depicted in many churches.

Baldwin's use of "disreputable" was also not intended as an insult. In fact, coming from Baldwin, this was high praise. What Baldwin was trying to say was that Jesus was "disreputable" to the authorities of his time. He was, in short, a rebel—Baldwin's kind of guy. In fact, "disreputable" was the word Baldwin often used to describe himself.[13] One searches in vain for so much as a cross word *about* Christ—who Baldwin frequently called the most betrayed human being in the history of the world—in the thousands of pages Baldwin wrote over the course of his career. Throughout his life, Baldwin would often refer to himself as a Christian, while acknowledging that his religious views were unorthodox to be sure.

The final and most important point worth making about Baldwin's description of Jesus is this: his central aim in the offending passage was to *exonerate* Jesus from the many crimes that would be committed in his name. It is clear that Baldwin had no love for the apostle Paul, and there is no doubt that this was offensive to the devoutly Catholic Buckley. They did not engage in a debate about the virtues and vices of Paul, but the crucial point is that Buckley misrepresented and fundamentally misunderstood Baldwin's attitude toward Jesus.[14]

Buckley was right, though, to say that Baldwin was a severe critic of "the Christian church," which he said had "operated with an unmitigated arrogance and cruelty." Although Baldwin offered several historical examples in *Fire* to support this claim, the one that was especially appalling to Buckley was, as he put it at Cambridge, "that Dachau was the natural consequence of the teachings of St. Paul and Jesus." Again, Buckley distorted and seems to have misunderstood Baldwin's point. There are two passages in *Fire* that inspired Buckley's assertion. First, Baldwin wrote that "the terms 'civilized' and 'Christian' begin to have a very strange ring . . . when a Christian nation surrenders to a foul and violent orgy, as Germany did during the Third Reich." Second, Baldwin declared that "the fact of the Third Reich alone makes obsolete forever any question of Christian superiority, except in technological terms."[15] Based on what I argued above, it seems apparent that Baldwin saw a clear distinction between "the teachings of Christ" and what he variously called "the Christian church," "Christendom," "the Christian world," and "Christianity." To the extent that the concentration camps at Dachau and elsewhere were the "natural consequence" of any one particular thing, Baldwin was not arguing that thing was the teaching of Jesus.

What Baldwin found objectionable about the historical record of the Christian church, though, was that it had all too often used "the authority of the true faith" as "justification" for a politics of conquest and domination, and its leaders had frequently refused to see the evil deeds of others. Baldwin was careful to acknowledge the "integrity" and "heroism" of some Christian missionaries and ministers who believed they were doing their "spiritual duty" through the "spreading of the Gospel," but he believed that people of sincere faith had all too often been *used* by those who were motivated by a desire to overtake and oppress others.[16] This perverse morality of conquest had, Baldwin contended, been blended with the doctrine of white supremacy to animate incredible cruelty over the course of history, and the Christian church, all too frequently, "sanctified" this cruelty with the imprimatur of holiness or turned a blind eye when it was politically convenient.

And so when "for the crime of their ancestry, millions of people in the middle of the twentieth century, and in the heart of Europe—God's citadel—were sent to a death so calculated, so hideous, and so prolonged that no age before this enlightened one had been able to imagine it," Baldwin was "frightened" yet not "astounded." His lack of surprise was *not* due to the fact, as Buckley claimed at Cambridge, that the Holocaust was the "natural consequence" of the "teachings of Jesus" but rather because so many people had behaved so inhumanely in Christ's name. The "foul and violent orgy" of the Third Reich made "obsolete forever any question of *Christian* superiority," but it had little to do with the teachings of Jesus, as Baldwin understood them.

As Buckley continued to develop his case before the students at Cambridge, he asked what the implications of Baldwin's views might be for "the library around here." "Shall we descend on it and uproot all the literature that depends in any way on the teachings of Plato and Aristotle because they justified slavery?" Here again, the influence of Wills is evident. "When a Dachau happens," Wills wrote in his review of *Fire*, "are we—as Baldwin suggests—to tear up all the Bibles, disband the police forces, take crowbars to the court buildings and the libraries?" Buckley, like Wills, was under the impression that Baldwin was urging a complete "overthrow" of "Western civilization." Once again, Buckley and Wills were oversimplifying Baldwin's position, which was far more nuanced.

Perhaps the most revealing reflections Baldwin offered on his relationship to the "Western tradition" was in his 1953 essay "Stranger in the Village." "Stranger" is the piece in which Baldwin described the bizarre experience of spending time in a Swiss Village (Loèches les Bains) where, as far as he could tell, "no black man had ever set foot." The six hundred villagers reacted to Baldwin as though he was a "living wonder," and as noted earlier, he used the experience to reflect not only on the peculiarities of spending time there but also on the sense in which he was a "stranger" in the village of "the West." Even though many of the villagers would never "see more of Europe than the hamlet at the foot of their mountain," they moved, Baldwin wrote, "with an authority which I shall never have; and they regard me, quite rightly, not only as a stranger in their village but as a suspect latecomer, bearing no credentials to everything they have—however unconsciously—inherited." Baldwin supported this claim by explaining that even the "most illiterate" of the villagers "is related, in a way that I am not, to Dante, Shakespeare, Michelangelo, Aeschylus, Da Vinci, Rembrandt, and Racine." Their ancestors had the power to make the modern world and write the histories: "Go back a few centuries," Baldwin wrote, "and they are in their full glory—but I am in Africa, watching the conquerors arrive."[17]

Baldwin's juxtaposition of the "makers" of the modern world and the image of European conquerors and enslavers arriving on the shores of Africa set up his discussion of where "the idea of white supremacy"—which he called "the very warp and woof of the heritage of the West"—fits within all this. The idea, he explained, "rests simply on the fact that white men are the creators of civilization . . . and therefore civilization's guardians and defenders." Although Baldwin was more deeply engaged with the treasures of Western culture than most whites ever would be, he confessed in "Stranger" that he would always feel a sense of estrangement from them.

A little over a decade later, Baldwin published a short piece called "Why I Stopped Hating Shakespeare" in the *Observer*. The piece captures some of the ways his reflections on his relationship to "the West" evolved over time. In the essay, Baldwin admitted that he once held Shakespeare in contempt "as one of the authors and architects of my oppression." As he matured, though, he realized that when he read Shakespeare in those early years, he had "missed the point entirely" because he failed "to go behind the words . . . to what the poet was saying."[18] When Baldwin began to hear Shakespeare's voice, he realized that the themes with which the poet was grappling were universal; they were Baldwin's themes too. Once he began to appreciate this, he saw the ways in which Shakespeare's ideas were alive and often revelatory.

Baldwin's evolving views of Shakespeare were part of a broader "quarrel with the English language," which was rooted in the fact that "the language reflected none of my experience." Rather than rejecting the language as it had been developed by the makers of the Western tradition, Baldwin "began to see the matter in quite another way." "Perhaps the language was not my own," he wrote, "because I had never attempted to *use* it, had only learned to imitate it." As he explored how he might put the language to work to tell the truth about his own experiences, he looked to many models, including his "black ancestors, who evolved the sorrow songs, the blues, and jazz," but also to Shakespeare, who "found his poetry where poetry is found: in the lives of the people." In the end, Baldwin came to love Shakespeare because he thought he was a "responsible" writer in the sense that he "tried not to lie about what he saw."[19]

This brief detour into some of Baldwin's reflections on his relationship to "the West" help us to see that Buckley's characterization was shallow and misguided.[20] Baldwin was not interested in ripping up the Bibles, as Wills had suggested, or descending on the library to "uproot" all the classics of the Western tradition, as Buckley had claimed. Indeed, just the opposite may be true. Baldwin believed there was much one could learn—both good and bad—from books such as these and fell in love with many canonical works. When Baldwin was asked to name his literary influences in author questionnaires, he invariably listed the King James Bible, Charles Dickens, Henry James, Fyodor Dostoyevsky, and Marcel Proust. When he delivered his "In Search of a Majority" speech in 1960, he relied on a quotation from Plato as a key framing device and did the same with Friedrich Nietzsche in the "stump speech" he delivered all over the country in 1963.[21] Baldwin was interested in critically engaging the Western tradition, not in jettisoning it. In the words of Podhoretz, "Jimmy did not want to overthrow the Western tradition. Henry James is a part of the Western tradition and he certainly did not want to overthrow Henry James!"[22]

While Buckley was asking the students to imagine Baldwin leading a band of radical marauders ransacking the libraries of Cambridge, a student stood up to be called on. Just after Buckley delivered his "Plato and Aristotle" line, he acknowledged the student, who said, "You keep asking what we *should* do and then you are telling us what we *should not* do." "I'll tell you in due course," Buckley shot back quickly and then relied, once again, on an argument from Wills to demonstrate why Baldwin's alleged desire to overthrow "our civilization" was unjustified. Buckley asked the students to reason analogically with him for a moment:

> Now I suggest that anybody who argued, as indeed it may have been argued at this very house, for all I know, in this very chamber, the very fact that Jews and Catholics . . . were not allowed to vote in England as late as 1828, suggested that English civilization ought to have been jettisoned. I suggest that the *other possibility* ought to be considered, that precisely the reason they *did* get the vote was because English civilization was *not* jettisoned.

With these lines, Buckley put rather eloquently what Wills had argued somewhat abstrusely in "What Color Is God?" Buckley was asking a question of enduring relevance for political life: If a civilization is failing to deliver justice to those in its midst, does the civilization itself have the resources (intellectually, politically, socially, economically, etc.) to rectify this injustice, or is the civilization itself an obstacle to such rectification? *If* Baldwin was indeed calling for an overthrow of "our civilization"—a doubtful claim to be sure—we ought to be open to "the other possibility": that such an overthrow would move us further away from justice for all than when we started.[23] If we are awake to this possibility, Buckley told the students, we might resist the temptation to "so immanetize our own misgivings as to rush forward to jettison and to overthrow our civilization because we don't live up to its higher ideals."[24]

At this point in the speech, Buckley picked up a thread he had left hanging a few minutes earlier. After acknowledging that the psychic humiliations suffered by American blacks were "dastardly," he hinted at what *should* be done before he launched into his explanation and critique of what he took to be Baldwin's answer to that question. How can we diminish the likelihood of humiliation on the basis of race? "Obviously," Buckley told the students, "the first element is concern. We've got to care that it happens, we have got to do what we can to change the warp and woof of moral thought in society in such a fashion as to try to make it happen less and less." After warning the students against Baldwin's revolutionary aims, Buckley returned to the theme of concern. "Let me urge this point to you which I can do with authority," Buckley said while jabbing his finger in the air. "In the United States there *is* a concern for the Negro problem." Although Buckley did not mean for this to be a "laugh line," the chamber was filled with a cacophony of chuckles, chortles, and guffaws. Why did the students think this line was so funny? Perhaps they were mocking Buckley for stating the obvious. "The Negro problem" in the United States was, at that moment, on the front pages of newspapers around the world, and as a result, was a matter of concern—in one way or another—to all Americans and many people abroad. As the students laughed and clapped, Buckley stared down at the floor and thought up a witty comeback that might put the students in their place. As he did so, he edged closer to Baldwin and eventually leaned over to move the water pitcher that was on the table dividing the aisle between them. Once the pitcher was out of the way, Buckley casually sat on the table and delivered lines that he hoped would serve as the rhetorical pinprick needed to deflate the moral egos of the undergraduates:

> If you get up to me and say, well now, is it the kind of concern that we, the students of Cambridge, would show if the problem were our own? All I can say is: I don't know. It may very well be that there has been *some sort of sunburst of moral enlightenment* that has hit this community so as to make it predictable that if you were the governors of the United States the situation would change overnight.

Many students began laughing when Buckley delivered the "moral enlightenment" line that was oozing with sarcasm, but he really brought down the house when he concluded the thought by turning to Fullerton and saying, "I am prepared to grant this as a form of courtesy, Mr. President."

Sitting a few rows behind Baldwin, Earl Hopper was getting anxious. Hopper was a young American instructor of sociology who had come to Cambridge to teach after completing graduate school at Washington University in Saint Louis, Missouri. When Hopper had gotten word of the Baldwin-Buckley debate, he made arrangements to bring many of his students to view the clash between the two famous Americans. What worried Hopper as he sat among the students was that they might be charmed by Buckley's wit and humor. As one of the few Americans in the chamber, Hopper also worried about how the audience reaction to Buckley might make Baldwin feel. Indeed, Hopper reported later that he was terrified that Buckley might actually win the debate. What would Baldwin (and those watching on both sides of the Atlantic) think of Cambridge *then*? Hopper began to think about what he might be able to do to prevent this result from coming to pass.[25]

The substance behind Buckley's witty comment about the moral enlightenment of the Cambridge students had its roots deep in his earliest reflections on the American racial situation. From the beginning, he had resisted the notion that the questions of segregation and civil rights were *moral* issues; they were instead, he insisted, *political* matters. In one of his first editorials on *Brown v. Board of Education*, for example, Buckley said that the "moral fervor attached to the Court decision itself is unconvincing and, at worst, hypocritical."[26] At Cambridge too, Buckley thought the students' sense of moral superiority was unconvincing and hypocritical. It was unconvincing to Buckley because he thought the students, like many northern liberals, were operating under the mistaken assumption that the "Negro problem" could be solved by following the dictates of some moral truth such as the idea that all human beings are "born Equal."[27] In fact, Buckley argued, political action on the basis of this abstract principle could prove to be morally disastrous for everyone involved. What was needed, he asserted, was a humane morality that was tempered by the tough-minded realism of men like Kilpatrick and Weaver.

Buckley thought the students' sense of moral superiority was hypocritical for reasons that are related to the luridities of oppression line of argument from earlier in his speech. The students were, like northern liberals in the United States, turning their ire to the blatant luridities of southern racial oppression, at least in part, as a way to avoid reflecting on the luridities for which they were more directly responsible. By pointing *"down there"* at the spectacle of Connor's forces brutalizing men, women, and children in the streets of Birmingham, they were able to divert attention away from the more subtle system of oppression in their own backyards. As noted above, this critique of moral hypocrisy was one matter on which Buckley and Baldwin were in complete agreement.[28]

"I am saying to you," Buckley continued, "that the engines of concern are working in the United States."[29] Then he decided to revert back to the personalized attack with which he began his speech: "The presence of Mr. Baldwin here tonight," Buckley said while looking down at Baldwin and pointing at him, "is in part a reflection of that concern." Buckley was suggesting explicitly what he had implied at the beginning of his speech: Baldwin's books were as popular as they were and he was greeted so warmly on college campuses *because he was black.* His blackness was the primary reason he was treated with such "unction" and afforded "protections" not available to whites. If the Cambridge students treated Baldwin the way he deserved to be treated, Buckley thought, they would have never hosted him in the first place and certainly would not have offered him a standing ovation.[30]

Buckley concluded his "engines of concern" line of argument by reminding the students that not only was Baldwin the "toast of the town" on practically every college campus in the United States but the problem that he represented—the "Negro problem"—had also preempted "practically all other problems of public policy." In devoting themselves so thoroughly to their "primary policy of concern for the Negro," Buckley contended, Americans were doing something unprecedented in the history of the world: "I challenge you to name another civilization anytime, anywhere, in the history of the world in which the problems of a minority is as much the subject of dramatic concern as it is in the United States." As Buckley delivered this challenge, he was looking at the crowd seated facing Fullerton in the president's chair. As he spoke, he had his right hand outstretched, and his eyebrows bounced up and down with the cadence of his words.

One has to wonder what Baldwin might have been thinking about Buckley's engines of concern argument. My guess is that he greeted it with skepticism. For almost two decades, he had been critical of the assumptions built into the very idea of "the Negro problem." First of all, "the Negro," he insisted, was an invention that white Americans had used for centuries in order to avoid confronting historical and moral realities that terrified them. Second, the racial "problem" was really a "white problem," not a "negro problem." The problem will persist, he maintained, until white people "ask themselves precisely why they found it necessary to invent the nigger" in the first place and are willing to act on an honest answer to that question.[31]

It is also worth mentioning that Baldwin was skeptical of the emphasis on "concern," which was the typical liberal response to the American racial nightmare. He was not, of course, opposed to people feeling a sense of concern for one another, but this was insufficient to achieve justice. Such concern, he argued, was all too often rooted in the reduction of other human beings to the status of symbols rather than an authentic respect for their humanity. As he said near the end of his speech that night, "I am not a ward of America, I am not an object of missionary charity, I am one of the people who built the country." Black people, he insisted again and again, are not "something exotic [and] bizarre. . . . We are human too."

Instead of pushing the engines of concern argument any further, Buckley revived his attack on Baldwin's radicalism. Before describing the next phase in his assault, it is worth noting what is revealed by this rhetorical choice. As he had demonstrated time and again throughout his career, he was far more comfortable on the attack than he was when he attempted to build an affirmative case for his views. If he had chosen to defend his claim that the United States was providing a world historical model of how to treat minority groups, he would have had to confront many uncomfortable questions. Was it true that the United States was showing "dramatic concern" for "the Negro problem"? If so, what did the policy of concern entail, and what problem, precisely, was being addressed? Was the American example *really* unprecedented in the history of the world? And perhaps most interestingly—assuming for a moment that Buckley was right about these matters—it would be worth asking *why* and *how* this policy of concern was activated and sustained. Was it primarily because of the enlightened humanitarianism of those in power or because of the radicalism of freedom fighters?

As a conservative who had been dragging his feet on civil rights for more than a decade, serious attention to these questions would have put Buckley in an awkward position. To the extent that the United States was giving "the problems of a minority" exceptional concern, it was *in spite of* the intransigence of Buckley, writers he commissioned to write for *National Review*, and political candidates he supported. He likely surmised that he had better not dwell too long on what was animating "dramatic concern" for the Negro problem or whether he was personally devoted to this "primary policy of concern." If the engines of concern had been working in the United States, it was no thanks to Buckley and his allies.

As Buckley returned to the attack, he told the students that Baldwin's radical agenda was not limited to matters philosophical and religious; he also had his sights set on the overthrow of the US government. Like Hoover, who Buckley had met in 1951, he apparently thought Baldwin was nothing less than a threat to American national security.[32] "The Americans are not willing," Buckley told the students, "to desert the constitutional system," "desert the idea of the rule of law," and "the idea of the individual rights of the American citizen" in order to meet Baldwin's demands. At this point, another student stood up to say something that was apparently on the minds of many others in the chamber. When Buckley ceded the floor to him, he said, "I wonder if you can point out to me any one of Mr. Baldwin's writings in which he actually said he wants to get rid of civilization." This request was met with rapturous applause and some laughter, but Buckley, as always, was ready with a clever comeback. "I don't know your rules intimately enough to know whether or not

I should have been forbidden from reading Mr. Baldwin's books before arriving here. I understand it is part of the purpose of this program to *promote* the reading of Mr. Baldwin's books." Many of the students laughed and applauded Buckley's witty retort before he attempted to provide a more substantive response to the question. "I quote you exactly a passage from Mr. Baldwin," he said, "which I would have thought would have traversed the Atlantic Ocean in which he says, 'The only thing that whites have that the Negroes should want is *power*.'" This line and the description of Jesus appear to be the two sentences that did the most to *define* Baldwin in Buckley's mind. The line about power comes from the final part of "Down at the Cross" and it is certainly a provocative one, which reads in full, "The only thing white people have that black people need, or should want, is power—and no one holds power forever." Before considering what Baldwin might have meant by this, we must address how Buckley thought it was related to his claim that Baldwin was hell-bent on overthrowing Western civilization, the US Constitution, and individual rights. Interestingly enough, Baldwin himself might supply the key to unlocking why Buckley found this line so offensive. "The idea of white supremacy," Baldwin had written in "Stranger in the Village," "rests simply on the fact that white men are the creators of civilization and are therefore civilization's guardians and defenders."[33] This describes *precisely* how Buckley thought about the meaning of conservatism. Indeed, if we alter Baldwin's sentence slightly, we capture the core of Buckley's creed: "The idea of [conservatism] rests simply on the fact that [men have created a civilization worth preserving] and [conservatives] are therefore civilization's guardians and defenders." What is not stated in my imagined Buckley version of this statement, but is there implicitly in his consternation at Baldwin's line about power, is this: white people are the possessors of civilization, which is what black people really need and should want, prior to any claim to power. Buckley had said this explicitly enough in many of his writings on race, from the infamous "Why the South Must Prevail" editorial to his more recent columns on the fight for voting rights in Mississippi. For Buckley, whiteness was—usually but not always—synonymous with civilization and blackness was suggestive of its absence.[34] Thus, what Buckley wanted black people to seek was not power but rather civilization, and it was the duty of white people to help them get it. Once *they* are civilized, Buckley said, then *we* will be willing to start talking about sharing some of *our* power.

In order to make sense of what Baldwin meant by the line about power that so rankled Buckley, it is helpful to return to the context in which it appears in "Down at the Cross." Baldwin included the line in the midst of many rhetorical flourishes in the last part of the essay. Interestingly, Baldwin's goal in the offending section was to cast doubt on the idea that "equality" was a sufficiently capacious moral concept for the civil rights revolution. When people called for equality, Baldwin was quick to ask, Equal to what? He was, of course, committed to the ideas of equal rights and equality before the law, but he was dead set against the idea that all people lived equally praiseworthy lives. When he heard "equality" used as a rallying cry in the civil rights movement, he reminded people that the goal ought to be to surpass the sorts of lives led by many whites. The goal in Birmingham, for example, should not simply be to wrest power away from Connor but also to rethink the nature of that power so that it might be exercised in a way that respects the dignity of all within its reach. As he put it in the sentence just after the one that so offended Buckley, we are sorely in "need of new standards, which will release [us] from [our] confusion and place [us] once again in fruitful communion with the depths of [our] own being."[35]

Baldwin thought, for instance, that the young people standing up to Jim Crow throughout the South were doing something revolutionary in the deepest sense of the word. They were, of course, challenging long-standing moral, political, social, and economic structures, but they were also reviving and reimagining the meaning of what Baldwin would later refer to as the "first principles" of moral life.[36] As such, these revolutionaries were doing something that was in a sense deeply conservative: they were the ones keeping the teachings of Christ, the spirit of the US Constitution, and the rights of American citizens alive in "our civilization," and it was the so-called conservatives who were doing the most to undermine our commitment to these things. As he put it in his debate with Kilpatrick in late 1962, "You say you are protecting Western values. And I say you are destroying them. I think that if you really take seriously such things as the Bill of Rights, the whole European journey, the Western journey, then you are under obligation, you are under the necessity, you have the duty at no matter what cost to you and yours to expand this concept to include black men."[37]

As Buckley was nearing the end of his speech, he turned back to his notes, clenched his right fist, lifted it just above his waist, and knocked it lightly on the lectern as he said, "Let me say finally, ladies and gentlemen, this: there is no instant cure for the race problem in America, and anybody who tells you that there is, is a charlatan and ultimately a boring man." This last assertion generated some laughter and murmuring from the students. Was Buckley, yet again, engaging in ad hominem attack? Was he suggesting that Baldwin was a "charlatan" and "boring man"? Some of the students seemed to interpret it that way, and although they did not know it, Buckley's writings on Baldwin supported their presumption. In "The Call to Colorblindness," for example, Buckley had mocked Baldwin's longing for the "evanescence of color" as a simplistic and unachievable cure for racial problems. It was a mistake, Buckley argued, to think through this problem—or any other political problem for that matter—by way of appeal to "the kind of abstractions that do not relate to the human experience." All political problems, he insisted, were too complex to be solved by such abstractions, and the race "trouble" was "very complicated" indeed. From his earliest writings on race, Buckley confessed that there was no conservative solution to the "race problem" because it was a problem that was fundamentally "insoluble."[38] This was a convenient posture for a conservative to assume. If one's primary objective is to preserve the status quo, it makes sense to cast doubt about the solvability of various problems with the status quo. A conservative like Buckley took it to be his role to remind would-be reformers of the complexities of political life and dangers of social change.

In this particular case, Buckley explained, those who have "an actual rather than a purely ideologized interest" in the "race problem in America" realize that the matter is "extremely complex as a result of an unfortunate conjunction of two factors: one is the dreadful efforts to perpetuate discrimination by many individual American citizens," and the other is the "result of the failure of the Negro community itself to make certain exertions which were made by other minority groups during the American experience." Buckley's use of "unfortunate" was a subtle way to suggest that the extreme complexity of the problem was due to bad luck, rather than the deliberate creation and perpetuation of institutions and norms that sustained racial hierarchy. Although Buckley conceded that blacks were victims of discrimination, he was sure to emphasize that this was the result of the "dreadful efforts" of "many *individual* American citizens." This is telling because it exemplifies a common rhetorical strategy employed by conservatives in discussions of racial inequality. The stress is almost always on the aberrant behavior of *individuals*—"a few bad apples," it is frequently said—in order to draw attention away from the historical and structural conditions that empowered these individuals in the first place. In addition, Buckley suggested that there has been a "failure of the Negro community." What is interesting here is that he shifted from an emphasis on the individual in his discussion of the *perpetrators* of racial discrimination to a focus on the community in his discussion of the *victims* of racial discrimination. Why not say that "many individual American Negroes" had failed to make "certain exertions" instead of saying this is true of "the Negro community"? I would like to suggest that Buckley was quite deliberate in these rhetorical choices. Just as the decision to highlight the individual's culpability in racial discrimination diverted attention away from structural inequality, the decision to claim failure by "the Negro community" was meant to direct attention away from the historical and societal roots of racial inequality, and toward the apparent shortcomings of a particular group of people, abstracted from the context that created the conditions in which they live.

As Buckley started in on his explanation of "this unfortunate conjunction of two factors," his focus was on the second and not the first. In order to explain the second factor, he appealed to the work of Professor Nathan Glazer, whom he described as a "prominent, Jewish intellectual."[39] In his book *Beyond the Melting Pot*, Glazer had argued that blacks had failed to take advantage of the opportunities made available to them throughout American history. In support of this claim, Glazer pointed out that there were only four hundred more black doctors in the United States in 1960 as there were in 1900. This was not, Buckley suggested by way of Glazer, because there were no opportunities to advance in the medical field. To the contrary, there were *more* opportunities by 1960. It was because, Buckley explained, black people had failed to exert "particular energy" to take advantage of these opportunities. If one of the major factors causing "the Negro problem" was the failure of African Americans to exert sufficient energy toward the right social and economic goals, Buckley surmised, the solution was simple enough: "We should focus on the necessity to animate [the] particular energy" in the black community that has served other minority groups well throughout American history.

Buckley capped off this self-help argument by imagining a role for leaders like Baldwin to play in the promotion of racial progress:

> And what should James Baldwin be doing rather than telling us that we should renounce our civilization? Baldwin, in my judgment, should be addressing his own people and urging them to at least take advantage of those opportunities that exist, and urging us, as he has been doing, to make those opportunities wider and better than those that exist.

Buckley wanted Baldwin to adopt the posture of a latter-day Booker T. Washington by urging blacks to "cast down their buckets" and make the most of whatever opportunities those in power decided to bestow on them.[40] As for those in power, Buckley encouraged a spirit of charity. This was not a new argument in his repertoire. Even in the infamous "Why the South Must Prevail" editorial, Buckley had concluded by insisting that whites must resist the temptation to "exploit Negro backwardness to preserve the Negro as a servile class." Instead, white southerners had an obligation to employ "humane and charitable means" to promote "genuine cultural equality."[41]

One final thing is noteworthy about Buckley's discussion of the "unfortunate conjunction" that made the racial problem so complex. In this part of the speech, his use of "us" and "them" is particularly striking. The obligation rests with "us," he told the crowd of elite university students, to make more opportunities available to "them." If Baldwin was permitted to interrupt, he might have asked, "How did *you* earn the right to decide which opportunities *we* deserve?" Earlier in the speech, Buckley addressed this question, in part, by dismissing the idea that the structures of power that existed in the world were the result of exploitation. "My great grandparents worked too," he said to the students, "[and] presumably yours did also."[42] By personalizing the matter in this way, Buckley wanted to deflate the impact of Baldwin's historical argument and suggest that those who had the power to allocate opportunity in the world were entitled to that power.

Buckley began his conclusion by asking the students to look toward the future. The civil rights movement, he conceded, had "done a great deal to agitate a moral concern, but where do they go now?" The greatest danger, Buckley suggested, was that they might "reach out for some sort of radical solution" that is less concerned with "the advancement of the Negro than the regression of white people." As Buckley delivered these lines, he moved around the speaker's area and directed his attention to all sides of the chamber. As he turned back to the lectern he saw a young, bespectacled man with dark hair standing up, hoping to be acknowledged for a question. This was Hopper, the American sociologist mentioned above. Hopper had started developing his question during Buckley's "what shall we do" refrain in the middle of his speech. When Buckley pointed at Hopper in a fashion much like a fencer's lunge, the young professor shouted his question loud enough for everyone in the chamber to hear him: "One thing you might do, Mr. Buckley, is let them vote in Mississippi!" Hopper's comment inspired applause and shouts of "Here! Here!" from around the chamber. As the audience clapped, Buckley leaned on the lectern, looked down, nodded, and said quietly, "I agree. I agree." Once the applause died down, Buckley added, "I couldn't agree with you more." Before Buckley could utter another word, the students filled the room with a wave of laughter far more "withering" than anything they had directed at Burford, and this stopped the godfather of American conservatism dead in his tracks. Although few—if any—of the students had read Buckley's writings on civil rights, they suspected there was something absurd and disingenuous about his claim to be in wholehearted agreement with Hopper. As Buckley gathered himself and thought about his counterattack, it must have occurred to him that he had indeed said something he did not really believe in his initial reaction.

As the laughter was subsiding in the chamber, Buckley allowed his true colors to come shining through and, in Fullerton's words, "brought the house down" in the process.[43] "Lest I appear too ingratiating," he said, "which is hardly my objective here tonight, I think actually what is wrong in Mississippi, sir, is not that not enough Negroes are voting but that too many white people are voting." Many of the students and even Hopper had to laugh at this clever retort.

What the students did not know was that Buckley's response to Hopper was more than just a crafty comeback; this revised reply was what he really believed. Buckley proceeded to make this clear to Hopper and the students. "It is much more complicated, sir," Buckley said as he crossed his arms and glared in Hopper's direction, "than simply giving them the vote. If I were myself a constituent of the community of Mississippi at this moment, what I would do is vote to lift the standards of the vote"—as Buckley said this he raised his right hand in the air before waving it to the side to indicate a sweeping away—"so as to disqualify 65 percent of the white people who are presently voting." Many of the students may have thought Buckley said this as a comedic follow-up to his original comment, but again, he was being quite serious. He believed the ideal state of affairs would be to have conservative elites dominating not only southern but national politics too.[44] In the South, for example, he longed for the political ascendance of people with Kilpatrick's cast of mind: "nonracist" but not reflexively egalitarian; charitable but realistic; and constitutionalist but willing to bend the law when the preservation of civilization required it. In sum, Buckley's position was hostile to both democratic and liberal values. He was far less concerned with the demand that all human beings should have a say in their political destiny, or that all individuals have rights that ought to be protected, than he was with the idea that those who were best suited to preserve civilization were authorized to do what was necessary to achieve this goal.

After his recovery from the Hopper interruption, Buckley returned to his conclusion. He repeated his claim that there were "two sets of difficulties." First, there was the "racial narcissism" of white people, who like "brown people and black people" act so as to "maximize their own power" and "protect their own vested interests."[45] Buckley then turned to the students directly behind him to remind them that the other set of difficulties had to do with "the Negro people" themselves, who must be told "that their best chances are in a mobile society, and the most mobile society in the world today, my friends, is the United States of America." It was the responsibility of leaders like Baldwin to encourage "his people" to take advantage of the opportunities made possible by this "mobile society."

Baldwin's failure to offer this sort of encouragement, Buckley insisted, was further evidence of the danger he posed. Rather than urging "his people" to take advantage of the opportunities made possible by "the American dream," Baldwin had nothing to offer but "cynicism" and "despair." Buckley was right to say that Baldwin was not the sort of leader likely to offer a "pull-yourself-up-by-your-bootstraps" sort of message. For Buckley, this was an indication of Baldwin's irresponsibility. After all, was it not incumbent on leaders like Baldwin to encourage his audiences to take advantage of opportunities to advance, limited though they may be? Was not his failure to do so only deepening the despair of the oppressed?

Baldwin was not one to denigrate those leaders who offered the sort of affirmative message Buckley wanted to hear. Indeed, Baldwin was fascinated by Booker T. Washington and interested in writing a biography that would free him from common misunderstandings.[46] Furthermore, the "improbable aristocrats" Baldwin praised in "Down at the Cross" were the sorts of people who worked behind the scenes to enhance the opportunities made available to those left out of the American dream.[47] But it is also true that Baldwin was suspicious of arguments that suggested explicitly or implicitly that black people were to blame for their lot in the United States. The key to understanding Baldwin's skepticism is the idea of "demoralization," a term he used repeatedly in his speeches and essays. In the context of the American racial nightmare, it was nearly impossible to escape a feeling of hopelessness, which was rooted in experience that taught black people that they could work hard and play by the rules, and yet stay stuck in the same cycle of despair that had ensnared the generation before them. Baldwin certainly wanted to encourage "his people," but he wanted to do so in an honest way. Perhaps the best model of his attitude on this matter is the letter to his fourteen-year-old nephew that he published in the *Progressive* magazine in late 1962 and reprinted as part of *The Fire Next Time*. In the letter, Baldwin lamented that the "country set you down in a ghetto in which, in fact, it intended that you should perish," but he implored his nephew to resist despair and accept white people "with love." Before black people would be able to take advantage of the opportunities Buckley imagined they were neglecting, the country had to liberate itself from the racial myths that had animated it for so long. In 1965, Baldwin was still hopeful that might happen, although his hope was eroding by the minute.

As Buckley was drawing his speech to a close, he was confronted with a choice: Should he take the path of conciliation or the path of confrontation? Based on what he had said so far, it is not surprising that he chose the latter course. What is somewhat startling, however, is just how far he was willing to go down the path of confrontation. "One thing I can tell you I believe with *absolute authority*," he said as he gestured emphatically with his right hand and opened his eyes wide, "is that where the United States is concerned, if it ever comes to a confrontation"—as he got to this last word, he raised his voice slightly, and squinted his eyes— "between a continuation of our sort of idealism . . . [and the] overthrow [of] that civilization which we consider to be the faith of our fathers, the faith indeed of your fathers . . . , we will fight the issue not only in the Cambridge Union, but we will fight it as you were once recently called to do on the beaches and on the hills and on mountains and on landing grounds."[48] There is no mistaking what Buckley was suggesting with this invocation of Churchill's famous wartime oratory. If "radical solutions" were pursued in response to "the Negro Problem," "Americans" would be prepared to fight a war of resistance.

There are several things to unpack here. First, just what qualified, in Buckley's mind, as a "radical solution"? Based on what he had said earlier in the speech, he might have had in mind the overthrow of "the constitutional system," the "rule of law," "individual rights," "Judeo-Christian civilization," and "our entire Hellenic background." It turns out, though, that this characterization of Baldwin's aims was more deeply rooted in

Buckley's imagination than anything Baldwin actually said or wrote. One wonders if it might in fact be more accurate to say that Buckley believed the more modest solutions being pursued—for instance, the desegregation of schools and enfranchisement of African Americans—were sufficiently radical to merit suppression by force. After all, in both early 1956 *and* late 1964, Buckley had written columns in which he refused to condemn Faulkner's threat of violence in defense of southern racial intransigence. Was white southern resistance a model of "fight[ing] the issue" in order to preserve "the faith of our fathers"?[49]

This brings us to another crucial question: Just what did Buckley mean by "the faith of our fathers"? Again, it is tempting to turn to the list of things he claimed to see as threatened by the radical Baldwin. The story, though, is quite a bit more complicated than that. In addition to all the problems with Buckley's interpretation of Baldwin discussed above, Buckley's own commitments to the items on that list were—at least in the context of civil rights—suspect. For more than a decade, he had insisted that racial questions could not be answered by "merely consulting a catalogue of rights of American citizens, born Equal."[50] The systematic deprivation of the rights of African Americans does not appear to have been enough to activate Buckley's "libertarian" streak, but what about his devotion to "our constitutional system"? Here again, the record is ambiguous. It is true that Buckley may have had some constitutional ground to stand on when he raised concerns about federal overreach, but it is also true that by 1965, he had still not completely given up on the idea that the Civil War and Reconstruction amendments—abolishing slavery, and guaranteeing due process, equal protection, and the right to vote—were "inorganic accretions" of lesser legitimacy than the rest of the Constitution.[51] And finally, what about Buckley's commitment to the "rule of law"? Even on this matter, the record is somewhat murky. His recently published editorial on Mississippi was a case in point. In the piece, he acknowledged that the rule of law did not really exist for blacks in the state, but he refused to accept the idea that much of anything could be done about it. Although he offered pragmatic and constitutional reasons in support of his reluctance, this can hardly be counted as a stirring defense of the rule of law.

All the above points us to the conclusion that Buckley was not *really* worried about the overthrow of the Judeo-Christian civilization, constitutional system, individual rights, or rule of law. What he was worried about was reimagining these things in a way that would threaten the arrangements of power that he preferred.[52] He was not against adaptation to fit new circumstances per se; he was worried about any changes that might empower those he considered to be unworthy.

Two points about the international and historical contexts are also worth keeping in mind as we reflect on Buckley's pledge to fight Baldwin to the death, if need be. First, although it is not explicit, Buckley's anti-Communism seems evident here. He delivered his words in a Cold War context and—along with most of his *National Review* colleagues— worried about Communist infiltration of the civil rights movement. Communism would be one radical solution that Buckley believed we ought to be willing to fight to the death. "Better to be dead than red," he and other anti-Communists were fond of saying. Second, Buckley's invocation of Churchill's call to fight the Nazis must have been startling to the students, many of whom had grown up with stories of relatives and family friends who fought and died in the Second World War. Although Buckley intended for his words to inspire the sort of patriotic spirit that animated the generation that preceded that of the students, a moment's reflection must have caused the spirit to dissipate that night in Cambridge. What was most surprising about Buckley's comparison was that he had cast figures like Baldwin and Rustin in the roles of, say, Joseph Goebbels and Hermann Göring. Just three months after an election in which Buckley would chafe repeatedly over comparisons of his candidate to the Nazis, here he was warning that the civil rights movement might prove to be the Trojan horse of fascism in the United States.[53] Farfetched though this claim may be, it is not altogether surprising that Buckley made it. Nearly a decade and a half later, he was still the Manichaean who wrote *God and Man at Yale*, in which Dewey appeared cheek by jowl with Hitler in Buckley's list of enemies that ought to be "deflated" by Yale professors. Baldwin was, as far Buckley was concerned, every bit as dangerous as these men.

As Buckley imagined it, the radical confrontation that might happen would be between "the United States" or "the Americans" and "the Negro people." In this framing, "the Negro people" are not counted as real Americans. This way of thinking was nothing new for Buckley. It was suggested in the very title of his infamous "Why *the South* Must Prevail" piece nearly a decade earlier.[54] In his formulation, black people were not actually part *of* "the South"; they were merely a problem that existed *in* the South. By framing matters in this way, Buckley was demonstrating the truth of what Baldwin considered to be his most damning indictment: "the country which is your birthplace, and to which you owe your life and identity," he had told the students earlier that night, "has not in its whole system of reality evolved any place for you."

Before Buckley sat down, he offered a final thought that he hoped might serve as moral redemption for his threat of a race war. If forced to fight such a war, he said, "we will be convinced that just as you won the war against a particular threat to civilization, you were nevertheless waging a war in favor and for the benefit of Germans, your own enemies"— as Buckley said these words, he had his back to Baldwin and jabbed his right hand in the air repeatedly to add emphasis to his words—"just as we are convinced that if it should ever come to that kind of a confrontation, our own determination to win the struggle will be a determination to wage a war not only for whites," Buckley paused and looked down before he delivered the final four words of his speech, "but also for Negroes."

With this, Buckley turned, retrieved his clipboard, and went to his seat next to Burford while the students applauded politely for almost half a minute. As Buckley leaned back in his seat and crossed his legs, he shot a glance across the aisle at Baldwin, who was not clapping. Baldwin's eyes were directed at Fullerton in the president's chair and then he looked toward Buckley. Their eyes met for the briefest of moments before Baldwin looked away as quickly as he could.

By the time Buckley sat down, the debate had been going on for about ninety minutes. Heycock and Burford had each spoken for exactly fifteen minutes, Baldwin had spoken for twenty-four minutes, and Buckley had

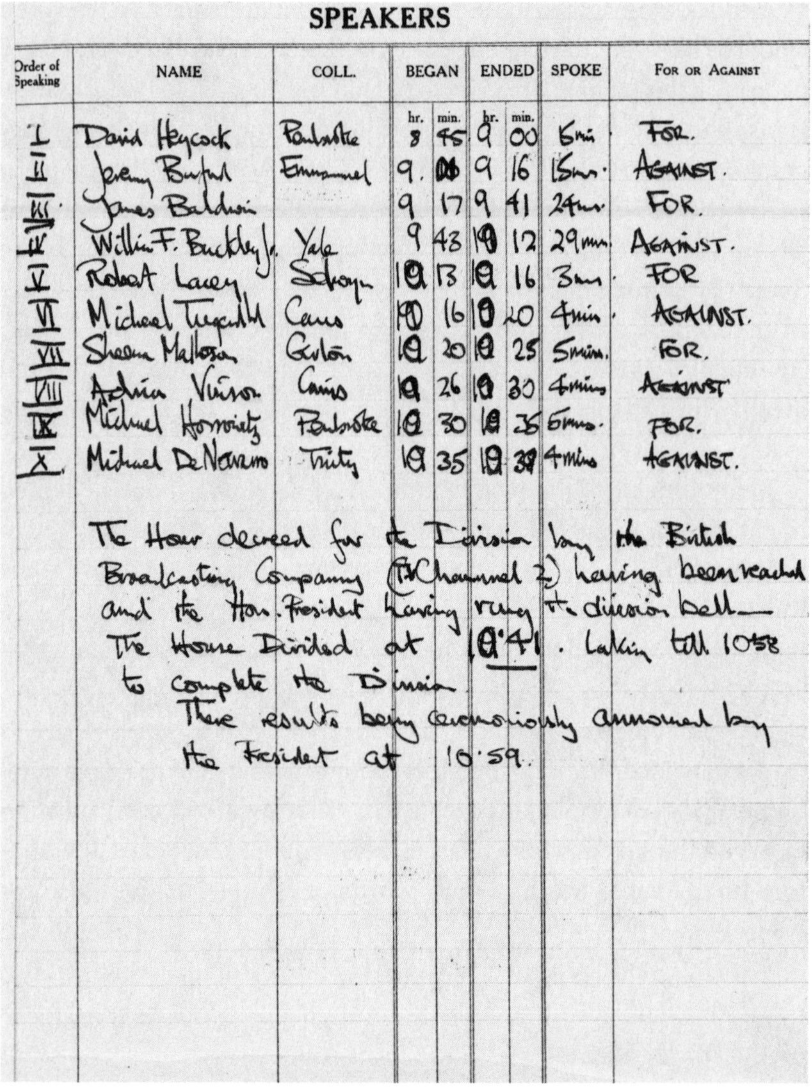

SPEAKERS

Order of Speaking	NAME	COLL.	BEGAN hr.	min.	ENDED hr.	min.	SPOKE	FOR OR AGAINST
I	David Heycock	Pembroke	8	45	9	00	6min	FOR.
II	Jeremy Buford	Emmanuel	9	00	9	16	15min.	AGAINST.
III	James Baldwin		9	17	9	41	24min	FOR.
IV	William F. Buckley Jr.	Yale	9	43	10	12	29min.	AGAINST.
V	Robert Lacey	Selwyn	10	13	10	16	3min.	FOR
VI	Michael Tugendhat	Cauis	10	16	10	20	4min.	AGAINST.
VII	Sheena Mallison	Girton	10	20	10	25	5min.	FOR.
VIII	Adrian Vinson	Caius	10	26	10	30	4mins	AGAINST
IX	Michael Horrowitz	Pembroke	10	30	10	35	5mins.	FOR.
X	Michael DeNavarro	Trinity	10	35	10	39	4mins	AGAINST.

The Hour decreed for the Division by the British Broadcasting Company (BBChannel 2) having been reached and the Hon. President having rung the division bell — The House Divided at 10·41. Taking till 10·58 to complete the Division

These results being ceremoniously announced by the President at 10·59.

FIGURE 7.1. Official Cambridge Union paperwork listing speakers and length of speeches (Cambridge University)

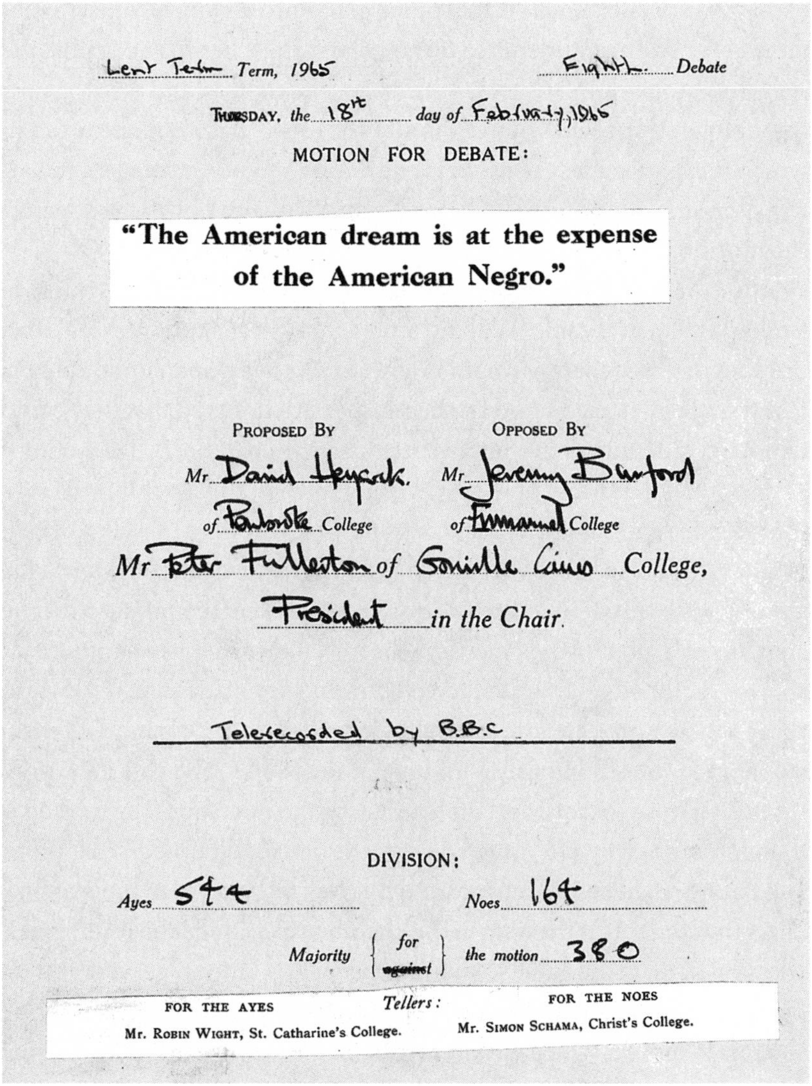

Lent Term Term, 1965 — Eighth Debate

THURSDAY, the 18th day of February, 1965

MOTION FOR DEBATE:

"The American dream is at the expense of the American Negro."

PROPOSED BY — Mr David Heycock of Pembroke College

OPPOSED BY — Mr Jeremy Burford of Emmanuel College

Mr Peter Fullerton of Gonville Caius College,

President in the Chair.

Telerecorded by B.B.C

DIVISION:

Ayes 544 — Noes 164

Majority for ~~against~~ the motion 380

Tellers:

FOR THE AYES — Mr. Robin Wight, St. Catharine's College.

FOR THE NOES — Mr. Simon Schama, Christ's College.

FIGURE 7.2. Official Cambridge Union results for the Baldwin-Buckley debate (Cambridge University) spoken for twenty-nine. At this point in the proceedings, Fullerton invited several other students to deliver short speeches for or against the motion. A total of six students—three for the motion and three against it—delivered speeches of five minutes or less.[55] Based on the order in which these speeches are listed in the Union records, it appears Fullerton alternated back and forth between students speaking for and against the motion.[56]

After the last of the student speeches from the floor, Fullerton rose from his chair and said, "Will the tellers take their places please?" This directed the two tellers—Robin Wight (for the ayes) and Simon Schama (for the noes)—to go stand by their respective doors so that they could count the students as they exited the debating chamber.[57] Their choice of door would indicate how they wished to vote; those wishing to vote for the side represented by Heycock and Baldwin were to walk through Wight's door, and those wishing to vote for Burford and Buckley's side were to walk through Schama's door. It took seventeen minutes for the students to file out of the chamber. The line, it turned out, was quite a bit shorter for those who wanted to vote for Buckley's side than the line for those who wanted to vote for Baldwin's side. At 10:59 p.m., Fullerton stood up to "ceremoniously announce" the results: "The vote in favor of the motion 544 persons and the vote against 164 persons. The motion is therefore carried by 380 votes. I declare the house adjourned."[58] Heycock and Baldwin had bested Burford and Buckley by better than three to one.

As the students remaining in the chamber applauded the result, Baldwin smiled up at the gallery where his sister and entourage were seated, before he stood up with Heycock to bask in the glow of victory. Buckley shot up to his feet with a Cheshire grin on his face. Sure, he had lost the battle with Baldwin, but he knew the loss could prove quite useful in the ideological war he would fight until the day he died.

Chapter 8

Lighting the Fuse

As students and guests filed out of the debating hall, Buckley and Baldwin found themselves surrounded by reporters eager to get their reactions. Buckley lit a large cigar as he fielded questions while Baldwin started in on the first of several cigarettes.[1] Baldwin told a reporter from the *Guardian* that he and Buckley "didn't have enough in common to debate at all." David Broad, the reporter for the university paper, *Varsity*, asked each man if he enjoyed the debate. "I wouldn't say I enjoyed the debate," Baldwin responded, "but I was glad to be here." "No," Buckley said, "I didn't enjoy debating the racial issue. It's so emotionally overloaded. My preference is to write about the problem."[2] With these words, Buckley began what would end up being a decades-long project to vindicate his performance that night. He lost so badly, he was suggesting, not because Baldwin had superior arguments but rather because he had succeeded in manipulating the emotions of students. A reporter from the *New York Times* was also on hand to report on Baldwin's "English Ovation." That reporter had done her best to transcribe what Baldwin and Buckley had said, and that attempt would soon become a subject of controversy in its own right.[3]

After fielding a few questions, Buckley made a hasty exit so that he could return to London to get a few hours of sleep before traveling back to Zurich to rejoin his injured wife. Baldwin and his entourage stuck around Cambridge for drinks with several students and professors.[4] None of the witnesses I interviewed remembers anything about what interactions—if any—Buckley and Baldwin had after the debate. If they spoke or shook hands, the interaction was likely brief and unremarkable.

The morning after the debate, Baldwin was back in London with his sister to continue with the hectic itinerary arranged by Kolins, including a visit to the BBC to sit for an interview. By Saturday, he would have received word of the latest trouble in Marion, Alabama, where civil rights protesters had been assaulted by police and Jimmie Lee Jackson lay mortally wounded. On Sunday, Baldwin and Davis had a rare opportunity to take a break so they decided to treat themselves to a "really fancy, friendly dinner" at their hotel. Years later, Baldwin described what happened as they enjoyed their dinner:

> There we were, at the table, all dressed up, and we'd ordered everything, and we were having a very nice time with each other. The headwaiter came, and said there was a phone call for me, and Gloria rose to take it. She was very strange when she came back. . . . Well, I've got to tell you because the press is on its way over here. They've just killed Malcolm X.[5]

When the reporters caught up with Baldwin, he was livid. Although he had butted heads with Malcolm over the years, and they still differed on some fundamental issues, he believed Malcolm had played an important role and was evolving in significant ways. Baldwin, like so many others, sensed that Malcolm's departure from the NOI—which had occurred the previous year—might unleash his potential as a leader. In just a few days, he was scheduled to sit down with Malcolm, King, and Kenneth Clark to discuss the next phase of their common struggle.[6] Baldwin wondered what Malcolm might become now that he was liberated from the NOI and overbearing presence of Muhammad. The bullets that killed Malcolm would prevent Baldwin—and everyone else—from ever finding out.

"You did it!" Baldwin shouted at the white reporters who surrounded him at the London Hilton. "It is because of you—the men who created white supremacy—that this man is dead! You are not guilty, but you did it!"[7] This statement was met with ridicule and backlash because it was being reported that Malcolm had been killed by black men who were associated with the NOI.[8] "The British press," Baldwin explained later, "said that I accused innocent people of this murder." This, he said, was based on a misunderstanding of his accusation. "Whatever hand pulled the trigger," he explained, "did not buy the bullet. That bullet was forged in the crucible of the West, that death was dictated by the most successful conspiracy in the history of the world, and its name is white supremacy."[9]

At a press conference the next day and during a visit to the Oxford Union the day after, Baldwin kept his anger at bay as he reflected on the significance of Malcolm's role in the civil rights revolution. At the press conference, he spoke slowly and just barely succeeded in holding back tears:

> In the northern streets . . . Malcolm was a kind of hero. . . . He was the only person who was describing, making vivid, making a catalog of the actual situation of the American Negro. That is to say when he talked about the situation in which we all find ourselves—the actual situation of being a Negro father, son, or daughter, a Negro woman—nobody could contest it; it was all true. That was a very important function and now he's gone. . . . It's a very sinister event, that's all I can say.[10]

Baldwin's explanation of the assassination of Malcolm was not, in fact, very different from his reaction to the assassination of Evers. In the Evers case, he was less interested in the hand that pulled the trigger—that is, the hand of Beckwith—than he was in the circumstances out of which the assassin emerged. Here too, Baldwin's focus was on the context in which Malcolm was killed, and what "moral assumptions" dominated the atmosphere in which he lived and died.[11] What made it likely, Baldwin was always asking, for organizations like the NOI or Citizens' Council to arise in the first place? How did the "circumstances" and "conditions" in which Malcolm forged his identity, Baldwin asked the students at Oxford, "make him into the man he had become?"[12] Baldwin was far less interested in the actual innocence or guilt of particular people for crimes such as these than he was in the ways in which our collective "innocence" made such crimes possible.

The day after the Oxford speech, Kolins sent Baldwin a note bidding him farewell and thanking him for his "sustained effort during these last few days." "You have really been an incredible success," he wrote, "and have made a very deep impression on us all." Kolins noted that he was especially pleased to see Baldwin receive yet another standing ovation when he spoke at Oxford and wished him luck in Stockholm, where Baldwin would be traveling next to attend the opening of *Blues for Mister Charlie* in the city.[13]

On February 26, Lantz wrote to Baldwin with some exciting news. Representatives from *Playboy* had seen the *New York Times* story about the debate and were interested in reprinting his speech on "The Negro and the American Dream." The last time Baldwin had published in *Playboy*—December 1964—the magazine had paid him $4,000 for his efforts, and Lantz was confident he could get even more this time around because there was competition for the piece. Representatives from McGraw-Hill Publishing had also seen the article about the debate and wondered if "there would be a book in it."[14]

While Baldwin and his representatives were contemplating what to do next with his Cambridge speech, Buckley was busy coming up with his explanation of what happened that night. On February 27, the space of his syndicated newspaper column was devoted to an essay called "The Negro and the American Dream." Buckley's thesis in the piece was that although he lost the *vote* by "about 3 to 1," he did not lose the *debate*. For one thing, it was not really a debate. It was, rather, an elaborate setup for an evening of "the kind of boozy anti-Americanism that so many urban Britishers find so stimulating."[15] Baldwin, he claimed—falsely—"received enormous ovations both at the beginning and at the end of his talk."[16] Baldwin delivered his speech, he told his readers, in "English accents," by which he meant that he had refrained from using the time allotted to him to "call for the destruction of that civilization which, he promised us in his evangelistic essay, would be given over to the fire next time." Buckley noted that the crowd booed and hissed when he made the

"English accents" accusation, and a few minutes later he reached a sudden revelation: "The gentlemen in the audience were quite literally unaware that Mr. Baldwin's indictment of our society is total, that he does not acknowledge that the American dream is defensible, let alone exalted."[17] The Cambridge students in the Union that night, he explained, were totally ignorant of Baldwin's works and treated him with such unalloyed enthusiasm because he was black. This, Buckley declared, was something he refused to do because he "respected him enough to take his arguments seriously, and to fight back with him as I would against a man whose skin was white."[18]

Buckley lost the vote that night, in sum, because his audience was biased, ignorant, and eager to placate Baldwin "simply, as a Negro." If the Cambridge students had retained possession of their "rational faculties," Buckley argued, they would have seen that the facts presented by his side made "shreds of Mr. Baldwin's proposition." Even if it was true that the success of *some* Americans was the result of racial exploitation, it did not follow "that the pursuit of the American dream *depends* on the subordination of the Negro." Buckley acknowledged that "American injustice to Negroes may be the blackest of our sins," but he refused to accept that racial exploitation was inextricably bound up with the American dream itself.[19]

Buckley also offered some reflections on what he thought was another underlying cause of what happened at Cambridge: anti-Americanism. The resolution was framed the way it was, Buckley asserted, so that the students would have the opportunity to go beyond merely condemning American failures in the area of civil rights. It was a resolution that allowed them to "censure America" root and branch. Baldwin was merely an "eloquent" weapon brought into the chamber that night to arm the "young Anglo-Saxon aristocrats" with reasons to bash their "big powerful" cousins across the pond.[20]

This perceived anti-Americanism really miffed Buckley. After all, he explained, the British had "relative good fortune" when it came to "racial problems" because they were able to simply run down "the Union Jack" and turn "over the seals of office to the dissenters." The United States had no such luck. We "cannot simply turn over the dissident minority to

James Baldwin or to Adam Clayton Powell," he said. We are stuck with them. This line of argument echoed the southern traditionalists— Davidson, Harrigan, and Weaver especially—who said time and again that they were simply "tough-minded pragmat[ists]" doing their best to grapple with a problem they would rather not have.[21]

Buckley concluded the piece with a sentence that was meant to simultaneously jab Baldwin and his British hosts:

> It is only important for Americans to pursue the demands of their own conscience, and smile courteously, if a little absent-mindedly, at the inflamed interventions of our cousins who chatter their preoccupations over our moral deficiencies while returning vast areas of the world to the conditions from which American Negroes were rescued years ago, at the very beginning of their American ordeal.[22]

Buckley's choice of the word "rescued" put a rhetorical exclamation point on a piece that made it entirely clear how he would deal with his overwhelming defeat at the hands of Baldwin. For some, defeat can be humbling; for Buckley, it was infuriating.

As soon as the ink was dry on his Cambridge piece, Buckley began circulating it to those who had written to him about the debate.[23] One of his most notable correspondents in this period was Michael Tugendhat, the Cambridge student who was responsible for his participation in the debate in the first place. Buckley sent Tugendhat a thank you letter and enclosed a copy of "The Negro and the American Dream." A few days later, Tugendhat wrote back to Buckley to thank him and offer "a short piece I wrote for my own amusement after reading your article."[24] In the official Union paperwork for the debate, Tugendhat is listed as one of the speakers who delivered brief comments in support of Buckley's side after the "paper speakers" (Heycock, Burford, Baldwin, and Buckley) had delivered their remarks. Their correspondence after the debate, though, indicates that Tugendhat may have had a change of heart. Although Tugendhat's "short piece" on the debate is lost to history, Buckley kept a copy of his detailed rebuttal.[25] Without Tugendhat's original piece, it is difficult to make sense of every argument in Buckley's eight-point rebuttal letter (which runs almost two, single-spaced, typewritten pages), but some are worth noting. First, it appears Tugendhat challenged Buckley's characterization of the motivations animating the students who voted for Baldwin's side (e.g., racial bias in favor of blacks and anti-Americanism). In response, Buckley contended that some of the Cambridge students simply did not know what they were doing (since they had not read Baldwin's writings), and others voted the way they did "to express solidarity with the Negroes" or because they were "seduced by the Neo-Marxist resolution." Second, Buckley complained that Tugendhat and the other students were underplaying the importance of the phrase "*at the expense of*" at the heart of the resolution. Buckley claimed that these four words were crucial to his decision to accept the invitation to participate. Had the resolution been framed as "Resolved, That the American Negro, though he has contributed to the realization of the American dream, has not been permitted to participate in it," Buckley wrote, "I would not have consented to participate in [the debate]." Third, it appears that Tugendhat objected to the final line of Buckley's editorial, in which he said "American Negroes were rescued" from Africa when they were enslaved. Tugendhat thought this line was a bit too "slick." "Slick or not, pal," Buckley wrote in response, "it is a perfectly fair observation, logically, morally, and historically. One does not have to approve the means by which something was done in order to observe that the thing was in fact done and that the results are desirable." To bolster his case, Buckley confessed that he had moral qualms about the "atom bombing of Japan" and "saturation bombing of Germany," but he thought "bombs, atomic or otherwise, rescued the Japs and the Germans from Tojo and Hitler."[26]

Baldwin attempted to put the finishing touches on his short story collection *Going to Meet the Man* while traveling around Europe to various openings of *Blues for Mister Charlie* and *The Amen Corner*. He followed the news from Alabama closely and knew that before long the call of duty would bring him back to the United States. Selma had become the focal point of the struggle to secure a federal voting rights bill—the most urgent goal for civil rights leaders who hoped for a law that would finally deliver on the Fifteenth Amendment's promise that the right to vote would "not be denied or abridged . . . on account of race, color, or previous condition of servitude." The reality in the American South was far from the ideal spelled out in this almost one-hundred-year-old text. Southern states had successfully excluded most African Americans from voting for decades, and there was desperate need for section 2 of the act— "The Congress shall have power to enforce this article by appropriate legislation"—to be mobilized to make the right to vote meaningful.

The murder of Jackson heightened the sense that Selma would be the site of the next dramatic clash in the black freedom struggle. As the white power structure—from Governor Wallace down to the lowliest member of the Citizens' Council—dug in, a coalition of civil rights groups led by the SCLC and SNCC plotted a challenge. The time had come, as Reverend James Bevel put it, to "go see the King!" By this he meant that it was time to confront Wallace—who had become the face of intransigent white supremacy—by delivering Jackson's casket to the door of the state capitol building in Montgomery, but this idea was rejected in favor a fifty-four-mile march from Selma to Montgomery.

In the early afternoon on March 7, 1965, a group of about six hundred activists—led by John Lewis of SNCC and Hosea Williams of the SCLC—began their march from Selma to Montgomery. In order to get to Montgomery from Selma, it was necessary to cross the Edmund Pettus Bridge over the Alabama River. As the marchers crossed the bridge, they were confronted by a wall of hundreds of law enforcement officers, who were armed to the teeth with guns, tear gas, clubs, bull whips, and rubber tubing wrapped in barbed wire.[27] Also on hand was the news media, and this time, there would be plenty of cameras rolling to capture the horror of what happened next.

The commanding officer of the troopers ordered the marchers to turn around and told them they had two minutes to do so. As the leaders of the march discussed what to do next, the troopers moved in unison toward them. Lewis and Williams did not flinch until the troopers were on them, at which point they were pushed back toward Selma by the force of the charging officers. That is when the screaming began. As most of the marchers attempted to run away, police on foot and horseback swung their clubs, whips, and barbed wire relentlessly and indiscriminately. Soon thereafter tear gas was fired into the crowd. As the fog of the gas lifted, several injured marchers could be seen writhing in pain on the ground. Dozens were injured, and many had to be hospitalized. March 7, 1965, would forever be known as "Bloody Sunday."

Bloody Sunday proved to be a day when many Americans—whether they liked it or not—were confronted with the country's ongoing racial tensions. Readers of the Sunday *New York Times* opened up the magazine section to see a large image of Baldwin and Buckley speaking at the Cambridge Union under the headline "The American Dream and the American Negro." Under a brief introduction, the *Times* provided what was purported to be a "transcript, slightly condensed, of the Baldwin-Buckley arguments" that occurred just over two weeks earlier.[28]

The number of eyes that saw the *Times* transcript of the Baldwin-Buckley debate, though, was miniscule when compared to the forty-eight million Americans who were watching the television premiere of *Judgment at Nuremberg*, the Academy-Award-winning film about the prosecution of Nazi war criminals, that night and had their viewing interrupted by fifteen minutes of gruesome footage from Selma.[29] It must have been striking to many of these viewers to see the images of people being beaten down on the Edmund Pettus Bridge while watching a film about human beings who, in the words of one character, had deluded "themselves into the commission of crimes and atrocities so vast and heinous as to stagger the imagination."[30]

The same day Jackson was mortally wounded in Alabama, Buckley published a syndicated column on "The Issue at Selma." In the piece, he reiterated many of the arguments he had made for over a decade. The key issue at Selma, he insisted, was not whether blacks ought to have the vote but rather how the vote might be further restricted in order to empower more responsible political leaders.[31] Jackson, like Schwerner, Goodman, and Chaney, would die, as far as Buckley was concerned, in an unworthy cause.

Buckley made the decision to rerun "The Issue at Selma" in the edition of *National Review* that would hit newsstands two days after Bloody Sunday. As fate would have it, the date on the cover of that issue of *National Review*—March 9, 1965—would mark yet another murder in Selma in the name of white supremacy. James Reeb, a young Unitarian minister from Boston, had traveled to Selma just a day earlier in response to King's call for support in the city. As Reeb and a few fellow ministers walked to dinner, they were attacked by a group of men who had saw them as "outside agitators." The thugs shouted, "Hey you niggers!" and "Here's what it feels like to be a nigger down here!" as they assaulted the ministers. One of the men struck Reeb with a bat, mortally wounding the father of four.[32]

For most writers, the coincidence of the publication of "The Issue at Selma" with the murder of two civil rights activists would constitute an incredibly embarrassing one-two punch of bad timing. But this was not true for Buckley. In fact, he probably took a considerable amount of pride in the fact that his piece ran in the shadow of the horrors in Alabama. Such things would not happen, we can imagine him saying, if southerners were governed by reasonable conservatives like Kilpatrick, and if blacks were led by men more prudent than King and Baldwin. The bloodshed in Selma, he would say, proved his point. Just days earlier he had devoted his syndicated column to thoughts on "How to Help the Negro," in which he highlighted Kilpatrick's work to "set up an organization whose ambition it is to take out insurance against the burning of any Negro church." What was ingenious about this idea (which was Buckley's own), he wrote, was that it showed one need not be an "immoral madman" to support segregation. In fact, it demonstrated to the world a distinction Buckley had been insisting on for as long as he had been writing about race: there are disreputable "primitives" whose support for segregation is rooted in racial animus, and there are respectable conservatives who are "opposed to coercive integration" as a matter of principle, and it was the duty of this latter group to "instruct their deranged supporters in the most basic rules of the game."[33] The connections between Buckley's arguments in "How to Help the Negro" and "The Issue at Selma" are not difficult to see. In order to empower responsible conservatives like Kilpatrick in the South and disempower racist demagogues like Wallace, Buckley contended that what was needed was not an expansion of the franchise but rather greater restriction of it. The best hope for improvement of race relations, Buckley thought, was less democracy, not more. So long as the sorts of men who were willing to firebomb churches were allowed to vote, they would support leaders like Wallace who were ill equipped to deal with the agitation of activists like King. What was needed to defeat King—and that *was* Buckley's objective—*National Review* concluded in an unsigned editorial on "The Selma Campaign," were leaders of greater "intelligence and flexibility."[34]

Baldwin greeted the news from Selma very differently. One can imagine his head being filled with a mix of disgust and wonder that such things could be happening, as he said at Cambridge, "not one hundred years ago, but in 1965, in a country" that claimed to lead the "free world." Baldwin was exhausted, and seemed to be longing to find refuge in his fictional writing and dramatic productions of his work, but he would not allow himself that escape, at least not yet.

As Baldwin traveled around Europe in the weeks after the debate, he kept in touch with various contacts in the movement as they plotted the next phase in the struggle. In early February, King had received assurances from President Johnson that a voting rights bill would be coming "very soon."[35] In the aftermath of the Jackson murder and Bloody Sunday, King was getting impatient. He returned to Selma in order to mobilize another march. While King huddled with local leaders, other SCLC officials, and activists from SNCC, he simultaneously pursued a federal court action to protect the marchers and negotiated with representatives from the White House. SNCC leaders were urging King to push the administration harder, and the administration was pleading with him to slow things down. On Tuesday, March 9, federal judge Frank Johnson issued a ruling prohibiting another Selma to Montgomery march until Thursday, March 11. King knew this delay would not sit well with the SNCC activists so he and the administration brokered what one historian has aptly called "an awkward compromise." King would lead a march that day, but when the marchers reached the barricade of law enforcement on the Edmund Pettus Bridge, they would kneel and pray before turning around and marching back to Selma.[36]

Just hours after this compromise march, Reverend Reeb was murdered and Johnson stepped up efforts to reach out to Governor Wallace through intermediaries. These negotiations led to a contentious, three-hour Oval Office meeting between the two men, during which the six-foot-four Johnson stood over the five-foot-seven Wallace and asked him if he would rather be remembered with a marble monument erected that read "George Wallace, He Built," or a "little piece of scrawny pine board" that read "George Wallace, He Hated." After the meeting, Johnson concluded that Wallace was a "very treacherous" and "no-good son of a bitch" who could not be trusted to provide protection for the marchers when they were finally permitted to start their trek on March 21.[37]

Two days after his meeting with Wallace, Johnson delivered an address on voting rights to a joint session of Congress. "I speak tonight," he began, "for the dignity of man and the destiny of democracy." After laying out the reasons why the issue of voting rights was such an urgent one, Johnson appropriated the protest rhetoric of the movement when he said, "Because it's not just Negroes, but really it's all of us, who must overcome the crippling injustice of bigotry. And we shall overcome."[38]

Neither Baldwin nor Buckley was particularly impressed by President Johnson's speech. Baldwin's distrust of politicians ran deep, and he was especially skeptical when he heard Johnson use the phrase "we shall overcome." While others saw this as a promising convergence of protest and elite rhetoric, Baldwin worried that speechifying and superficial policy changes might lull progressives into a false sense of victory and security. "What is crucial," he told the journalist Nat Hentoff, "is that none of these slogans—'War on Poverty,' 'The Great Society'—mean anything unless there are basic changes in the redistribution of wealth and power. The vote by itself does not mean anything if you don't know how you are going to eat and if you don't know how you're going to get a job in an age of cybernation."[39]

Buckley had different reasons to be skeptical of the push for voting rights. Baldwin's point, of course, was *not* that the voting rights bill was unnecessary. His point was that it was insufficient to meet the task at hand. Buckley, on the other hand, was convinced that the push for voting rights was not just unnecessary but harmful too. "What are the Negroes in Alabama being asked to believe will happen," Buckley queried in a column published after Johnson's speech, "once they have the vote?" Do they really believe that the vote would provide them with "peace and plenty on earth"? He then recycled a line he had used in his debate with Baldwin: "Will they, having been taught to despise George Wallace, learn, like their enfranchised Northern cousins, to adore Adam Clayton Powell Jr.?"[40]

While Buckley was expressing skepticism about the objectives of the "Selma campaign," he was also orchestrating a double-barreled attack on the voting rights bill. Much like his response to Baldwin's "Letter from a Region in My Mind," Buckley invited one of his trusted contributors—in this case, Kilpatrick—to write a long piece on the bill, and while Kilpatrick's piece was being edited at *National Review*, Buckley would devote his syndicated column to a shorter version of the argument. Buckley's piece was called "Constitutional Chaos," and he gave Kilpatrick's cover story the title "Must We Repeal the Constitution to Give the Negro the Vote?"[41] The pieces differ in style and some details, but they reach the same conclusion: the voting rights bill is unconstitutional and should be replaced by an alternative piece of legislation. Buckley and Kilpatrick's proposal anticipated what would become a central strategy in the conservative program to hollow out the achievements of the civil rights movement. Law, Buckley and Kilpatrick now insisted, must be colorblind. The federal government, they had now decided, had a constitutional duty to intervene if a state denied the right to vote on the basis of race. If, however, the state prescribed and enforced racially neutral voter qualification laws that *just so happened* to exclude a disproportionate number of racial minorities, that would be perfectly fine. This approach would accomplish two goals that Buckley and Kilpatrick had long sought. First, it would prevent the yielding of "political control" to "a mass of relatively uneducated Negro voters, easily led, [and] unequipped for public administration." Second, it would disenfranchise many of the "deranged" and "immoral" southerners who supported demagogues like Wallace and Barnett. "Doubtless it is futile to stand in the way of this jihad," Kilpatrick confessed, but he and Buckley were playing the long game.[42]

In the midst of this back and forth over the voting rights bill, the *New York Times* transcript of the Baldwin-Buckley debate was fast becoming a controversy in its own right. When Baldwin's agent, Lantz, opened his *Times* on the morning of Sunday, March 7 and saw it featured in the magazine, he was not pleased. He wrote to Baldwin to say he wished he would have "retained control of it because—a) your text, when printed, should always be edited from the spoken word, and no outsider should have permission to cut and edit it—and, b) when anybody prints anything of yours, you should be paid for it."[43]

A few days later, Buckley returned from Europe and was contacted by Baldwin's lawyers about the *New York Times* transcript. Baldwin had apparently gotten in touch with Lantz to let him know he did not consent to the transcription and publication, and with this information, his representatives reached out to Buckley, whose first reaction to the controversy was to reach out to Harvey Shapiro at the *Times* to complain. "I did not give permission to have my remarks transcribed, let alone published," asserted Buckley, "and would not have given permission if it had been sought, for the reason that what I said was wholly extemporaneous, calculated, or if you prefer, miscalculated, to fit the rhetorical and logical urgencies of the moment."[44] Buckley said he was "dumbfounded" by the *Times*' behavior, and informed Shapiro that he and Baldwin had found something about which they agreed: the newspaper screwed up.

A few days after the debate, the reporter representing the *Times* sent the transcription to the offices in New York. On receipt, it did occur to Lewis Bergman in the New York office to contact Heather Bradley of the *Times* Sunday department in London to see if permission might be needed. Bradley wrote a one-sentence reply: "It's perfectly okay to reprint [the] Cambridge Union debate since there's no question of copyright."[45] Baldwin's representatives disagreed, and called the *Times* "to complain that [they] had intended to sell the thing elsewhere" and the March 7 publication undermined those plans.[46] Then Buckley's letter to Shapiro arrived to add to Bergman's worries. His first thought was to cut Baldwin and Buckley checks as if they had coauthored a piece for the Sunday magazine. The going rate in those days was $400 for a solo-authored piece so it seemed reasonable to him that Buckley and Baldwin should get $200 each.[47] But before he mailed the checks, it occurred to him that he ought to confer with the *Times* legal department. He wrote to *Times* in-house general attorney James C. Goodale to explain the situation and ask, "What's our position? What should we tell them?"[48]

A few days later, Thomas R. McMullin of the *Times* legal department circulated a memo regarding "Copyright Protection Available to Messrs. Baldwin and Buckley in Speech Delivered before the Cambridge Union Society and Subsequently Printed in the Times Magazine." The four-and-a-half-page memo is dense and full of legal jargon, but the punch line was straightforward: "I was amazed to find," McMullin wrote, "that the law is now well established—that the delivery of a speech before the public does not constitute publication of that speech so as to deprive the speaker of a copyrightable interest in his work." In other words, "I conclude that Messrs. Buckley and Baldwin may have a substantial claim against the *Times* under the common law of copyright for the publication in the *Times* of their debate."[49]

General counsel Goodale, though, thought the *Times* might have an out. "Public speeches," he argued, are more easily covered by copyright than "extemporaneous remarks," and Buckley had admitted that his remarks fell into the latter category. Goodale suggested to Bergman that he send Buckley a half-hearted apology letter on the letterhead of Sunday editor Daniel Schwarz—to make Buckley believe that "his complaint" had been given "consideration at the highest level"—and he made sure to discourage Bergman from including a check, which might imply guilt and make Buckley think the *Times* was trying "to buy him off."[50]

At some point over the next few weeks, "there was a mix-up in the Sunday Department" and Baldwin's agent was mailed a check for $200 from the *Times* for his client's contribution to the debate. The check was then forwarded to Theodore R. Kupferman, Baldwin's high-powered attorney (who would be elected to Congress in 1966). Kupferman was not impressed. Just as the *Times* lawyers had predicted, Kupferman acknowledged the payment as "evidence of your indebtedness" and said there was one major problem with the gesture. "In view of the fact that we were negotiating [with *Playboy*]," he told representatives of the *Times*, "for payment of $10,000.00 for a magazine reproduction of the talk, your check is just $9,800.00 too little." Kupferman returned the check and told the *Times* to lawyer up.[51]

Goodale was beginning to get a bit nervous so he reached out to the company's general counsel, Louis M. Loeb, at the firm of Lord, Day & Lord. He explained the situation to Loeb, who wrote to Kupferman immediately. Loeb rejected the claim that the check represented an admission of wrongdoing, reported that the $10,000 request was "completely out of question," and said the *Times* was well within its rights to publish the "full texts of statements or documents which it believes to be newsworthy."[52] Far from being "harmed" by the publication of the transcript, Loeb claimed that Baldwin benefited by "having his considered views on the subject made available to the readers of the *New York Times*."[53]

In the end, neither Baldwin nor Buckley decided to pursue legal action against the *Times*. Buckley was satisfied with an assurance from the editors that they would never do it again, and wrote to Kupferman and the *Times* to inform them that he had "no interest under the circumstances of pressing for any financial recovery," and wished to "disengage . . . from [Baldwin's] pending action."[54] Kupferman let Buckley's mention of a "pending action" hang over the *Times*' head for a couple of months before finally informing its attorneys that Baldwin had "no desire to sue the *Times*," but that it seemed reasonable for the paper to pay Baldwin "the *highest* figure that the *Times Magazine* has paid for contributions."[55] In response, the *Times* offered to double its initial offer, from $200 to $400, for Baldwin's contribution, and Kupferman accepted on his behalf.

A week later, Schwarz wrote to Buckley to inform him of the agreement reached with Baldwin and tell him it seemed "only fair" that he should be paid the same amount "even though you were gracious enough to withdraw your claim." Schwarz could not resist concluding his letter to Buckley with a zinger at Baldwin's expense: "If Mr. Baldwin has to pay half of his fee to his lawyer, this will be only further proof that virtue is rewarded."[56] By that time, Buckley was in the thick of a third-party bid for the mayoralty of New York City, but he found time to write a clever two-sentence response to Schwarz: "How very good of you. If I win by $400 worth of votes, I promise to give credit to the *New York Times* in putting me over the top!"[57]

<hr />

After the dust settled in the back and forth between King, Governor Wallace, President Johnson, and the federal courts, the march from Selma to Montgomery was scheduled to begin on Sunday, March 21, and culminate in a rally at the state capitol building on Wednesday, March 25. In order to ensure that the event could happen without interrupting "public order," an agreement was reached that only three hundred marchers would participate along the highway, but that thousands would be permitted to take part in Montgomery.

Baldwin traveled to Alabama (along with thousands of others) to participate in the conclusion of the march and the rally in Montgomery. He was joined by other artists including Belafonte, Leonard Bernstein, Sammy Davis Jr., Nina Simone, Odetta, Tony Bennett, Dick Gregory, Mike Nichols, and Nipsey Russell.

The atmosphere was joyous and triumphant as the crowd applauded the speeches and sang freedom songs. When it was King's turn to speak, he said, "Our feet are tired, but our souls are rested. They told us we wouldn't get here. We are here before the forces of the State of Alabama and telling them that we aren't going to let anyone turn us back."[58]

FIGURE 8.1. Baldwin at the Montgomery rally at conclusion of Selma march, 1965.
Bayard Rustin, A. Philip Randolph, and John Lewis can be seen applauding Baldwin.
(Archive Photos / Getty Images)

A few hours after President Kennedy delivered the address that many identified as a significant shift in elite attitudes toward civil rights, an assassin gunned down Evers. Just two weeks after the momentous March on Washington, six young black people were killed by whites in Birmingham. Hours after the poet of the civil rights revolution triumphed over one of that revolution's greatest critics at the oldest debating society in the world, Jimmie Lee Jackson was murdered by a state trooper in Marion. Two days after peaceful marchers endured Bloody Sunday to remind the world of the work still to be done, Reverend James Reeb was bludgeoned to death in the streets of Selma. And so in the wake of the elation that must have followed the Montgomery rally, veterans of the civil rights struggle must have been worried. They had good reason to be. After the rally, Viola Liuzzo, a thirty-nine-year-old mother of five who had traveled south from Detroit to aid the marchers, was gunned down by members of the Ku Klux Klan.[59]

About two weeks after the murder of Liuzzo, Buckley found himself standing in the Hilton's Grand Ballroom in front of almost six thousand officers of the New York Police Department (about a quarter of the total force). The occasion was the annual police communion breakfast of the Holy Name Society, a Catholic community organization. Late in 1964, Buckley received an invitation from Father Joseph A. Dunne, the monsignor of Saint Stephen's Church and the spiritual director of the society, to address the group.[60] Dunne was a subscriber and financial supporter of *National Review*, and it is clear from his correspondence that he was tickled to have one of his political heroes speak to "our men." Two days after the *Times* transcript was published, Dunne wrote to Buckley to tell him ticket sales were going well and assure him, "The vote here is opposite that of Cambridge!"[61]

Buckley's speech to the Holy Name Society, which was attended by New York City mayor Robert Wagner and many other important city officials, would set off a political firestorm, but before we consider what he said, it is important to pause for a moment to reflect on the context in which he said it. At the start of his speech, Buckley took note of "the general atmosphere of hostility towards the police force." The proximate cause of this hostility was obvious enough. Over the course of the last few weeks, millions of Americans had been deeply disturbed by images of southern police officers brutalizing adults and children in the streets of the South. But it is also critical to remember that Buckley stood before the Holy Name Society less than a year after the Harlem riots of 1964. The shooting of a fifteen-year-old black teenager by an off-duty white police officer sparked the riots themselves, but the powder keg of discontent had been decades in the making. The relationship between the residents of Harlem and law enforcement had long been strained, with frequent accusations of brutality and unfair treatment. Since the 1930s, members of the community had been calling for a "Civilian Review Board" that would allow citizens to have their complaints about law enforcement officers heard by oversight panels that included members of the community in addition to members of the police department.[62] The demands for these safeguards were intensified in the months prior to the riots due to the enactment of a new "stop-and-search" law that enhanced police authority to search people in public spaces as well as a new "no-knock search warrant" bill that provided police with greater power to conduct searches.[63] "There was a great hue and cry against [these laws] in Harlem," NAACP spokesman Basil Patterson said in the wake of the riots, but "they were passed under the aegis of the law enforcement officials."[64]

Against this backdrop, Buckley left no doubt whose side he was on. "Nobody is more sacrosanct these days," he declared at the Holy Name Society breakfast, "than the man who strikes the policeman," and "no man more guilty than the policeman who strikes a defensive blow; or that for that matter who enforces the law or who uses his ingenuity to apprehend his lawbreaker." To be convinced of these points, Buckley said, we need look no further than Bloody Sunday. The "most dramatic part" of what happened that day was not "the sight of the policemen swinging their sticks with considerable purpose on the bodies of the demonstrators" but rather the "twenty long minutes, 1,200 seconds, freighted with tension, when two camps stood facing each other, between the moment the sheriff told the demonstrators to return, which order the demonstrators refused by standing there in defiance of it, until the moment when the human cordite was touched—who threw the lighted match?" Given these circumstances, what was most remarkable was *not* the violence that ensued but instead the tremendous "restraint" shown by the officers over the course of those "twenty long minutes." When the officers did act, Buckley conceded, they acted "excessively," "but were ever the excesses criticized of those who *provoked* them beyond the endurance that we tend to think of as human?"[65]

The most obvious and glaring problem with Buckley's version of events is his claim that officers demonstrated "restraint" for "twenty long minutes." In fact, the amount of time that elapsed between the order to turn around and the attack was about two minutes.[66] This gross misstatement of a crucial fact is absurd to be sure, but it is not clear that it is essential to Buckley's argument. Two minutes or twenty minutes, Buckley was committed to the view that the law enforcement officers in Selma had acted—for a time—with superhuman restraint, and as to "who threw the lighted match," he made it clear he believed the officers were "provoked" by the marchers.

As if his quasi defense of Alabama law enforcement actions on Bloody Sunday was not provocative enough, Buckley then proceeded to offer a few unorthodox reflections on Liuzzo, the Detroit mother of five who had gone down to Alabama to volunteer in support of the Selma to Montgomery marchers only to be murdered by the Ku Klux Klan. Buckley conceded the propriety of mourning Liuzzo's death, but wondered why the press was making such a big deal about it. Liuzzo, Buckley explained, "drove down a stretch of lonely road in the dead of night, ignoring the protection that had been given her, sharing the front seat with a young Negro identified with the protesting movement; and got killed." What was "unusual" or "unexpected" about that? "Didn't the killing," he asked rhetorically, "merely confirm precisely what everyone has been saying about certain elements of the South? About the intensity of its feelings? . . . Who could have been surprised by this ghastly episode?"[67]

While Buckley's comments on Liuzzo proved to be shocking to many, they were not a departure from what he had been saying about racial violence for a decade. Since the mid-1950s, he had been arguing that the use of force against civil rights protesters was the natural consequence of attempts to "tamper with [the] organic growth" of "deeply rooted folkways and mores."[68] This is not to say that Buckley thought such violence was morally *acceptable*; he always made it clear that he did not. He did, though, insist time and again that such violence was *understandable*. As he put it in his essay on the Freedom Riders, civil rights protests are a challenge to the southern regime, and such challenges would be "met, inevitably, by a spastic response. By violence."[69] Indeed, in the midst of his reflections on Liuzzo in the Holy Name Society address, he recycled the analogies he had used in earlier writings by comparing the civil rights activists in Alabama to Ku Klux Klan activists visiting Harlem or American Nazis visiting Washington Square. These comparisons drew laughter and applause from the police officers in the audience, many of whom undoubtedly agreed with Buckley's central conclusion: "the demands of law and order" sometimes trump the "right to demonstrate."[70]

But there is another thing that is seldom noted in the many things written about Buckley's Holy Name Society speech. In the midst of his musings on Liuzzo, Buckley twice mentioned "the *unprovoked* killing of a
policeman in Hattiesburg, Mississippi" by a "young Negro" just two days
after the Liuzzo murder. Buckley found it jarring and disturbing that the
killing of the policeman "who stopped [a] car to ask a question" was not
deemed "outrageous" enough to "occupy greater space in the newspapers," and perhaps even inspire federal officials to offer condolences or
appear at the funeral. We are, Buckley claimed, "unconcerned" with "dead
policemen."[71] Buckley's comparison of the Liuzzo case with the shooting of Constable Fredrick "Cotton" Humphrey is quite revealing, though
not quite in the way he anticipated. What Buckley largely ignored in the
Holy Name Society address were the background conditions of racial
subordination in which the deaths of Liuzzo and Humphrey took place.
While it is true that Buckley acknowledged that Liuzzo found herself in
Alabama due to "conditions of injustice to Negroes and a general lawless
disregard for their rights and honor," the thrust of his argument was the
same as it had been for years: "the South" ought to be left alone to sort
out its own racial problems. What was left unsaid here is of vital importance. "The South" he thought should decide these questions was
still, nearly a decade after he published "Why the South Must Prevail,"
a South of white elites who he hoped would lead the region toward a more
humane future. The agency of African Americans in deciding what this
future ought to look like was, for Buckley, of little significance.

What Buckley left unsaid about the Humphrey case is also telling.
While he thought it was worth explaining to the thousands of law enforcement officers gathered at the Holy Name Society breakfast that the
assailant in the case was a "young Negro," he did not deem it necessary
to identify the racial identity of Humphrey. Neither he nor anyone in the
audience had any doubt that the officer was white. The fact that this need
not be said exposes the assumption of racial hierarchy that dominated
the minds of those assembled in that room. Furthermore, Buckley's description of the Humphrey killing as the "unprovoked" murder of "a
policeman who stopped the car to ask a question" was rooted not only
in a questionable comprehension of the facts of the case—this was far

from a routine traffic stop—but more important, it demonstrates his failure to appreciate what the case uncovers about the workings of white supremacy.

Constable Humphrey was among the officers in Hattiesburg who had, in the words of historian Patricia Michelle Boyett, "earned reputations for 'shaking down' black club owners and beating blacks for sport." Cloudies Shinall, the shooter in this case, had been the victim of a police beating less than a year before his encounter with Humphrey. On the night in question, witnesses reported that both men were inebriated when Shinall drove a car into a ditch and refused to comply with Humphrey's command to exit his vehicle. Here is how Boyett describes what happened next: "The constable approached the driver's side, shined his flashlight into the window, aimed his gun at Shinall, and ordered, 'Get out you nigger, I ought to kill you.' Shinall grabbed his pistol, aimed it at the officer, and shot him in the throat."[72] None of this excuses Shinall—morally or legally—from killing Humphrey, but Buckley's description of the shooting sheds further light on the key concept in his Holy Name Society speech: provocation. The Selma to Montgomery marchers, he left no doubt, "provoked" the police officers who attacked them on the Edmund Pettus Bridge, and while he stopped short of saying Liuzzo provoked her killers, Buckley made it clear that he did not think she ought to have been surprised that her actions led "unrestrained members" of southern society "to resort to violence."[73] But a white police officer, who had earned a reputation for plunder and brutality against black people, points his gun at a black man and says, "Get out you nigger, I ought to kill you," was the victim, in Buckley's mind, of a killing completely "unprovoked."[74]

"My friends," Buckley concluded, "we live in a world in which order and values are disintegrating"; a world in which "the wrath of the unruly falls with special focus on the symbols of authority, of continuity, of tradition." It was no surprise, in "an age infatuated with revolution and ideology," that law enforcement should be so "despised." The police officer's "lot," Buckley contended, was a "galling" one because they must stand "silently" while wave after wave of unfair criticism comes crashing over them. "You must know that you will be hated for doing your duty," Buckley told the officers, but he asked them to bear this abuse with pride. In doing their duty and bearing unjust abuse silently, they would be following in the footsteps of "the author of all values . . . during His own days on earth."[75] With these words, Buckley turned from the podium and was greeted with a standing ovation. Since this crowd was nearly eight times the size of the one at the Cambridge Union, he might have taken some satisfaction in just how much more rapturous his ovation was than the one Baldwin had received a few weeks earlier.

In the 1980s, Buckley told biographer John Judis that he decided to run for mayor of New York City within forty-five minutes of the ovation he received at the Holy Name Society breakfast.[76] As we shall see in a moment, the precise timeline of Buckley's decision making seems to have been more complicated, but his comment to Judis is telling. There was something about that moment that stood out in Buckley's mind as pivotal in his decision to run. This was not the first standing ovation Buckley had received so it would be too simple to conclude that he was inspired by the enthusiasm of the crowd, and he knew he stood no chance of winning the election so the allure of power does not explain it either. The significance of the Holy Name Society speech is instead to be found in its concluding paragraph, in which he called on the police officers to fulfill their "duty" even if it meant they would be "reviled" and "hated" for doing so. Since his Class Day oration at Yale, Buckley had tried to answer his own call to his classmates to fulfill their "responsibility" of "preserving the framework that supports the vaster bounties that make our country an oasis of freedom and prosperity."[77] In Buckley's worldview, law enforcement officers were doing their part to preserve this framework in the face of those "infatuated with revolution and ideology."[78] As they fulfilled this vital duty, Buckley saw intellectual and political elites around him showering scorn and disapproval on them. Someone in the chattering classes had to stand up to defend them against this barrage of criticism. As Buckley saw throngs of police officers cheering him enthusiastically on that April morning, he could not help but think, Why not me?

~~~

"The next day all hell broke loose." So begins Buckley's account of the aftermath of his address to the Holy Name Society. The *New York Herald Tribune* ran an article in which the reporter claimed to quote extensively from the speech (he did not do so very accurately), and perhaps more important, the *Tribune* and *New York Post* reported that the officers in the audience laughed and cheered when Buckley spoke of Liuzzo, and the "Hilton's Grand Ballroom rocked with applause" when he talked about the "restraint" demonstrated by the Selma officers.[79] The following evening, the *New York Times* ran a headline that read, "Buckley Praises Police of Selma; Hailed by 5,600 Police Here as He Cites 'Restraint.'"[80] On reading these stories, Mailer wrote to Buckley to tell him "you are finally going to displace me as the most hated man in American life."[81] Several civic leaders and celebrities—including New York Supreme Court justice Samuel Hofstadter, NAACP executive director Roy Wilkins, the entertainer Artie Shaw, and baseball great Jackie Robinson—denounced Buckley and called on Mayor Wagner to do the same.[82]

Buckley was incensed. Not only did he believe the press was distorting his argument, but he did not think their reporting of the audience reaction was accurate.[83] In a white heat, he filed suit against the *Tribune*, and pounded out this statement and sent it to the *Times*:

> I am shocked in turn at the ease with which a routine job of misrepresentation by the press of a public speech can cause distinguished public figures to believe the unbelievable, namely that at a Communion Breakfast sponsored by the Holy Name Society of the Catholic Church, bigotry was applauded. I did not on the occasion in question breathe a word of prejudice against any people. I spoke sympathetically about the plight of the Negroes in the South. I deplored the violence in the South and the attitude of lackadaisical white Southerners towards it. I did criticize the general tendency of some of the noisiest elements in our public life to

jump to false and contumacious conclusions about policemen. The trigger-willingness, shown today, to impute to the police sympathy with bigotry is exactly the kind of thing I had in mind.[84]

The *Times* published an edited version of Buckley's complaint, and the *Tribune*—after Buckley held a press conference in which he played an audio recording of the speech—issued a partial apology for the misquotations and qualified its claims about the audience reactions. The reporter stood by his claims, but had to admit that the applause at key moments could not be detected on the audio recording. The partial apology led Buckley to withdraw plans to sue the *Tribune*, but he then set out on a quest to get more apologies.

Perhaps the most interesting exchange in the aftermath of the Holy Name Society address was between Buckley and NAACP executive director Wilkins. The *Tribune* had reported that Wilkins had telegraphed Mayor Wagner in the aftermath of the speech demanding that he "rebuke" Buckley, "who condemned the peaceful demonstrators and praised the tear gas and club attacks on them by Selma police." Buckley thought that perhaps the misquotations and contested accounts of audience reaction may have given Wilkins a false sense of his argument, so he sent him the full text of the speech. On reading the full and accurate text, Buckley suggested he would be surprised "if there is a sentence in it with which you disagree."[85] Wilkins responded by saying that reading the full text led him to a greater "cause for alarm."[86] He complimented Buckley on his mastery of the English language and skill in communicating his ideas, but he found the substance of what Buckley had to say to be deeply troubling and, notably, not very conservative. Buckley's suggestion that the nonviolent protesters "provoked" the police in Selma did not serve the cause of "law and order" or "conservatism" but rather "repression and retrogression."[87]

The Buckley-Wilkins exchange reveals the considerable gap between Buckley's self-conception and the perception of others that he was a racist. In the days while he waited for the Wilkins reply, this issue was at the forefront of his mind so he decided to devote one of his syndicated columns to the question "Are You a Racist?" Rather than focusing on the aftermath of the Holy Name Society address, Buckley took an alternative approach. He began the piece by saying that he "recently heard a man denounced as a racist for having observed that the rate of illegitimacy in New York is fourteen times as high among the Negro population as among the white."[88] Who knows if Buckley *actually* heard a man denounced for making this observation, but he was ready with a reply: if that is racist, then Nathan Glazer, "a prominent liberal Jewish sociologist," and Daniel Patrick Moynihan, "an Irish Catholic," must be racists too since they make the same observation in their book *Beyond the Melting Pot*.[89] This, Buckley thought, was absurd. A Jewish person (especially a liberal one) simply making a descriptive claim about the world cannot be deemed a racist, right? Because the answer was so obviously no in Buckley's mind, he had to look elsewhere for an explanation of the misuse of the term "racist." The answer, he concluded, was that the word "racist" was being used "licentious[ly]" and "indiscriminately," and therefore its meaning was becoming "diluted." This was a problem, Buckley insisted, because it undermined our ability to distinguish between the Glazers of the world and the Hitlers. Buckley was not, of course, really concerned with protecting the reputations of liberal sociologists. He was also sure at the end of the piece to point out how this applied to conservatives: "If everyone who believes in states' rights is automatically set down as a racist, then the word will further dilute in meaning."[90]

Buckley's "Are You a Racist?" essay is a document that can deepen our understanding of the protean nature of right-wing racial politics in response to the civil rights revolution. In the face of the Voting Rights Act, Buckley began promoting the idea of color blindness in order to undermine the potential of the law to challenge racial hierarchy. As he sensed the battle changing from a focus on political rights to questions of social and economic equality, he started to adapt his rhetoric accordingly. He thought that conservatives would do well, now that the ground had shifted beneath their feet, to admit that injustice and discrimination had played *some* role in producing racial inequality, but it was absolutely vital to begin drawing on the work of social scientists like Glazer to argue that some of the blame for inequality should be aimed at oppressed groups themselves.[91]

While Buckley was reflecting on the meaning of racism in the aftermath of his Holy Name Society speech, Baldwin was back in New York preparing for the Broadway opening of his play *The Amen Corner* and attempting to get one of his works turned into a major motion picture. When Nat Hentoff visited Baldwin at his West End apartment during the second week in April, the journalist thought the writer "looked unusually rested and relaxed." The reason was not hard to find: Baldwin seemed focused on his "works in progress" and less "consumed" with his duties as a "Public Figure." Hentoff reported that Baldwin was "brimming with pleasure" as he spoke about his short stories, plays, novels, theatrical productions, and potential film adaptations of his work. He seemed, to Hentoff, like a man who had begun shifting the "balance" in his life back toward the "writer within." But Baldwin's dual aspirations had always been to be "an honest man *and* a good writer," so he could not forget about the sense of responsibility he felt to engage in public life. Part of being an "honest man" meant fulfilling his role in the vanguard of the civil rights revolution. "It's a fact of my life," he told Hentoff before smiling broadly and taking a puff on his cigarette. "I'm looking forward to middle age. I'll be 41 in August. I'm amazed I've lasted so long."[92]

Baldwin told Hentoff he had come to terms with the fact that he would "from time to time" have to enter the public arena, and an invitation to do just that came when David Susskind, one of the kings of television, reached out to see if Baldwin would appear on *Open End* with none other than Buckley. In all likelihood, Susskind and his associates were inspired to make this proposal by the publication of the *Times* transcript of the Cambridge debate and the fact that both men had recently made the headlines.[93] With the Holy Name Society address still making waves, Susskind suggested a theme of "The Abuses of Police Power" as well as some discussion of "crime in America, the voting rights bill, and the future of the civil rights bill."[94]

Susskind knew both Buckley and Baldwin. He had hosted Buckley on his show before and considered him to be one of the few entertaining conservatives in the country. Although he was a committed liberal, he appreciated Buckley's style and presence. The two were well enough acquainted that they had placed a wager on the outcome of the 1964 election (Buckley lost).[95] Buckley was sufficiently charmed with Susskind that when he launched his own television show in 1966, *Firing Line*, he hosted Susskind as one of his first guests.[96] Baldwin and Susskind ran in many of the same circles on New York's cultural scene, and had collaborated on a number of projects. They were usually allies, but occasionally butted heads when Baldwin criticized "white liberals."[97]

Buckley must have been thrilled to receive the invitation from Susskind. He was probably tantalized by the prospect of avenging his loss to Baldwin at Cambridge and to be given an opportunity to vindicate himself in the wake of the Holy Name Society controversy. Baldwin, on the other hand, had less reason to be eager to share the stage with Buckley. As noted above, his agent, Lantz, did not like the idea of Baldwin appearing with Buckley "because he gets under your skin," and Lantz worried that Baldwin would lose his "cool" since he was "never cool and amused about the world's problems, he was always aroused."[98] Given the format of *Open End*, Lantz had good reason to be concerned. Unlike the Cambridge debate, which was structured in a way that allowed Baldwin to avoid any direct back and forth with Buckley, *Open End* was just that: open-ended. The idea of the show was to get interesting people to sit with Susskind and talk, and talk and talk, until they had nothing left to talk about. Since the show was the last thing on at night, the guests could literally keep talking for hours (until 1967, when it was capped at two hours). With this format, Buckley would have plenty of opportunity to get under Baldwin's skin.

An additional concern was raised by one of Baldwin's lawyers, Tom Michaelis. Susskind proposed to discuss concrete issues such as police brutality, crime, and the voting rights bill. Baldwin was a versatile thinker, but he was no policy wonk. Michaelis worried that Baldwin might be set up to fail. Buckley's thrice-weekly newspaper column and editorial duties forced him to follow policy debates fairly closely, but Baldwin was a frenetic bohemian whose engagement with American politics was sporadic and uneven. The stage seemed to be set for Buckley to get his revenge.

Baldwin listened to the concerns of his associates, yet once again, he would not be deterred. He had mopped the floor with Kilpatrick in 1962, and triumphed over Buckley at Cambridge. What reason did he have to fear an appearance on *Open End*? When Baldwin accepted the invitation, though, Michaelis insisted on prepping him with facts and statistics that he thought might be relevant. As research assistant David Leeming watched Michaelis try to fill Baldwin's head with this sort of information, he could not help but worry that such an approach might backfire. Jimmy's style was Jimmy's style, he thought; there was no use trying to change it now.[99]

On the morning of Friday, May 28, Baldwin and Buckley arrived at the MGM Telestudios on the corner of Broadway and Forty-Second Street to sit down with Susskind to record an episode of *Open End*. The set of the show was deliberately minimalist. There was a coffee table with three chairs around it, and in the background were the sorts of things one associates with television production (stage lighting rigs, ladders, etc.). The minimalism of the set was meant to communicate something about the nature of the show: it was driven by the personalities sitting in the chairs and ideas they were there to espouse. This was going to be "Baldwin v. Buckley," as they would soon begin advertising it—no props needed, and no holds barred.

One of the great tragedies of television history is that many shows of this era were simply taped over for new episodes because the cost of preservation was so high.[100] This seems to be the case with the "Baldwin v. Buckley" episode of *Open End*. Many of the major museums and archives of moving images continue to search for a copy, but as I write, none has been discovered, and the producers of the show were not in the habit of keeping verbatim transcripts of episodes. Therefore, everything we know about the "Baldwin v. Buckley" episode of *Open End* is from a one-page

FIGURE 8.2. David Susskind on the set of the *Open End*, circa 1965 (Getty Images)

document of notes taken by someone on the set the day of the recording, press accounts, fan mail each man received after the episode aired in June, the memories of people who watched the show, and each man's own reflections on the experience.[101]

When Baldwin and Buckley arrived on the set, it is difficult to imagine that they had much to say to each other. At the conclusion of the Cambridge debate, Baldwin seemed to avert his eyes when Buckley looked his way, and Buckley must have wondered if Baldwin had read his "Negro and the American Dream" column. If there was any small talk, it seems likely the two men would have discussed the controversy over the *New York Times* transcript of the debate. As they settled into their chairs, they would have seen a coffee table full of plenty of caffeine and nicotine—staples of the *Open End* experience.

According to *New York Daily News* television critic Ben Gross, the conversation lasted two hours and featured a "torrid exchange of arguments" from "the two great debaters." The back and forth, Gross reported, was "heated" but "intellectual."[102] If Baldwin did try to cite the statistics and facts Michaelis provided, these attempts were not particularly memorable to those who saw the program. Instead, it seems that Baldwin's approach was to focus on the moral and psychological questions raised by the very existence of "police power." Baldwin argued that the proper role of the police was to protect "life," "limb," and "property," but law enforcement in places like Harlem failed to do that well, and in fact, often threatened the lives, limbs, and property of the people living there. Baldwin's explanation of *why* this was happening echoed many themes from his 1960 essay "Fifth Avenue, Uptown." In that piece, he argued that "the only way to police a ghetto is to be oppressive," and he returned to this theme on *Open End*, telling Buckley that "the role of the police in the life of Puerto Ricans and Negroes is oppressive," and that many officers are guilty of "persecution" on the basis of race.[103] Black and brown people, Baldwin explained, "are forced to live" in the ghetto, and the "cops" are charged with the task of keeping them there. The police officers were identified as "the enemy," Baldwin said, because they were was a symbol of one's oppression *and* a threat to one's safety and freedom.[104] Baldwin's conclusion was that the police role in the ghetto constituted a great "moral crime." In response to what ought to be done to combat this "moral crime," Baldwin called for a "more civilized police force" and argued in favor of "civilian review boards" to empower members of the community to hold the police accountable.[105]

In response to Baldwin's repeated claims that the New York Police Department was an oppressive force, Buckley, according to Gross, "demanded that his opponent provide documentation."[106] In addition, Buckley insisted that any incidents of brutality were the exception, not the rule. He told Baldwin that "90% of the police are responsible and proud public servants." When the conversation shifted to Buckley's recent Holy Name Society address, he repeated his claim that "the police in Selma were provoked."[107]

Based on the existing sources, it seems Buckley focused his attention on several matters other than the theme of the show: "Abuses of Police Power." From his perspective, such abuses were rare, and the power of the police, far from being excessive, was actually lacking in society. The major question in his mind was, Why is there so much policing to be done in the ghetto? From Buckley's point of view, there were three major reasons: one economic, one moral, and one political. Buckley did not deny that the economic situation in places like Harlem was bleak, and proposed to ameliorate it by suspending all "taxes for Negroes and Puerto Ricans."[108] On the question of morality, he asserted that the "Negro is ungrateful to all of the people who have worked on his behalf," and black Americans should appreciate that they are "better off than the Negro in Africa," and he expressed worry about "morale fatigue among the Negroes."[109] Leaders like Baldwin deserved plenty of the blame for the problems afflicting the black community because they tended to be "destructive instead of instructive." After making this point, Buckley asked Baldwin to contribute to a political solution by telling "Negroes in New York not to vote for anyone who will not emancipate them." In response to this request, Baldwin said, "I will do that."[110] I imagine that if Baldwin smiled at all during the two-hour meeting, it may have been when he uttered these words because he knew he and Buckley had such dramatically different views of emancipation.

There is also evidence to suggest that Baldwin and Buckley crossed swords over the issue of religion. Precisely how this topic was introduced into the conversation is lost to history, but it seems likely that Buckley confronted Baldwin about some of the passages that so offended him in *The Fire Next Time*. Baldwin repeated his claim that "one of the architects of Negro oppression is the Christian church," and Buckley questioned how someone could be "a good Christian and against Negroes." This response may have been inspired by something Buckley had written a few weeks earlier in "Are You a Racist?" In that piece, Buckley contended that a true Christian could not be a racist because Christianity requires a commitment to "the inherent equality of all men" before God.[111] Whatever the truth of this statement as a matter of doctrine, Baldwin retorted, Christians have frequently fallen short of living by this belief. "Black people who become Christians," he said in an argument that echoed something he had said to Kilpatrick, "become Christians *in spite* of the example of white Christians."[112]

Finally, it appears that Baldwin made several statements on *Open End* in order to try to explain his worldview. This may be due to the fact that Buckley accused him of being a Marxist during the proceedings.[113] Baldwin denied this claim and explained that his views are rooted in a belief that some people are born with "a terrible disadvantage," and that this disadvantage is often inextricably bound with the question of color. The "Negro in this country," he told Buckley and Susskind, "will pass [their] life in this country struggling to become free." This is an uphill battle, he noted, because the "system of reality" of many Americans depends on the denial of freedom to "the Negro." It is up to the American people, Baldwin said, to face up to their history before it "destroys us." "This society," he said toward the end of the show, "is in a terrible state of chaos [because] we don't look at it as it is. We are in great danger."[114]

About two weeks after the taping, the *Open End* episode aired on stations from coast to coast. Almost immediately, viewers began to send letters to Buckley and Baldwin. Buckley received a postcard from the prominent University of Chicago economist Milton Friedman, who wrote, "Your performance on OPEN END against Baldwin was *magnificent*. Congratulations." Friedman, ever the economic policy stickler, did have one complaint to make: "However your proposal to suspend taxes for Negroes and Puerto Ricans is indefensible." Friedman proceeded to provide a brief economics lesson on the problems with "racial tariffs."[115] A man from Long Beach, California, wrote to say he enjoyed the "fine joust with the emotional Mr. Baldwin, who thinks entirely with his thalamus. You were, as usual, clear, concise and supra-logical."[116] A woman from Brooklyn wrote to applaud Buckley's performance. "Mr. Baldwin," she wrote, "has concocted an elaborate fiction in his stories and essays and you have the good sense to see that behind his glittering fiction lies a dull intellect. It was laid bare on *Open End* and I hope the viewers saw what I saw."[117]

Baldwin's "fan mail" in response to the *Open End* episode was a mixed bag. A writer from San Francisco was pleased with Baldwin's performance on *Open End* and in the Cambridge debate, which many stations aired on back-to-back nights. The viewer, much like Lantz, was worried about the idea of Baldwin going on *Open End* with Buckley. "It caused me to tremble," she wrote, "because this incredible man has reduced many experienced people to tatters." She then proceeded to provide a description that many of Buckley's debate opponents would describe as all too accurate: "They fell into the trap of his rapid-fire innuendos; somehow, his tongue is like a long fine lash with innumerable little, very sharp, fish hooks on it, in which he slyly ensnares his opponent. They usually fall right into it." But Baldwin, she said, "did not. God bless you. . . . You were more than a match for him."[118]

Other letters Baldwin received were more critical in nature. One letter from New York begins, " 'I am not a Marxist.' These were your words to William Buckley on *Open End*." The writer then proceeded to explain in great detail why Baldwin should embrace Marxism as "the key to the solution to the Negro's plight."[119] Another critical writer thought Baldwin seemed off his game when he sparred with Buckley on *Open End*. His letter is worth quoting at length because he identified something Baldwin himself believed about the encounter:

> I just turned off the TV set after watching, and hearing, you and William F. Buckley on David Susskind's program. I was distressed by what I saw and heard, by Buckley's cool and vicious and deliberate (and subtle) misemphasis and slanting of the facts, by his insidious sophistry in lifting things out of context, and almost equally by your apparent inability to make your position clear, something you have done so movingly in writing. . . . [I]t seemed you were appalled at the sophistry that was being used against you, fascinated dumb by its smoothness, and, realizing you had to combat it with some noise, spoke whatever words would come to you.

In a postscript to this long letter, the author said that since writing it, he was able to watch Baldwin and Buckley square off at Cambridge, and Baldwin's performance "cancels what I've said."[120]

In order to understand why this last fan letter seems to have captured part of the truth, it is necessary to consider what Buckley and Baldwin themselves had to say about the *Open End* appearance. Just days after the show aired, Buckley devoted his syndicated newspaper column to the episode. It appears that his original title for the piece was "When, Oh When?," but it also appeared under the titles "Negroes Harmed by

Extreme Militancy," "America Haters—Threat to Negroes," and—in the version included in Baldwin's growing FBI file—"The Baldwin Syndrome." Buckley began the piece thus:

> James Baldwin, the author and playwright whose reputation is in part owing to his fine writing, in part to the implacability of his theme (Hate the System), said a couple of discouraging things on a television program in which I participated. To wit:
>
>> That as regards the Negro, "things couldn't be worse." And that Negroes who throw their garbage out on the streets are doing so—legitimately, he suggests—as a form of protest against their plight.[121]

This opening introduces two statements not mentioned in other accounts of the *Open End* episode, but there is reason to believe that Buckley's depiction—especially of the second statement—is more or less accurate.[122] As Baldwin would later describe it, "I said people who live in the ghetto don't own it, it's white people's property. *I* know who owns Harlem. He said, 'Do the landlords tippy-toe uptown and throw the garbage out the windows?' "[123] Buckley would find this "rhetorical joust-about" over garbage (as he would portray it decades later) to be an extremely useful weapon in his rhetorical arsenal, and it would cause Baldwin, as we will see later, to reach some important conclusions about Buckley.[124]

It would not be surprising if Baldwin did indeed tell Buckley and Susskind that "things couldn't be worse" for black people. During his *New York Times* interview with Hentoff just a few weeks earlier, Baldwin expressed great pessimism about the possibility that the high tide of liberalism in the country would actually change the lot of most people at the margins of society. To Buckley, this was absolutely flabbergasting and may have been what prompted him to say he thought black people were "ungrateful." As he put it in his "When, Oh When?" piece, "If the Negroes' lot is not improved by the kind of sympathy he receives and has received—sympathy registered in legislation, editorials, columns, books, sermons, catechisms, [and] welfare payments—then what are we to do?"[125]

And so we see revealed before our eyes one of the great chasms that would forever separate Baldwin and Buckley. As the liberal politics of concern marched forward, Baldwin could not help but support the march while Buckley, as we have seen, resisted it tooth and nail. As progress was made, though, Baldwin was forever dissatisfied because such steps did not alter the fundamental structure of American racial hierarchy. Yes, it was better, he thought, to have a Civil Rights Act, Voting Rights Act, President Johnson instead of President Goldwater, and so on, yet these things only did minor damage to the fortress of white supremacy. As Buckley lost his battles against the Civil Rights Act, Voting Rights Act, and election of Johnson, he threw up his hands and said, What more do you want? "When, oh when," to borrow the title of his column, will "we" have done enough for "the Negroes"?[126]

All this led Buckley to wonder what, specifically, Baldwin did want. He was not the first, nor the last, to want more detail from Baldwin on this front. In 1964, *Commentary* editor Norman Podhoretz had invited Baldwin to appear alongside Clark, Gunnar Myrdal, Sidney Hook, and Glazer at a symposium on Liberalism and the Negro in order to try to force him to go beyond moralism into the realm of public policy.[127] "I purposely got Jimmy to the seminar," Podhoretz told *Esquire* reporter Marvin Elkoff, "to get him off that personal kick and make him talk about solutions and programs. It didn't work."[128] Baldwin's unwillingness to commit himself to an ideology or political program led Buckley to conclude that he must be hiding something. Buckley's first theory, which he emphasized again and again in "The Call to Lynch the White God" as well as the Cambridge debate, was that Baldwin was a violent revolutionary intent on overthrowing the whole of Western civilization. This theory reared its ugly head again in "When, Oh When?" when Buckley accused Baldwin of "threatening us with The Fire Next Time" if we dared disagree with any of his "poetical locution[s]." But during the *Open End* appearance, Buckley decided to pursue an avenue of suspicion that was being explored by the FBI: perhaps Baldwin was a Communist or fellow traveler:

> On our program, Mr. Baldwin said that he was neither a socialist nor a Marxist. Let us take him at his word—but I wonder how, intellectually, he can reconcile these statements with his behavior. In his writing he

deplores the capitalist system, which he holds institutionally responsible for enslaving the Negro. In his political associations, he makes common cause with, for instance, the editors of the magazine *Dissent*, which explicitly identifies itself as an organ of socialist dissent.[129]

As Buckley points out, Baldwin declined to accept the labels of either Marxist or socialist. From the earliest days of what he called his "political life," in fact, Baldwin had been a political iconoclast. When he was young, you will recall, he did join the Young People's Socialist League, but soon became a "Trotskyite—so that I was in the interesting position (at the age of nineteen) of being an anti-Stalinist when America and Russia were allies." As Baldwin reflected on this period later, he wrote, "My life on the Left is of absolutely no interest. It did not last long. It was useful in that I learned that it may be impossible to indoctrinate me."[130] Early in his career, when he was asked in an author questionnaire to comment on "what things or people annoy you most," he said he was "distrustful of the doctrinaire, and terrified by those who are never troubled by doubt."[131] Baldwin's writings from "The Crusade of Indignation" to the night he met Buckley on *Open End* lend credence to this self-conception. Baldwin was many things; ideologue was not one of them.

But does the evidence Buckley garnered—that Baldwin blamed the Negro's ordeal on capitalism and the claim that he "associated" with socialists—lend support to the idea that Baldwin was some sort of doctrinaire leftist? Baldwin was certainly sympathetic to the view that the mythology of racial hierarchy proved to be quite useful to those pursuing economic exploitation, but one need not embrace Marxism to accept this insight. What bothered Baldwin most about Marxist explanations of racial exploitation was their simplicity. As he put in his critique of the Marxist Daniel Guérin in "The Crusade of Indignation":

A man whose vision of the world remains as elementary as Mr. Guérin's can scarcely be trusted to help us understand it. It is true enough, for example, as far as it goes, that slavery was established and then abolished for economic reasons; but slavery did not come into the world along with capitalism any more than race prejudice did; and it need scarcely be said, at this late date, that where capitalism has been abolished slavery and race prejudice yet remain.[132]

Buckley's accusation that Baldwin associated with the editors of *Dissent* is a bit odd and difficult to take seriously. Its oddness is rooted in the fact that Baldwin never seems to have published a piece in *Dissent*. It is difficult to take seriously because Buckley produced no explanation of what the editors of *Dissent* might have believed, and no evidence that Baldwin shared these unnamed beliefs.

After this bit of speculation about what Baldwin was *really* after, Buckley concluded his essay with a call to "the voices of moderation" within the civil rights movement to "dissociate themselves" and "turn their backs" on the likes of "Mr. James Baldwin and his coterie of America-haters." So long as they fail to do so, the American people will be skeptical of those advocating "equality for the Negroes" because they will wonder if the movement is committed to "maintaining the American system" or replacing it with some radical alternative. Buckley ended the piece in the strongest language he could muster:

> How long, one wonders, before the Baldwins will be ghettoized in the corners of fanaticism where they belong? The moment is long overdue for someone who speaks authentically for the Negroes to tell Mr. Baldwin that his morose nihilism is a greater threat by far to prospects for the Negroes in America than anything that George Wallace ever said or did.

Here Buckley provided the reader with the second meaning of the title of his essay: when, oh when, will Roy Wilkins and Thurgood Marshall condemn "the swollen irrationalities" of Baldwin?[133]

⁓

The days between the taping of *Open End* on May 28 and its airing during the second week in June proved to be eventful for Buckley. On May 13, liberal Republican congressman John V. Lindsay announced that he would be a candidate for mayor of New York City. Buckley was not a fan of Lindsay, who was among the most liberal Republicans in Congress and

had committed the mortal sin (as far as Buckley was concerned) of refusing to support Goldwater in the 1964 presidential election. But
Buckley's disdain for Lindsay cut deeper than ideology. Many biographers of Lindsay and Buckley have looked for the roots of this contempt
in a sense of "class betrayal"—Lindsay was a well-to-do Yale man who had
become a liberal—and there may be something to that. There was something else, though: Buckley was appalled by Lindsay's style. By "style,"
I do not have in mind how Lindsay looked; Buckley conceded he was
"tall," "handsome," and "glamor[ous]." The style that Buckley loathed
was rhetorical. "John Lindsay tends to sound," Buckley wrote in his
column on Lindsay's declaration of candidacy, "like a Commencement
Address," and not in a good way. Lindsay spoke in moralistic platitudes
that hovered far above the solid ground of what Buckley called "political realism." Lindsay, he thought, was driven by a sense of moral righteousness and a desire to be "the People's Aristocrat" rather than by a
genuine desire to tell truth about the city's problems and do something
about them.[134]

A little over a week after Lindsay's announcement and just days before the *Open End* encounter with Baldwin, Buckley published a column
called "Mayor, Anyone?" In it, he presented a "packaged program" for
anyone who desired to run for mayor of a large city. Before doing so, he
was sure to mention Lindsay, whose central campaign plank seemed to
be "the brilliance of his teeth." Buckley then proposed a ten-point program that included everything from the decriminalization of drugs and
gambling to the busting of unions and elimination of the minimum wage
for minors. He also made several proposals that are especially central to
the themes of this book, including a plank against school busing to achieve
racial balance, the "suspension of property and income taxes for all Negro
or Puerto Rican entrepreneurs who establish businesses in those areas
that have . . . been denominated as depressed areas," the creation of community "watchmen" to patrol the streets, the incarceration of juvenile
delinquents, and welfare reform that would require any welfare recipi-
ent not looking after children to "report for duty at 8:00 AM every morning for street cleaning and general prettification work. No workee, no
dolee."[135]

When Buckley and his *National Review* editorial staff met soon after to put together the next issue, they decided to reprint the column. Buckley's sister Priscilla, who was the magazine's managing editor, proposed a diagonal headline on the cover of the issue that read, "Buckley for Mayor."[136] This caught the eye of New York Conservative Party chair J. Daniel Mahoney, who called Meyer to see if Buckley might be pondering a run. Meyer and his wife, Elsie, gave Mahoney some hope for what would be a major boon for his relatively tiny party: "Frank couldn't put his finger on anything specific, but his wife Elsie, he reported, intuited a definite Buckley interest in running." Mahoney then checked with Conservative Party legal counsel Jim Leff to see if Buckley, who lived and voted in Stamford, Connecticut, would be eligible to run for the office. The short answer was yes. Buckley still had time to take up residence in New York to meet the legal qualification to run. With this information in hand, Mahoney got in touch with Buckley, with whom he had been acquainted for several years. Buckley acted surprised at the suggestion, but Mahoney hung up the phone confident that he would run. Sure enough, a few days later Buckley told Mahoney that he was in. Mahoney was thrilled. "Bill Buckley was, after all," he wrote later, "one of the biggest figures in American conservatism," and his "candidacy had simply dropped into the lap of the Conservative Party."[137]

On the evening before Buckley called Mahoney to inform him of his decision, he sat down to write a speech for an upcoming rally to "commemorate an anniversary of Public Action, Inc."—a right-wing activist organization—"and to honor its octogenarian founder, Mrs. Seth Milliken." The rally was to take place in New York City, and the crowd on hand was expected to be upward of three thousand people so Buckley began to think of what he was writing as a first crack at a "stump speech." Before a crowd that included Senator John Tower of Texas and many conservative benefactors, Buckley opened with a comedic jab at the press coverage of his Holy Name Society address: "I suppose I should point out for the benefit of the *Tribune* reporter, that Mrs. Milliken, whom we are here to honor, is *not* a member of the Selma police force." He then proceeded to expand on several of the proposals he had made in "Mayor, Anyone?" As Buckley provided the crowd his answer to the question,

"What is wrong with New York?" it would not be too much to say that his answer was, in short, that too many people think like Baldwin when they reflect on the city's problems:

> It is no answer to the problem of crime to assume that every criminal merely midwifes a social imperative. That every criminal has been visited by a social incubus that you and I are responsible for, which, having impregnated him, requires, by the laws of nature, the birth of a crime. James Baldwin told me the other day that he does not blame the residents of Harlem for throwing garbage out their windows, that that is their form of social protest. Would we, by the same token, be entitled to throw our garbage out the window when John Lindsay passes by?

In response to this line, the *Tribune* reported, the right-wing "audience screamed with delight." As the waves of laughter washed over him, Buckley prepared himself to make a serious point. The "spirit of the age," he continued, "asks us to diffuse the responsibility for human aberration out among the veins and capillaries of the whole society," but what about the "victims" of their transgressions? "James Baldwin—and his followers, and his mentors—are there, always there, to hold society up as the imprisonable entity: and we are asked to punish our institutions, rather than the transgressors against our institutions."[138] What New Yorkers needed, Buckley concluded, were leaders who might be brave enough to stand up to the likes of Baldwin.

Buckley's encounters with Baldwin may not have *led him* to run for mayor of New York City, but the stuff at the core of his disdain for Baldwin was one of the pillars of his candidacy. Buckley's run was not a serious one in electoral terms; he had no illusions about his chances of getting elected. It was, though, deadly serious in ideological terms. Buckley was determined to run in order to put the spotlight on several of his ideas, and his views on race were absolutely central to this quest. When Buckley thought about what was wrong with the American racial situation in 1965, Baldwin came to the forefront of his mind. In the week prior to his decision to run, the day of his decision to run, and the week after, he was attacking Baldwin (first on television, then at the Public Action, Inc. rally, and then in print). When the time came to officially announce his candidacy, on June 24, 1965, it should not be surprising, then, that he brought Baldwin's name with him to the podium of the Overseas Press Club in Manhattan:

> In New York, the principal enemies of the Negro people are those demagogues of their own race before whom our politicians grovel. . . . Those leaders of the Negro people who cherish resentments, who refuse to deplore misconduct among their own people, who feed on the demoralization of the Negro race, ought to be publicly and explicitly disavowed by the political leaders of the City. It is the ultimate act of condescension to suppose that merely because a man is a Negro, it is hardly surprising that he is a poor husband, or an absent father, or a delinquent child. Mr. James Baldwin has said that the Negroes in Harlem who throw garbage out on the streets do so as a form of social protest. It is a much higher form of social protest to denounce such reasoning and the men who make it.[139]

Baldwin, Buckley had told readers of his column just a few days earlier, was a demagogue who posed a greater threat to black people than segregationists like Wallace. It was the obligation of responsible political leaders to stand up and say so. In that hot, packed room at the Overseas Press Club, Buckley was announcing his intention to do just that.[140]

Buckley's mention of Baldwin was no mere side note in his declaration of candidacy. The speech—and subsequent campaign—was shot through with explicit and implicit references to racially charged issues in the city. Historian Timothy J. Sullivan was only being slightly hyperbolic when he claimed that "all . . . Buckley's policy proposals . . . involved the issue of race."[141] As Buckley explained the issues that cause many in New York City to "seethe with frustration," the three at the top of his list were at the heart of the city's racial tensions. The first issue was "crime," and Buckley expressed a desire to create "a much larger police force, enjoined to lust after the apprehension of criminals," and most pointedly for the racial politics of the moment, declared, "Under no circumstances must the police be encumbered by such political irons as civilian review boards" that might undermine "law and order."[142]

Buckley then proceeded to reflect on what he took to be the second major issue in the city: "the ill-feeling that exists between the races." It was in the midst of this discussion that he attacked Baldwin, but it is also worth mentioning that he conceded that "white people owe a debt to the Negro people against whom we have discriminated for generations." Like so many other moments in his career when he appeared to be stepping in a liberal direction on race, he quickly qualified his remarks in important ways. The "debt" that white people owe to "the Negro people," he explained, should be discharged in accordance with conservative principles. We need not look far to know what Buckley might have meant by this since just weeks prior he had written about "How to Help the Negro." The central theme of that column, you may recall, is that the historical debt that is owed to black people *ought* to be paid in various ways, but such payment must be *voluntary*, not coerced by the state.[143]

Buckley's third major topic was "turmoil in the City's schools." After making a few general comments about his philosophy of education, he declared his opposition to the "synthetic integration" of the schools—a fancy way of saying that he was against busing to promote racial balance in the city's schools. The centrality of this anti-busing plank in the Conservative Party platform was solidified a couple weeks later when Rosemary Gunning was selected to run on the citywide ticket for president of the city council. Gunning's claim to fame at that moment in her career was as the "guiding figure in Parents and Taxpayers," a leading anti-busing organization. Buckley offered his "enthusiastic concurrence" to the selection of Gunning as his running mate.[144]

Buckley's entry into the race made headlines across the city and beyond. A great deal of attention was paid to the mirth of the question-and-answer period with the press. When Buckley was asked if he *wanted* to be mayor, he responded, "I have never considered it." When he was asked, "conservatively speaking," how many votes he expected to receive, he replied, "Conservatively speaking, one" (that of his longtime secretary, Gertrude Vogt). What the laughter generated by these quips obscured was the serious mission on which Buckley had just embarked. He was about to launch a campaign that would, in some ways, provide a useful model to future political candidates. While there is little question that no one would ever replicate *how* Buckley ran for public office, the substance of *what* he ran on was instructive indeed: the best way to grow the conservative coalition, he demonstrated, was to find what was causing people to "seethe with frustration" and exploit the hell out of it.

Baldwin's disappointment in his performance on *Open End* must have been compounded when he read headlines about Buckley's run for mayor. Just a week before these headlines first started to appear, Baldwin had his chance to expose Buckley on national television and failed to do so. Or at least he thought he did. As Lantz had predicted, Buckley had gotten under his skin, and rather than losing his "cool" (as Lantz worried he might), he "tuned out."[145]

As Baldwin reflected on his second encounter with Buckley, he received a surprise invitation to put his thoughts on paper. On June 9, less than two weeks after the *Open End* taping and just a few days after rumors of Buckley's candidacy were front-page news, Baldwin got a short note from Ponchitta Pierce at *Ebony* magazine.[146] Pierce was putting together an issue on "the white problem in America" and hoped Baldwin might contribute. She asked for fifteen hundred words for $1,000 and apologized profusely for the deadline she proposed: just eleven days later. Baldwin accepted the gig and sat down to write "The White Man's Guilt."[147]

Although Buckley's name does not appear in the "The White Man's Guilt," the timing and arguments of the essay suggest that he was on Baldwin's mind as he wrote.[148] Baldwin had been invited to write about the "white problem in America," and his thesis was that the white problem was rooted in the "white man's guilt," which "remains, more deeply rooted, more securely lodged, than the oldest of trees." The trouble with the "white man's guilt," he explained, is that he must confront it in order to become a free and honorable human being, but his fear prevents him from doing so. People will go to great lengths to avoid this confrontation.

"And to have to deal with such people," Baldwin confessed, "can be un-utterably exhausting, for they, with a really dazzling ingenuity, a tireless agility, are perpetually defending themselves against charges which one, disagreeable mirror though one may be, has not, really, for the moment, made."[149]

Until white Americans are willing to confront the source of their guilt—the historical record that has produced the world in which we live—they will remain trapped in a web of delusions. In order to escape this trap, white people must develop the ability to listen—an ability, it is worth noting, that Baldwin thought was conspicuously absent in the capacious skill set of Buckley:[150]

> White man, hear me! History, as nearly no one seems to know, is not merely something to be read. And it does not refer merely, or principally, to the past. On the contrary, the great force of history comes from the fact that we carry it within us, are unconsciously controlled by it in many ways, and history is literally *present* in all that we do. It could scarcely be otherwise, since it is to history that we owe our frames of reference, our identities, and our aspirations.[151]

In this passage, Baldwin slid into the prophetic mode that he used so powerfully at Cambridge. His use of "hear me!" evokes Jeremiah—"O land land land, hear the word of the lord!"[152] In this case, Baldwin was calling on the white power structure to hear his call to confront history and take responsibility for it.

Baldwin recognized that the idea of accepting the "force of history" in one's own life was a terrifying one. It was to invite nothing short of an existential confrontation within one's soul. The "pain and terror" invited by such a project was, though, the price one had to pay in order to be free. Echoing a theme that he had been trumpeting for almost two decades of writing, Baldwin declared:

> In great pain and terror . . . one enters into battle with that historical creation, Oneself, and attempts to re-create oneself according to a principle more humane and more liberating: one begins the attempt to achieve a level of personal maturity and freedom which robs history of its tyrannical power, and also changes history.[153]

Here Baldwin put in philosophical terms a description of the battle Gabriel had been unwilling to wage in *Mountain* and David had refused to fight in *Giovanni*. It was also Baldwin's battle throughout his own life, as he sought to liberate himself from the bitterness of his father, and learn how to love and teach others to do the same.

Rather than wrestling with a false sense of self that ignores history, Baldwin argued, most white Americans live in a state of denial. Much like Buckley at Cambridge, those in denial plead with the "disagreeable mirror":

> Do not blame *me*, I was not there. I did not do it. My history has nothing to do with Europe or the slave trade. Anyway, it was *your* chiefs who sold *you* to *me*. . . . I was not present on the middle passage . . . or the cotton fields of Mississippi. . . . I *also* despise the governors of Southern states and the sheriffs of Southern counties.[154]

Through such pleading, white people hope to keep their moral distance from those who really did, they are now willing to admit, commit grave injustices against people of color. *They* are guilty, of course, but *we* weren't there, and *my* great-grandparents, as Buckley was sure to point out at Cambridge, worked hard, and their success was not dependent on "Negro travail."

Whatever the literal truth of such statements, Baldwin argued, there was something false about them. The fact that one was not actually "present on the middle passage" does not separate that person from the social, political, and economic legacies of the slave trade. The fact that one's great-grandparents worked hard and achieved success that does not seem connected to "Negro travail" does not place one outside the historical forces that created the conditions of inequality that shape the nature and scope of opportunity afforded to those living in the present. To pretend otherwise, Baldwin declared, was to evade responsibility.

Baldwin wondered about the sincerity of those who apologized for the sins of their forbearers. Sure, that's what they say to me, he thought, but what do they say "in the most private chamber" of their hearts? Baldwin suspected that many a confessor of the sins of his ancestors "remains proud of that history for which he does not wish to pay, and from which materially, he has profited so much."[155] Such a man, Baldwin guessed, must thank God, his lucky stars, and fate that history has played out the way it has.

Baldwin then considered a more "awful" possibility: the idea that beyond feeling fortunate or unfortunate that history has played out this way or that, an individual convinces oneself that they *deserve* what history has given them. It is here that Baldwin cut to the heart of his dispute with Buckley. During the encounter on *Open End*, Baldwin had said that one of "the problems with a place like Harlem is that the people who live there do not own it."[156] It was at this point that Buckley engaged him in the "rhetorical joust-about" over garbage in the streets of Harlem. "Do the landlords," Buckley asked Baldwin, "tippy-toe uptown and throw the garbage out the windows?" It was this line—the line that Buckley would cite time and again during his mayoral campaign—that led Baldwin to "tune out." Buckley was saying, Baldwin explained later, that "Negroes deserved their fate, they stink."[157]

Just what was it that Baldwin heard Buckley saying the people in the ghetto deserved? In "The White Man's Guilt," he answered this question. At the same moment a white man might be swelling with pride about the ways in which history had rewarded him, "the black American finds *himself* facing the terrible roster of his lost: The dead, black junkie; the defeated black father; the unutterably weary, black mother; the unutterably ruined, black girl."[158] Baldwin's added emphasis on "*himself*" in the original is telling. The "terrible roster" that this man confronts is not only about the legacies of "the middle passage" or the cotton fields of Mississippi; it is about the human beings he sees all around him. But the weight of history also bears down on this man's shoulders: this roster has been in the making for so long, it grows ever longer before his eyes, and seems destined to continue to grow forever.

The moment one begins to believe one "*deserve[s]*" this "terrible roster" of loss, Baldwin continued, the "seeds of destruction" are planted. This destruction claims the bodies of many marginalized people, and those who do not perish physically, he explained, often perish spiritually.[159] The collective impact of the destruction of a people's sense of self-worth is the death of morale—a concept that was forever on Baldwin's mind.

Baldwin also expressed concern—as he had so many times before—about the impact on the moral lives of those who were the apparent beneficiaries of historical injustice. "White people," he wrote, "fall into the yet more stunning and intricate trap of believing that they deserve *their* fate, and their comparative safety and that black people, therefore, need only do as white people have done to rise to where white people now are." Someone who adopts such a point of view—and this is certainly an apt description of Buckley—will not "dare to open" an honest "dialogue" about history. Such a dialogue would require a "personal confession" that such a man dreads giving. This confession would have to be a "cry for help and healing," and this is a cry few men have the courage to make, but until they do, they will be unable to accept the simple facts that a "man is a man, a woman is a woman, [and] a child is a child."[160]

Just a few days before "The White Man's Guilt" hit the newsstands, Buckley was in the thick of one of the many racially incendiary moments of his mayoral campaign. On Tuesday, July 27, he and the other candidates participated in a "round-robin style" interview conducted by the Committee of 100, a group of prominent African Americans in the city. Buckley denied that "the American conservative is animated by hostility to the legitimate aspirations of the Negro race" and conceded, in an awkward way, that African Americans "suffer disadvantages that the white man did not suffer": "The Jew with his crooked nose, the Italian with his accent, the Irishman with his drunkenness or whatever—they had a difficult time. But it was nothing like the great disadvantage you have suffered and which we white people need to face as a charge upon our conscience that we need to expatiate." Not surprisingly, Buckley's reliance on racial stereotypes to make this point did not go over well. The Anti-Defamation League and one of Buckley's business associates, Henry Elmark, got in touch to ask him to explain himself. Like in the case of the Holy Name Society address, Buckley blamed the incompetence and maliciousness of the reporters who covered the event. "I described," he explained to Elmark and the representative from the Anti-Defamation League, "three dominant prejudices against three major ethnic groups" and then explained "notwithstanding these prejudices, they rose swiftly in America." The main point of the remark, though, was to draw attention to the fact that the "prejudice against the Negro" was "far more obstinate" and therefore imposed a greater moral responsibility on society to counteract it.[161]

After the "crooked nose" argument, Buckley spelled out in greater detail what this moral responsibility entailed. His explanation reveals the remarkable consistency of his views from his earliest writings on race to the moment he confronted the Committee of 100:

> But here is where I would disappoint you because I take a different view of government from the view you do. It would be inconceivable for me as a conservative, who believes in the integrity and inviolability of the individual, to take any contrary position. . . . I maintain that if you put every politician in New York who appears before you groveling and unctuous and prepared to turn the entire apparatus of New York and put it at your disposal on a silver tray—you will not substantially augment the happiness, the security, [and] the sense of accomplishment of your own people.[162]

Like his arguments against desegregation, the Civil Rights Act, and the Voting Rights Act, Buckley maintained that the problems confronting the black community must be met not by government coercion but rather by the voluntary cooperation of well-meaning individuals. Yes, wrongs had been done, and yes, expiation was necessary, but it would be inconsistent with "the integrity and inviolability of the individual" to force anyone to participate. The violation of the integrity and inviolability of people of color by both state and nonstate actors was a deeply rooted American tradition, but it would be illegitimate, Buckley insisted, for the state to redress those wrongs in a heavy-handed way.

Those in the crowd who had been following the campaign closely mustn't have been surprised by what Buckley said next. By then, he had his stump speech on race down to a science. First, acknowledge that injustices had been done. Next, point out that government cannot—and should not—be relied on to rectify these injustices. Third, explain that the problems in the black community are primarily moral in nature. And finally, say something nasty about Baldwin:

> What is it a government is supposed to do, for instance—*you* tell *me*—to keep people from throwing garbage out of their windows in Harlem? I asked James Baldwin why some people do that, and he said, "Why that's a form of social protest." This is an answer that is inexplicable to me. Why should people throw garbage out the windows?—in order themselves to wallow in it.[163]

The following week, President Johnson signed the Voting Rights Act of 1965 into law. In addition to reiterating the Fifteenth Amendment's prohibition on exclusion from voting on the basis of race, the Voting Rights Act sought to undermine the institutions and practices that southern states had used to keep people from the polls (e.g., "literacy tests"). Furthermore, the act empowered the Justice Department to intervene when racial discrimination by state and local officials was suspected. The act, King declared in a letter to President Johnson, was nothing less than a "second and final Emancipation Proclamation."[164]

Like so many other landmark moments in the history of the civil rights movement, the celebratory mood was soon squelched by the outbreak of violence. Just five days after King looked on as President Johnson signed the Voting Rights Act into law, the city of Watts, California, was in a state of rebellion. The match that lit the fuse in this case was, like so many other urban uprisings, a clash between black residents and white police officers, but the powder keg was decades in the making. In addition to widespread complaints of police brutality and racial discrimination in employment, the neighborhoods of Los Angeles, like those of most American cities, were deeply segregated. Racially restrictive covenants had long kept people of color from renting or buying housing in many areas. By the 1940s, people of color were barred from living in most

Los Angeles neighborhoods, and the California Fair Housing Act of 1963 was enacted in order to break down some of these barriers to residential freedom. Although the scope of the law was quite narrow, the California Real Estate Association acted quickly to spearhead a referendum effort to repeal it. On November 3, 1964, President Johnson carried California over Goldwater by almost twenty points. On the same ballot, California voters passed Proposition 14, which overturned the Fair Housing Act, by an even wider margin.[165]

So when a white California Highway patrolman pulled over a black motorist named Marquette Frye in Watts on August 11, 1965, racial discontent had been brewing in the city for quite a long time. The scene of Frye's arrest became a flash point for this discontent. As the officers attempted to take Frye into custody, a crowd gathered and clashed with the police. After one of the officers assaulted a black woman whose outfit (a barber's smock) made many witnesses believe she was pregnant, "the crowd erupted by pelting the police with bricks, stones, and bottles."[166]

Over the next five days, Watts was in a state of turmoil. By the time it was over, thirty-four people (almost all black) were dead, more than one thousand were injured, and more than $200 million in property damage had been done. In the aftermath of the rebellion, Los Angeles chief of police William A. Parker said he believed the civil rights movement was partly to blame for the disaster. Black people, he complained, are constantly being told by their leaders, "You are dislocated, you are abused because of your color. Your progenitors were oppressed. You haven't been given the share of materialistic things you are entitled to." This sort of "political pandering," he explained, deepened black discontent, and once it was combined with the doctrine of "civil disobedience," which "erodes respect for all law," the stage was set for trouble. "Is the law unjust," he asked, "because I want a pair of shoes and they are in that store, and I haven't got the money to buy them so I can steal them? In fact, it was amazing to me in the inquiry we had in the council when the councilman said, 'Why were these people shot, they were only stealing?' "[167]

When Buckley sat down at his typewriter to reflect on the Watts uprising, his diagnosis was not all that different from the one offered by Chief Parker. His language, though, was far more strident. How could this be blamed on "interracial frictions"? After all, the "explosion occurred just at the moment a major civil rights bill was passed"—a victory that should have led to a sense of "satisfaction" at securing "an unconditional surrender" from "Southern whites." After rejecting that explanation, Buckley looked for other reasons why "they all, in the Watts district, or rather a substantial number of them, *became animals.*" Although Buckley admitted there was no "single basic cause of disruptions of civilization," the prime mover seemed to him to be the "destructive lawlessness" promoted by figures like King. "The best way to guarantee what happened at Los Angeles *shall* happen again," he concluded, "is to moon over the affair and yelp about injustices by whites to Negroes, the guilt of the white slave trader, and the rest of it."[168]

When a black resident of Watts was asked to describe why he thought many of his neighbors (thirty-five thousand by one estimate) were in a state of rebellion, he offered a different explanation from the ones given by Chief Parker and Buckley:

> I think it started four hundred years ago, and things kept building up, building up. . . . They're tired. They're hungry. They are more educated. They know what's going on in the world. They see millions and billions of dollars spent on rockets . . . that are sent overseas, and here in their own country, they are hungry. They are out of a job.[169]

During summer and fall 1965, Baldwin was globe-trotting—to Vienna, the Netherlands, Italy, Germany, and Israel—to support productions of *The Amen Corner.* When he was not on the road for the play, he was spending a lot of time in Turkey, where he devoted himself to artistic projects—fiction, theater, and film—and tried to resolve some long-standing issues in his personal life. Baldwin seemed to be seeking refuge from the fires that were burning in the United States. During the previous three years, he had driven himself to the point of exhaustion as he fulfilled his duties as a "Public Figure" and was ready, as he had indicated to Hentoff months before, to reestablish his private life as a writer. As he turned inward, Baldwin felt a strong sense of guilt about distancing himself from the movement, but his mental, physical, and spiritual health required it.[170]

Although Baldwin was doubtless asked by journalists to comment on the situation in Watts, he did not pen an essay on the rebellion in late 1965. About a year later, though, he would offer some reflections on the unrest in "all our Harlems" in "A Report from Occupied Territory" for the *Nation* magazine. Although there is no evidence to suggest that Baldwin read Buckley's reactions to Watts, his "Report" is a stinging rebuke of the sort of conservative response to urban upheaval that Buckley was offering. Places like Harlem and Watts, he argued, are best understood as "occupied territories" where the residents are confronted with police who are charged with the task of "keep[ing] the Negro in his place and protect[ing] white business interests." Under such circumstances, Baldwin explained, "any act of resistance" can and often is met with "the full weight of the occupying forces." With "No Knock" and "Stop and Frisk" laws in place, these forces were empowered to exert control in all public and private spaces. This is what it means to live in "occupied territory."[171]

Under such conditions, Baldwin had no patience for talk of "civilization," "morality," and "law and order." "Where is the civilization," he asked, "and where, indeed, is the morality which can afford to destroy so many?" The "pious calls to 'respect the law,'" he declared, when the "ghetto explodes" are nothing short of "obscene." "The law," he insisted, "is meant to be my servant and not my master, still less my torturer and my murderer. To respect the law, in the context in which the American Negro finds himself, is simply to surrender self-respect." To resist the law under such circumstances is nothing less than "an exhibition of the spirit of '76."[172]

On the eve of the New York mayoral election, Bobby Kennedy was on the stump campaigning for Democratic candidate Abraham Beame and could not resist having some fun at Buckley's expense. "Did you hear about Bill Buckley?" Kennedy asked a crowd "consisting chiefly of

FIGURE 8.3. Candidate Buckley surrounded by supporters on the eve of the 1965 New York City mayoral election (AP Photo / Marty Lederhandler)

teenagers and parochial school students." "If he gets in," Kennedy answered, "he'll make you go to school on Saturdays and he'll make the nuns hit you with a ruler. Let's hear some really loud boos for Bill Buckley!"[173]

The next day, most voters—87 percent of them to be exact—registered their boos for Buckley by supporting his opponents (Lindsay with 46 percent, and Beame with 41 percent), yet Buckley could not help but feel vindicated. "What *is* significant" about my campaign, he declared, "is the crystallization of a vote of responsible protest."[174] What was most telling about Buckley's campaign was not the size of this protest vote

(13 percent in a liberal city) but rather where these voters came from. The core of his support was not from "the WASPs of Manhattan"; it was from the "white ethnics" of the outer boroughs.[175] Buckley staffer Neil McCaffrey issued—in a private memorandum—what historian Jonathan B. Schoenwald aptly calls "one of the more lucid analyses" of the race when he wrote:

> The pattern unfolds. George Wallace polls primary totals last year that rival, *up North and among Dems only*, Barry [Goldwater's] total vote in the same areas. The Wallace votes weren't from Klansmen. They were from the same fed-up, disenfranchised, basically conservative Dems who had earlier switched to Ike and cheered for Joe [McCarthy]. I don't mean to make you nervous, but Bill got Wallace Democrat votes.[176]

Although Buckley must have bristled about being placed in the company of Wallace, he must also have smiled at the irony of this discovery. Few figures in the United States held more elitist views than Buckley, and in his one foray into electoral politics, he emerged as the populist protest candidate.[177] Once again, Buckley's loss in a particular battle would be the story that would get the headlines. In the midst of the fog of the battle that was occupying the attention of most observers, though, Buckley marched toward victory in his ongoing war to move the country to the right.[178]

The Fire Is upon Us

In the decades after the Cambridge debate, Buckley told the same story again and again about his first encounter with Baldwin. He would claim—falsely—that Baldwin "received a standing ovation" before "he had uttered a single word," and would explain that the vote was so lopsided because Baldwin "was a black; he hated America; [and] he was a religious skeptic and a homosexual."[1] The students voted for Baldwin, Buckley surmised, not because he was right or offered superior arguments but because they wanted to affirm his identity and join him in "deplor[ing] the United States."[2]

But it would be a mistake to think that Buckley was ashamed of his performance at Cambridge. He was actually quite proud of what happened that night. It is fitting that Buckley provided the most detailed explanation of this pride to Wills, who published a profile of him in *Esquire* in January 1968. Wills, after all, had done so much to shape Buckley's understanding of Baldwin, and it would not be long after the *Esquire* piece was published that Buckley's intransigence on civil rights (as well as the other protest movements of the 1960s) led Wills to sever ties with *National Review* and the conservative movement. "The most satisfying debate I ever had," Buckley told Wills, "was the one I lost by the heaviest margin—in Cambridge." Wills asked his mentor to explain why he found the experience so rewarding:

> Well, it was planned as an orgy of anti-Americanism, a kind of intellectual masturbation; but they made it clear to me, in many ways, that I could personally get off with some of the laurels if, just slightly, I went along with the game and ingratiated myself. But I didn't give them one gaw-damn-*inch*! They were infuriated. [Wills describes Buckley smiling at this point, "savoring the memory," before he concluded,] I lost four to one. But I walked out of there tall so far as self-respect goes.[3]

With these musings, Buckley captured the essence of his conservative ethos, reduced to one sentence: don't "give them one gaw-damn- *inch*!"

Later in 1968, Baldwin was asked by journalist C. Robert Jennings to reflect on his encounters with Buckley. On that occasion, Baldwin reminisced about the *Open End* meeting rather than his triumph at Cambridge. I have already provided snippets of what Baldwin said to Jennings, but I now offer his comments in full:

> I was trying to do what Martin was doing. I still hoped people would listen. But Bill's a bully, he can't listen, he uses weapons I simply won't use. I said people who live in the ghetto don't own it; it's white people's property. *I* know who owns Harlem. He said, "Do the landlords tippy-toe uptown and throw garbage out the windows?" And I tuned out. If a cat said that to me in life, I'd simply beat the hell out of him. He was saying Negroes deserved their fate; they stink. To my eternal dishonor, I cooled it, I drew back and I lost the debate. I *should* have beat him over the head with the coffee cup. He's not a serious man. He's the intellectuals' James Bond.[4]

There is much that is revealing about how the tone and substance of Baldwin's ideas had changed in the three years since he had encountered Buckley. In the conclusion to his Cambridge speech, he told those assembled that "unless we can establish some kind of dialogue . . . we will be in terrible trouble." What "concerns me the most," he explained, is that unless "we can talk to each other" and "hear" each other, the days of reason are numbered. When reason loses its authority, violence fills the vacuum.

And so as Baldwin sat with Jennings in the Beverley Hills Hotel and thought about his encounters with Buckley, he could say—in what was perhaps a half joke that contained a serious point at its core—that Buckley deserved to be beaten over the head with a coffee mug on the set of *Open End* because he believed black folks living in the slums *deserved* their fate and refused to listen to anyone who challenged him on this point.[5]

By the time he was interviewed by Jennings, Baldwin's hope was in a precarious state. Just three months earlier, King was gunned down by a white supremacist in Memphis, Tennessee. "Since Martin's death," Baldwin explained later, "something has altered in me, something has gone away." That "something," he confessed, was his faith that people can be better than they are. King's death "forced me," Baldwin wrote, "into a judgment concerning human life and human beings which I have always been reluctant to make." Baldwin had spent decades trying to convince people to treat one another as "miracles" despite "the disasters" they had become, but after King's death he was finding it difficult to heed that advice.[6] It would be too much to say that the bullet that murdered King also killed Baldwin's hope, but it is fair to conclude that the event led him to undergo a radical transformation as a thinker and artist. Like all the other bloody moments in the history of the civil rights struggle, Baldwin's focus was not on the perpetrator of the crime but instead on the circumstances that produced him and led his life to intersect with King's. The moral corruption of a country that could produce this event, he thought, was beyond question. Baldwin had done all he could to avert the fire next time, but he was now accepting that the fire was upon us, and there was much that deserved to burn.

In the days and weeks after the King assassination, Buckley was appalled. What upset him was not the murder itself—horrific though it was—but rather the reaction to it. In an attempt to "atone for the crime against Martin Luther King," Buckley lamented, Americans were blaming themselves. In a speech to the American Society of Newspaper Editors called "Did You Kill Martin Luther King?" that Buckley delivered just two weeks after the assassination, his thesis was clear: those who, like Baldwin, thought the death of King revealed the corruption of the American soul were saying something that was "philosophically dangerous." By asking

Americans to reflect on their complicity in King's death, Buckley declared, Baldwin and his ilk were simply coming up with another way to promote their "Hate America" message. In the wake of these criticisms, Buckley said that moments like these made him swell with pride for his country. The big story, he argued, was not the alleged moral corruption that led to such an event but instead "that we bred the most widely shared and the most intensely felt sense of grief" in response to the murder. The most important thing one could do in the aftermath of an event like the King assassination, Buckley said, was to cling even tighter to one's faith in America. The country, he concluded, "needs us all as [the] devoted bodyguards" of her ideals and institutions.[7]

These disparate reactions to the King assassination bring into relief the gulf that forever separated Buckley and Baldwin, and continues to separate so many in American politics. This gulf can be explained by a fundamental disagreement between the two men about what it means to love one's country. Baldwin's reaction to the murder of King, Buckley believed, revealed his lack of love—indeed, his hatred—for the country. Buckley's reaction to the assassination, Baldwin believed, revealed the falseness and emptiness of his love for the country. For Buckley, love of country was displayed by one's gratitude for it, despite its flaws.[8] For Baldwin, one's love for the country was revealed by one's willingness to "criticize her perpetually."[9] Buckley's love was a love of devotion, much like a child's love for his parents. Baldwin's love was a love of confrontation. "Love is a battle," he insisted, "love is a war. Love is growing up."[10]

Buckley's name seldom passed Baldwin's lips in the years after the Jennings interview.[11] Late in life, though, as Baldwin found himself so deeply alienated from Ronald Reagan's America, Buckley was back on his mind.[12] During a discussion of "Blacks and Jews" in 1984, Baldwin explained that he felt a "certain bitterness" toward his Jewish "ex-running buddies" who had become "neoconservatives." Unlike "William Buckley, from whom obviously I expect nothing," Baldwin was disappointed by the fact that some American Jews had come under the spell of "a peculiarly vindictive form of American neofascism." Buckley's neofascism, Baldwin seemed to be suggesting, was to be expected; his "old running buddies" should have known better.[13]

In Baldwin's last book, *The Evidence of Things Not Seen*, he made reference to what was almost certainly his *Open End* appearance with Buckley.[14] "People can be defined by their color only by the beholder," he explained, "who, in order to arrive at this definition, must will himself blind." There is "not a racist alive," he continued, "who is not a liar and a coward, the proof being that they imagine reality to be at the mercy of their will—or, rather, of their terror." As an illustrative example of this phenomenon, Baldwin described what happened when he and Buckley left the set of *Open End*:

> I remember a very celebrated American patriot . . . proud issue of Yale, who, after a somewhat stormy TV interview on which we had both appeared, upon discovering one of my brothers and myself and a friend in the elevator, hurried, with his friends, down the stairs. He will say, of course, if challenged, that the elevator was crowded, but I remember the split second—the twinkling of an eye—in which he looked at me and he saw me looking at him. Okay. But *I* would have gotten on the elevator.[15]

Racist. Liar. Coward. These are the words that came into Baldwin's mind when he thought about Buckley.

———

From Baldwin's point of view, Buckley's moral failure was rooted in his unwillingness to see "the life, the aspirations, [and] the universal humanity hidden behind the dark skin."[16] Buckley often claimed that the inviolability of the individual was at the heart of his political philosophy, but this commitment was nowhere to be found in his reactions to the civil rights revolution. He worried about abstract individuals who might one day be violated by "Big Government" while paying little mind to the destruction of real individuals right in front of him. To respect the humanity of another, Baldwin argued, one must make a good faith effort to view the world through their eyes. This was something that Buckley was unwilling to do. When he discussed race matters, he failed—time and again—to think through issues from the standpoint of the oppressed. Even in moments when he seemed to concede the justice of their cause, Buckley invariably pivoted from this sympathy to a position of resistance. Yes, it's unfortunate that you are not allowed to send your children to that school, but you must wait until white parents feel comfortable with their sons and daughters being educated alongside yours. Yes, racially motivated violence is repulsive and the failure of the legal system to punish it is indefensible, but the federal government has no business doing anything about it. Yes, it is unfair that you are excluded from the right to vote because of your skin color, but should you really be voting anyway?[17]

Although Baldwin often displayed a tremendous amount of forgiveness for oppressors—for example, Sheriff Jim Clark—who he saw as more scared than evil, he had little patience for Buckley and his ilk. In Baldwin's view, men like Clark were trapped in a web of mythology they did not really understand and could not envision how to escape. What was happening to the moral lives of men such as these, Baldwin argued, was one of the most sinister things imaginable. He thought men like Buckley were in a different moral category. These men, he claimed, were not unwitting and frightened human beings trapped in webs of delusion; they were responsible for creating and maintaining these webs in order to advance agendas that had little to do with the well-being of Clark or anyone like him. Buckley, Baldwin believed, knew better and had the ability to exert a considerable amount of influence in the world. Indeed, Buckley's work as a guardian of white supremacy was, from Baldwin's perspective, more sinister than that of the most hardened racists in American politics. Time and again, Buckley's *ends* were the same as the racist demagogues he was always sure to condemn; his primary objection to these men was the *means* they chose to use on behalf of "the cause of white people."[18] For these reasons, Baldwin concluded, some of the blood shed as a result of the American racial nightmare was on Buckley's hands.

A critic may wonder if Baldwin's indictments of Buckley are fair. Did he not, in the end, recant the views at the heart of his decades-long debate with Baldwin? The answer, to put it simply, is not really. In interview after interview, Buckley insisted that the white supremacist thesis of "Why the South Must Prevail" was "absolutely correct."[19] As late as 2004, he argued that he had been right to say that blacks were not sufficiently "advanced" to receive the same rights and freedoms afforded to other Americans. He claimed to have accepted their status as human beings, but he was unwilling to accept their worthiness of full citizenship.

On the question of segregation, Buckley's musings late in life were muddled, contradictory, and downright confusing. In an interview with Terry Gross in 1989, he said he was "rather glad" to have lost the fight over the issue because he "welcomed the result," but just months later he was not so sure. As he wrote in the journal *Policy Review*, "Am I glad the civil-rights law (and its successor) passed? I don't find that question easy to answer."[20] In his meandering explanation of why, he expressed concern that the civil rights struggle helped establish the Supreme Court as "the principal moral tribunal of the American people" (although the question he had posed for himself was about two acts of Congress), and pointed out that "many" of those "who opposed the Civil War" did not do so in order to prolong slavery but rather "because they wished to avoid bloodshed *en route* to manumission." The same might be said, Buckley observed, of the position he and other conservatives took in opposition to civil rights. Even if the "ends" were "worthy" (something Buckley doubted at every turn), the "means" were troubling, and the "fallout" was certainly great.[21]

In 2004, Buckley came the closest to offering a public recantation of his position on segregation. The journalist James Carney asked him if any of his previously held positions were now a source of "regret." "Yes," Buckley responded, "I once believed we could evolve our way up from Jim Crow. I was wrong; federal intervention was necessary."[22] But it is important to note just what Buckley was admitting to being wrong about. His claim was a descriptive, not a normative, one. He was confessing his wrongness about what the country *could* have done, not saying anything about what he and others *should* have done. Buckley clung to the view that he was right as a matter of constitutional principle, and as a result, could never bring himself to offer anything resembling a full recantation or apology.[23]

The quibbling that Buckley's defenders and critics might do at the margins of these gestures of quasi regret misses a larger and far more important point. When it mattered and from a position of great influence in American political culture, Buckley resisted just about every step forward in the black liberation struggle. What is interesting is not whether Buckley may have, to borrow the words of political theorist Corey Robin, "made peace with some emancipations past," but why he reacted as he did "when those emancipations first arose."[24]

Throughout this book, I have attempted to show how his decades-long debate with Baldwin helps us answer that question. In sum, the answer consists of a blend of Buckley's assumption of white supremacy and his philosophical commitment to elite rule as well as the political instincts that led him to recognize the strategic value racial resentment could play in the achievement of conservative ascendancy. It is this political insight— and his tireless promotion of it—that has proven to be Buckley's most enduring legacy.[25] In the forty years that passed between Buckley's meetings with Baldwin and his death, Republicans became the conservative party, achieved almost total control of the South, won the White House in seven out of ten elections (losing only three to moderate southern Democrats), and movement conservatives were to be found wherever there was power to be had: in the judiciary, bureaucracy, think tanks, legislatures and statehouses, and corporate hierarchy as well as on the school boards. Buckley lost many battles over the years, but there was no doubt that racial politics helped him win the war.[26]

The price of victory, though, has been incredibly high. The American Right seems to be in much the same place today as where it found itself over half a century ago. To achieve overwhelming power, conservatives have had to rely on the political energy provided by racial resentment and status anxiety.[27] Much like Buckley, many conservative elites find reliance

FIGURE 9.1. Buckley with President Ronald Reagan in the Oval Office, 1988
(Wikimedia Commons)

on such energy unseemly, but they cling to it because they know it gives life to their agenda. For the American Right, the price of power has been a deal with the devil of white supremacy. This was true in Buckley's time, and it is true in our own.

Baldwin would likely ask Buckley and contemporary conservatives to reflect on just what it is that they have won. Has the cost of power—the staggering body count and destruction of so many moral lives—delivered to its beneficiaries all that they hoped? Baldwin had his doubts. "I don't see anything in American life—for myself—to aspire to," he told an interviewer not long before his death in 1987. "Nothing at all. It's all so very false, so shallow, so plastic, so morally and ethically corrupt."[28] With statements such as these, Baldwin was, in a sense, admitting that Buckley won the war for the American soul. Through their words and deeds, Baldwin and other civil rights revolutionaries laid bare the utter depravity of white supremacy, and yet decades later we find ourselves still caught in its merciless grip. The story of Baldwin and Buckley reminds us that moral righteousness is often not sufficient to gain political power. This is a sad truth, but it is a truth we ignore at our peril.

Baldwin's ultimate indictment of Buckley might be the one that would sting him the most: he was not a true conservative, or if he was, he was devoted to conserving the wrong things. Buckley's counterrevolutionary program led him to embrace a radical departure from several first principles he insisted were at the heart of his philosophy. He claimed to believe in the inviolability of the individual, but disregarded this truth when the individual in question happened to be black. He claimed to be devoted to the American Constitution and yet ignored it when it got in his way. He claimed to care about the American dream and yet, time and again, chose to side with those who were determined to deny many of their compatriots access to it. All this led Baldwin to wonder, Just what was it, really, that Buckley was trying conserve?

Baldwin might also add that it was he, not Buckley, who was engaged in a worthwhile conservative project. A few years after his debates with Buckley, Baldwin made this point explicitly during a dialogue with the anthropologist Margaret Mead:

> It is very difficult to ask people to give up the assumptions with which they have always lived and yet that's the demand one's got to make now of everybody. . . . I was a revolutionary at fifteen and I gave that up at the same time I left the church. I am another kind of revolutionary now, if I am revolutionary at all. I might even be described as a conservative, in terms of the things I think about and want to see honored and made viable for people's lives.[29]

What if, Baldwin asked, we actually lived as if "*all* men are the sons of God"?[30] What if our "national life" was truly animated by "the standard of human freedom with which we began"?[31] What if the promises of the American dream were really extended to all our fellows? These are the

FIGURE 9.2. Baldwin speaking in the age of Reagan, circa 1984 (Wikimedia Commons)

questions Baldwin thought someone who really cared about conserving the country ought to be asking.

———

For Baldwin, the bargain Buckley struck in the thick of the civil rights revolution and the one we are still striking today are but symptoms of much deeper problems. It is all too easy to focus our indignation on racist demagogues and their apologists.[32] Opposition to the most conspicuous guardians of the fortress of white supremacy is necessary, but it is not sufficient to meet the task at hand. Instead, Baldwin would tell us we must have the courage to examine what lies beneath the fortress. It is there that we will find, to borrow Baldwin's words at Cambridge, "the millions of details 24 hours of every day which spell out" that some lives matter to us more than others. The economic, educational, and health disparities across the color line did not happen, Baldwin would remind us, as a result of an act of God, nor did providence dictate that people of color be disproportionately victimized by mass incarceration and extrajudicial killing. These things happen because all of us allow them to happen, and until we summon the will to recognize this fact and do something about it, the American dream will remain a nightmare for many.

In the face of all this, it seems difficult to imagine where Baldwin might find hope. And yet he refused to accept despair. As long as one is breathing, he often said, one must search for hope. Baldwin is not the sort of thinker who provided an ideology or political program that promises to make the world a better place. Instead, he left us with a way of thinking and being in the world. He prescribed constant self-examination and brutal honesty in our relationships with others, and insisted that each of us has the capacity "to make life a little more human."[33] Baldwin was no utopian; there is nothing we can do that will, one fine day, make the world perfect. Our "salvation," he said late in life, "is never accomplished: it has to be reaffirmed every day and every hour."[34] And as he told Faulkner over half a century ago, "There is never time in the future in which we will work out our salvation. The challenge is in the moment, the time is always now."[35]

Acknowledgments

In the beginning, there was Sue McWilliams, who got me thinking seriously about Baldwin. A few years ago, Sue invited me to contribute to *The Political Companion to James Baldwin*, which she had been tapped to edit for the University Press of Kentucky. That invitation changed my life. I accepted, and devoted the next several months to reading every word Baldwin wrote and working my way, slowly but surely, to this book. My conversations with Sue over the years have taught me so much about Baldwin, and I will be forever in her debt.

Soon after my deep dive into all things Baldwin, I discovered his debate with Buckley, who had long been a source of fascination for me. I was raised in a staunchly Republican household and considered myself to be on the ideological Right into my early twenties. Among the many people I met at Cato Institute summer camps and in the halls of the Heritage Foundation (where I had an internship when I was in college), Buckley was identified as a hero. He seemed erudite, urbane, and aristocratic, and his presence on television was unforgettable.

My study of history and political science led me to grow up from conservatism, but when Buckley reentered my life through the study of Baldwin, I became mildly obsessed about the possibilities of thinking about the two of them together. The seeds of my own move up from conservatism were planted by my study of the black freedom struggle in the United States. I was coming to believe that the depth of Baldwin's thinking about that struggle was without parallel in American political thought, and Buckley, though certainly not the most serious American conservative intellectual, stood alone in his prominence as a promoter of right-wing political ideas, including opposition to civil rights. As these ideas swirled in my head, this book was born.

In order to actually write the book, though, I had to rely on a small army of interview subjects, archivists, colleagues, and student collaborators. In the early days of research, student collaborators Jillaine Cook, Ellie Forness, and Maggie Hawkins helped me track down the Cambridge students who hosted Baldwin and Buckley. This proved to be a challenging task until we got in touch with Christie Davies. Christie was eager to help, and after a couple of hours on the phone with him, I soon had the contact information of several of the key players in the debate. I am sad to say that Christie passed away before this book was completed, but I will forever be in his debt for helping me get in touch with Peter Fullerton, David Heycock, Earl Hopper, Adrian Vinson, and many others who witnessed the debate. All these gentlemen were so generous with their time and energy as they helped me reconstruct what happened that night, over five decades ago. I am also grateful to Lawrie Chickering, Lee Edwards, Gloria Karefa-Smart, David Leeming, Walter Lowe, Ponchitta Pierce, Norman Podhoretz, Dan Wakefield, and Garry Wills for speaking or corresponding with me as I attempted to solve the many historical mysteries at the heart of this project. Christopher Buckley was generous enough to grant me access to his father's vast papers at Yale. He knew that my project dealt with his father's views on race and civil rights, but he did not hesitate for a moment when I requested access to the papers. This reveals a commitment to history and scholarship that is admirable.

Before I started working on this book, I had a healthy amount of love and appreciation for librarians. That love and appreciation has increased tenfold as I have searched archive after archive to make sense of Baldwin and Buckley. I am especially grateful to the librarians at the William F. Buckley Jr. Papers at Yale and the James Baldwin Papers at the Schomburg Center for Black Culture. I am indebted especially to William Massa for his assistance with the Buckley papers and Tiana M. Taliep at the Baldwin Papers. I am also grateful to librarians at the Hoover Institution, James Jackson Kilpatrick Papers, Library of Congress, University of Albany, University of Texas, and New York Public Library. Librarians at my own institution—especially Susan Barnes-Whyte, Kent Cline, Bahram Rafaei, and Rich Schmidt—were also instrumental in this project. I want to single Rich out for special thanks as he helped me track down thousands of documents via interlibrary loan.

As I have proceeded with my research and writing, I have had the invaluable assistance of many Linfield students including Aspen Brooks, Madeline Colson, Jillaine Cook, Jade Everage, Ellie Forness, Pedro Graterol, Maggie Hawkins, Stella Mason, Morgan McCaslin, Hannah Roberts, and Chase Stowell. I also had the good fortune to spend many hours with the incredible students in my seminar on Frederick Douglass and Baldwin. You deepened my understanding of Baldwin in innumerable ways.

So many fellow scholars contributed to this project in myriad ways. My departmental colleagues—Pat Cottrell, Dimitri Kelly, and Dawn Nowacki—are the most kind and supportive friends and coworkers imaginable. Many other Linfield colleagues—especially Hillary Crane, Reshmi Dutt-Ballerstadt, Tom Mertes, Daniel Pollack-Pelzner, John Sagers, Chad Tillberg, Lissa Wadewitz, Joe Wilkins, and Megan Kozak Williams—have provided advice and support that has made me a wiser and stronger human being.

Beyond my campus, I have incurred many scholarly debts. In the early days of this project, Patrick Allitt, Lawrie Balfour, Will Barndt, Eddie Glaude, William Hogeland, Joseph Lowndes, and Susan McWilliams came to my campus to participate in a symposium to mark the fiftieth anniversary of the Baldwin-Buckley debate. During that symposium and in the many months since, their views of the debate had a deep impact on my own. Over the years I worked on this book, I also reached out to a number of scholars for insights and advice. On the Buckley side of the ledger, I am especially grateful to Carl Bogus, Alvin Felzenberg, and John Judis for sharing their wisdom. On the Baldwin side of things, David Leeming was beyond generous as I pestered him with question after question about his friend and former boss. A number of Baldwin scholars— especially Eddie Glaude, Susan McWilliams, Melvin Rogers, and Jack Turner—have answered many of my questions about Baldwin and provided valuable feedback on this manuscript.

The team at Princeton University Press has been terrific from the start. My editor at Princeton, Rob Tempio, has been a steady source of encouragement, good humor, and keen insight. Matt Rohal has been quick to answer my many questions about the editorial process. Several anonymous reviewers for Princeton have provided me with great advice about how to improve this book. It was painful to cut the thousands of words I cut, but I think the book is better as a result.

I am also grateful to the late Mark E. Kann and late Scott B. Smith, to whom this book is dedicated. Mark was my adviser at the University of Southern California, and taught me so much about teaching and scholarship. I wish Mark could read this book because I have tried to follow his model of writing political theory that is driven by a compelling story and not bogged down with jargon. Scott was my colleague at Linfield for a decade, and we had many conversations about this book. He was a first-class teacher and scholar, but I am especially indebted to him for modeling intellectual curiosity better than anyone I've ever met. Both Mark and Scott left this earth too soon. I am grateful for every moment I had the good fortune to spend in their presence.

This project has been a labor of love, and my devotion to it has often taken me away from the people that matter most to me in this world. My wife, Emily, has been patient, kind, and loving as I have worked on this book. Emily, you make everything better. I do not know where I would be without you. I am grateful to Luna and Brando, our beautiful children, who keep me silly and fill my heart with joy every single day. My mom and dad, Kathy and Tony, have done so much to mold me into the person I am today. Your love, support, and encouragement provide me with the foundation on which my life rests. I am so grateful. There are too many other friends and family members to name here, but you know who you are, and I want you to know how much I appreciate you.

Appendix

Transcript of the Baldwin versus Buckley Debate at the Cambridge Union

For decades, there has been a great deal of confusion about what was actually said when Baldwin and Buckley debated at the Cambridge Union on February 18, 1965. The confusion is rooted in the fact that the BBC recording of the debate was edited to fit within an hour time slot. The BBC recording includes the whole of Baldwin's speech, but only heavily edited versions of the speeches delivered by David Heycock, Jeremy Burford, and Buckley. This confusion was increased in March 1965 when the *New York Times* published what was purported to be a "condensed transcript" of the debate. The transcript contained many inaccuracies and included portions of Buckley's speech that were not included in the BBC recording. Excerpts from the debate have been anthologized from these two flawed sources, and scholars have been rightfully puzzled by what was actually said that night. The Cambridge Union did keep a reel-to-reel audio recording of the debate, but Union officials report that this recording was destroyed in a fire. One of the privileges afforded former presidents of the Union, though, is to request copies of the audio recordings of debates, and fortunately, Adrian Vinson, who was Union president after Peter Fullerton, requested a reel-to-reel copy of the Baldwin and Buckley speeches. When I was getting started with this project, Vinson was generous enough to ship this reel-to-reel copy from his home in England to my home in Portland, Oregon. After a couple failed attempts by audio specialists to transfer the reel-to-reel recording into digital form, Neil Wilburn and his staff at Limelight Video in Portland successfully digitized it. This recording provided me—and will provide future scholars—with access to the full Buckley speech for the first time. Portions of the student speeches by Heycock and Burford appear to be lost to history, but Buckley's speech—and the many interesting questions he got from students—is now available for analysis. In addition to the transcript provided below, Princeton University Press has made the audio recording available on its website {~?~URL to come}. Special thanks are due to Vinson for sharing the recording, Wilburn for digitizing it, and Linfield students Aspen Brooks, Maddy Colson, Jade Everage, Ellie Forness, Pedro Graterol, Maggie Hawkins, Morgan McCaslin, and Chase Stowell for their work on the transcription.

Beginning of Transcript

Union president Fullerton, other Union officers, student debaters Heycock and Burford, and guest debaters Baldwin and Buckley enter the Union debating hall to applause.

FULLERTON: The motion before the house tonight is: the American dream is at the expense of the American Negro, your proposer Mr. David Heycock of Pembroke College, and opposer Mr. Jeremy Burford of Emmanuel College. Mr. James Baldwin will speak third; Mr. William F. Buckley Jr. will speak fourth. Mr. Heycock has the ear of the house.

HEYCOCK: Mr. President, sir, it is the custom of the house for the first speaker in any debate to extend a formal welcome to any visitors to the house. I can honestly say, however, that it is a very great honor to be able to welcome to the house this evening Mr. William Buckley and Mr. James Baldwin. Mr. William Buckley has the reputation of possibly being the most articulate conservative in the United States of America. He was a graduate of Yale and he first gained a reputation for himself by publishing a book entitled *God and Man and Yale* [*sic*] [*audience laughter*]. Since then, he has devoted himself to the secular, and this has included Norman Mailer, Kenneth Tynan, and Mary McCarthy, and Fidel Castro, none of whom have come out of their confrontations unscathed. At present, his principal occupation is editing a right-wing newspaper in the United States entitled the *National Review*.

Mr. James Baldwin is hardly in need of introduction. His reputation both as a novelist and as an advocate of civil rights is international. His third novel, *Another Country*, has been published as a paperback in England today. Mr. Baldwin and Mr. Buckley are both very welcome to the house this evening.

[*Applause.*]

HEYCOCK: Imagine, Mr. President, a society which, above all, values freedom and equality. A society in which artificial barriers to fulfillment and achievement are unheard of. A society in which a man may begin his life as a rail-splitter and end it as president. A society in which all men are free in every sense of the word, free to live where they choose, free to work where they choose. Equal in the eyes of the law and every public authority, and equal in the eyes of their fellows. A society, in fact, in which intolerance and prejudice are meaningless terms.

Imagine, however, Mr. President, that a condition of this utopia has been the persistent and quite-deliberate exploitation of one-ninth of its inhabitants, that one man in nine has been denied those rights which the rest of that society takes for granted. That one man in nine does not have the chance for fulfillment or realization of his innate potentialities. That one man in nine cannot promise his children a secure future and unlimited opportunities. Imagine this, Mr. President, and you have what is, in my opinion, the bitter reality of the American dream.

A few weeks ago, Martin Luther King had to hold a nonviolent demonstration in Selma, Alabama, in his drive to register Negro voters. By the end of the week of his demonstrations, he was able to write, quite accurately, in a national fund-raising letter from Selma, Alabama, jail, "There are more Negroes in prison with me than there are on the voting rolls." When King wrote that letter, 335 out of 32,700 Negroes in Dallas had the vote: 1 percent of the Dallas population. After a mass march to the courthouse, 237 Negroes, King among them, were arrested. The following day, 470 children who had deserted their classrooms to protest against King's arrest were charged with juvenile delinquency [*audience laughter*]. Thirty-six adults on the same day were charged with contempt of court for picketing the courthouse while state circuit court was in session.

On the following day, 111 people were arrested on the same charge, despite their claim that they merely wanted to see the voting registrar. Four hundred students were arrested and taken to the armory, where many of them spent the night on a cold, cement floor. The following day the demonstration spread to Marion, Alabama. In Marion, Negroes outnumber whites by 11,500 to 6,000 people, and yet only 300 are registered to vote. Negroes in Marion were anxious to test the public accommodations section of the civil rights law. They entered a drugstore, and there they were served with Coca-Cola laced with salt and were told that hamburgers had risen to five dollars each. After the arrest of 15 Negroes for protesting against this treatment, 700 Negroes boycotted their classes next day and marched in orderly fashion to the jail. There they sang civil rights songs until they were warned by a state trooper that they would be arrested if they sung one more song. Of course, they sung another song, and of course all 700 were arrested.

American society has felt fit to use Negro labor. It has felt fit to use the blood of the Negro in two world wars. It has felt fit to listen to his music. It has felt fit to laugh at his jokes. And yet as far as I'm concerned, it has never felt fit to give the American Negro a fair deal, and for this reason, Mr. President, I would beg leave to propose the motion of the American dream is at the expense of the American Negro.

[*Applause.*]

FULLERTON: I now call Mr. Jeremy Burford of Emmanuel College to oppose the motion.

[*Applause.*]

BURFORD: Mr. President, sir, it is an honor to welcome two such distinguished speakers. James Baldwin is well known as one of the most vivid and articulate writers about the Negro problem in America. Mr. Baldwin had a difficult childhood, and he has personally himself suffered discrimination and ill treatment in the south of America, and I would like to say at this opportunity, at this time, that it is not the purpose of this side of the house to condone that in any way at all. It is not our purpose to oppose civil rights. It is our purpose to oppose this motion. And . . .

AUDIENCE MEMBER: Hear, hear!

[*Laughter.*]

Burford: Thank you, sir, come and collect your fee afterward.

[*Laughter and applause.*]

BURFORD: This side of the house denies that the American dream has in any way been helped by this undoubted inequality and suffering of the Negro. We maintain that in fact that it has hindered the American dream. And that if there had been equality, if there had been true freedom of opportunity, the American dream would be very much more advanced than it is now. If the American dream has made any progress, and I think it has, it has been made in spite of the suffering and inequality of the American Negro, and not because of it.

Now it is also implied from this motion that the American dream is encouraging and worsening the suffering of the American Negro. This is emphatically not the case. The American dream—the American economic prosperity and respect for civil liberties—has been the main factor in bringing about the undoubted improvement in race relations in America in the last twenty years. And Professor Arnold Rose, who is the author of *The Negro in America*, which is perhaps the definitive work on the subject, and who is also the contributor to what was called the *Freedom Pamphlet*—so I should imagine if he has any bias at all it is in favor of the Negro—he said that this improvement in race relations will be seen in years to come as remarkably quick, and he has put it down to three [*sic*] main causes: increased industrialization,

technical advance, the increased social mobility of the American
people, and the economic prosperity.

And I would put it to this house that industrialization and
economic prosperity are two of the main ingredients of the
American dream. And at the same time—again I do not want to say
that the American—the Negro in America is treated fairly—but at
the same time, the average per capita income of Negroes in America is exactly the same as the average per capita income of people
in Great Britain. Now I found that absolutely . . . [*audience laughter*]
I found that absolutely amazing, and I understand that . . . [*audience
laughter*] some of you do as well, so I have got the reference
here. From the *United States News and World Report* of July the
22nd, 1963, in which it points out—this will have to be the last
interruption I take because time is running short . . .

AUDIENCE MEMBER: Mr. President, on a point of information, is the
speaker talking of real income or money income?

[*Shouts of "hear, hear!" and applause.*]

BURFORD: I am talking of money income, I would not wish to
disguise that [*audience laughter*]. I would also say, that in terms of
this, there are only five countries in the world where the income is
higher than that of the American Negro, and they do not include
countries like West Germany and France and Japan. Now there are
in America, um, thirty-five Negro millionaires, there are Negro six
thousand doctors, and so on [*audience laughter*]. Now I do not, by
saying this, wish to emphasize that the Negro is fairly treated, I
merely wish to try and convey a more realistic and objective
account of the situation of the Negro [*audience laughter*]. I agree
that there are, um, Negroes who are very poor indeed, such as
the . . . [*audience laughter*] old gentleman in the South who was
talking about some of his wealthier brethren and he was saying,
"Yessir, some of these rich Negroes, they put on airs, dey like the
bottom figure of a fraction, the bigger they try to be, the smaller
they really are" [*audience laughter*].

I would repeat, Mr. President, sir, in the last minute I have, that this debate is not whether civil rights should be extended to American Negroes or not. If it were, it would be a very easy motion to argue for and a very easy motion to vote for. The debate tonight concerns whether the American dream is at the expense of the American Negro. That is, whether the American Negro has paid for the American dream with his suffering, or whether the American dream has furthered Negro inequality, and I would deny both those two precepts. I would say that Negro inequality has hindered the American dream, and I would say that the American dream has been very important indeed in furthering civil rights and in furthering freedom for the American Negro. Mr. President, sir, I beg to oppose the motion.

[*Applause.*]

FULLERTON: It is now with very great pleasure and a very great sense of honor that I call up Mr. James Baldwin to speak third to this motion.

[*Applause.*]

BALDWIN: Good evening. I find myself, not for the first time, in the position of a kind of Jeremiah. For example, I don't disagree with Mr. Burford that the inequalities suffered by the American Negro population of the United States has hindered the American dream. Indeed it has. I quarrel with some other things he has to say. The other, deeper element of a certain awfulness I feel has to do with one's point of view. I have to put it that way. One's sense, one's system of reality. It would seem to me the proposition before the house, when I put it that way, *is* the American dream *at* the expense of the American Negro, or the American dream *is* at the expense of the American Negro—is a question, hideously loaded—and that one's response to that question, one's reaction to that question, has to depend in effect—in effect on where you find yourself in the world. What your sense of reality is, what your system of reality is.

That is, it depends on assumptions which we hold, so deeply, as to be scarcely aware of them.

A white South African, or a Mississippi sharecropper, or a Mississippi sheriff, or a Frenchman driven out of Algeria, all have, at bottom, a system of reality which compels them to—for example, in the case of the French exiled from Algeria, to defend French reasons for having ruled Algeria. The Mississippi, or the Alabama, sheriff, who really does believe when he's facing a Negro, a boy or a girl, that this woman, this man, this child, must be insane to attack the system to which he owes his entire identity. Of course, for such a person, the proposition of which . . . which we are trying to discuss here tonight, does not exist.

And on the other hand, *I* have to speak as one of the people who have been most attacked by what we must now here call the Western, or the European, system of reality. What white people in the world . . . the doctrine of white supremacy, I hate to say it here, comes from Europe. That's how it got to America. Beneath then, what everyone's reaction to this proposition is, has to be the question of whether or not civilizations can be considered as such equal, or whether one civilization has the right to overtake and subjugate, and in fact to destroy, another.

Now what happens when that happens? Leaving aside all the physical facts which one can quote, leaving aside rape, or murder, leaving aside the bloody catalog of oppression—which we are, in one way, too familiar with already—what this does to the subjugated, the most private, the most serious thing this does to the subjugated, is to destroy his sense of reality. It destroys, for example, his father's authority over him. His father can no longer tell him anything because the past had disappeared, and his father has no power in the world.

This means, in the case of an American Negro born in that glittering republic, and in the moment you are born—since you don't know any better—every stick and stone, and every face, is white, and since you have not yet seen a mirror, you suppose that you are too. It comes as a great shock around the age of five or six or seven to discover the flag to which you have pledged allegiance, along with everybody else, has not pledged allegiance to you. It comes as a great shock to discover that Gary Cooper killing off the Indians, when you were rooting for Gary Cooper, that the Indians were you! [*Audience laughter*]

It comes as a great shock to discover the country which is your birthplace, and to which you owe your life and your identity, has not in its whole system of reality evolved any place for you. The disaffection, the demoralization, and the gap between one person and another only on the basis of the color of their skin begins there, and accelerates, accelerates throughout a whole lifetime, so at present that you realize you're thirty and are having a terrible time managing to trust your countrymen. By the time you are thirty, you have been through a certain kind of mill, and the most serious effect of the mill you have been through is, again, not the catalog of disaster—the policemen, the taxi drivers, the waiters, the landlady, the landlord, the banks, the insurance companies, the millions of details twenty-four hours of every day which spell out to you that you are a worthless human being—it is not that! It is by that time that you have begun to see it happening in your daughter, or your son, or your niece, or your nephew. You are thirty by now, and nothing you have done has helped you escape the trap. But what is worse than that, is that nothing you have done, and as far as you can tell, nothing you can do, will save your son or your daughter from meeting the same disaster and not impossibly coming to the same end.

Now we're speaking about expense. I suppose there are several ways to address oneself to . . . some attempt to find what that word means here. Let me put it this way, that from a very literal point of view, the harbors and the ports and the railroads of the country, the economy, especially of the southern states, could not conceivably be what it has become if they had not had—and do not still have, indeed—and for so long, so many generations, cheap labor. I am stating very seriously, and this is not an overstatement, *I* picked the cotton, and *I* carried it to market, and *I* built the railroads, under someone else's whip, for nothing. For nothing.

The southern oligarchy, which has until today so much power in Washington, and therefore some power in the world, was created by my labor and my sweat, and the violation of my women, and the murder of my children. This, in the land of the free and the home of the brave, and no one can challenge that statement, it is a matter of historical record.

In another way, this dream—and we'll get to the dream in a moment—is at the expense of the American Negro. You watch this in the deep South in great relief, but not only in the deep South. In the deep South you are dealing with a sheriff, or a landlord, or a landlady, or the girl of the Western Union desk. And she doesn't know quite who she's dealing with. By which I mean that if you're not a part of the town, and if you are a northern nigger, it shows in millions of ways. So she simply knows that it's an unknown quantity and she wants [to] have nothing to do with it so she won't talk to you, you have to wait for a while to get your telegram, OK, we all know this, we've been through it, and by the time you get to be a man it's very easy to deal with.

But what is happening in the poor woman, the poor man's mind, is this: they have been raised to believe, and by now they helplessly believe, that no matter how terrible their lives may be, and their lives have been quite terrible, and no matter how far they fall, no matter what disaster overtakes them, they have one enormous knowledge and consolation which is like a heavenly revelation: at least they are not black. Now I suggest that of all the terrible things that can happen to a human being, that is one of the worst. I suggest that what has happened to white southerners is in some ways, after all, much worse than what has happened to Negroes there.

Because, Sheriff Clark in Selma, Alabama, cannot be considered, you know, no one is . . . can be dismissed as a total monster. I'm sure he loves his wife, his children [*audience laughter*]. I am sure that, you know, he likes to get drunk. You know, he's, after all, one's got to assume, and is he visibly a man like me. But he doesn't know what drives him to use the club, to menace with a gun, and to use a cattle prod. Something awful must have happened to a human being to be able to put a cattle prod against a woman's breast, for example. What happens to the woman is ghastly. What happens to the man who does it, is, in some ways, much, much worse.

This is being done, after all, not a hundred years ago but in 1965, in a country which is blessed with what we call prosperity—a word we won't examine too closely—with a certain kind of social coherence, which calls itself a civilized nation, which espouses the notion of the freedom of the world. And it is perfectly true from the point of view now, simply of an American Negro, any American Negro watching this, no matter where he is, from the vantage point of Harlem—which is another terrible place—has to say to himself, in spite of what the government says—the government says, "We can't do anything about it"—but if those are white people being murdered in Mississippi work farms, being carried off to jail, if those are white children running up and down the streets, the government would find some way of doing something about it. We have a civil rights bill now. We had an amendment, the Fifteenth Amendment, nearly a hundred years ago. I hate to sound again like an Old Testament prophet, but if the amendment was not honored then, I have don't have any reason to believe that the civil rights bill will be honored now.

And after all, one's been there since before, you know, a lot of other people got there. If one has got to prove one's title to the land, isn't four hundred years enough? Four hundred years, at least three wars. The American soil is full of the corpses of my ancestors. Why is my freedom, or my citizenship, or my right to live there, how is it conceivably a question now? And I suggest further that in the same way the moral life of Alabama sheriffs, and poor Alabama ladies— white ladies—that their moral lives have been destroyed by the plague called color, that the American sense of reality has been corrupted by it.

At the risk of sounding excessive, what I always felt when I finally left the country and found myself abroad in other places, and watched Americans abroad, and these are my countrymen, and I do care about them. And even if I didn't, there is something between us. We have the same shorthand. I know when I look at a girl or a boy from Tennessee where they came from in Tennessee, and what that means. No Englishman knows that, no Frenchman, no one in the world knows that except another black man who comes from the same place. One watches these lonely people denying the only kin they have. We talk about integration in America as though it were some great, new conundrum. The problem in America is that we have been integrated for a very long time. Put me next to any African and you will see what I mean. And my grandmother was not a rapist.

What we are not facing is the results of what we've done. What one begs the American people to do for all our sakes is simply to accept our history. I was there not only as a slave but also as a concubine. One knows the power after all which can be used against another person if you've got absolute power over that person.

It seemed to me when I watched Americans in Europe that what they didn't know about Europeans was what they didn't know about me. They weren't trying, for example, to be nasty to the French girl, or rude to the French waiter; they didn't know they hurt their feelings. They didn't have any sense that this particular woman, this particular man, though they spoke another language, and had different manners and ways, was a human being. And they walked over them with the same kind of bland ignorance and condescension—charming and cheerful—with which they have always patted me on the head and called me "Shine," and were upset when I was upset.

What is relevant about this is that whereas forty years ago when I was born, the question of having to deal with what is unspoken by the subjugated, what is never said to the master, of having to deal with this reality, was a very remote, very remote possibility; it was in no one's mind. When I was growing up, I was taught in American history books that Africa had no history and neither did I. That I was a savage, about whom the less said the better, who had been saved by Europe and brought to America. And of course, I believed it. I didn't have much choice, those were the only books there were. Everyone else seemed to agree if you walk out of Harlem, ride out of Harlem, downtown, the world agrees what you see is much bigger, cleaner, whiter, richer, safer than where you are. They collect the garbage, people obviously can pay their life insurance, the children look happy, safe; you're not. And you go back home and it would seem that, of course, that it's an act of God that this *is* true, that you belong where white people have put you.

It is only since the Second World War that there's been a counterimage in the world, and that image had not come about through any legislation on the part of any American government, but through the fact that Africa was suddenly on the stage of the world and Africans had to be dealt with in a way they had never been dealt with before. This gave an American Negro, for the first time, a sense of himself beyond a savage or a clown. It has created, and will create, a great many conundrums.

One of the great things that the white world does not know, but I think I do know, is that black people are just like everybody else. One has used the myth of Negro and the myth of color to pretend and to assume that you are dealing, essentially, with something exotic, bizarre, and practically, according to human laws, unknown. Alas, that is not true. We are also mercenaries, dictators, murderers, liars. We are human too. What is crucial here, is that unless we can manage to establish some kind of dialogue between those people whom I pretend have paid for the American dream, and those other people who have not achieved it, we will be in terrible trouble.

I want to say at the end, at the last, is that that is what concerns me most. We are sitting in this room and we are all—at least we like to think we are—relatively civilized, and we can talk to each other at least on certain levels, so that we could walk out of here assuming that the measure of our enlightenment, or at least our politeness, has some effect on the world. It may not.

I remember, for example, when the ex attorney general Mr. Robert Kennedy said that it was conceivable that in forty years in America, we might have a Negro president. And that sounded like a very emancipated statement, I suppose, to white people. They were not in Harlem when this statement was first heard, and did not hear, and possibly will never hear, the laughter and the bitterness and the scorn with which this statement was greeted. From the point of view of the man in the Harlem barbershop, Bobby Kennedy only got here yesterday, and now he's already on his way to the presidency. We've been here for four hundred years, and now he tells us that maybe in forty years, if you're good [*audience laughter*], we may let you become president.

What is dangerous here is a turning away from, the turning away from anything any white American says. The reason for the political hesitation, in spite of the Johnson landslide, is that one has been betrayed by American politicians for so long. And I am a grown man, and perhaps I can be reasoned with, I certainly hope I can be. But I don't know, and neither does Martin Luther King, none of us know, how to deal with those other people whom the white world has so long ignored who don't believe anything the white world says, and don't entirely believe anything I or Martin say. And one can't blame them; you watch what has happened to them in less than twenty years.

It seems to me that the city of New York, for example—this is my last point—has had Negroes in it for a very long time. If the city of New York were able, as it has indeed been able for the last fifteen years, to reconstruct itself, tear down buildings and raise great new ones, downtown and for money, and has done nothing whatever except build housing projects in the ghetto for the Negroes. And of course the Negroes hate it. Presently the property does indeed deteriorate because it surely cannot bear it; they want to get out of the ghetto. If the American pretensions were based on more solid, a more honest assessment of life and of themselves, it would not mean for Negroes when someone may . . . says "urban renewal" that Negroes simply are going to be thrown out in the street, which is what it does mean now. It is not an act of God; we are dealing with a society made and ruled by men. If the American Negro had not been present in America, I am convinced that the history of the American labor movement would be much more edifying than it is.

It is a terrible thing for an entire people to surrender to the notion that one-ninth of its population is beneath them. And until that moment, until the moment comes, when we, the Americans, we the American people, are able to accept the fact that I have to accept, for example, that my ancestors are both white and black, that on that continent we are trying to forge a new identity for which we need each other, and that I am not a ward of America, I am not an object of missionary charity, I am one of the people who built the country. Until this moment there is scarcely any hope for the American dream because the people who are denied participation in it, by their very presence, will wreck it.

And if that happens, it's a very grave moment for the West. Thank you.

[*Applause that develops into standing ovation for Baldwin. The ovation lasts for just over one minute.*]

FULLERTON: I am now very grateful and very pleased to be able to call on Mr. William F. Buckley Jr. to speak forth to this motion.

[*Applause.*]

BUCKLEY: Thank you, Mr. President, Mr. Heycock, Mr. Burford, Mr. Baldwin, gentlemen. It seems to me that of all the indictments Mr. Baldwin has made of America here tonight and in his copious literature of protest, the one that is the most striking involves, in effect, the refusal of the American community to treat him other than as a Negro. The American community has refused to do this. The American community, almost everywhere he goes, treats him with a kind of unction, a kind of satisfaction at posturing carefully before his flagellations of our civilization, that indeed quite properly commands the contempt which he so eloquently showers upon it.

It is impossible, in my judgment, to deal with the indictment of Mr. Baldwin unless one is prepared to deal with him as a white man. Unless one is prepared to say to him, "The fact that your skin is black is utterly irrelevant to the arguments that you raise." The fact that you sit here as is your rhetorical device and lay the entire weight of the Negro ordeal on your own shoulders is irrelevant to the argument that we are here to discuss.

The gravamen of Mr. Baldwin's charges against America are not so much that our civilization has failed him and his people, that our ideals are insufficient, but that we have no ideals, that our ideals rather are some sort of a superficial coating which we come up with at any given moment in order to justify whatever commercial and noxious experiment we are engaged in. Thus Mr. Baldwin can write his book *The Fire Next Time* in which he threatens America . . . he didn't, in writing that book, speak with the British accents that he used exclusively tonight in which he threatened America with the necessity for us . . .

[*Coughing, scattered laughter, and a shout of "shame!" Fullerton admonishes the crowd to permit Buckley to speak.*]

BUCKLEY: . . . for us to jettison our entire civilization. "The only thing that the white man has that the Negro should want," he said, "is power." And he is treated from coast to coast of the United States with a kind of unctuous servitude which, in point of fact, goes beyond anything that was ever expected from the most servile Negro creature by a southern family.

I'm proposing to pay him the honor this night of saying to him, Mr. Baldwin, I'm going to speak to you without any reference whatever to those surrounding protections which you are used to in virtue of the fact that you are a Negro, and in virtue of the fact that your race has dreadfully suffered at the hands of my race.[1] I am treating you as a fellow American, as a person whose indictments of our civilization are unjustified. As a person who—if his counsels are listened to—would be cursed by all of his grandchildren's grandchildren in virtue of what he actually seeks to bring down upon America in pursuit of his neurotic mission.

Ladies and gentlemen, we may or may not as you like spend as much of the balance of this evening as you like in reciting these luridities of oppression. One hundred and twenty-five years ago this house was bitterly divided over the question of whether or not the same people in England who practiced the faith of Erasmus, your most distinguished graduate, should be allowed to vote. By a slim margin it was condescended that they ought to be allowed to do so. In other parts of this country, there are people who in virtue of their having been invited into the United Nations, we are now told, are not savages or clowns who, for instance, in the case of the Watusi are responsible for—according to statistics, I know statistics seem to disturb some of you—but according to these statistics, some 10,000 or 12,000 of them were killed over a six-week period. We know that class antagonism and even [unintelligible] are responsible for—to take the figures of the American federation of labor and CIO—are responsible for 22 million deaths over a period of two and a half years in Red China. We know that British Guyana, in which there are very few white people, has been engaged in an internecine war between Indians and Africans. We know that the [unintelligible] don't get on with the [unintelligible] and we know that the untouchables have a hard life in India. We know that there was more blood shed trying to bring emancipation to the Irish here in the British Isles than has been shed by all of the people, ten times the number of people who have been lynched as a result of the delirium of race consciousness, race supremacy, in the United States in the days since the Reconstruction.

Shall we devote the night to these luridities? Shall we devote the evening to examining the sociological facts of human nature? There is an endogamous instinct in the average person whether he be Irish or whether he be German, or whether he be French or whether English. Shall we discuss these class antagonisms in terms of race, in terms of economic standing? Shall we discuss the fate of the oiks in Eton College? Shall we discuss in effect the existential dilemma of humankind? That people do, in fact, group together, and that when they amass power, they often tend to ascertain that the English had done as the Irish had done. Let us ask the questions, sir . . .

[*Buckley calls on a questioner in the audience.*]

AUDIENCE MEMBER: Point of information, sir. Why don't we discuss the motion?

[*Laughter, applause, and shouts of "hear, hear!"*]

BUCKLEY: To respond to your question, I was not given your instructions on how to comport myself before being invited here.

[*Laughter and applause.*]

It is a fact, and let us stipulate, that the situation in America is as it is, that the situation in Africa is as it is, that the situation in India is as it is. The question before the house, as I understand it, is not ought we to have purchased slaves generations ago, or as we may be permitted to put it another way, ought the blacks who sold us these slaves, ought they to have sold them to us, but rather is there anything in the American dream, which intrinsically argues against some kind of a deliverance from a system that we all recognize as evil, as unsatisfactory, as arguing against the best impulses of a civilized society.[2]

And here we need to ask the question, What in fact shall we do about it, Mr. President? What shall we, in America, try to do, for instance, to eliminate those psychic humiliations which I join Mr. Baldwin in believing are the very worst aspects of this discrimination? You found it a source of considerable mirth to laugh away the statistics of my colleague Mr. Burford. I don't think they are insignificant; they are certainly not insignificant in a world which attaches a considerable importance to material progress. It is in fact the case that seven-tenths of the white income of the United States is equal to the income that is made by the average Negro. I don't think that this is an irrelevant statistic, ladies and gentlemen, but it takes the capitalization of fifteen, sixteen, seventeen thousand dollars per job in the United States. This was the capitalization that . . . that was not created exclusively as a result of Negro travail. My great-grandparents worked too; presumably yours worked also. I don't know of anything that has ever been created without the expense of something. All of you who hope for a diploma here are going to do that at the expense of a considerable amount of effort and I would thank you . . . [*audience laughter*] please not to deny the fact that a considerable amount of effort went into the production of a system which grants a greater degree of material well-being to the American Negro and that that is enjoyed by 95 percent of the other peoples of the human race. But even so, to the extent that your withering laughter suggested here, that you found this a contemptible observation, I agree! I don't think it matters that there are 35 millionaires among the Negro community, if there were 35, if there were 20 million millionaires among the Negro community of the United States, I would still agree with you, that we have a dastardly situation, but I am asking you not to make politics "as the crow flies," to use the fleeted phrase of Professor Oakeshott, but rather to consider what in fact is it that we Americans ought to do? What are your instructions that I am to take back to the United States, my friends? [*audience laughter*]. I want to know what it is that we should do, and especially I want to know whether it is time, in fact, to abandon the American dream as it has been defined by Mr. Heycock and Mr. Burford.

What in fact is it that we ought to do, for instance, to avoid due humiliations mentioned by Mr. Baldwin as being a part of his own experience during his lifetime. At the age of twelve, you will find on reading his book, he trespassed outside the ghetto of Harlem and was taken by the scruff of the neck by a policeman on Forty-Second Street and Madison Avenue, and said, "Here you nigger, go back to where you belong." Fifteen, twenty years later he goes in and asks for a scotch whiskey at the airport at Chicago, and is told by the white barman that he is obviously underage and under the circumstances cannot be served. I know! I know from your faces that you share with me the feeling of compassion and the feeling of outrage that this kind of thing should have happened. What in fact are we going to do to this policeman and what in fact are we going to do to this barman? How are we going to avoid the kind of humiliations that are perpetually visited on members of a minority race?

Obviously the first element is concern. We've got to care that it happens, we have got to do what we can to change the warp and woof of moral thought in society in such fashion as to try to make it happen less and less.[3] But the proposition before us tonight, as elaborated by Mr. Baldwin in his book *The Fire Next Time*, is we ought precisely to recognize that because the American civilization, and indeed the Western civilization, has failed him and his people, we ought to throw it over. He tells us that our civilization rests on the rantings of the Hebrew, sunbaked fanatic called Jesus—not, says he—reaching the depths of historical knowledge—truly the founder of the Christian religion. The founder of the Christian religion was actually Paul, whom he describes as a merciless fanatic. And as a result of the teachings of these people and notice, please, the soritic leap from that moment until this, we have Dachau. And Dachau forever foreclosed the notion and possibility that Christianity was a viable civilization. What is it appropriate for us to do under the circumstances if we assume that Dachau was the natural consequence of the teachings of Saint Paul and Jesus? What shall we do with the library around here to begin with? Shall we descend on it and uproot all the literature that depends in any way on the teachings of Plato and Aristotle because they justified slavery? Or shall we rather make the point, shall we . . . sir . . .

[*Buckley calls on a questioner in the audience.*]

AUDIENCE MEMBER: You keep asking what we should do and then you are telling us what we should *not* do.

BUCKLEY: I'll tell you in due course. The primary question before the house, as posed by the larger attitude taken by Mr. Baldwin, sir, is whether or not our civilization has shown itself so flawed as the result of the failure of its response to the Negro problem of the United States that it ought to be jettisoned. Now I suggest that anybody who argued, as indeed it may have been argued in this very house, for all I know, in this very chamber, 125 years ago, the very fact that Jews and Catholics were not given the vote, were not allowed to vote in England as late as 1828, suggested English civilization ought to have been jettisoned. I suggest that the other possibility ought to be considered: that precisely the reason they *did* get the vote was because English civilization was *not* jettisoned. That the whole point of our philosophical concern ought never to be to make that terrible fault that is made so frequently by the positivists, that we should so immanentize our own misgivings as to rush forward to jettison and to overthrow our civilization because we do not live up to its higher ideals.[4]

Let me urge this point to you which I can do with authority, my friends, the only thing that I can tonight [*scattered laughter*], and that is to tell you that in the United States, there is a concern for the Negro problem. Now if you get up to me and say . . . [*audience laughter*] if you get up to me and say, "Well now, is it the kind of concern that we, the students of Cambridge, would show if the problem were our own?" all I can say is I don't know. It may very well be that there has been some sort of a sunburst of moral enlightenment that has hit this community so as to make it predictable that if you were the governors of the United States, the situation would change overnight. I'm prepared to grant this as a form of courtesy, Mr. President [*audience laughter*].

But meanwhile I am saying to you that the engines of concern in the United States are working. The presence of Mr. Baldwin here tonight is in part a reflection of that concern [*scattered audience mumbling and shouting*]. You cannot go to a university in the United States, a university in the United States, presumably also governed by the Lord's spiritual as you are, in which Mr. Baldwin is not the toast of the town. You cannot go to a university of the United States in which practically all other problems of public policy are preempted by the primary policy of concern for the Negro. I challenge you to name another civilization anytime, anywhere, in the history of the world in which the problems of a minority which have been showing considerable material and political advancement is as much a subject of dramatic concern as it is in the United States.[5]

There is one thing that Americans are not willing to do. They are not willing, as a result of the exasperation of Mr. Baldwin to say that the whole American proposition was an unfortunate experiment. They are not willing to say that as a result of the fact that we have not accelerated faster the progress of the Negroes, we are going to desert the constitutional system, we are going to desert the idea of the rule of law, we are going to desert the idea of the individual rights of the American citizen, that we are going to burn all the Bibles, and turn our backs on Europe, and tell them that we want to reject our entire Judeo-Christian civilization and our entire Hellenic background because of the continuous persistence of the kind of evil that is so carefully and eloquently described by Mr. Baldwin.

[*Buckley calls on a questioner in the audience.*]

AUDIENCE MEMBER: I wonder if you can point out to me any one of Mr. Baldwin's writings in which he actually said he wants to get rid of civilization [*applause*]?

BUCKLEY: I don't know your rules intimately enough to know whether or not I should have been forbidden from reading Mr. Baldwin's books before arriving here. I understand it is part of the purpose of this program to promote the reading of those books [*audience laughter and applause*]. I quote you exactly a passage from Mr. Baldwin—which I would have thought would have traversed the Atlantic Ocean—in which he says, "The only thing that the whites have that the Negroes should want is power." If Mr. Baldwin chooses this electric occasion to renounce his own renunciation of civilization then I would think that you would have had a historic debate on your hands, Mr. President, and I do urge you to give Mr. Baldwin that opportunity and I hope he takes it.[6]

Let me just say finally, ladies and gentlemen, this: there is no instant cure for the race problem in America, and anybody who tells you that there is, is a charlatan and ultimately a boring man. Boring ... [*audience laughter and coughing*] precisely because he is then speaking in the kind of abstractions that do not relate to the human experience. The trouble in America where the Negro community is concerned is a very complicated one. I urge those of you who have an actual rather than a purely ideologized interest in the problem to read the book *Beyond the Melting Pot* by Professor Glazer, also coauthor of *The Lonely Crowd*, a prominent Jewish intellectual, who points to the fact that the situation in America where the Negroes are concerned is extremely complex as a result of an unfortunate conjunction of two factors. One is the dreadful efforts to perpetuate discrimination by many individual American citizens as a result of their lack of that final and ultimate concern which some people are truly trying to agitate. The other is as a result of the failure of the Negro community itself to make certain exertions, which were made by other minority groups during the American experience. If you can stand a statistic not of my own making, let me give you one which Professor Glazer considers as relevant; he says, for instance, "In 1900, there were 3,500 Negro doctors in America; in 1960, there were 3,900, an increase in 400." Is this because there were no opportunities, [as] has been suggested by Mr. Heycock and also by Mr. Baldwin, implicitly? No, says Professor Glazer, there are a great many medical schools, who by no means practice discrimination, who are anxious to receive ... to train Negro doctors; there are scholarships available to put them through. But in fact that particular energy, which he remarks was so noticeable in the Jewish community, and to a certain and lesser extent, in the Italian, Irish community, for some reason is not there.

We should focus on the necessity to animate this particular energy, but he comes to the conclusion which strikes me as plausible, that the people who can best do it, who can do it most effectively, are Negroes themselves.[7] And what should James Baldwin be doing rather than telling us that we should renounce our civilization. Rather in my judgment he should be addressing his own people, and urging them to take at least the advantage of those opportunities that exist, and urging us, as he has been doing, to make those opportunities wider and better than those that exist. Says Mr. Glazer: in relative terms, the Chinese community derives forty-five times as much income from the patronage of its own people as the Negroes do from the patronage of their own people. In fact, these problems do exist, and let us so sentimentalize the question as to assume they don't exist, because to do so is hardly to render any kind of creative fervor to the Negro problem.[8]

Let me conclude by reminding you, ladies and gentlemen, that where the Negro is concerned, the danger as far as I can see at this moment is that they will seek to reach out for some sort of radical solutions on the basis of which the true problem is obscured. They have done [a] great deal to focus on the fact of white discrimination against Negroes. They have great . . . done a great deal to agitate a moral concern, but where, in fact, do they go now? They seem to be slipping, if you will read carefully, for instance, the words of Mr. Bayard Rustin, towards some sort of a procrustean formulation which ends up less urging the advancement of the Negro than the regression of the white people. Fourteen times as many people in New York City born of Negroes are illegitimate as of whites. This is a problem. How shall we address it? By seeking out laws that encourage illegitimacy in white people? This, unfortunately, tends to be the rhetorical momentum that some of the arguments are taking.

[*Buckley calls on a questioner in the audience.*]

AUDIENCE MEMBER: One thing you might do, Mr. Buckley, is let them vote in Mississippi [*audience applause and shouts of "here, here!"*]!

BUCKLEY: I agree, I agree [*applause continues*]. I couldn't agree with you more. And for . . . [*audience laughter*]. Except, lest I appear too ingratiating, which is hardly my objective here tonight, I think actually what is wrong in Mississippi, sir, is not that not enough Negroes are voting but that too many white people are voting [*audience laughter and applause*].

Booker T. Washington said that the important thing where Negroes are concerned is not that they hold public office but that they be prepared to hold public office, not that they vote but that they be prepared to vote. What ought we to do with the Negroes having taught the Negroes in Mississippi to despise Ross Barnett? Shall we then teach them to emulate their cousins in Harlem and adore Adam Clayton Powell Jr.? It is much more complicated, sir, than simply the question of giving them the vote. If I were myself a constituent of the community of Mississippi at this moment, what I would do is vote to lift the standards of the vote so as to disqualify 65 percent of the white people . . . [*audience laughter*] who are presently voting [*audience laughter and applause*].

I say, then, that what we need is a considerable amount of frankness that acknowledges that there are two sets of difficulties: the difficulties of the white person who acts as white people and brown people and black people do all over the world to protect their own vested interests who have, as all of the races in the entire world have and suffer from a kind of a racial narcissism, which tends always to convert every contingency into such a way as to maximize their own power, that yes, we must do. But we must also reach through to the Negro people and tell them that their best chances are in a mobile society, and the most mobile society in the world today, my friends, is the United States of America.

AUDIENCE MEMBER: "Hear, hear!"

BUCKLEY: The most mobile society in the world is the United States of America, and it is precisely that mobility which will give opportunities to the Negroes which they must be encouraged to take, but they must not, in the course of their ordeal, be encouraged to adopt the kind of cynicism, the kind of despair, the kind of iconoclasm that is urged upon them by Mr. Baldwin in his recent works. Because of one thing I can tell you I believe with absolute authority, that where the United States is concerned, if it ever becomes a confrontation between a continuation of our own sort of idealism, the private stock of which, granted, like most people in the world we tend to lavish only every now and then on public enterprises, reserving it so often for our own irritations and pleasures, but the fundamental friend of the Negro people in the United States is the good nature and is the generosity, and is the good wishes, is the decency, the fundamental decency that do lie at the reserves of the spirit of the American people.

These must not be laughed at, under no circumstances must they be laughed at, and under no circumstances must America be addressed and told that the only alternative to the status quo is to overthrow that civilization which we consider to be the faith of our fathers, the faith indeed of your fathers. This is what must animate whatever meliorism must come because if it does finally come to a confrontation, a radical confrontation, between giving up what we understand to be the best features of the American way of life, which at that level is indistinguishable, so far as I can see, from the European way of life, then we will fight the issue, and we will fight the issue not only in the Cambridge Union, but we will fight it as you were once recently called to do on beaches and on hills, on mountains and on landing grounds. And we will be convinced that just as you won the war against a particular threat to civilization, you were nevertheless waging a war in favor of and for the benefit of Germans, your own enemies, just as we are convinced that if it should ever come to that kind of a confrontation, our own determination to win the struggle will be a determination to wage a war not only for whites but also for Negroes.

[Audience applause and scattered shouting for about half a minute.]

FULLERTON: Will the tellers take their places, please?

[*Members of the Union cast their votes by walking through the "aye" or "nay" door. After the votes are tallied, Fullerton rises to announce the results.*]

FULLERTON: Those voted in favor of the motion, the motion being that the American dream is at the expense of the Negro, those voted in favor of that motion 544 persons and against 164 persons. The motion is therefore carried by 380 votes. I declare the house to stand adjourned.

[*Applause.*]

Notes

Prologue

1. "A Tribute to the Union—150 Years," *Varsity*, February 13, 1965.

2. The BBC recording of the debate has been made available by the Riverbends Channel on YouTube, https://www.youtube.com/watch?v=oFeoS41xe7w.

3. Magdalena J. Zaborowska, *James Baldwin's Turkish Decade: Erotics of Exile* (Durham, NC: Duke University Press, 2008), 260.

4. *American Masters—Maya Angelou: And I Still Rise*, PBS documentary. References to Baldwin's "frog eyes" abound in the biographies. See, for example, William J. Weatherby, *James Baldwin: Artist on Fire, a Portrait* (New York: Dutton Adult, 1989), 7.

5. Rose Styron and R. Blakeslee Gilpin, eds., *Selected Letters of William Styron* (New York: Random House, 2012), 532.

6. Kevin Schultz, *Buckley and Mailer: The Difficult Friendship That Shaped the Sixties* (New York: W. W. Norton, 2015), 19.

7. James Baldwin, "Down at the Cross" (1962), in *James Baldwin: Collected Essays*, ed. Toni Morrison (New York: Library of America, 1998), 347.

8. William F. Buckley Jr., "Today We Are Educated Men," in *Let Us Talk of Many Things: The Collected Speeches* (New York: Forum, 2000), 4, 5, 6.

9. In the words of Garry Wills, Buckley was "not a reflective thinker. He was a quick responder. . . . His gifts were facility, flash, and charm, not depth or prolonged wrestling with a problem." Garry Wills, *Outside Looking In* (New York: Viking, 2010), 160.

10. Larry L. King, "God, Man, and William F. Buckley," *Harper's Magazine*, March 1967.

11. For more on Buckley's personal charm, see, for example, Wills, *Outside Looking In*, 151–52.

12. For a comparison of Buckley to Tomás de Torquemada, see Charles Lam Markmann, *The Buckleys: A Family Examined* (New York: William Morrow, 1973), 65.

13. Lee Edwards, *Standing Athwart History: The Political Thought of William F. Buckley Jr.* (Washington, DC: Heritage Foundation, 2010), 19.

14. Steve Fiffer and Adar Cohen, *Jimmie Lee & James: Two Lives, Two Deaths, and the Movement That Changed America* (New York: Simon and Schuster, 2015), 12–13.

15. Ibid., 16.

16. Ibid.

17. Ibid.

18. Taylor Branch, *Pillar of Fire: America in the King Years, 1963–65* (New York: Simon and Schuster, 1998), 593.

19. Ibid.

20. This ground has been covered well by each man's biographers. See, for example, John Judis, *William F. Buckley, Jr.: The Patron Saint of the Conservatives* (New York: Simon and Schuster, 1988); Alvin S. Felzenberg, *A Man and His Presidents* (New Haven, CT: Yale University Press, 2017); Carl Bogus,

Buckley (New York: Bloomsbury, 2011); David Leeming, *James Baldwin: A Biography* (New York: Arcade, 2015); Weatherby, *James Baldwin*.

21. It is worth noting that I approach this subject with the training of a political theorist, which is a field that occupies the ground—in the words of the late Judith Shklar—between history and ethics. In what follows, I go beyond mere description of the ideas of Baldwin and Buckley to offer some analysis of moral status of those thoughts.

22. The median income of white families is ten times that of black families. Pew Research Center, "How Wealth Inequality Has Changed in the U.S. since the Great Recession, by Race and Ethnicity," November 1, 2017, http://www.pewresearch.org/fact-tank/2017/11/01/how-wealth -inequality-has-changed-in-the-u-s-since-the-great-recession-by-race-ethnicity-and-income/.

White adults over twenty-five years old are far more likely to have bachelor's degrees or high school diplomas than their black counterparts. Pew Research Center, "On Views of Race and Inequality, Blacks and Whites Are Worlds Apart," June 27, 2016, http://www.pewsocialtrends.org/2016 /06/27/1-demographic-trends-and-economic-well-being/#blacks-still-trail-whites-in-college -completion. Black Americans are far less likely to own homes than are whites, and their applications for mortgage loans are denied at more than twice the rate. Pew Research Center, "Blacks and Hispanics Face Extra Challenges in Getting Home Loans," January 10, 2017, http://www.pewsocialtrends.org /2016/06/27/1-demographic-trends-and-economic-well-being/#blacks-still-trail-whites-in-college -completion.

23. Ibram X. Kendi, *Stamped from the Beginning: The Definitive History of Racist Ideas in America* (New York: Nation Books, 2016), 1. Blacks are 3.7 times more likely to be arrested for marijuana possession, for example, despite the fact that their usage rate is comparable to whites. See, in general, Ezekiel Edwards, Will Bunting, and Lynda Garcia, *The War on Marijuana in Black and White* (New York: American Civil Liberties Union, 2013).

Chapter 1. The Ghetto and the Mansion, 1924–46

1. James Baldwin, "The Harlem Ghetto" (1948), in *James Baldwin: Collected Essays*, ed. Toni Morrison (New York: Library of America, 1998), 42.

2. As noted in the prologue, this ground has been covered well by biographers of Baldwin and Buckley. See, for example, John Judis, *William F. Buckley, Jr.: The Patron Saint of the Conservatives* (New York: Simon and Schuster, 1988); Alvin S. Felzenberg, *A Man and His Presidents* (New Haven, CT: Yale University Press, 2017); Carl Bogus, *Buckley* (New York: Bloomsbury, 2011); David Leeming, *James Baldwin: A Biography* (New York: Arcade, 2015); William J. Weatherby, *James Baldwin: Artist on Fire, a Portrait* (New York: Dutton Adult, 1989).

3. See, in general, Jonathan Gill, *Harlem: The Four Hundred Year History from Dutch Village to Capital of Black America* (New York: Grove Press, 2011).

4. "The average Harlemite," historian Jonathan Gill has noted, "made under $18 per sixty-hour week," compared to whites, who were paid about $23 for a sixty-hour week." By "the early 1930s a quarter of all Harlem residents were out of work," and by the height of the Depression, the number of unemployed doubled to 50 percent of the Harlem population. Ibid., 283.

5. Baldwin, "Harlem Ghetto," 42.

6. Gill, *Harlem*, 284. All this corresponds with Baldwin's own recollections of the Harlem of his youth. As he looked back on those years, he remembered buildings that were "old and in desperate need of repair," "too many human beings per square block," rents "higher than anywhere else in the city," "jobs harder to get," and a realization that adequate food and clothing was anything but a given. Baldwin, "Harlem Ghetto," 42.

7. Gill, *Harlem*, 285. See also Roi Ottley and William J. Weatherby, *The Negro in New York* (Santa Barbara: Praeger, 1967), 270–71.

8. Ottley and Weatherby, *Negro in New York*, 270–71.

9. William Francis Buckley did not become William Frank Buckley Jr. until he decided to change his name at the age of five. More on this below.

10. For an extensive discussion of Aloïse Steiner Buckley's "Southern frame of mind," see Reid Buckley, *An American Family: The Buckleys* (New York: Threshold Editions, 2008), 76–83.

11. Felzenberg, *A Man and His Presidents*, 8. On the Buckley family connections to the Confederacy, see Garry Wills, *Outside Looking In* (New York: Viking, 2010), 157.

12. Bogus, *Buckley*, 61.

13. The older children were "supervised," as Buckley's brother Reid would put it, by a French governess called Mademoiselle Bouchex, and the younger kids were under the supervision of a woman they called their "Mexican Nana." English was spoken in the Buckley household, but so too was French and Spanish; Aloïse and the children were fluent in both, and Will, who had spent years living in Mexico, was also a fluent Spanish speaker. Buckley, *American Family*, 194.

14. William F. Buckley Jr., *Miles Gone By: A Literary Autobiography* (Washington, DC: Regnery Publishing, 2004), 4, 19.

15. Buckley, *American Family*, 215.

16. Bogus, *Buckley*, 66.

17. Aloise reports that the Buckley children received instruction in "apologetics, art, ballroom dancing, banjo, bird-watching, building boats in bottles, calligraphy, canoeing, carpentry, cooking, driving trotting horses, French, folk-dancing, golf, guitar (Hawaiian and Spanish), harmony, herb-gardening, horsemanship, history of architecture, ice-skating, mandolin, marimba, music appreciation, organ, painting, playing popular music, rumba, sailing, skiing, singing, Spanish, speech, stenography, swimming, tap-dancing, tennis, typing, and wood-carving." Priscilla L. Buckley and William F. Buckley Jr., eds., *W.F.B.: An Appreciation by His Family and Friends* (privately printed, 1959).

18. Aloise reported that her father, Will, was a dominant presence in these conversations. "At the foot of the table sits Papa," she wrote, "eating, talking, laughing, teasing, dominating the table with gust and vigor, the gaiety and the concentration on the moment at hand which, until his last illness, entered the house and left it only with him." See ibid., 202.

19. Buckley, *American Family*, 209.

20. Although I think it is important that we resist the temptation to conclude that the worldviews of Baldwin and Buckley were determined by the environments in which they were born and raised, we must not ignore the striking contrasts between the two scenes thus depicted. While Baldwin's childhood was marked by uncertainty over the security of basic necessities, Buckley was awash in abundance. While Baldwin found himself often placed in the position of caretaker of his younger siblings, Buckley had his every need met by a doting staff. The claustrophobia that Baldwin felt in the confines of the Harlem ghetto seems worlds away from the open air of the Connecticut countryside in which Buckley frolicked. The physical spaces that Baldwin and Buckley occupied in their early years did not determine the men they would become, but they certainly did a great deal to shape their perspectives. When Buckley would think later about what it was that he was trying to conserve, he would think of his idyllic childhood at Great Elm and feel grateful for the system that had made a life of such plenty possible. The sense of "captivity" that Baldwin felt in the streets of Harlem as a young man would inspire him to formulate a radical philosophy that might save future generations from the sort of childhood he endured.

21. Leeming, *James Baldwin*, 9.

22. Buckley, *Miles Gone By*, 27, 51, 52.

23. Ibid., 52.

24. Buckley, *American Family*, 79, 80.

25. Felzenberg, *A Man and His Presidents*, 9.

26. Ibid., 13–15.

27. For a detailed explanation of Buckley's ascent up from his father's anti-Semitism, see ibid., 22, 28–29.

28. Judis, *William F. Buckley, Jr.*, 27.

29. Albert Jay Nock, *The State of the Union* (Indianapolis: Liberty Fund, 2011), 133.

30. Felzenberg, *A Man and His Presidents*, 10.

31. King, "God, Man, and William F. Buckley."

32. According to Wills, Buckley's "supreme values" throughout his life were "Catholicism and the Market." See Garry Wills, "The Buckley Myth," *New York Review of Books*, August 11, 2015.

33. Buckley and Buckley, *W.F.B.*, 257.

34. Leeming, *James Baldwin*, 8.

35. Kenneth B. Clark, "A Conversation with James Baldwin," in *Conversations with James Baldwin*, ed. Fred R. Standley and Louis H. Pratt (Jackson: University Press of Mississippi, 1989), 38.

36. James Baldwin, "My Dungeon Shook" (1962), in *James Baldwin: Collected Essays*, ed. Toni Morrison (New York: Library of America, 1998), 291.

37. Fred R. Standley and Louis H. Pratt, eds., *Conversations with James Baldwin*, (Jackson: University Press of Mississippi, 1989), 39.

38. James Baldwin, "Notes of a Native Son" (1955), in *James Baldwin: Collected Essays*, ed. Toni Morrison (New York: Library of America, 1998), 64–65.

39. Ibid., 64.

40. James Baldwin, "Down at the Cross" (1962), in *James Baldwin: Collected Essays*, ed. Toni Morrison (New York: Library of America, 1998), 334.

41. Leeming, *James Baldwin*, 13. Indeed, Baldwin claims to have literally read every book in the neighborhood library.

42. For more on Baldwin's relationship with Cullen, see ibid., 21–26.

43. Ibid., 26.

44. Baldwin, "Down at the Cross," 305.

45. Ibid., 302, 301.

46. Ibid., 306–10.

47. Leeming, *James Baldwin*, 33.

48. James Baldwin, "On the Painter Beauford Delaney" (1965), in *James Baldwin: Collected Essays*, ed. Toni Morrison (New York: Library of America, 1998), 721.

49. Marcella Whalen, "Letters to the Editor," *National Review*, August 13, 1963, 120. More on the provenance of these letters below.

50. Felzenberg, *A Man and His Presidents*, 15; Bogus, *Buckley*, 67.

51. Bogus, *Buckley*, 67.

52. Buckley and Buckley, *W.F.B.*, 244.

53. Buckley, *American Family*, 210. Larry L. King, who profiled Buckley for *Harper's* in 1967, concluded that Buckley had "no suspicion that he could possibly be wrong about anything." Larry L. King, "God, Man, and William F. Buckley," *Harper's Magazine*, March 1967.

54. On Buckley's deferment, see Robert Sherrill, "William F. Buckley Lived off Evil as Mold Lives off Garbage," *Nation*, June 11, 1988, 829–36. Buckley spent some time at the University of Mexico during this period.

55. Lucille B. Milner, "Jim Crow in the Army," in *Reporting Civil Rights, Part One: American Journalism, 1941–1963*, ed. Clayborne Carson, David J. Garrow, Bill Kovach, and Carol Polsgrove (New York: Library of America, 2003), 54, 56.

56. William F. Buckley Jr. to Will Buckley, undated, William F. Buckley Jr. Papers (MS 576), Manuscripts and Archives, Yale University Library. The army was still officially segregated at the time Buckley wrote this letter so Buckley seems to be objecting to the very presence of black soldiers at the base.

57. Leeming, *James Baldwin*, 37.

58. James Baldwin, "Faulkner and Desegregation" (1956), in *James Baldwin: Collected Essays*, ed. Toni Morrison (New York: Library of America, 1998), 209.

59. James Baldwin, "Notes of a Native Son" (1955), in *James Baldwin: Collected Essays*, ed. Toni Morrison (New York: Library of America, 1998), 69.

60. Ibid., 70–71.

61. Ibid., 69, 72.

62. For more on the high incidence of lung disorders in Harlem, see Gill, *Harlem*, 285.

63. Leeming, *James Baldwin*, 44.

64. Ibid., 45–46.

65. When pressed later in life, Baldwin would describe himself as bisexual.

66. James Baldwin interview with Mavis Nicholson, https://www.youtube.com/watch?v=XZPmT3lk6cU.

67. James Baldwin, "The Price of the Ticket" (1985), in *James Baldwin: Collected Essays*, ed. Toni Morrison (New York: Library of America, 1998), 834.

68. Leeming, *James Baldwin*, 50.

69. Ibid., 49.

70. Baldwin, "Price of the Ticket," 834.

71. Baldwin suggests this understanding of Worth's demise in "The New Lost Generation" (1961), in *James Baldwin: Collected Essays*, ed. Toni Morrison (New York: Library of America, 1998), 659.

Chapter 2. Disturbing the Peace, 1946–54

1. See, in general, Fern Marja Eckman, *The Furious Passage of James Baldwin* (Lanham, MD: Rowman and Littlefield, 1966).

2. David Leeming, *James Baldwin: A Biography* (New York: Arcade, 2015), xii; Eckman, *Furious Passage of James Baldwin*, 13, 141.

3. Carl Bogus, *Buckley* (New York: Bloomsbury, 2011), 72.

4. Eckman, *Furious Passage of James Baldwin*, 13.

5. In what follows, I will not provide exhaustive analyses of everything Baldwin and Buckley ever published; they were far too prolific for that sort of treatment. Instead, I have chosen to discuss writings that I deem to be especially relevant to the debate at Cambridge.

6. Leeming, *James Baldwin*, 50, 293. See also James Baldwin, "Review of *The Best Short Stories* by Maxim Gorky," in *The Cross of Redemption: Uncollected Writings*, ed. Randall Kenan (New York: Pantheon Books, 2010), 291–93.

7. James Baldwin, "Smaller than Life" (1947), in *James Baldwin: Collected Essays*, ed. Toni Morrison (New York: Library of America, 1998), 577–78.

8. Ibid., 578. In this line of critique, we can see the influence of Baldwin's mother on his worldview. As noted in chapter 1, Berdis taught her children that true love required acceptance of not only a

person's virtues but also their shortcomings. Baldwin thought this was a worthwhile thing to remember for writers of fiction and nonfiction.

9. Ibid.

10. Sam Tanenhaus, "William F. Buckley Jr.: Founder," *Yale Alumni Magazine*, May–June 2008, 2.

11. William F. Buckley Jr., *Miles Gone By: A Literary Autobiography* (Washington, DC: Regnery Publishing, 2004), 95–96, 99.

12. Tanenhaus, "William F. Buckley Jr.," 1.

13. Charles Seymour, "Inaugural Address," Yale University, 1937, https://inauguration.yale.edu/sites /default/files/files/Seymour%2C%20Charles_PWJ.pdf.

14. John Judis, *William F. Buckley, Jr.: The Patron Saint of the Conservatives* (New York: Simon and Schuster, 1988), 59.

15. Buckley, *Miles Gone By*, 59.

16. Frederick D. Wilhelmsen and Willmoore Kendall, "Cicero and the Politics of Public Orthodoxy," in *Christianity and Political Philosophy*, ed. Frederick D. Wilhelmsen (Athens: University of Georgia Press, 1978), 26, 35–36. Among other things, Kendall believed that the idea of public orthodoxy not only legitimized the power of Athenians to "refuse Socrates' program" but also justified the right—and in fact the duty—of the Athenians "to refuse . . . to tolerate Socrates." Willmoore Kendall, "The People versus Socrates Revisited," *Modern Age* 3, no. 1 (Winter 58–59): 110. Although this piece was published after Buckley attended Yale, there can be little doubt based on Kendall's earlier writings that this was the sort of view he was teaching his students in the late 1940s.

17. George H. Nash, *The Conservative Intellectual Tradition in America since 1945* (New York: Open Road Media, 2006), 386.

18. Buckley, *Miles Gone By*, 58–59.

19. It is important to note that Kendall's trust in the "common man" led him to embrace various forms of majoritarianism throughout his career. This is a commitment Buckley was not able to make. While he would occasionally find appeals to majoritarianism politically useful, he was—at his core—an elitist. He would much rather see the public orthodoxy defined and enforced by a remnant of elites. For an excellent discussion of Kendall's evolving majoritarian views, see Nash, *Conservative Intellectual Movement*, 350–94.

20. Charles Lam Markmann, *The Buckleys: A Family Examined* (New York: William Morrow, 1973), 58, 62.

21. Buckley, *Miles Gone By*, 58.

22. James Baldwin, "Autobiographical Notes" (1955), in *James Baldwin: Collected Essays*, ed. Toni Morrison (New York: Library of America, 1998), 9.

23. Murray Friedman, ed., "Introduction: Commentary: The First 60 Years," in *Commentary in American Life* (Philadelphia: Temple University Press, 2005), 1.

24. James Baldwin, "The Harlem Ghetto" (1948), in *James Baldwin: Collected Essays*, ed. Toni Morrison (New York: Library of America, 1998), 42, 47, 44.

25. Ibid., 49–51

26. Ibid., 52, 54.

27. For evidence of the conservatism of Yale's student body, see Tanenhaus, "William F. Buckley Jr."

28. Alastair Horne, *A Bundle from Britain* (New York: St. Martin's Press, 1994), 175, 206.

29. Bogus, *Buckley*, 74.

30. Judis, *William F. Buckley, Jr.*, 62; Alvin S. Felzenberg, *A Man and His Presidents* (New Haven, CT: Yale University Press, 2017), 26.

31. Markmann, *Buckleys*, 63–64.

32. Clayborne Carson, ed., "Chronology, 1941–1973," in *Reporting Civil Rights, Part One: American Journalism, 1941–1963*, ed. Clayborne Carson, David J. Garrow, Bill Kovach, and Carol Polsgrove (New York: Library of America, 2003), 899.

33. Platform of the Democratic Party, 1948, http://www.presidency.ucsb.edu/ws/index.php?pid=29599.

34. Platform of the States' Rights Democratic Party, 1948, http://www.presidency.ucsb.edu/ws/?pid=25851.

35. Strom Thurmond, "Address by J. Strom Thurmond, Governor of South Carolina, Accepting the States' Rights Democratic Nomination for President of the United States" (speech given in Houston, TX, August 11, 1948).

36. Platform of the Progressive Party, 1948, http://credo.library.umass.edu/view/full/mums312-b121-i298.

37. Patricia Sullivan, "Henry Wallace's Campaign Foreshadowed the Movement as Well as the Rainbow," *Southern Changes* 10, no. 5 (1988): 11, 16–17.

38. Carson, "Chronology," 900.

39. James Baldwin, "Journey to Atlanta" (1948), in *James Baldwin: Collected Essays*, ed. Toni Morrison (New York: Library of America, 1998), 57–58.

40. Ibid., 54.

41. Ibid., 55.

42. Ibid., 59, 60.

43. I have been unable to find any evidence of Buckley devoting much thought to Thurmond's candidacy, but it seems likely he would have discussed it with his father, who would later tell Thurmond, "I don't know of any other man in public life whose views I entirely approve of." Joseph Crespino, *Strom Thurmond's America* (New York: Farrar, Straus and Giroux, 2012).

44. The apology, Buckley insisted, was merely an attempt to prevent leftists from utilizing "legal chicanery" to undermine the reputation of "a universally respected scholar." Markmann, *Buckleys*, 74; Felzenberg, *A Man and His Presidents*, 30–31.

45. According to Buckley biographer Alvin Felzenberg, "A poll of four hundred undergraduate and graduate students on election eve by the *Yale Daily News* put Dewey's support at 63 percent." Felzenberg, *A Man and His Presidents*, 29.

46. Markmann, *Buckleys*, 62.

47. Isaac Arnsdorf and Victor Zapana, "Editorials Presaged Authorial Style, Voice," *Yale Daily News*, February 28, 2008.

48. "For the Republican Conclave," *Yale Daily News*, April 30, 1949.

49. Arnsdorf and Zapana, "Editorials Presaged Authorial Style."

50. William F. Buckley Jr., *God and Man at Yale* (Washington, DC: Regnery Publishing, 1951), 14–15.

51. Tanenhaus, "William F. Buckley Jr.," 2.

52. Ibid., 8.

53. Bogus, *Buckley*, 78.

54. James Baldwin, "Everybody's Protest Novel" (1949), in *James Baldwin: Collected Essays*, ed. Toni Morrison (New York: Library of America, 1998), 11–12, 14.

55. Ibid., 15–16.

56. Ibid., 13.

57. Ibid., 12. It is worth noting here that this basic devotion to human dignity, which Baldwin articulates here in his mid-twenties, would continue to be the lodestar of his moral and political philosophy for the rest of his life.

58. Ibid., 12, 14–15.

59. Leeming, *James Baldwin*, 49.

60. Baldwin, "Everybody's Protest Novel," 18.

61. Buckley, *God and Man at Yale*, 208–9, 210.

62. It is difficult to say what might have happened if Buckley had been permitted to deliver his Alumni Day address in 1950. Buckley biographer Carl Bogus has suggested that the administration's recalcitrance inspired Buckley to pursue "a different means" of sending his message in the form of the book that would become *God and Man at Yale*. See Bogus, *Buckley*, 79.

63. William F. Buckley Jr., *Let Us Talk of Many Things: The Collected Speeches* (New York: Forum, 2000), 4, 5.

64. Ibid., 6.

65. James Baldwin, "Many Thousands Gone" (1951), in *James Baldwin: Collected Essays*, ed. Toni Morrison (New York: Library of America, 1998), 19.

66. Ibid. (emphasis added). The "voice" Baldwin adopted in some of these early essays proved confusing to some readers. Norman Podhoretz can recall arguing with his friends in the late 1940s about whether or not Baldwin was black or white. Norman Podhoretz, interview with the author, November 29, 2016.

67. Ibid., 19, 21, 20.

68. Ibid., 25, 26–27.

69. Ibid., 34.

70. Bogus, *Buckley*, 79. For more about Patricia Taylor Buckley, see, in general, Christopher Buckley, *Losing Mum and Pup: A Memoir* (New York: Grand Central Publishing, 2009).

71. For more on the roles played by Kendall and Chodorov, see Buckley, *Miles Gone By*, 58–59.

72. Buckley, *God and Man at Yale*, lxiii, lxv, lxiv.

73. Ibid., lxvi. In his autobiography, Buckley says that Kendall was "responsible for the provocative arrangement of [this] pair of sentences," which "got me into more trouble than any others in the book." Buckley, *Miles Gone By*, 59.

74. Buckley, *God and Man at Yale*, lxvii.

75. By "Manichaeanism," I mean that Buckley viewed the world in terms of a dualistic struggle between good and evil.

76. In chapter 5, I will discuss Buckley's failed attempt to produce a "big book" of political philosophy.

77. The relationship between relativism and the Manichaeanism described above is a complicated one, but it seems that Buckley was drawing a distinction between the status of truth in the realm of morality (where good and evil were clear to him) and the status of truth in the realm of politics (where the powerful are permitted to define truth).

78. I repurpose the philosophical-operational distinction from Kathleen Knight and Robert Erikson, "Ideology in the 1990s," in *Understanding Public Opinion*, ed. Barbara Norrander and Clyde Wilcox (Washington, DC: CQ Press, 1997), 286.

79. Buckley, *God and Man at Yale*, 4, 3–5, 7, 16.

80. Ibid., 42–43, 101.

81. Ibid., 104.

82. American Association of University Professors and the Association of American Colleges and Universities, *Statement of Principles of Academic Freedom and Tenure*, 1940, https://www.aaup.org/report/1940-statement-principles-academic-freedom-and-tenure.

83. Buckley, *God and Man at Yale*, 127.

84. Ibid., 133, 136.

85. Ibid., 138–39. Buckley also acknowledged that the "orthodoxy" Yale ought to enforce should be subject to revision, modification, and reinterpretation. The examination and criticism of Christianity and individualism, though, must be anchored in a general commitment to their preservation "until something better comes along" (in the case of individualism, at least).

86. Ibid., 161, 143.

87. Bogus, *Buckley*, 89.

88. Felzenberg, *A Man and His Presidents*, 46–47.

89. Bogus, *Buckley*, 89–90.

90. Buckley, *Miles Gone By*, 59; Bogus, *Buckley*, 84.

91. James Baldwin, "Stranger in the Village" (1953), in *James Baldwin: Collected Essays*, ed. Toni Morrison (New York: Library of America, 1998), 119.

92. I will return to some of the themes of this essay in chapter 7.

93. It is not possible to do this complex novel justice in the space available here so I will limit my analysis to themes that are most relevant to Baldwin's debate with Buckley.

94. James Baldwin, *Go Tell It on the Mountain*, in *Early Novels and Stories*, ed. Toni Morrison (New York: Library of America, 1998), 192.

95. Leeming, *James Baldwin*, 89.

96. Baldwin, *Go Tell It on the Mountain*, 32.

97. Ibid., 34.

98. Leeming, *James Baldwin*, 86.

99. Baldwin, *Go Tell It on the Mountain*, 153–55.

100. As David Leeming has pointed out, the characters in *Mountain* are "composites" of several people in Baldwin's life, including himself. See, in general, Leeming, *James Baldwin*, 84–89.

101. James Baldwin, "Down at the Cross" (1962), in *James Baldwin: Collected Essays*, ed. Toni Morrison (New York: Library of America, 1998), 347.

102. Baldwin, *Go Tell It on the Mountain*, 166.

103. Harry Truman, "Report to the American People on Korea," April 11, 1951, https://millercenter.org/the-presidency/presidential-speeches/april-11-1951-report-american-people-korea.

104. Joseph McCarthy, "Enemies Within" (speech delivered in Wheeling, West Virginia, February 9, 1950), https://liberalarts.utexas.edu/coretexts/_files/resources/texts/1950%20McCarthy%20Enemies.pdf.

105. For Truman's approval ratings, see "Presidential Approval Ratings—Gallup Historical Statistics and Trends," Gallup, http://news.gallup.com/poll/116677/presidential-approval-ratings-gallup-historical-statistics-trends.aspx.

106. "Truman Wrote of '48 Offer to Eisenhower," *New York Times*, July 11, 2003.

107. "Democrats Vote Today," *New York Times*, July 25, 1952.

108. See, in general, Mark V. Tushnet, *The NAACP's Legal Strategy against Segregated Education, 1925–1950* (Chapel Hill: University of North Carolina Press, 2012). The fund's strategy relied on these cases to build a legal rationale that could serve as the basis for broader challenges in the future and also wisely relied less on the hearts of southerners than on their pocketbooks. The reigning legal doctrine held that segregation was consistent with the Constitution's promise of equal protection if the separate facilities provided for blacks were equal. In most instances, of course, they were not, and in order to make them so, states and localities would have to start investing major amounts of taxpayer dollars to improve them—a political nonstarter to be sure.

109. Richard Brust, "The Court Comes Together," *ABA Journal* (April 2004).

110. Brown v. Board of Education, Topeka, Kansas, 347 U.S. 483 (1954).

111. James Poling, "Thurgood Marshall and the 14th Amendment," in *Reporting Civil Rights, Part One: American Journalism, 1941–1963*, ed. Clayborne Carson, David J. Garrow, Bill Kovach, and Carol Polsgrove (New York: Library of America, 2003), 150.

Chapter 3. Joining the Battle, 1955–61

1. Buckley's father encouraged him to "spend a couple of years in study . . . at Oxford or Cambridge" before "going into politics" or writing about "public questions" through journalism. Buckley did not heed his father's advice. See Priscilla L. Buckley and William F. Buckley Jr., eds., *W.F.B.: An Appreciation by His Family and Friends* (privately printed, 1959), 247.

2. William F. Buckley Jr., "Bad Little Black Sambo," *Freeman* (October 1952): 59–60. In this piece, Buckley objected to a proposal to ban "Little Black Sambo" from New York public schools.

3. Alvin S. Felzenberg, *A Man and His Presidents* (New Haven, CT: Yale University Press, 2017), 53.

4. It was also during this period that Buckley was appointed president of the Intercollegiate Society of Individualists, an educational foundation established to propagate right-wing ideas. Buckley held the post for only a short time, during which he reported that he was little more than a "figurehead." The organization would later be renamed the Intercollegiate Studies Institute and would play a key role in getting conservative ideas heard on college campuses. See George Thayer, *The Farther Shores of Politics: The American Political Fringe Today* (New York: Simon and Schuster, 1967), 284–88.

5. William F. Buckley Jr. and L. Brent Bozell Jr., *McCarthy and His Enemies* (Washington, DC: Regnery Publishing, 1954), vii.

6. Ibid., 6–7, 311.

7. Eisenhower, as we will soon see, did not pass their conservative muster.

8. Buckley and Bozell, *McCarthy and His Enemies*, 33, 333. The quotation within this citation is from James Burnham.

9. Ibid., 317. In a similar vein, the authors endorse and reject different conceptions of the idea based on what they "like" and "don't like," which is hardly the language of moral absolutism. On the question of political violence, for example, the authors objected to "Nazi conformity" in part because they "didn't like the fact that [the Nazis] violated persons who disagreed with them."

10. James Baldwin, "Introduction to *Notes of a Native Son*" (1984), in *James Baldwin: Collected Essays*, ed. Toni Morrison (New York: Library of America, 1998), 808.

11. For background, see, in general, Sol Stein, *Native Sons* (New York: One World, 2005).

12. James Baldwin, "Notes of a Native Son" (1955), in *James Baldwin: Collected Essays*, ed. Toni Morrison (New York: Library of America, 1998), 87, 90.

13. David Leeming, *James Baldwin: A Biography* (New York: Arcade, 2015), 103.

14. Baldwin, "Notes of a Native Son," 68, 73. Baldwin notes that the streets were so bad that parents could feel "a peculiar kind of relief" to find out that their children were being shipped overseas to fight in World War II.

15. Ibid., 78.

16. Ibid., 75, 113–14.

17. John Judis, *William F. Buckley, Jr.: The Patron Saint of the Conservatives* (New York: Simon and Schuster, 1988), 98.

18. William Schlamm would play a key role in the founding of the magazine, but it is beyond my scope to discuss him much here. For more on Schlamm, see William F. Buckley Jr., *Miles Gone By: A Literary Autobiography* (Washington, DC: Regnery Publishing, 2004), 282–85.

19. Carl Bogus, *Buckley* (New York: Bloomsbury, 2011), 105.

20. Ibid., 106–7.

21. It is beyond my scope to go into detail here about the interesting and deep roster of contributors Buckley recruited in the early years. For a great discussion of this, see Godfrey Hodgson, *The World Turned Right Side Up* (New York: Houghton Mifflin, 1978), 70–90.

22. William F. Buckley Jr., "Our Mission Statement," *National Review*, November 19, 1955, https://www.nationalreview.com/1955/11/our-mission-statement-william-f-buckley-jr/.

23. Chambers was a supporter of Eisenhower and sensed, quite rightly, that the magazine would be decidedly anti-Eisenhower. See, in general, Buckley, *Miles Gone By*, 299–317.

24. Buckley, "Our Mission Statement."

25. For more on Meyer, see Garry Wills, "Frank and Elsie," in *Confessions of a Conservative* (New York: Double Day, 1979), 38–48; Edwin J. Feulner, "Frank S. Meyer," in *The March of Freedom: Modern Classics in Conservative Thought* (Dallas: Spence Publishing, 1998). It is worth noting that Meyer was not a libertarian in the sense the term is used in the parlance of our times. He was designated as such because he was distrustful of state power in most matters outside national security and identified freedom as one of his central values.

26. See, for example, George H. Nash, *The Conservative Intellectual Movement in America since 1945* (New York: Open Road Media, 2006), 266–82.

27. Below I discuss the political utility of the fusionist philosophy in the context of civil rights.

28. See, for example, Leo Strauss, *Natural Right and History* (Chicago: University of Chicago Press, 1953); Eric Voegelin, *The New Science of Politics* (Chicago: University of Chicago Press, 1952).

29. It is worth noting that this objection to relativism is at odds with my interpretation of Buckley's arguments in *God and Man at Yale* and *McCarthy and His Enemies*. It is clear that Buckley did not conceive of his own position as relativist, but I think there is reason to doubt whether he was right about that.

30. Buckley, "Our Mission Statement."

31. Kirk, like Chambers, refused to be listed on the masthead of the magazine, but he became a regular contributor. Kirk's resistance was rooted in his distrust and disdain for libertarians like Meyer and Chodorov. See Bogus, *Buckley*, 109–11.

32. Buckley, "Our Mission Statement."

33. Ibid., 213.

34. Ibid.

35. Helen Taylor Greene and Shaun L. Gabbidon, eds., *Encyclopedia of Race and Crime* (Thousand Oaks, CA: Sage Publications, 2009), 467.

36. Murray Kempton, "He Went All the Way," *Reporting Civil Rights, Part One: American Journalism, 1941–1963*, ed. Clayborne Carson, David J. Garrow, Bill Kovach, and Carol Polsgrove (New York: Library of America, 2003), 214.

37. Richardson, "Charge Two with Lynch Death of 14-Year-Old," 212–13.

38. Dan Wakefield, "Justice in Sumner," in *Reporting Civil Rights, Part One: American Journalism, 1941–1963*, ed. Clayborne Carson, David J. Garrow, Bill Kovach, and Carol Polsgrove (New York: Library of America, 2003), 218, 220.

39. William Bradford Huie, "The Shocking Story of Approved Killing in Mississippi," *Reporting Civil Rights, Part One: American Journalism, 1941–1963*, ed. Clayborne Carson, David J. Garrow, Bill Kovach, and Carol Polsgrove (New York: Library of America, 2003), 239.

40. Taylor Branch, *Parting the Waters: America in the King Years, 1954–63* (New York: Simon and Schuster, 1988), 14.

41. Ibid., 128–29, 131.

42. For a description of the founding of the Montgomery Improvement Association and the selection of King to lead it, see ibid., 136–38.

43. Leeming, *James Baldwin*, 90, 95.

44. On the alternative title, see ibid., 95. *Giovanni's Room*, in the words of Baldwin biographer Leeming, "is not a bastard among the literary offspring of James Baldwin; it is one of the more impassioned expressions of the story he told all his life." Ibid., 123.

45. Ibid.,. 125.

46. James Baldwin, *Giovanni's Room*, in *Early Novels and Stories*, ed. Toni Morrison (New York: Library of America, 1998), 266–67.

47. For a brilliant account of the idea of freedom in *Giovanni's Room*, see Susan J. McWilliams, "James Baldwin and the Politics of Displacement," in *A Political Companion to James Baldwin*, ed. Susan J. McWilliams (Lexington: University Press of Kentucky, 2018), 94–115.

48. James Baldwin, "My Dungeon Shook" (1962), in *James Baldwin: Collected Essays*, ed. Toni Morrison (New York: Library of America, 1998), 294.

49. James Baldwin, "Down at the Cross" (1962), in *James Baldwin: Collected Essays*, ed. Toni Morrison (New York: Library of America, 1998), 337.

50. Leeming, *James Baldwin*, 116.

51. James Baldwin, "The Crusade of Indignation" (1956), in *James Baldwin: Collected Essays*, ed. Toni Morrison (New York: Library of America, 1998), 608.

52. Ibid., 609, 607.

53. Ibid., 609.

54. Ibid., 610–11.

55. James Baldwin, press conference at the University of California at Berkeley, https://www .youtube.com/watch?v=8klsr2TB5pA.

56. James Baldwin, "Autobiographical Notes" (1955), in *James Baldwin: Collected Essays*, ed. Toni Morrison (New York: Library of America, 1998), 9.

57. Baldwin, "Crusade of Indignation," 609.

58. James Baldwin, "Faulkner and Desegregation" (1956), in *James Baldwin: Collected Essays*, ed. Toni Morrison (New York: Library of America, 1998), 212.

59. Russell Warren Howe, "An Interview with William Faulkner," *London Sunday Times*, March 4, 1956.

60. Baldwin, "Faulkner and Desegregation," 210–11.

61. Ibid., 209, 211.

62. Ibid., 212–13. Baldwin doubted that this sense of moral superiority was justified.

63. Ibid., 213–14.

64. William F. Buckley Jr., "Voices of Sanity," *National Review*, April 4, 1956, 7.

65. William F. Buckley Jr., "Less Sound and Fury," *National Review*, March 28, 1956, 5–6.

66. Buckley, "Voices of Sanity," 7 (emphasis added).

67. Bogus, *Buckley*, 141, 150.

68. See, in general, Geoffrey Kabaservice, *Rule and Ruin: The Downfall of Moderation and the Destruction of the Republican Party, from Eisenhower to the Tea Party* (New York: Oxford University Press, 2012).

69. William F. Buckley Jr. to Jeffrey Hart, September 29, 1964, William F. Buckley Jr. Papers (MS 576), Manuscripts and Archives, Yale University Library.

70. I will explain this in greater detail later.

71. William F. Buckley Jr., "Why the South Must Prevail," *National Review*, August 24, 1957, 148–49.

72. William F. Buckley Jr., "Return to States' Rights," *National Review*, April 18, 1956, 263–64. Buckley would say later that "the principle of subsidiarity" was at the core of his political philosophy. That principle, he explained in 1961, held "that no public agency should undertake any job that a private agency should do, and that no public agency should undertake a job that a lesser public agency could do." See "An Interview with William F. Buckley Jr.," *Mademoiselle* 53 (June 1961): 121–27.

73. "Segregation and Democracy," *National Review*, January 25, 1956, 5. In "Behind the Filibuster Vote," Buckley and his colleagues accused the federal government of "despotic centralism" on civil rights issues.

74. "Segregation and Democracy," 5.

75. The three southern Democratic holdouts in the Senate were Albert Gore Sr. and Estes Kefeauver of Tennessee as well as Lyndon Johnson of Texas.

76. Southern Manifesto, http://americanradioworks.publicradio.org/features/marshall/manifesto.html.

77. Forrest Davis, "The Right to Nullify," *National Review*, April 25, 1956, 11. For more on Davis's biography, see John Chamberlain, "Forrest Davis," *National Review*, May 22, 1962, 357.

78. Davis, "Right to Nullify," 11. I will offer more on the Citizens' Council below.

79. George Lincoln Rockwell, *This Time the World* (Reedy, WV: Liberty Bell Publications, 2004), 205. Rockwell is a questionable source, but it does seem that he collaborated with Jones on various right-wing projects during the 1950s.

80. Joseph Crespino, *Strom Thurmond's America* (New York: Farrar, Straus and Giroux, 2012), 10.

81. Sam M. Jones, "South Carolina," *National Review*, February 29, 1956, 18.

82. Sam M. Jones, "A Voice of the South," *National Review*, July 27, 1957, 105–6.

83. *National Review* interoffice memos, 1958, William F. Buckley Jr. Papers (MS 576), Manuscripts and Archives, Yale University Library.

84. Buckley, "Return to States' Rights," 4.

85. In a journal entry dated March 12, 1953, Goldwater noted that both major parties had "New Dealers or Fair Dealers" who "feel that the federal government should have the power over everything." On "the other side," he observed, "you have members of both parties, particularly among the Southern Democrats, who believe in states' rights and who believe that the federal government should be out of the state and local government picture entirely, and out of the affairs of business as well." In a remarkably prescient insight, Goldwater concluded, "I sense here a realignment of Southern conservative Democrats with Democrats and Republicans of the West and Middle West." Donald T. Critchlow and Nancy MacLean, *Debating the American Conservative Movement: 1945 to the Present* (Lanham, MD: Rowman and Littlefield, 2009), 182.

86. The official name of the organization was the Citizens' Council, but it is often referred to as the "White Citizens' Council." See Neil R. McMillen, *The Citizens' Council: Organized Resistance to the Second Reconstruction, 1954–1964* (Urbana: University of Illinois Press, 1994).

87. Indeed, many biographers seem to have ignored or misunderstood the nature of Buckley's relationship with the Citizens' Council. Judis writes of "Buckley's disenchantment with segregationists" as a result of the rise of the "openly racist White Citizens' Councils," and Bogus wonders why Buckley as a "careful editor" did not "excise" Davis's praise for the councils in "Right to Nullify." This was not merely an editorial oversight; Buckley would soon privately indicate his common cause with the Citizens' Council and attempt to recruit their members into the conservative movement. See Judis, *William F. Buckley, Jr.*, 192; Bogus, *Buckley*, 154.

88. Within months, the membership grew to over sixty thousand in Mississippi and inspired the creation of similar organizations in nearly a dozen other states. The Citizens' Council was dubbed

"the uptown Klan" by the journalist Hodding Carter. Arnold Forster and Benjamin R. Epstein, *Danger on the Right* (Santa Barbara: Praeger, 1976), 107.

89. *Mississippi, U.S.A.*, produced by Scott Berner and Gene Allen, aired on WKY TV News, 1961, https://www.youtube.com/watch?v=qMa1-Jy5Er8. It is worth noting that in this comment and other council literature, he drew on a sentiment expressed by none other than Abraham Lincoln in one of his 1858 debates with Stephen A. Douglas.

90. Ibid.; Dan Wakefield, "Respectable Racism," in *Reporting Civil Rights, Part One: American Journalism, 1941–1963*, ed. Clayborne Carson, David J. Garrow, Bill Kovach, and Carol Polsgrove (New York: Library of America, 2003), 225.

91. *Mississippi, U.S.A.*

92. James Colaico, *Martin Luther King, Jr.: Apostle of Militant Nonviolence* (London: Macmillan, 1988), 14.

93. Historian Adam Nossiter has pointed out, for example, that the council "published the names of black petitioners in Yazoo City who demanded integrated schools; all faced economic ruin as a result." Adam Nossiter, *Of Long Memory: Mississippi and the Murder of Medgar Evers* (Reading, MA: Addison-Wesley, 1994).

94. Wakefield, "Respectable Racism," 224. Simmons was adamant that there was no relationship whatsoever between the Citizens' Council and the Klan. When asked how he felt about the Klan, he said, "I'm not exactly sure I know what they are. I've never been in touch with them." William J. Simmons file, James Jackson Kilpatrick Papers, University of Virginia Library, Accession #6626-b, box 48.

95. William P. Hustwit, *Salesman for Segregation* (Chapel Hill: University of North Carolina Press, 2013), 75. Kilpatrick was a regular contributor to the *Citizen*.

96. James Jackson Kilpatrick to William F. Buckley Jr., July 10, 1958, James Jackson Kilpatrick Papers, University of Virginia Library, Accession #6626-b, box 6.

97. For more on Simmons and his role in the Citizens' Council movement, see McMillen, *The Citizens' Council*, 122–23.

98. Critchlow and MacLean, *Debating the American Conservative Movement*, 188. See also W. J. Simmons to J. P. McFadden, assistant to the publisher, *National Review*, September 5, 1958, William F. Buckley Jr. Papers (MS 576), Manuscripts and Archives, Yale University Library.

99. For some discussion of the content of the *Citizen*, see Jesse Curtis, "Will the Jungle Take Over? *National Review* and the Defense of Western Civilization in the Era of Civil Rights and African Decolonization," *Journal of American Studies* (Spring 2018): 1–27.

100. Critchlow and MacLean, *Debating the American Conservative Movement*, 187.

101. In addition to Davis's praise of the Citizens' Council in "Right to Nullify," Anthony Harrigan spoke glowingly of the "astonishing revival of pamphleteering" led by "southwide resistance groups." Anthony Harrigan, "The South *Is* Different," *National Review*, March 8, 1958, 226. Harrigan's admiration for the Citizens' Council was reciprocated by its leader, Simmons, who described him to Kilpatrick as head and shoulders above just about every other southern journalist. William J. Simmons to James Jackson Kilpatrick, September 3, 1959, James Jackson Kilpatrick Papers, University of Virginia Library, Accession #6626-b, box 48.

102. In 1958, *National Review* had twenty-nine thousand subscribers and ran an operating deficit of $136,000. See William F. Buckley Jr., "Can a Little Magazine Break Even?," *National Review*, October 10, 1959, 393–94. According to George Thayer, "By its fifth birthday," *National Review* had "debts totaling $860,000." Thayer, *Farther Shores of Politics*, 166–73.

103. For some of the early correspondence in 1956 between Buckley and Kilpatrick, see James Jackson Kilpatrick Papers, University of Virginia Library, Accession #6626-b, box 6.

104. Hustwit, *Salesman for Segregation*, 73.

105. Nash, *Conservative Intellectual Movement*, 310.

106. The compatibility of the political philosophies of Buckley and Kilpatrick will become evident over the course of this book. In addition to similar racial views, Kilpatrick was deeply antiegalitarian and suspicious of the welfare state. For a fairly thorough statement of his political philosophy, see James Jackson Kilpatrick, "Conservatism and the South," in *The Lasting South*, ed. Louis D. Rubin and James Jackson Kilpatrick (Chicago: Regnery Publishing, 1957), 188–205.

107. James Jackson Kilpatrick to William F. Buckley Jr., January 9, 1957, William F. Buckley Jr. Papers (MS 576), Manuscripts and Archives, Yale University Library.

108. Hustwit, *Salesman for Segregation*, vi.

109. The editors of *National Review* were also sure to editorialize that the US Supreme Court was to blame for the "disintegrating effect of *Brown v. Board Education*. See "The Court Views Its Handiwork," *National Review*, September 21, 1957, 244–45.

110. James Jackson Kilpatrick, "Right and Power in Arkansas," *National Review*, September 28, 1957, 273.

111. In one of the first pieces in *National Review* on segregation, Buckley and his fellow editors referred to their position on the matter as "libertarian." See "Segregation and Democracy," 5.

112. Kilpatrick, "Right and Power in Arkansas," 273.

113. Ibid., 273. A few months after the Little Rock crisis, *National Review* reported that the Citizens' Council was producing stamps that said "Remember Little Rock" and depicted "soldiers with bayonets pointed at teenagers' backs." "For the Record," *National Review*, January 25, 1958, 74. In private correspondence, Kilpatrick also suggested that the Communists might have had something to do with the events at Little Rock. In a letter to Citizens' Council leader Simmons that was dated one day before his *National Review* piece was published, Kilpatrick said that "the Communists couldn't be any happier if they had planned every single step of this whole dreadful business. Maybe they did." James Jackson Kilpatrick to W. J. Simmons, September 27, 1957, James Jackson Kilpatrick Papers, University of Virginia Library, Accession #6626-b, box 48.

114. See, for example, William F. Buckley Jr. to W. E. Woodward, August 4, 1965, William F. Buckley Jr. Papers (MS 576), Manuscripts and Archives, Yale University Library.

115. George H. Nash, "The Influence of *Ideas Have Consequences* on the Conservative Intellectual Movement in America," in *Steps toward Restoration: The Consequences of Richard Weaver's Ideas*, ed. Ted J. Smith III (Wilmington, DE: Intercollegiate Studies Institute, 1998), 84. For more on Weaver, see Anthony Lejeune, "The Legacy of Richard Weaver," *National Review*, May 17, 1966, 473–74.

116. The content of this list is, of course, contestable, but these are the texts that seem most often mentioned by those in Buckley's circle.

117. Richard M. Weaver, *Ideas Have Consequences* (Chicago: University of Chicago Press, 1948), 1.

118. Nash, *Conservative Intellectual Tradition*, 381.

119. Nash argues that "Kendall ranked Weaver among the greatest contemporary conservative intellectuals." Ibid., 380–81.

120. Richard Weaver, "Integration Is Communization," *National Review*, July 13, 1957, 67. It is worth noting that the tactic of weaving together anti-Communist politics with resistance to the civil rights movement was a common one on the American Right. Indeed, one of the questions the government would often ask in order to determine whether or not someone might be a Communist was, "Do you ever entertain Negroes in your home?" See Constance Coiner, *Better Red: The Writing and Resistance of Tillie Olsen and Meridel Le Seur* (Urbana: University of Illinois Press, 1995), 83.

121. Richard M. Weaver, "The Regime of the South," *National Review*, March 14, 1959, 587.

122. Ibid., 587–88.

123. Ibid., 588.

124. Ibid., 589, 587.

125. Harrigan, "The South *Is* Different," 225. *National Review* made reprints of Harrigan's southern manifesto at fifteen cents each, or a hundred for ten dollars. See conclusion of Harrigan's article for details.

126. Donald Davidson, "The New South and the Conservative Tradition," *National Review*, September 10, 1960, 141–46. Davidson was the chair of the anti-integration organization known as the Tennessee Federation for Constitutional Government. In this capacity, he collaborated with both Kilpatrick and Citizens' Council leader Simmons. See Donald Davidson to William J. Simmons, December 7, 1958, James Jackson Kilpatrick Papers, University of Virginia Library, Accession #6626-b, box 48; William J. Simmons to Donald Davison, December 9, 1958, James Jackson Kilpatrick Papers, University of Virginia Library, Accession #6626-b, box 48.

127. William F. Buckley Jr. "Why the South Must Prevail," *National Review*, August 24, 1957, 357.

128. Sam Tanenhaus, "Original Sin," *New Republic*, February 9, 2013.

129. Buckley, "Why the South Must Prevail," 148–149. On Goldwater's role, see Rick Perlstein, *Before the Storm: Barry Goldwater and the Unmaking of the American Consensus* (New York: Hill and Wang, 2001).

130. Buckley, "Why the South Must Prevail," 148–49.

131. Ibid., 148–49. It appears that the numerical domination Buckley had in mind was of the national majority over the majorities that existed in southern states.

132. Ibid., 148–49. At no point did Buckley bother to offer any explanation of what he meant by "civilization" or "civilized standards."

133. Ibid., 148–49.

134. Ibid., 148–49. It is worth noting that Buckley also developed another version of the paternalist argument that focused on the danger of integration removing "the most talented and challenging members" of the black community from black schools, leaving "the mass of Negroes . . . more strictly ghettoized than ever." William F. Buckley Jr., "Solution for the South?," *National Review*, January 17, 1959, 446–47.

135. Buckley's naivete about human nature here is breathtaking and strains credulity. He claimed to be a "realist" who distrusted human beings to exercise power responsibly when unchecked, and yet he was willing to entrust white southerners with near-absolute power over blacks and the responsibility to determine when that power might be relinquished.

136. L. Brent Bozell Jr., "The Open Question," *National Review*, September 7, 1957, 196.

137. William F. Buckley Jr., "A Clarification," *National Review*, September 7, 1957, 199.

138. As the political scientist Joseph Lowndes has suggested, Buckley's "antiblackness" was part and parcel of his "antidemocracy." Joseph E. Lowndes, "William F. Buckley Jr.: Anti-blackness as Antidemocracy," *American Political Thought* 6, no. 4 (Fall 2017): 632–40.

139. For more on this journey, see Leeming, *James Baldwin*, 134–47.

140. James Baldwin, "A Fly in Buttermilk" (1958), in *James Baldwin: Collected Essays*, ed. Toni Morrison (New York: Library of America, 1998), 188, 192.

141. Ibid., 192.

142. Ibid.

143. Baldwin, "Notes of a Native Son," 78.

144. Baldwin, "Fly in Buttermilk," 191.

145. Ibid., 193–94

146. James Baldwin, "Nobody Knows My Name: A Letter from the South" (1959), in *James Baldwin: Collected Essays*, ed. Toni Morrison (New York: Library of America, 1998), 198–99.

147. Ibid.

148. Ibid., 204–5, 207–8.

149. Ibid., 207–8, 203.

150. William F. Buckley Jr., "Let Us Try, at Least, to Understand," *National Review*, June 3, 1961, 338.

151. Baldwin, "Nobody Knows My Name," 206.

152. Buckley, "Our Mission Statement."

153. William F. Meehan III, ed., *Conversations with William F. Buckley Jr.* (Jackson: University Press of Mississippi, 2009), 155, 64.

154. Baldwin, "Nobody Knows My Name," 208.

155. There has been a great deal of speculation and debate about precisely what Baldwin meant by "Nobody Knows My Name." The recent opening of his papers provides us with a definitive answer to this question. In a letter to John Fisher, the editor at *Harper's* for whom he was writing the piece, Baldwin said this about the essay: "It's my answer, anyway—let's say—to the moderate position which weeps for the death of the old South and the marvelous relationships which obtained therein. Any relationship which has, as it's indispensable cornerstone, the denial of the manhood of another man is marvelous indeed and I'd like to say something about it. I'd like to call it Nobody Knows My Name—it's a line from the blues and it's also something that was said to me by an old Negro porter in Birmingham." James Baldwin to John Fisher, "Correspondence," James Baldwin Papers, Schomburg Center for Research in Black Culture, Manuscripts, Archives and Rare Books Division, New York Public Library.

156. Gayle v. Browder, 352 U.S. 903 (1956).

157. For a discussion of King's meetings with Nixon, see Branch, *Parting the Waters*, 214, 218–20.

158. James Baldwin, "The Dangerous Road before Martin Luther King" (1961), in *James Baldwin: Collected Essays*, ed. Toni Morrison (New York: Library of America, 1998), 638.

159. Ibid., 638–39, 641.

160. Ibid., 645, 651.

161. James Baldwin, "Many Thousands Gone" (1951), in *James Baldwin: Collected Essays*, ed. Toni Morrison (New York: Library of America, 1998), 20.

162. Ibid.

163. Ibid., 657, 656.

164. Richard Weaver, "Relativism and the Crisis of Our Times," http://www.mmisi.org/mp3/lectures/weaver1.mp3.

165. Branch, *Parting the Waters*, 272.

166. James Baldwin, "They Can't Turn Back" (1960), in *James Baldwin: Collected Essays*, ed. Toni Morrison (New York: Library of America, 1998), 629. Again, Baldwin used letters to protect the anonymity of his subjects.

167. Ibid., 629, 633, 631, 636–37.

168. This Week, *National Review*, March 14, 1956.

169. William F. Buckley Jr., "Foul," *National Review*, April 18, 1956, 6. Buckley and his colleagues would repeat this argument almost a year later in another article. "If it is a matter of principle to them," they declared, "that they ride in separate sections from Negroes, let them prove their devotion to principle by shouldering the cost of private, all-white buses, and allow Negroes to run their own buses." "How Much Is It Worth?," *National Review*, January 19, 1957, 55.

170. Buckley, "Foul," 7.

171. For information on the economic situation in Montgomery in 1950 and 1960, see https://www.census.gov/prod/www/decennial.html.

172. A. B. H., "The Two Faces of Dr. King," *National Review*, January 31, 1959, 482. For a more philosophically sophisticated development of this idea, see Frank S. Meyer, "The Violence of Nonviolence," *National Review*, April 20, 1965, 357.

173. A. B. H., "Two Faces of Dr. King," 482.

174. William F. Buckley Jr., "Distinguamus," *National Review*, March 26, 1960, 193. This was an unsigned editorial that was later revealed to be the work of Buckley.

175. James T. Patterson, *Grand Expectations: The United States, 1945–1974* (Oxford: Oxford University Press, 1997), 312.

176. See, in general, Peter Carlson, *K Blows Top: A Cold War Comic Interlude, Starring Nikita Khrushchev, America's Most Unlikely Tourist* (New York: Public Affairs, 2010).

177. Judis, *William F. Buckley, Jr.*, 175. Buckley's antics during the Khrushchev visit proved to be a last straw for Chambers, who officially separated from *National Review*. William F. Buckley Jr., *Odyssey of a Friend* (Washington, DC: Regnery Publishing, 1987), 260–63.

178. Judis, *William F. Buckley, Jr.*, 176. For Buckley's remarks, see William F. Buckley Jr., "The Damage We Have Done to Ourselves," *National Review*, September 26, 1959, 349–51.

179. See, for example, Louis Hartz, *The Liberal Tradition in America* (New York: Mariner Books, 1955).

180. Buckley's title pays homage to Booker T. Washington's autobiographical *Up from Slavery*, but this too is a strange fit since Buckley never had the sensation of seeing the world through liberal eyes and Washington was indeed born into slavery. *National Review* contributor Weaver had published a similarly titled essay. Richard Weaver, "Up from Liberalism," *Modern Age* 3, no. 1 (Winter 1958–59): 22.

181. William F. Buckley Jr., *Up from Liberalism* (New York: McDowell, Obolensky, 1959), 37.

182. Ibid., 37, 66.

183. Ibid., 156–57.

184. Judis, *William F. Buckley, Jr.*, 192.

185. Buckley, *Up from Liberalism*, 157–58.

186. Allan J. Lichtman, *White Protestant Nation: The Rise of the American Conservative Movement* (New York: Atlantic Monthly Press, 2008), 227.

187. Ibid., 218–19.

188. Buckley, "Our Mission Statement."

189. See, in general, Buckley, *Odyssey of a Friend*.

190. Buckley, *Up from Liberalism*, 221. "That is what conservatives must decide," Chambers wrote to Buckley: "how much to give in order to survive at all; how much to give in order not to give up the basic principles." Lee Edwards, *Standing Athwart History: The Political Thought of William F. Buckley Jr.* (Washington, DC: Heritage Foundation, 2010), 7.

191. Buckley, *Up from Liberalism*, 222.

192. Ibid., 223, 229.

193. Unbeknownst to Buckley, Liebman was a closeted gay man who had, as fate would have it, befriended Baldwin in Greenwich Village in the 1940s. See Marvin Liebman, *Coming Out Conservative* (San Francisco: Chronicle Books, 1992), 54.

194. Judis, *William F. Buckley, Jr.*, 189.

195. For an extraordinarily detailed account of the Sharon summit and Young Americans for Freedom in general, see Wayne Thorburn, *A Generation Awakes: Young Americans for Freedom and the Creation of the Conservative Movement* (Ottawa, IL: Jameson Books, 2010); Gregory Schneider, *Cadres for Conservatism: Young Americans for Freedom and the Rise of the Contemporary Right* (New York: NYU Press, 1999). See also Thayer, *Farther Shores of Politics*, 166–73.

196. Lee Edwards, interview with the author, December 7, 2016.

197. Schneider, *Cadres for Conservatism*, 34.

198. For more on Medford Evans's place in the "chain of seniority" of the Citizens' Council movement, see McMillen, *Citizens' Council*, 125–26.

199. Felzenberg, *A Man and His Presidents*, 66.

200. For the full Sharon Statement, see Thorburn, *A Generation Awakes*, 543.

201. Lee Edwards, interview with the author, December 7, 2016. Wayne Thorburn reports that "language strongly supporting states' rights" was one of several points that did occasion "debate and discussion" among the participants. See Thorburn, *A Generation Awakes*, 28. Unfortunately, Thorburn does not provide any evidence for the claim. Gregory Schneider speculates about various reasons why civil rights were "of little concern to YAF [Young Americans for Freedom] Members." Schneider, *Cadres for Conservatism*, 58–60.

202. In the next issue of *National Review*, Buckley wrote a glowing piece about the new organization. "What is so striking in the students who met at Sharon," he remarked, "is their appetite for power." This comment proved to be quite prescient. Many of those who attended the Sharon meeting would go on to become key figures in the burgeoning conservative movement. For details, see Thorburn, *Generation Awakes*, 30–38. Young Americans for Freedom would, in the words of George Thayer, become primarily an "action group" that maintained a conservative speakers bureau, produced films, and distributed conservative literature. Thayer, *Farther Shores of Politics*, 170–71.

203. For more on Baldwin's time at the Styron home, see Sam Tanenhaus, "The Literary Battle for Nat Turner's Legacy," *Vanity Fair*, August 3, 2016.

204. For a brilliant discussion of Baldwin on American "mobility," see McWilliams, "James Baldwin and the Politics of Disconnection."

205. In Baldwin's collections, "In Search of a Majority" is listed as an address given in February 1960, but later research has revealed the talk was given in November. For more information, see http://ohla.info/engaging-the-wisdom-oral-history-project/.

206. James Baldwin, "In Search of a Majority" (1960), in *James Baldwin: Collected Essays*, ed. Toni Morrison (New York: Library of America, 1998), 217.

207. Ibid., 218, 216.

208. Ibid., 218.

209. Ibid., 218–19.

210. James Baldwin, "Fifth Avenue, Uptown: A Letter from Harlem" (1960), in *James Baldwin: Collected Essays*, ed. Toni Morrison (New York: Library of America, 1998), 179.

211. James Baldwin, "The Discovery of What It Means to Be an American" (1959), in *James Baldwin: Collected Essays*, ed. Toni Morrison (New York: Library of America, 1998), 139.

212. Baldwin, "In Search of a Majority," 218.

213. James Baldwin, "Color" (1962), in *James Baldwin: Collected Essays*, ed. Toni Morrison (New York: Library of America, 1998), 672.

214. Baldwin, "Fifth Avenue, Uptown," 176, 179. In a "Postscript" to this letter, published in the *New York Times Magazine* a few months later, Baldwin asked his readers to do more than "walk through Harlem." He also wanted them to ask themselves two questions: "The first question is: Would *I* like to live here? And the second question is: Why don't those who now live here move out?" James Baldwin, "East River, Downtown: Postscript to a Letter from Harlem" (1961), in *James Baldwin: Collected Essays*, ed. Toni Morrison (New York: Library of America, 1998), 180–81.

215. Baldwin, "Fifth Avenue, Uptown," 175.

216. James Baldwin, "The Creative Process" (1962), in *James Baldwin: Collected Essays*, ed. Toni Morrison (New York: Library of America, 1998), 669.

217. Baldwin, "Discovery of What It Means to Be an American, 142.

218. Baldwin, "Fifth Avenue, Uptown," 177.

219. For more on Baldwin's idea of freedom as nondelusion, see Nicholas Buccola, "What William F. Buckley Jr. Did Not Understand about James Baldwin," in *A Political Companion to James Baldwin*, ed. Susan J. McWilliams (Lexington: University Press of Kentucky, 2017), 116–48.

220. Baldwin, "Creative Process," 669. You will recall the lessons that Baldwin drew from what he took to be his friend and mentor Delaney's role as an artistic witness.

221. Ibid., 670, 672.

222. Baldwin, "In Search of a Majority," 220.

Chapter 4. Taking Responsibility, 1961–62

1. Stuart H. Loory, "Reporter Tails 'Freedom' Bus, Caught in Riot," *Reporting Civil Rights, Part One: American Journalism, 1941–1963*, ed. Clayborne Carson, David J. Garrow, Bill Kovach, and Carol Polsgrove (New York: Library of America, 2003), 573.

2. Ibid.

3. Bob Duke, "2 Mob Victims Ready to Die for Integration," *Reporting Civil Rights, Part One: American Journalism, 1941–1963*, ed. Clayborne Carson, David J. Garrow, Bill Kovach, and Carol Polsgrove (New York: Library of America, 2003), 587.

4. According to Rockwell biographer Frederic Simonelli, "Rockwell was a contract subscription salesman for Buckley's [the] *National Review*" for a short period. In the years after their acquaintance, Rockwell frequently mailed Buckley his anti-Semitic pamphlets and screeds. Buckley, to his credit, told Rockwell, "The things you sent me physically appalled me. . . . I can only pray that some day they will sicken you too." Later, Buckley arranged for Rockwell to visit a priest, who he hoped might counsel Rockwell to abandon his odious views. This experiment failed. Frederic J. Simonelli, *The American Fuehrer: George Lincoln Rockwell and the American Nazi Party* (Urbana: University of Illinois Press, 1999), 31.

5. William F. Buckley Jr., "Let Us Try, at Least, to Understand," *National Review*, June 3, 1961, 338.

6. As noted above, Buckley was philosophically absolutist but operationally relativist. It was important to him to maintain the facade of belief in universal moral truths, but on civil rights matters these commitments fell by the wayside.

7. Ibid. Buckley's relativism is on display here.

8. Ibid. Buckley made a similar argument in a 1956 piece on a mob attack on Autherine Lucy, a black student attempting to enroll at the University of Alabama. In that piece, Buckley contended that we should not be surprised by violent backlash against integration because it upset "deeply-rooted folkways and mores." See William F. Buckley, "The Assault on Miss Lucy," *National Review*, February 22, 1956, 5.

9. Buckley, "Let Us Try, at Least, to Understand," 338.

10. James Baldwin, "Fifth Avenue, Uptown: A Letter from Harlem" (1960), in *James Baldwin: Collected Essays*, ed. Toni Morrison (New York: Library of America, 1998), 177.

11. John Judis, *William F. Buckley, Jr.: The Patron Saint of the Conservatives* (New York: Simon and Schuster, 1988), 202. I will discuss *Revolt against the Masses* in greater detail in chapter 5 of this book.

12. C. Eric Lincoln, *The Black Muslims in America* (Grand Rapids, MI: Wm. B. Eerdmans Publishing Co., 1994), 12, 14.

13. James Baldwin, "Down at the Cross" (1962), in *James Baldwin: Collected Essays*, ed. Toni Morrison (New York: Library of America, 1998), 325.

14. Lincoln, *Black Muslims in America*, 17.

15. Baldwin, "Fifth Avenue, Uptown," 177.

16. Malcolm objected to this label because the NOI did not, properly speaking, have a second in command.

17. *The Hate That Hate Produced*, directed by Mike Wallace and Louis Lomax, 1959, https://www .youtube.com/watch?v=BsYWD2EqavQ.

18. Baldwin, "Fifth Avenue, Uptown," 171.

19. For more on these groups, see, in general, Clayborne Carson, *In Struggle: SNCC and the Black Awakening of the 1960s* (Cambridge, MA: Harvard University Press, 1995).

20. For Baldwin on Schuyler, see James Baldwin, "The Harlem Ghetto" (1948), in *James Baldwin: Collected Essays*, ed. Toni Morrison (New York: Library of America, 1998), 48. This may have been the first time Baldwin actually met Malcolm. In "No Name in the Street," Baldwin reported said he "saw Malcolm before I met him," and proceeded to describe giving a speech in Harlem and seeing Malcolm—who he knew by legend—"sitting in the first or second row of the hall, bending forward at such an angle that his long arms nearly caressed the ankles of his long legs, staring up at me." Baldwin then talks about meeting Malcolm in April 1961, during the media appearances described here. James Baldwin, "No Name in the Street" (1972), in *James Baldwin: Collected Essays*, ed. Toni Morrison (New York: Library of America, 1998), 411.

21. "The Black Muslims in America: An Interview with George S. Schuyler, Malcolm X, C. Eric Lincoln, and James Baldwin" (1961), transcribed in *Race(ing) to the Right: Selected Essays of George S. Schuyler*, ed. Jeffrey Leak (Knoxville: University of Tennessee Press, 2001), 74, 76–77.

22. Ibid., 76–77.

23. Ibid., 79.

24. Baldwin, "Down at the Cross," 320.

25. "Black Muslims in America," 83.

26. The name of the student activist is occasionally reported as LaVerne McCummins, but Mc-Cummings is the correct spelling. When Baldwin reflected on this second exchange with Malcolm years later, he recalled that he had been invited by WBAI to serve as a "moderator" for the discussion because the representatives at the station were worried "that Malcolm would simply eat [McCummings] alive." As Baldwin remembered the exchange years later, he said that this concern was totally misplaced because Malcolm treated McCummings with "extraordinary gentleness." Perhaps Baldwin's memory of the point of his appearance is correct—that the station was concerned that the young sit-in activist needed "back up"—but the program does not come across the way Baldwin described it. It seems clear that WBAI's John David is the "moderator," and Malcolm and Baldwin end up dominating the conversation, with McCummings playing the minor—but important—role of explaining what things are like "on the ground" in the South. As for Baldwin's recollection of Malcolm's "extraordinary gentleness" toward McCummings, I would say that this is a matter of interpretation. I tend to disagree with Baldwin's reading of Malcolm in this encounter, but it is worthwhile to listen to the program to decide for yourself. There are many edited versions of the conversation available on the internet (most of which cut McCummings out altogether). The full recording is available at pacificaradioarchives.org/recording/bb5322. For Baldwin's interpretation of the encounter, see Baldwin, "No Name in the Street," 410.

27. Malcolm X, James Baldwin, and LaVerne McCummings, "Black Muslims vs. the Sit-ins," WBAI, April 25, 1961, pacificaradioarchives.org/recording/bb5322.

28. Ibid.

29. Ibid.

30. Ibid.

31. Ibid.

32. Ibid.

33. Ibid.

34. For the King-Kilpatrick debate, see https://kinginstitute.stanford.edu/encyclopedia/king -debates-james-j-kilpatrick-nations-future.

35. X, Baldwin, and McCummings, "Black Muslims vs. the Sit-ins."

36. It is worth noting that this critique of Henry is yet another example of Baldwin's rejection of equality as a sufficiently capacious moral concept. We can aspire to something morally better, he was telling his audience, than the status achieved by Henry and other so-called American heroes.

37. Ibid.

38. William J. Maxwell, ed., *James Baldwin: The FBI File* (New York: Arcade Publishing, 2017), 37, 207.

39. Baldwin was due to be in Chicago to be interviewed by Studs Terkel. For his fascinating interview with Terkel, see https://studsterkel.wfmt.com/programs/interviewing-novelist-and-fighter -civil-rights-all-james-baldwin.

40. Baldwin, "Down at the Cross," 322.

41. Ibid., 321, 316.

42. Ibid., 324, 331–32.

43. Susan Currie Sivek, "Editing Conservatism: How *National Review* Magazine Framed and Mobilized a Political Movement," *Mass Communication and Society* 11, no. 3 (2008): 247–74. See also Lee Edwards, *Standing Athwart History: The Political Thought of William F. Buckley Jr.* (Washington, DC: Heritage Foundation, 2010), 12–14.

44. A few years later, Buckley commissioned Wills to write a critique of Rand. In the piece, Wills argued that "the narrow fixations of Miss Rand . . . should meet with more strenuous opposition from conservatives than from any other group of thinkers; especially when such chaos takes to itself the unearned title of conservatism." See Garry Wills, "But Is Ayn Rand Conservative?," *National Review*, February 27, 1960, 139. Indeed, later in life Buckley reported that Rand made it a practice whenever invited to a party to contact the host to be sure that Buckley was not on the guest list. Anne Heller, *Ayn Rand and the World She Made* (New York: Random House, 2009), 285.

45. Carl Bogus, *Buckley* (New York: Bloomsbury, 2011), 186.

46. William F. Buckley Jr., *Up from Liberalism* (New York: McDowell, Obolensky, 1959), 157.

47. John Judis, *William F. Buckley, Jr.: The Patron Saint of the Conservatives* (New York: Simon and Schuster, 1988), 192.

48. Jeffrey Hart, *The Making of the Conservative Mind* (Wilmington, DE: Intercollegiate Studies Institute, 2006), 103. Buckley was also continuing to publish essays and book reviews in *National Review* that left open the possibility that a "specifically biological inheritance" was to blame for racial inequality. See, for example, Willmoore Kendall, "Light on the American Dilemma?," *National Review*, November 5, 1960, 281–82.

49. William F. Buckley Jr., "Desegregation: Will It Work? No," *Saturday Review*, November 11, 1961, 21–22.

50. William F. Buckley Jr., "Can We Desegregate, Hesto Presto?," in *Rumbles Left and Right: A Book about Troublesome People and Ideas* (New York: G. P. Putnam's Sons, 1963), 122.

51. Ibid., 124.

52. Ibid., 125–27.

53. William F. Buckley Jr. to Ramon Castroviejo, February 14, 1962, William F. Buckley Jr. Papers (MS 576), Manuscripts and Archives, Yale University Library. Several years later, of course, Buckley would utter a homophobic slur to Vidal's face during their famous debates at the 1968 Democratic National Convention. This letter to Castroviejo, written over six years prior to that incident, reveals

that Buckley's slur was not a one-off occurrence inspired by the heat of that particularly tense moment.

54. For all of Buckley's syndicated columns via a searchable database, see https://cumulus .hillsdale.edu/Buckley/.

55. For discussion of Buckley's peculiar manner of speaking, see, for example, Sam Tanenhaus, "Q&A on William F. Buckley Jr.," *New York Times*, February 27, 2008, https://artsbeat.blogs.nytimes .com/2008/02/27/qa-with-sam-tanenhaus-on-william-f-buckley/.

56. Alvin S. Felzenberg, *A Man and His Presidents* (New Haven, CT: Yale University Press, 2017), 118, 116.

57. Buckley's extensive speaking commitments may have buoyed *National Review*'s financial fortunes, but they undermined his ability to devote as much time to editing the magazine. In his absence, his sister Priscilla and James Burnham picked up most of the editorial slack.

58. Buckley's papers at Yale contain many letters from his liberal fans. In one especially remarkable letter, a writer declares, "I am a liberal, and you are not likely to change that, but you are indeed a most remarkable, honest man. One can only be grateful for your presence. . . . You are a bird of paradise, Mr. Buckley. How I wish you were on our side!" David Gilbert to William F. Buckley Jr., July 21, 1965, William F. Buckley Jr. Papers (MS 576), Manuscripts and Archives, Yale University Library.

59. See Kevin Schultz, *Buckley and Mailer: The Difficult Friendship That Shaped the Sixties* (New York: W. W. Norton, 2015), 19–24.

60. William F. Buckley Jr., *Let Us Talk of Many Things: The Collected Speeches* (New York: Forum, 2000), 51.

61. See, in general, James Baldwin, "The Black Boy Looks at the White Boy" (1961), in *James Baldwin: Collected Essays*, ed. Toni Morrison (New York: Library of America, 1998), 269–90; Norman Mailer, "The White Negro," *Dissent* (Fall 1957); William J. Weatherby, *Squaring Off: Mailer vs Baldwin* (New York: Mason/Charter, 1977); Fern Marja Eckman, *The Furious Passage of James Baldwin* (Lanham, MD: Rowman and Littlefield, 1966), 141.

62. Eckman, *Furious Passage of James Baldwin*, 141–42; William J. Weatherby, *James Baldwin: Artist on Fire, a Portrait* (New York: Dutton Adult, 1989), 222.

63. Eckman, *Furious Passage of James Baldwin*, 141–42. See, in general, Schultz, *Buckley and Mailer*.

64. James Baldwin, "Letters from a Journey" (1963), in *The Cross of Redemption: Uncollected Writings*, ed. Randall Kenan (New York: Pantheon Books, 2010), 235.

65. *Another Country* is an extraordinarily complex novel in which Baldwin elaborates on themes he explored in *Mountain* and *Giovanni*. For a brilliant reflection on the philosophical significance of the novel, see, in general, Joel Schlosser, "Socrates in a Different Key," in *A Political Companion to James Baldwin*, ed. Susan J. McWilliams, (Lexington: University Press of Kentucky, 2017).

66. David Leeming, *James Baldwin: A Biography* (New York: Arcade, 2015), 206.

67. Norman Podhoretz, "My Negro Problem and Ours," *Commentary*, February 1, 1963, 93–101. Given the complexity just described, the idea of reconstructing the major arguments of "Cross" seems like a fool's errand. Such an attempt must be made, though, because the essay casts a heavy shadow over the debate at Cambridge. "Cross" is the essay that did the most to shape Buckley's perception of Baldwin and it is the piece that the students at Cambridge—if they'd read any Baldwin—had most likely encountered. Finally, a reconstruction of the major arguments in the essay is necessary because it—more so than anything else he ever wrote—captures the essence of Baldwin's worldview.

68. Baldwin, "Down at the Cross," 297–302.

69. Ibid., 299.

70. Ibid., 299–300.

71. Ibid., 304–6.

72. Ibid., 304, 301, 305–6.

73. Baldwin's attitude toward the historical Jesus and the doctrines he preached proved to be rather complicated. I discuss it below.

74. Ibid., 303, 306.

75. Ibid., 307. In response to his father's shunning of his Jewish friend, Baldwin declared defiantly, "He's a better Christian than you are."

76. Ibid., 309.

77. Sharifa Rhodes-Pitts, *Harlem Is Nowhere: A Journey to the Mecca of Black America* (New York: Little, Brown and Company, 2011), 107.

78. Baldwin, "Down at the Cross," 312–13.

79. Ibid., 308. Baldwin's reference here is to the 1935 military campaign of Italy against Ethiopia.

80. Ibid., 314.

81. Norman Podhoretz, *Breaking Ranks: A Political Memoir* (New York: Harper and Row, 1979), 124.

82. Norman Podhoretz, interview with the author, November 29, 2016.

83. In the recently opened James Baldwin Papers at the Schomburg Center for Research in Black Culture, there are two early drafts of "Down at the Cross." The first draft is only about a third of the length of the final one, and it appears to be a combination of some of the early church experience material from part I of the essay and some of the NOI material from part II.

84. Baldwin, "Down at the Cross," 314.

85. Ibid., 315.

86. Ibid., 325, 319.

87. Ibid., 313–14, 316–17.

88. Ibid., 342, 317–18, 315.

89. Ibid., 321–22, 324.

90. Ibid., 300.

91. Ibid., 317, 299, 341.

92. Ibid., 299.

93. Ibid., 334. It is interesting to note the allusion to a variation of the golden rule here—"do unto others as you would have them do unto you." In this instance, Baldwin offers a negative formulation of the idea: "do not do unto others as you would not have them do unto you."

94. Ibid., 310–11, 343.

95. For a brilliant account of Baldwin and the blues, see Ed Pavlic, *Who Can Afford to Improvise? James Baldwin and Black Music, the Lyric and the Listeners* (New York: Fordham University Press, 2015). For further reflections on this idea of his, see James Baldwin, "The Uses of the Blues" (1964), in *The Cross of Redemption: Uncollected Writings*, ed. Randall Kenan (New York: Pantheon Books, 2010), 70.

96. Baldwin, "Down at the Cross," 343. It is important to keep in mind that Baldwin considered black and white to be "political," not "biological," categories. He was fond of referring to black and white as "states of mind." Understood in this way, Baldwin's call to draw on the wealth of "black history" might be read rather broadly to include people of all colors who have modeled the virtues he describes in this passage.

97. Ibid., 343–44.

98. It is also worth noting that Baldwin believed the inverse to be true: in order to love, we must be free.

99. Ibid., 335, 341.

100. Ibid., 339, 346–47.

101. Baldwin, "Letters from a Journey," 242.

102. The manuscript was officially submitted to the *New Yorker* by Baldwin's agent, Mills, on September 27, 1962. In the attached letter, Mills told Shawn that he would soon see why Baldwin had "considerable trouble" finishing the piece, which turned out to be far more than a report about the NOI. It was also a report on the "the Negro in America, and perhaps beyond that, a report on the United States today." Mills recognized that the piece was not a conventional fit for the magazine, but he believed that Shawn's "patience with Jimmy" entitled him to a "first look." Robert P. Mills to William Shawn, December 27, 1962, Robert Park Mills Papers, Harry Ransom Humanities Research Center, University of Texas at Austin. According to biographer Weatherby, it was Baldwin—not his agent— who was to blame for the literary betrayal of *Commentary*. Indeed, Mills "lectured Baldwin about his treatment of Commentary" not long before Baldwin dismissed him as his agent. See Weatherby, *James Baldwin*, 237–38.

103. On October 22, 1962, Mills would receive a check for $6500 for Baldwin's "Letter from a Region in My Mind." Milton Greenstein to Robert P. Mills, October 22, 1962, Robert Park Mills Papers, Harry Ransom Humanities Research Center, University of Texas at Austin.

104. Norman Podhoretz, interview with the author, November 29, 2016.

105. Thomas Jeffers, *Norman Podhoretz: A Biography* (Cambridge: Cambridge University Press, 2010), 85.

106. Ibid.

107. Norman Podhoretz, interview with the author, November 29, 2016.

108. On December 19, 1962, Podhoretz wrote to Baldwin to tell him that his *New Yorker* piece was "superb" and "maybe the best thing you've ever written." He also informed Baldwin that the piece inspired him to write a sort of "counter statement that I'm going to publish in the February issue of *Commentary* (which may, as a result, be the last issue of *Commentary* that the world will ever see)." Norman Podhoretz to James Baldwin, December 19, 1962, *Commentary* Magazine Archive, Harry Ransom Humanities Research Center, University of Texas at Austin. On January 4, 1963, Podhoretz wrote to Baldwin with a copy of "My Negro Problem and Ours" enclosed. In the attached note, Podhoretz told Baldwin he was "very curious to know how it will strike you" and eager to get a note from Baldwin "commenting on the effect this kind of candor is likely to have on the struggle for Negro rights." Norman Podhoretz to James Baldwin, January 4, 1963, *Commentary* Magazine Archive, Harry Ransom Humanities Research Center, University of Texas at Austin.

109. James Baldwin, interview, 1963, https://www.youtube.com/watch?v=LmP41sPPF90.

110. Christine M. Bochen, ed., *The Courage for Truth: The Letters of Thomas Merton to Writers* (New York: Farrar, Straus and Giroux, 2008), 245.

111. Hannah Arendt Papers, Manuscript Division, Library of Congress, Correspondence, Letters under BA-.

112. The editors at the magazine knew already that within a few weeks, Baldwin would be publishing the essay along with a short piece called "My Dungeon Shook" as the book *The Fire Next Time*, so they sent this news back to the many readers who requested extra copies (along with their checks).

113. *New Yorker* Records, Manuscripts and Archives Division, New York Public Library.

114. Ibid.

115. Ibid.

116. Garry Wills to William F. Buckley Jr., January 7, 1963, William F. Buckley Jr. Papers (MS 576), Manuscripts and Archives, Yale University Library. It is also worth noting that the Baldwin review was a bit peculiar in that it was born in the wake of the *New Yorker* essay (before the book *The Fire Next Time* existed). The genesis of the review was therefore unconventional.

117. One exception was F. W. Dupee, "James Baldwin and 'The Man,'" *New York Review of Books*, February 1, 1963.

118. In April 1963, Weaver would die suddenly of a heart attack at the age of only fifty-three. Joseph Scotchie, *Barbarians in the Saddle: An Intellectual Biography of Richard M. Weaver* (New Brunswick, NJ: Transaction, 1997), 15.

119. William F. Buckley Jr. to James Jackson Kilpatrick, January 16, 1961, William F. Buckley Jr. Papers (MS 576), Manuscripts and Archives, Yale University Library. Wills also worked for Kilpatrick for a short time at the *Richmond News Leader*.

120. Garry Wills to William F. Buckley Jr., January 7, 1963, William F. Buckley Jr. Papers (MS 576), Manuscripts and Archives, Yale University Library.

121. Garry Wills to William F. Buckley Jr., undated letter from early 1963, William F. Buckley Jr. Papers (MS 576), Manuscripts and Archives, Yale University Library.

122. William F. Buckley, "A Call to Lynch the White God," syndicated column published on March 3, 1963.

123. Garry Wills to William F. Buckley Jr., February 27, 1963, William F. Buckley Jr. Papers (MS 576), Manuscripts and Archives, Yale University Library.

124. No copy is present in the vast collections of the William F. Buckley Jr. Papers at Yale, and Wills did not retain a copy.

125. Garry Wills to William F. Buckley Jr., March 9, 1963, William F. Buckley Jr. Papers (MS 576), Manuscripts and Archives, Yale University Library.

126. Hart, *Making of the Conservative Mind*, 105. At least one reader of *National Review* shared Meyer's assessment. After the piece was published, he wrote a letter—which the magazine published—that read, "It would appear that Garry Wills is something of another defender of James Baldwin; Wills assuredly is not a refuter of what Baldwin says." "To the Editor," *National Review*, July 16, 1963.

127. William F. Buckley Jr. to Harold Hayes, 1968, William F. Buckley Jr. Papers (MS 576), Manuscripts and Archives, Yale University Library.

128. Garry Wills, "What Color Is God?," *National Review*, May 1963, 410.

129. Ibid.

130. Ibid.

131. Ibid., 410–11.

132. Ibid., 416.

133. Ibid., 417.

134. Interview with Charles Childs, 1964, James Baldwin Papers, Schomburg Center for Research in Black Culture, Manuscripts, Archives and Rare Books Division, New York Public Library.

135. John Beecher, "If You Are a Negro," *Reporting Civil Rights, Part One: American Journalism, 1941–1963*, ed. Clayborne Carson, David J. Garrow, Bill Kovach, and Carol Polsgrove (New York: Library of America, 2003), 401.

136. Ross Barnett, "Address to the People of Mississippi," September 13, 1962, http://microsites .jfklibrary.org/olemiss/controversy/doc2.html.

137. Walker had been present at the Little Rock integration crisis in 1957 in his capacity as a member of the US Army. Now he was excited to participate in a different way: "I have been on the other side in such situations in a place called Little Rock," he told his radio audience, "and I was on the wrong side. This time I will be in . . . Mississippi, on the right side." Frank Lambert, *The Battle of Ole Miss* (New York: Oxford University Press, 2010), 122.

138. Ibid.

139. George B. Leonard, T. George Harris, and Christopher S. Wren, "How a Secret Deal Prevented a Massacre at Ole Miss," in *Reporting Civil Rights, Part One: American Journalism, 1941–1963*, ed. Clayborne Carson, David J. Garrow, Bill Kovach, and Carol Polsgrove (New York: Library of America, 2003), 696. See also Yasuhiro Katagiri, *The Mississippi State Sovereignty Commission: Civil Rights and States' Rights* (Oxford: University Press of Mississippi, 2001), 112–14.

140. Medford Evans, "An Interview with Citizen Edwin A. Walker," *National Review*, December 16, 1961, 411. Just months before the events at Ole Miss, Buckley declared himself to be "a great personal admirer of General Walker" in correspondence. William F. Buckley Jr. to Major General E. E. Westbrook, May 10, 1962, William F. Buckley Jr. Papers (MS 576), Manuscripts and Archives, Yale University Library.

141. Adam Nossiter, *Of Long Memory: Mississippi and the Murder of Medgar Evers* (Reading, MA: Addison-Wesley, 1994).

142. Kilpatrick was covering the story for *Human Events*. After Buckley read Kilpatrick's work a few weeks later, he complimented his friend on "a superb job of reporting" and added, "You scoundrel, why didn't you do it for us?" William F. Buckley Jr. to James Jackson Kilpatrick, February 15, 1963, James Jackson Kilpatrick Papers, University of Virginia Library, Accession #6626-b, box 6.

143. Kilpatrick had begun—along with "thousands of Southerners"—to "see the Negro in a way they never saw him before" as the result of the recent upheaval, but he remained as intransigent as ever on the question of civil rights. See James Jackson Kilpatrick, "The South Sees through New Glasses," *National Review*, March 11, 1961, 141.

144. William P. Hustwit, *Salesman for Segregation* (Chapel Hill: University of North Carolina Press, 2013), 114–15.

145. William Doyle, *An American Insurrection: James Meredith and the Battle of Oxford, Mississippi, 1962* (New York: Anchor Books, 2001), 57.

146. Hustwit, *Salesman for Segregation*, 116. See also Doyle, *An American Insurrection*, 56.

147. Hustwit, *Salesman for Segregation*, 117.

148. Norman Podhoretz, interview with the author, November 29, 2016.

149. See, in general, Hustwit, *Salesman for Segregation*.

150. "Is There a Case for School Segregation?," transcription, *The Open Mind*, NBC Television, October 14, 1962, James Baldwin Papers, Schomburg Center for Research in Black Culture, Manuscripts, Archives and Rare Books, New York Public Library, box 5, folder 11.

151. Ibid. In *The Southern Case for School Segregation*, Kilpatrick had written, "A really massive, significant change in race relations will not come until the Negro people develop leaders who will ask themselves the familiar question, 'Why are we treated as second-class citizens?' and return a candid answer to it: 'Because all too often that is what we are. . . . The Negro says he's the white man's equal; *show me*." L. Brent Bozell Jr., "To Mend the Tragic Flaw," *National Review*, March 12, 1963, 199.

152. "Is There a Case for School Segregation?"

153. Ibid.

154. James T. Patterson, *Grand Expectations: The United States, 1945–1974* (Oxford: Oxford University Press, 1997), 500.

155. Alabama was, of course, effectively a one-party state, and most of its black citizens were not able to exercise their right to vote.

156. Dan T. Carter, *From George Wallace to Newt Gingrich: Race in the Conservative Counterrevolution, 1963–1994* (Baton Rouge: Louisiana State Press, 1996), 3.

157. George C. Wallace, "Inaugural Address of George C. Wallace," Montgomery, AL, January 14, 1963, http://digital.archives.alabama.gov/cdm/ref/collection/voices/id/2952.

158. Taylor Branch, *Parting the Waters: America in the King Years, 1954–63* (New York: Simon and Schuster, 1988), 528–44.

159. Ibid., 420–25.

Chapter 5. In the Eye of the Storm, 1963–64

1. For more on this tour of the South, see "Baldwin on Tour for CORE," *Muhammad Speaks*, February 4, 1963, https://issuu.com/muhammadspeaks/docs/we_seek_truth_and_justice_february_.

2. Morris H. Rubin to James Baldwin, June 20, 1962, Robert Park Mills Papers, Harry Ransom Humanities Research Center, University of Texas at Austin.

3. James Baldwin, "My Dungeon Shook" (1962), in *James Baldwin: Collected Essays*, ed. Toni Morrison (New York: Library of America, 1998), 291, 293–94.

4. William J. Weatherby, *James Baldwin: Artist on Fire, a Portrait* (New York: Dutton Adult, 1989), 237. Baldwin's contract with Dell Books provided him with a guaranteed advance of $35,000, with the possibility of an increase to $75,000 depending on sales. Robert P. Mills to James Baldwin, December 5, 1962, Robert Park Mills Papers, Harry Ransom Humanities Research Center, University of Texas at Austin.

5. "Invitations to Speak," James Baldwin Papers, Schomburg Center for Research in Black Culture, Manuscripts, Archives and Rare Books Division, New York Public Library. It is also worth noting that Baldwin's agent at the time, Mills, was getting concerned about the impact of Baldwin's many speaking commitments on his ability to concentrate on his writing. Robert P. Mills to James Baldwin, September 20, 1962, Robert Park Mills Papers, Harry Ransom Humanities Research Center, University of Texas at Austin. Baldwin's brother, David, reported, "If Jimmy accepted all the speaking invitations that come across his desk, he'd be speaking for three years and never write." Weatherby, *James Baldwin*, 169.

6. Martin Luther King Jr., "Letter from a Birmingham Jail," April 13, 1963, http://www.africa.upenn.edu/Articles_Gen/Letter_Birmingham.html.

7. *Eyes on the Prize, Volume 4: No Easy Walk (1962–1966)*, directed by Callie Crossley and James A. DeVinney, February 11, 1987, https://www.youtube.com/watch?v=6YYaaEffMFk.

8. "Birmingham and Beyond: The Negro's Push for Equality," *Time*, May 17, 1963.

9. Eve Auchincloss and Nancy Lynch, "Disturber of the Peace: James Baldwin—An Interview," in *Conversations with James Baldwin*, ed. Fred R. Standley and Louis H. Pratt (Jackson: University Press of Mississippi, 1989), 69. This interview is reported in the book to have occurred in 1969, but it is clear from the matters discussed that it took place some time in early 1963. Baldwin makes reference, for example, to his "recent" trip to Mississippi to meet with Evers. Ibid., 68. See also Fern Marja Eckman, *The Furious Passage of James Baldwin* (Lanham, MD: Rowman and Littlefield, 1966), 180.

10. For Kennedy's remarks on the Ole Miss crisis, see http://microsites.jfklibrary.org/olemiss/confrontation/doc10.html.

11. David Leeming, *James Baldwin: A Biography* (New York: Arcade, 2015), 222.

12. Ibid., 223.

13. Arthur M. Schlesinger Jr., *Robert Kennedy and His Times*, (New York: Mariner Books, 1979), 332.

14. James Baldwin, "Lorraine Hansberry at the Summit" (1969), in *The Cross of Redemption: Uncollected Writings*, ed. Randall Kenan (New York: Pantheon Books, 2010), 137.

15. According to Schlesinger, it was Baldwin who raised the question of whether or not he would be willing to fight for his country. Schlesinger, *Robert Kennedy and His Times*, 332. I am making an interpretive claim when I say that Baldwin raised this in order to appeal to Kennedy's instincts as a

cold warrior. I think there is a strong case to be made for this interpretation because Baldwin had insisted for years that the American racial situation was a tremendous gift to our Soviet adversaries.

16. Ibid.

17. Baldwin, "Lorraine Hansberry at the Summit," 137.

18. Burke Marshall interview by David B. Filvaroff, transcript, April 7 and 8, 1967, David B. Filvaroff and Raymond E. Wolfinger Papers, State University of New York at Buffalo, box 22, 8.

19. Baldwin, "Lorraine Hansberry at the Summit," 137–38; Schlesinger, *Robert Kennedy and His Times*, 333.

20. Baldwin, "Lorraine Hansberry at the Summit," 138.

21. Schlesinger, *Robert Kennedy and His Times*, 334.

22. Ibid.

23. Burke Marshall interview by David B. Filvaroff, transcript, April 7 and 8, 1967, David B. Filvaroff and Raymond E. Wolfinger Papers, State University of New York at Buffalo, box 22.

24. Schlesinger, *Robert Kennedy and His Times*, 335.

25. Larry Tye, *Bobby Kennedy: The Making of a Liberal Icon* (New York: Random House, 2016), 198.

26. Kenneth Clark, "Conversation with James Baldwin, A; James Baldwin Interview," May 24, 1963, http://openvault.wgbh.org/catalog/V_C03ED1927DCF46B5A8C82275DF4239F9.

27. William F. Buckley Jr., "The Mess in Mississippi," *National Review*, October 23, 1962, 304.

28. Ibid.

29. Buckley would later break with the JBS as an organization, but he would wait until it was no longer deemed useful to the accomplishment of his immediate political ends. See, for example, William F. Buckley Jr., "The Birch Society," syndicated column published on August 5, 1965; William F. Buckley Jr., "And Finally on John Birch," syndicated column published on August 17, 1965.

30. William F. Buckley Jr., "The Mess in Mississippi," syndicated column published on October 7, 1962.

31. Erik von Kuehnelt-Leddihn, "Letter from Africa," *National Review*, April 9, 1960, 232; Erik von Kuehnelt-Leddihn, "Katanga's Cure," *National Review*, August 13, 1960. For Buckley's description, see "Erik Ritter von Kuehnelt-Leddihn," *Religion and Liberty* 9, no. 5 (July 20, 2010).

32. Anthony Lejeune, "Letter from Ghana," *National Review*, May 21, 1960, 330.

33. *Truth and Reconciliation Commission Report of South Africa*, volume 3, October 29, 1998, 397.

34. William F. Buckley Jr., "Deadend in South Africa," *National Review*, April 23, 1960, 255.

35. Dan Wakefield, "Portrait of a Complainer," *Esquire*, January 1961, 49–52.

36. John Judis, *William F. Buckley, Jr.: The Patron Saint of the Conservatives* (New York: Simon and Schuster, 1988), 185. See also Austin C. Wehrwein, "Talk by Buckley Angers Students," *New York Times*, August 23, 1961, 30.

37. William F. Buckley Jr., "Letter from Capetown," syndicated column published on November 25, 1962. A segregationist writer who had published in *National Review*, Anthony Harrigan, wrote to congratulate Buckley on his "Letter from Capetown," which Harrigan called "very good." Anthony Harrigan to William F. Buckley Jr., December 5, 1962, William F. Buckley Jr. Papers (MS 576), Manuscripts and Archives, Yale University Library. For more on Harrigan, see Marc Henrie, "Anthony Harrigan," *First Principles*, https://www.firstprinciplesjournal.com/articles.aspx?article=833&theme=home&loc=b.

38. William F. Buckley Jr., "Must We Hate Portugal?," syndicated column published on December 2, 1962.

39. William F. Buckley Jr., "South African Fortnight," *National Review*, January 14, 1963, 17–23. Kilpatrick wrote to Buckley to tell him that his "South African Fortnight" essay was "an absolute beauty" and perhaps "one of the best things" he had ever written. James Jackson Kilpatrick to William F.

Buckley Jr., January 10, 1963, James Jackson Kilpatrick Papers, University of Virginia Library, Accession #6626-6, box 6. It is worth noting that Buckley's reflections on apartheid strengthen my case that he was a moral relativist. When it came to race, Buckley was unwilling to pass moral judgment and objected to others doing so.

40. William F. Buckley Jr., "Birmingham and After," syndicated column published on May 11, 1963.

41. Ibid. Buckley would repeat this argument later in "The Haynesville Dilemma," a syndicated column published on May 13, 1965. In that piece, which was about the acquittal of the murderer of a civil rights volunteer in Alabama, Buckley declared that it "is the final irony that individual Southerners may prove responsible for the major impulse that is being given to the preemption by the federal government of local laws."

42. Buckley, "Birmingham and After."

43. Burke Marshall interview by David B. Filvaroff, transcript, April 7 and 8, 1967, David B. Filvaroff and Raymond E. Wolfinger Papers, State University of New York at Buffalo, box 22.

44. William F. Buckley Jr., "The Vote in the South," *National Review*, June 4, 1963, 437.

45. In the "Clarification" he wrote in response to Bozell's critique of "Why the South Must Prevail," Buckley had endorsed color-blind disenfranchisement. William F. Buckley Jr., "A Clarification," *National Review*, September 7, 1957, 199.

46. Ibid.

47. William F. Buckley Jr., "The Call to Colorblindness," syndicated column published on June 8, 1963. This is a caricature of Baldwin's position. Baldwin recognized that human beings are able to see all sorts of differences in their physical characteristics. His hope was to free people from the myth that those physical differences had moral significance.

48. Ibid.

49. Ibid. A few weeks later, Buckley would expand on the dangers of unrealistic expectations in an essay called "Enter Muhammed [*sic*]?" In the piece, he argued that the likely beneficiary of the unrealized hopes of the demand of "Freedom Now" from leaders like King and Baldwin would be Muhammad and the NOI. As "other programs fail, which they will," Buckley declared, Muhammad's "program will loom larger and larger." William F. Buckley Jr., "Enter Muhammed [*sic*]?" *National Review*, July 2, 1963, 519–20.

50. Buckley, "Call to Colorblindness." Not long after Buckley published "The Call to Colorblindness," *National Review* published a letter by Marcella Whalen, who was Baldwin's English teacher and adviser at DeWitt Clinton High School. Whalen wrote to *National Review* in order to challenge Baldwin's claim that New York was a "hostile" place to grow up. In order to support her argument, Whalen cited several "character cards" in which Baldwin's teachers spoke of his success as editor of the *Magpie*, the school's literary magazine. Marcella Whalen, "Letters to the Editor," *National Review*, August 13, 1963, 120.

51. William J. Maxwell, *James Baldwin: The FBI File* (New York: Arcade Publishing, 2017), 52–54, 59, 81.

52. See Robert P. Mills to Burke Marshall, May 28, 1963, Robert Park Mills Papers, Harry Ransom Humanities Research Center, University of Texas at Austin. In the letter to Assistant Attorney General Burke Marshall about this matter, Mills reminded him that Baldwin "stands ready to confer or assist in any way he can in the future." Baldwin biographer Eckman interviewed Marshall about the matter as well. Eckman, *Furious Passage of James Baldwin*, 196.

53. Baldwin also spoke about the possibility of writing a book exploring the "work of the FBI in the South . . . during recent civil rights incidents." Maxwell, *James Baldwin*, 10.

54. George C. Wallace, "Statement and Proclamation of Governor George C. Wallace," University of Alabama, June 11, 1963, http://www.archives.state.al.us/govs_list/schooldoor.html.

55. John F. Kennedy, "Address by President John F. Kennedy," June 11, 1963, https://www.jfklibrary.org/Asset-Viewer/LH8F_oMzvoe6Ro1yEm74Ng.aspx.

56. Maxwell, *James Baldwin*, 167; James Baldwin Papers, Schomburg Center for Research in Black Culture, Manuscripts, Archives and Rare Books Division, New York Public Library.

57. Cohen reports that "the assassination made such a book impossible, and we, me and my publisher, Macmillan, dropped the idea as unbearably ironic." Jacob Cohen, email to the author, July 22, 2017.

58. Claude Sitton, "N.A.A.C.P. Leader Slain in Jackson; Protests Mount," in *Reporting Civil Rights, Part One: American Journalism, 1941–1963*, ed. Clayborne Carson, David J. Garrow, Bill Kovach, and Carol Polsgrove (New York: Library of America, 2003), 832–34.

59. I am indebted to David Leeming for the idea of thinking about these works as eulogies for Evers.

60. It is worth noting, though, that Governor Barnett condemned the murder at first, but later appeared—alongside Major General Walker—at the assassin's trial, where they could be seen shaking his hand and hugging him. Stephanie Rolph, *Resisting Inequality: The Citizens' Council, 1954–1989* (Baton Rouge: Louisiana State University Press, 2018), 143.

61. "Nothing Personal" contains many themes Baldwin developed in what we might call the "stump speech" he used during his 1963 lecture tour around the country.

62. James Baldwin, "Nothing Personal" (1964), in *James Baldwin: Collected Essays*, edited by Toni Morrison (New York: Library of America, 1998), 693, 698.

63. Ibid., 694, 698–99.

64. Ibid., 702, 704, 700. This idea echoes something Baldwin had written nearly a decade earlier in *Giovanni's Room*: "But people can't, unhappily, invent their mooring posts, their lovers and their friends, any more than they can invent their parents. Life gives these and also takes them away and the great difficulty is to say Yes to life." James Baldwin, *Early Novels and Stories*, ed. Toni Morrison (New York: Library of America, 1998), 222.

65. James Baldwin, *Blues for Mister Charlie: A Play* (New York: Vintage Books, 1964), x.

66. Ibid., 11.

67. Ibid., 4.

68. It is important to note that according to Clay Risen's excellent history of the Civil Rights Act of 1964, by "mid-June 1963, more than a hundred major civil rights bills sat before the House, many of them Republican-sponsored, and many of them in the Judiciary Committee." Clay Risen, *The Bill of the Century: The Epic Battle for the Civil Rights Act* (New York: Bloomsbury Press, 2014), 86.

69. Ibid., 88, 91.

70. William F. Buckley Jr., *National Review* interoffice memos, 1963, William F. Buckley Jr. Papers (MS 576), Manuscripts and Archives, Yale University Library.

71. Memo from William F. Rickenbacker to William F. Buckley Jr., June 21, 1963, William F. Buckley Jr. Papers (MS 576), Manuscripts and Archives, Yale University Library.

72. Frank S. Meyer, "The Negro Revolution," *National Review*, June 18, 1963, 496. For more on Meyer's views of the civil rights movement, see Frank S. Meyer, "The Violence of Nonviolence," *National Review*, April 20, 1965, 327.

73. Meyer, "Negro Revolution."

74. Frank S. Meyer memo to William F. Buckley Jr., June 1963, William F. Buckley Jr. Papers (MS 576), Manuscripts and Archives, Yale University Library.

75. Lee Edwards, *Goldwater: The Man Who Made a Revolution* (Washington, DC: Regnery History, 1995), 230.

76. William P. Jones, *The March on Washington: Jobs, Freedom, and the Forgotten History of Civil Rights*, (New York: W. W. Norton, 2013), xvii. According to Jones, the "initial proposal for the 1963 March on Washington came from the Negro American Labor Council (NALC), a largely forgotten organization that Randolph and other black trade unionists created to highlight the economic crisis caused by black workers' exclusion from skilled jobs and unions." Ibid.

77. Executive Order 8802, issued in June 1941, https://www.ourdocuments.gov/doc.php?flash =true&doc=72.

78. William F. Buckley Jr., "The Other Way of Looking at It," syndicated column published on August 3, 1963.

79. William F. Buckley Jr., "Count Me Out," syndicated column published on August 17, 1963, and reprinted with slight alterations as "When the 'Plaints Go Marching In," *National Review*, August 27, 1963, 140. It is worth noting that Buckley also enlisted his segregationist colleague Kilpatrick to offer a constitutionalist critique of the civil rights bill. See, in general, James Jackson Kilpatrick, "Civil Rights and Legal Wrongs," *National Review*, September 24, 1963, 231.

80. Buckley, "Count Me Out." A few months later, Buckley would encourage readers to abandon the leadership of figures like Baldwin, King, and Rustin, who wanted to "purge all congressmen who do not vote for their version of the Civil Rights Bill," and endorse instead the leadership of an "American Negro . . . who will call for the advancement for the Negro within the context of a free and decentralized society." William F. Buckley Jr., "Leftward March," *National Review*, January 14, 1964, 11–12.

81. Frank Meyer, "The Twisted Tree of Liberty," in *Freedom and Virtue: The Conservative/Libertarian Debate*, ed. George W. Carey (Wilmington, DE: ISI Books, 1998), 17.

82. Ibid.

83. Leeming, *James Baldwin*, 227–28.

84. Burt Lancaster would read the Paris petition aloud at the March on Washington. See https://www.youtube.com/watch?v=U54KWuNolIE

85. Taylor Branch, *Parting the Waters: America in the King Years, 1954–63* (New York: Simon and Schuster, 1988), 831.

86. Malcolm X, "Message to the Grassroots," November 10, 1963, http://teachingamericanhistory .org/library/document/message-to-grassroots/. Branch reports that Baldwin was indeed excluded from the list of speakers, and that he was none too pleased when he received this news. Branch, *Parting the Waters*, 878.

87. Leeming, *James Baldwin*, 228. Rustin was permitted to speak, but played a lesser role "out front" than seems appropriate given his central role in organizing the event.

88. Thomas Chatteron Williams, "Breaking into James Baldwin's House," *New Yorker*, October 28, 2015.

89. D. Quentin Miller, "James Baldwin: America's Prophet, Resurrected," WBUR, February 24, 2015, http://www.wbur.org/cognoscenti/2015/02/24/james-baldwin-black-prophet-d-quentin-miller.

90. James Baldwin, "No Name in the Street" (1972), in *James Baldwin: Collected Essays*, ed. Toni Morrison (New York: Library of America, 1998), 439.

91. Claude Sitton, "Birmingham Bomb Kills 4 Negro Girls in Church; Riots Flare; 2 Boys Slain," *New York Times*, September 16, 1963, in *Reporting Civil Rights, Part Two: American Journalism, 1963–1973*, ed. Clayborne Carson, David J. Garrow, Bill Kovach, and Carol Polsgrove (New York: Library of America, 2003), 20.

92. Baldwin, "No Name in the Street," 440.

93. Like many other crimes of this sort, Baldwin was quick to point to our collective responsibility for creating a society where it was likely things like this could happen. His point was not, of course, to absolve the perpetrators of their responsibility but rather to get the rest of us to accept ours.

94. Alvin Felzenberg, *A Man and His Presidents* (New Haven, CT: Yale University Press, 2017), 121.

95. Biographer Charles Lam Markmann reported that Buckley wept when he learned of the Birmingham bombing. Markmann does not provide a source for this claim, but it appears he interviewed Buckley, many members of the Buckley family, and many Buckley associates as part of the research for his book. Charles Lam Markmann, *The Buckleys: A Family Examined* (New York: William Morrow, 1973), 271. For a list of Markmann's interviews for the project, see ibid., xi–xiv.

96. *National Review Bulletin* 15, no. 13 (October 1, 1963): 1.

97. Ibid. (emphasis added). In his discussion of this editorial, Felzenberg did not include Buckley's use of "widely assumed," and these two words are crucial to understanding how he could possibly proceed to suggest that "a Communist" or "deranged Negro" may be to blame. Indeed, after offering these alternative explanations, Buckley even goes on to say, "Some circumstantial evidence lends a hint of plausibility to [the crazed Negro] notion, especially the ten-minute fuse (surely a white man walking away from the church basement ten minutes earlier would have been noticed?)." Ibid.

98. Ibid.

99. *Revolt against the Masses* file, William F. Buckley Jr. Papers (MS 576), Manuscripts and Archives, Yale University Library.

100. See Judis, *William F. Buckley, Jr.*, 214–15.

101. *Revolt against the Masses* file, William F. Buckley Jr. Papers (MS 576), Manuscripts and Archives, Yale University Library.

102. According to Wills, Buckley never finished his "big book" because "he realized in time that this was not his métier. He was not a reflective thinker. He was a quick responder." Garry Wills, *Outside Looking In* (New York: Viking, 2010), 160. Hart echoed this sentiment when he said that Buckley abandoned the project because it "would require serious work over an extended period, for which he was disinclined." Jeffrey Hart, "Right at the End," *American Conservative*, March 24, 2008, https://www.theamericanconservative.com/articles/right-at-the-end/.

103. For the anti-Kennedy handbill, see https://news.utexas.edu/2013/11/18/why-jfk-died-in-dallas.

104. Leeming, *James Baldwin*, 230.

105. Eckman, *Furious Passage of James Baldwin*, 220.

106. James Baldwin Papers, Schomburg Center for Research in Black Culture, Manuscripts, Archives and Rare Books Division, New York Public Library, box 56, folder 14. For more on Baldwin's reaction to the assassination of Kennedy, see Eckman, *Furious Passage of James Baldwin*, 220–21.

107. William F. Buckley Jr., "The Morning After," *National Review*, December 17, 1963, 512. A few weeks after the assassination, Buckley utilized his syndicated column in order to push back against those critics who accused the American Right of creating "an atmosphere of hatred" that laid the groundwork for the murder. Buckley believed this was unfair to conservatives because Oswald was a man of the Left; American rightists seldom make "calls to violence," and it was really men of the Left— including King—who have "defied law and order" as well as created a culture of "lawlessness" in which something like this was more likely to happen. William F. Buckley Jr., "Do They Really Hate to Hate?," *National Review*, December 31, 1963, 558–59.

108. Donald T. Critchlow and Nancy MacLean, *Debating the American Conservative Movement: 1945 to the Present* (Lanham, MD: Rowman and Littlefield, 2009), 182.

109. See, in general, Rick Perlstein, *Before the Storm: Barry Goldwater and the Unmaking of the American Consensus* (New York: Hill and Wang, 2001).

110. Ibid., 51.

111. William F. Buckley Jr., *Did You Ever See a Dream Walking?* (New York: Bobbs-Merrill, 1970).

112. William F. Buckley Jr., "If Goldwater Were President," *Coronet*, July 1961, 156–62.

113. Ibid., 160.

114. See, in general, Lee Edwards, *Goldwater: The Man Who Made a Revolution* (Washington, DC: Regnery History, 1995).

115. William F. Buckley Jr. to James Jackson Kilpatrick, January 21, 1963, William F. Buckley Jr. Papers (MS 576), Manuscripts and Archives, Yale University Library. See also James Jackson Kilpatrick Papers, University of Virginia Library, Accession #6626-b, box 6.

116. James Jackson Kilpatrick to William F. Buckley Jr., January 23, 1963, James Jackson Kilpatrick Papers, University of Virginia Library, Accession #6626-b, box 6.

117. Perlstein, *Before the Storm*, 260.

118. Felzenberg, *A Man and His Presidents*, 145. See also Judis, *William F. Buckley, Jr.*, 222.

119. Lyndon Baines Johnson, "Address before a Joint Session of Congress," American Presidency Project, University of California at Santa Barbara, November 27, 1963, http://www.presidency.ucsb.edu/ws/?pid=25988.

120. Schlesinger, *Robert Kennedy and His Times*, 638–42.

121. It is worth noting that Republicans in Congress had been overwhelmingly supportive of the Civil Rights Acts of 1957 and 1960. See Perlstein, *Before the Storm*, 135.

122. William F. Buckley Jr., "Goldwater: Profile in Courage?," syndicated column published on June 25, 1964.

123. Ibid.

124. William F. Buckley Jr., "A White Revolt?," syndicated column published on April 16, 1964.

125. William F. Buckley Jr., "The Obliging Disappearance of George Wallace," syndicated column published on July 28, 1964.

126. Dan T. Carter, *From George Wallace to Newt Gingrich: Race in the Conservative Counterrevolution, 1963–1994* (Baton Rouge: Louisiana State Press, 1996), 114.

127. Joseph E. Lowndes, *From the New Deal to the New Right: Race and the Southern Origins of Modern Conservatism* (New Haven, CT: Yale University Press, 2008), 7.

128. William F. Buckley Jr., "The *Brown* Decade," *National Review*, June 2, 1964, 433–34.

129. "A Program for the Goldwater Administration," *National Review*, July 1964. Buckley asked other members of the staff to do all that they could to promote the special edition at the convention by distributing copies to delegates and arranging for a *National Review* banner to "float over San Francisco" during the proceedings. He even suggested that the contributors to the supplement be invited to appear before the party platform committee.

130. For a detailed discussion of Jaffa's role in the drafting of Goldwater's convention speech, see Edwards, *Goldwater*, 267–69.

131. Goldwater chose the anti–Civil Rights Act congressman William Miller of New York instead. Behind the scenes, Buckley friend and benefactor Roger Milliken served as an intermediary between the Goldwater and Wallace camps with hopes that he might convince the Alabama governor to join the GOP. Rick Perlstein, *Before the Storm*, 431.

132. James Jackson Kilpatrick, "Goldwater Country," *National Review*, April 9, 1963, 281. See also James Jackson Kilpatrick, "The South Goes Back Up for Grabs," *National Review*, December 17, 1963, 523–24.

133. William Rusher, "GOP at a Crossroads," *National Review*, February 12, 1963, 109–12.

134. Clayborne Carson, "Chronology, 1941 to 1973," in *Reporting Civil Rights, Part Two: American Journalism, 1963–1973*, ed. Clayborne Carson, David J. Garrow, Bill Kovach, and Carol Polsgrove (New York: Library of America, 2003), 899.

135. William Bradford Huie, "The Search for the Missing," in *Reporting Civil Rights, Part Two: American Journalism, 1963–1973*, ed. Clayborne Carson, David J. Garrow, Bill Kovach, and Carol Polsgrove (New York: Library of America, 2003), 160.

136. William F. Buckley Jr., "Mississippi," *National Review,* July 14, 1964, 574.

137. For a detailed and riveting account of the events preceding the Harlem riot, see Michael W. Flamm, *In the Heat of the Summer: The New York Riots of 1964 and the War on Crime* (Philadelphia: University of Pennsylvania Press, 2016), 10–17.

138. Lez Edmond, "The Long, Hot Summer," in *Reporting Civil Rights, Part Two: American Journalism, 1963–1973,* ed. Clayborne Carson, David J. Garrow, Bill Kovach, and Carol Polsgrove (New York: Library of America, 2003), 138. Edmond reports that Gilligan "said the kid had a knife and was going at him. That didn't mean much to the people of Harlem. You don't shoot a kid twice to get rid of his knife." Ibid. A grand jury would later disagree with that sentiment and excuse Gilligan from any wrongdoing. Schuyler, the black conservative who had jousted with Baldwin and Malcolm X years before, was among those on the grand jury that excused Gilligan.

139. Jonathan Gill, *Harlem: The Four Hundred Year History from Dutch Village to Capital of Black America* (New York: Grove Press, 2011), 381. While most Americans were transfixed by the spectacle of the events at the Cow Palace and riots in Harlem, Buckley was not. On the evening Goldwater was nominated, July 15, his younger sister, Maureen, suffered a cerebral hemorrhage. She would die two days later at the age of only thirty-one. As Buckley waited to take a red-eye flight back to the East Coast, his colleagues watched their ebullient leader slip into devastation. "Her death was shattering to him," his sister Patricia reported. "It didn't occur to me before," he said later, "that someone thirty-one years old could die." Judis, *William F. Buckley, Jr.,* 229–30.

140. Perlstein, *Before the Storm,* 401; James T. Patterson, *The Eve of Destruction: How 1965 Transformed America* (New York: Basic Books, 2012), 6.

141. Perlstein, *Before the Storm,* 403.

142. Steven F. Hayward, *The Age of Reagan: The Conservative Counterrevolution, 1980–1989* (New York: Random House, 2009), 51. See, in general, William F. Buckley Jr., "The Vile Campaign," *National Review,* October 6, 1964.

143. Hayward, *Age of Reagan.*

144. Maxwell, *James Baldwin,* 246.

145. Arnold Forster and Benjamin R. Epstein, *Danger on the Right* (Santa Barbara: Praeger, 1976).

146. In 1963, the prominent Columbia University sociologist Daniel Bell edited a similar collection titled *The Radical Right.* Buckley was so infuriated to be placed in the company of fringe elements on the American Right that he threatened to sue Bell and his publishers. In the end, Buckley decided against legal action, but lambasted Bell for his "intellectual slovenliness." William F. Buckley Jr. to Daniel Bell, April 3, 1963, William F. Buckley Jr. Papers (MS 576), Manuscripts and Archives, Yale University Library.

147. Alvin S. Felzenberg, "How William F. Buckley Jr. Changed His Mind on Civil Rights," *Politico,* May 13, 2017, https://www.politico.com/magazine/story/2017/05/13/William-f-buckley-civil-rights-215129.

148. William F. Buckley Jr., "The Impending Defeat of Barry Goldwater," in *Let Us Talk of Many Things: The Collected Speeches* (New York: Forum, 2000), 74.

149. "Special Report: The Race Issue and the Election," *National Review,* September 22, 1964.

150. Ibid.

151. Perlstein, *Before the Storm,* 431.

152. William F. Buckley Jr., "Strom Thurmond Makes It Official," syndicated column published on September 20, 1964.

153. In order to expedite matters, Buckley proposed that the Republican Party pledge to honor the seniority of any member of the Democratic Party willing to come across the aisle. See, in general,

Earl Black and Merle Black, *The Rise of the Southern Republicans* (Cambridge, MA: Belknap Press of Harvard University Press, 2001); Lowndes, *From the New Deal to the New Right*.

154. William F. Buckley Jr., introduction to "Special Report: The Race Issue and the Election," *National Review*, September 22, 1964.

155. Garry Wills, "Who Shall Overcome?," *National Review*, September 22, 1964. These ideas were expressed, though in a slightly different spirit, by Baldwin in "Down at the Cross."

156. For one of many descriptions of Buckley as "tablet keeper," see Alvin S. Felzenberg, "He Stood Athwart History," interview, *National Review*, February 27, 2013, https://www.nationalreview.com/2013/02/he-stood-athwart-history-interview/.

157. Whittaker Chambers, "Big Sister Is Watching You," *National Review*, December 28, 1957, 594–96; Garry Wills, "But Is Ayn Rand Conservative?," *National Review*, February 27, 1960, 139; William F. Buckley Jr., "The Question of Robert Welch," *National Review*, February 13, 1962, 83–88; Susan Currie Sivek, "Editing Conservatism: How *National Review* Magazine Framed and Mobilized a Political Movement," *Mass Communication and Society* 11, no. 3 (2008): 247–74.

158. It is worth noting that in Buckley's own account of his role as the "gatekeeper" of conservatism, he does not include racists among those he felt duty bound to extricate from the movement. In "Notes toward an Empirical Definition of Conservatism," Buckley gave his own of account of the "people and ideas with which [the] *National Review* has had trouble making common cause." He included sections on the Randians, "Murray Rothbard and his merry anarchists," the JBS, and atheists. William F. Buckley, "Notes toward an Empirical Definition of Conservatism," in *What Is Conservatism?*, ed. Frank S. Meyer (Wilmington, DE: Intercollegiate Studies Institute, 2015), 211–16. One of the leading court historians of the conservative movement, Edwards, reaches a conclusion similar to mine in his reflections on Buckley's role "defining" the conservative movement. Buckley is to be credited, Edwards argues, for excising Randians, Birchers, and anti-Semites, but "Buckley and the magazine did not acquit themselves well on the issue of civil rights." Lee Edwards, *Standing Athwart History: The Political Thought of William F. Buckley Jr.* (Washington, DC: Heritage Foundation, 2010), 12–14. It is also noteworthy that some of Buckley's contemporaries were urging him to make a more "unequivocal statement" about the racist fringe of the American Right. Steve Allen to Frank Meyer (Buckley cc'ed), January 13, 1965, William F. Buckley Jr. Papers (MS 576), Manuscripts and Archives, Yale University Library.

159. Buckley also reported that he was rethinking his views of race privately in correspondence with his mother in 1963. I have been unable to find evidence of this correspondence in the vast William F. Buckley Jr. Papers at Yale University. Buckley reported on an exchange with his mother about race in his obituary of her, which he reworked and published in his books, *Nearer, My God* and *Miles Gone By*. Buckley claims that he confronted his mother about how "she could reconcile Christian fraternity with the separation of the races." William F. Buckley Jr., *Miles Gone By: A Literary Autobiography* (Washington, DC: Regnery Publishing, 2004), 52. See also William F. Buckley Jr., "Saying Goodbye: Aloise Steiner Buckley, R.I.P.," *National Review*, April 19, 1985, 20–21.

160. Two letters from 1964 capture the awkward position in which Buckley found himself. Carleton Putnam, who was a notoriously racist writer and lecturer, submitted a manuscript for publication in *National Review*. In response, Buckley wrote to his sister Priscilla, who was the managing editor at the magazine: "Carleton Putnam is a racist. . . . Give him a wide berth but try not to antagonize him. Under no circumstances run his manuscript." William F. Buckley Jr. to Priscilla Buckley, January 24, 1964, William F. Buckley Jr. Papers (MS 576), Manuscripts and Archives, Yale University Library. Putnam later submitted some of his material for publication as an advertisement in *National Review*. Buckley consulted, among others, Ernest van den Haag to get advice on whether or not to publish the advertisement. Ernest van den Haag to William F. Buckley Jr., May 27, 1964, William F.

Buckley Jr. Papers (MS 576), Manuscripts and Archives, Yale University Library. Just a few months later, Buckley wrote to Kilpatrick—who was an enthusiastic champion of Putnam's work and still thick as thieves with the Citizens' Council's Simmons—to ask him if he would do him the "honor" of serving as an associate editor of *National Review*. William F. Buckley Jr. to James Jackson Kilpatrick, October 5, 1964, William F. Buckley Jr. Papers (MS 576), Manuscripts and Archives, Yale University Library. To get a sense of the breadth and depth of the collaboration between Kilpatrick and the Citizens' Council, one need only examine his extensive correspondence with Simmons, which is available in the James Jackson Kilpatrick Papers at the University of Virginia. The two men socialized with each other, sought professional advice from one another, and collaborated on numerous projects over many years. For Kilpatrick's enthusiasm for Putnam's work, see Robert Goldwin, ed., *100 Years of Emancipation* (New York: Rand McNally, 1963), 115. Simmons refers to Putnam as "our mutual friend." William J. Simmons to James Jackson Kilpatrick, August 4, 1964, James Jackson Kilpatrick Papers, University of Virginia Library, Accession #6626-b, box 48. It is worth noting that Simmons and Kilpatrick did have some significant disagreements during this period. Kilpatrick, Simmons had noticed, had "a definite bias . . . against any white youths who reacted physically to integration." Simmons was much more comfortable with such violence, which he thought was acceptable in the face of threats to segregation. "War is not pretty," Simmons told Kilpatrick. William J. Simmons to James Jackson Kilpatrick, August 4, 1964, James Jackson Kilpatrick Papers, University of Virginia Library, Accession #6626-b, box 48. Whatever concerns Buckley had about racism in the early 1960s, he kept them private in order to do what he believed to be politically expedient. The best way forward politically, he had concluded by the end of 1964, was to avoid antagonizing racists like Putnam, solidify ties with less virulently racist states' righters like Kilpatrick, and pursue an aggressive campaign to exploit the latent racial resentments and fears of working- and middle-class white voters outside the South.

161. William F. Buckley Jr. to Barry Goldwater, November 3, 1964, William F. Buckley Jr. Papers (MS 576), Manuscripts and Archives, Yale University Library.

162. Buckley wrote a telegram to Goldwater the day after the election in which he stated, "I wish to express my gratitude as an American for the gallant work you did for all your countrymen. I have no doubt that history will one day reward you." William F. Buckley Jr. to Barry Goldwater, November 4, 1964, William F. Buckley Jr. Papers (MS 576), Manuscripts and Archives, Yale University Library.

163. William F. Buckley Jr. to David Susskind, 1964, William F. Buckley Jr. Papers (MS 576), Manuscripts and Archives, Yale University Library.

164. William F. Buckley Jr., "The Defeat of Barry Goldwater," syndicated column published on November 7, 1964; William F. Buckley Jr., "Realignment," *National Review*, December 1, 1964, 1047.

Chapter 6. "What Concerns Me Most": Baldwin at Cambridge

1. David Leeming, *James Baldwin: A Biography* (New York: Arcade, 2015), 238.

2. Philip Roth, "Channel X: Two Plays on the Race Conflict," *New York Review of Books*, May 28, 1964.

3. Leeming, *James Baldwin*, 238.

4. In one of many interesting coincidences in this story, the writer Charles Lam Markmann—who would go on to write a book on the Buckley family—wrote to Baldwin to offer a small amount of financial support for *Blues for Mister Charlie*. James Baldwin Papers, Schomburg Center for Research in Black Culture, Manuscripts, Archives and Rare Books Division, New York Public Library.

5. Robert Brustein, "Everybody Knows My Name," *New York Review of Books*, December 17, 1964.

6. I think Brustein is right to say that *Nothing Personal* falls short of the standard of prose Baldwin established for himself in *Notes of a Native Son, Nobody Knows My Name*, and *The Fire Next Time*, but I do not think Baldwin's prose in the book falls quite as flatly as Brustein argues. Brustein either ignored or was unaware of the ways in which the text was inspired by the deaths in the South. This background, which I discussed above, seems to give the prose a richness it might otherwise lack.

7. Brustein, "Everybody Knows My Name." Even Avedon privately expressed reservations about Baldwin's essay. "It reads more like a scalding sermon," he said, "a diatribe. Jimmy had 'murder in his heart'—*his words*." Norma Stevens and Steven M. L. Aronson, *Avedon: Something Personal* (New York: Random House, 2017), 194.

8. James Baldwin, "Fifth Avenue, Uptown: A Letter from Harlem" (1960), in *James Baldwin: Collected Essays*, ed. Toni Morrison (New York: Library of America, 1998)," 172.

9. William J. Maxwell, *James Baldwin: The FBI File* (New York: Arcade Publishing, 2017), 237–38.

10. James Baldwin Papers, Schomburg Center for Research in Black Culture, Manuscripts, Archives and Rare Books Division, New York Public Library, box 64, file 7.

11. Fern Marja Eckman, *The Furious Passage of James Baldwin* (Lanham, MD: Rowman and Littlefield, 1966), 167.

12. William F. Buckley Jr., speech at the University of California at Los Angeles, December 8, 1964.

13. Mississippi Department of Archives and History, Forum Films Collection, 195566, reel 009. For more on van den Haag's promotion of segregation, see John P. Jackson Jr., *Science for Segregation: Race, Law, and the Case against Brown v. Board of Education* (New York: NYU Press, 2005), 141–45.

14. William F. Buckley Jr., "Footnote to *Brown v. Board of Education*," *National Review*, March 11, 1961, 137.

15. Ernest van den Haag, "NEGROES, INTELLIGENCE, AND PREJUDICE," *National Review*, December 1, 1964, 261. The proximate inspiration for the van den Haag essay was a UNESCO report prepared by Melvin Tumin, a sociologist at Princeton University. Melvin Tumin, *Race and Intelligence: A Scientific Evaluation* (New York: Anti-Defamation League of B'nai B'rith, 1963).

16. Ibid.

17. Daniel Bell to William F. Buckley Jr., November 25, 1964, William F. Buckley Jr. Papers (MS 576), Manuscripts and Archives, Yale University Library. It is interesting to note that Buckley himself had made this point in private correspondence with critics of his discussion of race in *Up from Liberalism*.

18. Irving Kristol to William F. Buckley Jr., November 23, 1964, William F. Buckley Jr. Papers (MS 576), Manuscripts and Archives, Yale University Library. Again, Buckley made much the same point about Jews in his private correspondence with critics of his discussion of race in *Up from Liberalism*.

19. William F. Buckley Jr., "Mississippi Dilemma and 'The Best Part of Life,'" syndicated column published on December 19, 1964.

20. Ibid.

21. This is also reminiscent of Buckley's reaction the Sharpeville massacre in South Africa, though in that case he offered more explicit moral critique. See William F. Buckley Jr., "Deadend in South Africa," *National Review*, April 23, 1960, 254–55.

22. The precise date of Kolins's initial contact with the Cambridge Union is lost to history, but it appears likely that it took place some time in January. The debate was not added to the Union schedule until early February, although this may have been due to the fact that Fullerton was working to come up with a resolution and find an opponent for Baldwin.

23. Peter Fullerton, interview with the author, September 28, 2015.

24. Leeming, *James Baldwin*, 243.

25. Letter from Gloria Davis to Bill Kolins, January 28, 1965, James Baldwin Papers, Schomburg Center for Research in Black Culture, Manuscripts, Archives and Rare Books Division, New York Public Library.

26. Percy Cradock, *Recollections of the Cambridge Union, 1815–1939* (Cambridge, UK: Bowes and Bowes, 1953), 5.

27. Fullerton, interview. It would have not been unusual for Fullerton to consult other officers of the Union as he attempted to come up with a suitable resolution, but he does not recall doing so.

28. Ibid.

29. David Birmingham, *The Decolonization of Africa* (Athens: Ohio University Press, 1995), 1, 5.

30. Clive Webb, "Brotherhood, Betrayal, and Rivers of Blood: Southern Segregationists and British Race Relations," in *The Other Special Relationship: Race, Rights, and Riots in Britain and the United States*, ed. Robert D. G. Kelley and Stephen Tuck (New York: Palgrave Macmillan, 2015), 232–33.

31. Kennetta Hammond Perry, "U.S. Negroes, Your Fight Is Our Fight: Black Britons and the 1963 March on Washington," in *The Other Special Relationship: Race, Rights, and Riots in Britain and the United States*, ed. Robert D. G. Kelley and Stephen Tuck (New York: Palgrave Macmillan, 2015), 13.

32. Stephen Parkinson, *Arena of Ambition: The History of the Cambridge Union* (London: Icon Books, 2009), 163. *National Review* weighed in on the Griffiths election in Colm Brogan, "Alabama, Here We Come," *National Review*, March 9, 1965, 195–96.

33. Paul Danaher, "March Will Greet Griffiths," *Varsity*, January 16, 1965; Paul Danaher, "No Action after Riot Misfires," *Varsity*, January 23, 1965.

34. Fullerton does not recall precisely how he came up with the resolution for the debate, and the details of this process appear to be lost to history. My thoughts on what may have happened should be read as speculation based on what Fullerton can recall about the process. Fullerton, interview.

35. James Baldwin, "Down at the Cross" (1962), in *James Baldwin: Collected Essays*, ed. Toni Morrison (New York: Library of America, 1998), 337.

36. Parkinson, *Arena of Ambition*, 16. The introduction of outside speakers, Union historian Stephen Parkinson reports, "changed the nature of Union debates: they became less closed, and attracted attention from the outside world, particularly as those eminent figures who came up to Cambridge to speak in them spread the word to their colleagues on their return." While some within the Union resented this change and pushed for various reforms to bring the students back to the center of activity, the costs of the inclusion of these "visiting dignitaries" proved to be a well worth paying for many Cambridge Students as they "eased the passage from the Union to Westminster or to other echelons of the Establishment for those young men who dined with them, sat alongside them in the chamber, or challenged them in debate with carefully prepared speeches."

37. Fullerton, interview.

38. Michael Tugendhat, email exchange with the author, September 21, 2015.

39. See, in general, Brustein, "Everybody Knows My Name."

40. William F. Buckley Jr., "Hate America," syndicated column published on January 21, 1965.

41. James Baldwin to Robert Lantz, February 1, 1965, James Baldwin Papers, Schomburg Center for Research in Black Culture, Manuscripts, Archives and Rare Books Division, New York Public Library.

42. For Buckley's description of Pat's ski accident, see William F. Buckley Jr. to John Kenneth Galbraith, September 8, 1965, William F. Buckley Jr. Papers (MS 576), Manuscripts and Archives, Yale University Library.

43. Helen Merrill to James Baldwin, February 1965, James Baldwin Papers, Schomburg Center for Black Culture, Manuscripts, Archives and Rare Books Division, New York Public Library.

44. Ibid.

45. Robert Lantz to Bill Kolins, February 11, 1965, James Baldwin Papers, Schomburg Center for Research in Black Culture, Manuscripts, Archives and Rare Books Division, New York Public Library.

46. William J. Weatherby, *James Baldwin: Artist on Fire, a Portrait* (New York: Dutton Adult, 1989), 315.

47. Eckman reports that Baldwin once told Mailer that "he'd rather spend his time with a white racist than a white liberal, since with the racist he knew at least exactly where he stood." Eckman, *Furious Passage of James Baldwin*, 141.

48. David Leeming, interview with the author, December 10, 2015.

49. Fullerton regrets his decision to consent to this request. Given the fact that it came from a publicist within a week of the event, though, it is not surprising that he felt some pressure to go along with what Kolins asked. Fullerton, interview.

50. "Baldwin Tackles Rightist," *Varsity*, February 13, 1965.

51. Leeming, *James Baldwin*, 244.

52. Ibid.

53. William F. Buckley Jr. to Colm Brogan, February 19, 1965, William F. Buckley Jr. Papers (MS 576), Manuscripts and Archives, Yale University Library.

54. Ibid.

55. William F. Buckley Jr., "What Says the South?," *National Review*, October 20, 1964, 898–99.

56. James Jackson Kilpatrick, "Shame of the South," *Richmond News Leader*, February 1965.

57. James Jackson Kilpatrick to William F. Buckley Jr., February 11, 1965, William F. Buckley Jr. Papers (MS 576), Manuscripts and Archives, Yale University Library.

58. William F. Buckley Jr. to James Jackson Kilpatrick, February 18, 1965, William F. Buckley Jr. Papers (MS 576), Manuscripts and Archives, Yale University Library.

59. Fullerton, interview.

60. Buckley biographers Carl Bogus and Kevin Schultz report that Baldwin was joined by the actor Sidney Poitier. Neither the press reports of the debate nor the eyewitnesses I have interviewed support these claims.

61. Eckman, *Furious Passage of James Baldwin*, 167.

62. David Broad, "Crowds Pack Union for Baldwin," *Varsity*, February 20, 1965, 1.

63. For more on Buckley's relationship with Horne, see, in general, Alistair Horne, *A Bundle from Britain* (New York: St. Martin's Press, 1994); Alvin S. Felzenberg, *A Man and His Presidents* (New Haven, CT: Yale University Press, 2017), 16–18.

64. William F. Buckley Jr., *On the Firing Line: The Public Life of Our Public Figures* (New York: Random House, 1989), 53.

65. For the BBC recording of the debate, made available by the Riverbends Channel on YouTube, see https://www.youtube.com/watch?v=oFeoS41xe7w. It is important to note that the BBC recording is incomplete. Baldwin's speech is included in its entirety, but at least of a third of Buckley's speech was cut from the final recording. In the appendix of this book, I provide a full transcript based on a reel-to-reel audio recording of the Baldwin and Buckley speeches given to me by Adrian Vinson, who was a Cambridge student at the time. Audio recordings of the Baldwin and Buckley speeches in their entirety are available on the Princeton University Press website.

66. Parkinson, *Arena of Ambition*, 231–32.

67. Both Bogus and Schultz have mistakenly reported that the only blacks in the Union that night were Baldwin and his friend Poitier, who they report was there as the author's guest. There are two problems with this account. First, the BBC recording of the debate reveals that there were several other blacks in the Union that evening. The Cambridge students I interviewed suggest that these were likely Cambridge students who hailed from Africa. Second, there does not seem to be any solid evidence that Poitier was indeed present. He was a friend of Baldwin's and may have been on location in London at the time, but in my interviews and research, I have been unable to corroborate this account. Neither Bogus nor Schultz provide citations for the Poitier claim. Carl Bogus, *Buckley* (New York: Bloomsbury, 2011), 170; Kevin Schultz, *Buckley and Mailer: The Difficult Friendship That Shaped the Sixties* (New York: W. W. Norton, 2015), 116.

68. Unfortunately, a full account of what Heycock and the other student speakers said that night is lost to history. The BBC edited the speeches of the two "paper speakers"—Heycock and Burford—significantly and did not retain an unedited recording of the proceedings, and the Cambridge Union did not retain a transcript or recording of the full speeches. And the audio recording retained by Vinson only contains the Baldwin and Buckley speeches. Therefore, all that is known about the student speeches is what was captured in the BBC broadcast.

69. Christie Davies, interview with the author, August 30, 2015; "Union Man Comes Second," *Varsity*, April 25, 1965.

70. Parkinson, *Arena of Ambition*, 32.

71. For an audio recording of the 1970 Buckley-Galbraith debate at the Cambridge Union, see https://www.youtube.com/watch?v=U2OV-vu-0r0. Buckley repeated this claim at Vanderbilt University in 1968: "When Mr. James Baldwin arose to speak, he received a standing ovation," and again in *On the Firing Line*, where he reported, "Before [Baldwin] uttered a single word, he received a standing ovation from most of the house."

72. The fact that there was no standing ovation is revealed by viewing the BBC recording of the debate, and in order to verify that the "standing ovation" Buckley remembered was not edited out, I have asked all the witnesses I interviewed for this book, and everyone agrees: Baldwin received one standing ovation, and it came at the *end* of his speech.

73. I suspect that the best explanation is likely some combination of these two things. It may be the case that Buckley imagined a standing ovation for Baldwin at the start of his speech as a way to cope with what happened that night. It is also possible that Buckley thought the story—though apocryphal—was "true" in the sense that it captured the spirit of the crowd.

74. All quotations from the Baldwin and Buckley speeches are taken from an audio recording of the two speeches. A full transcript of the speeches is provided as the appendix in this book. The BBC recording of the debate includes the entirety of Baldwin's speech, but a good deal of Buckley's speech (as well as several audience questions and comments) has been edited out. The *New York Times* "transcript" of the debate—which will be discussed below—is abridged and contains many inaccuracies.

75. The "typical" Union speech is a mixture of intellectual seriousness, jocularity, and performance art. It was a genre Buckley had mastered over decades of practice and that was totally unfamiliar to Baldwin. Baldwin was a preacher down to his toes and so preached that night.

76. See, in general, Sacvan Bercovitch, *American Jeremiad* (Madison: University of Wisconsin Press, 1978); George Schulman, *American Prophecy* (Minneapolis: University of Minnesota Press, 2008).

77. Jeremiah 6:10–11.

78. See, in general, Sacvan Bercovitch, *American Jeremiad* (Madison: University of Wisconsin Press, 1978); George Schulman, *American Prophecy: Race and Redemption in American Political Culture* (Minneapolis: University of Minnesota Press, 2008). Leeming argues that Baldwin remained a preacher—of one sort or another—throughout his life. Leeming, *James Baldwin*.

79. Buckley, *On the Firing Line*, 53.

80. Leeming was working as a research secretary for Baldwin at the time of the Cambridge debate. He reports that the author seldom carried detailed notes or prepared texts when he took the stage to speak. Like at Cambridge, he usually carried just a few handwritten notes with him and seldom referred to them once he began to speak. Leeming, interview.

81. Davies, interview.

82. Indeed, Baldwin inspired great laughter from his audience in a speech he delivered in 1963 when he said, "The American Negro . . . did the dirty work. Hoed the cotton. Do you hoe cotton? Chopped the cotton. Picked the cotton. Whatever it is you do with cotton!" For an audio recording of this speech, see https://www.youtube.com/watch?v=EMYgOfcgMaI.

83. David Blight, "The Civil War and Reconstruction Era, 1845–1877," Open Yale Courses, lecture 27, iTunes.

84. See Lawrie Balfour, "Hideously Loaded: James Baldwin's History of the American Dream" (lecture delivered at the Symposium on James Baldwin, William F. Buckley, and the American Dream, Linfield College, McMinnville, OR, May 2015), http://digitalcommons.linfield.edu/douglass/11.

85. James Baldwin, "Faulkner and Desegregation" (1956), in *James Baldwin: Collected Essays*, ed. Toni Morrison (New York: Library of America, 1998), 209. Schultz accuses Baldwin of "faux-generosity" in his arguments about the moral cost of racial oppression for white people. I think this interpretation is deeply flawed. Throughout his career, Baldwin insisted on this point. He may have been wrong, but there was nothing "faux" about his position. Schultz, *Buckley and Mailer*, 125.

86. James Baldwin, "My Dungeon Shook" (1962), in *James Baldwin: Collected Essays*, ed. Toni Morrison (New York: Library of America, 1998), 294.

87. These concepts are, of course, intimately related. Indeed, in the essay on Faulkner, Baldwin used the term "moral identity" to address these issues.

88. James Baldwin, "Everybody's Protest Novel" (1949), in *James Baldwin: Collected Essays*, ed. Toni Morrison (New York: Library of America, 1998), 12.

89. James Baldwin, "Many Thousands Gone" (1951), in *James Baldwin: Collected Essays*, ed. Toni Morrison (New York: Library of America, 1998), 20.

90. James Baldwin, "We Can Change the Country" (1963), in *The Cross of Redemption: Uncollected Writings*, ed. Randall Kenan (New York: Pantheon Books, 2010), 63.

91. Baldwin, "Down at the Cross," 337.

92. James Baldwin, "Letters from a Journey" (1963), in *The Cross of Redemption: Uncollected Writings*, ed. Randall Kenan (New York: Pantheon Books, 2010), 235.

93. See *Take This Hammer*, directed by Richard O. Moore, National Educational Television, 1963, https://www.youtube.com/watch?v=A-x7TP4z3fA.

94. By 1965, Baldwin was already getting a sense that figures like himself and King were being looked on with suspicion by a younger generation of those fighting for black liberation. Baldwin was proven right when, a couple of years after the Cambridge debate, he would have the experience of being shouted down by crowds that did not deem him sufficiently radical. See, for example, Jonathan Gill, *Harlem: The Four Hundred Year History from Dutch Village to Capital of Black America* (New York: Grove Press, 2011), 398.

95. Fullerton, interview.

Chapter 7. "The Faith of Our Fathers": Buckley at Cambridge

1. The BBC recording of the debate that is available on YouTube is missing about a third of Buckley's speech. Thanks to an old, reel-to-reel audio recording of the Baldwin and Buckley speeches that the Cambridge Union provided to former Union president Adrian Vinson, I have been able to prepare a transcript of the speech as the appendix in this book.

2. It is worth noting that the speeches of both Heycock and Burford seemed to agree with this sentiment.

3. Garry Wills, "What Color Is God?,"*National Review*, May 1963, 409.

4. James Baldwin, "The Crusade of Indignation" (1956), in *James Baldwin: Collected Essays*, ed. Toni Morrison (New York: Library of America, 1998), 609.

5. James Baldwin, "Nobody Knows My Name: A Letter from the South" (1959), in *James Baldwin: Collected Essays*, ed. Toni Morrison (New York: Library of America, 1998), 208.

6. James Baldwin, "Down at the Cross" (1962), in *James Baldwin: Collected Essays*, ed. Toni Morrison (New York: Library of America, 1998), 337.

7. Ibid., 341.

8. Buckley was careful to focus what concern he did express in the speech on "psychic" matters as opposed to economic, political, and social inequalities.

9. Michael Oakeshott, "Rationalism in Politics," in *Rationalism in Politics and Other Essays* (Indianapolis: Liberty Fund, 1991).

10. Baldwin, "Down at the Cross," 312.

11. B. W. Bennington to James Baldwin, February 16, 1965, James Baldwin Papers, Schomburg Center for Research in Black Culture, Manuscripts, Archives and Rare Books Division, New York Public Library, box 66, folder 3.

12. Baldwin, "Down at the Cross," 312.

13. See, for example, Marvin Elkoff, "Everybody Knows His Name," *Esquire*, August 1964. Baldwin told Elkoff that he was "thoroughly disreputable, and I intend to remain so." Ibid.

14. It is beyond my scope to enter into the debates others have had about the man Baldwin called "the real architect of the Christian church."

15. Baldwin, "Down at the Cross," 316.

16. Ibid.

17. James Baldwin, "Stranger in the Village" (1953), in *James Baldwin: Collected Essays*, ed. Toni Morrison (New York: Library of America, 1998), 117.

18. James Baldwin, "Why I Stopped Hating Shakespeare" (1964), in *The Cross of Redemption: Uncollected Writings*, ed. Randall Kenan (New York: Pantheon Books, 2010), 65.

19. Ibid., 67.

20. There is more to be said about Baldwin's recovery of other aspects of the Western canon.

21. James Baldwin, "In Search of a Majority" (1960), in *James Baldwin: Collected Essays*, ed. Toni Morrison (New York: Library of America, 1998); James Baldwin, "We Can Change the Country" (1963), in *The Cross of Redemption: Uncollected Writings*, ed. Randall Kenan (New York: Pantheon Books, 2010).

22. Norman Podhoretz, interview with the author, November 29, 2016.

23. Judis has argued that Wills liberalized Buckley's position on civil rights in the 1960s. My own review of the record does not lend much credence to this claim on a political level, but there may be something to Judis's argument on a philosophical level. In the context of discussions of race after "What Color Is God?" was published, Buckley would often invoke Wills's argument about the

relevance of the Christian conception of dignity to the civil rights struggle. For Judis's discussion of Wills's influence, see John Judis, *William F. Buckley, Jr.: The Patron Saint of the Conservatives* (New York: Simon and Schuster, 1988), 191–92.

24. Buckley's use of immanentize is a reference to the political philosopher Eric Voeglin, who famously warned against the temptation to "immanentize the eschaton" or attempt to realize utopia on earth. "Conservatives believe that there are rational limits to politics," he wrote in *The Unmaking of a Mayor*, "that politics should not, in the lofty phrase of Voeglin, attempt to 'immanentize the eschaton.' " William F. Buckley Jr., *The Unmaking of a Mayor* (New York: Viking, 1966), 196–97. Buckley and the *National Review* crowd adopted this as a kind of slogan in later years.

25. Earl Hopper, interview with the author, October 6, 2015.

26. William F. Buckley Jr., "Less Sound and Fury," *National Review*, March 28, 1956, 5–6.

27. William F. Buckley Jr., "Why the South Must Prevail," *National Review*, August 24, 1957, 148–49.

28. Their agreement, of course, was limited to the diagnosis of the problem; they did not agree much at all about what ought to be done about it.

29. For a brilliant exploration of the ambiguous status of "engines" in Buckley's rhetoric, see Will Barndt, "William F. Buckley Jr. and America's 'Engines of Concern,' " *American Political Thought* 6 (Fall 2017): 648–56.

30. It is not clear if Buckley had already convinced himself that Baldwin was *greeted* with a standing ovation.

31. James Baldwin, "The White Problem" (1963), in *The Cross of Redemption: Uncollected Writings*, ed. Randall Kenan (New York: Pantheon Books, 2010), 97. See also Kenneth Clark, "A Conversation with James Baldwin," in *Conversations with James Baldwin*, ed. Fred R. Standley and Louis H. Pratt (Jackson: University Press of Mississippi, 1989), 45.

32. For more on Buckley meeting Hoover, see Alvin S. Felzenberg, *A Man and His Presidents* (New Haven, CT: Yale University Press, 2017), 45–46.

33. Baldwin, "Stranger in the Village," 127.

34. Joseph E. Lowndes, "William F. Buckley Jr.: Anti-blackness as Anti-democracy," *American Political Thought* 6, no. 4 (Fall 2017): 632–40.

35. Baldwin, "Down at the Cross," 342.

36. James Baldwin, "White Racism or World Community" (1968), in *James Baldwin: Collected Essays*, ed. Toni Morrison (New York: Library of America, 1998), 752.

37. "Is There a Case for Segregation?," *Open Mind* transcript, James Baldwin Papers, Schomburg Center for Research in Black Culture, Manuscripts, Archives and Rare Books Division, New York Public Library.

38. Ibid.

39. One wonders why Buckley thought Glazer's religious background was relevant to the argument. After all, he had made a point early in his speech to criticize the notion that the identity of an individual is relevant to the merit of the arguments they defend. I suspect, however, that Buckley mentioned Glazer's religious background in order to inform the students that he, as a member of a minority group, was attentive to the sorts of concerns that animated those fighting for the rights of African Americans. William F. Buckley Jr., "Are You a Racist?," syndicated column published on April 15, 1965.

40. Booker T. Washington, *Up from Slavery* (New York: Double Day, 1901).

41. Buckley Jr., "Why the South Must Prevail," 148–49.

42. Ibid.

43. Peter Fullerton, interview with the author, September 28, 2015.

44. On the national scene, Goldwater had struck just the right note for Buckley on race matters. Goldwater was against aggressive federal intervention on civil rights on constitutional grounds and convinced that moral suasion, not legal coercion, was the best way to address racial problems. Outside the United States, Buckley had made it entirely clear that he was comfortable with entrusting apartheid leaders with power so long as they wielded it in the name of "civilization."

45. It is worth noting that once again, Buckley conceded white culpability while at the same time exonerating whites from any exceptional wrongdoing. Yes, whites practiced racial narcissism, but so too did everyone else.

46. On Baldwin's intention to write a biography of Washington, see David Leeming, *James Baldwin: A Biography* (New York: Arcade, 2015), 116–17.

47. Baldwin, "Down at the Cross," 343–44.

48. For more on Buckley's use of "faith of our fathers," see Susan J. McWilliams, "On the Faiths of (and in) Our Fathers," *American Political Thought* 6, no. 4 (Fall 2017); Jeffrey R. Dudas, *Raised Right: Fatherhood in Modern American Conservatism* (Palo Alto, CA: Stanford University Press, 2017), 2.

49. It is also worth remembering Buckley's refusal to find a morally clear position on the use of violence by the South African apartheid regime. William F. Buckley Jr., "Deadend in South Africa," *National Review*, April 23, 1960, 254–55.

50. Buckley, "Why the South Must Prevail," 148–49.

51. William F. Buckley Jr., "A Clarification," *National Review*, September 7, 1957, 199.

52. This reading echoes the interpretation of the Right more generally that is found in Corey Robin, *The Reactionary Mind: Conservatism from Edmund Burke to Sarah Palin* (New York: Oxford University Press, 2013).

53. It is worth mentioning that the portrayal of the civil rights movement as fascist was also a theme in the 1948 States' Rights Democratic Party presidential nomination acceptance speech of Buckley family friend Thurmond. See Strom Thurmond, "Address by J. Strom Thurmond, Governor of South Carolina, Accepting the States' Rights Democratic Nomination for President of the United States" (speech given in Houston, TX, August 11, 1948).

54. Emphasis added.

55. According to Union records, additional speeches for the motion were delivered by Robert Lacey, Sheena Mattheson, and Michael Horowitz, and additional speeches against the motion were delivered by Michael Tugendhat, Adrian Vinson, and Michael DeNavarro.

56. In one of Buckley's recollections of the debate, he reported that "one of the students assigned to endorse my position shook the very foundations of orthodoxy by announcing as he got up to speak, that he had changed his mind; that he was moved on consideration to agree with Baldwin." William F. Buckley Jr., *On the Firing Line: The Public Life of Our Public Figures* (New York: Random House, 1989), 53. None of the Cambridge students I interviewed have any recollection of this happening, and none of the historical or journalistic accounts of the debate corroborate Buckley's recollection. There are two possible explanations for this discrepancy. First, it is possible Buckley remembered something that other witnesses and participants did not. Second, it is possible that Buckley "misremembered" this occurrence in a manner similar to his "misremembering" of a standing ovation for Baldwin before the beginning of his speech. The story of the defecting student speaker fit Buckley's narrative of a hostile climate, and it is certainly easy to imagine an undergraduate feeling compelled or pressured to "switch sides" in that environment, but without corroboration of Buckley's claim, I think it is wise to view it with a healthy dose of skepticism.

57. This was indeed the same Schama who would become a famous scholar and public intellectual.

58. It is interesting to note that the total number of votes cast—708—is significantly lower than the total reported in the Griffiths debate earlier that term: 878 (Griffiths's proposition carried by a vote of 552 to 326). It may be for this reason that Union historian Stephen Parkinson has concluded that the Griffiths debate had the highest attendance of the term. This is possible, but it seems unlikely that there were nearly two hundred more people crammed into the Union for the Griffiths debate. It seems more likely that the attendance totals were close to the same, but there were more visitors to the Union—who were not eligible to vote—on the night Baldwin met Buckley.

Chapter 8. Lighting the Fuse

1. Although I have not seen any press or eyewitness accounts indicating that Baldwin lit up a cigarette at this point, it seems quite likely. He was a chain-smoker and had just been forced to forego smoking for nearly two hours.

2. David Broad, "Crowds Pack Union for Baldwin," *Varsity*, February 20, 1965, 1. Broad also filed a story a week later about an American student at Cambridge, Stephen Skjei, who "left the Baldwin debate last week determined to put undergraduate opinion to the test" by raising money for the University of Selma. David Broad, "Negroes—All Talk, No Action," *Varsity*, February 27, 1965.

3. "English Ovation for James Baldwin," *New York Times*, February 19, 1965. There is no author listed for the article. Heather Bradley is the *Times* representative who seems to have been the point person on the story in the London office.

4. Peter Fullerton, interview, September 28, 2015. The cocktail party after the debate was at the flat of Neil McKendrick, one of Fullerton's professors.

5. James Baldwin, "To Be Baptized" (1970), in *James Baldwin: Collected Essays*, ed. Toni Morrison (New York: Library of America, 1998), 425.

6. David Leeming, *James Baldwin: A Biography* (New York: Arcade, 2015), 245.

7. "Baldwin Blames White Supremacy," *New York Post*, February 22, 1965.

8. For a discussion of Malcolm's assassination, see Manning Marable, *Malcolm X: A Life of Reinvention* (New York: Viking, 2011), 450–57.

9. Baldwin, "To Be Baptized," 425.

10. For Baldwin's discussion of Malcolm's assassination, see https://www.youtube.com/watch?v =M55tlX32KEw.

11. Baldwin used the term "moral assumptions" in his Oxford Union address.

12. Mike Adler, "James Baldwin at the Union," *Isis at a Comprehensive School*, March 6, 1965, 26–27.

13. Bill Kolins to James Baldwin, February 24, 1965, James Baldwin Papers, Schomburg Center for Research in Black Culture, Manuscripts, Archives and Rare Books Division, New York Public Library.

14. Robert Lantz to James Baldwin, February 26, 1965, James Baldwin Papers, Schomburg Center for Research in Black Culture, Manuscripts, Archives and Rare Books Division, New York Public Library. The same morning Lantz sent this missive to Baldwin, President Johnson ordered his Department of Defense to mobilize the first two American combat battalions to South Vietnam. Within a week, American forces would begin Operation Rolling Thunder, a series of massive air strikes against the North Vietnamese that would continue for eight long years. Yet another chasm in American political culture would develop as a result of this escalating war, and Baldwin and Buckley would soon find themselves on opposite sides of it.

15. William F. Buckley, "The Negro and the American Dream," syndicated column published on February 27, 1965.

16. Ibid. As noted earlier, this is a misstatement Buckley would repeat over and over again during the next forty years.

17. Ibid. Once again, Buckley seems not to have noticed that he was speaking to an audience that consisted of both men *and* women.

18. Ibid. Buckley also remarked that the Cambridge student reaction probably did more "to hurt" Baldwin's "feelings and persuade him of the truth of his lament that nobody knows his name."

19. Ibid.

20. Ibid.

21. Ibid. See, for example, Donald Davidson, "The New South and the Conservative Tradition," *National Review*, September 10, 1960, 145.

22. Buckley, "The Negro and the American Dream."

23. In his correspondence following the debate, Buckley also complained—quite reasonably—about the fact that the BBC presentation left Baldwin's speech completely intact while it "ran only twelve minutes out of the thirty I spoke." See William F. Buckley Jr. to M. C. Shumiatcher, April 13, 1965, William F. Buckley Jr. Papers (MS 576), Manuscripts and Archives, Yale University Library.

24. Michael Tugendhat to William F. Buckley Jr., March 10, 1965, William F. Buckley Jr. Papers (MS 576), Manuscripts and Archives, Yale University Library.

25. In his letter back to Tugendhat (dated March 24, 1965), Buckley notes that he returned the original of Tugendhat's piece "annotated, in the event you did not keep a copy." William F. Buckley Jr. to Michael Tugendhat, March 24, 1965, William F. Buckley Jr. Papers (MS 576), Manuscripts and Archives, Yale University Library. In a final response to Buckley, Tugendhat said they "shall have to agree to disagree." Michael Tugendhat to William F. Buckley Jr., April 28, 1965, William F. Buckley Jr. Papers (MS 576), Manuscripts and Archives, Yale University Library.

26. William F. Buckley Jr. to Michael Tugendhat, March 24, 1965, William F. Buckley Jr. Papers (MS 576), Manuscripts and Archives, Yale University Library.

27. James T. Patterson, *The Eve of Destruction: How 1965 Transformed America* (New York: Basic Books, 2012), 78–79.

28. "The American Dream and the American Negro," *New York Times Magazine*, March 7, 1965, 22. The *Times* transcript was rife with inaccuracies, but it contained some material that was not included in the BBC edit of the debate. These inaccuracies and diverging editorial choices have led to a great deal of confusion for scholars over the years. As mentioned earlier, the full transcript included as an appendix in this book is based on an audio recording of the Baldwin and Buckley speeches.

29. Patterson, *Eve of Destruction*, 79.

30. *Judgment at Nuremberg*, directed by Stanley Kramer, Universal Studios, 1961.

31. William F. Buckley Jr., "The Issue at Selma," syndicated column published on February 18, 1965.

32. Steve Fiffer and Adar Cohen, *Jimmie Lee & James: Two Lives, Two Deaths, and the Movement That Changed America* (New York: Simon and Schuster, 2015), 125–27.

33. William F. Buckley Jr., "How to Help the Negro," syndicated column published on March 4, 1965. The other proposal highlighted by Buckley in the column is a "National Committee on Tithing Investment" promoted by Congressman Donald Fraser of Minneapolis that would have the purpose of funding "inter-racial construction projects." Buckley thought both this program and the Richmond project were laudable because they were voluntary and did not rely on extensive government action.

34. "The Selma Campaign," *National Review*, March 23, 1965, 227–28.

35. Michael Beschloss, *Reaching for Glory: Lyndon Johnson's Secret White House Tapes, 1964–1965* (New York: Simon and Schuster, 2001), 216.

36. Patterson, *Eve of Destruction*, 80–81.

37. Beschloss, *Reaching for Glory*, 231, 237. For Buckley's take on the negotiations between President Johnson, Governor Wallace, and King, see William F. Buckley Jr., "The Open Questions," syndicated column published on March 18, 1965.

38. Lyndon Baines Johnson, "Address to a Joint Session of Congress," March 15, 1965.

39. Nat Hentoff, "James Baldwin Gets 'Older and Sadder,'" *New York Times*, April 11, 1965.

40. William F. Buckley Jr., "Constitutional Chaos," syndicated column published on March 23, 1965. At Cambridge, he used Barnett rather than Wallace as his example of a southern demagogue.

41. William F. Buckley Jr. to James Jackson Kilpatrick, March 25, 1965, William F. Buckley Jr. Papers (MS 576), Manuscripts and Archives, Yale University Library.

42. James Jackson Kilpatrick, "Must We Repeal the Constitution to Give the Negro the Right to Vote?," *National Review*, April 20, 1965, 319.

43. Robert Lantz to James Baldwin, March 10, 1965, James Baldwin Papers, Schomburg Center for Research in Black Culture, Manuscripts, Archives and Rare Books Division, New York Public Library.

44. William F. Buckley Jr. to Harvey Shapiro, March 16, 1965, William F. Buckley Jr. Papers (MS 576), Manuscripts and Archives, Yale University Library; William F. Buckley Jr. to Harvey Shapiro, March 16, or 1965, *New York Times* Papers, Manuscripts and Archives Division, New York Public Library.

45. Heather Bradley to Lewis Bergman, n.d., *New York Times* Papers, Manuscripts and Archives, New York Public Library.

46. Lewis Bergman to James C. Goodale, March 18, 1965, *New York Times* Papers, Manuscripts and Archives, New York Public Library.

47. In later correspondence, Goodale claimed that Baldwin's "agent had agreed to accept $200 (one-half of the regular Sunday rate) as satisfactory payment." James C. Goodale to Louis M. Loeb, memo re: Baldwin-Buckley debates, April 19, 1965, *New York Times* Papers, Manuscripts and Archives, New York Public Library. I have discovered no corroborating evidence to support this claim, and given Baldwin's going rate in those days, it seems highly unlikely that his representatives would have accepted this as satisfactory.

48. Lewis Bergman to James C. Goodale, March 18, 1965, *New York Times* Papers, Manuscripts and Archives, New York Public Library.

49. *New York Times* legal department memorandum re: "Copyright Protection Available to Messrs. Baldwin and Buckley in Speech Delivered before the Cambridge Union Society and Subsequently Printed in the Times Magazine," March 25, 1965, *New York Times* Papers, Manuscripts and Archives, New York Public Library.

50. Memo from James C. Goodale to Lewis Bergman re: Baldwin-Buckley Debate, March 29, 1965, *New York Times* Papers, Manuscripts and Archives, New York Public Library.

51. Thedore Kupferman to the *New York Times*, April 12, 1965, *New York Times* Papers, Manuscripts and Archives, New York Public Library. I have been unable to discover any independent verification of Kupferman's claim that Baldwin had been offered $10,000 by *Playboy*. In 1963, *Playboy* had paid Baldwin $4,000 for the publication of one of his speeches. Robert P. Mills to Ingo Preminger, August 16, 1963, Robert Park Mills Papers, Harry Ransom Humanities Research Center, University of Texas at Austin.

52. Ibid.

53. Louis Loeb to Theodore R. Kupferman, April 19, 1965, *New York Times* Papers, Manuscripts and Archives, New York Public Library.

54. William F. Buckley Jr. to Daniel Schwarz, June 18, 1965, William F. Buckley Jr. Papers (MS 576), Manuscripts and Archives, Yale University Library; William F. Buckley Jr. to Theodore Kupferman,

June 18, 1965, William F. Buckley Jr. Papers (MS 576), Manuscripts and Archives, Yale University Library.

55. Theodore Kupferman to Louis Loeb, August 24, 1965, *New York Times* Papers, Manuscripts and Archives, New York Public Library.

56. Daniel Schwarz to William F. Buckley, September 24, 1965, *New York Times* Papers, Manuscripts and Archives, New York Public Library.

57. William F. Buckley Jr. to Daniel Schwarz, September 27, 1965, William F. Buckley Jr. Papers (MS 576), Manuscripts and Archives, Yale University Library. For more on Buckley's run for mayor, see below.

58. Jack Mallon, "Rev. Martin Luther King Jr. and the Demonstrators Reach Montgomery from Selma," *New York Daily News*, March 26, 1965.

59. Patterson, *Eve of Destruction*, 86.

60. Right Reverend Monsignor Joseph A. Dunne to William F. Buckley Jr., December 9, 1964, and December 16, 1964, William F. Buckley Jr. Papers (MS 576). Manuscripts and Archives, Yale University Library.

61. Right Reverend Monsignor Joseph Dunne to William F. Buckley Jr., March 9, 1965, William F. Buckley Jr. Papers (MS 576), Manuscripts and Archives, Yale University Library.

62. Samuel Walker, *Police Accountability: The Role of Citizen Oversight* (Belmont, CA: Wadsworth Publishing Company, 2000), 2–3.

63. See, in general, Michael D. White and Henry F. Fradella, *Stop and Frisk: The Use and Abuse of a Controversial Policing Tactic* (New York: NYU Press, 2016).

64. "Who Speaks for Harlem?," July 25, 1964, WNYC Archive.

65. William J. Buckley Jr., *The Unmaking of a Mayor* (New York: Viking, 1966), 311–14 (emphasis added)..

66. Ibid. Buckley claimed later that he was misinformed. Ibid., 14.

67. Ibid., 311–14.

68. William F. Buckley Jr., "The Assault on Miss Lucy," *National Review*, February 22, 1956, 5.

69. William F. Buckley Jr., "Let Us Try, at Least, to Understand," *National Review*, June 3, 1961, 338.

70. Buckley, *Unmaking of a Mayor*, 311–14.

71. Ibid. (emphasis added).

72. Patricia Michelle Boyett, *Right to Revolt: The Crusade for Racial Justice in Mississippi's Central Piney Woods* (Oxford: University Press of Mississippi, 2015), 113–17. Boyett describes the event based on testimony given in the litigation that followed Shinall's arrest. Shinall v. State, 199 So. 2d 251 (1967).

73. Buckley, *Unmaking of a Mayor*, 311–14.

74. I am not suggesting that Buckley knew much about the facts of the Humphrey-Shinall case. In fact, I would be shocked if he did. I do think it is revealing, though, that he did not deem it worthwhile to do some additional digging into the facts of the case, especially since he chose to make particular claims about it (e.g., that the officer stopped the assailant "simply to ask a question" and the shooting was completely "unprovoked").

75. Ibid., 313.

76. John Judis, *William F. Buckley, Jr.: The Patron Saint of the Conservatives* (New York: Simon and Schuster, 1988), 236–37.

77. William F. Buckley Jr., "Today We Are Educated Men," in *Let Us Talk of Many Things: The Collected Speeches* (New York: Forum, 2000), 6.

78. Buckley, *Unmaking of a Mayor*, 314.

79. Ibid., 11, 25.

80. "Buckley Praises Police of Selma; Hailed by 5,600 Police Here as He Cites 'Restraint,'" *New York Times*, April 5, 1965. Buckley even received a letter from an admirer who reported that the Soviet newspaper *Pravda* ran a story on the speech titled "Police Applaud Racists." Dr. Paolo Cella to William F. Buckley Jr., April 27, 1965, William F. Buckley Jr. Papers (MS 576), Manuscripts and Archives, Yale University Library.

81. Norman Mailer to William F. Buckley Jr., April 20, 1965, William F. Buckley Jr. Papers (MS 576), Manuscripts and Archives, Yale University Library.

82. Buckley, *Unmaking of a Mayor*, 16–20.

83. Dunne, who had invited Buckley to deliver the address, thought it was terrific, and sent a glowing thank you note along with "a check which we are forwarding to you for the important work you are doing and in appreciation for your labors on our behalf." Joseph A. Dunne to William F. Buckley Jr., April 5, 1965, William F. Buckley Jr. Papers (MS 576), Manuscripts and Archives, Yale University Library.

84. Buckley, *Unmaking of a Mayor*, 12.

85. Ibid., 18, 16. See also William F. Buckley Jr. to Roy Wilkins, April 6, 1965, William F. Buckley Jr. Papers, Sterling Library, Yale University.

86. Roy Wilkins to William F. Buckley Jr., April 1965, William F. Buckley Jr. Papers (MS 576), Manuscripts and Archives, Yale University Library.

87. Buckley, *Unmaking of a Mayor*, 17.

88. William F. Buckley Jr., "Are You a Racist?," syndicated column published on April 15, 1965.

89. Ibid. It is worth noting that Buckley had made a point of citing *Beyond the Melting Pot* during his speech at Cambridge, and that when he did, he was sure to tell the students that Glazer was indeed "a prominent Jewish sociologist."

90. Ibid.

91. Buckley was shifting, to borrow the terminology of Ibram X. Kendi, from a "segregationist" to an "integrationist" form of racism. For a brilliant exposition of segregationist versus integrationist racism, see, in general, Ibram X. Kendi, *Stamped from the Beginning: The Definitive History of Racist Ideas in America* (New York: Nation Books, 2016).

92. Hentoff, "James Baldwin Gets 'Older and Sadder,'" 1.

93. Buckley as a result of his Holy Name Society speech, and Baldwin as a result of his return to Broadway.

94. "Baldwin v. Buckley" press release, David Susskind Papers, University of Wisconsin at Madison Libraries.

95. William F. Buckley to David Susskind, 1964, William F. Buckley Jr. Papers (MS 576), Manuscripts and Archives, Yale University Library.

96. The episode was on "The Prevailing Bias." See https://www.youtube.com/watch?v=7UeSeZlXxqc.

97. In 1962, Baldwin and Susskind agreed to collaborate on a "TV spectacular" based on "A Letter to My Nephew." The "TV spectacular" never came off due to Baldwin's extensive commitments throughout 1962 and 1963. Leonard Lyons, "The Lyons Den," *New York Post*, June 29, 1962, 39. For a letter explaining why the television project did not happen, see Robert P. Mills to David Susskind, October 31, 1962, Robert Park Mills Papers, Harry Ransom Humanities Research Center, University of Texas at Austin. In 1963, Susskind engaged in a nasty public fight with Bennett Korn, the owner of the WNEW television station, when Korn objected to Susskind featuring Baldwin and Belafonte on an episode of *Open End* called "The American Negro Speaks His Mind." Korn insisted Susskind expand the panel to provide more perspectives, and Susskind refused. This led to Susskind's firing from

WNEW, but he wanted Baldwin and Belafonte to record the show anyway so it could be aired on other stations around the country. In the midst of the back and forth between Susskind and WNEW, Baldwin and Belafonte backed out of the appearance, but their relationship with Susskind remained cordial. Stephen Battaglio, *David Susskind: A Televised Life* (New York: Macmillan, 2010), 121–22. See Robert P. Mills to David Susskind, Robert Park Mills Papers, Harry Ransom Humanities Research Center, University of Texas at Austin.

98. William J. Weatherby, *James Baldwin: Artist on Fire, a Portrait* (New York: Dutton Adult, 1989), 315.

99. David Leeming, interview with the author, December 10, 2015.

100. For more on the most wanted lost treasures of this era, including the "Baldwin v. Buckley" episode of *Open End*, see David Everitt, "On the Trail of Television's Lost Treasures," *New York Times*, April 29, 2001.

101. I devoted more hours than I would care to admit in search of a recording or transcript of this program. Along the way, I incurred debts to dozens of archivists who joined me in my quest. I hope that one day, a recording or dusty copy of a transcript turns up somewhere. Due to the fact that no verbatim transcript exists, all the quotations from the show notes must be read as the best record we have, but not the complete record we want.

102. Ben Gross, "Baldwin-Buckley Debate Old Stuff but Exciting," *New York Daily News*, June 14, 1965.

103. "Baldwin v. Buckley" show notes, David Susskind Papers, University of Wisconsin at Madison Libraries.

104. Ibid. Baldwin's argument here is reminiscent of his analysis of the black perception of Jews in Harlem in "The Harlem Ghetto."

105. Ibid.

106. Gross, "Baldwin-Buckley Debate Old Stuff but Exciting."

107. "Baldwin v. Buckley" show notes, David Susskind Papers, University of Wisconsin at Madison Libraries.

108. Ibid. This is what was recorded in the "show notes," but a postcard Buckley received from the economist Milton Friedman (discussed below) as well as proposals Buckley would make during his mayoral campaign indicate that his proposal may have been a bit more nuanced than a suspension of all taxes for blacks and Puerto Ricans.

109. Ibid. What was recorded as "morale" in the notes may have been a typing error. "Moral" might make more sense.

110. Ibid.

111. Buckley, "Are You a Racist?" It is also worth mentioning that Buckley's invocation of this idea may have been inspired by some of Wills's arguments in "What Color Is God?" More specifically, you may recall that Wills argued that Baldwin ought not reject Christianity because it provided useful moral arguments—most notably the idea of equality before God—in the struggle against racial oppression.

112. "Baldwin v. Buckley" show notes, David Susskind Papers, University of Wisconsin at Madison Libraries.

113. More on this below.

114. Ibid.

115. Milton Friedman to William F. Buckley Jr., June 13, 1965, William F. Buckley Jr. Papers (MS 576), Manuscripts and Archives, Yale University Library.

116. Ed Dieckman to William F. Buckley Jr., June 16, 1965, William F. Buckley Jr. Papers (MS 576), Manuscripts and Archives, Yale University Library.

117. Dorothy Schein Diamond to William F. Buckley Jr., June 16, 1965, William F. Buckley Jr. Papers (MS 576), Manuscripts and Archives, Sterling Yale University Library.

118. Letter from Jean McGowan to James Baldwin, June 15, 1965, James Baldwin Papers, Schomburg Center for Research in Black Culture, Manuscripts, Archives and Rare Books Division, New York Public Library.

119. Letter from Frederick Vogelsang to James Baldwin, June 13, 1965, James Baldwin Papers, Schomburg Center for Research in Black Culture, Manuscripts, Archives and Rare Books Division, New York Public Library.

120. Paul Matthews to William F. Buckley Jr., June 13, 1965, James Baldwin Papers, Schomburg Center for Research in Black Culture, Manuscripts, Archives and Rare Books Division, New York Public Library.

121. William F. Buckley Jr., "When, Oh When?," syndicated column published on June 17, 1965. Also published as William F. Buckley Jr., "Negroes Harmed by Extreme Militancy," *Beaver County Times*, June 18, 1965; William F. Buckley Jr., "America Haters—Threat to Negroes," *New York Journal American*, June 17, 1965; "Buckley on 'The Baldwin Syndrome': June 1965," *Washington Daily News*, June 18, 1965, in *James Baldwin: The FBI File*, ed. William J. Maxwell (New York: Arcade Publishing, 2017), 259–61.

122. More on this below.

123. C. Robert Jennings, "Warning for Mister Charlie," *Los Angeles Times West Magazine*, July 7, 1968, 18. Gore Vidal corroborates the back and forth between Buckley and Baldwin on garbage in the following way: "During a television exchange with Buckley, James Baldwin blamed the white owners of the black slums for their condition. Buckley's response: And I suppose the white landlords go pitty-pat uptown and throw garbage out the windows?" Gore Vidal, "A Distasteful Encounter with William F. Buckley Jr.," *Esquire*, September 1969.

124. Brian Lamb, "William F. Buckley Jr.: Happy Days Were Here Again," in *Conversations with William F. Buckley Jr.*, ed. William F. Meehan III (Jackson: University Press of Mississippi, 2009), 99.

125. Buckley, "When, Oh When?"

126. Ibid.

127. See "Liberalism and the Negro: A Roundtable Discussion," *Commentary*, March 1, 1964.

128. Harold Cruse, *The Crisis of the Negro Intellectual: A Historical Analysis of the Failure of Black Leadership* (New York: New York Review of Books, 1967).

129. Buckley, "When, Oh When?"

130. James Baldwin, "The Price of the Ticket" (1985), in *James Baldwin: Collected Essays*, ed. Toni Morrison (New York: Library of America, 1998), 833–34.

131. James Baldwin, author questionnaire, Robert Park Mills Papers, Harry Ransom Humanities Research Center, University of Texas at Austin.

132. James Baldwin, "The Crusade of Indignation" (1956), in *James Baldwin: Collected Essays*, ed. Toni Morrison (New York: Library of America, 1998), 608.

133. Ibid.

134. William F. Buckley Jr., "Lindsay in the Ring," syndicated column published on May 18, 1965.

135. William F. Buckley Jr., "Mayor, Anyone?," syndicated column published on May 22, 1965. Although some of these proposals were not explicitly racialized in "Mayor, Anyone?," Buckley would soon make it quite clear that his racial views inspired many of the proposals.

136. Buckley, *Unmaking of a Mayor*, 93.

137. J. Daniel Mahoney, *Actions Speak Louder* (New York: Arlington House, 1968), 268–69. For more on the history of the New York Conservative Party, see George Thayer, *The Farther Shores of Politics: The American Political Fringe Today* (New York: Simon and Schuster, 1967), 206–9.

138. Buckley, *Unmaking of a Mayor*, 94, 97–98.

139. Buckley, *Unmaking of a Mayor*, 104–9.

140. For a general description of Buckley's announcement of his candidacy, see Richard L. Madden, "William Buckley in Race for Mayor," *New York Times*, June 25, 1965.

141. Timothy J. Sullivan, *New York State and the Rise of Modern Conservatism: Redrawing Party Lines*, (Albany: State University of New York Press, 2009), 62. Some of Buckley's proposals (e.g., on parking and taxis) do not seem to fit into this category.

142. Buckley, *Unmaking of a Mayor*, 107.

143. Buckley, "How to Help the Negro."

144. His other running mate in the race, for the office of comptroller, was Hugh Markey of the Staten Island Zoo. Mahoney, *Actions Speak Louder*, 283. A few months before Buckley's run, *National Review* had praised Gunning in its "Special Report on the Race Issue and the Campaign," and in a "Sonnet to Mrs. Gunning" by W. H. von Dreele had concluded, "If mothers can bring mayors to their knees, perhaps there's hope for us majorities." W. H. von Dreele, "Sonnet to Mrs. Gunning," *National Review*, October 6, 1964, 859.

145. More on this in the epilogue. As noted above, Baldwin received letters from sympathetic viewers who shared this assessment, and intellectuals across the political spectrum would later concur. It is also worth noting that journalist C. Robert Jennings thought Baldwin "lost" the debate that occurred on *Open End*. George Thayer referred to the *Open End* appearance when he wrote that Buckley can "reduce such advocates of liberalism as Norman Mailer and James Baldwin—both articulate when not under stress—to the point where they become incoherent." Thayer, *The Farther Shores of Politics*, 294–95. An admirer of Buckley named William R. Kaelin—who would soon be a supporter of his mayoral campaign—even wrote to the Cambridge Union in order to encourage it to screen the *Open End* debate for the students in order to provide them with the opportunity to see "Buckley and Baldwin under other auspices." William R. Kaelin to the president of the Cambridge Union, William F. Buckley Jr. Papers (MS 576), Manuscripts and Archives, Yale University Library. When the radical feminist Andrea Dworkin reflected on the *Open End* episode, she recalled that "Buckley was elegant and brilliant and *wrong*; Baldwin was passionate and brilliant and wore his heart on his sleeve—he was also right. But Buckley won the debate; Baldwin lost it." Andrea Dworkin, *Heartbreak: The Political Memoir of a Feminist Militant* (New York: Basic Books, 2002), 72. Conservative Shelby Steele also remembered seeing the program and reached conclusions similar to Dworkin about the outcome, though different ones about the moral of the story. "Buckley scalpeled his way through Baldwin's arguments with utter aplomb," Steele recalled, leaving Baldwin looking "overwhelmed, as flat as unleavened bread." Shelby Steele, *Shame: How America's Past Sins Have Polarized Our Country* (New Yorks: Basic Books, 2015), 192. Steele wrongly remembered the encounter occurring at Cambridge University (and that Buckley had announced it on *Firing Line*). Since the Cambridge debate took place in 1965 and *Firing Line* was not launched until 1966, this is not possible. Steele also refers to "Baldwin's performance in that *interview*." While it would be relatively easy to misremember the *Open End* appearance as an "interview," it would be impossible to remember the Cambridge debate that way. Leeming offered perhaps the most positive interpretation. He admits that Baldwin's "emotional approach was less effective against Buckley's carefully researched statistics and facts," but that "Baldwin held his own." Leeming, *James Baldwin*, 249.

146. The first *New York Times* story about the possible Buckley candidacy ran on June 4, 1965. Baldwin received the invitation from *Ebony* on June 9, 1965. Ponchitta Pierce to James Baldwin, June 9, 1965, James Baldwin Papers, Schomburg Center for Research in Black Culture, Manuscripts, Archives and Rare Books Division, New York Public Library.

147. When *Ebony* would publish this collection as a book in 1966, Baldwin would rename his essay "Unspeakable Crimes, Unnameable Objects."

148. I concede that this is an interpretative and not a factual claim. I am unable to prove that Buckley was on Baldwin's mind, but I believe that the timing and evidence make this a plausible interpretation.

149. James Baldwin, "The White Man's Guilt" (1965), in *James Baldwin: Collected Essays*, ed. Toni Morrison (New York: Library of America, 1998), 722. Entertaining the possibility that Baldwin had Buckley in mind, "dazzling ingenuity" and "tireless agility" seem like precisely the sorts of things Buckley's friends, colleagues, and admirers would say about him. Buckley's wife, Pat, also described him as "exhausting." Pat Buckley makes this claim in the documentary film, *Best of Enemies*.

150. In a 1968 interview with Jennings, Baldwin said of Buckley, "He can't listen." Jennings, "Warning for Mr. Charlie," 18.

151. Baldwin, "White Man's Guilt," 722–23.

152. Jer. 22:29.

153. Baldwin, "White Man's Guilt," 723.

154. Ibid. The "show notes" from the *Open End* appearance indicate that Buckley made comments along these lines during the program.

155. Ibid., 724.

156. "Baldwin v. Buckley" show notes, David Susskind Papers, University of Wisconsin at Madison Libraries.

157. Jennings, "Warning for Mr. Charlie," 18. This account is corroborated by Vidal: "During a television encounter with Buckley, James Baldwin blamed the white owners of black slums for their condition. Buckley's response: And I suppose the white landlords go pitty-pat uptown and throw the garbage out the windows." Vidal, "Distasteful Encounter with William F. Buckley Jr."

158. Baldwin, "White Man's Guilt," 724.

159. Ibid.

160. Ibid., 724, 726.

161. Buckley, *Unmaking of a Mayor*, 146–47.

162. Ibid., 147.

163. Ibid., 148.

164. Stephen Tuck, "Making the Voting Rights Act," in *The Voting Rights Act: Securing the Ballot*, ed. Richard M. Valelly (Washington, DC: CQ Press, 2006), 77.

165. Shana Bernstein, *Bridges to Reform: Interracial Civil Rights Activism in Twentieth-Century Los Angeles* (New York: Oxford University Press, 2011).

166. Patterson, *Eve of Destruction*, 180.

167. *Watts: Riot or Revolt?*, CBS Reports, December 1965, https://www.c-span.org/video/?327579 -1/reel-america-watts-riot-revolt-1965.

168. William F. Buckley Jr., "What Happened?," syndicated column published August 19, 1965.

169. *Watts: Riot or Revolt?* Buckley weighed in again on the Watts rebellion a month later in "Watts, Where Is That?" In that piece, he emphasized the importance of more aggressive police tactics to deal with lawbreakers. William F. Buckley Jr., "Watts, Where Is That?," syndicated column published on September 21, 1965.

170. Leeming, *James Baldwin*, 257.

171. James Baldwin, "A Report from Occupied Territory" (1966), in *James Baldwin: Collected Essays*, ed. Toni Morrison (New York: Library of America, 1998), 734–35.

172. Ibid., 731, 734–35.

173. Oliver Ramsay Pilat, *Lindsay's Campaign: A Behind-the-Scenes Diary* (Boston, MA: Beacon Press, 1968), 332.

174. Buckley, *Unmaking of a Mayor*, 307.

175. Buckley received 12,549 votes in Queens (or 17.2 percent of those cast in that county), 20,427 votes in Richmond (25.1 percent), 62,988 in the Bronx (13.8 percent), 97,115 in Brooklyn (12.5 percent), and 38,048 in Manhattan (only 7.3 percent, well below the 13 percent overall vote he received). Thayer, *The Farther Shores of Politics*, 207.

176. Jonathan M. Schoenwald, *A Time for Choosing: The Rise of Modern American Conservatism* (New York: Oxford University Press, 2001), 186. The *New York Times* agreed with McCaffrey's analysis of Buckley's support. "Behind the elegant banter . . . was an uglier strain of appeal to group passions, to the vein of hate Mr. Buckley has often deplored in his own strictures against the John Birch Society." "The Buckley Vote," *New York Times*, November 3, 1965, 38. See also Peter Kihss, "Analysis of Conservatives' Vote Implies Equality with Liberals," *New York Times*, November 6, 1965, 1.

177. Although Buckley would never become a fan of Wallace (who he called a "welfarist-populist"), he would admit in 1968 that the Alabama governor was "on to something, and if that something isn't unconstitutional, it is the right of the people to have it if that is what they want." Buckley could be a populist, when populism suited his ends. See William F. Buckley Jr., "Nixon and Wallace," syndicated column published on October 1, 1968. See also William F. Buckley Jr., "An Hour with George Wallace (I)," syndicated column published on February 24, 1968; William F. Buckley Jr., "An Hour with George Wallace (II)," syndicated column published on February 27, 1968.

178. I am indebted to Lawrie Balfour for the idea of thinking about the Baldwin-Buckley clash in terms of battles and wars.

Epilogue. The Fire Is upon Us

1. William F. Buckley Jr., *On the Firing Line: The Public Life of Our Public Figures* (New York: Random House, 1989), 53. For similar accounts, see William F. Buckley Jr., "The Negro and the American Dream," syndicated column published on February 28, 1965; William F. Buckley Jr., *Cruising Speed: A Documentary* (New York: G. P. Putnam's Sons, 1971), 101. Buckley also provided this account in numerous speeches, including his next visit to the Cambridge Union to debate Galbraith.

2. Buckley, *On the Firing Line*, 53.

3. Garry Wills, "Buckley, Buckley, Bow Wow Wow," *Esquire*, January 1968, 159. The vote was actually about three to one.

4. C. Robert Jennings, "Warning for Mister Charlie," *Los Angeles Times West Magazine*, July 7, 1968, 18.

5. I am grateful to Chip Turner for helping me make this point more precisely. Someone sent Buckley a copy of the *West* magazine in which Baldwin made these comments and he published a brief response in *National Review*, in which he repeated many of his usual thoughts about the Cambridge debate before he shared some reflections on Baldwin's response to the *Open End* encounter. First, he said he was unsure what "weapons" Baldwin was "not prepared to use." Second, he argued that Baldwin's anger about the garbage discussion had more to do with "the logical limitations of his own analysis" than with the "sadistic racism" of Buckley's position. Third, Buckley said that Baldwin's urge to violence put him in the company of "that regrettable class of people in the South" who believe that "the way to argue with dissidents is to 'beat the brains out of that uppity nigger.'" Finally, Buckley responded to Baldwin's dismissal of his seriousness with, of course, a joke. William F. Buckley Jr., "This Week," *National Review*, August 13, 1968. Reprinted in William F. Buckley Jr., *Cancel Your Own Goddam Subscription*, 12–14.

6. James Baldwin, "Take Me to the Water," in *James Baldwin: Collected Essays*, ed. Toni Morrison (New York: Library of America, 1998), 357.

7. William F. Buckley Jr., "Did You Kill Martin Luther King?," in *Let Us Talk of Many Things: The Collected Speeches* (New York: Forum, 2000), 121–23.

8. Gratitude was of no small importance to Buckley. Indeed, he would write an entire book on the subject. William F. Buckley Jr., *Gratitude: Reflections on What We Owe to Our Country* (New York: Random House, 1990).

9. James Baldwin, "Autobiographical Notes" (1955), in *James Baldwin: Collected Essays*, ed. Toni Morrison (New York: Library of America, 1998), 9.

10. James Baldwin, "In Search of a Majority" (1960), in *James Baldwin: Collected Essays*, ed. Toni Morrison (New York: Library of America, 1998), 220.

11. This statement is true at least in terms of Baldwin's published works, public utterances, and the letters of his that are available to the public. A significant portion of Baldwin's correspondence will not be available for public view until 2037.

12. There is a third mention I will not discuss here. In *The Evidence of Things Not Seen*, Baldwin mentions Buckley in passing in a section about the exploitation of the developing world. Baldwin suggests that Buckley was perfectly comfortable with such exploitation and "should certainly know" who benefits from it. James Baldwin, *The Evidence of Things Not Seen* (New York: Henry Holt, 1985), 29.

13. James Baldwin, "Blacks and Jews" (1984), in *The Cross of Redemption: Uncollected Writings*, ed. Randall Kenan (New York: Pantheon Books, 2010), 174.

14. Baldwin does not mention Buckley by name, and for that reason, I concede that this is a speculative, not a factual, claim. The description he provides is strongly suggestive of his second encounter with Buckley. Walter Lowe, one of Baldwin's editors for the project, agrees with my assessment that he likely had Buckley in mind. Walter Lowe, email to the author, August 8, 2018.

15. Baldwin, *Evidence of Things Not Seen*, 100.

16. James Baldwin, "A Fly in the Buttermilk," in *James Baldwin: Collected Essays*, ed. Toni Morrison (New York: Library of America, 1998), 194. This particular passage was not about Buckley but rather the "middle of the road" southern principal Baldwin interviewed in North Carolina in the early 1960s.

17. After losing several battles over civil rights legislation, Buckley called for a moratorium. See William F. Buckley Jr., "Time for a Hiatus," syndicated column published on October 4, 1966.

18. The phrase "cause of the white people" comes from Buckley's reflections on the Birmingham church bombing in 1963. *National Review Bulletin* 15, no. 13 (October 1, 1963): 1. Buckley made similar arguments in many instances, including his critiques of Governor Barnett in Mississippi and the juries that failed to convict in the Liuzzo murder case.

19. In an interview with Terry Gross on *Fresh Air*, Buckley said the following when asked about "Why the South": "I think that's absolutely correct. If you believe . . . that you should not vote unless you are literate and if you are prepared to admit the South was very heavily neglecting the education of black people, then under the circumstances you would have a much higher incidence of white people than black people voting. You have to remember we lived then in an age in which people—including myself—contributed to something called the National Association for the Advancement of Colored People. Well, if you acknowledge that you want to advance colored people, you acknowledge that they were not at that point as advanced as other people." "Buckley on *Fresh Air*," NPR, 1989, https://www.npr.org/templates/story/story.php?storyId=87761086. Buckley also said the following in an interview with Deborah Solomon in the *New York Times*:

> SOLOMON: In the '50's, you famously claimed that whites were culturally superior to African-Americans.

BUCKLEY: The point I made about white cultural supremacy was sociological. It reflected, in a different but complementary context, the postulates of the National Association of Colored People.

SOLOMON: What are you talking about?

BUCKLEY: The call for the "advancement" of colored people presupposes they are behind. Which they were, in 1958, by any standards of measurement.

Deborah Solomon, "The Way We Live Now, 7/11/04: Questions for William F. Buckley; Conservatively Speaking," *New York Times*, July 11, 2004, https://www.nytimes.com/2004/07/11/magazine/way-we-live-now-7-11-04-questions-for-william-f-buckley-conservatively-speaking.html. It should be noted that Buckley's interpretation of the purpose of the NAACP is a controversial one.

20. In the same letters section, Senator Thurmond—one of the country's most infamous segregationists—found it much easier than Buckley to answer this question in the affirmative.

21. William F. Buckley, "Was the Right Wrong on Rights?," *Policy Review* (Spring 1989): 93.

22. James Carney, "10 Questions for William F. Buckley," *Time*, April 5, 2004, http://content.time.com/time/magazine/article/0,9171,607805,00.html. Unfortunately, this comment came in the "10 Questions" in *Time*, which features only one- to two-sentence responses for each question.

23. In the interview with Gross in 1989, Buckley said he "welcomed the result," but that he had been right that it constituted a "constitutional disruption." "Buckley on *Fresh Air*."

24. Corey Robin, *The Reactionary Mind: Conservatism from Edmund Burke to Sarah Palin* (New York: Oxford University Press, 2013), 28.

25. Buckley's defenders will dispute this claim and say that his most lasting legacy is in his contributions to the Cold War. That is an argument for another day, but even if I were to concede the point, I would contend that Buckley's racial politics constitute his most enduring legacy for domestic politics. See, in general, "George Will and William F. Buckley Jr.," ABC News, October 9, 2005, https://abcnews.go.com/ThisWeek/TheList/story?id=1281875.

26. Buckley died several months before the election of Barack Obama.

27. See, for example, Joseph E. Lowndes, *From the New Deal to the New Right: Race and the Southern Origins of Modern Conservatism* (New Haven, CT: Yale University Press, 2008); Christopher S. Parker and Matt A. Barreto, *Change They Can't Believe In: The Tea Party and Reactionary Politics in America* (Princeton, NJ: Princeton University Press, 2013); Arlie Hochschild, *Strangers in their Own Land: Anger and Mourning on the American Right* (New York: New Press, 2016).

28. Fred R. Standley and Louis H. Pratt, eds., *Conversations with James Baldwin* (Jackson: University Press of Mississippi, 1989), 286.

29. Margaret Mead and James Baldwin, *A Rap on Race*, 1971, https://www.youtube.com/watch?v=3WNO6f7rjE0. Baldwin's comment about his conservatism occurs at about 1:10:25.

30. James Baldwin, "White Racism or World Community" (1968), in *James Baldwin: Collected Essays*, ed. Toni Morrison (New York: Library of America, 1998), 752.

31. James Baldwin, "Nobody Knows My Name: A Letter from the South" (1959), in *James Baldwin: Collected Essays*, ed. Toni Morrison (New York: Library of America, 1998), 208.

32. Buckley's defenders would be sure to point out that he was no fan of Donald Trump. A careful reading of his critique of Trump, however, reveals that his primary concerns about Trump had to do with his narcissism, not his ideology. William F. Buckley Jr., "Insights: Politics—The Demagogues Are Running," *Cigar Aficionado* (March–April 2000), https://www.cigaraficionado.com/article/insights-politics-the-demagogues-are-running-7081. I am indebted to conversations with Chase Stowell about how Baldwin might think through the Trump era.

33. James Baldwin, "Uses of the Blues" (1964), in *The Cross of Redemption: Uncollected Writings*, ed. Randall Kenan (New York: Pantheon Books, 2010), 81.

34. James Baldwin, "To Crush a Serpent" (1987), in *The Cross of Redemption: Uncollected Writings*, ed. Randall Kenan (New York: Pantheon Books, 2010), 203.

35. James Baldwin, "Faulkner and Desegregation" (1956), in *James Baldwin: Collected Essays*, ed. Toni Morrison (New York: Library of America, 1998), 214.

Appendix

1. This is the first cut—after the word "Negro"—in the BBC recording of Buckley's speech. I will note below where the recording resumes.

2. The BBC recording resumes here.

3. This is the second point at which the BBC recording cuts Buckley's speech. I will make a note below of where the recording resumes.

4. The BBC recording resumes after this sentence.

5. The third BBC cut to Buckley's speech occurs here. I will note below where the recording resumes.

6. The BBC recording resumes after this sentence.

7. The fourth cut in the BBC recording of Buckley's speech occurs here. I will note below when the recording resumes.

8. The BBC recording resumes here.

Bibliography

Archives

Arendt, Hannah. Papers. Manuscript Division, Library of Congress, Washington, DC

Baldwin, James. Papers. Sc MG 936, Schomburg Center for Research in Black Culture, Manuscripts, Archives and Rare Books Division, New York Public Library.

Buckley, William F., Jr. Papers (MS 576). Manuscripts and Archives, Yale University Library.

Commentary. Magazine Archive. Harry Ransom Humanities Research Center, University of Texas at Austin.

Filvaroff, David B., and Raymond E. Wolfinger. Civil Rights Acts Papers, 1957–2000. University Archives, State University of New York at Buffalo.

Kilpatrick, James Jackson. Accession #6626-b, Special Collections, University of Virginia Library, Charlottesville, VA.

Mills, Robert Park. Papers. Harry Ransom Humanities Research Center, University of Texas at Austin.

New York Times Papers. Manuscripts and Archives Division, New York Public Library.

New Yorker. Records. Manuscripts and Archives Division, New York Public Library.

Susskind, David. Papers. 1935–87. University of Wisconsin at Madison Libraries.

Books, Articles, and Other Media

A. B. H. "The Two Faces of Dr. King." *National Review*, January 31, 1959, 482.

Adler, Mike. "James Baldwin at the Union." *Isis at a Comprehensive School*, March 6, 1965, 26–27.

"The American Dream and the American Negro." *New York Times Magazine*, March 7, 1965, 32–33, 87–89.

American Masters—Maya Angelou: And I Still Rise. PBS documentary, 2017.

Arnsdorf, Isaac, and Victor Zapana. "Editorials Presaged Authorial Style, Voice." *Yale Daily News*, February 28, 2008.

Auchincloss, Eve, and Nancy Lynch. "Disturber of the Peace: James Baldwin—An Interview." In *Conversations with James Baldwin*, edited by Fred R. Standley and Louis H. Pratt, 64–83. Jackson: University Press of Mississippi, 1989.

"Baldwin Blames White Supremacy." *New York Post*, February 22, 1965.

Baldwin, James. "Autobiographical Notes." In *James Baldwin: Collected Essays*, edited by Toni Morrison, 5–9. New York: Library of America, 1998.

———. "The Black Boy Looks at the White Boy." In *James Baldwin: Collected Essays*, edited by Toni Morrison, 269–90. New York: Library of America, 1998.

———. "Blacks and Jews." In *The Cross of Redemption: Uncollected Writings*, edited by Randall Kenan, 171–94. New York: Pantheon Books, 2010.

———. *Blues for Mister Charlie: A Play*. New York: Vintage Books, 1964.

———. "Color." In *James Baldwin: Collected Essays*, edited by Toni Morrison, 673–77. New York: Library of America, 1998.

———. "The Creative Process." In *James Baldwin: Collected Essays*, edited by Toni Morrison, 669–72. New York: Library of America, 1998.

———. "The Crusade of Indignation." In *James Baldwin: Collected Essays*, edited by Toni Morrison, 606–13. New York: Library of America, 1998.

———. "To Crush a Serpent." In *The Cross of Redemption: Uncollected Writings*, edited by Randall Kenan, 195–206. New York: Pantheon Books, 2010.

———. "The Dangerous Road before Martin Luther King." In *James Baldwin: Collected Essays*, edited by Toni Morrison, 638–58. New York: Library of America, 1998.

———. "The Discovery of What It Means to Be an American." In *James Baldwin: Collected Essays*, edited by Toni Morrison, 137–42. New York: Library of America, 1998.

———. "Down at the Cross." In *James Baldwin: Collected Essays*, edited by Toni Morrison, 296–347. New York: Library of America, 1998.

———. *Early Novels and Stories*. Edited by Toni Morrison. New York: Library of America, 1998.

———. "East River, Downtown: Postscript to a Letter from Harlem." In *James Baldwin: Collected Essays*, edited by Toni Morrison, 180–86. New York: Library of America, 1998.

———. "Everybody's Protest Novel." In *James Baldwin: Collected Essays*, edited by Toni Morrison, 11–18. New York: Library of America, 1998.

———. *The Evidence of Things Not Seen*. New York: Henry Holt, 1985.

———. "Faulkner and Desegregation." In *James Baldwin: Collected Essays*, edited by Toni Morrison, 209–14. New York: Library of America, 1998.

———. "Fifth Avenue, Uptown: A Letter from Harlem." In *James Baldwin: Collected Essays*, edited by Toni Morrison, 170–79. New York: Library of America, 1998.

———. *The Fire Next Time*. New York: Vintage International Edition, 1993.

———. "Fly in Buttermilk." In *James Baldwin: Collected Essays*, edited by Toni Morrison, 187–96. New York: Library of America, 1998).

———. *Giovanni's Room*. In *Early Novels and Stories*, edited by Toni Morrison, 217–360. New York: Library of America, 1998.

———. *Go Tell It on the Mountain*. In *Early Novels and Stories*, edited by Toni Morrison, 1–216. New York: Library of America, 1998.

———. "The Harlem Ghetto." In *James Baldwin: Collected Essays*, edited by Toni Morrison, 42–53. New York: Library of America, 1998.

———. Interview. 1963. Available at https://www.youtube.com/watch?v=LmP41sPPF90.

———. "Introduction to *Notes of a Native Son*." In *James Baldwin: Collected Essays*, edited by Toni Morrison, 808–13. New York: Library of America, 1998.

———. "Journey to Atlanta." In *James Baldwin: Collected Essays*, edited by Toni Morrison, 54–62. New York: Library of America, 1998.

———. "Letters from a Journey." In *The Cross of Redemption: Uncollected Writings*, edited by Randall Kenan, 189–98. New York: Pantheon Books, 2010.

———. "Lorraine Hansberry at the Summit." In *The Cross of Redemption: Uncollected Writings*, edited by Randall Kenan, 109–13. New York: Pantheon Books, 2010.

———. "Many Thousands Gone." In *James Baldwin: Collected Essays*, edited by Toni Morrison, 19–34. New York: Library of America, 1998.

———. "My Dungeon Shook." In *James Baldwin: Collected Essays*, edited by Toni Morrison, 291–95. New York: Library of America, 1998.

———. "The New Lost Generation." In *James Baldwin: Collected Essays*, edited by Toni Morrison, 659–68. New York: Library of America, 1998.

———. "No Name in the Street." In *James Baldwin: Collected Essays*, edited by Toni Morrison, 349–476. New York: Library of America, 1998.

———. "Nobody Knows My Name: A Letter from the South." In *James Baldwin: Collected Essays*, edited by Toni Morrison, 197–208. New York: Library of America, 1998.

———. "Notes of a Native Son." In *James Baldwin: Collected Essays*, edited by Toni Morrison, 63–84. New York: Library of America, 1998.

———. "Nothing Personal." In *James Baldwin: Collected Essays*, edited by Toni Morrison, 692–706. New York: Library of America, 1998.

———. "On the Painter Beauford Delaney." In *James Baldwin: Collected Essays*, edited by Toni Morrison, 720–21. New York: Library of America, 1998.

———. "The Price of the Ticket." In *James Baldwin: Collected Essays*, edited by Toni Morrison, 830–44. New York: Library of America, 1998.

———. "A Report from Occupied Territory." In *James Baldwin: Collected Essays*, edited by Toni Morrison, 728–38. New York: Library of America, 1998.

———. "Review of *The Best Short Stories* by Maxim Gorky." In *The Cross of Redemption: Uncollected Writings*, edited by Randall Kenan, 291–93. New York: Pantheon Books, 2010.

———. "In Search of the Majority." In *James Baldwin: Collected Essays*, edited by Toni Morrison, 215–21. New York: Library of America, 1998.

———. "Smaller than Life." In *Collected Essays*, edited by Toni Morrison, 577–78. New York: Library of America, 1998.

———. "Stranger in the Village." In *James Baldwin: Collected Essays*, edited by Toni Morrison, 117–36. New York: Library of America, 1998.

———. "Take Me to the Water." In *James Baldwin: Collected Essays*, edited by Toni Morrison. New York: Library of America, 1998, 353–403.

———. "They Can't Turn Back." In *James Baldwin: Collected Essays*, edited by Toni Morrison, 622–37. New York: Library of America, 1998.

———. "The Uses of the Blues." In *The Cross of Redemption: Uncollected Writings*, edited by Randall Kenan, 70–81. New York: Pantheon Books, 2010.

———. "We Can Change the Country." In *The Cross of Redemption: Uncollected Writings*, edited by Randall Kenan, 59–64. New York: Pantheon Books, 2010.

———. "The White Man's Guilt." In *James Baldwin: Collected Essays*, edited by Toni Morrison, 722–27. New York: Library of America, 1998.

———. "The White Problem." In *The Cross of Redemption: Uncollected Writings*, edited by Randall Kenan, 88–97. New York: Pantheon Books, 2010.

———. "White Racism or World Community?" In *James Baldwin: Collected Essays*, edited by Toni Morrison, 749–56. New York: Library of America, 1998.

———. "Why I Stopped Hating Shakespeare." In *The Cross of Redemption: Uncollected Writings*, edited by Randall Kenan, 65–69. New York: Pantheon Books, 2010.

"Baldwin on Tour for CORE." *Muhammad Speaks*, February 4, 1963. https://issuu.com /muhammadspeaks/docs/we_seek_truth_and_justice_february.

"Baldwin Tackles Rightist." *Varsity*, February 13, 1965.

Balfour, Lawrie. "Hideously Loaded: James Baldwin's History of the American Dream." Lecture delivered at the Symposium on James Baldwin, William F. Buckley, and the American Dream, Linfield College, McMinnville, OR, May 2015. http://digitalcommons.linfield.edu/douglass /11.

Barndt, Will. "William F. Buckley Jr. and America's 'Engines of Concern.'" *American Political Thought* 6 (Fall 2017): 648–56.

Barnett, Ross. "Address to the People of Mississippi." September 13, 1962. http://microsites .jfklibrary.org/olemiss/controversy/doc2.html.

Battaglio, Stephen. *David Susskind: A Televised Life*. New York: Macmillan, 2010.

Beecher, John. "If You Are a Negro." In *Reporting Civil Rights, Part One: American Journalism, 1941–1963*, edited by Clayborne Carson, David J. Garrow, Bill Kovach, and Carol Polsgrove, 395–405. New York: Library of America, 2003.

Bercovitch, Sacvan. *American Jeremiad*. Madison: University of Wisconsin Press, 1978.

Bernstein, Shana. *Bridges to Reform: Interracial Civil Rights Activism in Twentieth-Century Los Angeles*. New York: Oxford University Press, 2011.Beschloss, Michael. *Reaching for Glory: Lyndon Johnson's Secret White House Tapes, 1964–1965*. New York: Simon and Schuster, 2001.

Birmingham, David. *The Decolonization of Africa*. Athens: Ohio University Press, 1995.

"Birmingham and Beyond: The Negro's Push for Equality." *Time*, May 17, 1963.

Black, Earl, and Merle Black. *The Rise of the Southern Republicans*. Cambridge, MA: Belknap Press of Harvard University Press, 2001.

"The Black Muslims in America: An Interview with George S. Schuyler, Malcolm X, C. Eric Lincoln, and James Baldwin." Transcribed in *Race(ing) to the Right: Selected Essays of George S. Schuyler*, edited by Jeffrey Leak, 74–79. Knoxville: University of Tennessee Press, 2001.

Blight, David. "The Civil War and Reconstruction Era, 1845–1877." Open Yale Course, Lecture 27, iTunes.

Bochen, Christine M., ed. *The Courage for Truth: The Letters of Thomas Merton to Writers*. New York: Farrar, Straus and Giroux, 2008.

Bogus, Carl. *Buckley*. New York: Bloomsbury, 2011.

Boyett, Patricia Michelle. *Right to Revolt: The Crusade for Justice in Mississippi's Central Piney Woods*. Oxford: University Press of Mississippi, 2015.

Bozell, L. Brent, Jr. "To Mend the Tragic Flaw." *National Review*, March 12, 1963, 199.

———. "The 1958 Elections: Coroner's Report." *National Review*, November 22, 1958, 335.

———. "The Open Question." *National Review*, September 7, 1957, 209.

Branch, Taylor. *Parting the Waters: America in the King Years, 1954–63*. New York: Simon and Schuster, 1988.

———. *Pillar of Fire: America in the King Years, 1963–65*. New York: Simon and Schuster, 1998.

Broad, David. "Crowds Pack Union for Baldwin." *Varsity*, February 20, 1965, 1.

———. "Negroes—All Talk, No Action." *Varsity*, February 27, 1965.

Brogan, Colm. "Alabama, Here We Come." *National Review*, March 9, 1965, 195–96.

Brown v. Board of Education, Topeka, Kansas, 347 U.S. 483 (1954).

Brust, Richard. "The Court Comes Together." *ABA Journal* 90, no. 4 (April 2004): 40–44.

Brustein, Robert. "Everybody Knows My Name." *New York Review of Books*, December 17, 1964.

Buccola, Nicholas. "What William F. Buckley Jr. Did Not Understand about James Baldwin." In *A Political Companion to James Baldwin*, ed. Susan J. McWilliams, 116–48. Lexington: University Press of Kentucky, 2017.

Buckley, Christopher. *Losing Mum and Pup: A Memoir*. New York: Grand Central Publishing, 2009.

Buckley, Priscilla L., and William F. Buckley Jr., eds. *W.F.B.: An Appreciation by His Family and Friends*. New York: Privately printed, 1959.

Buckley, Reid. *An American Family: The Buckleys*. New York: Threshold Editions, 2008.

Buckley, William F., Jr. "America Haters—Threat to Negroes." *New York Journal American*, June 17, 1965.

———. "Are You a Racist?" Syndicated column published on April 15, 1965.

———. "The Assault on Miss Lucy." *National Review*, February 22, 1956, 5.

———. "Bad Little Black Sambo." *Freeman* (October 1952): 59–60.

———. "The Baldwin Syndrome," *Washington Daily News*, June 18, 1965.

———. "The Birch Society." Syndicated column published on August 5, 1965.

———. "Birmingham and After." Syndicated column published on May 11, 1963.

———. "The *Brown* Decade." *National Review*, June 2, 1964, 433–34.

———. "The Call to Colorblindness." Syndicated column published on June 8, 1963.

———. "A Call to Lynch the White God." Syndicated column published on March 3, 1963.

———. "Can a Little Magazine Break Even?" *National Review*, October 10, 1959, 393–94.

———. "Can We Desegregate, Hesto Presto?" In *Rumbles Left and Right: A Book about Troublesome People and Ideas*, 122–27. New York: G. P. Putnam's Sons, 1963.

———. "The Civilian Review Board." Syndicated column published on July 10, 1965.

———. "A Clarification." *National Review*, September 7, 1957, 199.

———. "Constitutional Chaos." Syndicated column published on March 23, 1965.

———. "Count Me Out." Syndicated column published on August 17, 1963.

———. *Cruising Speed: A Documentary*. New York: G. P. Putnam's Sons, 1971.

———. "The Damage We Have Done to Ourselves." *National Review*, September 26, 1959, 349–51.

———. "Deadend in South Africa." *National Review*, April 23, 1960, 254–55.

———. "The Defeat of Barry Goldwater." Syndicated column published on November 7, 1964.

———. "Desegregation: Will It Work? No." *Saturday Review*, November 11, 1961, 21–22.

———. *Did You Ever See a Dream Walking?* New York: Bobbs-Merrill, 1970.

———. "Did You Kill Martin Luther King?" In *Let Us Talk of Many Things: The Collected Speeches*, 117–23. New York: Forum, 2000.

———. "Distinguamus." *National Review*, March 26, 1960, 193.

———. "Do They Really Hate to Hate?" *National Review*, December 31, 1963.

———. "Enter Muhammed [sic]?" *National Review*, July 2, 1963, 519–21.

———. "And Finally on John Birch." Syndicated column published on August 17, 1965.

———. "Footnote to *Brown v. Board of Education*." *National Review*, March 11, 1961, 137.

———. "Foul." *National Review*, April 18, 1956, 6.

———. *God and Man at Yale*. Washington, DC: Regnery Publishing, 1951.

———. "Goldwater: Profile in Courage?" Syndicated column published on June 25, 1964.

———. *Gratitude: Reflections on What We Owe to Our Country*. New York: Random House, 1990.

———. "Harlem Is in New York City." *National Review*, November 2, 1965, 978–79.

———. "Hate America." Syndicated column published on January 21, 1965.

———. "The Haynesville Dilemma." Syndicated column published on May 13, 1965.

———. "An Hour with George Wallace (I)." Syndicated column published on February 24, 1968.

———. "An Hour with George Wallace (II)." Syndicated column published on February 27, 1968.

———. "How to Help the Negro." Syndicated column published on March 4, 1965.

———. "If Goldwater Were President." *Coronet*, July 1961, 156–62.

———. "The Impending Defeat of Barry Goldwater." In *Let Us Talk of Many Things: The Collected Speeches*, 74–77. New York: Forum, 2000.

———. "Insights: Politics—The Demagogues Are Running." *Cigar Aficionado* (March–April 2000. https://www.cigaraficionado.com/article/insights-politics-the-demagogues-are-running-7081.

———. Introduction to "Special Report: The Race Issue and the Election." *National Review*, September 22, 1964, 813–21.

———. "The Issue at Selma." Syndicated column published on February 18, 1965.

———. "Leftward March." *National Review*, January 14, 1964, 11–12.

———. "Less Sound and Fury." *National Review*, March 28, 1956, 5–6.

———. "Let Us Try, at Least, to Understand." *National Review*, June 3, 1961, 338.

———. "Letter from Capetown." Syndicated column published on November 25, 1962.

———. "Lindsay in the Ring." Syndicated column published on May 18, 1965.

———. "Mayor, Anyone?" Syndicated column published on May 22, 1965.

———. "The Mess in Mississippi." Syndicated column published on October 7, 1962.

———. "The Mess in Mississippi." *National Review*, October 23, 1962, 305.

———. *Miles Gone By: A Literary Autobiography*. Washington, DC: Regnery Publishing, 2004.

———. "Mississippi." *National Review*, July 14, 1964, 573–54.

———. "Mississippi Dilemma and 'The Best Part of Life.'" Syndicated column published on December 19, 1964.

———. "The Morning After." *National Review*, December 17, 1963, 512.

———. "Must We Hate Portugal?" Syndicated column published on December 2, 1962.

———. "The Negro and the American Dream." Syndicated column published on February 27, 1965.

———. "Negroes Harmed by Extreme Militancy." *Beaver County Times*, June 18, 1965.

———. "Nixon and Wallace." Syndicated column published on October 1, 1968.

———. "Notes toward an Empirical Definition of Conservatism." In *What Is Conservatism?*, edited by Frank S. Meyer, 211–16. Wilmington, DE: Intercollegiate Studies Institute, 2015.

———. "The Obliging Disappearance of George Wallace." Syndicated column published on July 28, 1964.

———. *Odyssey of a Friend*. Washington, DC: Regnery Publishing, 1987.

———. *On the Firing Line: The Public Life of Our Public Figures*. New York: Random House, 1989.

———. "The Open Questions." Syndicated column published on March 18, 1965.

———. "The Other Way of Looking at It." Syndicated column published on August 3, 1963.

———. "Our Mission Statement." *National Review*, November 19, 1955. https://www.nationalreview.com/1955/11/our-mission-statement-william-f- buckley-jr/.

———. "The Question of Robert Welch." *National Review*, February 13, 1962, 83–88.

———. "Realignment." *National Review*, December 1, 1964, 1047.

———. "Return to States' Rights." *National Review*, April 18, 1956, 263–64.

———. "Saying Goodbye: Aloise Steiner Buckley, R.I.P." *National Review*, April 19, 1985, 20–21.

———. "Solution for the South?" *National Review*, January 17, 1959, 446–47.

———. "South African Fortnight." *National Review*, January 14, 1963, 17–23.

———. Speech at the University of California at Los Angeles. December 7, 1964. Mississippi Department of Archives and History, Forum Films Collection, 1955–66, reel 009.

———. "Strom Thurmond Makes It Official." Syndicated column published on September 20, 1964.

———. "Time for a Hiatus." Syndicated column published on October 4, 1966.

———. "Today We Are Educated Men." In *Let Us Talk of Many Things: The Collected Speeches*, 3–6. New York: Forum, 2000.

———. *The Unmaking of a Mayor*. New York: Viking, 1966.

———. *Up from Liberalism*. New York: McDowell, Obolensky, 1959.

———. "The Vile Campaign." *National Review*, October 6, 1964, 853–56.

———. "Voices of Sanity." *National Review*, April 4, 1956, 7.

———. "The Vote in the South." *National Review*, June 4, 1963, 437.

———. "Was the Right Wrong on Rights?" *Policy Review* (Spring 1989): 93.

———. "Watts, Where Is That?" Syndicated column published on September 21, 1965.

———. "What Happened?" Syndicated column published on August 19, 1965.

———. "What Says the South?" *National Review*, October 20, 1964, 898–99.

———. "When, Oh When?" Syndicated column published on June 17, 1965.

———. "When the 'Plaints Go Marching In." *National Review*, August 27, 1963, 140.

———. "A White Revolt?" Syndicated column published on April 16, 1964.

———. "Why the South Must Prevail." *National Review*, August 24, 1957, 148–49.

Buckley, William F., Jr., and L. Brent Bozell Jr. *McCarthy and His Enemies*. Washington, DC: Regnery Publishing, 1954.

Buckley, William F., Jr., and John Kenneth Galbraith. *National Review Presents the Cambridge Union Debate, Wm. F. Buckley vs. J. K. Galbraith*. New York: National Review, 1970.

"Buckley on *Fresh Air*. NPR, 1989. https://www.npr.org/templates/story/story.php?storyId=87761086.

"Buckley on 'The Baldwin Syndrome': June 1965." *Washington Daily News*, June 18, 1965. In *James Baldwin: The FBI File*, edited by William J. Maxwell, 259–61. New York: Arcade Publishing, 2017.

"Buckley Praises Police of Selma; Hailed by 5,600 Police Here as He Cites 'Restraint.'" *New York Times*, April 5, 1965.

"The Buckley Vote." *New York Times*, November 3, 1965.

Carlson, Peter. *K Blows Top: A Cold War Comic Interlude, Starring Nikita Khrushchev, America's Most Unlikely Tourist*. New York: Public Affairs, 2010.

Carney, James. "10 Questions for William F. Buckley." *Time*, April 5, 2004. http://content.time.com/time/magazine/article/0,9171,607805,00.html.

Carson, Clayborne. "Chronology, 1941 to 1973." In *Reporting Civil Rights, Part Two: American Journalism, 1963–1973*, edited by Clayborne Carson, David J. Garrow, Bill Kovach, and Carol Polsgrove, 885–907. New York: Library of America, 2003.

———. *In Struggle: SNCC and the Black Awakening of the 1960s*. Cambridge, MA: Harvard University Press, 1995.

Carson, Clayborne, ed. "Chronology, 1941–1973." In *Reporting Civil Rights, Part One: American Journalism, 1941–1963*, edited by Clayborne Carson, David J. Garrow, Bill Kovach, and Carol Polsgrove, 897–919. New York: Library of America, 2003.

Carter, Dan T. *From George Wallace to Newt Gingrich: Race in the Conservative Counterrevolution, 1963–1994*. Baton Rouge: Louisiana State University, 1996.

Chamberlain, John. "Forrest Davis." *National Review*, May 22, 1962, 357.

Chambers, Whittaker. "Big Sister Is Watching You." *National Review*, December 28, 1957, 594–96.

Clark, Kenneth B. "A Conversation with James Baldwin." In *Conversations with James Baldwin*, edited by Fred R. Standley and Louis H. Pratt, 38–46. Jackson: University Press of Mississippi, 1989.

———. "Conversation with James Baldwin, A; James Baldwin Interview." May 24, 1963. http://openvault.wgbh.org/catalog/V_C03ED1927DCF46B5A8C82275DF4239F9.

Coiner, Constance. *Better Red: The Writing and Resistance of Tillie Olsen and Meridel Le Seur*. Urbana: University of Illinois Press, 1995.

Colaico, James. *Martin Luther King, Jr.: Apostle of Militant Nonviolence*. London: Macmillan, 1988.

"The Court Views Its Handiwork." *National Review*, September 21, 1957, 244–45.

Cradock, Percy. *Recollections of the Cambridge Union, 1815–1939*. Cambridge, UK: Bowes and Bowes, 1953.

Crespino, Joseph. *Strom Thurmond's America*. New York: Farrar, Straus and Giroux, 2012.

Critchlow, Donald T., and Nancy McLean. *Debating the American Conservative Movement: 1945 to the Present*. Lanham, MD: Rowman and Littlefield, 2009.

Cruse, Harold. *The Crisis of the Negro Intellectual: A Historical Analysis of the Failure of Black Leadership*. New York: New York Review of Books, 1967.

Curtis, Jesse. "Will the Jungle Take Over? *National Review* and the Defense of Western Civilization in the Era of Civil Rights and African Decolonization." *Journal of American Studies* (Spring 2018): 1–27.

Danaher, Paul. "March Will Greet Griffiths." *Varsity*, January 16, 1965.

———. "No Action after Riot Misfires." *Varsity*, January 23, 1965.

Davidson, Donald. "The New South and the Conservative Tradition." *National Review*, September 10, 1960, 141–46.

Davis, Forrest. "The Right to Nullify." *National Review*, April 25, 1956, 9–11.

"Democrats Vote Today." *New York Times*, July 25, 1952.

Doyle, William. *An American Insurrection: James Meredith and the Battle of Oxford, Mississippi, 1962.* New York: Anchor Books, 2001.

Dudas, Jeffrey R. *Raised Right: Fatherhood in Modern American Conservatism.* Palo Alto, CA: Stanford University Press, 2017.

Duke, Bob. "2 Mob Victims Ready to Die for Integration." In *Reporting Civil Rights, Part One: American Journalism, 1941–1963,* edited by Clayborne Carson, David J. Garrow, Bill Kovach, and Carol Polsgrove, 585–88. New York: Library of America, 2003.

Dupee, F. W. "James Baldwin and 'The Man.'" *New York Review of Books*, February 1, 1963.

Dworkin, Andrea. *Heartbreak: The Political Memoir of a Feminist Militant.* New York: Basic Books, 2002.

Eckman, Fern Marja. *The Furious Passage of James Baldwin.* Lanham, MD: Rowman and Littlefield, 1966.

Edmond, Lez. "The Long, Hot Summer." In *Reporting Civil Rights, Part Two: American Journalism, 1963–1973,* edited by Clayborne Carson, David J. Garrow, Bill Kovach, and Carol Polsgrove, 138–56. New York: Library of America, 2003.

Edwards, Ezekiel, Will Bunting, and Lynda Garcia. *The War on Marijuana in Black and White.* New York: American Civil Liberties Union, 2013.

Edwards, Lee. "Flag Waver's Memoir." *Policy Review* (Spring 1989), 58–65.

———. *Goldwater: The Man Who Made a Revolution.* Washington, DC: Regnery History, 1995.

———. *Standing Athwart History: The Political Thought of William F. Buckley Jr.* Washington, DC: Heritage Foundation, 2010.

Elkoff, Marvin. "Everybody Knows His Name." *Esquire*, August 1964, 59–64, 120–23.

"English Ovation for James Baldwin." *New York Times*, February 19, 1965.

"Erik Ritter von Kuehnelt-Leddihn." *Religion and Liberty* 9, no. 5 (July 20, 2010). https://acton.org/pub/religion-liberty/volume-9-number-5/erik-ritter-von-kuehnelt-leddihn.

Evans, Medford. "An Interview with Citizen Edwin A. Walker," *National Review*, December 16, 1961, 411.

Everitt, David. "On the Trail of Television's Lost Treasures." *New York Times*, April 29, 2001.

Eyes on the Prize, Volume 4: No Easy Walk (1962–1966). Directed by Callie Crossley and James A. DeVinney. February 11, 1987. https://www.youtube.com/watch?v=6YYaaEffMFk.

Felzenberg, Alvin S. "He Stood Athwart History." Interview in *National Review*, February 27, 2013. https://www.nationalreview.com/2013/02/he-stood-athwart-history-interview/.

———. "How William F. Buckley Jr. Changed His Mind on Civil Rights." *Politico*, May 13, 2017. https://www.politico.com/magazine/story/2017/05/13/william-f-buckley-civil-rights-215129.

———. *A Man and His Presidents.* New Haven, CT: Yale University Press, 2017.

Feulner, Edwin J. "Frank S. Meyer." In *The March of Freedom: Modern Classics in Conservative Thought.* Dallas: Spence Publishing, 1998.

Fiffer, Steve, and Adar Cohen. *Jimmie Lee & James: Two Lives, Two Deaths, and the Movement That Changed America.* New York: Simon and Schuster, 2015.

Flamm, Michael W. *In the Heat of the Summer: The New York Riots of 1964 and the War on Crime*. Philadelphia: University of Pennsylvania Press, 2016.

"For the Record." *National Review*, January 25, 1958, 74.

"For the Republican Conclave." *Yale Daily News*, April 30, 1949.

Forster, Arnold, and Benjamin R. Epstein. *Danger on the Right*. Santa Barbara: Praeger, 1976.

Friedman, Murray, ed. "Introduction: Commentary: The First 60 Years." In *Commentary in American Life*, 1. Philadelphia: Temple University Press, 2005.

"George Will and William F. Buckley Jr." ABC News, October 9, 2005. https://abcnews.go.com/ThisWeek/TheList/story?id=1281875.

Gill, Jonathan. *Harlem The Four Hundred Year History from Dutch Village to Capital of Black America*. New York: Grove Press, 2011.

Goldwin, Robert, ed. *100 Years of Emancipation*. New York: Rand McNally, 1963.

Greene, Helen Taylor, and Shaun L. Gabbidon, eds. *Encyclopedia of Race and Crime*. Thousand Oaks, CA: Sage Publications, 2009.

Gross, Ben. "Baldwin-Buckley Old Stuff but Exciting." *New York Daily News*, June 24, 1965.

Harrigan, Anthony. "The South *Is* Different." *National Review*, March 8, 1958, 226.

Hart, Jeffrey. *The Making of the Conservative Mind*. Wilmington, DE: Intercollegiate Studies Institute, 2006.

———. "Right at the End." *American Conservative*, March 24, 2008. https://www.theamericanconservative.com/articles/right-at-the-end/.

Hartz, Louis. *The Liberal Tradition in America*. New York: Mariner Books, 1955.

The Hate That Hate Produced. Directed by Mike Wallace and Louis Lomax. 1959. https://www.youtube.com/watch?v=BsYWD2EqavQ.

Hayward, Steven F. *The Age of Reagan: The Conservative Counterrevolution, 1980–1989*. New York: Random House, 2009.

Heller, Anne. *Ayn Rand and the World She Made*. New York: Random House, 2009.

Henrie, Marc. "Anthony Harrigan" *First Principles*. https://www.firstprinciplesjournal.com/articles.aspx?article=833&theme=home&loc=b.

Hentoff, Nat. "James Baldwin Gets 'Older and Sadder.'" *New York Times*, April 11, 1965.

Hochschild, Arlie. *Strangers in their Own Land: Anger and Mourning on the American Right*. New York: New Press, 2016.

Hodgson, Godfrey. *The World Turned Right Side Up*. New York: Houghton Mifflin, 1978.

Hogeland, William. "William F. Buckley and the Politics of Denial." *American Political Thought* 6, no. 4 (Fall 2017): 657–64.

Horne, Alistair. *A Bundle from Britain*. New York: St. Martin's Press, 1994.

"How Much Is It Worth?" *National Review*, January 19, 1957, 55.

Howe, Russell Warren. "An Interview with William Faulkner." *London Sunday Times*, March 4, 1956.

Huie, William Bradford. "The Search for the Missing." In *Reporting Civil Rights, Part Two: American Journalism, 1963–1973*, edited by Clayborne Carson, David J. Garrow, Bill Kovach, and Carol Polsgrove, 157–75. New York: Library of America, 2003.

———. "The Shocking Story of Approved Killing in Mississippi." In *Reporting Civil Rights, Part One: American Journalism, 1941–1963*, edited by Clayborne Carson, David J. Garrow, Bill Kovach, and Carol Polsgrove, 232–40. New York: Library of America, 2003.

Hustwit, William P. *Salesman for Segregation*. Chapel Hill: University of North Carolina Press, 2013.

"An Interview with William F. Buckley Jr." *Mademoiselle* 53 (June 1961): 121–27.

"Is There a Case for Segregation?" *Open Mind* Transcript, James Baldwin Papers, Schomburg Center, New York Public Library.

Jackson, John P., Jr. *Science for Segregation: Race, Law, and the Case against Brown v. Board of Education*. New York: NYU Press, 2005.

Jeffers, Thomas. *Norman Podhoretz: A Biography*. Cambridge: Cambridge University Press, 2010.

Jennings, C. Robert. "Warning for Mister Charlie." *Los Angeles Times West Magazine*, July 7, 1968, 18–20, 22–23.

Johnson, Lyndon Baines. "Address before a Joint Session of Congress." American Presidency Project, University of California at Santa Barbara, November 27, 1963. http://www.presidency.ucsb.edu/ws/?pid=25988.

———. "Address to a Joint Session of Congress." March 15, 1965.

Jones, Sam M. "South Carolina." *National Review*, February 29, 1956, 18.

———. "A Voice of the South." *National Review*, July 27, 1957, 105–6.

Jones, William P. *The March on Washington: Jobs, Freedom, and the Forgotten History of Civil Rights*. New York: W. W. Norton, 2013.

Judgment at Nuremberg. Directed by Stanley Kramer. Universal Studios, 1961.

Judis, John B. *William F. Buckley, Jr.: Patron Saint of the Conservatives*. New York: Simon and and Schuster, 1988.

Kabaservice, Geoffrey. *Rule and Ruin: The Downfall of Moderation and the Destruction of the Republican Party, from Eisenhower to the Tea Party*. New York: Oxford University Press, 2012.

Katagiri, Yasuhiro. *The Mississippi State Sovereignty Commission: Civil Rights and States' Rights*. Oxford: University Press of Mississippi, 2001.

Kuehnelt-Leddihn, Erik von. "Katanga's Cure." *National Review*, August 13, 1960.

———. "Letter from Africa." *National Review*, April 9, 1960.

Kempton, Murray. "He Went All the Way." In *Reporting Civil Rights, Part One: American Journalism, 1941–1963*, edited by Clayborne Carson, David J. Garrow, Bill Kovach, and Carol Polsgrove, 214–16. New York: Library of America, 2003.

Kendall, Willmoore. "Conservatism and the Open Society." In *The Conservative Affirmation in America*. Chicago: Henry Regnery Company, 1963.

———. "Light on the American Dilemma?" *National* Review, November 5, 1960, 281–82.

———. "The People versus Socrates Revisited." *Modern Age* 3, no. 1 (Winter 1958–1959): 110.

Kendi, Ibram X. *Stamped from the Beginning: The Definitive History of Racist Ideas in America*. New York: Nation Books, 2016.

Kennedy, John F. "Address by President John F. Kennedy." June 11, 1963. https://www.jfklibrary.org/Asset-Viewer/LH8F_oMzvoe6Ro1yEm74Ng.aspx.

———. "President's Original Speech with Notes: The James Meredith Case." John F. Kennedy Presidential Library and Museum, September 30, 1962. http://microsites.jfklibrary.org/olemiss/confrontation/doc10.html.

———. "Report to the American People on Civil Rights." John F. Kennedy Presidential Library and Museum, June 11, 1963. https://www.jfklibrary.org/Asset-Viewer/LH8F_oMzvoe6Ro1yEm74Ng.aspx.

Kihss, Peter. "Analysis of Conservatives' Vote Implies Equality with Liberals." *New York Times*, November 6, 1965.

Kilpatrick, James Jackson. "Civil Rights and Legal Wrongs." *National Review*, September 24, 1963, 231.

————. "Conservatism and the South." In *The Lasting South*, edited by Louis D. Rubin and James Jackson Kilpatrick, 188–205. Chicago: Regnery Publishing, 1957.

————. "Goldwater Country." *National Review*, April 9, 1963, 281–82.

————. "Must We Repeal the Constitution to Give the Negro the Right to Vote?" *National Review*, April 20, 1965, 319–22.

————. "Right and Power in Arkansas." *National Review*, September 28, 1957, 273.

————. "Shame of the South." *Richmond News Leader*, February 1965.

————. "The South Goes Back Up for Grabs." *National Review*, December 17, 1963, 523–24.

————. "The South Sees through New Glasses." *National Review*, March 11, 1961, 141.

King, Larry L. "God, Man, and William F. Buckley." *Harper's Magazine*, March 1967, 53–61.

King, Martin Luther, Jr. "Letter from a Birmingham Jail." April 13, 1963. http://www.africa.upenn .edu/Articles_Gen/Letter_Birmingham.html.

"King Debates James J. Kilpatrick on 'The Nation's Future.'" November 26, 1960. https:// kinginstitute.stanford.edu/encyclopedia/king-debates-james-j-kilpatrick-nations-future.

Knight, Kathleen, and Robert Erikson. "Ideology in the 1990s." In *Understanding Public Opinion*, edited by Barbara Norrander and Clyde Wilcox. Washington, DC: CQ Press, 1997.

Lamb, Brian. "William F. Buckley Jr.: Happy Days Were Here Again." In *Conversations with William F. Buckley Jr.*, edited by William F. Meehan III, 99–118. Jackson: University Press of Mississippi, 2009.

Lambert, Frank. *The Battle of Ole Miss*. New York: Oxford University Press, 2010.

Leeming, David. *James Baldwin: A Biography*. New York: Arcade, 2015.

Lejeune, Anthony. "The Legacy of Richard Weaver." *National Review*, May 17, 1966, 473–74.

————. "Letter from Ghana." *National Review*, May 21, 1960, 330.

Leonard, George B., T. George Harris, and Christopher S. Wren. "How a Secret Deal Prevented a Massacre at Ole Miss." In *Reporting Civil Rights, Part One: American Journalism, 1941–1963*, edited by Clayborne Carson, David J. Garrow, Bill Kovach, and Carol Polsgrove, 671–701. New York: Library of America, 2003.

"Liberalism and the Negro: A Roundtable Discussion." *Commentary*, March 1, 1964, 25–42.

Lichtman, Allan J. *White Protestant Nation: The Rise of the American Conservative Movement*. New York: Atlantic Monthly Press, 2008.

Liebman, Marvin. *Coming Out Conservative*. San Francisco: Chronicle Books, 1992.

Lincoln, C. Eric. *The Black Muslims in America*. Grand Rapids, MI: Wm. B. Eerdmans Publishing Co., 1994.

Loory, Stuart H. "Reporter Tails 'Freedom' Bus, Caught in Riot." In *Reporting Civil Rights, Part One: American Journalism, 1941–1963*, edited by Clayborne Carson, David J. Garrow, Bill Kovach, and Carol Polsgrove, 573–79. New York: Library of America, 2003.

Lowndes, Joseph E. *From the New Deal to the New Right: Race and the Southern Origins of Modern Conservatism*. New Haven, CT: Yale University Press, 2008.

————. "William F. Buckley Jr.: Anti-blackness as Anti-democracy." *American Political Thought* 6, no. 4 (Fall 2017): 632–40.

Lyons, Leonard. "The Lyons Den." *New York Post*, June 29, 1962, 39.

Madden, Richard L. "William Buckley in Race for Mayor." *New York Times*, June 25, 1965.

Mahoney, J. Daniel. *Actions Speak Louder*. New York: Arlington House, 1968.

Mailer, Norman. "The White Negro." *Dissent* (Fall 1957). https://www.dissentmagazine.org /online_articles/the-white-negro-fall-1957.

Mallon, Jack. "Rev. Martin Luther King Jr. and the Demonstrators Reach Montgomery from Selma." *New York Daily News*, March 26, 1965.

Marable, Manning. *Malcolm X: A Life of Reinvention*. New York: Viking, 2011.

Markmann, Charles Lam. *The Buckleys: A Family Examined*. New York: William Morrow, 1973.

Maxwell, William J., ed. *James Baldwin: The FBI File*. New York: Arcade Publishing, 2017.

McCarthy, Joseph. "Enemies Within." Speech delivered in Wheeling, West Virginia, February 9, 1950. https://liberalarts.utexas.edu/coretexts/_files/resources/texts/1950%20McCarthy%20Enemies.pdf.

McMillen, Neil R. *The Citizens' Council: Organized Resistance to the Second Reconstruction, 1954– 1964*. Urbana: University of Illinois Press, 1994.

McWilliams, Susan J. "James Baldwin and the Politics of Displacement." In *A Political Companion to James Baldwin*, edited by Susan J. McWilliams, 94–115. Lexington: University Press of Kentucky, 2018.

———. "On the Faiths of (and in) Our Fathers." *American Political Thought* 6, no. 4 (Fall 2017), 624–31.

Mead, Margaret, and James Baldwin. *A Rap on Race*, 1971. https://www.youtube.com/watch?v =3WNO6f7rjE0.

Meehan, William F., III, ed. *Conversations with William F. Buckley, Jr.* Jackson: University Press of Mississippi, 2009.

Meyer, Frank S. "The Negro Revolution." *National Review*, June 18, 1963, 496.

———. "The Twisted Tree of Liberty." In *Freedom and Virtue: The Conservative/Libertarian Debate*, edited by George W. Carey, 13–19. Wilmington, DE: ISI Books, 1998.

———. "The Violence of Nonviolence." *National Review*, April 20, 1965, 357.

Miller, D. Quentin. "James Baldwin: America's Prophet, Resurrected." WBUR, February 24, 2015. http://www.wbur.org/cognoscenti/2015/02/24/james-baldwin-black-prophet-d-quentin -miller.

Milner, Lucille B. "Jim Crow in the Army." In *Reporting Civil Rights, Part One: American Journalism, 1941–1963*, edited by Clayborne Carson, David J. Garrow, Bill Kovach, and Carol Polsgrove, 52–61. New York: Library of America, 2003.

Nash, George H. *The Conservative Intellectual Movement in America since 1945*. New York: Open Road Media, 2006.

———. "The Influence of *Ideas Have Consequences* on the Conservative Intellectual Movement in America." In *Steps toward Restoration: The Consequences of Richard Weaver's Ideas*, edited by Ted J. Smith III, 81–124. Wilmington, DE: Intercollegiate Studies Institute, 1998.

National Review Bulletin 15, no. 13 (October 1, 1963): 1.

Nichols, David. *Ike and McCarthy: Dwight Eisenhower's Secret Campaign against Joseph McCarthy*. New York: Simon and Schuster, 2017.

Nock, Albert Jay. *The State of the Union*. Indianapolis: Liberty Fund, 2011.

Nossiter, Adam. *Of Long Memory: Mississippi and the Murder of Medgar Evers*. Reading, MA: Addison-Wesley, 1994.

Oakeshott, Michael. "Rationalism in Politics." In *Rationalism in Politics and Other Essays*. Indianapolis: Liberty Fund, 1991.

Ottley, Roi, and William J. Weatherby. *The Negro in New York*. Santa Barbara: Praeger, 1967.

Parker, Christopher S., and Matt A. Barreto. *Change They Can't Believe In: The Tea Party and Reactionary Politics in America*. Princeton, NJ: Princeton University Press, 2013.

Parkinson, Stephen. *Arena of Ambition: The History of the Cambridge Union*. London: Icon Books, 2009.

Patterson, James T. *The Eve of Destruction: How 1965 Transformed America*. New York: Basic Books, 2012.

———. *Grand Expectations: The United States, 1945–1974*. Oxford: Oxford University Press, 1997.

Pavlic, Ed. *Who Can Afford to Improvise? James Baldwin and Black Music, the Lyric and the Listeners*. New York: Fordham University Press, 2015.

Perlstein, Rick. *Before the Storm: Barry Goldwater and the Unmaking of the American Consensus*. New York: Hill and Wang, 2001.

Perry, Kennetta Hammond. "U.S. Negroes, Your Fight Is Our Fight: Black Britons and the 1963 March on Washington." In *The Other Special Relationship: Race, Rights, and Riots in Britain and the United States*, edited by Robert D. G. Kelley and Stephen Tuck, 7–24. New York: Palgrave Macmillan, 2015.

Pew Research Center. "Blacks and Hispanics Face Extra Challenges in Getting Home Loans." January 10, 2017. http://www.pewsocialtrends.org/2016/06/27/1-demographic-trends-and-economic-well-being/#blacks-still-trail-whites-in-college-completion.

———. "How Wealth Inequality Has Changed in the U.S. since the Great Recession, by Race and Ethnicity." November 1, 2017. http://www.pewresearch.org/fact-tank/2017/11/01/how-wealth-inequality-has-changed-in-the-u-s-since-the-great-recession-by-race-ethnicity-and-income/.

———. "On Views of Race and Inequality, Blacks and Whites Are Worlds Apart." June 27, 2016. http://www.pewsocialtrends.org/2016/06/27/1-demographic-trends-and-economic-well-being/#blacks-still-trail-whites-in-college-completion.

Pilat, Oliver Ramsey. *Lindsay's Campaign: A Behind-the-Scenes Diary*. Boston, MA: Beacon Press, 1968.

Podhoretz, Norman. *Breaking Ranks: A Political Memoir*. New York: Harper and Row, 1979.

———. Interview with the author. November 29, 2016.

———. "My Negro Problem and Ours." *Commentary*, February 1, 1963. https://www.commentarymagazine.com/articles/my-negro-problem-and-ours/.

Poling, James. "Thurgood Marshall and the 14th Amendment." In *Reporting Civil Rights, Part One: American Journalism, 1941–1963*, edited by Clayborne Carson, David J. Garrow, Bill Kovach, and Carol Polsgrove, 141–56. New York: Library of America, 2003.

"Presidential Approval Ratings—Gallup Historical Statistics and Trends." Gallup. https://news.gallup.com/poll/116677/presidential- approval-ratings-gallup-historical-statistics-trends.asp.

"A Program for the Goldwater Administration." *National Review*, July 1964.

Rhodes-Pitts, Sharifa. *Harlem Is Nowhere: A Journey to the Mecca of Black Amerca*. New York: Little, Brown and Company, 2011.

Richardson, Marty. "Charge Two with Lynch Death of 14-Year-Old." In *Reporting Civil Rights, Part One: American Journalism, 1941–1963*, edited by Clayborne Carson, David J. Garrow, Bill Kovach, and Carol Polsgrove, 211–13. New York: Library of America, 2003.

Risen, Clay. *The Bill of the Century The Epic Battle for the Civil Rights Act*. New York: Bloomsbury Press, 2014.

Robin, Corey. *The Reactionary Mind: Conservatism from Edmund Burke to Sarah Palin*. New York: Oxford University Press, 2013.

Rockwell, George Lincoln. *This Time the World*. Reedy, WV: Liberty Bell Publications, 2004.

Rolph, Stephanie. *Resisting Inequality: The Citizens' Council, 1954–1989*. Baton Rouge: Louisiana State University Press, 2018.

Roth, Philip. "Channel X: Two Plays on the Race Conflict." *New York Review of Books*, May 28, 1964. Rusher, William. "GOP at a Crossroads." *National Review*, February 12, 1963.

Schlesinger, Arthur M., Jr. *Robert Kennedy and His Times*. New York: Mariner Books, 1979.

Schlosser, Joel. "Socrates in a Different Key." In *A Political Companion to James Baldwin*, edited by Susan J. McWilliams, 219–46. Lexington: University Press of Kentucky, 2017.

Schneider, Gregory. *Cadres for Conservatism: Young Americans for Freedom and the Rise of the Contemporary Right*. New York: NYU Press, 1999.

Schoenwald, Jonathan M. *A Time for Choosing: The Rise of Modern American Conservatism*. New York: Oxford University Press, 2001.

Schulman, George. *American Prophecy: Race and Redemption in American Political Culture*. Minneapolis: University of Minnesota Press, 2008.

Schultz, Kevin. *Buckley and Mailer: The Difficult Friendship That Shaped the Sixties*. New York: W. W. Norton, 2015.

Scotchie, Joseph. *Barbarians in the Saddle: An Intellectual Biography of Richard M. Weaver*. New Brunswick, NJ: Transaction, 1997.

"Segregation and Democracy." *National Review*, January 25, 1956, 5.

"The Selma Campaign." *National Review*, March 23, 1965, 227–28.

Seymour, Charles. "Inaugural Address." Yale University, 1937. https://inauguration.yale.edu/sites/default/files/files/Seymour%2C%20C harles_PWJ.pdf.

Sherrill, Robert. "William F. Buckley Lived off Evil as Mold Lives off Garbage." *Nation*, June 11, 1988. https://www.thenation.com/article/squire-willie/.

Simonelli, Frederic J. *The American Fuehrer: George Lincoln Rockwell and the American Nazi Party*. Urbana: University of Illinois Press, 1999.

Sitton, Claude. "Birmingham Bomb Kills 4 Negro Girls in Church; Riots Flare; 2 Boys Slain." *New York Times*, September 16, 1963. In *Reporting Civil Rights, Part Two: American Journalism, 1963–1973*, edited by Clayborne Carson, David J. Garrow, Bill Kovach, and Carol Polsgrove, 19–22. New York: Library of America, 2003.

———. "N.A.A.C.P. Leader Slain in Jackson; Protests Mount." In *Reporting Civil Rights, Part One: American Journalism, 1941–1963*, edited by Clayborne Carson, David J. Garrow, Bill Kovach, and Carol Polsgrove, 831–35. New York: Library of America, 2003.

Sivek, Susan Currie. "Editing Conservatism: How *National Review* Magazine Framed and Mobilized a Political Movement." *Mass Communication and Society* 11, no. 3 (2008): 247–74.

Solomon, Deborah. "The Way We Live Now, 7/11/04: William F. Buckley; Conservatively Speaking." *New York Times*, July 11, 2004. https://www.nytimes.com/2004/07/11/magazine/way
-we-live-now-7-11-04-questions-for-william-f-buckley-conservatively-speaking.html.

"Special Report: The Race Issue and the Election." *National Review*, September 22, 1964.

Standley, Fred R., and Louis H. Pratt, ed. *Conversations with James Baldwin.* Jackson: University
Press of Mississippi, 1989.

Stanton, Mary. *From Selma to Sorrow.* Athens: University of Georgia Press, 2000.

Steele, Shelby. *Shame: How America's Past Sins Have Polarized Our Country.* New York: Basic
Books, 2015.

Stein, Sol. *Native Sons.* New York: One World, 2005.

Stevens, Norma, and Steven M. L. Aronson. *Avedon: Something Personal.* New York: Random
House, 2017.

Strauss, Leo. *Natural Right and History.* Chicago: University of Chicago Press, 1953.

Styron, Rose, and R. Blakeslee Gilpin, eds. *Selected Letters of William Styron.* New York: Random
House, 2012.

Sullivan, Patricia. "Henry Wallace's Campaign Foreshadowed the Movement as Well as the Rainbow." *Southern Changes* 10, no. 5 (1988): 11, 16–17.

Sullivan, Shannon and Nancy Tuana, eds. *Race and Epistemologies of Ignorance.* Albany: SUNY
Press, 2007.

Sullivan, Timothy J. *New York State and the Rise of Modern Conservatism: Redrawing Party Lines.*
Albany: State University of New York Press, 2009.

Take This Hammer. Directed by Richard O. Moore. National Educational Television, 1963.
https://www.youtube.com/watch?v=A-x7TP4z3fA.

Tanenhaus, Sam. "The Literary Battle for Nat Turner's Legacy." *Vanity Fair*, August 3, 2016.

———. "Original Sin." *New Republic*, February 9, 2013. https://newrepublic.com/article/112365
/why-republicans-are-party-white-people.

———. "Q&A on William F. Buckley Jr." *New York Times*, February 27, 2008. https://artsbeat
.blogs.nytimes.com/2008/02/27/qa-with-sam- tanenhaus-on-william-f-buckley/.

———. "William F. Buckley Jr.: Founder." *Yale Alumni Magazine*, May–June 2008, 1–8.

Thayer, George. *The Farther Shores of Politics: The American Political Fringe Today.* New York:
Simon and Schuster, 1967.

This Week. *National Review*, March 14, 1956.

Thorburn, Wayne. *A Generation Awakes: Young Americans for Freedom and the Creation of the Conservative Movement.* Ottawa, IL: Jameson Books, 2010.

Thurmond, Strom. "Address by J. Strom Thurmond, Governor of South Carolina, Accepting the
States' Rights Democratic Nomination for President of the United States." Speech given in
Houston, TX, August 11, 1948.

"To the Editor." *National Review*, July 16, 1963.

"A Tribute to the Union—150 Years." *Varsity*, February 13, 1965.

Truman, Harry. "Report to the American People on Korea." April 11, 1951. https://millercenter
.org/the-presidency/presidential-speeches/april-11-1951-report-american-people-korea.

"Truman Wrote of '48 Offer to Eisenhower." *New York Times*, July 11, 2003. https://www.nytimes .com/2003/07/11/us/truman-wrote-of-48-offer-to-eisenhower.html.

Truth and Reconciliation Commission Report of South Africa. Volume 3. October 29, 1998.

Tuck, Stephen. "Making the Voting Rights Act." In *The Voting Rights Act: Securing the Ballot*, edited by Richard M. Valelly, 77. Washington, DC: CQ Press, 2006.

Tumin, Melvin. *Race and Intelligence: A Scientific Evaluation.* New York: Anti-Defamation League of B'nai B'rith, 1963.

Tushnet, Mark V. *The NAACP's Legal Strategy against Segregated Education, 1925–1950.* Chapel Hill: University of North Carolina Press, 2012.

Tye, Larry. *Bobby Kennedy: The Making of a Liberal Icon.* New York: Random House, 2016.

"Union Man Comes Second." *Varsity*, April 25, 1965.

van den Haag, Ernest. "NEGROES, INTELLIGENCE, AND PREJUDICE." *National Review*, December 1, 1964.

Vidal, Gore. "A Distasteful Encounter with William F. Buckley Jr." *Esquire*, September 1969. https://classic.esquire.com/article/1969/9/1/a-distasteful-encounter-with-william-f -buckley-jr.

Voegelin, Eric. *The New Science of Politics.* Chicago: University of Chicago Press, 1952.

von Dreele, W. H. "Sonnet to Mrs. Gunning." *National Review*, October 6, 1964, 859.

von Kuenelt-Leddihn, Erik. "Letter from Africa." *National Review*, April 9, 1960, 232.

Wakefield, Dan. "Justice in Sumner." In *Reporting Civil Rights, Part One: American Journalism, 1941–1963*, edited by Clayborne Carson, David J. Garrow, Bill Kovach, and Carol Polsgrove, 217–21. New York: Library of America, 2003.

———. "Portrait of a Complainer." *Esquire*, January 1961. https://classic.esquire.com/issue /19610101.

———. "Respectable Racism." In *Reporting Civil Rights, Part One: American Journalism, 1941–1963*, edited by Clayborne Carson, David J. Garrow, Bill Kovach, and Carol Polsgrove, 222–27. New York: Library of America, 2003.

Wallace, George C. "Inaugural Address of Governor George C. Wallace." Montgomery, AL, January 14, 1963. http://digital.archives.alabama.gov/cdm/ref/collection/voices/id /2952.

———. "Statement and Proclamation by Governor George C. Wallace." University of Alabama, June 11, 1963. http://www.archives.state.al.us/govs_list/schooldoor.html.

Walker, Samuel. *Police Accountability: The Role of Citizen Oversight.* Belmont, CA: Wadsworth Publishing Company, 2000.

Washington, Booker T. *Up from Slavery.* New York: Double Day, 1901.

———. *Watts: Riot or Revolt?* CBS Reports, December 1965. https://www.c-span.org/video /?327579-1/reel-america-watts-riot-revolt-1965.

Weatherby, William J. *James Baldwin: Artist on Fire, a Portrait.* New York: Dutton Adult, 1989.

———. *Squaring Off: Mailer vs Baldwin.* New York: Mason/Charter, 1977.

Weaver, Richard M. *Ideas Have Consequences.* Chicago: University of Chicago Press, 1948.

———. "Integration Is Communization." *National Review*, July 13, 1957, 67.

———. "The Regime of the South." *National Review*, March 14, 1959, 587–89.

———. "Up from Liberalism." *Modern Age* (Winter 1958–59).

Webb, Clive. "Brotherhood, Betrayal, and Rivers of Blood: Southern Segregationists and British Race Relations." In *The Other Special Relationship: Race, Rights, and Riots in Britain and the United States*, edited by Robert D. G. Kelley and Stephen Tuck, 232–33. New York: Palgrave Macmillan, 2015.

Wehrwein, Austin C. "Talk by Buckley Angers Students." *New York Times*, August 23, 1961.

Whalen, Marcella. "Letters to the Editor." *National Review*, August 13, 1963, 120.

White, Michael D., and Henry F. Fradella. *Stop and Frisk: The Use and Abuse of a Controversial Policing Tactic*. New York: NYU Press, 2016.

"Who Speaks for Harlem?" July 25, 1964, WNYC Archive.

Wilhelmsen, Frederick D., and Willmoore Kendall. "Cicero and the Politics of Public Orthodoxy." In *Christianity and Political Philosophy*, edited by Frederick D. Wilhelmsen, 25–59. Athens: University of Georgia Press, 1978.

Williams, Thomas Chatteron. "Breaking into James Baldwin's House." *New Yorker*, October 28, 2015. https://www.newyorker.com/news/news-desk/breaking-into-james-baldwins-house.

Wills, Garry. "Buckley, Buckley, Bow Wow Wow." *Esquire*, January 1968. https://classic.esquire.com/article/1968/1/1/buckley-buckley-bow-wow-wow.

———. "The Buckley Myth." *New York Review of Books*, August 11, 2015. https://www.nybooks.com/daily/2015/08/11/william-buckley-myth/.

———. "But Is Ayn Rand Conservative?" *National Review*, February 27, 1960, 139.

———. "Frank and Elsie." In *Confessions of a Conservative*, 38–48. New York: Double Day, 1979.

———. *Outside Looking In*. New York: Viking, 2010.

———. "Reasoning on Race" *National Review*. August 26, 1961, 127.

———. "What Color Is God?" *National Review*, May 1963, 409–17.

———. "Who Shall Overcome?" *National Review*, September 22, 1964.

X, Malcolm. "Message to the Grassroots." November 10, 1963. http://teachingamericanhistory.org/library/document/message-to-grassroots/.

X, Malcolm, James Baldwin, and LaVerne McCummings. "Black Muslims vs. the Sit-ins." WBAI, April 25, 1961, pacificaradioarchives.org/recording/bb5322.

"Yet Another Country." *Observer*, February 21, 1965.

Zaborowska, Magdalena J. *James Baldwin's Turkish Decade: Erotics of Exile*. Durham, NC: Duke University Press, 2008.

Index